SHAKESPEARE SURVEY

66

Working with Shakespeare

EDITED BY

PETER HOLLAND

CAMBRIDGE
UNIVERSITY PRESS

CAMBRIDGE
UNIVERSITY PRESS

University Printing House, Cambridge CB2 8BS, United Kingdom

Published in the United States of America by Cambridge University Press, New York

Cambridge University Press is part of the University of Cambridge.

It furthers the University's mission by disseminating knowledge in the pursuit of
education, learning and research at the highest international levels of excellence.

www.cambridge.org
Information on this title: www.cambridge.org/9781107041738

© Cambridge University Press 2013

First published 2013

Printed in the United Kingdom by CPI Group Ltd, Croydon CR0 4YY

A catalogue record for this publication is available from the British Library

Library of Congress Cataloguing in Publication data
Shakespeare survey 66 : working with Shakespeare / edited by Peter Holland.
pages cm
Includes bibliographical references and index.
ISBN 978-1-107-04173-8 (hardback)
1. Shakespeare, William, 1564–1616 – Criticism and interpretation.
I. Holland, Peter, 1951 – editor of compilation.
PR2976.S33843   2013
822.3′3 – dc23   2013013113

ISBN 978-1-107-04173-8 Hardback

SHAKESPEARE SURVEY

66

Working with Shakespeare

ADVISORY BOARD

EDITOR'S NOTE

Volume 67, on 'Shakespeare's Collaborative Plays', will be at press by the time this volume appears. The theme of Volume 68 will be 'Shakespeare, Origins and Originality' and of Volume 69 will be 'Shakespeare and Rome'.

Submissions should be addressed to the Editor at The Shakespeare Institute, Church Street, Stratford-upon-Avon, Warwickshire CV37 6HP, to arrive at the latest by 1 September 2014 for Volume 68 and 1 September 2015 for Volume 69. Pressures on space are heavy and priority is given to articles related to the theme of a particular volume. Please send a copy you do not wish to be returned. Submissions may also be made as attachments to e-mail to pholland@nd.edu. All articles submitted are read by the Editor and at least one member of the Advisory Board, whose indispensable assistance the Editor gratefully acknowledges.

Unless otherwise indicated, Shakespeare quotations and references are keyed to *The Complete Works*, ed. Stanley Wells, Gary Taylor, John Jowett and William Montgomery, 2nd edition (Oxford, 2005).

Review copies should be addressed to the Editor as above. In attempting to survey the ever-increasing bulk of Shakespeare publications our reviewers inevitably have to exercise some selection. We are pleased to receive offprints of articles which help to draw our reviewers' attention to relevant material.

P.D.H.

CONTRIBUTORS

JANET BOTTOMS, *University of Cambridge*
MICHAEL CORDNER, *University of York*
HUGH CRAIG, *University of Newcastle, Australia*
PÉTER DÁVIDHÁZI, *Hungarian Academy of Sciences*
TOBIAS DÖRING, *Ludwig Maximilians University, Munich*
JOHN DRAKAKIS, *University of Stirling*
JAMES HIRSH, *Georgia State University*
TON HOENSELAARS, *Utrecht University*
RUSSELL JACKSON, *University of Birmingham*
M. LINDSAY KAPLAN, *Georgetown University*
HESTER LEES-JEFFRIES, *University of Cambridge*
SONIA MASSAI, *King's College, London*
RICHARD MEEK, *University of Hull*
MICHAEL NEILL, *University of Auckland*
SCOTT L. NEWSTOK, *Rhodes College*
REIKO OYA, *Keio University, Tokyo*
VARSHA PANJWANI, *University of York*
MICHAEL PAVELKA, *Propeller Theatre Company*
STEPHEN PURCELL, *University of Warwick*
CAROL CHILLINGTON RUTTER, *University of Warwick*
KIERNAN RYAN, *Royal Holloway, University of London*
DAVID SCHALKWYK, *Folger Shakespeare Library*
CHARLOTTE SCOTT, *Goldsmiths College, University of London*
JAMES SHAW, *University of Oxford*
ERICA SHEEN, *University of York*
TIFFANY STERN, *University of Oxford*
R. S. WHITE, *University of Western Australia*
RICHARD WILSON, *Kingston University*
CORDELIA ZUKERMAN, *University of Michigan*

CONTENTS

CONTENTS

ILLUSTRATIONS

LIST OF ILLUSTRATIONS

SERMONS, PLAYS AND NOTE-TAKERS: *HAMLET* Q1 AS A 'NOTED' TEXT

TIFFANY STERN

THE ACTOR-PIRATE

In the eighteenth century, when Shakespeare editors first came into being, only two texts of *Hamlet* were known, one printed in 1604 in quarto (now called Q2), and one in the Folio of 1623 (F). But in 1823 Sir Henry Bunbury discovered a third version of *Hamlet* 'in a closet at Barton'.[1] Dated 1603, it was the first and earliest printed text of the play (now known as Q1). It was also, as shocked scholars realized, the 'worst'. As one of the earliest commentators on the text, Ambrose Gunthio (probably J. P. Collier) asked, 'Can any one for a moment believe that Shakspeare penned this unconnected, unintelligible jargon?'[2] Since then, critics have repeatedly drawn attention to *Hamlet* Q1's incoherence, inconsistencies, ellipses, reworkings and loose ends, generally concluding, with G. R. Hibbard, that 'the text itself, . . . is a completely illegitimate and unreliable one'. So how did such a text come about – and why?[3]

Finding an answer is difficult, partly because the text is not equally 'bad' – or even 'bad' in the same way – throughout. Running at about 2200 lines (the other texts are Q2 *c.*3800 lines, F *c.*3570 lines) *Hamlet* Q1 is more filled with gaps and summaries than the other texts. Yet its earliest pages are fairly true to Q2 and F, while some later sections are quite accurately represented, including speeches by the Ghost and Horatio. Though some passages reflect their *Hamlet* counterparts almost line-by-line, even if full of synonyms and rephrasings, others are partially, and some entirely, 'new'.

Early explanations for *Hamlet* Q1 included the notion that it combines Shakespeare's *Hamlet* with

bits of the lost earlier text on which it was based, the '*Ur*' *Hamlet*; or that it is Shakespeare's rough draft. Yet *Hamlet* Q1 contains textual moments from *Hamlet* Q2, thought to be a pre-performance text, and F, thought to be a post-performance text – meaning that, in chronological terms, it seems to be the middle text of the three. Another early explanation was offered by 'Gunthio': that *Hamlet* Q1 must have been 'taken down piecemeal in the theatre, by a blundering scribe'.[4]

There were good reasons for believing that *Hamlet* Q1 had been constructed by scribes in the audience. Several sermons of the 1580s and '90s had been published not from authorial texts, but from notes taken down by the congregation in 'charactery', an early form of shorthand; if sermons could be 'taken' in this way, why not plays? Anthony Tyrrell's *A Fruitfull Sermon* of 1589, for instance, broadcasts on its title-page that it has been 'Taken by Characterye'; Stephen Egerton's *Ordinary Lecture* (1589) is, says its title-page, 'taken as it was uttered by characterie'. Henry Smith's *Sermon of the Benefite of Contentation* (1590) is also 'Taken by characterie'; while his *Fruit[full]*

Heartfelt thanks to David Scott Kastan, Holger Klein, Zachary Lesser, Ivan Lupic, Will Poole, Paul Menzer, Holger Schott Syme, Arlynda Boyer, Rhodri Lewis, John Staines and William St Clair for their invaluable feedback on this article.

[1] Sir Henry Bunbury, *The Correspondence of Sir Thomas Hanmer* (London, 1838), p. 80.
[2] Ambrose Gunthio, 'A Running Commentary on the Hamlet of 1603', *European Magazine*, 1:4 (1825), 339–47 at 340.
[3] G. R. Hibbard, ed., *Hamlet* (Oxford, 1987), p. 69.
[4] Gunthio, 'Running Commentary', 340.

Sermon (1591) 'being taken by characterie, is now published for the benefite of the faithfull'. So usual did it become to publish sermons from audience's shorthand 'characterical' notes in the 1590s that 'L.S.' had to explain, when he provided his own sermon text in 1593, that in this instance 'Taken it was not from the Preachers mouth by any fond or new found Characterisme'.[5]

It was the evidence of these sermons that led W. Matthews, in the 1930s, to learn 'charactery' in order to determine whether it really could be used to capture Shakespeare. He recorded his conclusions in a series of articles: that charactery has too few words – 550 (if particles are included) – to record a literary text; that it is too difficult a system to be used at speed; and that, using pictorial symbols to represent words – in principal it could be 'read' by a foreigner – it is anti-literary, recording only the meaning, not the sound, of any text.[6] He and other scholars then worked on the two further shorthands published before *Hamlet* Q1: brachygraphy (1590), which was also pictorial; and stenography (1602), the first phonetic shorthand. They found inadequacies in all of them, and dismissed the entire notion of scribes in the audience.

In 1941, G. I. Duthie, in *The 'Bad' Quarto of 'Hamlet'*, accepted Matthews's rejection of shorthand, adding that a shorthand writer, confronted with a word he did not know, would be brought to a standstill, and suggesting that visible note-takers in the audience would, anyway, have been caught and removed. He then offered his preferred explanation for the origin of *Hamlet* Q1. Summarizing ideas promoted by Dover Wilson, but originating with Tycho Mommsen in 1857, Duthie argued that *Hamlet* Q1 had been stolen by a traitor-actor who had been involved in the play's production. As Duthie saw it, the hireling who had played Marcellus and Lucianus 'stole' the text of *Hamlet*, reproducing his own part(s) and memorizing what he could of the others. Hence the reason, he said, that Marcellus's part was 'good'. Since Duthie, most scholars have accepted the idea that *Hamlet* was taken by a traitor-actor; in 1992 Kathleen Irace furthered it with her computer-based analysis of the part of Marcellus: she suggested, however, that

the Marcellus player was reconstructing an adapted form of *Hamlet* from memory.[7] As *Hamlet* Q1 had long been said to be a 'pirate' text, 'pirate' meaning, bibliographically, a work belonging to another which has been reproduced without authority, the actor-thief was said to have been a 'pirate' – picking up on a joke first made by Alfred Pollard in his *Shakespeare's Fight with the Pirates* (London, 1917). Over time, however, the joke has been forgotten, and the player of 'Marcellus' has come to be called the 'actor-pirate', despite the fact that a 'pirate' is a plunderer of ships, not a land thief.

The glamorous word 'pirate', and the confused notions that it accrued, may have kept alive the theory of the actor-thief. No longer was *Hamlet* Q1 a disappointingly inaccurate text; it was now an enthralling record of insubordination inside Shakespeare's very playhouse, run, or masterminded, by a rogue 'pirate' actor. Yet the actor-pirate theory is inherently problematic. Even in 1.1, Marcellus, as well as Horatio and Bernardo, 'make mistakes' and 'have recourse to synonyms'.[8] More damning still for an actor-based theory is the fact that 'Marcellus' misremembers his own cues. An actor's 'part' for Marcellus – the script that an actor would receive, consisting of his lines and cues – made from Q2/F would look like this, with the words 'desperate with imagination' cueing 'Let's follow':

―――――――――――[desperate] [with] imagination.
Let's follow; 'tis not fit thus to obey him.
―――――――――――[will] [this] come?
Something is rotten in the State of Denmarke.

But in Q1, Marcellus's part would look like this – with 'desperate with imagination' cuing 'something is rotten' and 'will this sort' cuing 'Lets

---

[5] L. S., *Resurgendum* (1593), A3r.

[6] W. Matthews, 'Shorthand and the Bad Shakespeare Quartos', *Modern Language Review*, 27 (1932), 243–62; W. Matthews, 'Shakespeare and the Reporters', *The Library*, 15 (1935), 481–500.

[7] Kathleen Irace, 'Origins and Agents of Q1 *Hamlet*', in Thomas Clayton, ed., *The Hamlet First Published* (Newark, 1992), pp. 90–122.

[8] Hibbard, ed., *Hamlet*, p. 80.

follow' – meaning that the cues are reversed and misremembered:

————————————[desperate] [with] imagination.
Something is rotten in the state of *Denmarke*.
————————————[will] [this] sort?
Lets follow, tis not fit thus to obey him.

Marcellus also does not remember to give out his cues to his fellow actor. Q2/F has

Mar. And Leedgemen to the Dane,
Fran. Give you good night.
Mar. O, farwell honest souldiers . . .

But Q1 has instead 'And leegemen to the Dane, / O farewell honest souldier', meaning that Marcellus neglects to stop at his cue for Francisco.[9] It is unfortunate for the actor-pirate theory that it does not take acting into account.

There are further problems with the actor-pirate explanation. All of the early pages of *Hamlet* Q1, not just Marcellus's part, are relatively 'good', but the more the play progresses, the more is sense, rather than word, recorded. This demands an actor who begins the play with verbal recall, but who, over time, becomes more retentive of sense than sound: a change particularly unlikely for an actor, who usually remembers sound over meaning. Moreover, though in Act 1 the text is sometimes better when Marcellus is on stage, that notion falls apart later in the play, as Paul Werstine points out. Not only are lines surrounding the putative actor-pirate often as bad as lines elsewhere, but also, conversely, sometimes 'Q1 . . . provides us with a better version of some Q2/F dialogue when the putative reporters are off than it . . . does when they are on.'[10] Attempts to explain this have resulted in casting the 'pirate' in ever more roles. Though on the one hand said to be a temporary, hireling actor, with no qualms about stealing the playhouse's property, the actor-pirate has, on the other, been said to have played Marcellus, Voltemand ('Voltemar'), Lucianus, Prologue, Second Gravedigger, Churlish Priest, an English Ambassador and a scattered selection of mutes – thus becoming one of the most continuously staged players in *Hamlet*.

The question of actor-piracy, moreover, depends on fusing two different ideas together: that actors might be textual thieves (for which there is no evidence); and that people with very good memories were able to steal plays (for which there is plenty of evidence). In Spain, there are records of men who could hold entire plays in their heads. Luís Remírez, in 1615, was said to be able to reproduce a *comedia* having heard it three times; while Lope de Vega in 1620 inveighs against audience-members who make their money 'by stealing the *comedias* . . . saying that they are able to memorize them only by hearing them'.[11] Maguire points out, however, 'in neither case are actors involved in the reconstruction'.[12] Both instances in fact bolster the argument for locating textual theft amongst the spectators. Moreover, the Spanish memorizers are praised, or blamed, for being unusual: not anyone could perform such feats of memory, and these men are said to have trained with textual theft in mind.

Recently, the more general idea that *Hamlet* Q1 comes directly from a single actor at all has been implicitly questioned by the work of Paul Menzer, who shows the text to be, because of its poor cues, unstageable; while Lene B. Petersen indicates that *Hamlet* Q1 is not simply 'memorial': its features of repetition and simplification, though reminiscent of folktales and ballads, render it neither fully authorial nor fully 'oral'.[13]

Given problems with the 'actor-pirate' theory, this article will return to the explanation for which there is historical evidence: audience notation.

---

[9] William Shakespeare, *The Tragicall Historie of Hamlet* (1604); William Shakespeare, *The Tragicall Historie of Hamlet* (1603). Unless otherwise noted, all textual references to *Hamlet* are to these versions, in their original printed states. All quotations that are essentially the same in Q2/F are quoted from Q2.

[10] Paul Werstine, 'A Century of Bad Shakespeare Quartos', *Shakespeare Quarterly*, 50 (1999), 310–33 at 320.

[11] Roger Chartier, *Publishing Drama in Early Modern Europe* (London, 1998), p. 29.

[12] Laurie Maguire, *Shakespearean Suspect Texts* (Cambridge, 1996), p. 106.

[13] Paul Menzer, *The Hamlets* (Newark, 2008), p. 24; Lene B. Petersen, *Shakespeare's Errant Texts* (Cambridge, 2010), p. 142.

This is an idea that has been revisited with respect to *King Lear* in P. W. K. Stone's excellent *The Textual History of King Lear* (London, 1980), which argues that *King Lear* Q1 is a reported, but not a shorthand, text, and Adele Davidson's *Shakespeare in Shorthand* (Newark, 2009), which argues conversely that *King Lear* Q1 *is* a shorthand text, and that it was copied from manuscript, not from an audience report. Both books deserve to be better known than they are, but both saddle themselves with a quarto that is particularly receptive to other explanations, and further limit themselves by insisting on one notation, shorthand or otherwise, for bringing the play about.

This article, changing the terms in which Matthews and Duthie originally asked and rejected the shorthand option for *Hamlet* Q1, will investigate not whether one person, using one form of shorthand, on one occasion, copied Q1 *Hamlet*, but whether some people, using any form of handwriting they liked, on any number of occasions, could have penned *Hamlet* Q1. It considers evidence that plays, like sermons, were noted during performance; it looks at what might constitute 'note traces' in the text of *Hamlet* and asks why watchers might want to capture in notes – and then publish – the uttered performances that they heard.

NOTERS AT CHURCHES AND PLAYHOUSES

As there is detailed evidence about the way congregations rendered the sermons they heard into written texts, this section will start by examining church practice; it will then turn to other oral performances captured in text – parliamentary speeches – before looking, finally, at plays. Did theatrical audiences sometimes transcribe what they heard?

Just as contemporary students are expected to take notes in lectures to facilitate their memorizing and learning, so congregations in early modern England were expected to take notes at sermons 'for the helping of their owne memories' while listening, and 'for their owne private helpe and edification' afterwards.[14] As Lady Hatton wrote to her son Christopher in Cambridge, 'Heare sermonns', enjoining him to 'strive to take notes that you may meditate on them'.[15] John Brinsley, in his educational treatise *Ludus Literarius* (1612), recommends instilling the note-taking habit in children as early as possible. In order to 'cause every one to learn something at the sermons' he suggests that young children, if they can write at all, 'take notes'. The distinction between partial 'notes' and whole sermons, however, was permeable; Brinsley goes on to suggest that children in the highest forms at school should 'set downe the substance exactly'.[16]

As literacy increased over time, churches became so full of noters as to resemble schoolrooms. In 1641 'boys' at sermons are castigated for turning the communion tables into a surface on which to write, 'fouling and spotting the linnen' in the process.[17] By 1644, Robert Baillie, participating in the Westminster Assembly, recorded that in England 'most of all the assembly write, as all the people almost, men, women, and children, write at preaching'; by 1651 Lodewijck Huygens went to church in Covent Garden and found 'In the box next to ours three or four ladies . . . writing down the entire sermon, and more than 50 other persons throughout the whole church . . . doing the same'.[18]

Preachers from the 1590s onwards had to decide what to think about the sea of 'noters' that confronted them. Stephen Egerton concluded, carefully, in 1592, that

I do not mislike the noting at Sermons, but rather wish it were more used then it is, so it were used to keepe the minde more attentive in the time of hearing, to

---

[14] Robert Rollock, *Five and Twentie Lectures* (1619), π4r; Stephen Egerton, *A Lecture* [1603], A6v-A7r.

[15] Edward Maund Thomson, ed., *Correspondence of the Family of Hatton* (London, 1878), p. 3.

[16] John Brinsley, *Ludus Literarius* (1612), p. 255.

[17] Ephraim Udall, *Tò Prepon Emchariotichòn* (1641), C2v.

[18] Robert Baillie, *Letters and Journals*, 2 vols. (1775), vol. 1, p. 414; Lodewijck Huygens, *The English Journal, 1651–1652*, ed. and trans. A. G. H. Bachrach and R. G. Collmer (Leiden, 1982), p. 55.

helpe the memorie after hearing, that men might be more able afterwards to meditate by themselves, and to conferre with others.[19]

He may have been affected by the fact that the popularity of preachers could be measured by the number of noters they attracted.

Naturally, notes of sermons by popular preachers had a tendency to make their way to the press. Sermons that are described as having been 'gathered', 'taken', or 'received' from 'the mouth' of a preacher, advertise that they are printed from notes and are not directly 'authorial'. John Dod's *The Bright Star* claims, on its title page, to have been '*gathered from the mouth of a faithfull pastor by a gracious young man*' (1603); William Crashaw printed sermons by William Perkins, 'taken with this hand of mine, from his owne mouth' (1605); while Robert Rollock's Scots *Certaine Sermons* (1599) were likewise printed from a text 'we / fand in the hand of sum of his Schollers quha wrait at his mouth'.[20] Such texts draw attention to the two body parts they manifest, mouth and hand, highlighting their inscripted orality, rather than their literary features.

One ramification of the noting habit was that notebooks needed to be created capable, in size terms, of recording about an hour's worth of preaching (sermons at the time being measured by the hour-glass).[21] Rather than taking to church the pens, ink, sand, knives, paper and blotting-paper that permanent text required, congregations seem often to have opted for 'tablebooks' – small notebooks that could be written on with graphite pencils or soft-metal pens. In 1625, Hall refers to the man who 'in the middest of the Sermon puls out his Tables in haste, as if he feared to leese that note' (in fact all he actually records is 'his forgotten errand, or nothing'): tablebooks were a stylish accoutrement, and some people wanted to draw attention to the fact that they had them.[22] Those who hoped to be 'noted' ('seen'), flourishing the writing implements that advertised their literacy and their piety, were the subject of a weak pun repeatedly used. The playwright Thomas Heywood, in a 1636 text he himself noted from utterance (it is 'taken' from the 'mouthes' of two

phoney-prophets), depicts a religious hypocrite as one who, 'In the time of the Sermon . . . drawes out his tables to take the Notes, . . . still noting who observes him to take them'.[23]

Tablebooks had several advantages: they encouraged continuous writing, as they were not reliant on dipping a pen in ink; they were portable – surviving examples are 16mos in 8s; and they were economical, as they could be wiped clean with damp bread or a wet sponge once their notes had been transcribed onto a permanent medium.[24] Daniel Featley depicts, using the well-worn pun, the '*noted noters* of sermons', as they prepare to attend a church: they 'cleanse their table-books, especially before your fast sermons'.[25]

A second ramification of the noting habit, especially for those who wished to take an entire sermon, was that speedy writing became a goal: the more swiftly one could write, the more sermon one could gather. As early as 1569, John Hart's *Orthographie* had recommended using italic rather than secretary hand when taking notes, and avoiding unsounded or unnecessary letters; in effect, he had created the first shorthand, though his was still reliant on the alphabet. From then on, ever more pictorial shorthands came into being, as 'by the benefite of speedy writing, the whole body of the Lecture, and sermon might be registred' while otherwise 'no more remaineth after the hower passed, then so much as the frailtie of memory

[19] Stephen Egerton in William Cupper, *Certaine Sermons* (1592), A7r.
[20] William Perkins, *M. Perkins, his Exhortation to Repentance* (1605), A7v; Robert Rollock, *Certaine sermons . . . Preached . . . at Edinburgh* (1599), A6r-v.
[21] Laurie Maguire, *Shakespearean Suspect Texts* (Cambridge, 1996), p. 97.
[22] Joseph Hall, *The Works* (1625), p. 187.
[23] Thomas Heywood, *A True Discourse of the Two Infamous Upstart Prophets, Richard Farnham . . . and John Bull . . . with their Examinations and Opinions taken from their Owne Mouthes* (1636), p. 3.
[24] H. R. Woudhuysen, 'Writing-Tables and Table Books', *eBLJ* (2004), 1–11 at 4; Peter Stallybrass et al., 'Hamlet's Tables and the Technologies of Writing in Renaissance England', *Shakespeare Quarterly*, 55 (2004), 379–419, 385.
[25] Daniel Featley, *Sacra Nemesis* (1644), p. 77.

carieth away'.[26] By the time charactery made its way into print in 1588, several other forms of shorthand were already extant, though 'none' of them, maintained charactery's inventor Timothie Bright, was 'comparable' with his own.[27] As Bright also patented his own system, ensuring no one could teach, print or publish any new form of 'character' for the next fifteen years,[28] other systems were forced underground. Edmond Willis, whose shorthand was not printed until 1618, for instance, had been using it for the previous twenty years; it was the method employed to note the sermons of Nicholas Felton between 1599 and 1602, as a surviving manuscript attests.[29] By the time Willis printed his *Abreviation of Writing by Character*, London was crammed not so much with shorthand books as with shorthand teachers who had 'with their *Bills* . . . be-sprinkled the posts and walls of this Citie'.[30]

Some shorthands never made it into print. Most, after *Orthographie*, whether logographic or phonetic, were reliant on new symbols, which meant that publication was expensive: the new characters needed to be carved onto special types, or engraved onto plates, or, as was the case with John Willis's *Stenographie*, which could be bought 'charactered' or 'uncharactered', inked in by hand on every page. So though by 1641 'short-hand writing' was 'usuall for any common Mechanick both to write and invent', it is impossible to tell how many systems there were at any particular period, and how they related to one another.[31] What can be said is that at least the following different shorthands were being discussed by name – each name representing a different 'brand' – in London by the 1650s: brachygraphy, brachyography, cryptography, polygraphy, radiography, semigraphy, semography, steganography, stenography, tachygraphy, zeiglography.

As Arnold Hunt in his brilliant *Art of Hearing* makes clear, however, texts that claim to have been taken by shorthand often contain mistakes traceable to longhand; shorthand involved longhand when that was necessary, and the shorthand-longhand distinction is not entirely useful.[32] Besides, as Richard Knowles reminds us, longhand itself also

remained popular for notes:[33] shorthand, after all, comes after the desire to note, and is a consequence of that desire, not a cause. Oliver Heywood, writing about the 1650s, records that his wife would take, at sermons, 'the heads and proofes fully and a considerable part of the inlargement'; she, he observes, 'writ long-hand and not characters', making clear that longhand might be sufficient – and that both long- and shorthand were 'usual' for sermon notes at the time.[34] Many were committed to the shorthand cause, however. In 1634, Samuel Hartlib, in an excess of zeal, proposed sending volunteer shorthand writers to every single sermon preached in London, with the aim of preserving all of them.[35]

Whether notes were gathered in longhand or shorthand, or a mix, they tended to end up in longhand. Notes taken during sermons were helps towards remembering an entire sermon later, and were often rewritten at home. Margaret Hoby, for instance, went to the popular 'Egertons sermons' in 1600, afterwards 'setting downe' – writing in a permanent medium – 'some notes I had Colected'; Gilbert Freville made a longhand commonplace book in 1604 from 'the notes, taken . . . at sev[er]all sermons of Mr. Stephen Egertons preached at

---

[26] Stephen Egerton, *An Ordinary Lecture* (1589), A2r.
[27] Timothie Bright, *Characterie* (1588), A8v. A 1586 shorthand letter preserves an earlier form of charactery than that printed by Bright. See Max Förster, 'Shakespeare and Shorthand', *Philological Quarterly*, 16 (1937), 1–29 at 11.
[28] Adele Davidson, *Shakespeare in Shorthand: The Textual Mystery of 'King Lear'* (Newark, 2009), p. 34.
[29] W. Matthews, 'A Postscript to "Shorthand and the Bad Shakespeare Quartos"', *Modern Language Review*, 28 (1933), 81–3 at 83.
[30] Edmond Willis, *An Abreviation of Writing by Character* (1618), A3r.
[31] John Wilkins, *Mercury, or, The secret and swift messenger* (1641), pp. 98–9.
[32] Arnold Hunt, *The Art of Hearing: English Preachers and Their Audiences, 1590–1640* (Cambridge, 2010), pp. 144–6.
[33] Richard Knowles, 'Shakespeare and Shorthand Once Again', *PBSA*, 104:2 (2010), 141–80.
[34] J. H. Turner, *The Rev Oliver Heywood, B.A., 1630–1702*, 4 vols. (Brighouse [England], 1881), vol. 1, p. 58.
[35] Vivian Salmon, *The Works of Francis Lodwick* (London, 1972), p. 62.

Black friers', his texts extending to up to two thousand words.[36] John Manningham's longhand surviving sermon records are fuller still: consisting of texts that are up to four thousand words long, they roughly match the length of the sermon itself.[37] Given the habit of rewriting sermon notes at home in order to free a tablebook for reuse, to expand shorthand for other readers, or to create the fullest *aide memoire*, the process of note-taking in whatever form easily became (re)writing. A final, written up, sermon might well come to seem the possession of the note-taker – for its gaps had been filled by the note-taker's words, and it had been inscribed, and reinscribed, in the note-taker's hand.

Perhaps this accounts not just for the regularity with which noters then published the sermons they had gathered but for their habit of boasting about it. Edward Philips's *Certaine Godly and Learned Sermons* proclaim on their title-page that they are provided 'as they were . . . taken by the pen of H. Yelverton of Grayes Inne Gentleman, 1605'; William Perkins's *A Cloud of Faithfull Witnesses*, brags on its title-page that it is *'published . . . by Will. Crashawe, and Tho. Pierson . . . who heard him preach it, and wrote it from his mouth'* (1608). Publishers too, were ready to reveal that the sermons they were issuing were published against the will of the preacher; this gave purchasers the delightful *frisson* of acquiring something that was morally improving and, as it was not designed for them, illicit. Of Henry Smith's *Sermon of the Benefite*, 'Taken by characterie', 'it were not the authors minde or consent that it shoulde come foorth thus' (1590); the doctrines in Dod's *The Bright Star* 'were received from his mouth, but neither penned nor perused by himselfe, nor published with his consent or knowledge' (1603).[38]

Though some preachers printed their own sermons, others, who suddenly discovered their sermons in print, were outraged, publishing correctives to 'bring this boate to land, which the owner never meant should see the shore'.[39] It is often only the correctives that reveal that the earlier texts were 'stolen' in the first place: 'Some (I know not who) . . . have presumed to printe the *Meane in Mourning*, altogether without true judgement,

or calling me to counsell therein' writes Playfere at the front of his revamped *Pathway to Perfection* (1596); in front of his new *Meane in Mourning* he records that 'this sermon hath been twise printed already without my procurement or privitie any manner of way. Yea to my very great griefe and trouble' (1596).[40] Preachers who did not mind their sermons being published never reveal the theft – meaning that probably more printed sermons of the period are 'taken' than is known about.

What is noticeable, however, is that Playfere's correctives, like those of his fellow preachers', are not hugely different in substance from the 'bad' texts that preceded them. Partly this is because preachers did not write entire texts before preaching, but spoke from notes of their own; the published 'bad' texts were the most complete records available of what had been preached.[41] But partly this is because the substance was fairly well represented – it was the verbal texture that had been lost. What is corrected the second time round by preachers is not so much content as style, which some think of as too full of flourishes, and others as not having flourishes enough – the point being, either way, that the text does not sound 'authorial'. Though Dod's *Plaine and Familiar Exposition* was first published 'By noters hand', explains 'E.C.', it is now revised by the author, and appears 'In grave and sober modest weede, not garishly bedeckt'.[42] Playfere is particularly explicit on the subject: the two previous, noted, editions of *The Meane in Mourning* 'were but wooden sheathes. Or if there

---

36 Matthews, 'Shakespeare and the Reporters', p. 492.

37 Matthews, 'Shakespeare and the Reporters', pp. 491–2, 494.

38 Henry Smith, *A Sermon of the Benefite of Contentation* (1590), A3r; John Dod, *The Bright Star* (1603), A2r.

39 Edward Philips, *Certaine Godly and Learned Sermons* (1605), A5r.

40 Thomas Playfere, *The Pathway to Perfection* (1596), A2r-v; Thomas Playfere, *The Meane in Mourning* (1596), A2r.

41 Mary Morrissey, 'From Pulpit to Press', *Politics and the Paul's Cross Sermons, 1558–1642* (Oxford, 2011).

42 E.C. 'A friendly counsell to the Christian reader, touching the Author and his booke', in John Dod, *A Plaine and Familiar Exposition* (1604), A3v.

were any mettall in them, yet it had not an yvorie but a dudgin haft, being blunt and dull, without any point or edge', an explanation that illustrates, in its very phrasing, the importance to him of the striking 'literary' image his sermons had lost.[43]

Naturally, Londoners, habituated to noting by education and church, responded not only to preachers but to other speakers by inscribing them: public utterance tended to lead to text. Note-takers filled parliament, relying on tablebooks to create records they would afterwards write up – William Holt, on 13 March 1607, attended parliament with 'tables in his hand, and was seen to write diligently'; Sir Francis Bacon, reporting on a conference he had attended about Scotland, 'professeth to omit some answers by reason that his tables failed him'.[44]

It will come as no surprise that spectators went to playhouses, too, with notebooks in their hands. Often, like the congregation show-offs, they were interested in waving their books around while collecting tiny snippets of text – which may explain why playwrights of the period so often wrote in sententiae and instantly quotable passages ('soundbites' in today's parlance). 'Gulls' in the theatre are described who 'will not let a merriment slip, but they will trusse it up for their owne provision':[45] they gather jokes from plays to repeat later as their own. Lawyers, too, in their most carefully designed choleric rants, were said to be making use of 'shreds and scraps dropt from some Stage-Poet, at the Globe or Cock-pit, which they have carefully bookt up'.[46] Many went to plays to gather the newest word into their tables, as Shakespeare parodies, when Holofernes in *Love's Labour's Lost* uses the word 'peregrinat' and the fascinated Nathaniel '*Draw[s] out his Table-booke*' to record it (TLN 1752–5).[47] What was collected at plays might include staging details, as well as dialogue, for these could function, like a theatre programme today, as a token or memento of performance. The playwright Cyril Tourneur writes about a man who saw an entertainment without writing equipment: 'Many . . . pretty *Figures* there were expressing the meaning of these *Maskers*', mourns the man, 'which, for lack of a note booke, are suddainlie slipt out of my memorie'.[48] But playwright Thomas Dekker writes of plays that were comprehensively gathered. Describing the accession of King James as a play, he declares: 'it were able to fill a hundred paire of writing-tables with notes, but to see the parts plaid . . . on the stage of this new-found world.'[49]

There was, then, nothing covert or hidden about noters in the audience; confident playwrights, like confident preachers, assumed the practice of noting reflected the worth of the play. Fletcher and Massinger, for instance

> dare looke
> On any man, that brings his Table-booke
> To write downe, what againe he may repeate
> At some great Table, to deserve his meate.[50]

Playwrights did, however, fear malicious noters in a way that preachers did not. Several refer to spectators who gather passages because they dislike them, or intend to misinterpret them later out of context: 'if there bee any lurking amongst you in corners, with Table bookes . . . to feede his ——— mallice on, let them claspe them up, and slinke away, or stay and be converted' suggests Beaumont.[51] Cordatus, spokesman for Ben Jonson, defensively turns upon the audience members he calls 'decipherers': '(where e're they sit conceald) let them know, the Authour defies them, and their writing-Tables'.[52] As noted passages, favourable and otherwise, would also have to be retranscribed at home to clear tablebooks, extant theatrical commonplace books are

---

[43] Playfere, *Pathway*, A3r.

[44] Chris R. Kyle, *Theater of State* (Stanford, 2012), p. 68.

[45] Barnaby Rich, *Faultes Faults, and Nothing Else but Faultes* (1606), B4v.

[46] Thomas Trescot, *The Zealous Magistrate* (1642), C3v.

[47] Non-*Hamlet* Shakespeare quotations are taken from Charlton Hinman's *Norton Facsimile* (New York: W. W. Norton, 1968) of the Folio, and use the through line numbering (TLN) of that edition.

[48] Cyril Tourneur, *Laugh and Lie Down* (1605), F2v.

[49] Thomas Dekker, *The Wonderfull Yeare* (1603), C1v.

[50] Frances Beaumont and John Fletcher, *Custom of the Country* in *Comedies and Tragedies* (1647), p. 25.

[51] Francis Beaumont, *The Woman Hater* (1607), A2r.

[52] Ben Jonson, *Every Man out of his Humor* (1600), H2r.

generally in longhand, though that reveals nothing about the gathering process.[53]

Early performances of *Hamlet* were, it seems, attended by noters, as a surviving passage suggests. In 1623 William Basse republished his popular book *A Helpe to Discourse*. Designed for the conversationally inadequate, the book provided a series of questions or riddles with their ideal answers. One of its new 'ideal' exchanges includes the following question (Q) and the perfect answer for it (A):

Q. What Birds are those that are called Prophets twice born?

A. The cock: first an egge from the Hen, after a Cock from the Egge: they foretell seasons and changes of weather, according to the Verse:

Some **say for** ever 'gainst that season comes,	say that Q1; sayes that Q2, F
Wherin our Saviours birth is celebrated,	
The Bird of dawning singeth all Night long,	
And then they say no spirit **dares walk** abroad,	
So **sacred** and so **hallow'd** is that **tune**.	dare walke Q1; dare sturre Q2; can walke F
W. Shakes[54]	gratious . . . hallowed Q1; hallowed . . . gratious Q2, F
	time Q1, Q2, F

Basse's passage differs verbally from all three printed *Hamlet* editions (they also all differ from one another, though the lines are spoken by the putative actor-pirate Marcellus); Basse also neglects to print altogether a couple of lines found, in some form, in all three texts: 'The nights are wholsome, then no plannets strike, / No fairy takes, nor witch hath power to charme' (Q2). Most telling, though, is the fact that Basse's version declares that it is the bird's 'sacred and hallow'd . . . tune' that prevents spirits walking, rather than the 'hallowed and gracious . . . time', Christmas, that keeps the spirits at bay. As 'tune' and 'time' are unlikely to be misheard, but are quite easy, through minim error, to be misread, Basse is almost certainly printing notes originally written at the theatre (the error is unlikely to be compositorial, as it is retained in subsequent reprintings of the book).[55] If so, his

notes may have been in longhand, as 'un'/'im' is an alphabetical error.

People did, though, also take notes using shorthand in the theatre – particularly when they were trying to capture a whole text. In a passage published in 1615, George Buc, Master of the Revels since 1610 (and granted its reversion in 1603), recorded of brachygraphy that 'by the means and helpe therof (they which know it) can readily take a Sermon, Oration, Play, or any long speech, as they are spoken, dictated, acted, & uttered in the instant'.[56] George Buc's profession will have made him particularly conscious of the way plays (and he specifies a 'play' rather than a 'passage' of play) were 'taken' in the theatre; he may too have seen the print consequences of brachygraphy, as, from 1606 onwards, he had been the licenser of playbooks for publication. He is joined by playwright Thomas Heywood who, in 1637, published a prologue that puffed the revival of his play *If You Know Not Me, You Know Nobody*. Heywood reminded the spectators that the version of the play that they had bought – first published in 1605 – had come about disingenuously: 'some', he charged, 'by Stenography drew / The plot: put it in print: (scarce one word trew:)'.[57] Heywood's new prologue assumes an audience that 'knows' that 'stealing' plays – or,

---

53 For more on the note-taking audience and their commonplace records, see Tiffany Stern, 'Watching as Reading: The Audience and Written Text in the Early Modern Playhouse', in *How to Do Things with Shakespeare* ed. Laurie Maguire (Oxford, 2008), pp. 136–59.

54 William Basse, *A Helpe to Discourse* (1623), pp. 249–50 (annotation mine; bold mine, here and throughout).

55 Though Basse may have deliberately adapted his text to fit his new, commonplace, context, his wrong sense that the entire passage is about birdsong – and hence his choice of it – seems itself to have its origins in mistranscription.

56 George Buck, *The Third Universitie of England* (1615), p. 984.

57 Thomas Heywood, '*A Prologue to the Play of Queene Elizabeth*', *Pleasant Dialogues and Dramma's* (1637), p. 249. Though G. N. Giordano-Orsini in 'Thomas Heywood's Play on The Troubles of Queen Elizabeth', *The Library*, series 4, 14 (1933–4), 313–38 at 338, suggested that the play had been pirated, he was jumping on the 'actor-pirate' bandwagon; even then he conceded that stenography may have been used 'supplemented from the memories (and perhaps from the "parts") of two or more of the actors'.

it is here suggested, their scenarios, to be filled with 'untrue' text later – through shorthand was possible in 1605; a 'noter' himself, as this article has shown, Heywood is likely to be particularly conscious of other note-takers. He had, in 1608, recorded that several of his plays had '(unknown to me, and without any of my direction) accidentally come into the Printers handes, . . . (coppied onely by the eare)':[58] these were plays taken, as sermons had been, against their author's will and, as Heywood emphasizes, not from any kind of written text, but from heard performance.

Other playwrights articulated in more roundabout ways their fear that what started as (shorthand) notes might end up as illegitimate printed text. John Webster writes a dialogue exchange concerning note-taking at court in *The Devils Law-Case*. 'You must take speciall care, that you let in / No *Brachigraphy* men, to take notes', says Sanitonella, explaining that the result will be 'scurvy pamphlets, and lewd Ballets'; his notion was that shorthand led to distasteful publication.[59]

Printed plays, however, do not habitually articulate the varying processes that brought them to the press, as sermons do, so it is harder to identify noted texts amongst them. This is partly because a company, rather than a playwright, was likely to 'own' a play manuscript – meaning that playbooks generally reached the press without authorial paratexts; they were, as one 1607 writer put it, usually 'published without Inscriptions unto particular Patrons (contrary to Custome in divulging other Bookes)'.[60] Nevertheless 'corrected' playtexts were sometimes released, presumably by companies, in the wake of errant ones: *Romeo and Juliet* Q2 explains on its title-page that it is 'newly corrected, augmented, and amended' (1599), thus casting aspersions on the previous text – a practice that also worked well as advertising: *I Henry IV* used it even though simply reprinting the earlier edition. Such printed title-pages are reminiscent of that for Henry Smith's rectified [*The*] *Affinitie of the Faithfull*, 'Nowe the second time Imprinted, corrected, and augmented' (1591). *Hamlet* Q2 is similarly 'Newly imprinted and enlarg'd to almost as much again as it was, according to the true and perfect Copy' (1604), strongly suggesting that *Hamlet* Q1 is defective, and not directly authorial. As to why a company might release a correct text when an incorrect one was doing the rounds – the answer is probably pragmatic: once a text was being sold anyway, it might as well be sold in its most accurate form. Besides, as playhouses were also sites where playbooks (and sermons) were offered for sale, there was some logic in being able to market, to the sitting audience, texts that advertised and promoted the theatre.[61]

The vocabulary used by sermons for illegitimate texts is matched by that adopted by some playtexts – suggesting a similar process is responsible for both. So sermons printed poorly from notes are often depicted as wounded bodies: they are 'maimed copie[s]', texts printed 'with intollerable mutilations', 'lame and unjoynted' or, taking the metaphor further, with 'whole lims cut off at once'.[62] Playtexts employ the same language. Beaumont's '*Philaster*, and *Arethusa*' had been 'mained [sic] and deformed', and then 'laine . . . long a bleeding, by reason of some dangerous and gaping wounds, . . . in the first Impression'.[63] Heminges and Condell, introducing Shakespeare's Folio, even adopt the 'limbless' metaphor when describing the earlier quartos (including *Hamlet* Q1, though they appear to extend their blame to all previous publications): '(before) you were abus'd with . . . copies, maimed, and deformed by the frauds and stealthes of injurious impostors, . . . those, are now offer'd to your view cur'd, and perfect of their limbes'.[64] As this vocabulary makes clear, the errant sermons and plays are damaged ('wounded') versions of the whole works

---

[58] Thomas Heywood, *The Rape of Lucrece* (1608), A2r.
[59] John Webster, *The Devils Law-case* (1623), H1v.
[60] *The Statelie Tragedie of Claudius Tiberius Nero* (1607), A3r.
[61] See Stern, 'Watching as Reading', pp. 136–59.
[62] *The True and Perfect Copie of a Godly Sermon* (1575), A1v; L. S., *Resurgendum* (1593), A3r; John Andrewes, *The Brazen Serpent* (1621), A3v; Henry Smith, *The Benefite of Contentation* (1591), A2r.
[63] Francis Beaumont, *Philaster* (1622), A2r.
[64] 'To The Great Variety of Readers', in William Shakespeare, *Comedies, Histories and Tragedies* (1623), A3r.

with which they are compared – they are, then, not described as preparatory drafts by authors, or direct transcriptions, but poor descendants of better, complete texts.

How such mangled texts reached the printer is also much more clearly addressed in sermons than in plays – though, again, shared vocabulary gestures towards a shared process. John White was forced into print when he learned his sermons were in danger of 'stealing out at a back dore', his comment playing on the double meaning of 'stealing' – surreptitiously creeping and being pilfered.[65] Later in time, friends of the Archbishop of Canterbury were outspoken on the subject: they fronted his sermons with a warning against versions published 'surreptitiously' and explained their origins:

Whereas several *Sermons* of His Grace *JOHN* late Lord Archbishop of *Canterbury*, Imperfectly taken from Him in *Short-hand*, may be surreptitiously Printed: This is to give Notice, That there is nothing of His Grace's design'd for the Press at present.[66]

It is that same vocabulary that is used, most famously, for Shakespeare's First Folio. There Heminges and Condell compare the 'cured' texts they are printing with the 'diverse stolne, and surreptitious copies' that have preceded them.[67] Though this passage is still variously interpreted – Heminges and Condell are at the very least exaggerating for publication purposes, as they actually use some of the preceding quartos as copy – they are nevertheless assuming a process of 'stealing' plays with which the reader will identify. Humphrey Mosley, the publisher, does likewise. In his edition of Beaumont and Fletcher's *Comedies and Tragedies*, he draws a distinction between the '*Spurious* or *impos'd*' preceding texts and what he is now printing, 'Originalls', which 'I had . . . from . . . the *Authours* themselves'.[68] Other plays claim to have been printed in a rush to forestall the publication of poor-quality stolen texts. The 1655 tragedy *Imperiale* was put in print 'chiefly to prevent a surreptitious publication intended from an erroneous Copy' – 'erroneous' again suggesting lack of authority in the circulating text.[69] The 1620 comedy *The Merry Milkmaids*,

meanwhile, had not been intended for a readership at all. 'Had not false Copies travail'd abroad', explains its introduction, 'this had kept in'; the play itself had been designed 'more for the Eye, then the Eare; lesse for the Hand, then eyther', the 'hand' berated here seemingly, as with sermons, that of the person who rendered performance into text.[70]

Theatres and churches were both sites of 'entertainment' for which entrance fees could be charged. Huygens describes a 1650s church in Covent Garden 'divided into boxes, just like a place where comedies are performed' for which 'Before one enters . . . one must pay a fee according to the position of the seat', and John Hurlebutt was given the right to charge entrance fees to Paul's Cross 'due . . . by use and ancient Custome'. Thus it would not be surprising if the noting that both encouraged led to publication too.[71] A congregation/audience, attending an entertainment it had paid for, may have felt it had purchased its experience, and had a right to 'take' it.

Given the longhand and shorthand notes taken in churches and theatres, seemingly in similar fashion and for similar reasons, it is worth exploring whether *Hamlet* Q1 might have its origins in a 'noted' text.

NOTE TRACES IN *HAMLET* Q1

How can 'note-taking' be recognized in a printed text? Scholars who look for a particular form of shorthand in Shakespeare's plays are often unconvincing: they have to spot shorthand behind a

---

[65] John White, *Two Sermons* (1615), A3r.
[66] John Tillotson, *The Last Sermon* (1695), A1v.
[67] 'To The Great Variety of Readers', A3r.
[68] 'The Stationer to the Readers', Beaumont and Fletcher, *Comedies and Tragedies* (1647), A4r. David Scott Kastan, *Shakespeare and the Book* (Cambridge, 2001), p. 77, argues that Heminges, Condell and Moseley enact 'the classic "before and after" advertiser's strategy' and cannot be taken as definitive accounts of the early texts themselves.
[69] *Imperiale, a Tragedy* (1655), A2r.
[70] John Cumber, *The Two Merry Milke-Maids* (1620), A2r.
[71] Huygens, *English Journal*, p. 55; Morrissey, *Politics and the Paul's Cross Sermons*, pp. 8–9.

printed, longhand word, and become loyal to a single brand of shorthand, ignoring the fact that longhand, or shorthands that no longer exist, may have been used by the audience. So this section will eschew shorthand itself, though its presence in a noted text is likely. Instead, it will look for the techniques taught around shorthand: 'swift writing'. These include methods for taking orations verbatim, and methods for taking them by contraction or summary. Comparison will, again, be made with 'noted' sermons. Can 'swift writing' be found in *Hamlet* Q1?

For catching words 'swiftly' as they were spoken 'verbatim', every manual advised noting by synonyms. Indeed, some early shorthand forms, like charactery and brachygraphy, depended on synonyms: in those systems, the noter learned a general symbol that stood for a noun – say, 'air' – and then placed a letter by that symbol to describe what variety it took: so 'air' plus 'b' would be 'breath', and 'air' plus 'm' would be 'mist'. Alternatively, as Bales put it, one was simply to 'take such a word in your [brachygraphy] Table as your selfe shall thinke to come . . . neere unto it . . . which words of like sense are called Synonimies'.[72] Other, later, systems, which were phonetic, and thus more directly related to longhand, still encouraged synonyms. W. Folkingham, for instance, thought there was 'good purpose' in substituting short words for long, recommending that instead of 'assistance, renowne, unadvised, communication' the noter opt for the shorter words 'ayde, fame, rash, talke'.[73]

Hamlet Q1 is known for its synonyms; commentators are often puzzled to see one word quite needlessly replaced by another. Q2/F's 'did sometimes march' is Q1's 'did sometimes / Walke', Q2/F's 'this marvile to you' is Q1's 'this wonder to you', Q2/F's 'a clout uppon that head' is Q1's 'a kercher on that head'. Sometimes almost every word is matched by a synonym, as when Q2/F's 'the first rowe of the pious chanson / will showe you more' is Q1's 'the first verse of the godly Ballet / Wil tel you all'. Synonyms, necessary for charactery and brachygraphy, and recommended by subsequent systems, would explain this habit of replacing words, and would explain, too, why the poetic

flourishes of Q2/F are often reduced or simplified by synonyms – as when Q2/F's 'My pulse, as yours, doth temperately keepe time' is, in Q1, 'my pulse doth beate like yours'. For an actor-pirate, trained to remember a text by sound and rhythm, a synonym is less obvious than the correct word; for a note-taker, however, synonyms are a habit of thought long learned and regularly advised in swift-writing systems.

Another aid to writing 'verbatim' was to note only so much of a word as was necessary to recall the whole. Bales suggests, 'take the two first letters of everie name, and so commit the rest to memorie'.[74] Again, one of the striking features of *Hamlet* Q1 is that, aside from entirely different names ('Corambis' and 'Montano' are covered in the conclusion to this article), many of its names recall the ones in Q2/F but are slightly different – Q2/F's Cornelius is Cornelia, its Voltemand is Voltemar, its Rosencrantz and Guildenstern are Rossencraft and Guilderstone; where, in Q2/F 'Sceneca cannot be too heavy, nor *Plautus* too light', in Q1 it is 'Plato' who cannot be 'too light', despite the fact that Plato was not a playwright. Of course, names at the time admitted of fluid spellings. Nevertheless, if an actor-pirate was playing Voltemand, it is surprising that, in addition to misrecalling his entrance in the last scene, he also cannot remember his name.

Another trick to help with verbatim writing was to 'rest' while rhyme was spoken. John Willis, in 1602, reminded the noter that he could omit 'the ende of a line answering in sound the end of some other line'.[75] That was because the rhyme itself would prompt and recall the other, matching, half. Again, *Hamlet* Q1 seems to bear traces of this: it is striking how often in that text one half of a rhyming couplet is presented with relative accuracy, while the other half differs entirely. Examples include the King's rhyming couplet that in Q2/F describes his inability to pray: as his guilt remains unexpiated,

[72] Peter Bales, *The Writing Schoolemaster* (1590), C3r.
[73] W. Folkingham, *Brachygraphie, Post-writt* (1622), p. 23.
[74] Bales, *Writing*, C3r.
[75] John Willis, *The Art of Stenographie* (1602), D4r.

only the sound, not the content, of his words can reach heaven.

> My words fly up, my thoughts remaine belowe
> Words without thoughts never to heaven goe.

In Q1, however, the King is unable to pray because God has taken against him:

> My wordes fly up, my sinnes remaine below.
> No King on earth is safe, if Gods his foe.

The rhyme, entirely against the tenor of the rest of the King's prayer, is preceded by the only semi-accurate line of the whole supplication ('My wordes fly up . . .'); it appears to have been collected in a different fashion from its surrounding dialogue, and rules for noting might explain why. Likewise Hamlet's lines in Q2/F refer to the Herculean task of restraining Laertes (while perhaps metatheatrically gesturing towards the Globe, the sign of which was Hercules shouldering the world):

> Let *Hercules* himself doe what he may,
> The Cat will mew, and Dogge will have his day.

In Q1 these are recorded as:

> I never gave you cause: but stand away,
> A Cat will meaw, a Dog will have a day.

As Laertes is already standing, and as it is Hamlet who then sweeps out, 'stand away' seems to have been brought about to fit the rhyme rather than for its meaning. (The capture of the second line here may reflect the fact that only the rhyme revealed with certainty that a couplet was being spoken.)

Note-taking, too, is suggested by aural errors in *Hamlet* Q1, for it would be surprising if an actor-pirate, shrewd enough about sense to recall synonyms, is also ignorant enough about sense to recall entirely wrong words that sound similar – whereas, as Willis warns, a noter might easily 'write one word instead of another, & take one word for another', particularly as it can be hard to think while capturing text verbatim.[76] Obvious aural errors include the fact that 'Norway' who in Q2/F is '**impotent** and bedred', is in Q1 '**impudent** / And bed-rid'; in Q2/F 'The Gloworme shewes the **matine** to be neere', while in Q1 'the Glo-worme

shewes the **Martin** To be neere'; in Q2/F 'Who this had seene, with tongue **in venom steept**', while in Q1 'Who this had seene with tongue **invenom'd speech**'. Amongst further examples that might be aural error are Q2/F's 'we did thinke it **writ downe** in our dutie / To let you knowe of it' which in Q1 is 'wee did thinke it **right done**, / In our dutie to let you know it'; J. P. Collier, however, himself a shorthand writer, pointed out that 'rt dn' would be alphabetic shorthand for both – it was, indeed, this instance that led him to conclude that *Hamlet* Q1 was a shorthand text.[77]

Sometimes in *Hamlet* Q1 there seem to be traces of memorial corruption. That, too, can be ascribed to note-taking, however, for when a speaker was 'very swift of deliverie', the noter was advised to 'write only the . . . Wordes essentiall to the speech delivered, reserving a space for the rest . . . to be supplied with Penne immediately after the speech is ended'.[78] There is no suggestion, then, that noting precludes memory – and, indeed, John Willis, as well as inventing stenography, also wrote a text on *The Art of Memory* (1621); for him stenography was memorialization in note form.

Often, in *Hamlet* Q1, a correct word is in the correct place in the play – but its meaning is different, as though it has been recorded 'verbatim', but the space surrounding it has been completed using inadequate memory later. Thus, there is the moment where 'course' in Q2/F means 'corpse', while in Q1 it means 'route' or 'movement forward', suggesting the word was marooned and a context has later been invented to house it:

> . . . tis a fault to heaven,
> A fault against the dead, a fault to nature,
> To reason most absurd, . . . who still hath cryed
> From the first **course**, till he that died to day
> This must be so . . . (Q2/F)
> It is a fault gainst heaven, fault gainst the dead,
> A fault gainst nature, and in reasons

---

76 Willis, *Abreviation*, A2v.
77 J. Payne Collier, '*The Edition Of 'Hamlet' In 1603*', *Athenaeum* (4 October 1856), 1220. I am grateful to Zachary Lesser for supplying this reference.
78 Willis, *Stenographie* (1602), E3v.

Common **course** most certaine,
None lives on earth, but hee is borne to die. (Q1)

Likewise, there is the section of Q2/F in which 'grave' means 'serious', and its matching section in Q1, where 'grave' remains *in situ* though context now renders it 'sepulchre' (here it is equally possible, of course, that the word 'grave' was 'correctly' guessed at through rhyme):

now most still, most secret, and most **grave**,
Who was in life a most foolish prating knave. (Q2/F)

Come sir, I'le provide for you a **grave**,
Who was in life a foolish prating knave. (Q1)

In the famously muddled text of 'To be or not to be', meanwhile, though in Q2/F Hamlet fears 'The undiscover'd country, from whose **borne** [frontier/terminus] / No travailer returnes'; in *Hamlet* Q1 he fears the moment 'when wee awake, / And **borne** [carried] before an everlasting Judge'. As these and other instances suggest, 'the judicious Wryter' (the noter) has made 'what hee had overtaken, to coheare, the best hee could'.[79] While an actor is likely to remember a word *because* he remembers its context, rather than entirely separately from it, a writer might easily find him or herself with a tablebook containing a stranded word without its surrounding logic.

Books of shorthand, having devoted some pages to teaching the 'verbatim' capture of words, then teach a contrary skill. They show how meaning may be preserved when none of the original words are kept. 'For, The great triangled Iland in the West' suggests Willis, 'write England.'[80] Often, they suggest that a lengthy idea can be reduced to its quintessential meaning or 'epitome' – which can have a particularly devastating effect on poetry, as one of Willis's contractions illustrates. He starts with the full text, supplying a passage from Spenser's *Faerie Queene*:

At last the gold Orientall gate,
Of greater Heaven gan to open faire,
And Thebus fresh, as Bridegroome to his mate,
Came daunsing foorth shaking his deawie haire,
And hurles his glistering beames through gloomie aire.

He suggests it can be 'Contracted thus: At last the Sunne arose'.[81] Willis's expectation that a 'noter' will need to contract verse anticipates, of course, a listener hearing a lot of poetry (a reader can copy verse verbatim). A play is the most obvious event at which noters are deluged with verse.

At various points, *Hamlet* Q1 appears to show contraction, its poetic lists being often reduced to bland summaries of their contexts. In Q2/F Gertrude describes how Ophelia came to the willow with 'fantastique garlands' consisting of:

Crowflowers, Nettles, Daises, and long Purples
That liberall Shepheards give a grosser name,
But our cull-cold maydes doe dead mens fingers call
  them.

In that same passage in *Hamlet* Q1 she explains how Ofelia came 'Having made a garland of sundry sortes of floures'. Here an actor might be expected to recall the elongated 'long Purples', the bawdy 'grosser name', or the prescient 'dead mens fingers'. But a summarizer, using the rules of contraction, reduces the text irrespective of verbal texture. Of the same kind is the section that in Q2/F reads:

Is it not monstrous that this player heere
But in a fixion, in a dreame of passion
Could force his soule so to his owne conceit
That from her working all the visage wand,
Teares in his eyes, distraction in his aspect,
A broken voyce, and his whole function suting
With formes to his conceit; and all for nothing,
For Hecuba.

In Q1 this reads, 'Why these Players here draw water from eyes: / For Hecuba'. These Q2/F lines in particular, might be expected to stick in the mind of an actor, for they are about the trade of playing; for a contracting noter, however, they breezily summarize the sense, though not the emotions, of the discourse.

Other passages that bespeak a noter are stage directions. Well-known unique and elaborate stage

---

[79] David Dickson, *A Short Explanation, of the Epistle of Paul to the Hebrewes* (1635), π3v.
[80] Willis, *Stenographie* (1602), E3r.
[81] Willis, *Stenographie* (1602), F1v.

directions in Q1 supply or record visually striking details of the production – '*Enter the ghost in his night gowne*', '*Enter Ofelia playing on a Lute, and her haire downe singing*'. These seem to preserve the experience of watching *Hamlet*, at least as much as they tell actors what to do. Indeed, so conscious is the *Hamlet* Q1 text of visual happenings on stage that actions sometimes end up recorded as part of the dialogue: Hamlet says to his mother in the closet that he'll talk to her 'but first weele make all safe'; a Q1 only line, this seems to indicate that Hamlet checks and perhaps locks the door. Action, written down, seems also to be visible when the Queen reports, using the historic present, how Hamlet 'throwes and tosses me about', a recollection of the lurid closet scene we have just seen, and also unique to Q1.

Even the play's frequent mislineation is more easily traced to a noter than an actor. A noter trying to capture rapid spoken text, would probably take down the words as spoken, without recording line-division at all; an actor, whose skill relied on his choice of 'pointing' using correct pronunciation and emphases, is likely to have been conscious of line endings – he needed to observe, particularly, when they were enjambed – which would have been an aid to memorization.

How, though, to explain the larger oddities of *Hamlet* Q1: the fact that the order of *Hamlet* Q1 is different from the order of Q2/F? That might, of course, reflect the version of the play that Q1 records. Yet significant reordering is a feature of noted sermons, explained by the fact that the noter wants to preserve as much text as possible, but has not always recorded how it connects together. 'Although the Pen-man' of Philips's *Certaine Godly and Learned Sermons* 'in setting downe these Sermons, have not precisely kept the divisions of them . . . as placing more in some one Sermon then was uttered at one time, and lesse in some other: yet in the whole . . . thou shalt find nothing wanting'.[82]

Some of the transposed sections in *Hamlet* Q1 seem to have been resituated with what might be a noter's logic. Material of a similar kind tends to be pooled together. Hamlet's conversation with Ophelia about the jig-maker and the hobby-horse,

for instance, is not spoken before the dumbshow (as in Q2/F), but is incorporated into their similar, later conversation about 'the puppets dallying' after the entry of Lucianus. Hamlet's comparison of Rosencrantz to a sponge, which in Q2/F is in 4.2, in Q1 follows from his equivalent lecture to Guildenstern about the recorder. A similar explanation may even account for the play's largest transposition. In Q2/F, the 'to be or not to be' speech and its subsequent nunnery scene occur after the arrival of the players at court; in Q1 they are placed a day earlier, just before the 'fishmonger' scene. The problem *may* arise from an attempt to group like with like again. In Q2/F Hamlet enters the stage for the 'fishmonger' scene with a book in his hands; later, Ophelia is 'loosed' to Hamlet with a book in her hands for 'to be or not to be' and nunnery scene. Q1, however, introduces Hamlet with his book, immediately flanked by Ophelia and her book; matching book with book may be the cause for the scene's new placement – perhaps prompted by the fact that Polonius, in all texts, has said that he will go with Ophelia 'to the king', even though in Q2/F he then actually goes to the court by himself. Immediate fulfilment of what Polonius had promised, by means of two bookish tragic heroes, may be the cause for this transposition.

Additions, too, were usual in noted texts, heard of in sermons both when the noter boasts that he or she will not need to have recourse to them – 'I have added nothing of mine owne'; 'what is . . . by mee published under his name, shall not be . . . made up with additions, and alterations of my owne' – and in sermons when the noter feels addition is appropriate: '*we let these Sermons passe forth as they were delivered by himselfe, in publicke, without taking that libertie of adding or detracting, which, perhaps, some would have thought meete*'.[83] Yet the comparison of sermons to patchworks reveals that passages between notes were often the noter's creation: 'coppies of this Sermon, . . . were . . . (patched as it seemeth) out of some borrowed notes'; 'in some places the

---

82 Philips, *Certaine Godly and Learned Sermons*, A8v.
83 Richard Sibbs and John Davenport in John Preston, *The Saints Daily Exercise* (1629), A2v.

minde of the Author [is] obscured, in other some the sentences [are] unskilfully patched together'.[84] *Hamlet* Q1 can most obviously be seen to be a series of notes stitched together when it uses poetic lines from other plays to solder its gaps. Laertes in *Hamlet* Q1 says 'Revenge it is must yeeld this heart releefe', which picks up Hieronimo's lines in *The Spanish Tragedy* 'in revenge my hart would finde releefe';[85] Corambis' wise saw in Q1, 'Such men often prove, / Great in their wordes, but little in their love', repeats Viola's sentiment in *Twelfth Night*, 'We men' who 'Prove / much in our vowes, but little in our love' (TLN 1005–7); even the oft-derided 'To be, or not to be, I there's the point' may echo a crucial line in *Othello*, Iago's 'I, there's the point' (TLN 1855). A noter who has records of several productions has reason to be conscious of their similarities; an actor may have various productions in his head – but needs to observe their differences to avoid switching the performance to the wrong play.

Other *Hamlet* Q1 additions consist of the same line repeated over and over again. 'To a nunnery go', for instance, becomes something of a refrain in the nunnery scene, which speaks to its power as a phrase, but which again argues against an actor-pirate, whose consciousness of 'parts' is likely to have mitigated against a text that would yield Ofelia a 'virtually unplayable' part like this:[86]

─────────────────────[never] [loved] you.
You made me beleeve you did.
─────────────────────[a] [Nunnery] goe.
O heavens secure him!
─────────────────────[Wher's] [thy] father?
At home my lord.
─────────────────────[a] [Nunnery] goe.
Help him good God.
─────────────────────[a] [Nunnery] goe.
Alas, what change is this?
─────────────────────[a] [Nunnery] goe.
Pray God restore him.
─────────────────[a]   [Nunnery]   goe.
                                            exit.
Great God of heaven, what a quicke change is this?

Larger additions in *Hamlet* Q1 simplify the play and are partly responsible for its short length. In the most major addition, Horatio relates to the Queen a letter he has received telling of Hamlet's escape from the ship taking him to England. The Queen then declares her disillusionment with the King and loyalty to Hamlet. This addition compresses 4.6 and 5.2, dispenses with some additional characters, and makes the Queen, who 'was the character that lent itself most readily to . . . simplification with the least loss of subtlety', less complex and more sympathetic.[87] This section, then, may have been designed; on the other hand, it may have been created to fill a gap, as the Queen then does nothing to substantiate her new allegiances, and the play returns to the plot of Q2/F again.

Finally, *Hamlet* Q1 is filled with gaps, in which sections are so clearly missing that 'some passages in Q1 make sense only to someone familiar with Q2 or F, a clear indication that Q1 was derived from a longer version'.[88] Examples include the moment when Horatio says 'Heere my lord' though Hamlet hasn't called for him; the moment when 'the flood' is seen to 'beckle [beetle?] ore his bace into the sea' (because the line about 'the dreadful summit of the cliff' is missing); the moment when Hamlet forces the king to drink the wine, 'here lies thy union here', though the king has never thrown a union into the cup. Gaps, it will hardly be surprising to discover, are features of noted sermons. Smith's *Benefite* had been 'abused in Printing, as it were with whole lims cut off at once, and cleane left out'; and Rich recorded how regularly noters 'in the midst of discourse, when the tongue of the Speaker hath out-run the pen of the Writer . . . strike saile and lie becalm'd, not knowing where to stay, nor which way to goe'.[89] As a whole, then, what Gouge said about troubles in the

---

[84] Henry Smith, *The Wedding Garment* (1590), A2r; Henry Smith, *The Pride of King Nabuchadnezzer* (1591), A2r.

[85] Thomas Kyd, *Spanish Tragedie* (1592), D3v.

[86] Menzer, *The Hamlets*, p. 65.

[87] Giorgio Melchiori, '*Hamlet*: The Acting Version and the Wiser Sort', in Clayton, *Hamlet First Published*, p. 202.

[88] Kathleen Irace, 'Origins and Agents of Q1 *Hamlet*', in Clayton, *Hamlet First Published*, p. 91.

[89] Smith, *Benefite* (1591), A2r; Jeremiah Rich, *Semigraphy, or, Arts Rarity* (1654), p. 3.

worst recorded sermons could also be said about some sections of *Hamlet* Q1:

Many have beene much wronged...by the Short-writers omissions, additions, mis-placings, mistakings. If severall Workes of one and the same Author (but some published by himselfe, and others by an Exceptor) be compared together, they will easily be found in matter and manner as different, as Works of different Authors.[90]

What is extraordinary about *Hamlet* Q1, however, is not that it is universally 'bad', but that it is not. *Hamlet* Q1 consists of relatively accurate 'verbatim' noting early on, and relatively inaccurate generalized noting later – with the odd 'verbatim' passage again. It is as though the noter is sharp and obtuse, fast and slow, led by the word and led by the meaning. But explanations for that, too, can be supplied, first by looking at performers, and second by looking at noting habits.

Firstly, the clarity of the performer affected the quality of the notes. As Willis presents the problem in dialogue:

Schol. May we be able to take any mans speech verbatim by this Art?

Mast. No. If the speaker be of a treatable and sober delivery, we may write after him verbatim: if hee be slow of speech, we may write faster then hee can speake: but if he be of a swift volubility of tongue, then we cannot doe it; but must...content our selves to take the substance of his speech.[91]

Preachers whose texts had been inadequately represented, often attributed the problem to their own fluency. Egerton maintains that 'the swiftest hand commeth often short of the slowest tongue', though 'often' allows for the remote possibility that some writers may keep up. Nevertheless, he stresses his point by explaining how his own words have been imperfectly 'penned' despite the fact that he is 'constrained thorough the straightnes of my breast, & difficulty of breathing, to speake more laysurely then most men doe'.[92] 'R.C.', a noter, excuses his own inadequacies by asking 'what hand or memorie can follow so fast the fluent speech of an eloquent Preacher, as to set downe all in the same forme and elegancie wherein it is delivered?'[93]

What that actually meant was that a speaker would impact the accuracy of the noter – always bearing in mind that ambient and background noise might also affect his ability to be heard. James I, for instance, slowed one of his speeches to parliament: 'because I see many writing and noting I will hold you a little longer by speaking the more distinctly for fear of mistaking'; Perkins the preacher 'observed his auditors, and so spake, as a diligent Barve [sic: 'Brave'] might write verbatim al that was spoken'.[94] Some players will, in their natures, and some by choice, have spoken more slowly and distinctly than others. At least one reason why some speeches, and some characters – in order of accuracy, Lucianus, Prologue, 'Voltemar', Marcellus, Barnado, Ghost – are more clearly captured than others may be that the speakers themselves were louder or clearer.

Noting habits, however, also affected the quality of the record. The swifter the hand, the more it could take, obviously. Cupper's sermons were 'mangeled...according to the slow hand...of him that tooke them'; Sabine Staresmore, the noter of Ainsworth's sermons, writes 'so farr as my slow hand could extend to compasse' explaining 'the fullnes of his words I professe not to report'.[95]

There was, however, an obvious solution to the problem of slow noters, and troubled hearing: more notes. Noters, for this reason, often combined their various texts. One reporter of a parliamentary speech, for instance, described the way he sought further notes to improve his own: 'I did diligently employ my tables, and made use of the like collection of two gentlemen of the lower house who had better brains and swifter pens than I.'[96] In this instance, one putatively 'slow' and two putatively 'fast' texts were combined, though each had been separately penned. A similar

---

90 William Gouge, *A Recovery from Apostacy* (1639), A3r.

91 Willis, *Stenography* (1628), A5r.

92 Egerton, *A Lecture*, A5v.

93 'R.C.', in Dod, *Bright Star*, A2r-A2v.

94 Kyle, *Theater of State*, p. 67; Perkins, *Satans Sophistrie*, A8v.

95 Cupper, *Certaine Sermons*, A7r; Henry Ainsworth, *Certain Notes* (1630), A6r.

96 Kyle, *Theater of State*, p. 68.

combination is projected by Crashaw when he prints a plea for more good accounts of Perkins's sermons. He requests that:

all who have any *perfect* Coppies of such as are in my *owne handes*, that they would either helpe *me* with theirs, or rather take *mine* to helpe them. That by our joynt powers and our forces layd together: the walles of this worthy building, may goe up the fairer & the faster.[97]

Sometimes, alternately, groups of people seem to have arranged to attend a sermon together and combine notes afterwards. Symon Presse dedicates his 1596 sermon 'To his loving parishioners Mr. F. Cooke, R. Johnson, W. Walton, R. Knight, J. Gyllyver, & R. Slygh', because the six men have conjointly taken such 'paines in conferring together', and 'penning . . . to make my simple skill liked'.[98] If a group attended together, intending to share their work later, they could distribute the task of note-taking between them, either noting in relay, or divvying up features like structure and content according to their skills. In an intense version of this, orphans in 1690s Germany were told to transcribe 10–12 words of a sermon in turn; the whole was then reconstructed from their notes later.[99]

If *Hamlet* Q1 is a text combined from the notes of two or more people, then the reason for its 'good' earlier section, and poor later sections is explained: they bespeak two or more separate noters, the early 'good' one being more given to verbatim methods of copying, and perhaps using good longhand or phonetic shorthand, the later, less good one (or more) tending towards contraction and epitome, and perhaps reliant on less good longhand or pictorial shorthand. The sudden good speeches later would then be traceable either to actors who spoke more clearly, or to a noter supplying freestanding verbatim 'passages' to be combined with someone else's 'whole' text later. There are certainly reasons for thinking *Hamlet* Q1 a combination of different people's work, rather than a text made by one person. Some sections are 'right', then 'wrong', and then 'right' again, as when the internal dumbshow consists of 'the King and the Queene', while the play it flanks calls the same people 'the Duke and Dutchesse', though in that play Lucianus is still described as 'nephew to the King'. A combined text would explain how this, and similar right/wrong moments, came about – not least because, as in Q2 'Gonzago is the Duke's name', a version of the play visited by one of the noters might have had a Duke and Duchess instead of a King and Queen.

It should also be remembered that amongst the noters of a combined text just might be a 'memorizer'. Willis, in his book on memory, writes of 'divers unlettered persons' who can 'retaine much more then the . . . Penman',[100] and a few of *Hamlet* Q1's signs of memory may relate to such a person – though too many features of *Hamlet* Q1 recall the note-taking process to explain the whole text as the product of audience-memory. Jesús Tronch-Pérez, for instance, writes a thoughtful article in which he examines the relationship between the suspect 'memorized' text of Lope de Vega's *La Dama Boba* and the actual text, comparing it to the relationship between *Hamlet* Q1 and Q2/F; he finds *Hamlet* Q1 oddly lacking in the signs of memory that typify *La Dama Boba*.[101]

Combined texts naturally required an 'amender' to massage the various scripts together. The printers of one 1623 sermon, for instance, are amenders: having received a text 'miserably written', they did what they could to make sense of it: 'Being loth, to leave out any sentence, or piece of a sentence, which we could make English of, we put some words downe at a venture.'[102] More often amenders were fans of the original text, and tried to create as accurate a representation of it as possible. Rollock's 1619 sermons were gathered by Sir William Scott of Ely 'from the handes of *SCHOLLERS*, that wrote them: and by your exspenses they were written over and over againe:

---

97 Perkins, *Exhortation to Repentance*, *8v.

98 Symon Presse, *A Sermon Preached at Eggington* (1596), A1v.

99 Ann Blair, 'The Rise of Note-taking in Early Modern Europe', *Intellectual History Review*, 20 (2010), 303–16.

100 William Basse, *A Helpe to Memory* (1630), B1v.

101 Jesús Tronch-Pérez, 'A Comparison of the Suspect Texts of Lope de Vega's *La Dama Boba* and Shakespeare's *Hamlet*', *Shakespeare Yearbook*, 13 (2002), 30–57.

102 Samuel Hieron, *Aarons Bells a-Sounding* (1623), 2***v.

without you they had never beene revised and corrected: without you they had not beene made meet for the *PRESSE*'; John Preston's 1629 sermons, taken from his mouth, are then 'prepared' by those 'that had the Coppies'; others who possess notes are asked not to 'be hastie . . . to publish them, till we, whom the Author put in trust, have perused them'.[103]

An 'amender' has long been imagined for *Hamlet* Q1, usually denigrated by the term 'hack' or 'inferior poet'. And, as Q1 is a play rather than a sermon, such a person will have been able to visit the theatre more than once, though the fact that there were no play runs in the period, added to the level of corruption in Q1, may suggest he/she did not attend many times. Nevertheless, Stephen Urkowitz, as part of a different argument, draws attention to the moment in *Hamlet* Q1 where two questions and two replies seem to have become confused:

King. How now son Hamlet, how fare you, shall we have a play?
Ham. Yfaith the Camelions dish, not capon cramm'd, feede a the ayre.
   I father: My lord, you playd in the Universitie.

He suggests that 'how fare you' is supposed to be followed by 'Yfaith the Camelions dish', and 'shall we have a play' should be followed by 'I ['aye'] father'.[104] An amended text that was something of a palimpsest, with additional moments squeezed in as they were heard, might result in difficulties of this kind – though 'combination' without revisiting the theatre might produce similar results.

On some occasions, the printed play of *Hamlet* Q1 may even gesture towards its method of construction. It has, as is often pointed out, a few sections specifically highlighted by inverted commas – for instance, Corambis' wise saws:

      . . . my blessing with thee
And these few precepts in thy memory.
"Be thou familiar, but by no meanes vulgare;
"Those friends thou hast, and their adoptions tried,
"Graple them to thee with a hoope of steele . . .

These inverted commas have been identified as markers of *sententiae*, drawing the reader's attention to passages primed for extraction into commonplace books. Thus *Hamlet* Q1, in published form, has been said to proclaim itself, through layout, the first 'literary' drama.[105] This is entirely possible. It is equally likely, however, that the lines are marked as coming *from* commonplacing, showing not what a reader should do, but what a noter did. If this is the case, they may illustrate a section supplied by a different noter, or from a separate source, like the passage in Erasmus' *Seven Dialogues* (1606) which 'followeth after this marke *' because it is 'not in Erasmus'.[106] Alternatively, the marks may witness a passage that an amender, revisiting the theatre, observed had been cut. In sermons, inverted commas often signify the least important passages: those not spoken during the preaching – 'I was forced [while preaching] to cut off here and there part of what I had penned: which . . . I here present . . . distinguished from the rest with this note (,,) against the lines.'[107] In the later history of the *Hamlet* text, too, inverted commas signal cuts as they do in playbooks throughout the late seventeenth and eighteenth centuries, the 1676 edition explaining:

THis Play being too long to be conveniently Acted, such places as might be least prejudicial to the Plot or Sense, are left out upon the Stage: but that we may no way wrong the incomparable Author, are here inserted according to the Original Copy with this Mark "[108]

And the lines it chooses for omission? They include:

" . . . my blessing with thee,
"And these few precepts in thy memory
"Look thou character: . . .

---

[103] Rollock, *Five and Twentie Lectures*, π4r; John Preston, *The New Covenant* (1629), A3v.

[104] Steven Urkowitz, 'Back to Basics', in Clayton, *Hamlet First Published*, p. 204.

[105] Zachary Lesser and Peter Stallybrass, 'The First Literary *Hamlet* and the Commonplacing of Professional Plays', *Shakespeare Quarterly*, 59 (2008), 371–420.

[106] Desiderius Erasmus, *Seven Dialogues both Pithie and Profitable* (1606), H3r.

[107] Robert Sanderson, *Two Sermons* (1622), A4r.

[108] William Davenant, *The tragedy of Hamlet, Prince of Denmark* (1676), A2r.

"Be thou familiar, but by no means vulgar:
"Those friends thou hast and their adoption tried,
"Grapple them unto thy soul with hoops of steel . . . [109]

It is possible, then, that the lines in inverted commas are not the most important sections of play, but the least. Whatever is the case, the passages marked by inverted commas in *Hamlet* Q1 reveal some sections to be 'different', but whether that is because of reading habits, or because of gathering habits, depends on who is preparing the text – and what the text is.

One way in which *Hamlet* Q1 seems to flirt with the very idea of noters is in one if its unique passages. In Q1, Hamlet, having complained about the clown who speaks more than is set down for him, illustrates how predictable the clown's 'extemporized' jokes actually are:

> Gentlemen quotes his jeasts downe
In their tables, before they come to the play as thus:
Cannot you stay till I eate my porrige? and, you owe me
A quarters wages: and, my coate wants a cullison . . .

These are jests – actually catchphrases – so obvious that people record them in tablebooks not during but *in advance* of performance. 'Sly' does something similar in the Induction to *The Malcontent*, when he explains that he has 'seene this play often . . . I have most of the jeasts heere in my table-booke'.[110] Maybe this passage is Shakespearian and ironic: the only 'clown' who brings these bad jokes into the play is Hamlet himself. Maybe this is an actor's interpolation designed to level further insults at an irritatingly unoriginal 'improviser'. But perhaps this is a reference to the process that brought *Hamlet* Q1 about. The very jests said to be unfit for a serious play (such as *Hamlet*), and to belong only to tablebooks, enter here into the *Hamlet* text – showing how lines from tablebooks can indeed, with the aid of a noter, become passages of plays.

WHY PUBLISH NOTES?

If *Hamlet* Q1 is a noted text, however, its pathway to the press has to be explained. Why would a noter or noters choose to publish private records – and why might a publisher accept them? Sermons, again, suggest answers to both questions.

There were several self-serving reasons for giving noted texts to the press. One was for the money; it was the noter, rather than the preacher/playwright, who would receive payment. Egerton maintains that 'hungrie Schollers and preposterous noters of Sermons' publish noted texts 'beguiled with hope of gaine', and bemoans the quest for 'filthy lucre' that brought his sermons to print, while William Crashaw wishes that 'men would not be so hastie . . . to commend to the world, their *unperfect notes*, upon a base desire of a little gaine'.[111] If money was the goal of printing *Hamlet* Q1, of course, then, provided the whole work was good enough to sell, it had served its purpose.

Printing notes also enabled the noter to see 'his' words published. John Winston, a noter, disingenuously confesses to having 'nothing of mine owne of any worth whereby to testifie my unfained thankefulness', explaining that 'I have borrowed of others for this purpose, and withal annexed my hand-writing.'[112] That urge to reach print, even without anything to say, could lead noters to add traces of themselves into the noted text. Thomas Taylor criticizes those scribes who 'make the grounds of the authors serve their owne discourses'; and the preacher William Gouge maintains that 'some' had 'attempted in the Authors name to publish their owne notes'.[113] Noters, in these instances, obtrude to bear witness to their hand, or to mingle their words with their hero's. If *Hamlet* Q1 passed through the hands of a noter with 'authorial' leanings, it might record the creativity of its scribe or scribes as well as Shakespeare.

---

[109] Davenant, *Hamlet*, C3r.
[110] John Webster, Induction to John Marston, *The Malcontent* (1604), A3r.
[111] Egerton in Cupper, *Certaine Sermons*, A7r; Egerton, *Lecture*, A3v; 'W. C.' in William Perkins, *Exhortation to Repentance*, *7r-*7v.
[112] John Winston in John Dod, *Ten Sermons* (1609), π4r.
[113] Thomas Taylor in William Perkins, *A Godlie and Learned Exposition* (1606), A4r; William Gouge, *A recovery from apostacy* (1639), A3r.

Even nobler reasons for bringing notes to the press mitigated against their accuracy. Yelverton published Philips's sermons, to 'quicken' the voice of the preacher that would otherwise 'perish in the ayre or in the eare'; 'A.B.' likewise printed Stoughton's sermons because the 'precious labours of godly men . . . are not fit to vanish into the air, or to be buried in obscurity'.[114] But these instances draw attention to the oral nature of the text; what is being trapped is not a text for the page but a performance rendered into words. Printing *Hamlet* Q1, when no one knew any other *Hamlet*s would ever be made public, rescued the play for posterity, but what was being preserved may have been captured utterance; the gaps, segues and startling moments of vivid action that differentiate it from an authorial 'literary' text might in fact be a proud display of its performance heritage.

Many of the reasons for publishing a text from notes, then, were also reasons for inaccuracy. Only if the scribe's noting ability were at issue was a text likely to have accuracy as a goal. Egerton's *Lecture* was brought to the press, said its preacher, 'by one who . . . respected the commendation of his skill in Charracterie, more than the credit of my ministery'; and Tyrrell feared that the youth who wanted to print his sermon 'did it but to shew his skill and cunning in the dexteritie of his owne handewriting'.[115] For such writers, precision may have been important. Indeed, shorthand teachers even seem to have used 'their' texts as advertisements: Burrough's 1654 sermons contain a printed puff for the noter: 'these Sermons have been very happily taken by the pen of a ready writer, Mr. *Farthing*, now a Teacher of Shortwriting'.[116] *Hamlet* Q1, is, however, too varied in quality to be by a single 'good' noter. It could, however, reflect the varying skills of, for example, a teacher flanked by his students learning the noting trade; Phillips some years later, denigrates 'Pamphlets . . . rak'd from the simple collections of Short hand prentices'.[117]

If notes, then, were likely to be inaccurate, and often came without authorial sanction, what made them interesting to publishers? One answer is to do with 'ownership'. As the publisher, not the author, would 'own' the text he had had printed,

his authority residing in his entrance of the text into the Stationers' Register, acquiring and printing a 'bad' copy gave him publishing rights to any subsequent 'good' copy. Preacher Henry Smith grudgingly agreed to 'correct' *The Wedding Garment* and publish it with William Wright, who had issued the text twice already from notes, 'To controll those false coppies of this Sermon, whiche were printed without my knowledge . . . and to stoppe the Printing of it againe without my corrections, as it was intented, because they had gotte it licensed before'.[118] As this makes clear, Smith was obliged to keep Wright as his publisher, because Wright already had the license for Smith's sermon. 'Bad' sermons could flush out good ones. E. Edgar published both Perkins' *Satans Sophistrie Answered* (1604) and 'The second edition much enlarged by a more perfect copie', now named *The Combat betweene Christ and the Divell Displayed* (1606). Andrew Wise, meanwhile, who was fined for publishing Playfere's *A Most Excellent and Heavenly Sermon upon the 23 Chapter of the Gospell by Saint Luke* (1595) without authority (he had not entered it into the Stationers' Register), still became its publisher when that same sermon was set out 'a new' by its preacher and renamed *The Meane in Mourning* (1596). Wise also then published Playfere's *The Pathway to Perfection*, allowing him to add in that text that 'if any one who hath cast away his money upon the former editions [of *Meane in Mourning*], wil bestow a groate upon the true copie now set out by my selfe, hee may have this sermon with it for nothing' – the result being that Wise was able to sell one 'bad' sermon twice while acquiring two separate good texts from Playfere.[119] In all these instances, the first 'bad' text is from notes; the

---

114 H. Yelverton in Philips, *Certaine Godly . . . Sermons*, A5r; 'A.B.' in John Stoughton, *A Forme of Wholsome Words* (1640), A4r.
115 Egerton, *A Lecture*, A3v; Anthony Tyrrell in *A Fruitfull Sermon, Taken by Charracterye* (1589), A6v-A7r.
116 Jeremiah Burroughs, *The Saints Treasury* (1654), A4r.
117 John Phillips, *Sportive Wit* (1656), A3v.
118 Smith, *Wedding Garment*, A2r.
119 Playfere, *Meane in Mourning*, A3r; Playfere, *Pathway*, A3r.

second is authorial. Though the familiar argument is that publishers did not care about the 'goodness' of a text, the fact that they spent money to reprint the texts once they had acquired them in 'good' form suggests something different. Expedience or desire may have led publishers to take on a text in noted form *in order* to force the 'real' version from the author. Most telling in this respect is the fact that publisher Nicholas Ling was able to acquire 'good' sermons and plays through printing 'bad' ones. He produced two editions of Henry Smith's *The Affinitie of the Faithfull* (1591) before publishing [*The*] *Affinitie of the Faithfull . . . the Second Time Imprinted, Corrected, and Augmented*. As Nicholas Ling was also publisher both of *Hamlet* Q1, and the text that responded to it a year later, *Hamlet* Q2 – perhaps, as Melnikoff suggests, financing both as part of his expansion into the world of play publishing[120] – he may have paid for a noted *Hamlet* Q1 in the hope of acquiring *Hamlet* Q2 as a result. If that is so, *Hamlet* Q1, for Ling, is a form of blackmail – and, again, accuracy is not in question here. Indeed, the more inaccurate the text, the more the company is likely to release a corrective.

CONCLUSION

If *Hamlet* Q1 is a noted, audience, text, rather than a text taken by an actor-pirate, how should that affect our understanding of the play? In some ways, what has hitherto been concluded about the play remains unchanged: it is still a 'performance text', though it is no longer a direct one, as it has no relationship to players in the production itself. Nevertheless, it remains as a misty record of staged performance, offering, through its stage directions, additional information about the production. Textual oddities visible through or behind the noting process still remain interesting witnesses to a different moment in the life of *Hamlet*. For instance, when Q1 renders what in Q2/F is '& must th'inheritor himselfe have no more' as 'and must / The honor lie there?' it is obvious that 'honor', which makes no sense, misrepresents the word said on stage, presumably 'owner'. If, however, the noter mishears a word, that also gives us a performance variant, 'owner'

being what the player said, and perhaps, though not necessarily, what Shakespeare once intended. *Hamlet* Q1, here, may preserve the aural experience – the sound and, in mishearing, even the pronunciation – of performance. Other instances, too, seem to record specific performance variants. Polonius is in Q1 called Corambis, and Reynaldo is called Montano. As Hibbard points out, Robert Pullen ('Polenius' in Latin) was Oxford University's founder, and John Reynolds was the President of Corpus Christi College, Oxford: *Hamlet* Q1, the only professional play of the period to boast Oxford performance on its title-page, may record the play, or aspects of the play, in a localized version.[121]

Where differences emerge, if this is a noted play, is in the fact that the text need not be the record of a single performance. One noter may have attended the production on more than one occasion, or several noters might have taken texts on different days of performance, combining them later. The title page of *Hamlet* Q1, which promises the play 'as it hath been diverse times acted' in London, Oxford and Cambridge, already makes an 'incongruous offer of a solitary record of multiple events', and may, then, even broadcast that it is an interposition of several overlaid performances.[122] If that is the case, the playbook represents simultaneously an effort to reconstruct *Hamlet*s in performance and – in its choice of what to capture, what to drop, what to render accurately, and what inaccurately – an interpretation of them.

---

[120] For more on this, see Kirk Melnikoff, 'Nicholas Ling's Hamlet', in *Shakespeare's Stationers* ed. Marta Straznicky (Philadelphia, 2013). Confusingly, John Roberts was first to enter the play into the Stationers' Register; Melnikoff summarizes the reasons why this may have happened.

[121] Hibbard, ed., *Hamlet*, p. 74. As the university is unlikely to have sanctioned performance within its colleges, this play was probably put on at 'the tavern' in Oxford owned by theatre-loving John Davenant. John Aubrey relates that Shakespeare stayed at this tavern and that Davenant's son, William Davenant, claimed to have been sired by Shakespeare, presumably on one such occasion (see John Aubrey's *Brief Lives* ed. Oliver Lawson Dick (London, 1949), pp. 85–8).

[122] Menzer, *The Hamlets*, p. 111.

Finally, if *Hamlet* Q1 is a 'noted' text, then other plays may be too. Noting is not, of course, the only way a text might illegitimately reach the press; copies transcribed by actors or by the playwright's friends clearly sometimes circulated and were published. But the plays that do not seem to be direct transcriptions, and that were once called 'bad quartos', should perhaps be re-examined. We, these days, have eschewed the word 'bad', and have limited to 'suspect' those texts containing obvious features of memory, such as external echoes and internal repetitions − because of a belief that memorial reconstruction was the way they came about. But some of the play quartos that lack significant memorial features, and so have been repatriated as 'good', should perhaps be redefined as 'bad' again − or, rather, not 'bad' but 'noted', created, like their sermon counterparts, from 'broken notes, penned from the mouth . . . mingled perhaps with the weake conceits of some illiterate Stenographer'.[123]

Whatever is the case, this article has argued that *Hamlet* Q1 is less likely to have been taken by an actor-pirate than an audience. That is true of 'pirated' products today, of course. Rogue audiences film blockbusters and put the results on the internet; film stars do not. 'Pirating', these days, is an audience phenomenon. Perhaps it always has been.

---

[123] Jeremiah Dyke, *Divers Select Sermons* (1640), A4v–A5r.

EQUIVOCATIONS: READING THE SHAKESPEARE/MIDDLETON *MACBETH*

CORDELIA ZUKERMAN

I

'Faith, here's an equivocator'   – Porter, *Macbeth*

When Shakespeare's Lady Macbeth walks onstage reading a letter, the audience becomes privy to a complex series of textual collaborations. Although Macbeth has written the letter, its contents include his transcription of others' spoken text: 'All hail, Macbeth! Hail to thee, Thane of Glamis! . . . Thane of Cawdor! . . . that shalt be king hereafter!' (1.3.46–48). That text travelled into Macbeth's letter in the following way: when it first was spoken – by three 'weird sisters' Macbeth did not know – he was unsure how to construe it. Then, upon learning that he had indeed been named Thane of Cawdor, he interpreted the weird sisters' equivocal text as a prophecy – and thus well worth sharing with his wife. So he wrote the letter, filtering the text through his own (editorial?) consciousness and inviting her to (re)read, (re)interpret it. When Lady Macbeth reads the letter onstage, she becomes Macbeth's textual collaborator; after reading it, she determines to take action to make the prophecy it speaks come true. As an independent reader of Macbeth's adaptation of the weird sisters' text, Lady Macbeth therefore plays a critical role in determining that text's meaning: one could argue that through the force of her action and her influence on Macbeth, she author-izes the text as prophecy. Who, then, is the text's author? Who is the author of Duncan's murder? Given how its events unfold, this play suggests that there is no clear singular author. Rather, texts are dynamic entities that are only realized through a series of collaborations among speakers, writers, editors and readers.[1]

In order to explore more fully the kinds of collaborative relationships involved in creating texts, I want to look at how a controversial scholarly edition of *Macbeth* – *The Tragedy of Macbeth*, edited by Gary Taylor for the 2007 Oxford critical edition of *Thomas Middleton: The Collected Works* – calls attention to them and to the reader's collaborative inputs in constructing a text. Relying on extensive scholarship, Taylor's edition attempts to recreate *Macbeth* as Middleton adapted it from Shakespeare's (supposed) 'original'. The editorial decisions Taylor makes and the readerly work the edition invites and requires ultimately demonstrate the centrality of the editor's and the reader's collaborative inputs in the construction of a text.[2]

Earlier versions of this essay were presented at conferences hosted by the Theatre Students of the Graduate Center of the City University of New York in May 2010 and the University of Michigan Early Modern Colloquium in October 2011. I am grateful to the organizers and participants of both events. I also thank Barbara Hodgdon and William Ingram for their generous attention to the manuscript at various stages of preparation.

[1] As D. F. McKenzie argues, since 'forms effect meaning', we should describe 'not only the technical but the social processes of [texts'] transmission . . . their physical forms, textual versions, technical transmission, institutional control, their perceived meanings, and social effects', *Bibliography and the Sociology of Texts* (Cambridge, 1999), p. 13. He adds that 'an author disperses into his collaborators, those who produced his texts and their meanings' (p. 27).

[2] Throughout this essay I use the term 'text' according to the definition that Joseph Grigley provides, whereby a 'work',

The notion that Middleton contributed significantly to *Macbeth* has been accepted in most editorial circles for over a century.[3] According to Taylor, whose textual analysis closely follows the work of prior editors, Middleton was most likely responsible for cutting perhaps as much as a quarter of Shakespeare's original text and for adding a Hecate character and extra scenes with the witches, including two songs that also appear in his play *The Witch*. In Taylor's estimation, these additions amount to about eleven per cent of the adapted text.

Middleton's version has had a long theatrical life, most notably as an important source for William Davenant's 1674 popular adaptation of *Macbeth*, and for Giuseppe Verdi's 1847 opera.[4] Taylor's project in including *Macbeth* in Middleton's *Collected Works* is to point out Middleton's role as a collaborator on and adapter of one of the most famous and popular plays in the English language, and perhaps as the authorial voice that had the most influence on *Macbeth*'s afterlife. If this indeed is the case, Taylor's project has considerable import, not just because it accords Middleton his authorial rights but also because it dismantles some of the historical construction of Shakespeare as an 'autonomous self' and acknowledges, at least in part, the collaborative environment of early modern dramatic production.[5] How Taylor goes about doing this, however, becomes increasingly complicated, for in order to reconstruct one early modern collaborative process, Taylor ends up occluding, even denying, a slew of others.

Taylor calls his version of *Macbeth* a 'genetic' text; the goal of his editorial practice is to allow a reader to trace on her own the way the text changed – evolved, developed – over time.[6] Taylor therefore reconstructs, and distinguishes typographically through two-text editing, the adaptive process that Middleton supposedly pursued with *Macbeth*. In describing how a reader should understand the text's typography, he writes:

Passages apparently added or rewritten by Middleton are printed in bold type; passages apparently deleted or intended for deletion are printed in grey; transposed passages are printed in grey where Shakespeare probably placed them, and in bold where Middleton apparently moved them.[7]

Reading the text, then, becomes a process of mentally adding and deleting passages, sometimes rereading passages that have been moved, and perhaps even flipping through pages to compare the placement of scenes. The unusual typography, with its constant visual reminders to consider Middleton's hand, asks a reader to interrogate the play's structure and analyse the overall effect of

---

such as Shakespeare's *Tempest*, is 'defined by [an] accretion' of textual events of that work: for example, 'a copy of the First Folio represents one text of that work, just as a copy of Knight's illustrated edition is another text. Nor is it necessary to exclude performances from this formulation.' In Grigley's imagining, a work can be thought of in the following way: 'W —> $T_1, T_2, T_3, \ldots T_N$'. Joseph Grigley, *Textualterity: Art, Theory, and Textual Criticism* (Michigan, 1995), p. 100. Here, I consider Taylor's *Macbeth* to be one text of the work *Macbeth*.

[3] Inga-Stina Ewbank writes, 'the consensus of editorial and critical opinion, since the Clarendon edition of 1869, is that there are non-Shakespearean interpolations in the first printed text of *Macbeth*, the 1623 Folio; and recent scholarship points unmistakably to Middleton as the author of these', in 'Introduction', *The Tragedy of Macbeth*, by William Shakespeare and Thomas Middleton, ed. Gary Taylor, in *Thomas Middleton: The Collected Works*, ed. Taylor and John Lavagnino (Oxford, 2007), p. 1165. Not all scholars, however, agree with Taylor's estimation, or indeed his entire editorial project. For example, Brian Vickers, in his scathing review of the Middleton *Macbeth*, systematically rebuts the scholarship that points to Middleton as the adapter of the play: 'Disintegrated', *Times Literary Supplement* 5591 (28 May 2010). Vickers's work, while highly compelling, is not fully relevant to my concerns. I hope to use the Middleton *Macbeth* to make a broader point about the relationship between texts, editors and readers; ultimately the question of whether or not Middleton actually adapted the text is not as important for my project as thinking about how the modern-day editorial process affects texts and readers.

[4] 'Introduction', *Macbeth*, ed. Taylor, p. 1165.

[5] Margreta de Grazia, *Shakespeare Verbatim: The Reproduction of Authenticity and the 1790 Apparatus* (Oxford, 1991), p. 10.

[6] Taylor, 'The Tragedy of Macbeth: A Genetic Text', in *Thomas Middleton and Early Modern Textual Culture*, ed. Taylor and John Lavagnino (Oxford, 2007).

[7] Taylor, ed. *Macbeth*, p. 1170n.

Middleton's changes.[8] Consider the following lines, in which one can see significant differences in the characterization of the witches:

> Banquo.   what are these
> fairies or nymphs **so withered and** so wild in their
> attire   (1.3.37–8)[9]

According to this passage, Shakespeare's original characterization of the witches seems to have been less sinister and more feminized than the characterization that ultimately appeared in the Folio – and that has since influenced countless readers. Moreover, this passage suggests that without Middleton's adaptive hand, the play would have differed significantly in how it imagines and represents the spiritual world.

In highlighting Middleton's raw adaptive process, and reconstructing what (and where) Shakespeare may have written originally, such two-text editing seems invaluable for any reader interested in examining either writer's work or the relationship between the two. However, since no extant manuscripts of *Macbeth* unquestionably identify it as Shakespeare's or Middleton's, this text does not represent Middleton's actual adaptation: rather, it is *Taylor's* adaptation – one based on strong but not irrefutable evidence.[10] Taylor's frequent use of hedge words such as 'probably' and 'apparently' in his editorial apparatus signal the speculative nature of his project. And when he adds never-before-seen material, such as the arrival of Edward the Confessor at the end of the scene between Malcolm and Macduff (4.3), he is careful to label it 'a rough, minimal, and conjectural reconstruction' of a moment that '*might* have been the climax of Shakespeare's scene'.[11] What becomes quite clear to any reader attempting to engage with the Middleton *Macbeth* is that Taylor himself is an adapter who shares a near-equivalent (or perhaps an equivocal) authority with Shakespeare and Middleton.

Taylor's adaptive role does not stop with his reconstructive typographic efforts regarding particular words and scenes. He also makes two important choices that significantly qualify his claim that he is recreating an 'original' text: he modernizes the spelling and omits all punctuation.[12] Both choices – in different ways – attempt to create an unmediated text that resembles, as closely as possible, an 'ideal original text' of Shakespeare and Middleton. Both choices, however, occur at the expense of a historicized understanding of early modern dramatic textual production. Moreover, the text as a whole requires extensive readerly work to fill in important gaps usually filled by editorial fiat: in short, rather than being as unmediated as possible, Taylor's text merely shifts the mediating force from editor to reader. Ultimately, then, the Middleton *Macbeth* demonstrates the impossibility of actually reconstructing a lost text – especially

---

8   This kind of two-text editing is designed to highlight 'the process of adaptation': John Jowett, 'Addressing Adaptation: *Measure for Measure* and *Sir Thomas More*', in Lukas Erne and Margaret Jane Kidnie, eds., *Textual Performances: The Modern Reproduction of Shakespeare's Drama* (Cambridge, 2004), p. 63. For a full discussion, see Jowett's article (pp. 63–76). See also Taylor, 'Genetic Text'.

9   Taylor, ed. *Macbeth*. All subsequent quotations from *Macbeth* are from this edition.

10   Vickers, indeed, has done much to refute this evidence. See his review ('Disintegration'), and the website for the London Forum for Authorship Studies (http://ies.sas.ac.uk/events/seminars/LFAS/index.htm).

11   Taylor, ed. *Macbeth*, p. 1194 (note, emphasis added).

12   Opinions on what is and what is not considered punctuation vary widely: it can be anything from 'marks of punctuation' to 'any and all distinction' between figures on a page. John Lennard, 'Mark, Space, Axis, Function: Towards a (New) Theory of Punctuation on Historical Principles' in *Ma(r)king the Text: The Presentation of Meaning on the Literary Page*. ed. Joe Bray *et al.* (Ashgate, 2000), pp. 4–5; see Lennard's article for a full discussion (pp. 1–11). For the purposes of this essay I follow Taylor's lead when I use the word 'punctuation'. Taylor is primarily concerned with omitting any marks whose presence would fix the text's meaning in a potentially non-authorial way. Therefore, he considers as punctuation, and omits from his text, the following elements: commas, colons, semicolons, exclamation marks, periods, question marks, parentheses, and others of their kind, as well as the capitalization of initial words in verse-lines. Taylor does not omit from his text the following elements: apostrophes, capitalization of names, capitalization of the pronoun 'I', and divisions between verse-lines. The elements he retains do not, in his view, present a threat to the kind of ambiguity he seeks. See Taylor, 'Genetic Text', p. 691. Here, I use the word 'punctuation' to signify the typographic elements that Taylor deliberately omits from his text because of his desire to enhance ambiguity.

when that text may never have existed at all. What it does achieve, by turning the reader into a fellow collaborator, is the kind of fluid, multi-authored textual production that its editorial apparatus seems to deny.

II

'[O]n a forgotten matter we can hardly make distinction of our hands.'
— Maria, *Twelfth Night*

Throughout the editorial apparatus of *Macbeth*, Taylor appears to intuit compositional process – or reimagine it – and to assume knowledge of intentionalities. These assumptions appear to have guided his editorial choices. Taylor writes at length about his choice to modernize spelling and eliminate punctuation, asserting that it is simply impossible to tell what specific preferences Shakespeare and Middleton had in these areas, as opposed to what would have been chosen by others during the publishing process. He writes: 'In the several known stages of the text's transmission and adaptation, there was plenty of opportunity for human error.'[13] Although many people besides the author(s) were involved in the life of any given printed work in the early modern period – including colleagues, scribes, printers and compositors[14] – to call the input of these people 'human error' misrepresents the particularities of early modern textual production.

For in using the term 'human error', Taylor suggests a very particular story about the text of *Macbeth*: it was first written, in its entirety, by William Shakespeare. At some later time, Thomas Middleton came along, took Shakespeare's manuscript, and made changes to it. Then, over the course of the manuscript's life, as it was copied multiple times, sometimes from non-original copies, and finally sent to press, it underwent unauthorized alterations by negligent scribes and compositors, who buried signs of original authorship beneath their own non-authorial spelling and punctuation choices. This story is compelling, especially in a culture like ours that, at least at the popular level, continues to uphold the myth of singular

authorship, idealizing the lone genius who produces, unaided, a 'perfect' text.[15] However, much recent historical work has suggested that the real story is far more complicated.

Recent scholarship has done much towards reconstructing the particularly collaborative environment of early modern theatre and printing houses, in which the idea of a singular authoritative author may not have existed.[16] Margreta de Grazia has demonstrated how the notion of Shakespeare as an individual author was constructed during the Enlightenment through the editorial practices of Edmond Malone, who projected the values of his day onto the playwright whose work he was editing.[17] Peter Stallybrass has argued that early seventeenth-century England did not even have a stable understanding of the word 'individual', much less the notion of an individual author (in our twenty-first-century definition) whose intent mattered down to the details of spelling and punctuation.[18] Moreover, he asserts, 'Instability was inscribed in the material means of reproduction' of texts; in other words, instability was part of the textual process, not an accidental

---

13 Taylor, 'Genetic Text', p. 691.
14 For a discussion of the process of publication from beginning to end, see William Proctor Williams and Craig S. Abbott, 'A Text and Its Embodiments', in *An Introduction to Bibliographical and Textual Studies* (New York, 2009).
15 This is perhaps an oversimplification of contemporary English/American values. Ezra Pound's revisions/adaptations of T. S. Eliot's *The Waste Land* provide one powerful counter-example among many – but, like many oversimplifications, there is some basis for it.
16 For more detailed discussions, see Peter Stallybrass and Margreta de Grazia, 'The Materiality of the Shakespearean Text', *Shakespeare Quarterly*, 44 (1993), 255–83; Jeffrey Masten, *Textual Intercourse: Collaboration, Authorship, and Sexualities in Renaissance Drama* (Cambridge, 1997); Paul Werstine, 'Close Contrivers: Nameless Collaborators in Early Modern London Plays', in *Elizabethan Theatre XV* (Toronto, 2002), pp. 3–20; and Wendy Wall, 'Editors in Love? Performing Desire in *Romeo and Juliet*', in *A Companion to Shakespeare and Performance*, ed. Barbara Hodgdon and W. B. Worthen (Blackwell 2005), pp. 197–211.
17 de Grazia, *Shakespeare Verbatim*.
18 Peter Stallybrass, 'Shakespeare, the Individual, and the Text', in *Cultural Studies*, ed. Lawrence Grossberg, Cary Nelson and Paula A. Treichler (Routledge, 1992), pp. 593–612.

perversion of it that only happened occasionally.[19] Along these lines, Simon Palfrey and Tiffany Stern contend that many early modern plays may never even have existed in single continuous manuscripts before publication, suggesting a high degree of instability as the norm.[20] And Jeffrey Masten argues for 'the presence of more corporate forms of textual production' in the early modern period than we might assume today.[21] These scholars, and others working along the same lines, suggest that the idea of a kind of corporate author, made up of all the people who necessarily worked on a text in the process of its writing and transmission, might be a more appropriate way to understand early modern textual production. In the early modern period, therefore, it seems to have been *expected* that others besides the person who wrote the original manuscript would be involved in the life of the text.

Michel de Montaigne, who wrote and revised his *Essais* in France in the 1570s and 1580s, addressed this idea head-on, writing, 'I do not concern myself with spelling, and simply order them to follow the old style; or with punctuation; I am inexpert in both. He adds that he 'would rather write as many more essays again than subject myself to going over these again for such childish correction'.[22] Here Montaigne, who generally has a highly developed sense of his authorial presence, claims to have no interest in controlling the spelling and punctuation of his text. Paying attention to such textual elements, he insists, is simply not worth his time; he would much rather cede authority to others involved in the publication process.[23] According to Montaigne, then, there is no strictly authorial spelling or punctuation in the published editions of the *Essais* – and it was his authorial decision to have it that way.

All of this suggests that even if early modern authors had particular spelling or punctuation preferences – and it is not entirely clear that they did[24] – there was not necessarily an expectation that those preferences would be carried over into a printed text.[25] Concerns such as line-justification tended to take precedence when a compositor was putting together a printed page: a single compositor might

[19] Stallybrass, 'Individual', p. 608. Similarly, Leah Marcus notes that the written versions of the speeches of Elizabeth I are characterized by often significant variability. For Marcus, such variability demonstrates that each version was carefully calibrated to the particular audience it was likely to reach. Therefore variability, far from being a nuisance, was an effective tool that people could harness. 'From Oral Delivery to Print in the Speeches of Elizabeth I', in *Print, Manuscript & Performance*, ed. Arthur F. Marotti and Michael D. Bristol (Columbus, OH, 2000), pp. 33–48.

[20] Simon Palfrey and Tiffany Stern, *Shakespeare in Parts* (Oxford, 2007); see also Tiffany Stern, *Documents of Performance in Early Modern England* (Cambridge, 2009).

[21] Masten, *Textual Intercourse*, p. 9.

[22] Michel de Montaigne, *The Complete Essays of Montaigne*. trans. and ed. Donald Frame (Stanford, 1958), III.9; p. 737. The French reads: 'Je ne me mesle ny d'ortografe, et ordonne seulement qu'ils suivent l'ancienne, ny de la punctuation; je suis peu expert en l'un et en l'autre . . . . je redicterois plus volontiers encore autant d'essais que de m'assujettir à resuivre ceux-cy, pour cette puerile correction' in Michel de Montaigne, *Les Essais*, ed. Pierre Villey and Verdun L. Saulnier (Presses Universitaires de France, 1978), III.9; p. 965.

[23] One might choose not to take Montaigne's statement at face value, of course, and there is a sense in which he could be using it to blame others for any problems that may occur in the text. The full context is as follows: 'Do not blame me, reader, for those [faults] that slip in here through the caprices or inadvertency of others: each hand, each workman, contributes his own. I do not concern myself with spelling, and simply order them to follow the old style; or with punctuation; I am inexpert in both. When they wholly shatter the sense, I am not much troubled about it, for at least they relieve me of responsibility; but when they substitute a false meaning, as they do so often, and twist me to their view, they ruin me. However, when the thought is not up to my strength, a fair-minded man should reject it as not mine. Anyone who knows how little I like to work, how much I am formed in my own way, will easily believe that I would rather write as many more essays again than subject myself to going over these again for such childish correction' (Montaigne, *Essays*, p. 737). The French reads: 'Ne te prens point à moy, Lecteur, de celles [fautes] qui se coulent icy par la fantasie ou inadvertance d'autruy: chaque main, chaque ouvrier y apporte les siennes. Je ne me mesle ny d'ortografe, et ordonne seulement qu'ils suivent l'ancienne, ny de la punctuation; je suis peu expert en l'un et en l'autre. Où ils rompent du tout le sens, je m'en donne peu de peine, car au-moins ils me deschargent; mais où ils en substituent un faux, comme ils font si souvent, et me destournent à leur conception, ils me ruynent. Toutesfois, quand la sentence n'est forte à ma mesure, un honeste homme la doit

choose, for example, a shorter or longer version of the same word depending on spatial needs.[26] Therefore, rather than 'authorial' authority taking precedence in decisions about spelling and punctuation marks, the only kind of authority we can be sure an early modern printed text would have is the authority of its original cultural moment, when flexibility, rather than standardization, prevailed.

In choosing modern spelling, Taylor strives for a textual presentation that adequately reflects the absence of an original manuscript with authorial spelling. He writes that modern spelling, with its 'prescribed, formal, and relatively invariant' qualities, presents 'the least intrusively interpretive system available' in this situation. He adds, 'Of course, the resulting orthography is not authoritative, but that is part of its point: there *is* no authority in these matters.'[27] In writing this, Taylor assumes that the authority of Shakespeare and Middleton – the text's authors – is the only kind of authority of consequence when attempting to recover a lost original text. Since their individual spelling preferences – or at least those of Shakespeare – are irrecoverable, the least intrusive approach is to neutralize all the spelling with modern forms. Of course, in making this decision, Taylor assumes that early modern authors had individual spelling preferences, that those spelling preferences mattered, and that, in their absence, modern spelling presents a neutral alternative.

I have already touched on Taylor's first two assumptions. As for the third, modernized spelling is far from a neutral alternative. It is essentially just as informed by a particular cultural and historical moment as were early modern variations in spelling; it only *seems* neutral because twenty-first-century readers are accustomed to reading it. As David Bevington argues, modernized spelling 'exacts a measurable cost in terms of verbal resonances, multiple plays of meaning, metre, characterization of speaker, dialectical speech, and still more'.[28] Peter Stallybrass writes at length about what it might have been like to write and read in a culture that had no rules for standardized spelling. He argues that there was often no one-to-one correlation between a word and whatever it signified. Thus the words 'one', 'won', 'on', 'owne', and other variations, could all stand in for each other; each distinct spelling did not connote the distinct word that appears to modern eyes accustomed to standard forms. Stallybrass points to 'the inadequacy of our own terms (pun, word-play, and so on) to examine the constant *conflation of signifiers* that characterizes Renaissance texts'.[29] In making his own decisions about spelling without reference to the way the words were actually spelled in the early seventeenth century, Taylor privileges his own

---

refuser pour mienne. Qui connoistra combien je suis peu laborieux, combien je suis faict à ma mode, croira facilement que je redicterois plus volontiers encore autant d'essais que de m'assujetir à resuivre ceux-cy, pour cette puerile correction' (Montaigne, *Les Essais*, p. 965). Here Montaigne's statement presents the idea that people such as scribes and compositors could be susceptible to human error in their work, and such error could be disastrous for the integrity of the *Essais*; however, his meaning can be distinguished from what Taylor assumes by the term 'human error'. Taylor seems to conceive of 'error' as anything that was not authorial, while Montaigne seems to think of it as anything that endangers the integrity (albeit authorial) of the text. According to Montaigne's logic, a punctuation schema that best preserves his 'authorial intentions' would be one that appropriately conveys the meaning of the text, not his actual punctuation marks.

24 See Stallybrass, 'Individual'; Stallybrass and de Grazia, 'Materiality'; and Jaffrey Masten, 'Pressing Subjects: Or, the Secret Lives of Shakespeare's Compositors', in *Language Machines: Technologies of Literary and Cultural Production*, ed. Masten, Stallybrass and Nancy Vickers (London, 1997), pp. 75–107.

25 Antony Hammond writes that 'no printed play has a punctuation pattern particularly like any of the surviving manuscripts, which themselves differ radically according to their date, scribe, and purpose' ('The Noisy Comma: Searching for the Signal in Renaissance Dramatic Texts', in *Crisis in Editing: Texts of the English Renaissance*, ed. Randall McLeod (New York, 1994), p. 212).

26 Masten, 'Pressing Subjects', pp. 81–2.

27 Taylor, 'Genetic Text', p. 691.

28 David Bevington, 'Modern Spelling: The Hard Choices', in Erne and Kidnie, eds., *Textual Performances*, p. 157. For more in-depth consideration of this issue, see Stanley Wells, *Re-Editing Shakespeare for the Modern Reader* (Oxford, 1984).

29 Stallybrass, 'Individual', pp. 600–1 (emphasis in original).

era over the era in which the text originated – hardly, it would seem, an appropriate strategy for recovering a lost original.

As with spelling, Taylor assumes a singular, unrecoverable authorial intention when it comes to punctuation. He writes:

[JAGGARD's, the First Folio's] punctuation bears little, if any, relation to Shakespeare's (or Middleton's) intentions; it reflects the preferences of two different compositors, working from a scribal manuscript which was itself copying, probably, another (annotated) scribal manuscript. On the evidence of the Hand D pages of *Sir Thomas More*, Shakespeare's own manuscripts contained virtually no punctuation, and what punctuation there was would be unlikely to survive into a printed text, or would there be surrounded by so much non-authorial punctuation that the identity and function of any such authorial relics would be irrecoverable. Thus, every [punctuation mark] in JAGGARD (and every subsequent edition) represents an act of interpretation, not an act of preservation or restoration.[30]

Taylor's solution to the perceived problem of rampant 'non-authorial punctuation' is the opposite of his solution to the spelling problem: instead of imposing his own standardized preferences, he chooses to omit all punctuation marks. He does this presumably because, while written words must be spelled in some way in order to exist on a page, a written text can still exist without any punctuation marks. According to Taylor's logic, omitting punctuation, like modernizing the spelling, is apparently 'the least intrusively interpretive system available'. However, choosing not to include punctuation is just as intrusive an editorial decision as anything else Taylor reasonably could have done, for, while it may seem neutral under a particular editorial logic that ignores the reading process, it certainly does not appear so for anyone actually reading the text.

Punctuation marks as written symbols – marks that identify boundaries between syntactic units within a text – evolved over time to aid the reading process. In *Pause and Effect*, which details the history of Western punctuation, Malcolm Parkes writes that the practice of writing punctuation only began to develop as silent reading became more

widespread. Before that, written language was primarily 'a record of the spoken word'. Texts were usually read aloud, and an orator would be able to decide how to punctuate a text that, in its written form, might not even have visual divisions between words, let alone marks indicating different types of pauses between them. When, however, 'writing came to be regarded as conveying information directly to the mind through the eye' rather than through the medium of the orator, written punctuation steadily developed. The primary function of written punctuation, Parkes writes, is to 'resolve structural uncertainties in a text, and to signal nuances of semantic significance which might otherwise not be conveyed at all, or would at best be much more difficult for a reader to figure out'.[31] Punctuation, therefore, contributes to determining the meaning of a text. Moreover, it is not neutral: Parkes writes that punctuation can also 'modify the emphases, and hence the "meaning", embodied in a text, and has been used to communicate particular interpretations to readers'.[32]

Parkes's study brings up some important points relevant to the Middleton *Macbeth*. The idea that punctuation is not a neutral force, that it actually contributes to the construction of meaning, seems to corroborate Taylor's choice to omit it altogether in his edition of the play. If, after all, what we want is Shakespeare and Middleton's play, we should avoid anything not strictly written by Shakespeare and Middleton – anything that would blunt or work against 'authorial' authority. But complicating this idea is Parkes's other point: a text written primarily for an orator might not have much, or any, written punctuation. When writing this, Parkes does not mean that such a text would be unpunctuated; instead, he means that the punctuation would be provided by the orator rather

---

[30] Taylor, 'Genetic Text', p. 691. For a discussion of why the Hand D pages of *Sir Thomas More* might not even be very good evidence for Shakespeare's handwriting, see Stallybrass and de Grazia, 'Materiality', pp. 277–8.

[31] Malcolm Beckwith Parkes, *Pause and Effect: An Introduction to the History of Punctuation in the West* (Menston, 1992), p. 1.

[32] Parkes, *Pause and Effect*, p. 4.

than the author or the scribe or any other person setting down the text in written form.

In the period under consideration here, the early seventeenth century, written punctuation was still in the process of being standardized. This process was largely dependent on the influence of the printing press and its ability to disseminate particular fonts, which 'subsequently led to the adoption of a single graphic symbol for each [punctuation] sign'.[33] Not only were punctuation marks themselves still in flux, but cultural assumptions about the relationship between oral/aural and written culture were as well.[34] Leah Marcus, whose work on the speeches of Elizabeth I highlights the variability of their written forms, argues that in this period 'writing was not authoritative in itself, but only insofar as it served as a record of speech, with the oral *prototypon*, evanescent though it was, retaining primary authority'.[35] In a culture that often privileged the spoken over the written word, written punctuation marks, whose function is to preserve meaning for a reader in the absence of an orator, would not have been necessary or even desirable in texts written for oral performance.

Working along those lines, Simon Palfrey and Tiffany Stern show that extant acting parts of early modern plays 'are lightly punctuated (as are all remaining manuscript plays)' and that 'punctuation varies markedly from script to script (in a far greater way than words do)'. Pointing to this evidence as well as to contemporaneous written commentary on sermons, they conclude that, when a text in this period was intended for some kind of spoken performance, punctuation was decided by the speaker. Of course, in the absence of original manuscripts there is no specific proof of this for *Macbeth*, but it is unlikely that *Macbeth* would have proved the exception to a fairly wide-spread practice. Moreover, Palfrey and Stern argue, 'when actors were praised, it was for carefully selecting and isolating moments of punctuation and highlighting them with the use of appropriate action'.[36] Antony Hammond points to a negative example, the moment in *A Midsummer Night's Dream* when Theseus criticizes Peter Quince's prologue because the actor 'doth not stand upon points' – in other words, fails to punctuate the text appropriately (5.1.118).[37] Since making the words come alive seems to have been the player's prerogative rather than the playwright's, a playwright in this period would most likely have used very little written punctuation in a manuscript version of a play – and might not necessarily have expected a player to retain any that was there.

A compositor, however, setting the play for a reading public – the segment of readership Taylor omits from his thinking – would know that without at least some punctuation, a text would be very difficult to parse. Far from human error, then, the work of people such as compositors could be considered an art in itself: indeed, the late-seventeenth-century writer Joseph Moxon referred to both the '*Authors* Genius' and the '*good natural Genius*' of the compositor.[38] As Jeffrey Masten writes, rather than being 'an intruding perverter in the ideally unmediated transmission of the text, . . . the good compositor orients himself in two directions, toward the author and toward the reader'.[39] Similarly, Hammond argues that the compositor 'was at his most creative as a

---

[33] Parkes, *Pause and Effect*, p. 87.

[34] For a thoughtful discussion of this relationship, see the chapter, 'Acting in the Passive Voice: *Love's Labour's Lost* and the Melancholy of Print' in Carla Mazzio's *The Inarticulate Renaissance: Language Trouble in an Age of Eloquence* (Philadelphia, 2008), pp. 142–74.

[35] Marcus, 'From Oral Delivery to Print in the Speeches of Elizabeth I', p. 46.

[36] Palfrey and Stern, *Shakespeare in Parts*, pp. 318–20.

[37] Hammond points out that 'For the joke to work, the passage must have been carefully punctuated by Shakespeare, and it is a reasonable inference that he marked up his manuscript in such a way that the theatrical copyist (and subsequently, the compositors) would, contrary to their normal practice, reproduce the punctuation of the foul papers. This inference is strengthened by the fact that the Folio text of the [speech], though it contains six spelling variants from Q1, changes only one punctuation mark' ('The Noisy Comma', p. 217). This suggests that whenever authorial punctuation really mattered, it was possible to transmit the desired punctuation in such a way that it appeared in the printed version of the text.

[38] Moxon, *Mechanick Exercises*, 2:220, 2:197, quoted in Masten, 'Pressing Subjects', p. 95.

[39] Masten, 'Pressing Subjects', p. 95.

collaborator in the production of a text'.[40] The work of compositors seems to have served a necessary mediating function between author and reader. In his analysis of the punctuation problem, therefore, Taylor sets up a false dichotomy between authorial and non-authorial punctuation: perhaps, as with spelling, there is no original authorial punctuation to recover.

Nevertheless, Taylor's overarching goal in his decision about punctuation is to filter out anonymous, non-authorial hands in order to avoid muddying the authorial waters with any textual work not specifically executed by Shakespeare or Middleton. He writes: 'We have tried, here, to restore the *actual words* which we believe Shakespeare and Middleton wrote . . . without supplying the apparatus of punctuation, capitalization, indentation, commentary, and arbitrary orthography which usually accompany those words.'[41] With this language, Taylor claims to present the reader with a text that is as editorially neutral – as unmediated between Middleton/Shakespeare and the reader – as possible. But as Jerome McGann tells us, there is no such thing as a neutral editor: 'editing, including critical editing, is more an act of translation than of reproduction. When we edit we change, and even good editing . . . necessarily involves fundamental departures from "authorial intention," however that term is interpreted.'[42]

In claiming to restore Shakespeare and Middleton's 'actual words', and to rescue their authorial work from the muddied waters of time and sloppy editing, Taylor makes the significant editorial decision to value words more than anything else – a choice that cannot fully encompass whatever original text we might be talking about, and is, moreover, already muddied by his decision to impose his own spelling preferences.[43] Therefore, while claiming to liberate the text from the interpretive punctuation choices of early modern printers and compositors, Taylor neglects to mention that his own choice not to include punctuation is also an act of interpretation. Perhaps we do not have Shakespeare's or Middleton's original punctuation, and perhaps they never wrote down any punctuation, but they undoubtedly expected that their

texts would be punctuated – whether by player's voice or printer's mark. In aligning his editing practice so carefully with one type of authorial 'intention' – specific spelling and punctuation marks – Taylor loses sight of another: the idea of having a punctuated text.[44] And what he calls the 'actual' Shakespeare/Middleton text is really a product of significant 'non-authorial' collaborative work, on Taylor's part and, ultimately, on the reader's.

III

'You shall yourself read . . . / After your own sense'
Duke of Venice, *Othello*

Critical editions, especially of early modern works, rely heavily on editorial decisions that shape, even *re-wright*, the texts that appear on the page. As Joseph Grigley asserts, for a critical edition, 'It is . . . difficult to say where Shakespeare's text ends and the Other's adapt[at]ion begins, because each

---

40 'The Noisy Comma', p. 213.

41 Taylor, 'Genetic Text', p. 691 (emphasis added).

42 Jerome J. McGann, *The Textual Condition* (Princeton, NJ, 1991), p. 53. As regards authorial intention, McGann suggests that critical editing traditionally has been based on the idea of recovering an author's final 'intentions', and is careful to point out, and explore, how vexed that term is. For a more detailed discussion, see his chapter, 'What is Critical Editing?', in *The Textual Condition*, pp. 48–68.

43 The idea that words are the only thing that matters in a text has been criticized rightly by a number of scholars who argue that bibliographical elements such as layout, typeface, paratextual elements, and, of course, punctuation, are important conveyors of meaning in a text and should not be ignored by critical editors. For an overview of some of this scholarship, see McGann's chapter 'The Socialization of Texts', in *The Textual Condition*, pp. 69–87, and McKenzie, *Bibliography and the Sociology of Texts*.

44 As an example of a text that can be true to one kind of authorial 'intentions' while being a 'travesty' of others, McGann points to David V. Erdman's edition of *The Complete Poetry and Prose of William Blake*, which reproduces in type Blake's handwritten text *Jerusalem*. Erdman's typed text thus preserves layout, word choices, spelling etc., while neglecting handwriting and illustrations, among other elements. Erdman's edition won the Modern Language Association's editorial seal of distinction, yet some Blake scholars refuse to teach from it (*Textual Condition*, pp. 52–6).

new text is in a sense an adapt[at]ion.'[45] Hammond writes that 'All editors are, or try to be, collaborators.'[46] And McGann ultimately attributes all the qualities of authorship to a critical editor, when he writes, 'All critical editions . . . reflect certain "intentions" of the author in the present [in this case, Taylor] rather than the author in the past [in this case, Middleton/Shakespeare].'[47] I have discussed above how Taylor serves as a collaborator or adapter alongside Middleton and Shakespeare. But as it turns out, the Middleton *Macbeth* is not just a product of Taylor's collaborative work: because of his choice regarding punctuation, the text ultimately becomes the reader's adaptation just as much as Taylor's. While seeking to 'lower the temperature of editorial interference', Taylor has adapted the text in such a way that it requires heightened readerly interference: effectively, it forces the reader to collaborate on the text herself by re-voicing and re-punctuating it.[48]

Many theorists have written at length about the role of reader response in determining meaning in texts. McGann, for example, writes: 'Texts vary from themselves (as it were) immediately, as soon as they engage with the readers they anticipate.'[49] Roland Barthes goes so far as to assert that 'the true place of the writing . . . is reading'.[50] A written sentence, under these theoretical approaches, should be thought of as an event rather than a physical object. Grigley, following the lead of Stephen Mailloux, writes:

The event is a moment of encounter: the text meets the reader, and the reader in turn decides . . . the text's essence. In a way the text is absolved of its textuality; it becomes absorbed by (and by default possessed by) the reader, which in turn gives rise to [Stanley] Fish's lemma: '[T]he reader's response is not *to* the meaning; it *is* the meaning.'[51]

Essentially, then, every reader encountering a text will create that text anew according to her particular way of being in the world. As McGann tells us, every text 'comprises an interactive mechanism of communicative exchange'; there is, therefore, no objective, neutral, physical text, but only moments of interaction between a text and a reader.[52]

Any early modern text, and especially a text using complex editorial practices such as two-text editing, will require a twenty-first-century reader to spend some energy working through meaning. Taylor's unpunctuated text, however, goes much further, to the extent that the reader is regularly required to make significant interpretive choices that shape the meaning of the play down to the level of the line or phrase. The problem is, of course, that a text can only remain fully unpunctuated if one considers it to be an inert object in the same category as, say, a chair. In order to make any sense at all – in order to exist in a way that has meaning for its textual user as part of a textual event – a text invites, even requires, punctuation. And it is through this punctuation process that the reader of the Middleton *Macbeth* takes on the most strenuously collaborative role.

When reading the unpunctuated text, the reader's only guides are the ending of verse-lines, the meter of iambic pentameter, and the use of speech prefixes to assign different roles. In some situations, such as the following example, these guides are enough to produce a meaningful understanding of the text without a reader's active interpretive input:

Lady.	I heard the owl scream and the crickets cry	
	did you not speak	
Macbeth.	when	
Lady.	now	
Macbeth.	as I descended	
Lady.	ay	(2.2.15–19)

This passage is hardly affected by its lack of written punctuation marks, since a reader can gain a strong sense of basic and more abstract meaning through

---

45 Grigley, *Textualterity*, p. 99.
46 Hammond, 'The Noisy Comma', p. 235.
47 McGann, *Textual Condition*, p. 53.
48 Jowett, 'Addressing Adaptation', p. 69.
49 McGann, *Textual Condition*, pp. 9–10.
50 Roland Barthes, 'The Death of the Author', in *Image Music Text*, Stephen Heath, trans. (London, 1977), p. 147.
51 Grigley, *Textualterity*, p. 114.
52 McGann, *Textual Condition*, p. 10.

the form of the text on the page. (It is worth noting that in versifying this exchange as a single iambic pentameter line, Taylor follows editorial tradition rather than the First Folio – the oldest extant text of the play.) Basic meaning – divisions between coherent syntactic units – is signalled either by a change from one character's speech to another's, as in 'did you not speak/when/now', or by a change from one verse-line to another, as in 'I heard the owl scream and the crickets cry/did you not speak.' This works, of course, because this passage contains only short units of thought; there are no subordinate clauses, for example. The short, clipped statements also contribute to creating a more abstract meaning, the intense agitation the Macbeths feel at this moment. Here Macbeth and his wife, having just plotted and carried out the murder, are uneasy and over-alert, their words following each other at a rapid pace, or even overlapping, as they react to the smallest ambient sounds. Because of the way the text appears on the page, it is nearly impossible to read it without picking up on this sense of unease.

Many other passages, however, present greater challenges to determining basic and abstract meaning. One example occurs during Macbeth's 'dagger' speech; the relevant lines in Taylor's edition read:

> witchcraft celebrates
> pale Hecate's offerings and withered murder
> alarumed by his sentinel the wolf
> whose howl's his watch thus with his stealthy pace
> with Tarquin's ravishing strides towards his design
> moves like a ghost   (2.1.51–6)

The complicated syntax of this passage initially obscures its meaning. A reader attempting to make sense of it might read it several times, perhaps focusing on the phrase 'whose howl's his watch' as the most complex and difficult to parse. After working through the text, the reader might choose to punctuate it mentally in the following way:

> witchcraft celebrates
> pale Hecate's offerings and withered murder.
> Alarumed by his sentinel, the wolf,
> whose howl's his watch, thus with his stealthy pace,

> with Tarquin's ravishing strides, towards his design
> moves like a ghost.

In this interpretation, the personified witchcraft is celebrating both Hecate's offerings and withered murder. Simultaneously, the wolf, alarmed by either his own or witchcraft's sentinel (the pronoun makes it unclear), is moving towards his design like a ghost. Reading the speech this way, the reader focuses on the wolf, who takes on a significant amount of agency in the sentence and the speech as a whole. The image of the wolf striding stealthily through the night is powerful and eerie, contributing substantially to the supernatural aura of the play.

But another reader might see the text differently, and might not even see the first reader's interpretation at all. This other reader might punctuate the passage thus:

> witchcraft celebrates
> pale Hecate's offerings; and withered murder,
> alarumed by his sentinel the wolf,
> whose howl's his watch, thus with his stealthy pace,
> with Tarquin's ravishing strides, towards his design
> moves like a ghost.

In this interpretation, the wolf slides into a supporting role as the sentinel to murder, and murder itself becomes the subject of the lengthy sentence, and ultimately an important agent in the speech. Murder, and not the wolf, is striding towards his design like a ghost – a fitting image for a man to summon as he contemplates an imminent murder. Both interpretations share a common trait: Macbeth displaces his own agency onto a supernatural figure, refusing to take full blame for the action he is about to commit.

A case can be made for each interpretation, just as a case can be made for any other interpretation a reader might make that divides this speech into meaningful syntactic units. And the interpretive possibilities do not end there, since even when a reader is fairly confident about syntactic units – either because they are unambiguous or because the reader believes strongly in her own choices – there are still numerous possibilities for individual punctuation marks that would affect a reader's overall understanding of the passage. For example, in the earlier exchange between Macbeth and his wife, even though the places where end punctuation is required may seem unambiguous, a reader has interpretive latitude with regard to what kind of end punctuation to imagine. The lines 'Did you not speak?/When?/Now./As I descended?/Ay.' read very differently from 'Did you not speak?/When?/Now!/As I descended?/Ay!' whose exclamation marks create an added sense of hysteria and might influence a reader's interpretation of Lady Macbeth's character. The implication of Taylor's editorial choice to omit punctuation altogether is that since Shakespeare's and Middleton's authorial punctuation cannot be recreated, all of the possible punctuation decisions a reader might make – on the level of syntax *and* specific marks – are equally valid.[53]

Is this really what Taylor is suggesting? I would posit that it is not; Taylor seems to be thinking not as much about the scene of reading as about his own role as an editor producing a historical object. John Jowett, another editor for the Oxford Middleton, articulates this notion when he writes:

The familiarity of [the play] in another context – the context of the Shakespeare canon – means that few readers will encounter the play in the Middleton edition for the first time ... This offers a unique opportunity for the editor to place less emphasis than usual on the responsibility to present the text for unpredetermined and various practices of reading and criticism.[54]

In other words, Taylor is under no obligation to produce a readable *Macbeth*; in fact, he writes explicitly that 'readers who want a more comfortable text can find it easily enough elsewhere'.[55] His text is not necessarily meant to be read, it would seem, by an individual reader who is easily discomforted by a complex typographic system – a reader whose primary interest is, for example, the story. Taylor's goal is rather to create a textual entity that demonstrates Middleton's adaptive process. The text, then, as Taylor seems to see it, is a physical object, made known to the world in 2007, representing a scholar's best approximation – based on available knowledge at the time of editing – of

the linguistic and structural variations between Shakespeare's text and Middleton's.

Although Taylor does not seem particularly interested in the site of individual reading, he does suggest an audience for this edition of *Macbeth* that might benefit significantly from using an unpunctuated text: an acting company. Taylor writes that he has included everything 'necessary to *stage* [Shakespeare and Middleton's] text'.[56] One can imagine a director, having decided to produce the newly reconstructed Middleton *Macbeth*, sitting down with a cast and spending several rehearsals working through the script, determining emphasis and punctuation together, and ultimately creating a strong and coherent interpretation of the play to perform for an audience.[57] Of course, in this

---

53 This includes punctuation choices that may have been rare or generally not used in the early modern period.

54 Jowett, 'Addressing Adaptation', p. 68. Jowett makes this statement in reference to another play in the edition, *Measure for Measure*, which, though it does have punctuation, is presented in the same two-text editing format that Taylor used for *Macbeth*. Although the statement does not actually refer to the punctuation of *Macbeth*, it is still apt for this discussion because it arises from the same editorial sentiment about readership.

55 Taylor, 'Genetic Text', p. 692. The question of audience comes up regularly in reviews of the Oxford Middleton, and there is a general consensus that this text is of interest primarily to advanced scholars. For example, William Proctor Williams writes, 'in its present physical form, it may be so unwieldy as to deter all but the most serious scholar': William Proctor Williams, 'Thomas Middleton: The Collected Works', *Notes and Queries* (March 2009), p. 148. Similarly, Mark Hutchings and Michelle O'Callaghan write, 'As a work of scholarship the Oxford Middleton is a considerable achievement and an invaluable resource for *specialists*, bringing up to date a range of issues surrounding both canon and content over the last few years' in 'Thomas Middleton: The Collected Works and Companion', *The Review of English Studies* 60 (2009), 319 (emphasis added). Moreover, according to Jowett, in their plans to edit *Macbeth* for the New Oxford Shakespeare Project, he and Taylor 'are very unlikely to repeat the unpunctuated editing in a Shakespeare edition *designed for a wider readership*': email conversation, 9 November 2011 (emphasis added).

56 Taylor, 'Genetic Text', p. 691 (emphasis added).

57 This practice is by no means unheard of. For example, Hammond writes of 'One celebrated actor at the Stratford Festival in Ontario' who 'prepares his part by having a copy of the

situation, the company of actors, like the orators before written punctuation, and like the early modern player, would be completely free to interpret and perform the text according to their own judgment. They would, in fact, be playing a collaborative role in creating the text.

This situation seems to be the only way Taylor envisions his text being read. And yet the imagined acting company's mutually agreed upon punctuation could not possibly be less 'intrusive' into the supposed ideal original text than any punctuation Taylor could have included as editor. The text, after all, needs to be punctuated to be understood. Taylor, in requiring his readers – no matter who they are – to insert punctuation themselves, moves the mediating force from the editor to the reader. And in the process, he ultimately creates an unfamiliar – but not necessarily new – way of understanding texts.

IV

'Is all our company here?'

Quince, *A Midsummer Night's Dream*

According to Parkes, the idea of a reader inserting her own punctuation into a written text has a long historical precedent. It developed from manuscript traditions in the Middle Ages, when scribes copying ancient texts often 'sought to present a neutral reading of a text' by restricting 'the use of punctuation to indicating only the most basic divisions of the text – paragraphs and *sententiae* [in this context, sentences] – leaving the rest unmarked'. Such a practice 'allows the reader freedom to assess for himself the semantic values which he wishes to attribute to individual words, phrases and clauses'.[58] Even with the rise of printing, readers in the sixteenth and early seventeenth centuries, in addition to inserting marginalia, often added their own punctuation to printed copies of texts. In fact, authors 'sometimes direct[ed] the reader to insert punctuation omitted by the printer, either from a list of errata, or according to the reader's own judgement'.[59] In the early modern period,

therefore, a text was imagined as an event, a moment of interaction.

In subsequent centuries, however, the practice of involving the reader in semantic decisions has fallen out of favour. Texts, rather than being considered interpretive events, have come to be viewed as objects that *seem*, at least, to be semantically stable. Ernst Honigmann asserts that twenty-first-century readers and editors 'are more likely to think of a play as a text, or an ideal text ("the author's fair copy") frozen in time', something very different from its original, early modern identity as a kind of 'living organism'.[60] In giving readers agency to interpret the semantic values of the text and create meaning themselves, Taylor is recovering an older, mostly forgotten, form of collaboration between author and reader.

Readers unfamiliar with reader response criticism or the latest debates in textual theory will probably read a comfortably punctuated text without thinking very much at all about their own role in creating that text through the act of reading. While such readers might expect to discuss various interpretations of a text in an English class, a majority, I would submit, assume that if two people are reading the same text, they are reading the same text. But a reader encountering the Middleton *Macbeth* becomes almost immediately aware that no reader of this text can possibly read exactly the same text as another, since each person is making too many obviously significant interpretive decisions with every textual encounter. A reader encountering the Middleton *Macbeth*, like Lady Macbeth reading her husband's letter, cannot help but think about her role as a player in developing textual meanings. Through struggling with the interpretive demands of an equivocal text and imagining other readers doing so as well, she may come to understand organically that 'the presence

---

play made for him from which all punctuation has been removed': 'The Noisy Comma', p. 211.

58 Parkes, *Pause and Effect*, pp. 71–2.

59 Parkes, *Pause and Effect*, p. 5.

60 Ernst Honigmann, 'The New Bibliography and its Critics', in Erne and Kidnie, *Textual Performances*, p. 86.

of a text as an object belies the absence of the text as an utterance of another time and place. That is to say, the fixedness of a text is as illusory as the fixedness of an interpretation; neither is final, neither is authorial.'[61] The process of reading the Middleton *Macbeth*, then, is less about recovering Middleton's adaptive work than about discovering one's own. Every reader becomes a collaborator.

The idea of an individual reader or an acting company working to create a text's meaning essentially dramatizes, or plays out, the original textual identity of the Shakespeare and Middleton *Macbeth* – the very identity that Taylor subsumes beneath his editorial apparatus in order to claim access to the lost original. In claiming to reconstruct the lost original of *Macbeth*, Taylor has, knowingly or unknowingly, managed to create a text that, by its very presentation on the page, recreates the kind of collaborative environment that characterized early modern textual production and reception. One of the most significant accomplishments of Taylor's text, then, has nothing to do with Middleton; rather, it is to guide the reader towards an understanding of her own participatory role in those moments of interaction that constitute textual events.

---

[61] Grigley, *Textualterity*, p. 108.

THE DATE OF *SIR THOMAS MORE*

HUGH CRAIG

The play *Sir Thomas More* survives in a single manuscript copy in the British Library. This document preserves an original version of the play and a series of revisions. The first draft is in a single hand, which scholars have identified as that of the writer and sometime anti-Catholic agent Antony Munday. The revisions, like the first draft, are anonymous, but evidently involve a series of dramatists, one of them, most likely, William Shakespeare. The original version is annotated by the Master of the Revels, Sir Edmund Tilney, who demands various changes.[1]

The date of the original version has been the focus of intense scholarly activity because of Shakespeare's probable involvement in the revisions. It is of great interest when Shakespeare made his additions, assuming they are his, and that in turn is related to the question of when the original play was composed. At various times scholars have argued for dates as early as 1586 and as late as 1605.[2] In one of the more striking pronouncements on this topic, A. W. Pollard declared that 'If [the play] *More* can be proved to be as late as 1599 . . . I should regard the date as an obstacle to Shakespeare's authorship of the three pages so great as to be fatal.'[3] (Pollard was thinking of theatre company allegiances as an obstacle to associating the play with Shakespeare in 1599; later commentators have offered alternative possibilities for the connections of the play and the revisions to acting companies, and maintained both a late date for the original version and Shakespeare as the author of some of the additions.)[4] William B. Long says 'Date is all important' for the study of the play.[5]

There is nothing decisive in terms of external evidence. There is no date on the manuscript, and its provenance only goes back to 1727, when it belonged to the collector Alexander Murray. It was sold Edward Harley, 2nd Earl of Oxford and Earl Mortimer. The third Earl then sold it to the British Museum with the rest of the family manuscript collection in 1753. The careers of Munday, the scribe, and Tilney, the annotator, do not serve to narrow the date range either. Munday was associated with plays and playwriting from as early as 1584 to as late as 1602. Tilney was Master of the Revels for an even greater span, from 1579 to 1610.

Scholars have sometimes sought clues to the date of *Sir Thomas More* from incidents which might have prompted the writing of the play, and from situations which might have deterred playwrights from tackling it. The play deals with the career of Sir Thomas More, beginning with his elevation to the Privy Council following his success as

---

[1] John Jowett, 'Introduction', in *Sir Thomas More*, Arden 3 (London, 2011), pp. 1–130 at 5–7.

[2] G. Harold Metz, '"Voice and Credyt": The Scholars and *Sir Thomas More*', in *Shakespeare and Sir Thomas More: Essays on the Play and Its Shakespearian Interest*, ed. T. H. Howard-Hill (Cambridge, 1989), pp. 11–44 at 25.

[3] Alfred W. Pollard, 'Introduction', in *Shakespeare's Hand in 'The Play of Sir Thomas More'*, ed. Alfred W. Pollard (Cambridge, 1923), pp. 1–32 at 31.

[4] T. H. Howard-Hill, 'Introduction', in *Shakespeare and 'Sir Thomas More'*, ed. Howard-Hill, pp. 1–9 at 2; Jowett, 'Introduction', pp. 100–3.

[5] William B. Long, 'The Occasion of *The Book of Sir Thomas More*', in *Shakespeare and Sir Thomas More*, ed. Howard-Hill, pp. 45–56 at 47.

under-sheriff of London in quelling the Ill May Day riots of 1517. Tilney says the writers must cut the scenes showing this riot and mention it only in a 'short report', 'at your own perils'.[6] The play also shows More's meeting with Erasmus and his refusal to sign articles as ordered by King Henry VIII, evidently the Oath of Succession recognizing Anne Boleyn's issue as heirs to the throne,[7] leading to More's execution. It would be obvious even without Tilney's annotations that the riot and the signing of the articles are sensitive matters. Vittorio Gabrieli and Giorgio Melchiori suggest that the writing of the play was stimulated by the xenophobic riots in London in 1592–3.[8] Looking more broadly, Gary Taylor argues that though there were also notable riots in London in 1595 and 1601, 1595 is ruled out because the suppression of the riots was so punitive that no playwright would have risked an allusion, and 1601 because the riots then were neither popular, as those in the play are, nor related to the presence of foreigners in London.[9]

Sources also offer evidence for dating. There is some indication that the writers of the play draw two episodes from Sir John Harington's satirical prose publication *The Metamorphosis of Ajax* (1596). This work seems to be the source for More's witty sayings about his urine sample and about his execution saving him the cost of being shaved.[10] Gabrieli notes '[t]he extraordinary verbal similarities between Harington and the play text' in the case of the first of the sayings.[11] If the authors of the play had used the printed version of Harington's satire, this would contradict an early date. Gabrieli, who favours the early date, counters this objection by quoting Melchiori's suggestion that Harington may have used the play, rather than the other way round, either after seeing it in the theatre or after reading the playbook.[12] Gabrieli also concedes that of all the surviving sources for the second anecdote 'Harington's wording is closest to the play', but then says that 'we could account for this in the same way as we did for the episode of the urinal', i.e. presuming that Harington had somehow seen a performance of the play or been shown the manuscript playbook.[13]

The other main plank for dating is Munday's handwriting. There are two other manuscripts in his hand, the entirety of the play *John a Kent and John a Cumber* and the preliminaries to the devotional work *The Heaven of the Mind*, and scholars have seen a progression from one to the other, with the hand of *Sir Thomas More* lying between and nearer to the stage represented by *John a Kent*.[14] *The Heaven of the Mind* is signed and dated 1602 by Munday, and *John a Kent* also bears a date (actually in a different hand, not Munday's). E. Maunde Thompson and W.W. Greg read this date as 1596 and this was orthodoxy in the first half of the twentieth century.[15] In 1955 I. A. Shapiro determined that it was in fact 1590.[16] This contributed to a consensus view of the early 1590s for the composition of the original play, maintained in an important volume of essays on the

---

[6] Long, 'The Occasion', p. 45.

[7] Tilney says the playwrights must 'alter' this section (Long, 'The Occasion', p. 46). Jowett in the Arden edition identifies the 'articles' with the Oath of Succession ('Introduction', p. 1), whereas in their Revels edition Vittorio Gabrieli and Giorgio Melchiori suggest they refer to the Oath of Supremacy (*Sir Thomas More*, ed. Gabrieli and Melchiori (Manchester, 1990) p. 161n).

[8] Gabrieli and Melchiori, 'Introduction', *Sir Thomas More*, pp. 1–53 at 11, 12 and 45 n40.

[9] Gary Taylor, 'The Canon and Chronology of Shakespeare's Plays', in *William Shakespeare: A Textual Companion*, eds. Stanley Wells, Gary Taylor, John Jowett, and William Montgomery (Oxford, 1987), pp. 69–144 at 139.

[10] Jowett, 'Introduction', pp. 60–1.

[11] Vittorio Gabrieli, '*Sir Thomas More*: Sources, Characters, Ideas', *Moreana*, 23 (1986), 17–43 at 29.

[12] On the date, see Gabrieli, '*Sir Thomas More*', pp. 24, 29; cf. Gabrieli and Melchiori, 'Introduction', p. 9.

[13] Gabrieli, '*Sir Thomas More*', p. 30.

[14] E. Maunde Thompson, 'The Autograph Manuscripts of Anthony Mundy', *Transactions of the Bibliographical Society*, 14 (1919), 325–53 at 334–5; W. W. Greg, 'The Handwritings of the Manuscript', in *Shakespeare's Hand in 'The Play of Sir Thomas More'*, ed. Pollard, pp. 41–56 at 49.

[15] MacDonald P. Jackson, 'Deciphering a Date and Determining a Date: Antony Munday's *John a Kent and John a Cumber* and the Original Version of *Sir Thomas More*', *Early Modern Literary Studies*, 15.3 (2011), paras. 1–24 at paras. 1 and n1.

[16] I. A. Shapiro, 'The Significance of a Date', *Shakespeare Survey* 8 (Cambridge, 1955), pp. 100–5.

manuscript edited by T. H. Howard-Hill in 1989,[17] and firmly espoused in the Gabrieli and Melchiori Revels edition of 1990. Gabrieli and Melchiori say 'It is now generally accepted – with a few extravagant exceptions – that the original version of the play was written in Munday's hand not later than 1593 and this view is supported by the topical relevance of the Ill May Day scenes to those years.'[18] They also note the *John a Kent* date and Scott McMillin's argument that only a company like the Lord Strange's Men, with a lead actor like Edward Alleyn, could have performed the play, with its unusually lengthy main part.[19] (Lord Strange died in 1594.) The Oxford Shakespeare second edition of 2005 also favours the early 1590s as the date for the original *More*, this time nominating 1592–3.[20]

Recently, however, MacDonald P. Jackson has challenged this consensus. He begins by arguing that 1596 is in fact the correct reading of the date on the *John a Kent* manuscript.[21] Jackson says the upward continuation past the beginning of the number forms a 6 rather than being a flourish on the 0.[22] Given that the formation of Munday's handwriting in the More play seems to lie between his style in the *John a Kent* play and his style in the 1602 manuscript, this reversion to the 1596 date narrows the possible date range for the original *Sir Thomas More* and brings it forward.

Jackson also adduces evidence about date from the play's high proportion of feminine endings, its pause patterns, its use of contractions and exclamations and the relative proportions of newer forms like *has* and *does* compared to older ones like *hath* and *doth*. He revives earlier theories like Levin L. Schücking's that placed the *More* play with three other plays set in Henry VIII's reign, two about Cardinal Wolsey and one about Thomas Cromwell, which all date from 1601–2.[23] All these factors put the composition of the play at 1600 or later.

John Jowett in his Arden edition of 2011 follows Jackson in proposing a date for the original version of *More* of 'in or around 1600'.[24] He notes that the play fits well with the fashion for city comedy at the end of the sixteenth century, and with the aforementioned group of plays about

Wolsey and Cromwell – who, like More, were at one time Henry's chancellors – performed in 1600 and 1601.[25] He also detects influence from late 1590s Shakespeare plays like *Julius Caesar* (1599) in *More*[26] and relies on Jackson's linguistic and metrical evidence.[27]

The main current contenders for the dates of the composition of the play are therefore 1593–4 and *circa* 1600. In what follows I offer a reassessment of the problem by attempting to make a model of the style of early 1590s plays compared to that of early 1600s ones. I take a group of 30 plays from the first of these half-decades and a second of about the same size separated by another half-decade and look systematically at broad differences in style. The degree of change is remarkable. Even among words one might assume to be very stable, the commonest ones, with essentially grammatical functions, there are startling shifts. Some

---

[17] Howard-Hill, 'Introduction' (p. 8), Long, 'The Occasion' (p. 54), and Scott McMillin, 'The Book of Sir Thomas More: Dates and Acting Companies' (pp. 57–76 at 71), all in *Shakespeare and Sir Thomas More*, ed. Howard-Hill.

[18] Gabrieli and Melchiori, 'Introduction', p. 12.

[19] Gabrieli and Melchiori, 'Introduction', p. 12; Scott McMillin, *The Elizabethan Theatre and 'The Book of Sir Thomas More'* (Ithaca and London, 1987), pp. 61–4.

[20] Stanley Wells, Gary Taylor, John Jowett, and William Montgomery, eds., *William Shakespeare: The Complete Works*, second edition (Oxford, 2005), p. 813.

[21] Grace Ioppolo, *Dramatists and Their Manuscripts in the Age of Shakespeare, Jonson, Middleton and Heywood: Authorship, Authority and the Playhouse* (London, 2006), p. 101, argues for the last digit as a 5, i.e. for the date as 1595.

[22] Jackson, 'Deciphering a Date', para. 6.

[23] Jackson, 'Deciphering a Date', paras. 22–3. The plays are *Thomas Lord Cromwell* (1600); Chettle, *The Life of Cardinal Wolsey* (1601); Chettle, Drayton, Munday and Smith, *The Rising of Cardinal Wolsey* (1601).

[24] John Jowett, 'Appendix 4: Authorship and Dates', in *Sir Thomas More*, pp. 415–60 at 430.

[25] Jowett, 'Appendix 4', p. 426.

[26] Jowett, 'Appendix 4', pp. 427–9.

[27] Jowett, 'Appendix 4', p. 430. Thomas Merriam, 'Date and Authorship of the Original Text of *Sir Thomas More*', *The Christian Shakespeare*, www.christianshakespeare.blogspot.com.au/2012/06/date-and-authorship-of-original-text-of.html, accessed 23 October 2012, reopens the case for an early-1590s date for the original version of *Sir Thomas More*.

may well reflect the way language was changing outside the theatre, but some seem to be better traced to collective changes in dramatic discourse. In the later period writers wanted their characters to strike different attitudes, and they gave them different preoccupations. The changes happened within the work of individual writers, and within genres, as well as in the whole sets. The word data gives us the opportunity to make a model of language change, something measurable to put beside a reader's intuition that characters in the 1600s plays have moved across a dramatic boundary and speak a recognizably different dramatic dialect. In the event the system works well in distinguishing early 1590s plays from early 1600s ones. When the tests are applied to the *More* play its affinities prove to be with the later group.

I chose two half-decades for analysis, 1590 to 1594 and 1600 to 1604, to match the two rival theories for the date of the original version of *Sir Thomas More*. The half-decade gap, the missing years 1595 to 1599, ensures that we are not comparing plays within a year or two, where we would hardly expect to be able to detect a difference. I use 30 plays from the first five-year period and 28 from the second, all edited from early printed versions (Appendix 1).[28] The dates come from Alfred Harbage and S. Schoenbaum's *Annals of English Drama*.[29]

I began with function words, words like *the* and *of* which have a structural rather than semantic role in language. These words have been the mainstay of computational stylistics, and have proved to be rich in stylistic information.[30] Despite a common-sense expectation that they are used much the same way by all speakers of a language, they turn out to vary in patterns that are very revealing about the stances of speakers. Since they are common, they provide abundant, evenly distributed data, well suited to locating broader currents of change in groups of texts, where such currents exist. I applied a statistical measure called the 't-test'[31] to each of 219 function word variables, to determine if any of them were differently used in the two groups of plays. I found that 28 of the 219 variables tested had t-test results suggesting very marked differences between the two groups (Illustration 1). This fits with the idea that the turn of the century marks a sharp change in dramatic style.[32]

As a comparison, I took the same 58 plays and created two new sets of 30 and 28 plays, this time randomly assigned from the original list. I looked for differences between the two new sets. There were no results which would have qualified for a list like that in Illustration 1.[33] Thus we can be confident that there are marked and consistent differences between the early 1590s and early 1600s plays, quite unlike those that might have come about by chance.

Illustration 2 shows just how stark the differences can be. In the early 1590s plays there are on average slightly more instances of *thou* and *thee* together than those of *you*. In the early 1600s ones this is reversed and *you* far outnumbers the combined counts of the other two.

The differences are starker still in the case of *doth* and *does* (Illustration 3). *Does* is very rare in the earlier group – the average is less than one a play, and 22 of the 30 plays have no instances at all – but it occurs regularly in the later group, about ten a play on average, with only three plays of the 28 having no instances.

The whole span is just fifteen years, well within a single playwriting career, and yet some of the

---

[28] The plays were edited so that all the function words listed in Appendix 2 could be counted separately. Variant spellings of other words were combined as modern-spelling headwords for counting with the help of specially designed software.

[29] Alfred Harbage and S. Schoenbaum, *Annals of English Drama 975–1700*, second edition (Philadelphia, 1964).

[30] The pioneer work in this area is John Burrows, *Computation into Criticism: A Study in Jane Austen and an Experiment in Method* (Oxford, 1987).

[31] This is the ratio of the difference between the means of two groups of samples for a given variable and the standard deviation of the whole set. See 'Student', 'The Probable Error of a Mean', *Biometrika*, 6 (1908), 1–25.

[32] See D. J. Lake, 'The Date of the *Sir Thomas More* Additions by Dekker and Shakespeare', *Notes and Queries*, 222 (1977), 114–16; and Macdonald P. Jackson, 'Linguistic Evidence for the Date of Shakespeare's Addition to *Sir Thomas More*', *Notes and Queries*, 25 (1978), 154–6 at 155.

[33] The strongest t-test result was $p = 0.003$, with just five results at $p < 0.05$.

More common in 1590–4 plays	More common in 1600–4 plays
although	a, an
and	could
art [verb]	does
doth	has
for [conjunction]	is
hast	it
hath	most
that [conjunction]	on [adverb]
thee	own
then	there
thou	too
thy	very
thyself	would
unto	you

1. Function-word variables much more common in 1590–4 plays compared to 1600–4 plays or the reverse.[34] For the plays used, see Appendix 1.

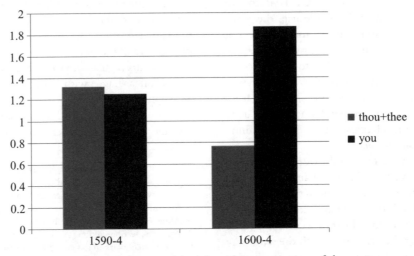

2. Average percentage of *thou+thee* and *you* in two groups of plays

basic fabric of the language had altered. Thus the playwrights did reflect the familiar changes taking place in early modern English, and (it seems) they did so with alacrity.

In cases like *thou* and *you* and *doth* and *does*, a more modern form is being substituted for an equivalent older one. There are also fluctuations among word frequencies which reflect changing structures rather than substitutions. *Very* is a word that comes to be used more often in the later plays. It adds emphasis and seems to belong to the redundancy and informality of everyday speech. The average for a 20,000-word play is 8 in the early

---

34 These are chosen from a list of 219 function words on the basis that for a t-test of the two play groups there is a probability of 0.0001 or less that they belong to the same parent population. The 219 words are listed in Appendix 2.

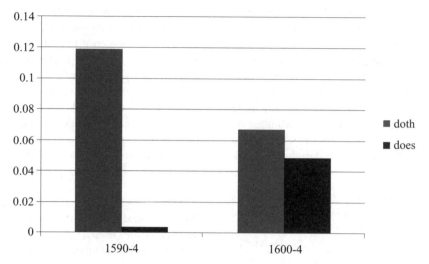

3. Average percentage of *doth* and *does* in two groups of plays

1590s, compared to 22 in the early 1600s. The difference holds good for comedies as a subset (11 in the early comedies, 23 in the later ones), for Shakespeare plays (11 to 31) and for Shakespeare comedies (19 to 31). Two of the early plays, *Dr Faustus* and *Orlando Furioso*, have no instances at all. In Marston's comedy *Dutch Courtesan* (1604),[35] with the second highest average, we hear 'a toy, a very trifle', 'Be very careful', ''tis very well spoken', ''tis very well', and 'very fine language'.[36] In *Hamlet* (1601) there are four instances in one soliloquy. Hamlet imagines the the player he has just heard would 'amaze indeed / The very faculty of eyes and ears' if he was in Hamlet's shoes (2.2.567–8), while he himself does no more than 'fall a-cursing like a very drab' (2.2.588). He recalls that guilty parties have been moved to confess 'by the very cunning of the scene' in some plays (2.2.592). It may be that the Ghost was in fact a creation of the devil, working on Hamlet's own melancholy, since the fiend 'is very potent with such spirits' (2.2.603). In his interview with Osric, Hamlet seems to mock the new fashion for the word. He tells Osric to put his hat back on. Osric replies:

Osric. I thank your lordship, 'tis very hot.
Hamlet. No, believe me, 'tis very cold. The wind is northerly.

Osric. It is indifferent cold, my lord, indeed.
Hamlet. Methinks it is very sultry and hot for my complexion.
Osric. Exceedingly, my lord. It is very sultry, as 'twere, – I cannot tell how. (5.2.95–102)

In less 'foregrounded' cases, a taste for judicious emphasis and an inclination towards amplification rather than pithiness seems to lie behind the increase in the use of the word. *Most* is also markedly more common in the later plays, for what seem to be similar reasons.

The indefinite articles *a* and *an* are much more widely used in the early 1600s plays (Illustration 1). This is not just a slight or occasional rise but a marked and consistent one. I have discussed elsewhere a remarkable upward trend in the use of these words in plays from the 1580s to the 1630s.[37] Speakers use *a* or *an* when referring to an entity considered as a member of a class rather than a particular instance – 'a priest' rather than 'the priest'. Jokes are often framed in terms of 'an Irishman',

---

[35] Dates for plays given in parentheses are from Harbage and Schoenbaum, *Annals of English Drama*.
[36] John Marston, *The Dutch Courtezan* (London, 1605), sigs. C3r, E2v, E3r, and F3v. Spelling has been modernized.
[37] Hugh Craig, '*A* and *an* in English Plays, 1580–1639', *Texas Studies in Literature and Language*, 53.3 (2011), 273–93.

and so on, and philosophical reflections turn on 'a precise statement' or 'a final cause'. One way to account for the increase in *a* and *an* is a new element of detachment in the 1600s plays. Generally, it seems that playwrights found more detached, more urbane, more reflective dialogue to serve their purposes better, to be more piquant, more of the moment. The lawyer Tangle in Middleton's comedy *The Phoenix* (1604) cites the Captain as a case in point to illustrate the multitude who seek his lawyerly services:

Why, thus am I sought after by all professions. Here's a weatherbeaten captain, who not long since new married to a lady widow, would now fain have sued a divorce between her and him... (4.244–7)[38]

Characters in the play talk of 'a pretty policy' (4.157) and 'an excellent stratagem' (4.158). Trends in the wider history of *a* and *an* discussed in my article help demonstrate the patterns of their use. *Platea* characters, like the Fool in *King Lear* and the Porter in *Macbeth*, relate directly to the audience, whereas *locus* characters remain within the time and place of the fiction. *Platea* characters use *a* and *an* more freely than *locus* characters.[39] Jokes, proverbs and word play bring with them an increase in instances.[40] Sardonic observers within the plays also have a marked recourse to these words. Flamineo and Bosola, for example, are in this group, and use *a* and *an* freely. G. K. Hunter places them with a generation of impoverished offspring of profligate landowners, graduates who worked their way through university and 'now relish with Montaignian detachment the immorality of the world in which they make their living'.[41]

Another of the changes in function word use that has larger implications is the increase in the modal auxiliaries *would* and *could*. They signal attention to motivation and possibility, to action considered more in terms of its human and social context. Once again the contrast between early 1590s and early 1600s plays belongs within a larger sweep from the 1580s to the 1630s, this time of a group of modal verbs. There are some purely grammatical factors at work, but it is also possible to see the expansion of the use of some modals as corresponding to an increased 'apprehension that the self is mobile, in play, and ambiguous', a 'new sense of a self suspended, provisional, negotiable, and constantly re-enacted'.[42]

Thus we can see a cultural drift as well as a linguistic drift in the overall changes in style. The scale of these changes is remarkable. They are as prominent as the expected changes in direct substitutes, *does* supplanting *doth*, *you* supplanting *thou*, and so on; and even there, the rapidity of the change is a surprise.

The dialogue of the earlier plays is more direct and straightforward. John Lyly's comedy *The Woman in the Moon* (1593) deals with the shaping of the first woman in creation, Pandora. In Act 3 Venus plays her part, teaching Pandora the tricks of love:

> Is she not young? then let her to the world,
> All those are strumpets that are over-chaste,
> Defying such as keep their company,
> 'Tis not the touching of a womans hand,
> Kissing her lips, hanging about her neck.
> A speaking look, no nor a yielding word,
> That men expect, believe me *Sol* 'tis more,
> And were *Mars* here he would protest as much.

Sol. But what is more than this is worse than
> nought,
> I dare not stay lest she infect me too.

> *Exit.*

Venus. What is he gone, then light foot *Ioculus*,
> Set me *Pandora* in a dancing vein,
Ioculus. Fair mother I will make *Pandora* blithe,
> And like a satyr hop upon these plains.

> *Exit*

---

38 Quotations from the play here and below are from Thomas Middleton, *The Collected Works*, ed. Gary Taylor and John Lavagnino (Oxford, 2007).

39 Craig, '*A* and *an*', pp. 277–83.

40 Craig, '*A* and *an*', p. 281.

41 G. K. Hunter, *English Drama 1586–1642: The Age of Shakespeare*, Oxford History of English Literature (Oxford, 1997), p. 476.

42 Hugh Craig, 'Grammatical Modality in English Plays from the 1580s to the 1640s', *English Literary Renaissance*, 30.1 (2000), 32–54 at 54.

Venus. Go Cupid give her all the golden shafts.
    And she will take thee for a forester.
Cupid. I will and you shall see her straight in love.[43]

Most of this dialogue is imperative and declarative, not much concerned with subjectivity. Action and straightforward statement are predominant. There is some general reference bringing instances of *a* but the overall effect is brisk and concrete.

Similarly, the anonymous comedy *Knack to Know a Knave* (1592) has dialogue with illustration and much detail, but stately and explicit rather than elliptical. In this speech the dying bailiff instructs his sons:

My sons you see how age decays my state,
And that my life like snow before the sun:
'Gins to dissolve into that substance now,
From whose enclosure grew my fire of life,
The earth I mean, sweet mother of us all,
Whom death authorised by heaven's high power,
Shall bring at last, from whence at first I came,
Yet ere I yield myself to death, my sons,
Give ear, and hear what rules I set you down,
And first to thee my son, that livest by wit,
I know thou hast so many honest sleights,
To shift and cozen smoothly on thy wit,
To cog and lie, and brave it with the best,
That 'twere but labour lost to counsel thee,
And therefore to the next, Walter, that seems in show a
    husbandman:
My son, when that thy master trusts thee most,
And thinks thou dealest as truly as himself,
Be thou the first to work deceit to him:
So by that means thou mayst enrich thyself,
And live at pleasure when thy master's dead:
And when to market thou art sent with wool,
Put sand amongst it, and 'twill make it weigh,
The weight twice double that it did before,
The overplus is thine into thy purse.[44]

There is just one instance of *a* in this passage, and none of *could* or *would*, or of *very* or *most*. The bailiff is generalizing, but in very specific terms, picturing fully realized commonplace situations. He does not concern himself with motivation or cognition.

By contrast here is a passage from *All's Well that Ends Well* (1602), with the staccato quality, the aspect of detachment, the focus on attitude and evaluation, and the more life-like padding and redundancy which characterize the new style:

Lafeu. They say miracles are past, and we have our philosophical persons to make modern and familiar things supernatural and causeless. Hence is it that we make trifles of terrors, ensconcing ourselves into seeming knowledge when we should submit ourselves to an unknown fear.
Paroles. Why, 'tis the rarest argument of wonder that hath shot out in our latter times.
Bertram. And so 'tis.
Lafeu. To be relinquished of the artists –
Paroles. So I say – both of Galen and Paracelsus.
Lafeu. Of all the learned and authentic Fellows –
Paroles. Right, so I say.
Lafeu. That gave him out incurable –
Paroles. Why, there 'tis, so say I too.
Lafeu. Not to be helped.
Paroles. Right, as 'twere a man assur'd of a –
Lafeu. Uncertain life and sure death.
Paroles. Just, you say well, so would I have said.
Lafeu. I may truly say it is a novelty to the world.
Paroles. It is indeed. If you will have it in showing, you shall read it in [*pointing to the ballad*] what-do-ye-call there.
Lafeu. [*reads*] 'A showing of a heavenly effect in an earthly actor'.
Paroles. That's it, I would have said the very same.

(2.3.1–26)

This is bookish talk, and yet colloquial, too, in its elliptical rhythms and recourse to fillers. It incorporates tendencies from both orality and literacy. The drama was learning to represent casual speech at the same time as it was absorbing the new profusion of written language in the age of the printed book.[45]

We can combine the counts for the 28 variables of illustration 1 and, with the help of a 'data reduction' procedure, Principal Components Analysis, find the two most important factors in the whole

---

[43] John Lyly, *The Woman in the Moone* (London, 1597), sig. C3v. Spelling has been modernized.

[44] *Knacke to Knowe a Knaue* (London, 1594), sigs. B1r-v. Spelling has been modernized.

[45] Lynne Magnusson, 'Language', *The Oxford Handbook of Shakespeare* (Oxford, 2012), pp. 239–57 at 248.

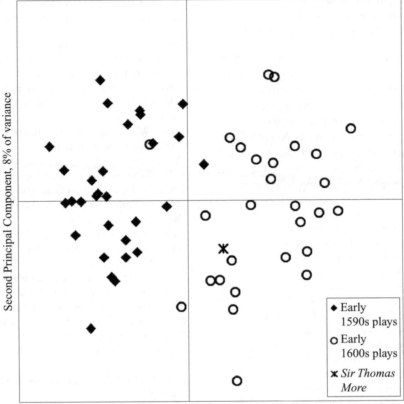

4. Principal Components Analysis of 28 word-variables from a list of 219 function words in two sets of plays and *Sir Thomas More*

table of 28 variables in 58 texts. The texts can then be arrayed along the two axes, as in Illustration 4.

The First Principal Component, along the X axis, arrays the plays largely by half-decade group. If we use the Y axis as a boundary, we find just one early play (a Shakespeare comedy, *The Taming of the Shrew*) to the right and two later plays (two non-Shakespeare comedies, William Haughton's *A Devil and his Dame*, higher up, and Thomas Heywood's *Four Prentices*, lower down) to the left. The selected word-variables give a basis for an almost complete separation of the two sets. Shakespeare is represented in both sets – the only author to be so, as it happens – but his plays remain within their separate half-decade clusters.[46] There is an imbalance in genres, as the listings in the table in

Appendix 1 show, with more history plays in the earlier set (12 out of 30 versus 2 out of 28, if we add together examples of 'History', 'Foreign History' and 'Legendary History') and more comedies in the later one (11 out of 30 versus 17 out of 28, this time including 'Romantic Comedy' and 'Domestic Comedy' as well as simply 'Comedy'). Yet the genre imbalance does not override the half-decade clustering. With the odd exception, early histories cluster with the other early plays, and late histories with other late plays, and the same with the comedies. *Sir Thomas More* is placed with the

---

[46] That is, the highest score for a 1590–4 Shakespeare play on the first principal component is still lower than the lowest score for a 1600–4 Shakespeare play.

1600–4 plays. It has a First Principal Component score higher than any of the 1590–4 plays, and well within the 1600–4 range, with five of the accredited 1600–4 plays scoring lower. This result supports Jackson's findings in his article on the date question. The approach here is combinatory and statistically driven, complementing Jackson's use of carefully specific, *a priori* markers drawn from prosody and accidence.

One doubt that arises, though, is whether the selection of words according to these particular plays means that the method is well adapted to separating these two sets, but would not work so well for a play freshly introduced which had not already been involved in the word selection. To test this, we can take out one of the plays in the sets, find a new set of words following the same rules as before, and then reintroduce the withdrawn play and check how things change.[47] We then return this play to its set and withdraw a second one, and repeat this until we have completed ten trials.[48] In these trials there was some movement of plays relative to each other along the first principal component, but within a narrow range.[49] In each case the play now treated as if it were of unknown provenance remained on the 'correct' side of the Y axis. Thus we can assume that the dating test using selected function words and PCA gives a reliable result for freshly introduced plays as well as for the ones used to establish the marker word lists. We might have feared that the position of *Sir Thomas More* in the chart was unstable because this text was not used to help define the marker words, but the experience with the test plays shows that this is not necessarily the case.

Illustration 4 and all that underlies it are a mathematical model of language shift. It tells us that there is undoubtedly change in the dialogue of plays of the early 1600s compared to the early 1590s, something both marked and consistent, much more than could be explained by a shift in genres or one author's idiosyncratic style compared to another's. The model can also serve as a classifier, to distinguish plays from one half-decade from plays from another. It places the original version of *Sir Thomas More* with the 1600–4 plays.

In taking two half-decades as reference points we are concentrating on just two stations on a much longer line. But the distance travelled is already significant. The later plays are more satirical, more reflective, more urbane, more courtly and more colloquially redundant. Their discourse is more attentive to individual motivation and cognition.

The function words in the full list of 219 contain some very common words indeed and, overall, instances of these words represent something close to 60 per cent of the total number of words in any set of plays.[50] As a separate test we can compile another set of words which may be less evenly distributed, and mostly less common overall, but also playing a part in style. I excluded the words in the list of 219 function words and then took the words that appear in at least half the plays in the set of 216 and selected those which are most different in use between the two half-decades (Illustration 5).

These are mostly lexical words, though some of the function words not in the list of 219 appear, such as *unless* and *wherefore* in the 1590–4 column and *betwixt* in the 1600–4 one. Some of the words in the left-hand column, those favoured in the earlier plays, are associated with the plays of conquest and barbaric triumph which predominate there, particularly *cursed*, *golden*, *mighty*, *slain*, and *will* as a noun. The words in the right-hand column are harder to link to one particular genre. There is a group of words applying to perceptual and cognitive functions: *appears*, *judgement*, *knowledge*, *memory*, *observe*

---

47 This is a bootstrapping method: see Bradley Efron, 'Bootstrap Methods: Another Look at the Jackknife', *The Annals of Statistics*, 7.1 (1979), 1–26.

48 The plays were randomly chosen, five from each half-decade. They are those identified as Nos. 7, 8, 13, 15, 26, 31, 35, 37, 40 and 46 in Appendix 1.

49 I correlated the play scores for the first principal component from the analysis using the marker words derived from the full play sets with the scores for the first principal component from each of the ten trials using marker words derived from the sets without a held-out play. The average correlation was 0.998, with the lowest being 0.997.

50 In a set of 216 plays of the period, the 219 word-variables have 2,391,146 instances out of a total word count of 4,159,893, or 57%.

More common in 1590–4 plays	More common in 1600–4 plays
came	action
content	appears
cursed	better
darest	betwixt
depart	bounty
golden	close
gracious	express
loving	form
mighty	friendship
modest	gallant
request	gentleman
reward	greatness
slain	judgement
sorrow	knowledge
trouble	memory
unless	motion
wherefore	natural
will [noun]	observe
	office
	patience
	pleased
	precious
	private
	protest
	raised
	remember
	respect

5. Word-variables not in the 219 list (Appendix 2), appearing in half or more of a set of 216 plays, and much more common in 1590–4 plays compared to 1600–4 plays and the reverse.[51] For the plays used, see Appendix 1. For the list of words from which these sets are drawn, see Appendix 3.

and *remember*. A second group belongs to the world of social and institutional arrangements: *friendship*, *gallant*, *gentleman*, *pleased* and *private*. The world of the plays is more concerned with the overt exercise of power in the early 1590s and more with the interior life and with a denser web of social relations in the early 1600s.

As before, I subjected a table of frequencies for these words in the two half-decade sets to a Principal Components Analysis (Illustration 6).

As with Illustration 2, there is an evident split along the First Principal Component between early 1590s and early 1600s plays. If we use the Y axis as a boundary, we find all plays bar one from the earlier set on the left-hand side, with lower scores, and all bar one of the later plays on the right-hand, higher side. *Sir Thomas More* again clusters with the later plays.

---

51 Using a t-test probability of 0.01 or lower.

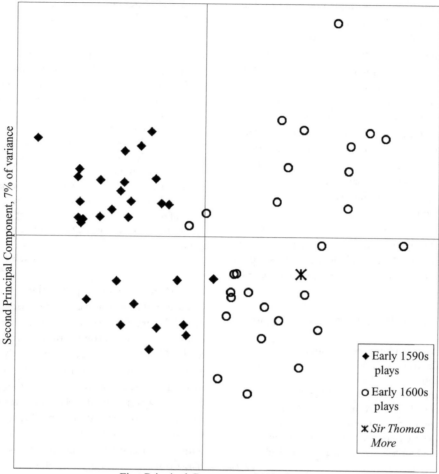

6. Principal Components Analysis using 45 words from a list of 234 common words in two sets of plays
and *Sir Thomas More*

As before, we need to test how well the method works with plays whose provenance we know, but which are presented to the system as though they were of disputed date. If we use the same ten plays as before as test cases, change the words according to the t-test results for each slightly modified play set, and correlate the new scores for plays with the old ones, we find that, though there is more change this time,[52] each of the ten plays selected for 'bootstrapping' remains correctly assigned to its half-decade group.

The strength of the case is in a quantitative analysis of the whole of *More* in relation to the broad sweep of the two play sets. To illustrate what this might mean in terms of style, we can take a

---

[52] The average correlation between the first principal component play scores for the analysis with markers drawn from the full sets and the same scores for analyses using markers drawn from the sets without a held-out play was 0.996, with the lowest 0.992.

passage from the play, while conceding that nothing can be proved from a short extract. For instance, there might be all sorts of more modern features in such a passage, for entirely local reasons, which could be entirely outweighed by patterns elsewhere. Alternatively, archaic elements might be explained by the fact that *More* is a history play, following a well-known series of events from the past, and the authors might have wished to emphasize at one point or another a sense of a setting in a historical era. However, identifying the words the analysis tells us are characteristic of the early-1600s plays in a short passage shows individual words in context and as an assemblage.

Half way through scene 13, when More is on the way to the Tower after his arrest, he meets a poor woman who had in his former life sought his help with a suit in Chancery. More recognizes her:

More. What, my old client, are thou got hither too?
　Poor silly wretch, I must confess indeed
　I had such writings as concern thee near,
　But the King
　Has ta'en the matter into his own hand;
　He has all I had. Then, woman, sue to him.
　I cannot help thee. Thou must bear with me.
Woman. Ah, gentle heart, my soul for thee is sad.
　Farewell, the best friend that the poor e'er had.

Exit

Gentleman Porter. Before you enter through the Tower gate,
　Your upper garment, sir, belongs to me.
More. Sir, you shall have it. There it is.
　He gives him his cap
Gentleman Porter. The upmost on your back, sir. You mistake me.
More. Sir, now I understand ye very well.
　He gives him his cloak
　But that you name my back,
　Sure else my cap had been the uppermost.
Shrewsbury. Farewell, kind lord. God send us merry meeting.
More. Amen, my lord.
Surrey. Farewell, dear friend. I hope your safe return.
More. My lord, and my dear fellow in the Muses,

Farewell. Farewell, most noble poet.
Lieutenant. Adieu, most honoured lords.

Exeunt Lords

More. Fair prison, welcome. Yet methinks
　For thy fair building 'tis too foul a name.
　Many a guilty soul, and many an innocent,
　Have breathed their farewell to thy hollow rooms.
　I oft have entered into thee this way,
　Yet, I thank God, ne'er with a clearer conscience
　Than at this hour.
　This is my comfort yet: how hard soe'er
　My lodging prove, the cry of the poor suitor,
　Fatherless orphan or distressed widow
　Shall not disturb me in my quiet sleep.
　On, then, i'God's name, to our close abode.
　God is as strong here as he is abroad.

Exeunt (14.36–70)[53]

In More's first long speech there is an instance of *too* and of *own* and two instances of *has*, all words more characteristic of the 1600–4 plays compared to the 1590–4 ones (Illustration 1). In his speeches to the Gentleman Porter More mostly uses *you* as his form of address and once uses *very*. He uses *most* in his farewell to Surrey, and the Lieutenant uses this word again immediately afterwards in his adieu to Surrey and Shrewsbury. In More's soliloquy at the end there are three instances of *a*, and one of *an*. This speech also has an instance of *too*, and one of *close* ('our close abode') from the list of early-1600s lexical words (Illustration 5).

Returning to the numerical evidence: going by dead reckoning on language patterns alone, and ignoring the indications from handwriting, theatre history, possible occasions, sources, and so on, we find *Sir Thomas More* placed in the 1600–4 band as opposed to the 1590–4 one. The early 1590s dating, favoured by most scholars before Jackson's article and the Jowett Arden edition, fares poorly

---

53 Text from *Sir Thomas More*, ed. Jowett. This is not identical with the text I have used for analysis, which is based on W. W. Greg, ed., *The Book of Sir Thomas More*, Malone Society Reprints (Oxford, 1911), which conveniently separates the original version from the additions.

in this comparison. Jackson modestly says his evidence 'falls short of *proving* that the play was written about the turn of the century'[54] and in this spirit one must concede that the trials presented here are a contribution to the discussion rather than a resolution of it, but there is definitely support for the later dating here.

A later date would decouple the composition of the play from the outbreak of anger against foreigners in London in 1592–3, proposed by Gabrieli and Melchiori and others as an important element in the occasion for writing *More*. On the other hand, it makes sense of the coincidences in theme with Munday's two-part play *The Life of Sir John Oldcastle* (1599–1600), which Gabrieli notes in his article on the sources of the play.[55] The *More* play moves into a context of other city comedy and plays about Cromwell and Wolsey, as already noted. The late date also means that the closeness in wording to Harington already discussed has a simpler explanation, i.e. that the authors of *More* read Harington's book in its printed form. A later date for the original play fits with the perceived influence of *Julius Caesar*. It also brings its composition closer to the latest generally supported date for the revisions. Original and revisions can be thought of as occurring at one historical moment.

Surprisingly, the frequencies of the two sets of words give a good fix on date for plays in bands separated by only five years. This implies that the language of the plays changed remarkably quickly and remarkably consistently. As playwrights composed their plays, imitated one another, tried to outdo one another, as companies and audiences exerted their influence, they all – whether they knew it or not – followed the same broad common path. This underlying collective movement in language gives us another tool to date plays where the usual sources like title-pages and records of performance are lacking. Philology can come to the aid of bibliography and theatre history.

---

[54] Jackson, 'Deciphering a Date', para. 24.
[55] Gabrieli, '*Sir Thomas More*', p. 24.

APPENDIX I

Plays used in the two half-decade sets. 'Date' and 'Genre' from A. Harbage and S. Schoenbaum, *Annals of English Drama 975–1700* (Philadelphia, 1964)

1590–4 plays

No.	Author	Title	Date	Genre	Copytext	Date of Copytext
1	Greene	*James IV*	1590	History	STC12308	1598
2	Greene	*Orlando Furioso*	1591	Romantic comedy	STC12265	1594
3	Lodge and Greene	*Looking Glass for London and England*	1590	Biblical moral	STC16680	1598
4	Lyly	*Love's Metamorphosis*	1590	Pastoral	STC17082	1601
5	Lyly	*Woman in the Moon*	1593	Comedy	STC17090	1597
6	Marlowe	*Doctor Faustus* (A text)	1592	Tragedy	STC17429	1604
7	Marlowe	*Edward II*	1592	History	STC17437	1594
8	Marlowe	*Massacre at Paris*	1593	Foreign history	STC17423	1600
9	Nashe	*Summer's Last Will and Testament*	1592	Comedy	STC18376	1600
10	Peele	*Edward I*	1591	History	STC19535	1593
11	Peele	*Old Wives Tale*	1590	Romance	STC19545	1595

(cont.)

(*cont.*)

No.	Author	Title	Date	Genre	Copytext	Date of Copytext
12	Shakespeare	*Comedy of Errors*	1592	Comedy	STC22273	1623
13	Shakespeare	*Richard III*	1593	History	STC22314	1597
14	Shakespeare	*Taming of the Shrew*	1594	Comedy	STC22273	1623
15	Shakespeare	*Two Gentlemen of Verona*	1593	Comedy	STC22273	1623
16	Shakespeare and others	*Henry VI Part 1*	1592	History	STC22273	1623
17	Shakespeare and others	*Henry VI Part 2*	1591	History	STC22273	1623
18	Shakespeare and others	*Henry VI Part 3*	1591	History	STC22273	1623
19	Shakespeare and Peele	*Titus Andronicus*	1594	Tragedy	STC22328	1594
20	Uncertain	*Arden of Faversham*	1591	Realistic tragedy	STC733	1592
21	Uncertain	*Edward III*	1590	History	STC7501	1596
22	Uncertain	*Fair Em*	1590	Romantic comedy	STC7675	1591(?)
23	Uncertain	*John of Bordeaux*	1592	Comedy	Malone Society	1936
24	Uncertain	*King Leir*	1590	Legendary history	STC15343	1605
25	Uncertain	*Knack to Know a Knave*	1592	Comedy	STC15027	1594
26	Uncertain	*Selimus Part 1*	1592	Heroical romance	STC12310a	1594
27	Uncertain	*Soliman and Perseda*	1590	Tragedy	STC22894	1592(?)
28	Uncertain	*George a Greene*	1590	Romantic comedy	STC12212	1599
29	Uncertain	*True Tragedy of Richard III*	1591	History	STC21009	1594
30	Wilson	*Cobbler's Prophecy*	1590	Comedy	STC25781	1594

1600–4 plays

No.	Author	Title	Date	Genre	Copytext	Date of Copytext
31	Chapman	*All Fools*	1604	Comedy	STC4963	1605
32	Chapman	*Bussy d'Ambois*	1604	Foreign History	STC4966	1607
33	Chapman	*Gentleman Usher*	1602	Comedy	STC4978	1606
34	Chapman	*May Day*	1602	Comedy	STC4980	1611
35	Chapman	*Monsieur d'Olive*	1604	Comedy	STC4984	1606
36	Chapman	*Sir Giles Goosecap*	1602	Comedy	STC12050	1606
37	Chettle	*Hoffman*	1602	Tragedy	STC5125	1631
38	Haughton	*Devil and his Dame*	1600	Comedy	Wing G1580	1662
39	Heywood	*Four Prentices*	1600	Heroical Romance	STC13321	1615
40	Heywood	*If You Know Not Me Part 1*	1604	History	STC13328	1605

No.	Author	Title	Date	Genre	Copytext	Date of Copytext
41	Heywood	*Wise Woman*	1604	Comedy	STC13370	1638
42	Heywood	*Woman Killed with Kindness*	1603	Tragedy	STC13371	1607
43	Jonson	*Cynthia's Revels*	1601	Comedy	STC14773	1601
44	Jonson	*Poetaster*	1601	Comedy	STC14781	1602
45	Jonson	*Sejanus*	1603	Tragedy	STC14782	1605
46	Marston	*Antonio's Revenge*	1600	Tragedy	STC17474	1601
47	Marston	*Dutch Courtesan*	1604	Comedy	STC17475	1605
48	Marston	*Jack Drum's Entertainment*	1600	Domestic comedy	STC7243	1601
49	Marston	*Malcontent*	1604	Tragicomedy	STC17481	1604
50	Marston	*What You Will*	1601	Comedy	STC17487	1607
51	Middleton	*Phoenix*	1604	Comedy	STC17892	1607
52	Shakespeare	*All's Well that Ends Well*	1602	Comedy	STC22273	1623
53	Shakespeare	*Hamlet*	1601	Tragedy	STC22276	1604
54	Shakespeare	*Merry Wives of Windsor*	1600	Comedy	STC22299	1602
55	Shakespeare	*Othello*	1604	Tragedy	STC22305	1622
56	Shakespeare	*Troilus and Cressida*	1602	Tragedy	STC22331	1609
57	Shakespeare	*Twelfth Night*	1600	Comedy	STC22273	1623
58	Shakespeare and Middleton	*Measure for Measure*	1604	Comedy	STC22273	1623

APPENDIX 2

219 function words

a + an, about, above, after, again, against, all, almost, along, although, am, among, amongst, and, another, any, anything, are, art, as, at, back, be, because, been, before, being, besides, beyond, both, but, by [adverb], by [fossil], by [preposition], can, cannot, canst, could, dare, did, didst, do, does, doing, done, dost, doth, down, durst, each, either, enough, ere, even, ever, every, few, for [adverb], for [conjunction], for [preposition], from, had, hadst, has, hast, hath, have, having, he, hence, her [adjective], her [personal pronoun], here, him, himself, his, how, I, if, in [adverb], in [preposition], into, is, it, itself, least, like [adjective], like [adverb], like [conjunction], like [preposition], many, may, me, might, mine, more, most, much, must, my, myself, neither, never, no [adjective], no [adverb], no [exclamation], no [fossil], none, nor, not, nothing, now, o, of, off, oft, often, on [adverb], on [preposition], one, only, or, other, our [royal plural], our [true plural], ours [royal plural], ours [true plural], ourselves, out, over, own, past, perhaps, quite, rather, round, same, shall, shalt, she, should, since, sith, so [adverb degree], so [adverb manner], so [conjunction], some, something, somewhat, still, such, than, that [conjunction], that [demonstrative], that [relative], the, thee, their, them, themselves, then, there, these, they, thine, this, those, thou, though, through, thus, thy, thyself, till, to [adverb], to [fossil], to [infinitive], to [preposition], too, under, until, unto, up [adverb], up [preposition], upon [adverb], upon [preposition], us [royal plural], us [true plural], very, was, we [royal plural], we [true plural], well, were, wert, what, when, where, which [interrogative], which [relative], while, whilst, who [interrogative], who [relative], whom, whose, why, will [verb], with, within, without, would, ye, yet, you, your, yours, yourself, yourselves.

APPENDIX 3

234 words appearing in half or more of a set of 216 plays, in order of t-test score for 1590–4 and 1600–4 play groups, highest first:

action, mighty, golden, observe, darest, reward, slain, loving, respect, wherefore, content, protest, greatness, judgement, natural, gallant, came, knowledge, pleased, unless, cursed, depart, bounty, private, memory, express, gracious, patience, sorrow, trouble, office, appears, betwixt, modest, form, motion, precious, remember, gentleman, request, raised, close, will [noun], friendship, better, famous, abused, blows, mirth, away, actions, takes, provide, account, unhappy, shadow, fruit, instant, jewel, creature, gifts, creatures, fatal, disgrace, second, freely, difference, virgin, easy, pleasure, presence, blame, forbear, empty, glory, ashamed, lawful, hereafter, told, buried, deceived, perfect, deadly, greater, lusty, flatter, holds, expect, choice, heavenly, changed, gentlemen, servant, forsooth, endure, glorious, farewell, willingly, news, age, answer, manners, making, bought, lately, miserable, example, art [noun], behind, kept, preserve, stranger, lips, dance, present, train, despair, subject, troubled, violence, sorry, going, vengeance, makes, purse, thunder, condition, courage, prisoner, innocent, increase, names, prepare, torment, forty, used, treason, large, report, today, early, acquainted, entreat, suffer, credit, thence, remedy, blessing, happiness, ruled, like [verb], maintain, goodly, graces, melancholy, remove, mischief, order, wretched, poison, meant, goes, sport, prepared, estate, necessity, pieces, satisfy, worlds, hazard, willing, otherwise, charge, patient, unknown, abuse, tells, knees, health, dearly, forgot, clouds, minute, sacred, longer, assured, becomes, envy, always, served, forever, passage, swift, noble, discourse, company, naked, faults, fame, undertake, month, spend, malice, divine, change, seldom, urge, runs, suddenly, stomach, dangerous, constant, ones, heartily, monstrous, visit, ancient, undone, presently, attempt, frame, knowing, two, quickly, thinking, beasts, strength, sooner, bones, dust, hardly, wounds, easily, prevent.

FILMING 'THE WEIGHT OF THIS SAD TIME': YASUJIRO OZU'S REREADING OF *KING LEAR* IN *TOKYO STORY* (1953)

REIKO OYA

Ozu was like an English poet. It was as if he was reflecting on the old castle in the estate of the manor. It was as if he was visualizing a disintegration of the family of the lord of the fief in the dispersal of the early-wintry leaves of a tall, stately tree.
—*Scriptwriter Tadao Ikeda's obituary of Ozu*[1]

CINEMA'S ARTISTIC REPRODUCTION: THREE SHOCHIKU *LEARS*

Japanese film director and scriptwriter Yasujiro Ozu was born in 1903 and, entering the major film and theatre company Shochiku in 1923, went on to make 54 films (34 silents and 20 talkies, of which the final 6 are in colour) as a studio director. Known for his rigorous cinematic style and ascetic restraint on the narrative contents of his films, this highly idiosyncratic filmmaker perfected his very own 'grammar' of cinema which includes consistently low and stationary camera position (no tilts or pans), adherence to just clean cuts for transition (no fades or dissolves), and very distinctive use of cutaways, eye-line mismatches and 360 degree space (instead of Hollywood's 180 degree).[2] Working with a single hand-picked film crew, Ozu tirelessly portrayed the disintegration of traditional family structures in contemporary Japan by casting his virtual stock company in only slightly (but decisively) modified roles with similar-sounding character names in film after film. Actor Chishu Ryu for instance appeared in all but two of the director's works, playing a father figure named Shukichi in many of them. Ozu's scripts and films in effect formed an extended family saga, where each new

piece critically and creatively revised the earlier interpretations. During the wartime years of the 1930s and '40s, tragic motifs of Shakespeare's *King Lear* came to be interlaced into this dense intertextual web of the director's family romance, paving the way to his 1953 masterpiece, *Tokyo Story* (*Tokyo monogatari*).

While Walter Benjamin regarded film as the paradigmatic art in the age of mechanical reproduction, this audio-visual medium is also characterized by its proclivity to 'artistic' reproduction and remaking. Films not only borrow their narrative, shooting, acting and editorial styles from one another but draw inspiration from existing literature and drama as well as from music, painting and other art forms. French film director Abel Gance (1889–1981) was certainly right when he proclaimed in 1927 that 'Shakespeare, Rembrandt, Beethoven will make films . . . All legends, all mythologies, and all myths, all the founders of religions, indeed, all religions . . . await their celluloid resurrection, and the heroes are pressing at the gates.'[3] Filmmakers, meanwhile, are not always

---

[1] 'A Poet of Film' [in Japanese], in *Scenario* (*Shinario*), 168 (1964), 39. In this article, unless otherwise specified, English translations of Japanese materials are mine.

[2] David Bordwell gives an excellent analysis of Ozu's cinematic style and technique in *Ozu and the Poetics of Cinema* (London and Princeton, N.J., 1988), pp. 5–179.

[3] '*Le Temps de l'image est venu!*' cited, with much misgiving, by Walter Benjamin, in *The Work of Art in the Age of its Technological Reproducibility, and Other Writings on Media*, ed. Michael W. Jennings, Brigid Doherty and Thomas Y. Levin; tr. Edmund Jephcott *et al.* (Stanford, 2008), p. 22.

rigorous in acknowledging their sources, and the borrowed materials routinely undergo a process of seemingly random selection and drastic mutation through many filmic generations. It is therefore often not easy to establish whether a particular motif is attributable to a specific source, or whether it is down to a more generalized, impersonal pattern of storytelling. Ozu's 1936 screenplay, along with two more *King Lear* lookalike pieces from the Shochiku emporium, is a case in point.

In Japan, commercial film production started and quickly matured in the first two decades of the twentieth century, already turning out six to eight hundred features per year in the 1920s. From the outset, Japanese filmmakers were engaged in largely uncredited artistic reproduction and, to them, the most important foreign source of inspiration was the literature and drama of nineteenth-century Europe. For instance, Ozu's close friend Kenji Mizoguchi (1898–1956) directed adaptations of Eugene O'Neill's *Anna Christie* (1921), E. T. A. Hoffmann's novella, *Mademoiselle de Scudéri* (1819) and Henrik Ibsen's *Peer Gynt* (1867) in the 1920s. Among his mature works, *Oyuki the Virgin* (*Maria no Oyuki*, 1935) and *The Straits of Love and Hate* (*Aienkyo*, 1937) were fairly straight adaptations respectively of Guy de Maupassant's *Ball of Fat* (1880) and Leo Tolstoy's *Resurrection* (1899), even though the final products featuring *geisha* girls and *samurai* look stereotypically Japanese.[4]

Shakespeare did not figure in any obvious way in Japanese cinema until 1957, when Akira Kurosawa (1910–98) scored a great artistic and critical success with his daring *Macbeth* adaptation, *The Throne of Blood* (*Kumonosu-jo*, 1957). From the early 1930s, however, the excellent scriptwriting team of Shochiku[5] sporadically wrote scenarios that incorporated, without credit, various thematic and morphologic traits of *King Lear*. In 1931, Ozu's senior colleague Yasujiro Shimazu (1897–1945) directed a big budget silent film, *Love and Humanity* (*Aiyo jinruito tomoni are*, in two parts, 1931), to mark the return of actor Sojin Kamiyama from a successful career in Hollywood. The film portrays an elderly industrialist Kokichi Yamaguchi (Kamiyama) and his four children, of whom the youngest revolts against the dictatorial father and is disinherited. Kokichi is deserted by his elder children when a forest fire destroys his empire and, suddenly alone and penniless, goes mad and tries to commit suicide, only to be rescued by the youngest rebel son.[6] The Shakespearian echoes in this commemorative piece seem more than a mere coincidence, as Lear was the very final role Kamiyama had played as stage actor before his departure for Hollywood in 1919.[7]

The second instance is Ozu's screenplay entitled *What a Cheerful Guy, This Mr Yasukichi* (*Tanoshiki kana Yasukichi-kun*), which was written in 1936 in cooperation with a professional scriptwriter Yasutaro Yagi. The story features an old patriarch Yasukichi, a mediocre office worker, who goes mad when he is forced to take early retirement and his dream of a comfortable old age is shattered.[8] Like Lear on the heath, Yasukichi wanders around in a storm with thunder and lightning and claims that he is the manager of the company from which he has already been made redundant. The script ends with the consignment of Yasukichi to a mental institution by his children.

A Broken Drum (*Yabure daiko*, 1949), a post-war comedy by Ozu's former assistant director Keisuke

---

[4] For Mizoguchi's sources, see Nobuo Chiba, 'Conversion, Representation and History: From *Peer Gynt* to *Ugetsu*' [in Japanese], in Inuhiko Yomota, ed., *Film Director Kenji Mizoguchi* (Tokyo, 1999), pp. 67–92. The most comprehensive study of the foreign sources of Japanese films is Kikuo Yamamoto's *The Influence of Foreign Films on Japanese Cinema* [in Japanese] (Tokyo, 1983).

[5] Shochiku set up an institute for scriptwriters in 1928 and trained young writers in-house. The institute was headed by Ozu's lifelong collaborator Kogo Noda.

[6] See *Film Centre* [in Japanese], vol. 24 (Special Issue: Yasujiro Shimazu) (1974). The existing print of the film is in the possession of the National Film Centre, Tokyo.

[7] *King Lear*, The Modern Stage Association (Kindaigeki kyokai), at Yurakuza, Tokyo (February 1919).

[8] The scenario was published in a literary magazine *Shincho* (August 1936), 201–45. The film's only existing print, which is heavily cut and misses the final scenes, is in the possession of the National Film Centre.

Kinoshita (1912–98), can be seen as a comic reincarnation of *King Lear*. The overbearing father of this film is the owner of a once profitable construction business. He is so intolerably bossy, even at home, that his children and his wife desert him. He even loses his fortune when his company goes bankrupt. While the misadventure of the father is analogous in part to that of Lear, his second musician son also elicits comparison with the king's Fool, as he stands by the father through his ordeals and cheers him by singing and playing the piano. Yet another nod to Shakespeare is the second daughter, who is rehearsing *Hamlet*'s nunnery scene for a school performance, which actually takes place towards the end of the film.

The Shakespearian credentials of these Shochiku *King Lears* deserve close scrutiny. In their appraisal of yet another ostensible Shakespearian offshoot, Kurosawa's *The Bad Sleep Well* (*Warui yatsu hodo yoku nemuru*, 1960), Ann Thompson and John O. Thompson put forward the concept of 'pertinent likeness' to the source text, alongside that of 'attested likeness' or real life documentation, to identify an adaptation. According to their proposal, pertinent likeness exists 'where both the likeness and the difference between source text and version text give rise to interesting thought, backwards and forwards' and 'where one can intuit how features of the version text wouldn't be there save for the original text'.[9] According to this criterion, the three Shochiku pieces are pertinently like *King Lear* in their respective portrayals of a despondent (and in two of them actually mad) patriarch and his children. In addition, in *What a Cheerful Guy*, Ozu gives a totally uncharacteristic direction for 'thunder and lightning' and 'wind' in a scene in which the deranged Yasukichi dashes out of his house and wanders in the streets.[10] As skies are permanently sunny and clear in Ozu's films, with only three rain scenes in the whole of his canon,[11] the cue for a storm with thunder and lightning in *What a Cheerful Guy* really is an anomaly and so pertinently *unlike* the director, that it strongly indicates its derivation from the 'Storm and tempest' and 'Storm still' in the comparable mad scenes in *King Lear*.[12]

While Shimazu's Lear actor and Kinoshita's *Hamlet*-within-a-film attest (if obliquely) to the two films' indebtedness to Shakespeare, Ozu's script does not refer to the Elizabethan playwright explicitly. The director's existing diaries and letters do not clarify when, if ever, he came to be interested in Shakespeare's tormented monarch, either.[13] Even the thunderstorm in *What a Cheerful Guy* might have derived from a completely different source. For instance, Teinosuke Kinugasa's *A Page of Madness* (*Kurutta ichi peiji*, 1926), an experimental Expressionist film inspired by Robert Wiene's *The Cabinet of Dr Caligari* (1920), also combined thunder and lightning with madness with spectacular effect. The question of the screenplay's connection with Shakespeare was left tantalizingly unsettled as, while Ozu originally intended to direct *What a Cheerful Guy*, he offered the script to fellow director Tomu Uchida in the end and left for China to serve in the Imperial Japanese Army before the completion of the film's shooting in 1937.[14] Although Ozu missed the opportunity to shoot thunder and lightning forever, the issue of the director's relationship with the Bard, and even the elusive thunderstorm, will loom up again when

---

9 Ann Thompson and John O. Thompson, 'Pertinent Likeness: Kurosawa's *The Bad Sleep Well* as a Version of Shakespeare's *Hamlet*,' *Shakespeare Studies* [Tokyo], 44 (2006), 17–27 at 17.

10 Ozu, *What a Cheerful Guy*, pp. 334–5.

11 They are in *The Story of the Floating Weeds* (*Ukigusa monogatari*, 1934) and its post-war remake *Floating Weeds* (*Ukigusa*, 1959), and in *Munekata Sisters* (*Munekata kyodai*, 1950). As for the Ozuian weather, see Shigehiko Hasumi, 'Sunny Skies', in David Desser, ed., *Ozu's 'Tokyo Story'* (Cambridge, 1997), pp. 118–29.

12 Quotations from *King Lear* are from the Folio text of the Complete Oxford modern spelling edition. The stage directions are given at 2.2.458, 3.1.1, 3.2.1, 3.4.4, 3.4.59, 3.4.95 and 3.4.153.

13 Ozu seems to have kept diaries fairly consistently from childhood, but many of them are lost. Extant diaries of his adult years are collected in *Complete Diaries* [in Japanese], ed. Masasumi Tanaka (Tokyo, 1993). I also consulted manuscript materials covering the years 1918 and 1921 in the possession of the Kamakura Museum of Literature.

14 Tomu Uchida revised and directed the story under the title *Unending Advance* (*Kagirinaki zenshin*, 1937).

he took up the theme of filial impiety in two of his own directorial works: *The Brothers and Sisters of the Toda Family* (*Todake no kyodai*, 1941) and *Tokyo Story*.

SLAPPING THE VILLAINS IN THE FACE: *THE BROTHERS AND SISTERS OF THE TODA FAMILY*

One watershed in Ozu's otherwise exceptionally consistent filmic career was his conscription into the army and his service for two years as an infantry corporal in the Second Sino-Japanese War (1937–45). Returning from China in 1939 and recalling the dire realities of the battlefield, Ozu somewhat paradoxically renounced the aesthetic of his earlier years as too cynical and negative about life,[15] and advocated a more life-affirming art.

I do not want to shoot sceptical pieces any more. After experiencing war, I cultivated what should be called an affirmative spirit, and want to cry out, from the bottom of my heart, that things out there are good as they are.[16]

This was a crucial moment in Ozu's filmic career and he would repeatedly voice his faith in optimism in art for the rest of his life.[17] The director's newly affirmative aesthetic would, however, undergo a further, and even more radical, transformation over the years, to which his second and third *King Lear* analogues would bear witness.

With the Second World War impending, Ozu, a real war veteran, was placed under immense political pressure to make a war film back in Japan and to support the cause of the Imperial Japanese Army. In 1941, he managed to disappoint the film authority and nationalistic critics alike by making a humanistic family drama: *The Brothers and Sisters of the Toda Family*. The film opens with an unexpected death of the patriarch of a bourgeois family who leaves a legacy of debts. Suddenly homeless and penniless, the matriarch Mrs Toda, along with her unmarried third daughter Setsuko, is shuttled between her inhospitable married children, in a way reminiscent of Shakespeare's patriarch Lear.

The second son Shojiro leaves for China to pursue a business career, but returns on the father's first anniversary and confronts the heartless elder siblings.

According to the co-scriptwriter Tadao Ikeda, *The Toda Family* is based on Harry F. Millarde's silent film *Over the Hill to the Poorhouse* (1920), an American motherhood melodrama which film historian Masasumi Tanaka regards as a version of *King Lear*.[18] However, the Toda story seems to have derived various plot elements and motifs directly from *King Lear* (rather than by way of *Over the Hill*), such as the dutiful son Shojiro's sojourn in a neighbouring country (China, instead of Cordelia's France).[19] Most crucially, the film resembles its Shakespearian prototype in its stark opposition of the dutiful children and the callous ones (or as Ikeda put it, 'between fair-spoken ones and those who put their love into real action').[20] It is markedly uncharacteristic of Ozu, too, as his

---

[15] The cynicism and pessimism of Ozu's films in the 1930s were noted, and often criticized, by contemporary critics. See for instance, Shintaro Miki, 'Some Notes on Yasujiro Ozu' [in Japanese], in *Studies in Filmic Art* (*Eiga geijutu kenkyu*), 2.9 (1933), 62–71.

[16] Yasujiro Ozu, *Complete Interviews and Table Talks* (1933–1945) [in Japanese], ed. Masasumi Tanaka (Tokyo, 1987), p. 106.

[17] For Ozu's similar statements, see *Interviews and Table Talks* (1933–1945), pp. 114, 118–19, 141–2; Ozu, *Post-war Interviews and Table Talks* [in Japanese], ed. Masasumi Tanaka (Tokyo, 1989), pp. 108, 115–16, 186, 272 and 317.

[18] Masasumi Tanaka, *An Excursion around the World of Yasujiro Ozu* [in Japanese] (Tokyo, 2003), p. 275. Eizo Tanaka translated into Japanese and novelized *Over the Hill*, as *The Story of 'Over the Hill'* (*oba ze hiru monogatari*, 1923), and published it at the time of the film's release in Tokyo. My discussion is based on Tanaka's rendition. For Ikeda, another source of inspiration was Chekhov's *The Cherry Orchard*. See 'Documentary History of Japanese Cinema: Tadao Ikeda Part 1' [in Japanese], *The Yomiuri Shimbun*, 21 May 1964 (evening issue).

[19] Other significant similarities are: the patriarch's anger at Shojiro's sabotage of a family ritual; the patriarch's dying words ('Pray you, undo this sash'); the division of the family property; withdrawal of marriage proposal by a suitor when Setsuko is left without legacy; the suffering women's taking refuge in a hovel; and the suggestion that Setsuko will eventually marry someone in China.

[20] 'Documentary History: Tadao Ikeda Part 1.'

pre-war pieces always avoided such contrastive dramaturgy. Indeed, the dutiful son's reprimand of his siblings on his return from China is, in its unforgiving denunciation, more like Cordelia's reproof ('Had you not been their father, these white flakes / Did challenge pity of them . . . Mine enemy's dog, though he had bit me, should have stood / That night against my fire,' 4.6.28–31), than anything in Ozu's earlier works:

Shojiro. Whether I'm here or not has nothing to do with it! It's a question of your sincerity. Don't tell me, since father died, you think mother's only in the way? Is that it, Sister? Don't think I don't know what's going on here. Maybe I trusted you too much. I should've taken care of mother and Setsuko myself. I should've decided earlier. Even a destitute family would have cared more for one another. But none of you have shown mother any warmth.

(*Toda Family*, Scene 83)[21]

After Shojiro's admonition, however, *The Toda Family* departs from the Shakespearian tragedy and ends on a triumphant note. Ozu puts his newly affirmative aesthetic into action by making Shojiro successfully tell off his siblings at the anniversary of the father's death and even slap one of his married sisters (Ayako) in the face.[22] While Shojiro is emphatically a civilian pursuing a business career in Tianjin, his unnervingly easy recourse to violence resonates with Japan's wartime aggression, as he adds: 'If you lived out there [i.e. in China] for a year, you'd learn that it is best to pack a hard punch.' Let us note that, with the wartime Film Law in force since 1939, it was a feat in itself that Ozu filmed a family drama devoid of crude warlike propaganda. Nevertheless, at this stage, the director's efforts to overcome nihilism and cynicism resulted in a rectification of evil by force, and Shakespeare's tragedy was transformed into a 'melodrama' in Peter Brooks's sense of the term: a bourgeois drama of emotional excess and stark ethical conflict.[23] When Ozu worked on the tragic motifs of *King Lear* for the third time, however, he would not only revise the 1941 film drastically, but also offer a searching insight into the architectonics of the Shakespearian tragedy.

'ISN'T LIFE DISAPPOINTING?': NORIKO'S AFFIRMATION IN *TOKYO STORY*

Soon after the Second World War, Ozu was reunited with his long-time co-scriptwriter Kogo Noda and went on to produce a string of masterpieces. *Tokyo Story*, which is recognized as one of the greatest films ever made in various international polls,[24] was the fifth outcome of their post-war collaboration. In it, the elderly Shukichi Hirayama and his wife Tomi make their first, and as it happens last, trip from Onomichi to distant Tokyo to visit their grown children. Their doctor son Koichi and beautician daughter Shige are somewhat grudging in their welcome and shuttle the parents between them, while their two grandchildren are spoilt and unresponsive. The only person who treats them with kindness and warm hospitality is Noriko, the widow of their second son Shoji, who has gone missing in the war and very probably died eight years ago. The parents are soon packed off by Koichi and Shige to an inexpensive inn at a nearby hot spring resort Atami (Illustration 7), but tormented by the noise of boisterous guests, return to Tokyo earlier than they are supposed to, only to be pushed out of their children's homes yet again. After the disappointing stay in Tokyo, Tomi falls ill on the way back to Onomichi and dies soon afterwards.

---

[21] For the ease of reference, the English translation of *The Toda Family* is based on the subtitles of the film in the BFI collection. I modified several expressions to render them more literally.

[22] In the original screenplay, Shojiro hit not only Ayako but also her spouse, but the latter was spared Shojiro's chastisement in the final script. After the end of WW2, the Shochiku Company edited Shojiro's slap out of the negatives, apparently to comply with the guidelines of the Allied Occupation. The existing negatives and prints therefore do not include the scene of Shojiro's violence.

[23] Peter Brooks, *The Melodramatic Imagination: Balzac, Henry James, Melodrama, and the Mode of Excess* (New Haven, 1976)

[24] *Tokyo Story* was awarded the first Southerland Prize in 1954. It has constantly been chosen as one of the top ten greatest films of all time in the British Film Institute's once-in-a-decade poll since 1992, and won the directors' poll in 2012.

7. Shukichi (Chishu Ryu, left) and Tomi (Chieko Higashiyama), in Atami. *Tokyo Story* by Yasujiro Ozu.

Filmed in 1953 and widely regarded as the apex of Ozu's filmic career, *Tokyo Story* not only recapitulates the elderly parent's pilgrimage to her married children in *The Toda Family* but also makes new reference to Shakespeare's *King Lear*: the old couple's sleepless stay in Atami (Scenes 75–90) resembles Lear's night on the heath, and the intoxicated father's reflection on the ingrate children on a drunken night out with two of his old pals (Scenes 98–101) is comparable to the mock trial by Lear, Fool and Mad Tom. However, Ozu gives filial impiety a highly nuanced aspect in *Tokyo Story*, as Koichi and Shige's discussion about the welcome dinner for their parents illustrates:

Shige. What shall we feed them? What about some meat? *Sukiyaki* maybe?
Koichi. That sounds good.

Fumiko. And some *sashimi*.
Koichi. We don't need that too, do we? What do you think?
Shige. That's enough. We'll just give them meat.

(*Tokyo Story*, Scene 25)[25]

The question here does not have the life-or-death, all-or-nothing urgency of *The Toda Family* or of *King Lear*, where the parent is reduced to utter destitution. Shukichi and Tomi are treated to some delicious *sukiyaki* after all. What is at issue is the vague sense of stinginess as seen in not *also* serving *sashimi*. Instead of obvious mistreatments, Ozu here

---

[25] Yasujiro Ozu and Kogo Noda, *Tokyo Story: The Ozu/Noda Screenplay*, trans. by Donald Richie and Eric Klestadt (Berkeley, 2003). Quotations from *Tokyo Story* are from this English version.

portrays unkindness and hypocrisy of which the children themselves are not quite aware.

A similar revision can be seen in the scenes in which the parents are thrown out of their children's houses. In the Toda piece, Kazuko, the wife of the eldest son, makes it absolutely clear that the mother and Setsuko need to vacate the house to make space for her own guests:

Kazuko. [To Setsuko] You know Mrs Tanimoto from Kobe, don't you? She's in town with her husband. I invited her over this evening. That's why I want you to go out with mother. I'll only vex mother if she stays in this evening. You don't have to stay out late, only till seven or eight. All right? Do that for me, then. Thanks.   (*The Toda Family*, Scene 46)

In a corresponding episode in *Tokyo Story*, Shige conveys her intentions in a subtler manner. When the parents make the mistake of returning from Atami too early, Shige ostensibly urges them fully to enjoy their stay in Tokyo, casually adding:

Shige. However, tonight I do have this meeting here with the other beauticians.
Tomi. Are many coming?
Shige. Well, it's my turn to provide the place.
Shukichi. We came back at the wrong time.
Shige. That's why I wanted you to stay at Atami. I should have told you so . . . (*Goes out.*)
                                    (*Tokyo Story*, Scene 93)

Unlike Kazuko, Shige shows her parents the door without actually telling them to go out. The parents in their turn accept the distressing situation with a faint smile, unlike Setsuko, who is visibly upset in the scene, let alone Lear, who rages and howls at the ingrate daughters.

Ozu further explores the parents' response to their children's indifference and ingratitude, if not outright cruelty, in a scene set in Osaka, where their youngest son Keizo lives. Tomi is indisposed during the train journey home and stops over at Keizo's. The old folks reflect on their children and grandchildren:

Shukichi. Some grandparents seem to like their grandchildren better than their own children. What about you?

Tomi. And you?
Shukichi. Well, I think I like my children better.
Tomi. Yes, that's true.
Shukichi. But I'm surprised at how children change. Shige, now – she used to be much nicer before. A married daughter is like a stranger.
Tomi. Koichi's changed too. He used to be such a nice boy.
Shukichi. No, children don't live up to their parents' expectations. (*They both smile*) But, if you are greedy then there is no end to it. Let's think that they are better than most.
Tomi. They are certainly better than average. We are fortunate.
Shukichi. Yes, fortunate. We should consider ourselves lucky.
Tomi. Yes, we are very lucky.   (*Tokyo Story*, Scene 116)

Shukichi and Tomi are aware of their children's heartlessness as acutely as Mrs Toda and Lear, but this does not stop them from loving them. The concept of happiness and unhappiness is also undermined, when the parents regard themselves as *relatively* happy, deflecting the black-and-white opposition. Moreover, the dialogue challenges the idea of human character as an unchanging entity. In *King Lear*, Cordelia knows the evil nature of her sisters from the outset ('I know you what you are,' 1.1.268), whereas Lear discovers the true character of his 'two pernicious daughters' (3.2.22) much later. Either way, the elder daughters are deemed essentially evil by nature and, in the words of Cordelia, 'Time shall unfold what pleated cunning hides' (1.1.280). Shukichi and Tomi on the other hand are 'surprised at how children change', pointing to the corrosive power of time and thereby questioning the existence of a 'true nature' itself.

After the sudden demise of Tomi, a 'division of the kingdom' takes place in the form of the distribution of her very humble belongings. Like Goneril and Regan, Shige speaks fairly in the presence of the father and gets what she wants:

Shige. You must take care of yourself, Father, and live for a long, long time.
Shukichi. Thank you. (*He gets up and goes out. All the rest are silent for a while.*)

8. Noriko (Setsuko Hara, right) and Kyoko (Kyoko Kagawa). *Tokyo Story* by Yasujiro Ozu.

Shige. I may seem a bit heartless to say so, but I do rather wish he had died first. Look, if Kyoko marries, then he'll be left all alone.

Koichi. Yes.

Shige. We could have looked after Mother in Tokyo. Kyoko, did Mother still have her gray summer sash?

Kyoko. Yes.

Shige. You know, I'd like it for a keepsake. All right?

Koichi. I suppose so.

Shige. And that linen kimono she used to wear in the summer. Did she still have that too?

Kyoko. Yes.

Shige. Well, I want that too. You know where it is?

(*Tokyo Story*, Scene 156)

The Cordelia figures in the story, the widow Noriko and the family's unmarried youngest daughter Kyoko, are noticeably silent during the dinner but have a heart-to-heart talk when they are alone (Illustration 8). Echoing Cordelia and Shojiro, Kyoko denounces the selfishness and cruelty of her elder siblings in no ambiguous terms ('They are selfish. Wanting her clothes right after her death. I felt so sorry for poor Mother. Even strangers would have been more considerate. That's no way to treat your parents.'). The other, slightly older Cordelia, however, understands the situation very differently:

Noriko. But, look, Kyoko. At your age I thought as you do. But children do drift away from their parents. A woman has her own life apart from her parents, when she is Shige's age. She meant no harm, I'm sure. It's only that everyone has to look after himself.

Kyoko. I wonder. Well, I won't ever be like that. That would be just too cruel.

Noriko. It is. But children get that way . . . gradually.

Kyoko. Then – you too . . .
Noriko. I may become like that. In spite of myself.
Kyoko. Isn't life disappointing?
Noriko. Yes it is.

(*Tokyo Story*, Scene 161)

It is a critical commonplace to contrast the heartless Shige and the rather saintly Noriko, just as Goneril and Regan are pitted against Cordelia. However, in this crucial dialogue, while Kyoko asserts that she is different from her elder siblings ('I won't ever be like that'), Noriko not only identifies her former self in Kyoko but recognizes her future self in Shige, thereby undercutting the tragic dramaturgy that is based on a contrast and conflict of different characters. In *The Toda Family*, Ozu put his affirmative spirit into action by making the hero defeat the antiheroes. In *Tokyo Story*, the opposition between good and bad characters is revoked, or in the words of Ozu:

The old parents of this story might feel sad when they are disillusioned with their own children. That is all. I do not intend to deny, or to emphasize, either the affection between the parents and their own children, or the one between them and their daughter-in-law.[26]

To Kyoko's question ('Isn't life disappointing?'), Noriko replies in the affirmative ('Yes it is'), signifying that the director's affirmative aesthetic is now conveyed not by the boisterous action of a dashing hero but by the quiet dignity and resilience of a sympathetic woman.

Motifs of the division of the kingdom are modified further in the dialogue between Noriko and her father-in-law. After Tomi's funeral, Shukichi thanks Noriko once again for the warm hospitality she extended during his and his late wife's stay in Tokyo. He notes just how much Tomi appreciated her kindness and, like his wife before him, warmly encourages the young widow to remarry and be happy again. Reworking Cordelia's declaration in the Quarto text, 'Sure, I shall never marry like my sisters, / To love my father all' (1.1.95–6), Noriko confesses that, eight years after her husband's very probable death, she does not love him 'all' any more, though she let Tomi entertain that impression so the mother's feelings should not be hurt:

Noriko. She overestimated me.
Shukichi. You're wrong, Noriko.
Noriko. She did. I'm not the nice woman she thought I was. If you see me like that – it embarrasses me.
Shukichi. No, it shouldn't.
Noriko. No, really. I'm quite selfish [*zurui*]. Whatever you may imagine, I'm not always thinking of your son.
Shukichi. I'd be happy if you'd forget him.
Noriko. There are days when I don't think of him at all . . . Then sometimes I feel that I just cannot go on like this. Sometimes at night I lie and wonder what will become of me if I stay this way. The days pass and nothing happens. I feel a kind of impatience. My heart seems to be waiting – for something. Oh, yes, I'm selfish [*zurui*].
Shukichi. You are not.
Noriko. Yes, I am. But I couldn't tell Mother this.
Shukichi. That's all right. You are a truly good woman. An honest woman.
Noriko. Not at all.

(*Tokyo Story*, Scene 163)

The word *zurui*, which is translated as 'selfish' here, would mean anything from crafty, deceitful, devious to dishonest, and signify a quality that is opposite to Cordelia's 'truth' ('So young, my lord, and true,' 1.1.107). Noriko is sorry that she was not 'true' to the mother, and that she does not love Shukichi's son 'all' any longer. Shukichi emphatically repudiates her self-doubt on both counts, assuring her that she is a 'truly good woman' and an 'honest woman'. Unlike Lear who disinherits Cordelia by making 'thy truth, then, be thy dower' (1.1.108), Shukichi rewards Noriko's truthfulness with a keepsake (Illustration 9).

(*Shukichi gets up and from a drawer brings a woman's watch.*)
Shukichi. This watch belonged to her. It's old-fashioned now but she began to wear it when she was your age. Please take this to remember her by.
Noriko. But, I —
Shukichi. Please accept it. (*He gives it to her.*) She'll be happy to know that you'll be wearing it. Take it for her sake.
Noriko. Thank you.

---

[26] Ozu, *Post-war Interviews and Table Talks*, pp. 192–3.

9. Shukichi (left) handing Tomi's watch to Noriko. *Tokyo Story* by Yasujiro Ozu.

Shukichi. Please believe me. I want you to be happy. I really, very sincerely, mean that. (*Noriko covers her face.*)
(*Tokyo Story*, Scene 163)

By receiving a timepiece Tomi used to wear when she was her age, Noriko is identified with her mother-in-law. Tomi, Shige, Kyoko and Noriko, who at first looked very different and even deliberately contrasted, finally emerge as temporarily differentiated manifestations of common humanity.

Though widely recognized as a master craftsman of cinema from the 1930s, Ozu has often been criticized for lack of social commitment. During the war, the director irritated the nationalistic critics by not making a propaganda film.[27] After the war, Ozu did not make any obviously 'democratic' film to renounce the military past, either. He simply did not film a single soldier, even as an extra,

in any of his works before, during or after the war. In the late 1950s and '60s, the 'new wave' filmmakers such as Nagisa Oshima (1932–2013) and Shohei Imamura (1926–2006) attacked Ozu as hopelessly conservative in theme and style, and out of touch with the turbulent real world. In the meanwhile, Anglo-American and European

[27] See Hideo Tsumura's critique of *The Brothers and Sisters of the Toda Family*, in 'On Yasujiro Ozu' [in Japanese], *Transformation (Kaizo)*, 23.7 (1941), 222–7. Ozu indeed took up two propaganda film projects at the request of the military government. In 1942, he wrote *The Faraway Country of My Parents* (*Haruka nari fubo no kuni*), in collaboration with Kosaku Akiyama and Ryosuke Saito, but the screenplay was deemed not warlike enough and was abandoned. In 1943, Ozu was sent to Singapore to shoot *On to Delhi* (*On tu Derii*), a documentary about the Indian National Army. The war ended before the project materialized.

critics and filmmakers such as Lindsay Anderson, Paul Schrader and Donald Richie, admire Ozu specifically because his films 'transcend' such historical contingencies and attain universality.[28] However, the foregoing comparison between *The Toda Family* and *Tokyo Story* has shown that, even though Ozu's films might appear to be always the same and ahistorical, the director repeated the plots and situations specifically to revise them and to realize his artistic vision, which his wartime experience crucially informed. Enmeshed in the intertext of *The Toda Family* and *Tokyo Story*, the tragedy of *King Lear* helped the director not simply to visualize his affirmative aesthetic, but also to interrogate and undermine Japan's, and his own, militarism and aggression through the sad wartime years.

A DISTANT STORM: THE DIRECTOR'S INTENT AND BEYOND

Authorial intention has long been a seriously discredited proposition in literary studies. In their 1946 essay 'Intentional Fallacy', W. K. Wimsatt, Jr and Monroe C. Beardsley emphasized poetic analysis and exegesis into internal and contextual evidence, while downplaying biographical and genetic enquiry of external facts.[29] According to their argument, even when the line 'I have heard the mermaids singing, each to each' in 'The Love Song of J. Alfred Prufrock' strikes you as somewhat similar to 'Teach me to heare Mermaides singing' in John Donne's 'Song', you should forbear writing to T. S. Eliot and asking him what he meant, or if he had Donne in mind. More recently, Linda Hutcheon challenged the assumption of such impersonal intertextuality between the adapted text and the adaptation. She tried to reinstate the author's intention in literary and cultural studies by defining an adaptation as the adapter's 'extended, *deliberate*, *announced* revisitation of a particular work of art'.[30]

For all the internal evidence *What a Cheerful Guy*, *The Toda Family* and *Tokyo Story* afford as to their connection with *King Lear*, coupled with the contextual evidence of the three films' relationship

to each other, the temptation to send a letter to Ozu and enquire about his awareness of Shakespeare remains very alluring. While the director carried the theme of filial impiety from one film to another and definitely *reread* the tragic motifs of *King Lear* on the way, we are ultimately left uncertain whether he actually *read* Shakespeare to make the films, as he always worked with the highly-trained co-scriptwriters of Shochiku who were perfectly capable of adapting, and playing with, Shakespeare.

It may not be appropriate to anchor the contributions made by Ozu's collaborators to the name 'Shakespeare', either. For instance, Kogo Noda, who co-wrote *Tokyo Story* with Ozu, studied drama at the English department of Waseda University, Tokyo, and was thoroughly versed in Shakespeare's plays. However, he was also a student of Georges Polti's theory of thirty-six dramatic situations[31] and had an encyclopaedic knowledge of world literature and theatre, making famously free use of the narrative and dramatic patterns thus collected to iron out script problems.[32] In Noda's taxonomic and impersonal scheme, to ascribe a script to Shakespeare may not be appropriate, even when motifs in it had actually originated in the works of the Elizabethan playwright.

The director's, and his collaborators', intention notwithstanding, Ozu's films, and *Tokyo Story* in particular, have been associated with Shakespeare by viewers, by critics (including Philip French,

---

[28] See Lindsay Anderson, 'Two Inches off the Ground', in *Sight and Sound* (Winter 1957), reprinted in Desser, *Ozu's 'Tokyo Story'*, pp. 145–51; Paul Schrader, *Transcendental Style in Film: Ozu, Bresson, Dreyer* (Berkeley, 1972); Donald Richie, *Ozu* (Berkeley, [1974]).

[29] W. K. Wimsatt, Jr and Monroe C. Beardsley, *The Verbal Icon: Studies in the Meaning of Poetry* (New York, 1958), pp. 3–18.

[30] Linda Hutcheon, *A Theory of Adaptation* (New York, 2006), p. 170 (italics mine).

[31] Georges Polti, *The Thirty-Six Dramatic Situations* [1916] (Franklin, Ohio, 1921). Noda often refers to Polti's taxonomy in his influential textbook for screenplay writers, *Structure of the Scenario* [in Japanese], new ed. (Tokyo, 1952).

[32] See Akira Iwasaki, 'Kogo Noda' [in Japanese], in Akira Shimizu et al., eds., *Noda Kogo Retrospective* (Tokyo, 1970), pp. 4–5.

whose review article on the 1953 film's rerelease in London in 2004 was entitled 'As Great as *King Lear*')[33] and, most curiously, by succeeding artists. The direction for 'a train passing' in the night sequence portraying Shukichi's drunken binge in *Tokyo Story* (Scene 99) illustrates this subtle interplay of authorial intention and the work's interpretation. The roaring sound and the flickering reflection of the light from the passing train, as they were deftly captured by Ozu's lifelong cinematographer Yuharu Atsuta, have since been 'mistaken' by many viewers for an indication of a subsiding, distant thunderstorm. The eminent poet Gozo Yoshimasu also made the mistake. To mark the 100th anniversary of the director's birth in 2003, he even wrote a poem 'A Whistle (from Beyond)', in which he muses,

How many times did I count the four puppies that went running through the unpaved (unpaved?) backstreet when the thunderstorm subsided in *Tokyo Story*?[34]

The direction for 'a train passing' was added at a very late stage in the film's production and was pencilled in the margin of Ozu's shooting script in his own hand. While the director, not his co-scriptwriter, was therefore definitely responsible for the cue in this case, we still cannot say whether he *intended* the audio and visual effects of a passing train to resemble the light and sound of a distant thunderstorm.[35] Regardless of the authorial intention (or un-intention), the Shakespearian lightning and thunder that Ozu had failed to shoot for *What a Cheerful Guy* finally materialized in Yoshimasu's tribute poem to the director.

In 2010, Ozu's films were linked to the Elizabethan playwright yet again by novelist Osamu Hashimoto, who had conceived a new

Shakespearian adaptation while watching *Ran* (1985), a *samurai* version of *King Lear* by Kurosawa. In his imagination, Hashimoto replaced Kurosawa's Lear (Tatsuya Nakadai) with Ozu's quintessential male actor, Chishu Ryu. The novelist postulated that, after impersonating countless fathers in Ozu's films (including Shukichi in *Tokyo Story*), Ryu's archetypal patriarch lived beyond the director's final effort *The Autumn Afternoon* (*Sanma no aji*, 1962), to see the turmoil over the United States–Japan security treaty and the students' rebellion in 1968. He accordingly penned a story of a Japanese bureaucrat and his three daughters, entitled *People of the Lear Household* (*Ria-ke no hitobito*, 2010), basing his Lear on Ryu and incorporating various episodes and motifs from Ozu's films.[36] The novel, whose final chapter is entitled 'Storm (*arashi*)', shows that the creative dialogue between Shakespeare and Ozu continues quite beyond the authorial intent, and that the thunder and lightning still linger fifty years after the master filmmaker's demise on his sixtieth birthday in 1963.

---

33 *The Observer* (18 January 2004).

34 'A Whistle (from Beyond)' [in Japanese] in Gozo Yoshimasu, *The Snake of Heaven, Purple Flowers* (*Tenjou no hebi, murasaki no hana*, Tokyo, 2005). Yoshimasu also discussed the 'thunderstorm' in *Tokyo Story* at length in a television programme, 'Ozu's Silent Resistance to War' [in Japanese] (NHK, 27 December 2003).

35 Ozu's shooting script, in the possession of Kawakita Memorial Film Institute, is reproduced in Masasumi Tanaka, ed., *Yasujiro Ozu's 'Tokyo Story' and Several Other Films* (Tokyo, 2001), pp. 141–278. The cue for 'a train passing' is on p. 220.

36 For Hashimoto's explanation of the origin of the novel, see his dialogue with playwright Akio Miyazawa in *Eureka* (*Yuriika*), 42.7 (2010), pp. 62–83.

CURSING TO LEARN: THEATRICALITY AND THE CREATION OF CHARACTER IN *THE TEMPEST*

DAVID SCHALKWYK

There is a decisive moment in *The Tempest*: it is a point of confrontation – intensely theatrical – when Caliban responds to Miranda's claim that he owes the gift of language to her. 'I pitied thee', she reminds him,

Took pains to make thee speak, taught thee each hour
One thing or other. When thou didst not, savage,
Know thine own meaning, but wouldst gabble like
A thing most brutish, I endowed thy purposes
With words that made them known.   (1.2.353–7)[1]

He replies, 'You taught me language, and my profit on 't / Is I know how to curse. The red plague rid you / For learning me your language!' (362–4).

'LANGUAGE' VS. 'YOUR LANGUAGE'

If character in drama is established by what characters say *to* each other, this is a strange interaction, if we can call it that. One character, who commands speech with a certain inborn ease that we all assume, speaks to another by reminding him (and the audience watching, overhearing) that he owes everything to her. Responding in her language and ours, he concedes that she gave him language, but then curses her for teaching him *her* language. 'Language' and 'your language': what is the difference?

Miranda begins with a straightforward, traditional, but fairly primitive notion of what it might mean to teach someone language as such: to give someone the capacity to speak is to teach them to distinguish, by degrees, painstakingly, 'one *thing* or another'. It is to teach someone the names of things. But she complicates that primitive idea by suggesting that language is a more powerful force than a mere collection of names – it reveals a person's inner self, it shapes and enables their purposes and desires, and allows them to 'know', as she puts it, 'their own meaning'. As a philosophy of language this is actually quite sophisticated: it suggests that a person's 'meaning' or 'purposes' exist already in some kind of inchoate form, within them, but words are required to make that inner self known to them. To teach someone language, then, is not merely to allow them to give names to the objects in their world, but also to teach them something previously unknown about their very selves. It is to provide them with what is now commonly called their subjectivity or, if we are to be old-fashioned, their character. This is what language – any language – does. It enables the subject to know him or herself: to place themselves in a world which includes other human beings, not as mere things, but as other forms of subjectivity, as other characters to whom one responds and who respond in turn to you.

Caliban appears to be singularly ungrateful for this gift. But it is not a straightforward gift. Caliban seems originally to have survived well enough without it. He does not appear to have needed the names of the things of the island – the 'crabs', the 'pig-nuts', the 'nimble marmoset', the 'clust'ring

---

[1] All references to *The Tempest* are to the Norton Critical Edition, ed. Peter Hulme and William H. Sherman (New York, 2004).

filberts', and the bewildering 'scamels'[2] – to feed himself or make the island his home. Indeed, the eloquent intruders are the ones who needed the dumb expertise of the local to survive, like the colonists of the New World.[3] What use would it have been to the isolated, sovereign subject of the island before Prospero's arrival, to have 'known his own meaning'? This prompts the question of whether Caliban did possess in some sense, a 'meaning', which he was unable to express or recognize before this gift of 'language' from Miranda. It means, perhaps, that he is not entirely shaped by the language that Miranda taught him: Miranda's language would in this sense have been a kind of translation of some sort of meaning that he already possessed, but not fully.

Herein lies one possible difference between 'language' and 'your language'. Caliban acknowledges that Miranda taught him language; but he curses her for teaching him 'your language'. The paradox, of which he is perfectly aware, is that the capacity to curse is precisely the gift of language. It is one of the powers with which language endows its subjects, allowing them to call upon its force against others. But what does it mean that, in addition to being taught language, which gives him the capacity to curse his teachers, Caliban has also been subjected to something alien: what he calls 'your language'. Are these two different things?

THE CHARACTER OF LANGUAGE AND THE LANGUAGE OF CHARACTER

Cursing is a speech act that is generally the property of Caliban. It marks his character, which means not some kind of mysterious hidden interiority for which we need an extensive sub-text, but rather it is his active, overt mobilization of the force of language for his own ends. Cursing is what the philosopher J. L. Austin calls a performative or an illocutionary speech act:[4] it does not describe anything, it cannot be true or false; instead it performs an action, it brings about something, it transforms a situation by mobilizing the conventional force

of language *in* the saying of something. Standard examples of performative speech acts are a promise, whereby I bind myself to a course of action in the future – the most consequential of which is perhaps saying 'I do' in a marriage ceremony, the mere uttering of which transforms my status and that of my partner – or the declaration 'guilty' by a judge in a court of law, or 'out' on a tennis court. All of these require what Austin calls 'felicity conditions' to be satisfied for the action to be performed: I must not be married already, and the person who declares 'guilty' or 'out' must be the properly appointed official with the requisite authority. The ball is not out if a spectator shouts the word; the man will not go to jail no matter how loudly and with what conviction his alleged victim pronounces him guilty. These speech acts require not merely a verbal form to be effective but also a set of established social conventions, conditions and agreements. This is all simple enough.

Cursing

Alongside relatively straightforward illocutionary acts like promising, declaring, urging, commanding, demanding and giving, curses are strange animals. Who has the authority to curse someone else? Well, anyone, just as anyone has the authority to make a promise. In this respect they are different from the judgments 'guilty' or 'out'. What happens when you curse someone? – 'The red plague rid you for teaching me your language!' Strangely, nothing much. One might incense or

---

[2] Editors have perennially been at a loss to find the meaning of this word. Is it possible that it is meant to be a remnant of Caliban's own, private language, untouched by Prospero and Miranda's teaching, and therefore a signal of his 'own meaning', which existed before the teaching of what is necessarily not language as such, but *their* language?

[3] See Peter Hulme's argument that Prospero's strange need of Caliban (given the reach of his magic powers elsewhere) for survival replicates the story of the earliest European travellers who depended upon the largesse and local knowledge of the indigenous people of North America to survive: *Colonial Encounters: Europe and the Native Caribbean, 1492–1796* (London, 1986), pp. 115–34.

[4] J. L. Austin, *How to Do Things with Words*, 2nd edn (Cambridge, MA, 1975).

frighten the person cursed, and that would be a rhetorical effect of the speech act, but neither of those reactions would be the result of the conventional force of the curse. This highlights an important distinction between two different kinds of performative speech act – what Austin calls illocutionary acts and perlocutionary acts: what we achieve *in* saying something and what we effect *by* saying something. Every illocutionary act (which carries a predictable, conventional force) will have perlocutionary effects. But those effects are not conventional (except insofar as all utterances are conventional merely by being part of a system of language) or entirely predictable or controllable. In saying, 'I promise you I'll be there', I commit myself to being there whatever my state of mind or intentions. But that relatively simple illocutionary act may have a variety of perlocutionary effects: you may believe me, or feel satisfied, or have an attack of scepticism. Saying 'I do' in a marriage ceremony has the conventional force of binding me to my wife – indeed of *transforming* us into husband and wife – but it may have a variety of unforeseen perlocutionary effects: my mother may burst into tears, my sister may beam at me happily, and my ex-fiancée may get up, shout 'You bastard!' and shoot me dead on the spot. So to distinguish between the two, I refer to the conventional, transformative *force* of an illocutionary speech act and the largely uncontrollable, contingent *effects* of a perlocutionary act, remembering that such forces and effects may be produced by the same act.

What is a curse? On the face of it, it is an act with illocutionary force: *in* saying 'the red plague rid you' – or even, more explicitly, 'I curse you' – I am performing the act. But what kind of act is it? What are its felicity conditions? Like a promise, it is open to anyone: one does not have to have a special status to be able to curse. But the curse has a curious dual time structure: I curse you now, but the effects of my curse are projected into the future, as a kind of wish. A curse is a projection of desire, and as such it is a kind of modal, an optative: it generally uses the jussive voice: '[May] the red plague rid you . . . ' or '[Let] all the charms

of Sycorax . . . light on you' (1.2.363 and 339–40). Furthermore, it mobilizes language to invoke an ineffable force; but it is simultaneously an admission of powerlessness. It is a projection of a world of desire rather than power: it conjures a possible world as we would like the present world to be, if we had the power to bring it into existence. What will bring about the effects of the curse? Unlike a promise, not anything the curser does in the future. My curse invokes something else, beyond me – the gods, fate, some sort of supernatural force – to come to my aid, to act on my behalf.

In a secular age, in the absence of fate or the gods, curses have, like challenging someone to a duel, lost their force: there are no longer any felicity conditions to make the act happy (or from the point of view of the cursed, unhappy). We no longer believe in the power of words to bring down awful (in the original sense of the word) effects on someone else. In other words, we no longer believe that curses will achieve their aims; but that does not mean that curses are empty. When I curse you, you are cursed, even though you may shrug it off as being of no consequence. There is an historical gap, then, between an age in which curses might make one quake in one's boots, and ours, when they would be amusing, or, at best, just insulting. This gap, I want to suggest, marks the strangeness of Caliban, who is marked by the curse in all senses, as a character to us, and it is a strangeness that is different from his alienation from Prospero and Miranda. For they would have reason to take Caliban's curses seriously: his mother was a witch, his father the Devil, and although Prospero may be secure in his belief that his own magic powers are greater than those of Sycorax, Caliban's curses ought to send just a little shiver down his spine and that of his daughter.[5]

---

[5] For a further discussion of the modalities of curses, oaths and wishes, see David Schalkwyk, 'Shakespeare's Speech', *Journal of Medieval and Early Modern Studies*, 40 (2010), 373–400; 'Text and Performance, Reiterated', *The Shakespearean International Yearbook: Special Section, The Achievement of Robert Weimann* (2010): 47–76; and Lynne Magnusson, 'A Play of

Commanding

Prospero brings us to a different speech act, which, just as cursing may be said to partially characterize Caliban, makes up Prospero's substance: ordering, commanding, instructing, directing and illocutionary acts of that ilk. In *How To Do Things with Words*, Austin illustrates the notion of infelicities that may befall a speech act with an example that is germane to *The Tempest*: 'On a desert island', Austin declares, 'you may say to me "Go pick up wood"; and I may say "I don't take orders from you" or "you're not entitled to give me orders" – I do not take orders from you when you try to assert your authority . . . on a desert island, as opposed to when you are a captain on a ship and therefore have genuine authority' (28). The example is so particular that Austin may have had Caliban in mind. Certainly, the events around the Bermuda shipwreck in 1609, which are generally thought to have been a source for *The Tempest*, highlight precisely a crisis of authority at the beginning of the English colonial enterprise, when the sailors shipwrecked on Bermuda began to question the extension of authority, and had to be held in check with the sheer exercise of brutal power in the form of an exemplary hanging or two.[6]

The Tempest itself opens with a brief but powerful staging of the conditional nature of authority, and its relation to its executive arm – the command or order. In preparation for this paper I used the programme DocuScope, with the generous assistance of Jonathan Hope and Michael Witmore, to count the relative prevalence of the imperative voice in *The Tempest* and its relative use across the Shakespeare canon.[7] I was particularly interested in this programme because it counts speech acts or instances of language in use, based on the pragmatics of linguists like Michael Halliday, and thus underwrote my own performative approach to language. I was surprised, however, that DocuScope registered the imperative as a minor component of the speech acts in *The Tempest*. That seemed utterly unintuitive. I looked at the opening scene, which comprises some sixty-three lines. DocuScope marked *two* instances of the imperative voice in the scene. A manual count reveals between thirty and forty instances, depending on whether one does or not count repetitions. That is almost a command a line.[8]

The opening move of *The Tempest* thus stages the imperative as such; and the theatricality of the moment forces us to attend to its illocutionary force and its felicity conditions. The opening exchanges establish the lines of authority on the ship: the master commands the boatswain to stir the mariners to action, which the latter obeys by in turn issuing

---

Modals: Grammar and Potential Action in Early Shakespeare'. *Shakespeare Survey* 62 (Cambridge, 2009), pp. 69–80.

[6] The classic essays are Francis Barker and Stephen Hulme, 'Nymphs and Reapers Heavily Vanish: The Discursive Contexts of *The Tempest*', in *Alternative Shakespeares*, ed. John Drakakis (London, 1985), pp. 191–205, and Stephen Greenblatt, 'Martial Law in the Land of Cockaigne', in *Shakespearean Negotiations: The Circulation of Social Energy in Renaissance England* (Berkeley, 1989), pp. 129–64.

[7] For an account of the way DocuScope works, see Jonathan Hope and and Michael Witmore, 'The Hundredth Psalm to the Tune of "Green Sleeves": Digital Approaches to the Language of Genre', *Shakespeare Quarterly*, 61 (2010), 357–90; also www.winedarksea.org.

[8] DocuScope's capacity for registering this particular rhetorical form is clearly compromised. I suspect two reasons for this. The first is due to a decision by its programmer to count each instance of language use only once, as a single instance of a particular language use. The second is that since there is no distinct and universal grammatical marker of the imperative, a program such as DocuScope finds it very difficult to distinguish this language use unambiguously from others. This difficulty goes to the heart of Ludwig Wittgenstein's radical transformation of philosophical analysis of language: Wittgenstein's philosophical therapy is founded on the idea that the grammatical form of an utterance does not give any secure indication of its logical form, or its effective use in practice. The same grammatical form can be used in radically different ways, and the problem with philosophers is that they took at face value what one could call the deep structure of the grammar of a sentence while ignoring the surface structure, in use, of the utterance. They see only the grammatical structure of a description when it in fact carries the rhetorical or performative structure of a command. Despite its dependence on pragmatic linguistics, which is derived from Wittgenstein's notion that the meaning of a word lies in its use, DocuScope seems, in this instance at least, to have fallen into an old, formalist conception of language. I must add that this is an aberration. I have found DocuScope very useful in other instances, and admire what Hope and Witmore have been able to do with it.

orders to the sailors under him, until the King of Naples, Alonzo, and his retinue appear on deck. The king tries to assume a position of authority via a series of interrogatories and orders, but is promptly rebuffed, not merely in the boatswain's refusal of his authority, but more radically, his issuing orders to the king for him and his subjects to leave the deck. The rest of the scene extends the contest between king and courtier on the one hand and master and mariner on the other under conditions which indicate absolutely clearly the suspension of the king's authority and the demonstration of the infelicity of his attempts to assume command. The contest between boatswain and courtier is completed as a conflict between the assumption of command by the chief mariner on the one hand and the degeneration of the courtier's speech into curses on the other. The boatswain's precise instructions to trim the sails in the face of the storm – 'Down with the topmast! Yare! Lower, lower! Bring her to try with maincourse' – are countered by Sebastian and Antonio's impotent invective: 'A pox o' your throat, you bawling, blasphemous incharitable dog' and 'Hang, cur, you whoreson insolent noisemaker' (1.1.37–8 and 39–40), in a prelude to the discursive relationship that will unfold in due course between Prospero and Caliban.

The staged questioning of the illocutionary force of the imperative and its provocation of a curse in return thus prepares the stage, literally, for the next scene, for which the audience will reflect critically on any casual assumption of the imperative voice. The imperative appears to be the speech act that best characterizes Prospero: his signature mode. He uses it more often than any other character in the play (although comparatively, the Boatswain, with twenty-five instances in sixty-three lines, by far outweighs Prospero's seventy-five uses across the whole play). Its iterative patterns, established in the opening scene, are transferred to Prospero early in the second scene of the play, precisely by the *challenges* against it that are mounted, in different ways, by his daughter, his slave and his bonded servant.

Miranda's challenge is not direct. She begins from a position of uncertainty, signalled by a conditional plea that has the grammatical form, but not the performative force, of a command – 'If by your art, my dearest father, you have / Put the wild waters into this roar, *allay them*' (1.2.1–2). Miranda's speech act is a plea that proceeds from compassion, made in the name of humanity, qualified by the modalities of uncertainty, desire and impotence: '*If . . . would* pour . . . who had *no doubt . . . had I . . . I would . . .* ere *it should*' (1–12). Prospero responds with a series of instructions designed both to allay her fears and justify himself: '*Be collected / No more amazement*: *Tell* your piteous heart / There's no harm done . . . *Lend they hand . . . pluck* my magic garment . . . *Lie there . . . Wipe . . .* thine eyes . . . *have comfort . . . sit down . . . obey* and *be attentive*' (14–38). All these orders are a stage setting for the piece of theatre that he is about to unfold, the narrative of which provides, for Miranda at least, the self-authorized felicity conditions of his assumption of authority.

In the process of complicating his initial, apparently rigid distinction between performative and constative or descriptive speech acts (the former being happy or unhappy whereas the latter are true or false), Austin makes the point that for a perfomative act to be happy, some things have to be true or false. For someone to be able to pronounce someone guilty in a court of law, it must be true that he or she is a properly appointed judge. The narrative that Prospero tells Miranda, as if it is the tale of Fate itself ('the hour's now come / The very minute bids thee ope thine ear' (36–7)), are the conditions that must be established as true for him to be able or empowered routinely to assume the imperative voice, for the authority of his commands to have any force. (Notice how his own imperative force is transferred to the greater authority of the 'very minute' which 'bids' Miranda to 'ope [her] ear'.) We are all acquainted with the story that Prospero not only tells Miranda, but which he elaborates in his attempt, with her help, to subdue Caliban and in due course pacify Ariel. The point has been made often enough that, far from being Shakespeare's story, this is in fact no more than Prospero's, and that it is an instance of the need to control history (in other words the force of constative or descriptive acts) in order to mobilize the performative force of those speech acts that are central to the exercise of political control.

I want to focus on only one small part of Prospero's tale: his account of the consequences of Prospero's own fatal illocutionary act – 'The government I cast upon my brother' (1.2.75):

> Thy false uncle . . .
> Being once perfected how to grant suits,
> How to deny them, who t' advance, and who
> To trash for overtopping, new-created
> The creatures that were mine, I say, or changed 'em,
> Or else new formed 'em; having both the key
> Of officer and office . . .   (77–84)

Illocutionary speech acts lie at the heart of this transfer of power (itself illocutionary), by which the subjects of the state are not merely issued commands from above, but *turned into* new subjects – subjected anew by the performative power of language. They are creatures – the subjects of creation and re-creation. Prospero is obsessive about the performative dimensions of his loss of his subjects: they have been 'new-created' or 'changed' or 'else new formed' by someone else who has taken his place. In order to change them back, he needs the office (and the officers) that will provide the felicity conditions for his own reshaping of his subjects through the performative speech acts appropriated by his brother.

Whatever specific, historical, geographic and political resonances *The Tempest* may have, it stages in an overtly theatrical manner the creation and formation of subjects through the performative power of illocutionary speech acts. In the first two scenes, the king and his courtiers are transformed in a matter of minutes from figures who presume to bear natural authority into blustering underlings. The masters of power are reduced from habitual command to improvisatory cursing: from being carriers of meaning to mere 'noisemakers'. Prospero is reduced from Duke of Milan to his poor cell, now able to lord it over a bare three creatures, by his brother's assumption of the illocutionary force of habitual rule. And Miranda, Caliban and Ariel are variously made to subject themselves

to the new master of the isle by the combination of Prospero's magical powers, the illocutionary acts that they enable, and the historical narrative that he shapes through the power of memory and iterative retelling. Constative (descriptive) and performative need and support each other in this process. These three figures are Prospero's creatures, new created, changed and new formed, just as his brother translated his previous subjects. And the power that enables him to do so is that which 'endows their purposes with words that made them known'.

The Tempest may mimic or represent this power, but it is also itself shaped or created by it. Prospero himself and all the creatures we count as the characters of the play are themselves no more than a conglomeration of speech acts. They are literally made up of, *characterized* by, the speech acts that are laid out, dialogically, in the text. As characters in *The Tempest* they are indeed 'new created' – formed out of nothing other than the interactive forces and effects of speech. I have argued elsewhere for a minimal or thin theory of character, by which character is the (at least by implication) embodied movement of a series of speech acts and their consequences.[9] In the analysis I have presented so far, habitual speech act and dramatic character have an essentially dialogical and sometimes even dialectical relationship. In the example of the imperative and the curse these two performative forces of language occur in response to or in productive tension with each other: the imperative, with its assumption of authority, is resisted by the curse, which implicitly acknowledges a degree of powerlessness as a mark of its character, but tries to overcome that powerlessness by projecting an imagined and wished for different world at some future point. Most important, the force of command needs to be sustained by the narrative of personal history.

Character is dynamically shaped by the interplay of speech act, its dialogical other, and the ways in which it is able to insert itself into and control the productive interplay of performative speech of

---

9 Schalkwyk, 'Shakespeare's Speech'.

narrative event and personal past. We have seen Prospero's relatively casual assumption of the right to give commands on the island as a whole; but also his need to recall, as objective memory, the events that imbue his commands with authority. We have also seen Caliban's response, as the subject of language and Prospero's political subject, with the curse rather than command as a sign both of resentment and impotence. But we should also note the way in which Prospero himself betrays his weakness before the challenges of both his slave and servant. That weakness is signalled by a further performative speech act. It is related to but not identical to Caliban's curses. It even bears the same name. In response to Caliban's reminders that the island, originally his, was taken away from him, Prospero bolsters his narrative of Caliban's incorrigible ingratitude and unruly lust with a series of uncontrolled curses. These do not take the form of Caliban's curses, but are what we call name-calling: 'Slave . . . earth . . . tortoise . . . lying slave . . . Filth . . . Hag-seed . . . malice' (1.2.313–64).[10]

Faced with similar resistance from Ariel, Prospero resorts to name-calling no different in kind from the curses he heaps upon Caliban: 'my Ariel' (188) is transformed into 'malignant thing' (257), 'servant' (187) into 'my slave' (270), and 'my brave spirit' (206) is turned into 'dull thing' (285). Prospero controls and diverts Ariel's relatively mild resistance by forcing him to endorse his master's version of memory, which Ariel is accused of wilfully forgetting. 'I must / Once in a month recount what thou hast been, / Which thou forget'st' (261–5), recalls the mode in which Prospero's own subjects were 'new formed' by the performative speech acts of his brother. What lies in that 'must'? Its resonance for us as audience lies in its ambiguity, its undecidable status between an obligation that Prospero bears from outside and his own voluntary imposition of an obligation upon his servant. Furthermore, its reiterative process, reminiscent of brain-washing, prompts us to ask whether the scene we have just seen enacted with Miranda, in which she is provoked into asking questions which, in Prospero's words, his 'tale provokes' (140) and then

put to sleep before she can ask uncomfortable questions ('Thou art inclined to sleep . . . I know thou canst not choose' (185–6)), is not the endless repetition of the same scene, iterated 'once in a month', to subject Miranda to Prospero's will and design, to 'new create' her repeatedly and literally as his creature. How often, we may ask, has Act 1 scene 2 of *The Tempest* been rehearsed, re-performed, re-enacted and repeated?

Prospero's name-calling, then, would itself be the rehearsal of two things: recalling the process whereby he engaged in the reiterative process of teaching Caliban the names for things (or *his* names for things), it would be a rehearsal of the God-given power to give things the names that correspond to their natures. This is not an exercise in the arbitrary nature of the sign, in which names bear no *natural* relation to the objects they name. Caliban is an anagram of cannibal (did Caliban know his own name when Prospero met him, or did his master *give* him that name?); the islander is, if Prospero is to be believed, *by nature* 'malice', 'earth', a 'tortoise', a 'lying slave', and 'hag-seed', just as Ariel as independent servant is a 'malignant thing', a 'slave', and a 'dull thing', and admired Miranda no more than her father's 'foot' (467). The grammatical form of Prospero's appellations invites us to believe that he is doing no more than recognizing Caliban, Ariel and Miranda by their proper names. He is simply calling them by name, by what they are. But the illocutionary force that we recognize in his name-calling betrays the fact that he is in fact *giving* them these names in an attempt to shape

---

[10] This is related, but not identical to, DocuScope's use of Principle Component Anaylsis (PCA) to isolate the predominant speech actions in a play by plotting frequent occurrences against infrequent ones. So, for example, DocuScope indicates that Shakespeare's comedies differ from his histories in inversely proportional aspects: the comedies use second-person pronouns frequently, but tend to avoid descriptions; the histories engage in references to the external world but avoid second-person pronouns. In my analysis of *The Tempest*, command and curses tend to have an inverse relation to each other – the one denoting power, the other impotence – but this is complicated by the fact that the power of the command depends upon the capacity to sustain a particular historical narrative.

them in his image of them. Such name-calling is paradoxically a simultaneous exercise of power and an acknowledgement of weakness – an attempt, in the face of resistance, to impose the names upon them in an act of defensiveness, not unquestioned authority.

The fact that *The Tempest* is a piece of theatre means that it calls us as witnesses to the double nature of such name-calling. We see both aspects of Prospero's name-calling, just as we recognize the uncertain nature of the felicity conditions upon which characters presume to enact their performatives.

UNMASQUEING *THE TEMPEST*

A great deal has been written about the the-atricality of *The Tempest*. Most commentary has focused on the degree to which, unlike most of Shakespeare's plays, *The Tempest* incorporates into itself a peculiar theatrical form that became especially popular in the court of James I and his son Charles: the court masque. The court masque was an elitist form of theatre performed only to and at the court. It reduced the essentially dialogical dynamic of the public theatre to a peculiarly truncated form of dialectic. It was directed at an ideal audience, the king and his family, who not only occupied the perfect, unique place of the gaze in physical space, but for whom the masque reflected back to his central gaze the perfect image of his authority. The masque was the king's dream wrought to perfection – not merely the complete fulfilment of his wishes, but also something public, which others in his circle could share, without the disturbing dream-work of condensation or displacement.

It is a commonplace that masques usually opened with a scene of disorder enacted by profes-sional actors who were quickly dispelled by the entrance of new *dramatis personae* resplendent in specially designed costumes, whose *fiat* at once restored a particular ideal vision of order, harmony and illusion. Actors in the masque proper were played by members of the court, especially Queen Anne and her attendant ladies, who, though they personated exotic characters, nevertheless in effect played themselves. The disparity between player and part of the antimasque having been banished from the stage, the ideal vision of the masque proper sought to forge an Edenic notion of actor and action, person and name, which are by nature indivisible. The Jacobean court masque thus pre-sented to the king and his court in all dimensions the formation or creation of an ideal order at whose centre they sat without drawing anyone's attention to the artificiality – the conditions and modes of production – of that vision. It was fundamentally narcissistic; it eschewed the essentially theatrical dialogism whereby each voice is rendered relative to another, to the response of which it shapes itself; and it cut off the progression of any dialectic by stopping its movement at the mere supersession of one voice and vision (the antimasque) by another, superior one (the masque) in a moment of final stasis.

There are two masques, or masque-like sequences, in *The Tempest*. The most obvious is the play staged by Prospero's spirits in Act 4 scene 1 – a wedding masque for Ferdinand and Miranda (and, if theatre historians are right, directed in at least one performance for the marriage of James's daughter to the Elector Palatine on 20 May 1613). Shakespeare wrote no masques for James's court. But like those of his contemporaries, Ben Jonson and Thomas Heywood, the masque of Ceres, Iris and Juno, which celebrates the chaste union of the young couple, and pointedly excludes Venus and Cupid while paradoxically celebrating fertil-ity, offers a selective, highly idealized and directed vision of reality. Its language is significantly charac-terized by the imperative voice, and its performa-tive directives and exclusions echo those that Pros-pero himself repeatedly directs at Ferdinand and Miranda. The other masque is the false banquet in Act 3 scene 3, in which the castaways are first invited to an elaborate banquet, before it is abruptly removed, and Ariel, acting as a harpy pretending to be a minister of fate, castigates them for their evil. It is striking that in both cases Shakespeare reverses the usual order of masque and antimasque, so that the symbolic order and vision of the masque do not supplant but are destroyed by the chaos of the antimasque.

The masques and antimasques of *The Tempest* have attracted a great deal of commentary. They represent for many the most theatrical moments in the play – the scenes in which Shakespeare draws attention to the histrionic artificiality of the masque as both an aesthetic and political event. David Bevington holds that they are examples of Shakespeare making available to a popular audience an elite, exclusive form that was the exclusive preserve of the court. Others, including David Lindley, Tom Bishop, John Gillies, Graham Holderness, Stephen Orgel and Glynne Wickham have variously argued that the masques of *The Tempest* show up the fragile ideological work of the court masque as the producer of illusion.[11] By disrupting the masque with the antimasque, and by revealing or staging the ways in which the illusions or fictions of the masque are artificially produced, Shakespeare demystifies the form of theatre (and its political or ideological work) to which his colleagues had migrated.

Linguistically speaking *The Tempest* is marked by a curious similarity, at least in broad usage, to the Jacobean masque, even if it is clearly itself no masque. DocuScope usefully reveals that masques by Jonson generally differ in a pronounced way both from the rest of his plays and from Shakespeare's. But in one respect the masques and *The Tempest* are alike: they both contain a high proportion of description – that is to say, they describe what the audience is seeing or has seen in a static fashion – and, in both, accounts of the future are offered from the standpoint of the present. This suggests that there are key linguistic aspects of the masque that are present in *The Tempest* as a whole: that at least in some ways not only the short masque-scenes but also the play itself contains elements of masque-like language.

Another linguistic form that marks *The Tempest* (but not necessarily the masque as such), is a high degree of the use of first-person pronouns, but not (unlike the romantic comedies) *interactive* personal pronoun uses.[12] This means that it lacks the comedies' dialogical dynamic, by

which personal relationships and identities are in conversational flux, the product of collaborative negotiations that involve uncertainty, risk, and a desire to achieve reciprocal relationships. The centrality of the 'I' in *The Tempest* underscores what we have already seen regarding its initiating speech acts: the command, the curse and descriptive narrative all assume a strong initiating self as their sources. But the theatricality of the play is not confined to the moments in the interaction of masque and anti-masque where either the directing forces are disrupted (as in Prospero's suddenly remembering, 'I had forgot . . . ', the conspiracy against him). Such theatricality, which stages the staging of theatre, is present throughout the play, and is one of its most fundamental features. We are made aware of the uncertainty of authority by the storm of the opening scene; we are invited to question the truth of Prospero's historical narratives both by the internal features of his magic, which allows him to provoke and cease Miranda's questioning at a whim, and the external challenges he faces from his servant and slave. These forces compel him to bolster the power and authority of his imperatives with a narrative that, by the very fact of its retelling, means that it has to be brought out into the open – it cannot be taken for granted as the silent ground of his speech acts – and also oblige him to resort to the weakness of name-calling. In other words, the theatricality of *The Tempest* is staged in the smallest units of language and in the shaping dynamics of character: in the construction of the 'I' that enables and is enabled by its speech acts.

---

[11] See David Bevington and Peter Holbrook, eds., *The Politics of the Stuart Court Masque* (Cambridge, 1999), which includes essays by Lindley, Bishop, Orgel and the editors. Also, Glynne Wickham, 'Masque and Anti-masque in *The Tempest*', *Essays and Studies*, 28 (1975), 1–14; John Gillies, 'Shakespeare's Virginian Masque', *English Literary History* 53 (1986), 673–707; Graham Holderness, Nick Potter, and John Turner, *Shakespeare: Out of Court: Dramatizations of Court Society* (London, 1990); and Glynne Wickham, 'Masque and Anti-masque in *The Tempest*', *Essays and Studies*, 28 (1975), 1–14.

[12] As revealed by DocuScope.

MODALS

I have done no more than sketch some of the linguistic features of the first two scenes of the play. I now wish to add another, rather different one: what we call modal auxiliary verbs: 'would', 'could', 'shall', 'will', 'can'. There are fewer instances of these than commands and descriptions, but they offer a crucial alternative pattern to the relative certainty and stability of the play's major illocutionary acts, and therefore of our notion of character. Act 2 scene 1 provides plenty of examples of modals at work, the most famous of which is Gonzalo's fantasy, after Montaigne, of how he would rule the island if he were in charge: '*Had* I a plantation of this isle, my lord . . . And *were* the king on't, what *would* I do? . . . I *would* by contraries / Execute all things . . .' (2.1.139–44). From the audience's point of view, the old courtier is imagining himself in Prospero's position. He is therefore offering an alternative possible world to the one already shaped and being shaped through the illocutionary force of language dominated up to this point by Prospero. This speech act enacts a performative contradiction, which the two cynical courtiers are all too ready to point out, but it is a contradiction that goes to the heart of the issues that we have already discussed: the power and authority to engage in certain speech acts, to change the world through speech. The modals in Gonzalo's speech mean that he is *entertaining* imaginatively the directives and imperatives that Prospero already commands as an alternative possibility: he would give orders that no more orders, no more authority will be exercised or needed. Of course, he cannot give such orders, but he does make us aware of the conditions that make orders as such possible, and also desirable or not.

The whole scene is set up so as to produce the island and its experiences as a series of modal possibilities or, in other words, a contradiction. It begins with Alonzo's regretful declaration, 'Would I had never married my daughter there . . .' (103–4), and continues with a series of contradictions regarding the nature of the island itself: Is the island inhospitable or of gentle temperance? Does the air breathe sweetly or is it perfumed like a fen? Are their garments drenched or fresh as the day of the wedding? Was Dido a widow or a whore? Is Carthage Tunis? At its most intense, it modulates into the series of modals through which Antonio and Sebastian entertain, in the mode of Gonzalo's speculations, the possibility of murdering the king and usurping the throne. 'What impossible matter will he make easy next?' is a reference to the possibilities that exist in language itself, especially in its modal forms: in the potentiality lurking in (wonderful ambiguity!) the simple word 'might': 'What might, / Worthy Sebastian, O, what might? – No more. / And yet methinks I see it in thy face, / What thou *shouldst* be' (200–3).

The modalities that language makes available is what allows men to make themselves anew; it is a 'sleepy language' that allows speakers to 'be asleep / With eyes wide open' (209–10). It is the language of dreams, wishes, desires, of making a world that is different, that lurks in the reality of language itself. Its darker sides are revealed in Antonio's capacity to recreate as his own creatures Prospero's subjects and his capacity to invite Sebastian to act on his desires. There is a play of light and dark in Prospero's own uses of it, or rather his capacity to hide the modalities of his own desires and power behind a façade of apparently straightforward command and narrative. It surfaces again in a slightly different key when Trinculo and then Stephano speculate (in all senses of the word) on how Caliban *might* make a man if he could be exhibited abroad. ('Were I in England now . . . and had but this fish painted, not a holiday fool there but would give a piece of silver. There would this monster make a man' (2.2.26–9)). But its creative power is most marked in that meeting of Miranda and Ferdinand, where both lovers negotiate their love for each other via the modalities of uncertain, vulnerable reciprocity. Miranda's uncertain sense of wonder at the sight of Ferdinand – 'I *might* call him / A thing divine, for nothing natural / I ever saw so noble' (1.2.415–17) – is matched by the prince's own stance, which assumes the form of a prayer: 'Vouchsafe my prayer / *May* know if you remain upon this island, / And that you will some good instruction give / How I *may* bear me here' (1.2.420–3).

The modalities of love

In a brilliant and pioneering analysis of the role of modals in Shakespeare, Lynne Magnusson writes that 'modals facilitate the fine calibration of relationships', bringing into play 'fine-tuned and culturally inflected estimations of ability, obligation, volition and knowledge as they relate to future actions, conflicts and negotiations in which we can recognize the mind in motion' – in her wonderful phrase – 'a psychology in the potential mode'.[13] This is precisely what we see in the interaction of Ferdinand and Miranda. Moreover, Magnusson's analysis of the effect of modal verbs in the creation of character can be very usefully supplemented by Stanley Cavell's extension of Austin's work on performative utterances in the form of what Cavell calls 'passionate utterances'.[14] Passionate utterances are perlocutionary acts through which people negotiate, invite or challenge each other into what Cavell calls 'the disorders of desire' (185). Cavell does not focus on the role of modals, but we can see in the interaction – the dialogue – between Ferdinand and Miranda the way in which modals allow them to position themselves in relation to each other in such a way that their independent (and isolated) selves are made available to (and also vulnerable to) the other.

Such negotiations are the predominant modes of the romantic comedies but in the very different linguistic landscape of *The Tempest* this interaction is remarkable. Ferdinand and Miranda's language is marked by uncertainty, a vulnerable openness that moves towards a set of new relationships and possibilities – a new world of reciprocity that stands in stark contrast to the world we have encountered up to now. For in contrast to the apparently secure modalities of the imperative, or the assumption of a certain discourse of narrative history, or even the insecure aggressiveness of the curse, the hesitant, exploratory language of love works in a world of possibilities rather than of obligation or necessity; but it nevertheless forges a sense of free commitment for itself out of a world of imposed, external

necessity. In Act 3 scene 1, Ferdinand begins by reflection of the difference that the world of love has committed him to: 'This my mean task / Would be as heavy to me as odious, but / The mistress which I serve quickens what's dead / And makes my labours pleasures' (4–7). Ferdinand's enforced slavery is displaced onto his willing service of his mistress, in an example of not merely a desired alternative world but one experienced or lived through. Moreover, in contrast to his conventional language of erotic service, his 'mistress' joins him in the modality of reciprocal suffering. 'I would the lightning had / Burnt up those logs that you are enjoined to pile' (16–17), Miranda remarks in sympathy, and even her offer of help is couched in the open, vulnerable conditional mode that seeks to make possible a different path to the future: 'If you'll sit down / I'll bear your logs the while: Pray give me that: / I'll carry it to the pile' (23–5).

A starker contrast to Prospero's habitual imperative voice it would be hard to find, although this is complicated by our awareness throughout, in another moment of the play's relentless metatheatricality, of Prospero's supposedly controlling figure, like that of a puppet-master, behind the scene. This is proceeding, he tells us, according to his grand design. But even if the couple act in accordance with his desires, the modality of their language is a constant reminder of how different their negotiations are from his habitual mode of speaking, and also that love cannot be commanded: it lies beyond the domain of the imperative, and so marks the limit of that mode of speech, which is thereby marked off as one mode among many rather than an act that commands the entire field. The most remarkable thing about the pledges of the lovers is the way in which they invert the usual modes by which Prospero controls the performative, the way they couch the uncertainties of subjunctive or conditional desire into the certainties of indicative fact: 'I am yours, if you'll marry

---

13 Magnusson, 'A Play of Modals', pp. 74, 79.
14 Stanley Cavell, *Philosophy the Day After Tomorrow* (Cambridge, MA., 2006), pp. 155–91.

me', Miranda declares, opening through the conditional, her transformation into Ferdinand's. Not, 'If you'll have me, I'll be your wife', but 'I am your wife . . .'.

IMPERATIVES AND DISTRIBUTED CHARACTER

One of the most striking things about the subtle plotting of *The Tempest* is that this scene is followed by one of the most comically burlesque in the play: the one in which Stephano, Trinculo and Caliban gather their plot against Prospero, and then fall out in a farce of mistaken confusion. The subtlety of the scene lies in its modulation of the kinds of language we have already encountered. It begins with Stephano's assumption of Prospero's imperative mode, rendered the more parodic by the fact that his kingdom and subjects are not a great deal more meagre than Prospero's. It may come as a surprise that Stephano's command of the imperative voice is second only to Prospero's: thirty-one instances against seventy-five. The butler begins with a relatively secure assumption of command, but the confidence of that stance is immediately undercut by a series of conditionals and projections that reveal a state in the making rather than achieved. This invites us to reflect on the way in which Prospero's state is constructed, performatively, rather than inherited as a fact of nature. Cross-cutting Stephano's imperatives (to Trinculo to shut up, to Caliban to drink to him, to Trinculo to stand further off, and so on), is a series of conditionals that undermine the felicity of Stephano's authority. Almost all the dialogue is conducted as a set of *potential* actions or events – projected into the future as if they were facts ('Thou *shalt* be lord of it' (3.2.55); 'She *will* become thy bed, I warrant, / And bring thee forth brave brood' (101–2); 'I *will* kill this man. His daughter and I *will be* king and queen, save our graces; and Trinculo and thyself *shall be* viceroys' (103–5)). Shakespeare reminds us through performatives like 'I warrant' and 'save our graces' that the events and the status that they entail require transformative speech acts underwritten by

broad social convention (what warrant does Caliban's voice have, and what force does Stephano's wishful, self-directed honorific carry?), which are not confined to the obviously powerless figures like the servants. They carry over into questions about Prospero's right, on his usurped, occupied plantation, to summarily assume the mantle of authority.

Especially interesting is the way in which Caliban moves from the linguistic position of servile supplication to an increasingly strident assumption of command, as he desperately but ineffectually tries to keep the wayward servants focused on their primary task. At the end of Act 4 scene 1 he begins to adopt Prospero's voice, shifting from the grammatically indistinguishable mode of the request ('Pray you, tread softly' (194)) to the derisive imperative ('Let it alone, thou fool, it is but trash' (223)). This linguistic shift betrays a whole way of seeing, evaluation and being in the world. It shows that if we attend to the linguistic building blocks of character the idea of an independent, wholly formed character prior to the unfolding of the play's speech acts is a false image of how character is formed, at least in Shakespeare. Character is produced *between* speakers, in potential. It is always on the move and, as the example of Caliban's unexpected assumption of the imperative here shows, it is a structural effect that can relate speakers in unexpected ways as well as distinguish them. In other words, the truth of the otherwise questionable claim that there are no people in fiction but only collections of words lies in a *distributed* notion of character. Caliban's world is separated from Prospero's in their opening encounter, and this is signalled by their respective, habitual speech acts: imperatives and name-calling by the master and curses by the slave. But Caliban's assumption of the imperative and name-calling in Act 4 – in the midst of his conspiracy – subtly aligns him more closely with his master than with the renegade servants he has undertaken to serve. It therefore prepares for his willingness to 'seek for grace'. Theatre doesn't merely present us with independent people; it also links and dissociates the characters it creates through a process of subtle linguistic and other patterning.

If Ferdinand and Miranda enter a linguistic realm of vulnerable negotiation and modal uncertainty, Prospero's control is reasserted in the masque of Act 4, where his characteristic imperative voice is redistributed via his servant, Ariel, among the mythical goddesses, Ceres, Iris and Juno. Prospero's art effects the celebration of a wedding, but it also represents the intensification of his jussive over their optative modes. People who fall in love open themselves to one another in a non-coercive mode, and their friends usually *wish* them well in their future navigation of their fragile relationship; Prospero's creatures take on his voice to *command* them to be well along the lines of his preconceived social and sexual order. Particularly striking for the *play's* audience is Prospero's restriction of the freedom of the *masque's* audience to take the show as they like it: 'No tongue! All eyes! Be silent!' (4.1.59). His insistent injunctions highlight our metatheatrical awareness of Prospero's manipulation, and underline our perception of the disjunction between Prospero's and Shakespeare's plays.[15] The relationships set up for the characters in the masque thus reflect those of its players and their master: they underwrite the demands of settled service and obedience. Iris's initial speech is a meandering, syntactically complex, transferred command dressed as a description, which consumes a dozen lines before coming to its point: 'the queen o' th' sky / Whose wat'ry arch and messenger am I / Bids thee leave these . . . Approach, rich Ceres, her to entertain' (70–5). The transfer of authority from Juno to Ceres matches perfectly a similar transmission from Prospero to Ariel, who plays the part of Ceres. And when Ceres appears in answer to this summons, her opening greeting to Iris underlines the obligations of duty and obedience: 'Hail; many-coloured messenger, that ne'er / Dost disobey the wife of Jupiter' (76–7). Grammatically the speech act has the form of a description, but it is in fact deontic: it stresses the general, natural order of unquestionable obedience. Enough has been said about the banishment of Venus and Cupid from the scene to require no further comment, other than that it conforms to a general linguistic characteristic of *The Tempest* to pass prescription off as description. This event is represented as having already happened; nobody actually witnesses the messy process of coercion and banishment of erotic desire (which is, of course, a fiction – a product of Prospero's 'present fancies' (122)).

'WOULD/SHOULD'

There is one more set of modals to be examined: the fascinating pair 'would/should'. Magnusson reminds us that modal auxiliary verbs were in a state of flux in Shakespeare's time, and therefore lent themselves to ambiguity that is instrumental in negotiating the complexity of interpersonal relations. Modals like 'may' hovered between epistemic modality and deontic modality.[16] Epistemic modality concerns the possible truth of a proposition, whereas deontic modality concerns relations of power, like obligation or permission. To use her example, declaring 'He may come tomorrow' is open to two possible interpretations: first, that it is uncertain whether or not he will come (we don't *know*), and second, that I am giving him permission or allowing him to come tomorrow (this is an interaction of wills or desires, not of knowledge).

There is a key moment when Ariel's report on the completion of his task turns into a more intimate relationship between himself and his master, in which the humanity of the master himself is suddenly at stake:

Ariel. Your charm so strongly works 'em
　　　That if you now beheld them, your affections
　　　Would become tender.
Prospero.　　　　Dost thou think so, spirit?
Ariel. Mine would, sir, were I human.
Prospero.　　　　　　And mine shall.
　　　　　　　　　　　　　　(5.1.17–20)

Ariel's first use of 'would' seems to be epistemic: he is predicting that Prospero will take pity on his enemies, if he saw them. Prospero's interrogation ('Dost thou think so, spirit'), with its grammatical

---

[15] The distinction between Prospero's and Shakespeare's plays is forcefully made by Peter Hulme in *Colonial Encounters*.
[16] Magnusson, 'A Play of Modals', p. 71.

reminder of both Ariel's non-human quality and his subordinate status, hovers between an enquiry as to his servant's state of mind or belief and a challenge. Ariel nimbly meets the challenge by turning his earlier epistemic 'would' into a deontic one: 'Mine would, sir, if I were human'. It remains epistemic at one level – a statement of what he would do if he were human – but it is itself a challenge or prescription directed at the human master: if even I should find pity (as a matter of fact), then so should you (as a matter of obligation). Tenderness of affection is not a quality displayed with any frequency by Prospero, so it is all the more telling that he should respond to Ariel's deontic challenge by accepting the obligation suggested by the subordinate as an undertaking in the future: 'And mine shall'. Note how clearly Shakespeare signals the distributive nature of character (and its ethical dimensions) here; the possessives that signal the essential separation of speakers – 'mine' (Ariel) and 'mine' (Prospero) – are finally combined in a mutual accommodation of a common humanity, effected by the *non*-human creature.

The next notable distribution of the modal 'would' occurs in a much-noted exchange between the lovers, Ferdinand and Miranda, when they are revealed by Prospero's theatrical gesture of disclosure:

(*Here Prospero discovers Ferdinand and Miranda, playing at chess*)

Miranda.   Sweet lord, you play me false.
Ferdinand. No, my dearest love,
    I would not for the world.
Miranda. Yes, for a score of kingdoms you should wrangle,
    And I would call it fair play.   (5.1.172–5)

Miranda's first words after her declaration of love in Act 3 is an accusation – a mode that we've come to associate with Caliban and Ariel. This is the first speech act *we* hear from her as a wife, a position conventionally conflated with those of servants in the Jacobean household. Yet to her husband's conventional denial – that he *would* not for the world – she confirms a strange, performative contradiction that both humanizes the strange inhumanity of the

wedding masque and negates its coercive idealism. 'Yes' – you *do* play me false. And 'no' – even if you did, I would not regard it as cheating, so I am not accusing you now. What is the force of 'would' and 'should' here? It's very hard to say, exactly. E. A. Abbott's *A Shakespearean Grammar* suggests that there is a usage that falls somewhere between entertained future action and obligation, in which the sense of 'if you were to' is combined with the meaning of 'you ought to'.[17] If that is so – if Miranda is not merely entertaining the conditional possibility of her response to Ferdinand's future actions, but suggesting not only that he will do them, but also ought to do them – then her own reflection on her response indicates a full-sighted knowingness that is somewhat different from the character we have seen so far. The crucial thing, however, is that these modes are ambiguous, and they therefore offer an enriched mixture of emotions and attitudes: knowingness, indulgence, wistfulness, tenderness, realism and love. The speech act is a kind of projected *occupatio*, a figure by which so many unsaid things are said: I would call your wrangling by a name that it is not, but by the very mode through which I undertake this I am pointing out its true quality. In her grammar, at least, Miranda sees the world with old eyes, but this is not a sign of the corruption of innocence. Or if it is, it is a corruption that is necessary for love as a force between people rather than mere figures in masque.

FINALLY . . .

We come to Prospero's epilogue, in which character is finally abandoned, the book drowned, his staff broken, as the actor pleads for the indulgence of the audience.

Prospero.
    Now my charms are all o'erthrown,
    And what strength I have's mine own,
    Which is most faint. Now 'tis true

---

[17] E. A. Abbott, *A Shakespearean Grammar* (London, 1869), 324.

I must be here confined by you,
Or sent to Naples. Let me not,
Since I have my dukedom got
And pardoned the deceiver, dwell
In this bare island by your spell.
But release me from my bands
With the help of your good hands.
Gentle breath of yours my sails
Must fill, or else my project fails,
Which was to please. Now I want
Spirits to enforce, art to enchant;
And my ending is despair
Unless I be relieved by prayer
Which pierces so, that it assaults
Mercy itself, and frees all faults.
As you from crimes would pardoned be,
Let your indulgence set me free.   (Epilogue, 1–20)

Who speaks this speech? The character or the actor? The First Folio tells us that it is 'spoken by Prospero'. It makes most sense to see this as an instance of the actor casting off his assumed authority and, from a position of weakness, directing a plea to the audience to be released by their applause. But its modalities are complex: it opens with a statement, an avowal of the truth of the actor's dependency upon the audience. Yet it is to *Naples* that the speaker, whose habitual home is the 'here' of the stage, wishes to be sent. And the modes of the speech move undecidably among statement, plea and imperative, all wrapped in an insistent conditionality. What force lies in the 'must' of 'gentle breath of yours my sails / *Must* fill', and what transformative power is carried by the appellation 'gentle', at the very point at which Prospero's assumed gentility slips from the body of the 'common player'? The final jussive, an apparent declaration of complete weakness, traps the audience through its conditionality: those who refuse the indulgence condemn themselves to damnation. Who wouldn't offer up his or her 'gentle breath', as a final endorsement of the figure who refuses to be confined to either 'assumed' character or 'real' actor?

LIKE AN OLYMPIAN WRESTLING:
SHAKESPEARE'S OLYMPIC GAME

RICHARD WILSON

THIS SHORT-GRASSED GREEN

The Opening Ceremony of the 2012 Olympic Games began on the evening of Friday 1 June with a massed choir singing 'Songs of Welcome' by folk artist Eliza Carthy based on traditional English melodies but also inspired, it was stated, by 'the values of the modern Olympic and Paralympic movements', before the spectacular entry of an actor dressed in historic royal costume. Courtesy of the palace, the gimmick of representing the sovereign as a good sport was doubtless intended to symbolize the inclusiveness celebrated in Carthy's refrain, 'We're all together again, singing all together again.'[1] In fact, as Leah Marcus has pointed out, King James originally gave permission for this mimicry, and donated his 'Hat and Feather and Ruff' to his impersonator, 'purposely to grace him and consequently the solemnity', as part of the patriarchal 'politics of mirth', the campaign to co-opt holiday pastimes to 'the symbolic language of Stuart power'.[2] 'A substitute shines brightly as a king' (*Merchant*, 5.1.93), however, and as Shakespearians know, English sovereigns started something they could not easily control when they played with 'the cease of majesty' (*Hamlet*, 3.3.15) by allowing their regalia to be used in sport.

The merry monarch who inaugurated the Midsummer Games of 2012 wore a get-up more in keeping with Shakespeare's Globe than any sporting fixture, because this was, of course, not London 2012, into which Queen Elizabeth was represented leaping by a parachutist wearing her signature pink

dress, but the Cotswold Olympics, founded in 1612, on the site of much older summer rites at Chipping Campden in Gloucestershire, by the lawyer Robert Dover, whose friend the courtier Endymion Porter arranged for him to preside over these Games of wrestling, stick-fighting, pole-vaulting, leap-frogging, javelin-throwing, jumping, hammer-tossing, gymnastics and shin-kicking, as well as hunting, horse- and greyhound-racing, dicing, dancing, chess (for the gentry) and drinking, in front of a toy mock-up of Dover Castle, in the royal clothes. Previously the Whitsun wake took place there, Michael Drayton recorded in *Polyolbion*, under the lead of a 'Shepherd King', whose flock had 'chanc'd that year the earliest lamb to bring'.[3] London 2012 had proudly cited its Jacobean precursor, however, in its bid to host the Games, and commenced on 27 July with the actor Kenneth Branagh, posed as the King of Engineers, Isambard Kingdom Brunel, reciting lines from *The Tempest*, exactly contemporary with

All quotations of Shakespeare are from the Norton Shakespeare, based on the Oxford text, ed. Stephen Greenblatt, Walter Cohen, Jean Howard and Katharine Eisaman Maus (New York, 2007).

[1] Eliza Carthy, 'Welcome Song', 'Robert Dover's Cotswold Olimpicks 2012' website.

[2] Leah Marcus, *The Politics of Mirth: Jonson, Herrick, Milton, Marvell, and the Defense of Old Holiday Customs* (Chicago, 1989), p. 5; 'purposely to grace him': Anthony à Wood, *Athenae Oxonienses*, repr. in Christopher Whitfield, *Robert Dover and the Cotswold Games: 'Annalia Dubrensia'* (London, 1962), p. 18.

[3] Michael Drayton, *Polyolbion*, 14th Song, 1:162.

Dover's Games, that were clearly meant to signal the same pastoral message about 'this green land' (*Tempest*, 4.1.130), that 'on this grass plot, in this very place' (73), there was for this special time nothing of which to be afraid:

Be not afeard. The isle is full of noises,
Sounds and sweet airs, that give delight and hurt not.
(3.2.130–1)

What frightened London's panoptic Olympic organisation, LOCOG, was the threat of an Islamist terrorist attack. But by winding the athletes' parade around one of the 'turfy mountains', complete with maypoles and 'nibbling sheep' (4.1.62), mentioned in Prospero's masque, a 'wanton green' like those into which the ancient Britons had supposedly cut 'the quaint mazes' that by Shakespeare's day were already said 'for lack of tread' to be 'indistinguishable' and 'filled with mud' (*Dream*, 2.1.98–100), the director Danny Boyle led his two billion TV audience a merry dance, to which Fox News was unable to provide a clue. So the outrage of the right-wing media was provoked as much by bemusement at its initiation into the semiotic labyrinth of 'this short-grassed green' (*Tempest*, 4.1.90) as by the subsequent pageant of Britain's National Health. Yet, 'How does your fallow greyhound, sir?' Shakespeare's Slender needles Page, 'I heard say he was outrun on Cotswold' (*Wives*, 1.1.73), prompting enthusiasts to cite the Bard himself as an eyewitness to the importance of the events on Dover's Hill.[4] The 'hilltop of sports and Merriments', one of the wags calls the site of 'Dover's Olympicks' in Richard Brome's *A Jovial Crew*.[5] And sports historians do, in fact, trace the modern Olympics in part to a visit paid in 1890 by their instigator, the French Baron Pierre de Coubertin, to the Wenlock Hills in Shropshire, where for forty years Dr William Penny Brookes convened an athletics festival inspired by the ancient Greek Olympics that took off from Dover's Games.[6]

Official Olympic history might prefer the heroics admired by the French aristocrat in the proto-fascism of Thomas Arnold's Rugby School; but by setting London's 'Olympic village' down upon

the hallowed turf of a 'nine-men's Morris' (*Dream*, 2.1.98), in the timeless springtime of an actual English village green, then planting the nations' flags on Fortune's 'high and pleasant hill' (*Timon*, 1.1.64), Boyle looked to be idealizing a disarmingly alternative genealogy, and a bucolic rather than heroic sporting culture that had lingered on Dover's Hill until 1851, when having become a 'trysting place of the lowest scum of the population which lived between Birmingham and Oxford', the Cotswold Games were officially suppressed.[7] The director had done his homework, for historian David Underdown has indeed correlated the English Civil War with a fault-line running through these parts between the chalk country that played the bloody melée of football, and rallied to the King, and the cheese country that preferred more mediated bat-and-ball games such as cricket, and sided with Parliament.[8] By hurling Her Majesty's lookalike into the air at the start, and then ending the Paralympic revels on September 2 with the Shakespearian knight Sir Ian McKellen as an abdicating Prospero, London 2012 thus appeared to be nodding not only to those summer kings who wore the monarch's clothes, but to a vision Shakespeare also worked into *The Tempest*, of an

---

4 See, for example, Peter Levi, *The Life and Times of William Shakespeare* (London, 1988), p. 28: 'I think the greyhound ... must have been in the unreformed version of the Cotswold Whitsun meeting ... and that Shakespeare knew these country sports ... The key that fits this door is Robert Dover. Shakespeare knew him as a boy from Barton in the Heath, and probably later at the Inns of Court.' But Whitfield points out that the reference in *Merry Wives* occurs only in the Folio, and suggests Shakespeare 'attended the games during the last few of his life' as 'one of a gathering of kindred, neighbours, cousins, and friends' (*Robert Dover*, pp. 23, 29).

5 Richard Brome, *A Jovial Crew. or the Merry Beggars*, ed. Ann Haaker (London, 1968), p. 39.

6 John Findling and Kimberly Pelle, eds., *Enclopaedia of the Modern Olympic Movement* (Westport, CT, 2004), p. 457.

7 E. R. Vyvian, ed., 'Introduction', *Cotswold Games: Annalia Dubrensia* (Cheltenham, 1878; repr. London, 1970), p. ix.

8 David Underdown, *Revel, Riot, and Rebellion: Popular Politics and Culture in England, 1603–1660* (Oxford, 1985), pp. 73–6.

island unperturbed by power, a pastoral place in a utopian time with 'no sovereignty' (2.1.160):[9]

> Had I a plantation of this isle...
> I'th'commonwealth I would by contraries
> Execute all things. For no kind of traffic
> Would I admit, no name of magistrate.
>
> (*Tempest*, 2.1.143–9)

Gonzalo's dream of an isle exempt from sovereignty is shot down by the cynics with brutal logic: 'No sovereignty. Yet he would be king on't' (148). Sovereign is he who decides the exception, however.[10] So when the self-mocking Queen 'welcomed all, served all' (*Winter's Tale*, 4.4.57) at the Olympic feast, she exemplified one of the contortions inherent in the Olympic ideal which Boyle struggled to negotiate: that, as Steven Connor observed in a timely sprint through the philosophy of sport, the exception of sport is set off from the sovereign decision 'by an act of pure decision, by the simple decision to mark out a space in which to decide' the game on its own terms.[11] For in contrast to the immemorial festive world of the 'Shepherd King', which François Laroque has shown to have been deeply integrated into both profane and sacred calendars, sport 'comes into being in the antagonism between absolute and immanent time', and is always governed by the desire 'to take the time to which one is subject and convert it into a time of which one is the subject', an ambition that saw its mad apogee in the timeless Test-matches of pre-War cricket.[12] It is this transcendence of real time that makes sport more than a pastime, Connor proposes. But what renders the Olympic concept truly exceptional, ever since Heracles, legendary founder of the Olympics, was said to have enforced the Sacred Truce, the *ekecheiria* or 'staying of hands', for an interregnum of sixteen days, is the invocation of sovereignty to suspend sovereignty, and so to subsume absolute time to play time absolutely, for the time of the Games.[13]

'Who durst assemble such a Troop as he', wondered one of Dover's admirers, 'But might of insurrection charged be?'[14] In fact, the 'Cotswold Hercules' said he could not recall where he got his idea

of reviving the Olympics: 'Nor can I give account to you at all, / How this conceit into my brain did fall.'[15] So it is not surprising that the contributors to *Annalia Dubrensia*, his 1636 *Festschrift*, were divided as to whether his politics amounted to subversion, encouraging shepherds to rise against the 'bad owners of enclosed grounds', or containment, bowing 'To's King'.[16] Nor that Dover's encomiasts were confused over whether his plan was to rehabilitate 'country Wakes', the 'Palm and rush-bearing, harmless Whitsun ales' of Old England, or introduce the Olympic spirit of the sporting festival as a transcendent event, in which case, someone predicted, 'those two days of thine will (perhaps) stir / Some Saints to wrath, cut out of the Calendar'.[17] Dover's modern editor Christopher Whitfield calls the Cotswold Games 'a little local makeweight put in on the side of compromise' in religion; yet Phebe Jensen is surely right to infer that the effect of the *Annalia* was to insulate sport from the contentiousness of religion altogether, 'by implying that English festivity originated not with

---

[9] For Dover's games and 'summer kings', see Sandra Billington, *Mock Kings in Medieval Society and Renaissance Drama* (Oxford, 1991), pp. 63 and 80–5.

[10] Carl Schmitt, *Political Theology: Four Chapters on the Concept of Sovereignty*, trans. George Schwab (Chicago, 2005) p. 5.

[11] Steven Connor, *The Philosophy of Sport* (London, 2011), pp. 52–3.

[12] François Laroque, *Shakespeare's Festive World*, trans. Janet Lloyd (Cambridge, 1991); Connor, *Philosophy of Sport*, p. 83.

[13] Nigel Spivey, *The Ancient Olympics* (Oxford, 2004), pp. 76–7, 189–90; Connor, *Philosophy of Sport*, pp. 78–82.

[14] Nicholas Wallington, 'To the Great Inventor and Champion of the English Olympicks', repr. in Whitfield, *Robert Dover*, p. 150.

[15] Robert Dover, 'A Congratulatory Poem to my Poetical and Learned Noble Friends'; 'Cotswold Hercules': Richard Wells, 'To his Worthy Friend Mr Robert Dover concerning his Dover Castle and Cotswold Olympicke', in Whitfield, *Robert Dover*, pp. 205, 223.

[16] Shackerley Marmion, 'To Mr. Robert Dover, Upon His Annual Sports at Cotswold', and Nicolas Wallington, 'To the Great Inventor', in Whitfield, *Robert Dover*, pp. 150, 210.

[17] John Trussell, 'To My Noble Friend, Mr. Robert Dover'; and Richard Wells, 'To His Worthy Friend, Mr. Robert Dover', in Whitfield, *Robert Dover*, pp. 105, 205.

the medieval church, but Grecian sports'.[18] In his *Sport, Politics and Literature in the English Renaissance* Gregory Semenza goes further: 'the invention of sport' in this poets' symposium, itself a panegyric competition, was also the inception of a liberal society with an autonomous aesthetic.[19] Dover's jostling cheerleaders concurred, affirming that his ulterior purpose in assembling 'such multitudes' from so many classes, conditions and confessions, in this 'Great Instauration' of the Games, was precisely 'to advance true love and neighbourhood', as Ben Jonson toasted, in a zone of innocent neutrality:

His Soldiers, though they every one dissent
In minds, in manners, yet his Merriment
Ones them: Lords, Knights, Swains, Shepherds, Churls,
    agree,
To crown his sports, Discords make Harmony.[20]

FLORAL WARS

New Historicists insist that while Renaissance writers like Sir John Harington recognize play as a defining human activity, 'whose only end is delight of the mind or the spirit', they ground their defence of sport in the prerogative of the gentleman, rather than any Kantian disinterestedness.[21] And to be sure, Dover's Olympics were as much a rich man's club as our own so-called Olympic 'family'. Yet read against the backdrop of the Wars of Religion, *Annalia Dubrensia* amounts to a universalist manifesto in which Gloucestershire's Olympic Committee legislates the rules of the game of neutralization a century and a half before an affectless Kantian aesthetic issued in the Enlightenment project of perpetual peace. For Dover's Games would indeed be applauded by Shakespeare's Stratford relation John Trussell (author of a poem on Helen) as a universal truce, when 'scorn / And pride' were 'wholly at that time forborne', as contestants strove 'to excel... In love and courtesy'. 'For though... thy sports most man-like bee, / Yet they are linked with peace and modestie', attested another of the poets: 'Here all in th'one and self-same sphere do move, / Nor strive so much to win

by force as love.'[22] So on Dover's Hill, according to this moralizing, a different ethic of sportsmanship from that of the country meets of old was emerging, which affirmed that what mattered was not the win or loss, but how the game was played:

... where men meet not for delight,
So much as for delight to meete,
And where, to make their pastime right,
They make it not so great, as sweete;
Where love doth more than gain invite,
Hands part at last as first they grete,
And loosers none, where all that's plaid,
With friendship won, may not be weighed.[23]

'The Pythian, Grecian, and the Trojan plays / Are hardly match to those that thou dost raise', affirmed Dover's cousin John Stratford, for 'Thy sports are merely harmless.' Thus, they would teach 'each man how to master passion', sermonized the lawyer Sir William Denny. Likewise, Drayton enthused how the Cotswold Games restored 'The golden Age's glories... As those brave Grecians in their

---

18 Whitfield, *Robert Dover*, p. 2; Phebe Jensen, *Religion and Revelry in Shakespeare's Festive World* (Cambridge, 2008), p. 203. See also Laroque, *Shakespeare's Festive World*, pp. 163–5.

19 Gregory Colon Semenza, *Sport, Politics and Literature in the English Renaissance* (Newark, 2003), p. 116.

20 Robert Dover, 'A Congratulatory Poem to my Poetical Learned Noble Friends'; Ben Jonson, 'An Epigram to my Jovial Good Friend, Mr. Robert Dover, on his great Instauration of his Hunting and Dancing at Cotswold'; Ben Jonson, 'An Epigram to my Joviall Good Friend, Mr. Robert Dover, on his Great Instauration'; and Nicholas Wallington, 'To the Great Inventor', repr. in Whitfield, *Robert Dover*, pp. 134, 223.

21 John Harington, 'A Treatise on Play', in *Nugae Antiquaae*, ed. Henry Harington (3 vols., 1779; repr. Hildesheim, 1968), vol. 2, p. 173; Louis Montrose, *The Purpose of Playing: Shakespeare and the Cultural Politics of the Elizabethan Theatre* (Chicago, 1996), pp. 41–2.

22 John Trussell, 'To the Noble and Disposed Ladies and Gentlewomen assembled in Whitsun-Week upon Cotswold'; John Mosson, 'To his Worthy Friend Mr Robert Dover, on his famous Yeerely Assemblies upon Cotswold', in Whitfield, *Robert Dover*, pp. 172, 199.

23 William Basse, 'To the Noble and Fayre Assemblies... and their Jovial Entertainer, my right Generous Friend, Master Robert Dover, upon Cotswold', in Whitfield, *Robert Dover*, pp. 166–7.

happy dayes / On Mount Olympus . . . Where then their able Youth Leapt, Wrestled, Ran', purely 'for the garland'.[24] It cannot be coincidence, then, that so many of Dover's reconcilers were Catholics, nor that he had himself trained with the Jesuits in the 'concentration camp for Catholics' at Wisbech Castle in Norfolk.[25] For these Pindarics extol his Games as a template for exactly the kind of 'Westphalian' coexistence that would, during the seventeenth century, displace the passions of sectarian conflict into what Carl Schmitt contemptuously termed a *theatre* of war: a war in form, whereby 'war became analogous to a duel, a conflict of arms between *personae morales* who contended on the basis of the *jus publicum Europaeum*'. The Cotswold project was indeed typical of all those 'masonic lodges, conventicles, synagogues, and literary circles', Schmitt blamed for sabotaging Hobbes's leviathan state with a myth of power as 'a plant, a growing tree, or even a flower', which 'left nothing to remind people of a "huge man"', and whose pacifism he identified not only with 'the restless spirit of the Jew', but also 'the humanist-rational superiority' of Shakespeare's Prospero:[26]

The Grecians next (a nation of great fame)
To stout Alcydes make the Olympic game,
Which Games each lustrum they with great expense
Perform'd with state, and true Magnificence.
Mycenae, and Argos, and prow'd Sparta hight,
From thence each Spriteful Lord and Active Knight
Went up Olympus Mountain Top, to try
Who in their Games could win the Victory.
Wrestling, Running, Leaping, were games of Prize,
Coursing with Chariots, a prime exercise.
Contention there, with Poets and Musicians,
Great emulation amongst the Rhetoricians;
And crown'd with garland from the Olive Tree
He was, in those Games, that won the Victory;
And to those Games came Nations far and nigh . . .
But when those noble games the Grecians left, they fly,
To ease, to Lust, from Lust to Luxury.
Then stepp'd the Soldier in, with Conquering Blade,
And in a moment of Greece Conquest made.[27]

It is the Catholicism of Dover's Olympians that exposes his disingenuousness in disclaiming any intellectual source. For the very first Renaissance study of the Olympic Games had recently been produced in an analogous culture of Christian humanism, with an identical subtext of ecumenical *détente*. Modern sports specialists are thrown by the 'muscular Catholicism' of the *Agonisticon*, published in 1592 by another French aristocrat Pierre du Faur, or Petrus Faber, and describe its 360 pages of Latin as 'disorganized, repetitive, and unclear'.[28] But du Faur's attempt to align gymnastics with Carlo Borromeo's spiritual exercises, and his moralization of the ancient Olympics as the foundation for a European peace, become intelligible within the Erasmian and Platonizing networks of the French Academies in which he moved, where as Frances Yates recounted, the programme of rationed toleration that would be sealed in the Edict of Nantes was thrashed out by the moderate Catholic 'politique' party to which most Academicians belonged.[29] Born in 1550 in Toulouse, and President of its Parliament, du Faur was in fact a leading light of the world's oldest surviving literary society, the city's august *Académie des Jeux Floraux*. So, if the modern Olympics have any single taproot, it is in the Floral Games played since 1323 by the troubadours of the Languedoc, in which

---

24 John Stratford, 'To my kind Cosen and Noble Friend Mr Robert Dover on his Sports upon Cotswold'; William Denny, 'An Encomiastick to his worthy Friend Mr Robert Dover on his Famous Annual Assemblies at Cotswold'; Michael Drayton, 'To my Noble Friend Mr. Robert Dover on his brave annuall assemblies upon Cotswold', in Whitfield, *Robert Dover*, pp. 102, 118, 179.

25 Whitfield, *Robert Dover*, p. 6.

26 Carl Schmitt, *The Nomos of the Earth in the International Law of the Jus Publicum Europaeum*, trans. G. L. Ulmen (New York, 2006), pp. 141–2; *The Leviathan in the State Theory of Thomas Hobbes*, trans. George Schwab (Chicago, 2008), pp. 60–3.

27 John Stratford, 'To My Kind Cosen and Noble Friend, Mr. Robert Dover, on his sports upon Cotswold', in Whitfield, *Robert Dover*, p. 179.

28 'Muscular Catholicism': Spivey, *The Ancient Olympics*, p. 240; 'disorganised, repetitive': Hugh Lee, 'Politics, Society, and Greek Athletics: Views from the Twenty-First Century', *Journal of Sport History* (2003), 168.

29 Frances Yates, *The French Academies of the Sixteenth Century* (London, 1988), pp. 68–76. For the religious politics of the *Agonisticon*, see Maurizio Zerbini, *Alle Fonti Del Doping* (Rome, 2001), p. 44.

flowers are awarded to the champions of the variegated literary forms, du Faur himself winning the junior prize of a carnation in 1572. For as Chancellor of this so-called 'gay science', the pink champion wrote his treatise on the Olympics, he stated in its Dedication, in order to continue these floral wars by other means:

I started this my *Agonisticon* a year ago, when the law had fallen silent in a city that had given itself over to war, and I had retired to my small estate on the outskirts, where I could not sit idly by on the side-lines, however, without using my experience to aid my fellow citizens.[30]

'In all our games', rejoiced one of Du Faur's Academicians, 'the fighting spirit of the Greeks is revived. Since fame is our only ambition, we do not aspire to win a crown, but limit ourselves to flowers'.[31] Thus, centuries before Jacob Burckhardt attributed Greek civilization to the 'agonistic spirit' of athletics, these Renaissance Gamesmakers had evolved the Neo-platonic notion of competitive sport as a demonstration that, since 'Discords make harmony', religious pluralism could also produce a complementary coincidence of opposites. Henceforth, sport would consume man's 'conflicts, joys, and agonies', as Roland Barthes put it, 'without ever letting anything be destroyed'.[32] Dover had probably studied the *Agonisticon* at Wisbech; but it seems unlikely, in any case, that he and his English *Pléiade* were unfamiliar with this French Olympianism, as they confabulated on how 'These Cotswold to th'Olympicke Games compare', considering how Shakespeare caught its cult of agonistic strife so accurately in the 'little academe' of Navarre in *Love's Labour's Lost*, where fame is the spur to a war waged not against enemies but 'the huge army of the world's desires' (1.1.1–15) and sublimated in a comparable way into the *Discordia concors* of 'Very reverend sport' (4.2.1).[33] The Bard knew as well as Samuel Beckett the importance of 'a very good bowler' (5.1.100). And whether or not the Cotswold Olympians had read the French tome, their fellow West Midlander certainly associated 'the glory that was Greece' with the ethical turn the *Agonisticon* described, when the Grecian 'Soldier with Conquering Blade' returned from the wars to institute a new age of peace and toleration in the garlanded *agôn* of the playing field, as Theseus was said to have founded the Isthmian Games 'In glory of (his) kinsman Hercules' (*Dream*, 5.1.47):

> Go, Philostrate,
> Stir up the Athenian youth to merriments,
> Awake the pert and nimble spirit of mirth . . .
> Hippolyta, I wooed thee with my sword . . .
> But I will wed thee in another key –
> With pomp, with triumph, and with revelling.
> (*Dream*, 1.1.12–19)

In *A Midsummer Night's Dream* the Queen of Fairies complains to the King that 'never, since the middle summer's spring, / Met we on hill, in dale, forest or mead . . . But with thy brawls thou hast disturbed our sport' (2.1.81–2); yet in Athens the duke hangs up his sword in a gesture that annuls such sovereign spoil-sporting in the true spirit of the Grecian Games. Editors warn us that whenever Shakespeare uses the term 'sport' it is in the earlier sense of the freakish or gratuitous act, the animal instinct to play that Roger Caillois distinguished from *ludus*, the regulation of rule-bound games, and that Gloucester seems to associate with the sadism of the Roman circus, when he bewails that 'As flies to wanton boys are we to the gods / They kill us for their sport' (*Lear*, 4.1.37–8). So, when in 1588 Montaigne mused that if I play with my cat, 'how do I know she is not playing with me?' he was reflecting not whimsy but an urgent new anxiety in the humanist mind about the danger to the aesthetic realm of that amoral and

---

[30] Pierre du Faur (Petrus Faber), *Agonisticon* (Lyons, 1592), 'Dedication', p. 1.

[31] Quoted in Isabelle Luciani, 'Floral Games and Civic Humanism in the 16th-Century City', in Nathalie Dauvois, ed., *Humanism in Toulouse: 1480–1595* (Paris, 2006), pp. 301–35 at 319–20. See also John Charles Dawson, *The Floral Games of Toulouse in the Renaissance: Etienne Dolet (1532–1534)* (New York, 1921).

[32] Roland Barthes, *What Is Sport?*, trans. Richard Howard (New Haven, 2007), p. 61.

[33] William Bellas, 'To the Heroick and Generous-minded Gentleman Mr Robert Dover, on his yeerely assemblies upon Cotswold', in Whitfield, *Robert Dover*, p. 162.

arbitrary *playfulness* which Marlowe, by contrast, perversely relished, when he dreamed of classical life as one long orgy of 'heady riots, incests, rapes'.[34] Of course, Andreas Höfele reminds us how difficult even Shakespeare found it to separate 'fencing, dancing, and bearbaiting' (*Twelfth Night*, 1.3.79–80), or theatre itself, from aristocratic blood sports such as hunting, 'the sport of kings', in which the game of killing 'game' is a 'playing with life – a playing with forces that might otherwise make you their plaything'.[35] So the stakes, in every sense, could not be higher as these plays turn persistently to a Greece where modernity seems to be in process of being defined as a paradigm-shift from the tragic necessity of such archaic sacrifice, through the proclamation of something approaching the mutual give-and-take of the 'Olympic Game', an Olympianism that, like Dover, Shakespeare can even imagine relocated as 'sport for ladies' (*As You Like It*, 1.2.114) on his own terrain:

> *Rosalind.* (*to* ORLANDO) Now Hercules be thy speed, young man!
> *Celia.* I would I were invisible, to catch the strong fellow by the leg.
>   [CHARLES *and* ORLANDO] *wrestle*
> *Rosalind.* O excellent young man!
> *Celia.* If I had a thunderbolt in mine eye, I could tell who should down.
>   [ORLANDO *throws* CHARLES.] *Shout*
> *Duke Frederick.* No more, no more.
>
>   (175–81)

FOOL'S PLAY

Clifford Leech long ago noticed how Greek settings 'gave Shakespeare special liberty', and that 'he felt curiously free' when he sailed to 'these golden shores' (*Merry Wives*, 1.3.70), as if he liked to believe that because 'we came into this world like brother and brother' we could still go 'hand in hand' (*Errors*, 5.1.426–7), and again 'think ourselves for ever perfect' (*Timon*, 1.2.83), as Timon imagines, for all the flaws of that 'imperfect man', the Athenian 'who dreamt of human brotherhood'.[36] So when the Trojan champion Hector fights Greek

Ajax in Shakespeare's version of the Troy story, and the entire war is displaced onto a match to test which of them is most like Pythagoras's son-in-law, the 'Bull-bearing Milo' (2.3.233) of Croton, a six-time Olympic wrestling champion, and five-time winner of the grand slam of all four panhellenic Games, it is what Achilles derisively calls 'A maiden battle' (4.6.89) without blood.[37] The 'order of the field' is that referees must decide if 'the knights / Shall to the edge of all extremity / Pursue each other, or be divided' (69–71): 'either to the uttermost / Or else a breath' (93–4). But as King Agamemnon smiles, 'The combatants being kin / Half stints their strife before their strokes begin' (94–5); and the flexing musclemen are no sooner in action than the umpires stop the fight, to finish it 'As Hector pleases' (4.7.3). This interruption is so abrupt that the Oxford editor, Gary Taylor, splits the scene in two to allow the bruisers to continue '*fighting*', as they do in Chapman's 1598 *Iliad*, until 'out gusht the blood'.[38] But that seems a misreading. For what is truly at stake here is the question on which both *Troilus and Cressida* and the Olympic movement turn, and that Homer gave to a war-weary Achilles at the end of his poem, of whether

---

34 Roger Caillois, *Man, Play and Games*, trans. Meyer Barash (Urbana, 2001), pp. 30–6; Michel de Montaigne, 'Apology for Raymond Sebond', in *The Complete Essays*, trans. M. A. Screech (Harmondsworth, 1991), p. 505; Christopher Marlowe, 'Hero and Leander', I: 144, in *The Collected Poems of Christopher Marlowe*, ed. Patrick Cheney and Brian Striar (Oxford, 2006), p. 200. See Robert Logan, 'Edward II, Richard II, the Will to Play, and an Aesthetic of Ambiguity', in *Shakespeare's Marlowe: The Influence of Christopher Marlowe on Shakespeare's Artistry* (Aldershot, 2007), pp. 83–116.

35 Andreas Höfele, *Stage, Stake, and Scaffold: Humans and Animals in Shakespeare's Theatre* (Oxford, 2011); Connor, *Philosophy of Sport*, p. 32.

36 Clifford Leech, 'Shakespeare's Greeks', in B. W. Jackson, ed., *Stratford Papers on Shakespeare* (Toronto, 1963), pp. 1–20 at 18–19.

37 Harold Arthur Harris, *Greek Athletes and Athletics* (London, 1952), pp. 110–13.

38 *The Norton Shakespeare*, ed. Stephen Greenblatt, Walter Cohen, Jean Howard and Katharine Maus (New York, 1997), pp. 1833–4, 1893; George Chapman, *The Iliad*, ed. Allardyce Nicoll (Princeton, 1998), 7: 232, p. 160.

'strife' can ever be 'stinted' 'among the men and gods'?[39]

As Shakespeare's most sustained engagement with the Greeks and their Games, *Troilus and Cressida* stages Schmitt's observation in his book *Hamlet or Hecuba* that while 'children and frisky cats play with special intensity, delighting in the fact that they do not play according to fixed rules but in perfect freedom', there is in 'the rules of the game . . . a fundamental negation of the critical situation': the 'unplayability' (*Unverspielbarkeit*) of the tragic 'ends where such play begins'.[40] So no wonder Aeneas nudges the two joshing jocks that 'There is expectation here from both sides / What further you will do' (30–1); nor that Hector explains to his opponent that the reason why 'I will no more' is that 'The obligation of our blood forbids / A gory emulation 'twixt us twain . . . the just gods gainsay / That any drop thou borrowed'st from thy mother, / My sacred aunt, should by my mortal sword be drained' (6–19). Achilles had joked about the sweaty amorousness of this match, confessing his 'woman's longing . . . To see great Hector in his weeds of peace' (3.3.230–2); and it is because Ajax is 'A cousin-german to great Priam's seed' (4.7.5) that 'The issue is embracement' (32) all round, so this war can be a *civil* one in every sense. But it is old Nestor, famed for the garrulousness of his own 'stretched-out life' (1.3.60), who recalls that this is how Hector has always operated, since 'the order of their fight' (4.6.92) permits these 'huge men' to 'stint' their 'strife' by treating their encounters as bloodless and unheroic extensions of the Olympic Games:

I have, thou gallant Trojan, seen thee oft,
Labouring for destiny, make cruel way
Through ranks of Greekish youth, and I have seen thee
As hot as Perseus spur thy Phrygian steed,
And seen their scorning forfeits and subduements,
When thou hast hung th'advancèd sword i'th'air,
Not letting it decline on the declined,
That I have said to some my standers-by,
'Lo, Jupiter is yonder, dealing life.'
And I have seen thee pause and take thy breath,
When that a ring of Greeks have hemmed thee in,
Like an Olympian, wrestling.   (4.7.67–78)

Nestor's anachronistic memory of Hector halting amid Greeks with 'high blood chafed' (*Pro.*2), to take breath like the great Olympic wrestler Milo, is prefigured in *3 Henry VI*, when Clarence promises his troops 'such rewards / As victors wear at the Olympian games' (2.3.52). Semenza considers that warfare is 'stinted' into chivalric 'sport royal' in all Shakespeare's Histories.[41] What we glimpse in this locker-room posturizing is something newer, however, that implicitly anticipates the disarmament Schmitt dreaded in all such schemes for a Christian Union or United Nations. For in Shakespeare's Olympics sport is already what George Orwell called it: a mock 'war without the bullets'.[42] So, whether or not the Bard ever frequented them personally, what Dover's classicized Cotswold Games provide is a discursive context for the humanist ideal to which *Troilus and Cressida* keeps returning: of Hector's Olympian pause as a literal *breathing space*, a life-dealing amnesty or moratorium from the deadliness of armed struggle, when 'during all question of the gentle truce' (4.1.12) sectarian 'strife' is sublimated into the godlike mutuality of live-and-let-live, an evacuation of pathos of the kind that Johann Huizinga maintained always underpins the rules of the game. Anthropologists now consider Huizinga's notion of *Homo Ludens* to be founded on an untenable distinction between play and reality, seriousness and sport, but in this drama that puts the grace of the 'Olympian' ideal under such pressure it is what inspires Shakespeare's Greeks and Trojans to dream of the zone of 'free play' as their soothing substitute for the murderous 'unplayability' of a tragic war:

. . . standing quite consciously outside 'ordinary' life as being 'not serious', but at the same time absorbing the player intensely and utterly. It is an activity connected with no material interest, and no profit can be gained by

---

[39] Homer, *Iliad*, 18: 107.

[40] Carl Schmitt, *Hamlet or Hecuba: The Intrusion of the Time of the Play*, trans. David Pan and Jennifer Rust (New York, 2009), p. 40.

[41] Semenza, *Sport, Politics and Literature*, p. 83.

[42] George Orwell, *Collected Essays. Journalism and Letters*, ed. Sonia Orwell (Harmondsworth, 1970), pp. 61–4.

it. It proceeds within its own boundary of time and space in an orderly manner and according to fixed rules.[43]

Since our knowledge of the Olympic truce comes largely from reports of its breach, classicists doubt the *ekecheiria* was as universal as modern Olympians think, and Schmitt even cited Pindar for the *Realpolitik* that the victor is he who cheats or violates the peace.[44] But the first lines of Shakespeare's drama suspend the action inside the 'fair play' of just such a demobilization, when Troilus commands: 'Call here my varlet. I'll unarm again. / Why should I war without the walls of Troy / That find such cruel battle here within' (1.1.1–3). Editors of *Troilus and Cressida* are stumped by the inconsistency of this 'dull and long-continued truce' (1.3.259) with its constant 'news from the field' and the 'war without the walls' (1.1.2;104). The preening parade of 'the flowers of Troy' as they are 'coming from the field' (1.2.164–71) is at odds with reports that in the stalemate they are 'resty grown' (1.3.260). Yet Dover's Olympians show how early modern readers could appreciate ancient civilization as a permanent *ludus* of such 'bloodless emulation'. What seems to trouble the dramatist, however, as it did Montaigne, is the tension between the level playing field of this rule-bound agonistic contest and the daylight robbery of chance, as his 'armed' Prologue (*Pro*.23) ominously sets the scene for 'sport abroad' (1.1.111) by relating how 'expectation, tickling skittish spirits / On one and other side, Trojan and Greek, / Sets all on hazard', in the capriciousness of a throw of dice: 'Like or find fault; do as your pleasures are; / Now good or bad, 'tis but the chance of war' (*Pro*.20–31). So there is wishful-thinking when Aeneas says the reason for 'the gentle truce' (4.1.12) is that this 'sportful combat', in which so much 'opinion dwells' (1.3.329–30), is precisely *not* to be a life-or-death struggle, but rather a friendly fixture the home team is just itching to play: 'Hark what good sport is out of town today... But to the sport abroad' (1.1.109–11).

Play is a neglected topic in current Shakespeare studies. Yet what must have intrigued the dramatist in his source is how Chaucer's *Troilus and Criseyde* performs its own game theory by constantly alluding to sporting events, like the 'queynte pley' in 'tyme / Of Aperil', when despite the siege Trojans insist 'Palladiones feste for to holde'.[45] For throughout Shakespeare's drama its characters struggle to hold a similar line between cruel chance and competitive sport, *alea* and *agôn*, as we are told how 'Hector in his blaze of wrath subscribes / To tender objects' (4.6.108–9); or that Diomedes will 'let Aeneas live, / If to [his] sword his fate be not [his] glory' (4.1.26–7).[46] As on Dover's Olympic Hill, the 'Contention' of 'the Soldier with Conquering blade' is appeased so long as the lethal passion of 'gory emulation' is subsumed into the innocuous agonistics of a 'pale and bloodless' sport. Thus, according to Troilus, even 'The seas and winds, old wranglers, took a truce' to assist Paris to 'do some vengeance on the Greeks', supposing the rape of Helen to be yet another playful charade, when 'for an old aunt whom the Greeks held captive / He brought a Grecian queen' (2.2.72–8). But if this war is one long siesta, the impatient stripling jeers, 'Let's shut our gates and sleep' (46). Instead, he prides himself he 'cannot sing, / Nor heel the high lavolt... Nor play at subtle games' (4.5.86–8). For as he portentously lectures his brother Hector, merely to 'play the hunter' (4.1.19) in this trivializing way, with sword suspended in a perpetual amnesty, 'Not letting it decline on the declined', may be sportsmanlike, but such a passionless 'vein of chivalry' (5.3.31) can never distinguish friend

---

[43] Johann Huizinga, *Homo Ludens: A Study of the Play Element in Culture*, trans. anon. (New York, 1950), p. 13. For Schmitt's equally problematic distinction between 'normal life' and the state of exception, see David Pan, 'Carl Schmitt on Culture and Violence in the Political Decision', *Telos*, 142 (Spring 2008), 49–72, especially 56–7.

[44] Spivey, *Philosophy of Sport*, p. 3; Schmitt, *The Nomos of the Earth*, pp. 69–77; discussed in Giorgio Agamben, *Homo Sacer: Sovereign Power and Bare Life*, trans. Daniel Heller-Roazen (Stanford, 1998), pp. 30–4. The citation is of Pindar, Fragment 169 (Heidegger's favourite), which refers to Hercules as law-founder despite his theft of Geryon's cattle.

[45] Geoffrey Chaucer, *Troilus and Criseyde*, ed. Barry Windeatt (London, 2003), 1:48–168.

[46] For the distinction between games of chance and competition, see especially Caillois, *Man, Play and Games*, pp. 14–19.

from foe, nor who is truly 'for Hector's match' (5.4.23):

Troilus. Brother, you have a vice of mercy in you,
    Which better fits a lion than a man . . .
    When many times the captive Grecian falls
    Even in the fan and wind of your fair sword,
    You bid them rise and live.
Hector. O, 'tis fair play.
Troilus.   Fool's play, by heaven, Hector . . .
    For th'love of all the gods,
    Let's leave the hermit Pity with our mother
    And when we have our armours buckled on,
    The venomed vengeance ride upon our swords,
    Spur them to ruthful work, rein them from ruth.
Hector. Fie, savage, fie!
Troilus. Hector, then 'tis wars.   (5.3.37–51)

FUNERAL GAMES

If the phenomenon of Renaissance pacifism that crystallized around 1600 in the Olympic revival 'is neither an anachronistic concept nor an ephemeral aberration', it is *Troilus and Cressida*, as Stephen Marx has noted, that marks the turning-point in Shakespeare's thinking, as he 'mounts an attack on classical war heroes and on the very arguments for going to war he had supported earlier'.[47] For here he pits the disarmament of the Olympic idea against the blood and guts of Chapman's *Iliad*, as he toys with the game when 'fair play' lets peace catch breath, and allows the mimicry of war to blunt the 'edge of steel', as though 'The time of universal peace' promised by Tudor and Stuart propagandists is truly 'near' (*Antony*, 4.6.4). The equilibrium of this 'good sport' is in itself nothing new, for, as Kiernan Ryan remarks, these plays are full of footloose warriors *killing time*: demobbed veterans 'spinning things out, keeping this breathing space open and holding time at bay'.[48] But what the universalism of the contemporary Olympic movement gave the author of *Hamlet*, it seems, was a cue to conceive an anti-tragic work in which *the entire history of the world* would be stalled 'in the fan and wind' of a tied 'time of pause' (4.5.34),

'this extant moment' (4.7.53) of deadlocked gamesmanship amid the anarchic destructiveness of 'pelting wars' (4.7.151), presided over by a 'honey-sweet queen' (3.1.131) of 'I spy' (3.1.86), the interminable and literally pointless nursery game of deliberately displaced mimetic desire, Helen herself:[49]

    Sweet Helen, I must woo you
To help unarm our Hector. His stubborn buckles,
With these your white enchanting fingers touched,
Shall more obey than to the edge of steel
Or force of Greekish sinews. You shall do more
Than all the island kings: disarm great Hector.
                              (3.1.139–44)

Shakespeare is always fascinated by the playhouse as a place to catch breath, and by performance as an inspirational 'breathing time' (*Hamlet*, 5.2.128), a means to 'eat the air, promise crammed' (3.2.85–6), in which players and playgoers are recharged by 'the animating and generative force of breath'.[50] But by inserting so many speechless 'periods in the midst of sentences' (*Dream*, 5.1.96), this 'master of ellipsis' seems also to be experimenting with something like 'the queer art of failure' that Judith Halberstam has identified on the faces of Olympic *losers*, the paradox insinuated in Danny Boyle's anti-triumph, that 'all our failures combined might just be enough to bring the winner down'.[51] If 'seeing the world as an aesthetic phenomenon' is one definition of camp, in Susan Sontag's famous formulation, in its undoing of male striving for paramountcy *Troilus and Cressida* might therefore even be considered the original

---

[47] Stephen Marx, 'Shakespeare's Pacifism', *Renaissance Quarterly*, 45:1 (1992), 49–95 at 55 and 59.

[48] Kiernan Ryan, *Shakespeare* (Basingstoke, 2004), pp. 123–4. See also Steven Marx, 'Shakespeare's Pacifism', *Renaissance Quarterly*, 45 (1992), 49–95, especially 71–5.

[49] Geoffrey Chaucer, *Troilus and Criseyde*, ed. Barry Windeatt (London, 2003), 1:148–68; 1:866–8; 4:1629; 5:304.

[50] See Carolyn Sale, 'Eating Air, Feeling Smells: *Hamlet*'s Theory of Performance', *Renaissance Drama*, 35 (2006), 145–68 at 163.

[51] 'Master of ellipsis': Harold Bloom, *The Anatomy of Influence* (New Haven, 2011), p. 49; Judith Halberstam, *The Queer Art of Failure* (Durham, 2011), pp. 120–1.

'campy' work of art.[52] What marks its 'stretched out' *détournement*, however, is that here these poetics of unsuccess succeed so well that, like one of those matches that absorb time into themselves by ineluctably generating a timed-out draw – 'After seven years siege' (*Troilus*, 1.3.11), 'Yet Troy walls stand', as though 'The wise and fool, the artist and unread, / The hard and soft seem all affined and kin' (1.3.11;23–4). And this neutralizing of distinctions between enemy and friend, 'when degree is shaked' (101) by the anodyne power of weakness, is personified by a *flâneur* who promises in his 'queer art' of substitution what Caillois terms a 'convulsion of simulation', and René Girard an epidemic of 'undifferentiation', when, as the Schmittian Ulysses winces, 'right and wrong, / Between whose endless jar justice resides... lose their names, and so should justice too' (116–18).[53]

A deconstructive figure of Derridean indeterminacy, like the assimilated Jew Schmitt despised, Pandarus is a kind-hearted fool 'who wants to make the bed for every couple', in Jan Kott's view; while, for Girard, in his voyeuristic desire for the universal mediation of indiscriminate 'Love, love, nothing but love' (3.1.105), he is a playwright, since 'all playwrights are panders... *Troilus and Cressida* is written and staged by Pandarus'.[54] His creator admits as much, giving him rights to address the playhouse as 'Pander's hall' (5.11.31), and to sell his niece to join 'the daughters of the game' (4.6.64). Thus, Cressida learns from her uncle what it means to 'play the tyrant' (3.2.108), becoming a model for what 'is, and is not' when 'a thing inseparate / Divides' (5.2.146–9) into the original and fake. 'Populuxe' is Paul Yachnin's Baudrillardian term for the pathological 'madness of discourse' (142) Pandarus thereby disseminates with his 'diseases' (5.11.31).[55] For what this poseur poses is the purposelessness of the aesthetic itself, the promiscuous reproduceability similarly personified by 'Achilles' male varlet' (5.1.15) Patroclus, who prostitutes theatre to pure 'sport and pleasure' (2.3.100) by caricaturing heroism in the queer histrionics of a 'pale and bloodless' simulacrum of 'mere oppugnancy' (1.3.111), making 'paradoxes' of 'Excitements to

the field or speech of truce', until 'at this sport / Sir Valour dies' (175–82). As Heather James comments in her study of Shakespeare's Troy, in presenting this scandalous playworld as symptomatic of 'the problem of "emulation" or rivalrous imitation', *Troilus and Cressida* thereby anticipates Walter Benjamin's worryingly Schmittian thesis in 'The Work of Art in the Age of Mechanical Reproduction', that the copy loses the *aura* of immediacy since 'the presence of the original is the prerequisite to the concept of authenticity':[56]

... like a strutting player whose conceit
Lies in his hamstring, and doth think it rich
To hear the wooden dialogue and sound
'Twixt his stretched footing and the scaffoldage.
(1.3.153–6)

The 'poor player / That struts and frets his hour upon the stage' haunts Shakespeare's Jacobean dramas as a figure for the false autonomy of the play as 'a tale / Told by an idiot, full of sound and fury, signifying nothing' (*Macbeth*, 5.5.23–7) in 'someone else's words'.[57] So what distances *Troilus and Cressida* from the plays it contains is that Shakespeare suddenly calls the ethical turn into question 'in terms of the morality of morality', by stressing that 'what is forgotten by the moralizing moralists', as Derrida conceded in his meditation on the Sacrifice of Isaac, is how such universalism unbolts the door to the 'universal wolf' (1.3.121) of sovereign violence.[58] 'It would be hard to imagine a quicker

---

[52] Susan Sontag, 'Notes on Camp', in *Against Interpretation: And Other Essays* (New York, 1966), p. 277.

[53] Caillois, *Man, Play and Games*, pp. 88–9; René Girard, *A Theater of Envy: William Shakespeare* (Oxford, 1991), pp. 157–8.

[54] Jan Kott, *Shakespeare Our Contemporary*, trans. Boleslaw Taborski (London, 1964); Girard, *A Theater of Envy*, p. 158.

[55] Paul Yachnin, '"The Perfection of Ten": Populuxe Art and Artisanal Value in *Troilus and Cressida*', *Shakespeare Quarterly*, 56 (2005), 306–27.

[56] Heather James, *Shakespeare's Troy: Drama, Politics and the Translation of Empire* (Cambridge, 1997), pp. 97–8.

[57] Thomas Betteridge, *Shakespearean Fantasy and Politics* (Hatfield, 2005), p. 142.

[58] Jacques Derrida, *The Gift of Death*, trans. David Wills (Chicago, 1995), pp. 68–9.

shift' than this old footballer's to the common sense that caring for *someone* is incompatible with caring for *everyone*, quips Jacques Rancière.[59] Likewise, the play seems abruptly to recall how, despite wearing his Olympic garland into battle, the golden athlete Milo was eventually eaten by a wolf.[60] For its neutralizing of friend and enemy in the endless substitutability of indifference to difference will finally be exposed as 'fool's play' when Hector encounters Achilles in a 'blaze of wrath', but 'scorning forfeits and subduements', hangs his sword in the air, just as he has his mortal foe at bay, to apply his usual 'trick of mercy' and allow the other to 'Pause if thou wilt' (5.6.14). All the text's 'Olympian' idealism is focused in this last 'staying of hands', that repeats as it predicts the 'interim' opened by Pyrrhus in *Hamlet* (5.2.73), when Achilles's son stood stalled 'as a painted tyrant', in an epitome of the aesthetic as pointed pointlessness, as his sword which was 'declining on the milky head / Of reverend Priam, seemed i'th'air to stick . . . And like a neutral to his will and matter / Did nothing' (*Hamlet*, 2.2.457–62); the ultimate Shakespearian play-within-the-play that is itself a word-picture of the suspense when the 'speechless' actor freezes during a performance at the Globe:[61]

> . . . as often we see against the storm
> A silence in the heavens, the rack stand still,
> The bold winds speechless, and the orb below
> As hush as death . . .   (*Hamlet*, 2.2.463–6)

As pretty as a picture, Shakespeare's image of Pyrrhus's blade hanging as if 'painted' evokes the countless depictions of Damoclean swords or emasculated warriors in actual Baroque paintings, where the mimicry of blood in paint inspires the redemptive idea of art as 'an antidote to violence' that would be most searchingly explored by Rembrandt in his own version of *The Sacrifice of Isaac*.[62] There the 'virtuoso of interruption' reveals the mediation when the angel stays the hand of Abraham to be a paradigm of the aesthetic as a transcendence of the imperative to sacrifice.[63] All the liberalism that caused Spinoza to be excommunicated by the rabbis is foretold in this hiatus. Likewise, in their episodes of indecision Shakespeare's killers

seem to represent the caesura of representation as 'a dream of passion' (2.2.529), a stalemate we might be relieved to think is indeed taking 'the time to which one is subject' and converting it into 'a time of which one is the subject', by 'signifying nothing'. The queer effect produced by beautifying these violent incarnations of sacrificial masculinity into such a 'painted' immobility is perhaps comparable to that of the photographs by Jewish artist Collier Schorr of young Nazi soldiers cradling flowers or fruit, which in Halberstam's view deconstruct the fascist equation of eros with terror.[64] Yet behind all these Shakespearian pauses hovers the hungry ghost of Marlowe, whose Aeneas recites Troy's holocaust story to Dido, and whose 'entire absorption in the game' carried him inexorably to the nihilistic irresponsibility of '*absolute* play', in Stephen Greenblatt's words, and an

---

[59] Jacques Rancière, 'Should Democracy Come? Ethics and Politics in Derrida', in Pheng Cheah and Suzanne Guerlac, eds., *Derrida and the Time of the Political* (Durham, 2009), pp. 274–90 at 286–7.

[60] Michael Poliakoff, *Combat Sports in the Ancient World* (New Haven, 1987), pp. 117–19, 182–3.

[61] The classic reading of the pause is Clifford Leech, 'The Hesitation of Pyrrhus', in *The Morality of Art: Essays Presented to G. Wilson Knight* (London, 1969), pp. 41–9. Christopher Pye views it as a 'model of autochthonic subjectivity' in *The Vanishing* (Durham, 2001), pp. 110–17; and for its Lacanian decoding as a mirror of Hamlet's hesitation, see Philip Armstrong, 'Watching *Hamlet* Watching: Lacan, Shakespeare and the Mirror / Stage', in *Alternative Shakespeares: 2*, ed. Terence Hawkes (London, 1996), pp. 223–6. But for antecedents, see Catherine Belsey, 'Senecan Vacillation and Elizabethan Deliberation: Influence or Confluence?' *Renaissance Drama*, 6 (1973), 65–88.

[62] 'An antidote to violence': Svetlana Alpers, *The Vexations of Art: Velázquez and Others* (New Haven, 2007), p. 129. See also Leo Bersani and Ulysses Dutoit, *Caravaggio's Secrets* (Cambridge, MA, 1998), pp. 98–9.

[63] 'Virtuoso of interruption': Simon Schama, *Rembrandt's Eyes* (London, 1999), p. 605. For the redemptive interpretation of Abraham's suspended knife and the face of the other in Rembrandt's 1635 painting, see Steven Shankman 'Justice, Injustice, and the Differentiation of the Monotheistic Worldview: Reflections on Genesis 17, 20, and 22', in *Differentiation and Integration of Worldviews: International Readings in Theory, History and Philosophy of Culture, No. 19* (St Petersburg, 2004), pp. 201–12.

[64] Halberstam, *The Queer Art of Failure*, pp. 162–71.

atrocious death in Deptford.[65] So in *Troilus and Cressida* the Marlovian Achilles will refuse to humour Hector's gentlemanly game, snarling 'I do disdain thy courtesy, proud Trojan' (5.6.15). As Caillois writes, the ethical turn ends and 'the corruption of the *agôn* begins at the point where no referee is recognised'.[66]

Instead of the Lévinasian ethic of 'fair play' Rembrandt could depict a generation later, in Shakespeare's Trojan War 'The bull has the game', as Thersites gleefully snipes: 'Now, bull! Now, dog!' (5.8.2–3). *Homo homini lupus*: by descending into the havoc of a bare Hobbesian life, in which man becomes 'an universal prey' (1.3.123), *Troilus and Cressida* trashes the Olympic ideal to reassert the terrifying affinity of the sovereign and the beast. Critics connect the resulting mayhem to the shock and awe of the Essex Revolt, and the intrusion of what Schmitt called its 'historical time' into the time of the play.[67] Whatever its context, *Troilus and Cressida* thereby simply confirms over the length of an entire play Montaigne's dark foreboding that 'players may be played; that as an object in the game, the player may be its stake'.[68] So when Hector ribs his nemesis that 'like a book of sport thou'lt read me o'er', Achilles's response is truly unsporting: 'Tell me, you heavens, in which part of his body / Shall I destroy him?' (4.7.126–7). For as the decisionist prince Troilus warns Cressida, if we mistake life for some Olympian 'book of sport' we will 'suddenly' discover that the irrational arbitrariness of 'chance . . . jostles roughly by / All time of pause' (4.5.32–4). A 'venomed vengeance' is the action on which this disillusioned romantic therefore decides, as 'Distinction with a loud and powerful fan . . . winnows the light away' (1.3.26–7); and the decider's words about the discriminating fall of his 'prompted sword' are almost exactly those of the avenging son of Achilles:

> Not the dreadful spout
> Which shipmen so the hurricano call,
> Constringed in mass by the almighty sun,
> Shall dizzy with more clamour Neptune's ear
> In his descent than shall my prompted sword
> Falling on Diomed.   (5.2.171–6)

'The end crowns all', Hector believed, hoping for a sporting chance to receive 'such a reward as victors wear at the Olympian games' from 'that old common arbitrator Time' (4.7.107–9), when the final 'trumpets sound' and 'stickler-like, the armies separate' (5.9.16–18). For even in sport, 'Everything is time', observes Connor, and 'All the time, the time is running out.'[69] In *Troilus and Cressida*, however, Father Time is an umpire who carries 'a wallet at his back' crammed with 'scraps' (3.3.140) of the scorecards he ignores. Thus, 'After so many hours, lives, speeches spent' (*Troilus*, 2.2.1), Hector has to decide whether to call time by returning Helen or to fight in earnest. He likens the warmongers to youths 'Aristotle thought / Unfit to hear moral philosophy' (2.2.165–6) for confusing war with a game. Aristotle *before* Homer!? This insane anachronism is Schmitt's 'terrible reality' intruding into the fiction, a shot at the Inns of Court, where the play was acted shortly after the students backed Essex's doomed rebellion, letting their 'hot passion' overrule a 'true decision' (168–72).[70] So, 'Hector's opinion / Is this in way of truth' (187–8). Yet merely for the puerile sensation of a shock 'to shriek amazement' (209), like that of the cat's claw Montaigne feared, the great champion of indecision succumbs to the irrationality of 'absolute play' by deciding 'to keep Helen still' (190), and so goes down to 'ugly night' (5.9.6) at the hands of Achilles and his storm-troopers. Such a catastrophe is 'but the chance of war'; yet the defile of Myrmidons, with 'balls of wildfire in their murderous paws, / Which made the funeral flame that burnt fair

---

[65] Stephen Greenblatt, *Renaissance Self-Fashioning: From More to Shakespeare* (Chicago, 1980), p. 220.

[66] Caillois, *Man, Play and Games*, p. 46.

[67] Schmitt, *Hamlet or Hecuba*, pp. 23–5, 44–5, *et passim*.

[68] Jacques Ehrmann, 'Homo Ludens Revisited', *Yale French Studies*, 41 (1968), 31–57 at 55.

[69] Connor, *Philosophy of Sport*, p. 77.

[70] Schmitt, *Hamlet or Hecuba*, p. 51. For the anachronistic allusion to Aristotle, see W. R. Elton, 'Aristotle's *Nicomachean Ethics* and Shakespeare's *Troilus and Cressida*', *Journal of the History of Ideas*, 58 (1997), 331–7; repr. in *Shakespeare's 'Troilus and Cressida' and the Inns of Court Revels* (Aldershot, 2000), pp. 183–9.

Troy', might have been scripted by Marlowe, or even Schmitt:[71]

Hector. I am unarmed. Forego this vantage, Greek.
Achilles. Strike, fellows, strike! This is the man I seek.
                    (*The Myrmidons kill Hector*)
So, Ilium, fall thou. Now, Troy, sink down.

                                        (5.9.9–11)

'Troy's lofty towers, which once ore-topped the clouds, / And menaced heaven, Helen's beauty shrouds / In cinders', but 'This turret swells as proud', proclaimed Dover's Olympians of his wooden castle.[72] It was Aeneas himself who had 'Revived those games . . . Amongst his wearied Trojans' that were 'now transferred over / Into our Cotswold by thee, worthy Dover', to endure for all time, the poets fantasized.[73] Of course, it was not to be. By 1643 ignorant armies were clashing 'Over the Cotswold Downs, where Dover's Games were', as the real fortress of nearby Campden House, 'which was so fair', burned to the ground.[74] 'Be not afeared', the Cotswold Olympians had poeticized. But even they could not hide their own fear of the Puritans. And in Shakespeare's Olympic drama too, what makes us truly afraid is the exception of the man who will not play the game, but instead turns sporting competition back to sacrifice. 'We know from the Hellenic context that it is common for sports to evolve from competitions to displays and back again (think of Olympic wrestling)',

comments Justin Smith, for 'it has long seemed that sports would be far more interesting if the losing team were truly punished'. The philosopher cites the Mayan ball game, in which the losers were slanghtered by being trussed and bounced from on high as balls themselves.[75] And such is the ferocity of *Troilus and Cressida* that Achilles proves the point, as 'in fellest manner' (5.7.6) he returns 'this short-grassed green' to something more 'sportive' or sovereign, with the potlatch of the oldest form of athletic display, the Homeric Funeral Game, when 'at the murderer's horse's tail / In beastly sort' the loser's body is dragged about 'the shameful field' (5.10.4–5), on the winner's lap of honour:

> Come, tie his body to my horse's tail;
> Along the field I will the Trojan trail.

                                        (5.8.21–2)

---

[71] Christopher Marlowe, *Dido Queen of Carthage*, 2.1.217–18, in *Complete Plays of Christopher Marlowe*, ed. Frank Romany and Robert Lindsey (London, 2003), p. 257.

[72] William Durham, 'To my Noble Friend Mr Robert Dover, on his Daucing Assembly upon Cotswold', in Whitfield, *Robert Dover*, p. 109.

[73] John Stratford, 'To my kind Cosen', in Whitfield, *Robert Dover*, pp. 179–80.

[74] Richard Symonds, *Diary of the Marches of the Royal Army* (London, 1859), p. 133.

[75] Justin Smith, 'Who Better to Punish Than the Innocent?' *Cabinet*, 46 (2012), 80–4 at 81.

'DOING SHAKESPEARE': HOW SHAKESPEARE BECAME A SCHOOL 'SUBJECT'

JANET BOTTOMS

Shakespeare, says Henry Crawford in *Mansfield Park*, 'is part of an Englishman's constitution'; 'one gets acquainted with him without knowing how'. Yet Crawford also denies having had a volume of Shakespeare in his hand since he was fifteen years old and is not sure that he has ever seen a performance. This early version of the claim for Shakespeare as the 'genius' of the nation is a pointer to one of the principal but often overlooked roots of the cult of Shakespeare – the schoolroom. Schoolmasters, governesses, teachers and, finally, examiners have been working with Shakespeare over a period of more than three hundred years. But the 'Shakespeare' seen from these perspectives has been shaped by ideas about his 'usefulness' in accordance with when, how and with whom he was to be so used. A thorough history of how teachers have worked with Shakespeare would have to take account of class, gender, the economics of publishing and political pressures, as well as changing views of the purpose of education, but to ignore the influence of the schoolroom on what Linda Colley has called 'the evolution of Shakespeare's reputation in these islands',[1] or indeed beyond them, is to be blind to one of the most powerful forces at work upon it.

SPEAK THE SPEECH

One result of the Renaissance in England was that plays – even plays in English – became recognized as a useful element in the education of a boy intended for church, law or secretarial employment. As William Malim, Headmaster of Eton

conceded, though 'the actor's art' might be a 'trifling one', yet 'for action in oratory and proper gestures and movement of the body there is nothing like it'.[2] There was also a vague belief that plays were, or could be, morally instructive, and a more specific argument that they offered a rich source of aphorisms and 'commonplaces' for use in public speaking. It was in this light that Shakespeare's own plays began to be seen almost immediately after the publication of Rowe's edition in 1709, with its convenient regularizing of act and scene divisions. The beginning of schoolroom Shakespeare may be marked by the appearance in the *Spectator* in 1711 of a letter outlining 'an ideal programme of study for a group of "British Youth"', including the suggestion that some of their leisure time might be usefully devoted to 'acting a Scene of *Terence*, *Sophocles*, or our own *Shakespear*'. From such exercises, it was said, 'the early Dawnings of their Imagination' might daily 'brighten into Sense, their Innocence improve into Virtue, and their unexperienc'd Good-nature be directed to a generous Love of their Country'.[3]

Though the reference to Imagination was rarely followed up in the next two centuries, both Virtue and Love of Country would figure largely in the choice of plays for use in schools. The earliest

---

[1] Linda Colley, *Shakespeare and the Limits of National Culture*, Hayes Robinson Lecture Series 2 (Egham, Surrey, 1999), p. 23.
[2] Wasey Sterry, *Annals of the King's College of Our Lady of Eton Beside Windsor* (London, 1898), p. 89.
[3] *The Spectator*, ed. D. F. Bond (Oxford, 1965), pp. 395–6.

known reference to an actual school performance is to a production of *Timon of Athens* by the master and boys of a Welsh charity school in Clerkenwell in 1711,[4] though the performance of *Julius Caesar* at St Paul's School in the following year was more typical of what was to follow. John Newbery included passages from this play in his *Art of rhetorick* (1746) – a work that, as Ian Michael says, provides us with 'a rare instance of a textbook passage being analysed' for indications of how Mark Antony's rhetoric worked in action;[5] and when Robert Dodsley published his *Preceptor . . . containing a general course of education* in 1748, his Shakespeare selections were also drawn largely from *Caesar* and the *Henry* plays, plus 'several Scenes from *Timon of Athens*, somewhat altered, and thrown into one'.[6] These set the pattern for much of the century, though we do hear of a production of *Romeo and Juliet* at Harrow in 1752.[7]

At first Shakespeare featured less often in the records of school performances than the more classically correct works of Dryden, Otway or Rowe, but the move from classicism to sentiment in the course of the century, which also brought a shift towards the tragedies, meant that when John Walker came to publish his *Elements of Elocution* (1781) he drew the majority of his examples from Shakespeare. 'Good poets', wrote Walker, 'are generally the best painters of the passions'; the greatest orators had always taken care to make themselves 'most conversant with the best poets';[8] and for Walker it was now incontrovertible that Shakespeare was the best poet, able to convey the widest range of emotions. Many schoolmasters seem to have agreed with this judgement. Emphasis on oratory did not mean, however, that the 'moral' of a play was regarded as unimportant, though this had to be carefully interpreted and the plays 'rendered more unexceptionable' by 'judicious emendation' or the addition of extra material. There was a natural preference for plays with few or no female roles, and they had certainly to include 'no scenes of love to tire the sickening ear'.[9] The *Merchant of Venice* performed at Reading School in 1802 was therefore 'altered' and lacked most of the final act. For the 1792 performance of *King Lear* at

Reading, which followed Nahum Tate in rewarding Cordelia, the Master wrote an Epilogue stressing the lessons to be learned from 'life's glass – the stage', where boys would be taught that 'sense of filial duty' which, combined with 'all the requisites of cultured mind', was so essential to guide them safely 'on youth's tempestuous tide'.[10] With such provisos school acting flourished in the second half of the eighteenth century, when some of the newer Academies as well as the great public schools such as Westminster and St Paul's drew large and fashionable crowds to their performances. Hackney Academy, commonly known as Newcome's, was 'especially famous for the dramatic performances of the boys'[11] and produced a play by Shakespeare every third year, though their repertoire was typically limited. *Macbeth* was chosen in 1739, and *King Lear* in 1783, but repeated performances of *Henry IV, Part 1* (1748, 1764, 1777) and *Julius Caesar* (1754, 1774) give an indication of the plays still considered most educationally useful.

'FOR THE IMPROVEMENT OF YOUTH'

Gradually the fashion for such large-scale productions waned as their 'inconveniences', and the amount of time taken from other studies, began to outweigh their usefulness. In public speaking, too, the 'polite' style of the gentleman was diverging from the language of the stage and critics such as

---

[4] K. M. Lobb, *The Drama in School and Church* (London, 1955), p. 53.

[5] Ian Michael, *The Teaching of English from the Sixteenth Century to 1870* (Cambridge, 1987), p. 164.

[6] Robert Dodsley, *The Preceptor: containing a general course of education . . . in twelve parts*, vol. 5 (London, 1748).

[7] T. H. V. Motter, *The School Drama in England* (London, 1929), pp. 183–4.

[8] John Walker, *Elements of Elocution*, vol. II (Menston, 1969), pp. 280–1.

[9] Richard Valpy, 'Prologue to King Lear', *Poems, Odes, Prologues, and Epilogues. Spoken on Public Occasions at Reading School* (London, 1804), pp. 125–6.

[10] Valpy, 'Epilogue to King Lear', p. 131.

[11] E. A. Jones, 'Newcome's Academy and Its Plays', *The Library*, 4th series, 3 (1934), 339.

Lord Shaftesbury condemned Shakespeare as suffering from a 'Deficiency in almost all the Graces and Ornaments of this kind of Writing', as well as wanting both 'Method and Coherence'.[12] At the same time, however, belief that 'English reading, speaking, and eloquence' were 'among the most important objects of education' was gaining ground among the middle classes,[13] where the popular voice was increasingly in favour of Shakespeare. A new focus on the idea of studying, as distinct from acting a text led to the publication of the earliest and most influential of the anthologies that would gradually give Shakespeare pre-eminence in the schoolroom at the same time as shaping the way he was read. The first of these, William Dodd's *Beauties of Shakespear Regularly Selected from each Play* (1752), was not originally intended for use in schools but appears by its title designed to challenge Gildon's 'Remarks on the Plays of Shakespear', which laid down the rules by which a reader should 'judge of the Mistakes of our Poet so far, as by his Authority not to be drawn into Imitation of his Errors, by mistaking them for Beauties'.[14] However, it quickly became both ubiquitous and widely imitated, and the third edition, in 1780, contained both an Index systematizing the chosen passages 'under Proper Heads' and General Observations on each play which begin to sound many of the notes to be found in later texts intended for the young. William Enfield's *The Speaker* and Vicesimus Knox's *Elegant Extracts* 'for the Improvement of Youth in Speaking, Reading, Thinking, Composing and in the Conduct of Life' were more obvious school texts. Knox specifically recommended that his 'poetical' selections be read as the classics were in the grammar schools – that is 'by explaining everything grammatically, historically, metrically, and critically; and then giving a portion to be learned by memory'.[15] It may well have been from Knox's anthology that Coleridge had those lessons which, as he said, 'required most time and trouble to *bring up*, so as to escape [the master's] censure';[16] and in fact Hazlitt was later to claim that Coleridge knew little more of Shakespeare than was to be found in *Elegant Extracts*.[17]

It was Enfield's *Speaker*, however, that proved most influential of all, being widely admired for the careful gradation and ordering of his extracts. As Mary Wollstonecraft wrote in an anonymous review:

Before the publication of Dr ENFIELD'S SPEAKER, a methodical order in the arrangement of the pieces selected was not attempted, or even thought of, though it is evidently the only way to render a book of this kind extensively useful; as whatever tends to impress habits of order on the expanding mind may be reckoned the most beneficial part of education.[18]

Shakespeare was particularly useful for Enfield's purpose because of the number of different modes to be found in his plays: Narrative and Didactic Pieces, Orations and Harangues, Dialogues, and Descriptive and Pathetic Pieces, especially the last. By the end of the century Shakespeare's place in the schoolrooms of the educated classes was assured. He had been made 'safe' for schools. His 'usefulness', however, was dependent on sentiments extracted from their dramatic context, causing Charles Lamb to complain that hearing Shakespeare '*spouted*' [italics original] by schoolboys out of '*Enfield Speakers*, and such kind of books' had made him 'utterly unable to appreciate that celebrated soliloquy in Hamlet . . . or to tell whether it

---

12 George Sewell, quoting Lord Shaftesbury in 'Preface', *The Works of Mr William Shakespear*, vol. VII (1725), p. xiv.

13 David Williams, *A Treatise on Education* (London, 1774), p. 145.

14 Charles Gildon, 'Remarks on the Plays of Shakespear', *The Works of Mr William Shakespear*, vol. VII, (London, 1710), p. 257.

15 William Enfield, *The speaker; or Miscellaneous pieces selected from the best English writers* (London, 1774). Vicesimus Knox, *Elegant Extracts: or Useful & Entertaining Pieces of Poetry* (London, 1781), p. viii.

16 S. T. Coleridge, *Biographia Literaria*, in J. Engell and W. J. Bate, eds., *Collected Works of Samuel Taylor Coleridge*, 2 vols. (Princeton, 1983), vol. I, p. 9.

17 From J. P. Collier's record of an evening at Lamb's, in R. A. Foakes, ed., *Coleridge on Shakespeare* (London, 1971), pp. 60–3.

18 Mary Wollstonecraft, *The Female Reader* (1789), in J. Todd and M. Butler, eds., *The Works of Mary Wollstonecraft*, 7 vols. (London, 1989), vol. IV, p. 55.

be good, bad, or indifferent, it has been so handled and pawed about by declamatory boys and men'.[19]

While the popularity of these anthologies continued, it was not long before a reaction set in as some teachers began to realize that for such study to be truly useful the chosen passages should relate in some way to the situation and expectations of the student. In particular, a growing belief in education for girls brought a new Shakespeare into being. Knox had recommended only 'Milton, Addison, and Pope' as the 'standing models in English' for girls,[20] and many people doubted the propriety of encouraging them to read Shakespeare at all, but a number of anthologies modelled on Dodd and Enfield, though with subtly gendered difference, now began to appear. *The Female Reader . . . for the Improvement of Young Women*, pseudonymously edited by Wollstonecraft for Johnson in 1789, paid tribute to Enfield's *Speaker* while at the same time suggesting that girls' needs were somewhat different. Wollstonecraft's extracts were generally longer than Enfield's and arranged in such a way as to give them some narrative coherence. They also privileged sensibility over rhetorical power, preferring, for example, 'pathetic pieces' focusing on Cordelia to Enfield's choice of Lear's 'Blow winds' speech.[21] Anna Barbauld's *The Female Speaker* (1811), another anthology modelled on Enfield's, also avoided his selections in favour of those chosen with 'a more scrupulous regard to delicacy' and relevance to 'the duties, the employments, and the dispositions of the softer sex'.[22] Each of her six extracts focused on a woman and the situations chosen predominantly depicted them as good, devoted daughters or wives.

Volumes of *Readings* and *Shakespeares* for girls now multiplied rapidly and soon the lack of context was overcome by combining them with the Lambs' *Tales* or other prose narrative versions, suitably redacted. 'The attention of young females, both in schools and families', wrote the editor of the 1822 *School Shakespeare*, was now being 'carefully directed to the study of our English Classics'; and the Preface to the 1828 *Juvenile Edition of Shakspeare* declared that 'a polite education' could no longer be considered complete without a knowledge of

'this excellent author'.[23] Dodd's or Enfield's collections, 'enfeebled' as they were by 'the total want of connexion', were no longer adequate, 'it being impossible duly to appreciate the excellencies of Shakspeare, without close and immediate reference to the characters and situations of his personages';[24] but this shift in focus was to lead to an almost exclusive emphasis on the female characters, along with the exclusion of comic scenes as being those 'least appreciable' by women and in which 'the greatest freedom of expression is to be found'.[25] 'For models of courtesy, gentleness, grace, and every combination of moral beauty', said the editor of *Select Plays* in 1836, 'witness Imogen, Desdemona, Ophelia, Perdita, Ariel, and a host of others. Ethereal Essences! Never has the human imagination bodied forth creations more pure, more lovely, and soul-subduing.'[26] Soon Shakespeare was well on the way to becoming the 'Girls' friend', as Mary Cowden Clarke called him, able to 'discern and sympathize with the innermost core of woman's heart',[27] while his plays, embodying 'a poet's view of their own sex', were designed to 'impress and captivate' them 'in early youth'[28] with the beautiful feeling and dignity of a Shakespeare heroine. Girls growing up with this feminized Shakespeare would in due course take him into the nursery and teach him to their children with the aid of the many

---

19 Charles Lamb, 'On the Tragedies of Shakespeare', in T. Hutchinson, ed., *The Works of Charles and Mary Lamb*, 2 vols. (London, 1924), vol. I, pp. 126–7.

20 Knox, *Liberal Education* (London, 1781), p. 234.

21 Wollstonecraft, *The Female Reader*, p. 55.

22 Anna Laetitia Barbauld, 'Preface', in *The Female Speaker* (London, 1811), p. v.

23 Caroline Maxwell, *The Juvenile Edition of Shakspeare* (London, 1828).

24 J. R. Pitman, 'Advertisement', in *The School Shakspeare*, (London, 1822).

25 Rosa Baughan, 'Preface', in *Shakespeare's Plays Abridged and Revised for the Use of Girls*, Bk.1 (London, 1863).

26 Edward Slater, *Select Plays From Shakspeare* (London, 1836), p. xi.

27 Mary Cowden Clarke, 'Shakespeare as the Girl's Friend', *The Girl's Own Paper*, VIII (1887), p. 562.

28 Anna Jameson, *Characteristics of Women, Moral, Poetical and Historical*, 2 vols. (London, 1832), vol. II, p. 98.

sanitized story book versions that flooded from the nineteenth-century presses.

THE EXAMINING METHOD

Those most interested in education at this period, however, had other concerns in mind than the appropriate reading matter for girls, and at the root of these lay class distinctions. While belief in the importance of educating the poor had grown, in some quarters, to such an extent that the government found it necessary to take an interest, others sensed a threat to the social order if the working classes were encouraged to become more literate than their social superiors. 'If the peasant's toe does not in this respect gall the courtier's kibe', wrote H. G. Robinson in an article titled 'Middle-Class Education', 'yet it assuredly presses somewhat unceremoniously on the farmer's and the shopkeeper's heel'.[29] As early as 1825 a writer to *The Times* was demanding that support given to elementary education should be matched by a strengthened system for 'effectively and multifariously teaching, examining, exercising and rewarding with honours in the liberal arts and sciences the youth of our middling rich people';[30] and the changes in the franchise which followed the 1832 Reform Bill further focused the minds of many on the importance of educating the voters.

One result of such concerns was the publication in the 1860s of three major Commissions of Inquiry into the state, respectively, of 'popular' education, the nine major public schools, and the so called 'middle-class' – a term that covered everything in between, from the minor professional classes to the 'respectable tradesman' or tenant farmer.[31] Obviously there was a wide difference between the kinds of education wanted by this disparate group, for though the professional class might still be desirous of a classical training, many of the 'mercantile classes' preferred modern and 'useful' subjects above 'any culture, however valuable otherwise', while the 'trades-class' wanted little more for their sons than a knowledge of arithmetic and the ability to write a good letter. The gentlemen of the third (Taunton) Commission therefore advocated three different grades of school, but refused to abandon their belief that even those in the lower classes ought to learn something of 'the value of a somewhat higher cultivation',[32] and if this was not to be classical it would have to be gained from English literature. There was precedent for the idea, since it was already a required part of the curriculum of government schools in British India, where the prescribed canon consisted mainly of Shakespeare, Bacon, Milton and Pope. There, as Gauri Viswanathan says, 'the administrative and political imperatives of British rule' charged the works of these authors 'with a radically altered significance, enabling the humanistic ideals of enlightenment to coexist with and indeed even support education for social and political control'.[33] Something of the same combination of aims may have been in the minds of the authors of the Taunton Report, though it was less easy to impose a curriculum on the more fluid and fragmented middle-class schools of the 'home country'. It would recur later in relation to elementary schools.

The 1860s were a turning point in the teaching of English literature and specifically of Shakespeare. On the one hand it was important to be able to answer the classicists' accusation that there was no 'work', no 'digging' in studying English;[34] on the other there was a need to persuade those who still saw little value in 'poetry' that its study could be of some practical or quantifiable benefit. It was at

---

[29] Hugh G. Robinson, 'Middle-Class Education in England', *The Museum: A Quarterly Magazine of Education, Literature and Science*, I (1861), p. 2.

[30] Letter to *The Times*, 1825, cited in F. J. C. Hearnshaw, *Centenary History of King's College, London* (London, 1929), p. 28.

[31] 'Report of the Royal Commission known as the Schools Inquiry Commision', in J. Stuart Maclure, ed., *Educational Documents: England and Wales 1816–1963* (London, 1965), pp. 89–97.

[32] Maclure, *Educational Documents*, pp. 93–5.

[33] Gauri Viswanathan, *Literary Study and British Rule in India* (London, 1990), p. 3.

[34] E. A. Abbott, quoting the objections of others in 'The Teaching of English' (1868) in Alan Bacon, ed., *The Nineteenth Century History of English Studies* (Aldershot, 1998), p. 175.

this point that the earlier focus on the plays as a tool for teaching oratory finally gave way to what would later be called 'desk bound' methods. 'We have passed the stage in which "elegant extracts" were used merely as a means of teaching to read or to declaim', wrote one schoolmaster in 1867.

The teacher of English does not now merely teach his pupils 'to read and write the English language with propriety' . . . but he uses the language and literature in combination as a valuable instrument of mental culture, and his professional status has risen proportionately with the elevation of his aims. The value and richness of our literature as such have always been admitted in theory; it has been reserved for the present generation to demonstrate the value of its study as a discipline.[35]

The reference to the teacher's status is significant. 'English studies' had to be dissociated from any suspicion that they were 'feminine' or lacked rigour, and Shakespeare's plays were particularly valuable from 'an educational point of view' precisely because they involved 'difficulties' which required 'research', and supplied 'materials for the exercise of a scholar's faculties'.[36] In fact, it was suggested, 'a mind formed on the study, the close and careful study, mark, of Shakespeare alone', might acquire 'such strength of thought and refinement of taste', as would entitle it to be compared with the results of any other process of training.[37]

This value was further enhanced by the institution of the 'examining method', as it was called, which began in the 1840s as a system of common examinations for graduates of the new training colleges for elementary school teachers, and was followed by proposals for government-sponsored examinations and certificates for those 'middle-class' boys not destined for either the army or the universities.[38] Finally, in 1858, the first Local Examinations authorized respectively by the Oxford Delegacy and the Cambridge Syndicate were launched, offering a choice of subjects, one of which soon came to be known as 'English Language and Literature'. At Senior level in that first year Oxford selected Bacon and *King Lear* while Cambridge offered Milton and *Julius Caesar*. Under the influence of the university Syndics,

the Shakespeare plays chosen for study naturally reverted to the classical and history plays or the less 'girly' tragedies such as *Macbeth*, and so the superior educational status of the middle classes, capable of ploughing a way through such verbal thickets, was assured as was the status of their teachers.

It did not take long for publishers to recognize a new market. In 1867 J. W. Hales prophesied that 'should English once take its place as a vulgar school-subject, innumerable text-books would quickly spring into existence'[39] and by 1890 one reviewer was commenting:

Editions of Shakespeare's plays come not single spies, but in battalions. Still we do not look upon them as sorrows. On the contrary, we heartily welcome them, because they prove that publishers (whose business it is to be well informed on the matter) believe that the study of Shakespeare is spreading rapidly in schools.[40]

Shakespeare texts produced especially for schools multiplied rapidly, adorned with 'Historical and Critical Introductions, Grammatical, Philological, and Miscellaneous Notes, &c.' (Nelson's School Series), or 'Copious Interpretation of the Text, Critical and Grammatical Notes, and numerous Extracts from the History on which the Play is founded' (Longman's), and often with the addition of examination questions and plans for preparation. While some concern for 'character', and what was called 'aesthetic criticism' crept in occasionally, as the influence of Coleridge made itself felt, emphasis on linguistics remained strong; and William Aldis Wright, editor of the officially approved Clarendon Press Shakespeare, firmly rejected 'aesthetic' questions on the grounds that 'sign post

---

35 'The Study of English Classics', *The Museum*, n.s. III (March 1867), p. 441.
36 'On the Teaching of the "English Language and Literature"', *The Museum*, n.s. IV (April 1867), p. 5.
37 'The Study of English Classics', p. 444.
38 John Roach, *Public Examinations in England 1850–1900* (Cambridge, 1971), pp. 56–8.
39 J. W. Hales 'The Teaching of English', in *Essays on a Liberal Education*, ed. F. W. Farrar (London, 1867), pp. 298, 301.
40 Anonymous Review, *The Journal of Education*, n.s. XII (January 1890), p. 30.

criticism' would interfere with 'the independent effort of the reader to understand the author' by feeding him with second-hand opinions.[41] The result was that pupils acquired, instead, second-hand ideas about etymology, sources and dating, and were given little encouragement to 'understand' Shakespeare in any other way.

By becoming an examinable 'subject', English literature had justified its practical and economic value, but once this had been established the demands of examiners began to constrict the way it was taught, with results they themselves found unsatisfactory. The annual reports to the Cambridge Syndicate, for example, refer repeatedly to candidates who had obviously learned the notes by heart but 'cited [them] without intelligence'; where 'the facts were known, their inferential value was utterly misunderstood' and 'the "aesthetic criticism" quoted had not been properly appreciated'.[42] The pupils were, naturally, no happier than the examiners. George Sampson was later to recall how 'the phantom of external examination brooded over' his adolescence. 'As examinations had to be passed, we spent our time in being examined so that we should be ready for examination.'[43] For girls it was even more discouraging. Though they had been officially permitted to sit the Cambridge examinations from 1865 the prescribed plays reflected the supposed interests of boys and were markedly lacking in female roles. Perhaps, too, the alienating effect of this system of teaching bore particularly heavily on them because of their longer tradition of reading Shakespeare in stories and linked extracts. 'I can't do my Shakespeare', complained one girl in 1886 – an early example of the word 'do' used in this context;[44] and another, just moved into the 'Senior Cambridge' form in 1895, demanded to know why one should 'learn Shakespeare' at all; what *was* there in him 'to make people rave about him'.[45]

From the many articles and letters that now began appearing in the educational journals it is clear that their teachers shared their frustration. 'Receipt for an Examination Paper on English Literature', wrote one in 1883: 'First catch your subject'. Shakespeare, being 'always in season', was best

as his text afforded more 'opportunity for the finding out of errors in English than that of cultured later-century writers'.

Keep your subject for some months (years would be better) in the most absolutely dry mental atmosphere you can find. Then choose about a dozen phrases, carefully strip them of context, and ask their meaning... Questions touching on any aesthetic criticism would entirely spoil the flavour, but a sprinkling of Anglo-Saxon or Meso-Gothic roots will add piquancy.[46]

For the first time claims began to be made for the value of imagination, and the importance of training it. In a lecture on education in 1883, F. G. Fleay urged that literature should be read 'as literature, not as exercises in grammatical and antiquarian pedantry, as it too often is in our schools'.[47] James Sully, Professor of Mind and Logic at University College London, complained that 'in these days of examinations even the beauties of our modern literature may be made too much a mere exercise of memory... and too little a cultivation of imaginative power'.[48] Many teachers turned to these new ideas with relief. The concept of teaching 'literature *as* literature', felt to be 'comparatively new' at the beginning of the '80s, was now repeatedly endorsed.[49] 'All we ought ever to ask our pupils to "do"', wrote one teacher, 'is to laugh and cry with Shakespeare, and in this they will not fail us,

---

41 W. Aldis Wright, Preface, *King Lear* (Oxford, 1875), p. xviii.
42 The Cambridge Local Examinations Syndicate, *Annual Report of the Syndicate* (Cambridge, 1892).
43 George Sampson, 'A Boy and His Books', *Seven Essays* (Cambridge, 1947), p. 50.
44 'Occasional Notes', *Journal of Education*, n.s. VIII (January 1886), p. 229.
45 Kathleen Knox, 'On the Study of Shakespeare for Girls', *Journal of Education*, n.s. XVII (1895), pp. 222–3.
46 'A Hint for Examiners', *The Journal of Education*, n.s. V (1883), p. 166.
47 F. G. Fleay, *Three Lectures on Education* (London, 1883), pp. 44, 11.
48 James Sully, 'On the Training of the Imagination', *Journal of Education*, n.s. VI (August 1884), p. 304.
49 Anonymous review of H. C. Bowen's *English Literature Teaching in Schools*, in *Journal of Education*, 274 (1892), 263.

if the plays are placed before them in any reasonable fashion.'[50] But what was a 'reasonable fashion'? If rhetoric, grammar, logic, philology and history were removed from the literature lesson 'as at present given' what would be left?[51] As the new century dawned, and after two decades of debate, a writer to *School World* admitted that 'it is because we do not know what it really means that we "teach" literature so badly'.[52] Nevertheless, there was no suggestion of abandoning Shakespeare. His place in middle-class education, bolstered by the examination system, seemed unassailable, and by the end of the century even some of the greater public schools had begun to find a place for him.

CULTURE FOR THE WORKING CLASS

Meanwhile, there was a growing body of opinion in favour of making education for the lower classes 'as liberal as prudence would permit',[53] and inspiring their teachers with 'a discriminating but earnest admiration for those gifts of great minds to English literature which are alike the property of the peasant and the peer'.[54] Some leading intellectuals such as Matthew Arnold were beginning to argue for the importance of promoting 'the spiritual and intellectual perfection' of the whole nation through 'culture'[55]— that civilizing and humanizing 'culture' needed to 'do away with classes' and 'make all men live in an atmosphere of sweetness and light'[56]— and the well-established position of Shakespeare as national poet and moral philosopher made his plays appear to many the most appropriate material on which to build 'community of feeling and interest among the different classes of society'.[57] Though the movement towards liberalizing the elementary school curriculum received a setback in the 'Revised Code' of 1862, which limited the curriculum to six clearly defined but narrow 'standards' in the three Rs,[58] it was not long before the Code was revised again to allow for 'extra subjects', one of which was called 'English Literature'. After 1880 every child was required to stay at school until Standard V, while new, higher grades were introduced, allowing

individual pupils to choose English as a 'Specific Subject', with the opportunity of reading a whole 'single play by Shakespeare'.[59] The introduction of Standard VII in 1883 made it possible to separate 'higher grade' schools from junior, and create a new educational category combining pupils in the advanced elementary classes with those from among the poorer of the so-called 'middle-classes'. We should not overestimate the effect of this since the higher classes were rarely large enough to justify the expenditure of much time or attention on them,[60] but the general direction was, nevertheless, towards a broadening of opportunity, especially after 1888 when a Royal Commission urged an improvement in the quality of teacher training and stressed the need for more 'women of superior social position and general culture' to take up elementary school teaching.[61] These, of course, would be women who had grown up with Shakespeare in their homes.

Shakespeare made his official entry into the elementary school curriculum at Standard V, the level at which pupils were required to read and

---

[50] 'Occasional Notes', p. 335.

[51] Kathleen Knox, 'Correspondence', *Journal of Education*, n.s. xvi (1894), p. 338.

[52] P. A. Barnett, 'English Literature A Great Discipline', *The School World*, 30 (1901), p. 201–3.

[53] John Arthur Roebuck, speaking in the Commons in 1833, quoted by H. C. Barnard, *History of English Education* (London, 1961), p. 69.

[54] James Kay-Shuttleworth, 'The Training School at Battersea', *Four Periods of Public Education* (Brighton, 1973), p. 339.

[55] Matthew Arnold, *A French Eton* (1864), in Peter Smith and Geoffrey Summerfield, eds., *Matthew Arnold and the Education of the New Order* (Cambridge, 1969), pp. 133, 151.

[56] Matthew Arnold, *Culture and Anarchy*, ed. J. Dover Wilson (Cambridge, 1932), pp. 69–70.

[57] Stephen Hawtrey, *A Narrative-Essay on a Liberal Education*, Appendix G, 'An Address to Parochial Schoolmasters' (London, 1859), pp. 99–100.

[58] Maclure, *Educational Documents*, p. 74.

[59] John Russell, ed., *The New Education Code for 1882–83 in England and Wales* (London, 1883), p. 53.

[60] David Vincent, *Literacy and Popular Culture: England 1750–1914* (Cambridge, 1989), pp. 90–1.

[61] From, 'Report of the Royal Commission on the Elementary Acts' [*The Cross Report*], in Maclure, *Educational Documents*, p. 129.

memorize a hundred lines of verse, though 'prudence' still operated in the choice of extracts. The Shakespeare encountered in the new *Standard* and *Grade Lesson Books* celebrated 'A Woodland Life' – 'Sweet are the uses of adversity', praised 'Mercy', and moralized on the 'Fall of Wolsey'.[62] The *Royal Readers* again taught the importance of mercy and that 'Submission to Heaven [is] Our Duty',[63] while *The Advanced Lesson Book*, 'for use in Advanced Classes in Schools and Institutes', offered 'The Praises of England' from *Richard II*, *Henry V* and the end of *King John*, along with more lessons on 'The Vicissitudes of Life' from Cardinal Wolsey, who had found 'the blessedness of being little' in his overthrow.[64] Stripped of their dramatic context, this small selection of passages for recitation could be attributed simply to the authority of the National Poet himself and soon became as well known to one social class as 'To be or not to be' was to another. It was not long, also, before publishers began to bring out new, simpler play texts for the higher grades, or abbreviated versions with titles such as The *'Ghost Scene' from 'Hamlet'*; *Arthur and Hubert*; and *Shakespeare's Queen Katharine and Wolsey*. These were unencumbered with notes but included 'a few short *sayings* of his critics and admirers' (italics original), to convince readers that Shakespeare was 'the greatest dramatist and poet that ever lived'.[65] The same years also saw new, selective versions of the Lambs' *Tales*, sometimes accompanied by short illustrative extracts from the plays themselves, intended to stress some 'essential truth of life' embodied in the story and show 'how Shakspeare solves the problems of life' and teaches us that that 'it is not material blessings, but human sympathy, that are necessary to human happiness'.[66]

Such notes were intended for the teachers rather than their pupils. Not many elementary teachers were qualified to help the children see beyond the mechanical task of memorization, and the circumstances in which they worked could not have offered much encouragement to do more. William Morris, recalling the depression he felt on the few occasions on which he had been inside a Board-school, questioned whether the 'mechanical drill that was too obviously being applied there to all

the varying capacities and moods' could possibly implant a taste for books in anyone's mind. 'My heart sank before Mr. M'Choakumchild and his method.'[67] Yet while some people saw only drudgery in the practice of 'learning lines by heart' Matthew Arnold defended it on the grounds that it did at least 'relieve the passive reception of knowledge', and that the child who was brought, 'as he easily can be brought, to *throw himself into* a piece of poetry [italics original]', had taken part in a 'creative activity quite different from the effort of learning a list of words to spell' and capable of 'affording a lively pleasure'.[68] One product of a London Board School recalled the chosen passage being 'copied on to a blackboard in weekly instalments' and repeated in chorus 'until everyone within earshot had had about enough of it'; yet his teacher also encouraged him to write an 'essay' on Shakespeare in which, 'trusting largely to hearsay', he 'lavished high praise upon the bard'. He appears to have enjoyed his Shakespeare until he gained a Junior County Scholarship to secondary school and encountered him 'in the lump', 'copiously mingled' with 'large dollops of boredom' about dates and sources.[69] There were also teachers who were genuinely motivated by a belief in the right of children of the lower classes to access 'the best' the country had to offer, and for these

---

62 E. T. Stevens and Charles Hole, eds., *The Grade Lesson Books in Six Standards* (London, 1863). J. S. Laurie, ed., *The 'Standard' Series of Elementary Reading Books* (London, 1863).

63 *The Royal Readers* (London, 1889), pp. 355–60.

64 E. T. Stevens and Charles Hole, eds., *The Advanced Lesson Book* (London, 1866), p. 97.

65 Preface, *Arthur and Hubert, From 'King John'*, Allman's English Classics for Elementary Schools, No. 28 (London, 1883).

66 Alfonzo Gardiner, 'Preface', *Tales from Shakspeare by Charles and Mary Lamb* (London, 1888), pp. 177, 22.

67 William Morris, 'Thoughts on Education under Capitalism', *Commonweal*, vol. 4, No. 129 (30 June 1888). Reproduced in *the informal education archives*, www.infed.org/archives/e-texts/william_morris_thoughts_on_education_under_capitalism.htm.

68 Arnold, 'Reports on Elementary Schools in 1880 and 1882', in P. Smith and G. Summerfield, eds., *Matthew Arnold and the Education of the New Order* (Cambridge, 1969), pp. 223–7.

69 Mark Grossek, *First Movement* (London, 1937), pp. 29, 84.

Shakespeare constituted the best. In the Preface to his *Shakspere Reading Book* (1881) Henry Courthope Bowen declared:

Those who have at heart the training and welfare of the pupils who attend our Middle Class Schools and Board Schools, and who, moreover, have some practical experience in the matter, are only too keenly aware how great a stumbling-block rough and inelegant speech is in the way of those whose advancement they are anxious to promote.

As much as their social superiors they were entitled to learn to speak with confidence from 'the very best models in prose and poetry which the language affords'.[70] Nor were they to be confined to 'Readers', or to learning and parroting the 'sayings' of critics, but to be encouraged genuinely to explore the play for themselves. Though the result, said Bowen, might be faulty and inferior to what a Coleridge, Lamb or Dowden would do, the activity would be both interesting and educationally valuable, especially in 'the constructiveness of the final stage'.[71]

Other influences were at work, particularly the introduction from the continent of the so-called 'New Education' – a term not easily defined but summed up in the words of R. H. Quick as treating the child less as a learner than as 'a doer and creator'. Others saw it as detaching education from 'the excessive bondage to books, and to learning from books' that had characterized the 'old education'.[72] There was a movement towards the return of acting in schools, seen by some as particularly valuable for 'the poorest class of children that go to a school of any kind', who should be allowed to 'learn through pure enjoyment that there is a power of healing in every lovely thing'.[73] Though many of these ideas might not appear compatible with the way Shakespeare was being taught, it was not long before the power of his name found a place for him, too, in the new movement. One enterprising schoolmaster of a small village school in Lincolnshire in the 1880s, after testing the waters with a few small concerts, finally dared to stage a production of the trial scene from *The Merchant of Venice*, one of the most popular plays with schools.

As his 'Shylock' was later to recall, 'I knew there were grave doubts about introducing Shakespeare in the village; ninety-nine out of a hundred people had never heard the name. Anyhow it came off and was perhaps the greatest success of any of the concerts.'[74] A few years later Harriet Finlay-Johnson, the headmistress of a school at Sompting in Sussex, was persuaded by the children themselves to move beyond little improvisations to the performance of the 'ready-made plays' they found in Shakespeare. 'It was not a case', wrote Finlay-Johnson, 'of the teacher telling the children to read so-and-so; but, on the contrary, it was the children who drew the teacher's attention to the fact that there were good plays which they could act in the volume of Shakespeare's plays which they kept on the library shelf.'[75] By such means Arnold's unifying 'culture' began to be disseminated through the school system.

A LIBERAL EDUCATION

By the end of the nineteenth century it was widely accepted that the education of the nation was a proper matter for government, and the 'imperfect condition' of its secondary education system required a thorough overhaul if it was to compete with its major continental rivals.[76] In the 1902 Education Act, the independent School Boards were therefore replaced by Local Education Authorities charged with maintaining and building new, secondary 'grammar' schools. Two years later, finding it necessary to clarify what was expected of the

---

[70] H. Courthope Bowen, *The Shakspere Reading Book* (London, 1881), pp. v–vi.

[71] H. Courthope Bowen, *English Literature Teaching in Schools* (London, 1891), pp. 30–1.

[72] R. H. Quick and H. T. Mark, cited in R. J. W. Selleck, *The New Education: 1870–1914* (London, 1968), pp. 102–3.

[73] H. Elrington, 'Acting in Schools and Its Affects', *Journal of Education*, n.s. xv (1893), p. 426.

[74] Fred Gresswell, *Bright Boots: An Autobiography* (London, 1956), p. 36.

[75] H. Finlay-Johnson, *The Dramatic Method of Teaching* (London, n.d.), pp. 103, 111–12.

[76] 'The Education Act, 1902', Maclure, *Educational Documents*, pp. 150, 153.

LEAs, the Board of Education published Regulations for Secondary Schools which, while avoiding 'any precise definition of the term Secondary Education', stated that such a school must offer 'each of its scholars, up to and beyond the age of 16, a general education, physical, mental and moral, given through a complete graded course of instruction'.[77] In 1917 a single, unified Secondary School Certificate was introduced 'to emphasize the principle that every secondary school should provide . . . a sound basis of liberal education'.[78] From this point the ways in which teachers worked with Shakespeare would be controlled, to a greater or lesser degree, by the demands, internal and external, of the timetable, central government and a centrally directed examination system.

It was by no means obvious to everyone that 'a general education' should include English Literature. There was still wide acceptance of the view, originally expressed by Herbert Spencer, that only when the forces of nature had been 'fully conquered to man's use' would the time be right for the pursuit of 'the fine arts, *belles-lettres*, and all those things which, as we say, constitute the efflorescence of civilization'.[79] The idea of 'technical instruction as a means for the formation of citizens capable of producing or distributing wealth' had also taken strong hold in both the old borough and new county councils,[80] and English teachers frequently found themselves having to defend the value of their subject against 'the peremptory demand for what is useful, for what pays'.[81] Literature, complained the Registrar of the Teachers' Guild in 1896, was 'the Cinderella of education', commonly being placed last in demand after science, mathematics, modern languages, classics and history, and treated as 'a subject which anybody is supposed capable of teaching'.[82] Against this, however, the Bryce Report of 1895, noting the 'dullness and barrenness', the lack of 'intellectual enjoyment' in the lives of many, had concluded that it was important for the 'moral strength' of the nation that its people be taught to draw their pleasure 'from the best sources',[83] and by this time 'the best sources' had become almost synonymous with 'Shakespeare'. The 1904 Regulations therefore specified 'English Literature' as one of the subjects to be taught for the full four years of a basic secondary school programme[84] and in an attached model, though not mandatory, scheme named Shakespeare as a subject for study in the third and fourth years. The corresponding new Elementary Code also directed that all children should be given some familiarity with the literature of their country, along with 'a taste for good reading' and 'a reverence for what is noble'.[85]

Even among the English teachers, however, not everyone was convinced that Shakespeare was a suitable subject for schools. Some questioned 'whether the benefit to the students from studying him is likely to be at all an approximate compensation for the time and labour expended',[86] while in many schools literature syllabuses were heavily weighted towards Scott, Kingsley or Tennyson, whose narratives of 'romance and adventure' were thought better suited to children and more likely to 'rivet their attention'.[87] When the English Association was established in 1906 one of it first acts, therefore, was to request from its members information on how Shakespeare was being taught. The responses show how every way in which

---

[77] 'Regulations for Secondary Schools', Maclure, *Educational Documents*, pp. 156–9.

[78] 'Report of the Consultative Committee of the Board of Education on Examinations in Secondary Schools (1911)', Maclure, *Educational Documents*, p. 166.

[79] Herbert Spencer, *Education, Intellectual, Moral and Physical*, ed. C. T. Smith (London, 1949), pp. 45, 47.

[80] 'Report of the Royal Commission on Secondary Education' (1895) (*The Bryce Report*) in Maclure, *Educational Documents*, p. 142.

[81] James Sully, 'On the training of the Imagination', *Journal of Education*, n.s. VI (August 1884), 304.

[82] Notes from a paper read by the Registrar of the Teachers' Guild, *Journal of Education*, n.s. XVIII (January 1896), 45.

[83] *The Bryce Report*, Maclure, *Educational Documents*, p. 148.

[84] 'Regulations for Secondary Schools, 1904', Maclure, *Educational Documents*, pp. 156–9.

[85] 'Elementary Code, 1904', Maclure, *Educational Documents*, p. 154.

[86] John D. Jones, 'Shakespeare in English Schools', *Jahrbuch der Deutschen Shakespeare Gesellschaft* (1906), 113–26 at 118.

[87] Francis G. Harmer, 'An English Literature Scheme', *The School World* (December 1905), 453–4.

Shakespeare had been used in the past centuries was still in operation somewhere. One teacher would read impressive passages aloud, 'very slowly', and then 'preach' on them; another laid 'great stress on the logical analysis of complex sentences';[88] while a third considered that 'first-class representation of the plays' was most valuable.[89] The belief in Shakespeare as a vehicle for morality continued to influence them strongly, though it was suggested that this aim should be concealed from the pupils, who were to 'imbibe the influence from literature as habit or experience'.[90] The headmaster of Leeds Middle Class School outlined an entire four-year curriculum beginning with the Lambs' *Tales* and Shakespeare's 'patriotic poetry', introducing 'Dramatic poetry', with the *Dream* and *The Tempest*, at thirteen, but putting off developing 'critical appreciation' until the third and fourth years, when pupils would be 'taught to realise the beauty of the lines', and to 'appreciate the general idea underlying the whole composition'.[91]

Efforts in the classroom were reinforced by the growth of acting companies with performances specifically intended for schools. This movement gained impetus during the years of the Great War with Ben Greet's matinees for schools at the Old Vic, and was consolidated in 1924 when the Board of Education declared that visits to the theatre in school hours were a legitimate aspect of education.[92] Inevitably, not everyone agreed. 'The effect on the children's written English is almost untraceable', commented one, while others were concerned about the moral influence of such full-blooded embodiments of the plays, which seemed to make them much less instructive and certainly less safe than the moralized or abbreviated classroom versions.[93] Most teachers, however, in the rather cryptic phrase used by Alice Woods summing up these reactions, felt that the effect of watching a play was to add 'culture to mere instruction'; and the Newbolt Committee, appointed to report on the teaching of English in England and Wales, defended the practice resoundingly on the grounds that 'the sooner a child becomes familiar with the best forms of theatrical amusement the

less likely is he to be permanently attracted by the worst'.[94]

THE PLAY WAY

Other influences were at work in the ferment of new educational theories and systems in the early decades of the century. In 1917 Henry Caldwell Cook published *The Play Way*, an account of his work at the Perse School in Cambridge, in which he claimed that the best way of teaching both language and literature to boys was to '*base all their English studies on their acting of the plays of Shakespeare*' (italics original). So inspired, they would themselves demand to know more, and by discovering for themselves the action implicit in the text would learn to understand motivation and to appreciate dramatic structure.[95] Nor was Cook the only teacher turning to the 'acting method' as the most productive approach to literature. 'The treatment of Shakespeare has vastly improved in recent years', wrote one in 1916. 'It has become more literary and more human; "the play's the thing" nowadays, and not grammar or philology.'[96] Sharwood Smith, headmaster of Newbury Grammar School, went so far as to argue that it was relatively unimportant whether the young actor consciously understood the words he was speaking;[97] and George Sampson, recalling a performance of *Richard II* in

---

[88] English Association, 'English Teaching in the Schools of Liverpool', *Bulletin*, 8 (1909), 13.

[89] English Association, *Bulletin*, 4 (1908), 6.

[90] Report of a speech by A. M. Williams, Principal of Glasgow Training College, *Bulletin*, 10 (1910).

[91] Harmer, 'English Literature Scheme', p. 453.

[92] Winifred Isaac, *Ben Greet and The Old Vic* (London, 1964), pp. 163–8.

[93] Alice Woods, *Educational Experiments in England* (London, 1920), pp. 211–12.

[94] Board of Education, *The Teaching of English in England* (London, 1921), p. 315.

[95] H. Caldwell Cook, *The Play Way: An Essay in Educational Method* (London, 1917), pp. 49, 219.

[96] *Journal of Education*, n.s. 38 (June 1916), 310.

[97] E. Sharwood Smith, 'English in Schools', *The Teaching of English in Schools*, ed. E. J. Morley, English Association Pamphlet, 43 (1919), pp. 29–30.

a London elementary school, remarked that 'boys or girls usually regarded as stupid, and incapable of learning' were discovered to have 'unsuspected ability in acting' and 'gained a new interest in themselves and their possibilities'.[98]

Enthusiasm for the 'acting method' took hold in influential circles. Shakespeare 'should be taught, as music is taught, by being performed', said an editorial in the *Times Educational Supplement* in 1916, since if pupils read him only from a sense of duty it would simply make 'prigs' of them.[99] Acting was the way to find that 'delight', that 'experience in creative reception' without which, Sampson declared, literature in schools must be a failure.[100] Some teachers might still complain that Shakespeare was 'not only difficult but archaic as well', making him 'doubly unsuitable for young readers',[101] but leading educational opinion was against them. 'Fortunately', declared Sampson, in words repeated verbatim in the Newbolt Report (1921), Shakespeare 'is saved for the schools by his wonderful power of re-telling a story in dramatic form, and his equally wonderful power of characterisation, and we may add his incomparable word-music'. 'We feel no call to dispute with those who tell us that Shakespeare is over the heads of children', concluded Newbolt. 'He is over the heads of us all. It is sufficient to say that in the schools Shakespeare proves an immense success.'[102]

The problem for teachers sharing these ideals was that, as even Cook himself admitted, the play way was 'not the easy way'. 'There is more hard work, even actual labour, attached to the Play Way schemes' – for both pupils and teachers – 'than there is in classroom "work".'[103] The effort involved was exacerbated for teachers struggling with small and ill-equipped classrooms, and with the financial constraints of the inter-war period as the Board of Education 'embarked on a policy designed to confine the activity of the L.E.A.s to "the provision of minimal statutory services"'.[104] Though many books of *Little Plays* or *Peeps Into Shakespeare* published between the wars reiterated that 'Shakespeare wrote for performance', and that 'every class-room is a little theatre',[105] in practice this seldom meant more than 'reading round'. In the elementary schools the main emphasis was still on the learning of 'familiar passages', with written exercises ranging from the factual – making a list of flowers, birds and animals mentioned – to noting Shakespeare's advice on such subjects as 'borrowing, quarrels, friends, obedience, good reputation, humility'.[106] In the secondary schools more emphasis was given to the systematic study of plot or character, but examples given in a handbook for teachers show how the teacher's view of 'the character' was likely to become an *a priori* definition for which illustration must be 'found' by the pupils. Debates might be permitted on 'suitable topics' such as 'Was Shylock fairly treated?' or 'Did Ophelia die by accident or commit suicide?' but 'mere word-spinning, mistiness of thought, imaginative kite-flying' were to be avoided.[107] The demands of rigid school timetables patrolled the boundaries of 'creative reception', and over everything lay the constraints of the examination system, criticized from all sides but apparently impossible to dispense with. Teachers' manuals began to focus again on the 'difficulty' of Shakespeare for the pupil and, by extension, the teacher. Though he might be worth studying because knowledge of his works was associated with 'success', the heart had gone out of any belief in his 'inward' or unifying value.

A CONTESTED FIELD

Of course, this is not the end of the story, but to continue it through the next fifty plus years is

98 George Sampson, *English for the English*, ed. D. Thompson, (Cambridge, 1970), pp. 114–15.
99 *Times Educational Supplement*, 4 April 1916, 47.
100 Sampson, *English for the English*, p. 106
101 Sampson, *English for the English*, p. 111.
102 Board of Education, *Teaching of English in England*, p. 86.
103 Cook, *The Play Way*, p. 181.
104 R. J. W. Selleck, *English Primary Education and the Progressives, 1914–1939* (London, 1972), pp. 130–2.
105 J. Dover Wilson, 'Preface', in *First Steps in Shakespeare* (Cambridge, 1931).
106 F. Thomson Smith, *A Little Book of Shakespeare* (London, 1925).
107 Margaret Steppat, *Shakespeare in the Classroom* (London, 1933), pp. 51, 36, 40–43.

outside the scope of this article. What must be obvious is that by this stage a great many different interests – political, commercial, pedagogic and media-led – are at work shaping the way Shakespeare is used in schools. It has been subject to changes in government, the educational system and the structure of a society evolving from a traditionally conservative and nationalistic one into one that is multicultural and multilingual. As Gunther Kress has said, 'Curriculum is inevitably a political matter. A curriculum projects an imagined subjectivity and, with that, an imagined social/cultural future, and it is therefore at once drawn into the field of contestation around other imagined social and cultural futures.'[108] Precisely because of the national and cultural status Shakespeare has been afforded, those working with him in a school context must often feel they are struggling on a darkling plain 'where ignorant armies clash by night'.[109] Despite it all, the plays live on, open to discovery in new ways that respond to their own needs by new young readers, performers and audiences.

---

[108] Gunther Kress, 'An English Curriculum for the Future', in *Writing the Future* (Sheffield, 1995), pp. 97–8.

[109] Matthew Arnold, 'Dover Beach', *Penguin Book of English Verse* (1956), pp. 344–5.

(MIS)ADVISING SHAKESPEARE'S PLAYERS

MICHAEL CORDNER

John Selden, the seventeenth-century lawyer scholar and linguist, delighted in exposing ill-founded traditions. A poet himself, and a friend of poets, he included in his intimate circle the dramatist Ben Jonson.[1] This did not, however, deter him from mocking Jonson's profession of playwriting. Selden argued that

'Tis a fine thing for Children to learne to make verse; but when they come to bee men they must speake like other folkes, or else they will bee laughed att. Tis ridiculous to speake or write or preach in verse.

He specifically applied this scepticism to writing for the stage:

There is noe reason playes should bee in verse, either in blank or Rhyme, Only the poett has to say for himself, That hee makes something like that wh^{ch} somebody made before him.

So, blind tradition has inertly sustained an indefensible convention. Anticipating that contemporary dramatists might cite ancient Greek theatre in their defence, Selden pre-empted that move:

The old poetts had noe other reason but this, Their verse was sung to Musick, otherwise it had been a senseless thing to have fetter'd upp themselves.[2]

In Jacobean theatre, on the other hand, where words usually stood alone, unsupported by music, decking them out in metre was absurd and perverse.

Selden knew he was being iconoclastic. In his lifetime, verse was the default mode for dramatic dialogue, while in the theatre prose was emphatically verse's junior partner. Our twenty-first century stages, however, are inundated by prose. Over the last century, few playwrights have sought to revitalize the traditions of verse drama, and those who have (from T. S. Eliot to Tony Harrison) have achieved only limited personal success and failed to attract disciples who might, in their turn, keep the torch alight. Consequently, contemporary actors can often feel ill-prepared, when asked to confront the challenges of verse dialogue, especially in scripts written four centuries ago. Their nervousness will often be increased by the infrequency with which this repertoire figures in most of their careers, and the small amount of time conservatoire programmes accord to training for it. They may accordingly wonder with Selden whether they are not confronting an inauthentic and arcane convention, which condemns its players to seeming not fully adult, and accordingly yearn to be allowed to 'speak like other Men'.

In an earlier, and different, version, this article formed the core of my inaugural lecture as Ken Dixon Professor of Theatre at the University of York. This revised and expanded version was read, in advance of publication, by Michael Billington, Clare Brennan, Tom Cantrell, Tom Cornford, Mark France, Barbara Hodgdon, Peter Holland, Genista McIntosh, Felicity Riddy and Richard Rowland. I am grateful to them for their comments and advice. Any errors which remain are my own.
[1] David Riggs, *Ben Jonson: A Life* (Cambridge, MA, 1989), pp. 16, 197–8, 204–7.
[2] John Selden, *Table Talk*, ed. Sir Frederick Pollock (London, 1927), pp. 95–6.

In recent decades numerous publications from directors, voice coaches and fellow actors have sought to allay such panic and offer practical advice on coping with this repertoire's special demands. A common reference point in much of this writing is the tradition of training actors in handling Shakespearian verse associated with the nascent Royal Shakespeare Company from its moment of origin, and still featured prominently in the company's representation of itself to its audiences today. Sir Peter Hall and John Barton are the two key figures who forged that tradition, and both have gone on record about the subject many times since. In addition to copious interview material, the prime texts are, for Hall, his Clark Lectures, *Exposed by the Mask: Form and Language in Drama* (2000) and his *Shakespeare's Advice to the Players* (2003), and, for Barton, the Channel 4 series, *Playing Shakespeare*, which he masterminded and fronted, and the book of the same title (1984), which was derived from it.[3] *Playing Shakespeare*, after numerous reprintings, was reissued in 2009 with an accompanying DVD, while *Shakespeare's Advice to the Players*, according to its publisher's proud publicity release, sold 10,000 copies in hardback before going into paperback. Contemporary conversations about how to equip actors to perform Shakespeare often treat the two men's contributions as a starting-point for future debate.

The closeness of their work together in the 1960s has frequently generated a presumption of near-identity of viewpoint between them. Indeed, in deciding which directors should receive chapter-length treatments in his *Routledge Companion to Directors' Shakespeare*, John Russell Brown, who was Hall's Literary Manager in the early years of the latter's tenure as Artistic Director of the National Theatre, rejected Barton's claims to inclusion on essentially those grounds. He admitted that Barton had satisfied all the criteria he had set, which included that a director's work should be 'innovative in its time' and that his productions should have influenced 'other directors or the expectations of later audiences'. In a vague formulation, however, he explained that the decisive factor for him had been that the two men had 'much in common',

adding (questionably) that Hall had enjoyed the 'longer and *more varied* career' (my emphasis) as a Shakespeare director. In effect, he absorbed Barton into Hall, even while conceding that there were 'clear differences' between them – 'differences' his collection would now neglect.[4]

In many ways the two directors are undeniably closely akin. They are of the same generation, only three years apart in age. Both are Cambridge-educated. While at Cambridge, both were associated with the Marlowe Society (the university drama society which specialized in early modern drama) and its *éminence grise*, the King's College fellow and Shakespeare guru George Rylands. For both Hall and Barton, directorial practice is inflected by scholarly interests. Barton is the more diffident of the two about professing these, but he held an academic post before being lured to the RSC by Hall and, when pressed, is willing to confess a fascination with Shakespearian bibliography.[5] His marriage to the Shakespearian scholar Anne Barton, and the intimacy with which her thinking informed some of his finest productions, also ensured a constant interplay between current scholarly investigations and his work in the rehearsal room.[6] Similarly, it is characteristic of Hall that, while under extreme pressure as Artistic Director of the National Theatre, he still

---

[3] Peter Hall, *Exposed by the Mask: Form and Language in Drama* (London, 2000); Peter Hall, *Shakespeare's Advice to the Players* (London, 2003); John Barton, *Playing Shakespeare* (London, 1984). Quotations from these three books are followed in the text by page references on the following pattern: '(*Exposed*, 44)'.

[4] John Russell Brown, 'Introduction', in John Russell Brown, ed., *The Routledge Companion to Directors' Theatre* (London, 2008), pp. x–xi. Hall's versatility as a director encompasses an impressive variety of different kinds of theatre, including work on new scripts, for which Barton's career offers no parallel. But, as Shakespeare directors, it is impossible to distinguish seriously between them either in terms of range of plays and genres explored or in the diversity of directorial styles experimented with.

[5] Michael L. Greenwald, *Directions by Indirections: John Barton of the Royal Shakespeare Company* (Newark, 1985), pp. 22–3.

[6] For a case-study of Anne Barton's influence on his 1980 *Hamlet*, for instance, see Greenwald, *Directions*, pp. 186–97.

found time to relish a *Theatre Quarterly* article on the Stanislavsky/Gordon Craig Moscow Arts Theatre *Hamlet* and interpret it as an 'object lesson in two different aesthetics both getting in the way of the play'.[7] Equally, he sometimes describes his own explorations with actors as, in effect, their own mode of research discovery. Rehearsing Marlowe's *Tamburlaine*, for example, made him convinced that 'no scholar has properly understood' the play's 'intricate mosaic of extreme emotions', with 'no bridge' between them, 'no Stanislavsky comfort' (*Diaries*, 240).

Similarly, in a professional world where many Shakespeare directors pay scant attention to his verse, Hall and Barton, in common with Rylands, have always placed the dramatic potentiality of Shakespeare's language at the heart of their directorial credos; and, while both have, on occasion, expressed a disinclination to be teachers, their shared desire to introduce professional actors to new approaches to performing Shakespeare have frequently led them to assume that role and to display considerable aptitude for it.

Accordingly, the text training they introduced for RSC actors has often been read as a transference of their Cambridge English Faculty training in close reading (and some of the pedagogical apparatus that went with it) to the world of professional theatre. For Janet Suzman, one of the company's leading actresses in the 1960s, what resulted was 'a universitarial sort of exercise, rather than a Guthriesque, theatrical one',[8] while Terry Hands, the RSC's third Artistic Director, who joined it in the mid-1960s, identified as the key policy initiative underpinning the company's foundation 'the application of university-trained men (and latterly women) to the study of Shakespeare – to living research, living academia, living literature'.[9] So, in Hands's view, academe had benignly invaded the theatre and instituted research-by-practice.

There was some initial resistance to this takeover. In his autobiography, Hall claims that, in 1960, 'it was a jibe that going to the RSC was like going back to university', but that, by 1965, 'the jibe had become affectionate'.[10] Along the way he had fielded, for example, a letter from his 1964

Falstaff, Hugh Griffith, railing at being forced to act for '*a mass of some, perhaps, nonentities; perhaps* scholars *and professors etc*', and Barton had faced a revolt by his first RSC cast, fuelled by, in Hall's account, the actors' distrust of 'the analytical and historical approach of academics' and Barton's difficulties in adjusting his methods from 'admonishing a student' to 'directing Peggy Ashcroft'.[11]

As early as 1962, however, Kenneth Tynan's review of Clifford Williams's *Comedy of Errors* hailed the arrival of a distinctive company style, the principal attributes of which included 'cogent, deliberate verse-speaking that discards melodic cadenzas in favour of meaning and motivation'.[12] Much praise to similar effect flowed from critics' pens across the next few years. Whatever birth pangs they might have endured, the new policies were judged to be producing palpable results. The credence accorded to the two directors' views about performing Shakespeare flows largely from the reputation for successful translation of theories into practice earned by them during these pioneer stages in the youthful RSC's history.

---

7 John Goodwin, ed., *Peter Hall's Diaries: The Story of a Dramatic Battle* (London, 1983), p. 258. Subsequent quotations from this book are followed in the text by page references on the following pattern: '(*Diaries*, 258)'.

8 Carole Zucker, *In the Company of Actors: Reflections on the Art of Acting* (London, 1999), p. 200.

9 'Terry Hands, Interviewed by Christopher J. McCullough', in Graham Holderness, ed., *The Shakespeare Myth* (Manchester, 1988), p. 125.

10 Peter Hall, *Making an Exhibition of Myself* (London, 1993), p. 158. Subsequent quotations from this book are followed in the text by page references on the following pattern: '(*Making*, 158)'.

11 Stephen Fay, *Power Play: The Life & Times of Peter Hall* (London, 1995, pp. 116, 168. Subsequent quotations from this book are followed in the text by page references on the following pattern: '(*Power*, 116)'.

12 Kenneth Tynan, 'Classical Style', *Observer Weekend Review* (16 September 1962), 20. Ironically, Hall initially failed to realize what had been achieved and reacted hostilely when he saw a run-through of the production. Hall's attitude towards the highly talented Williams, 'who was not part of the Cambridge circle', was always uncertain and uneasy (Colin Chambers, *Inside the Royal Shakespeare Company: Creativity and the Institution* (London, 2004), p. 20).

The purposeful accord between Hall and Barton during that period should not, however, mask from us the numerous ways in which their attitudes and approaches diverge.[13] One place to start is their contrasting attitudes to their Cambridge affiliations. Hall spent his childhood in or near Cambridge, but only the normal three years as an undergraduate at the university, whereas Barton progressed from his BA to embark on a research career and hold a King's College fellowship, before being lured to the RSC by Hall. Similarly, Hall's directorial career while at Cambridge concentrated on the modern repertoire. His links with the Marlowe, which specialized in performing plays from *c.*1600, were confined to playing middle-ranking parts in a few productions. Barton, in contrast, directed trend-setting productions for the Marlowe and was Rylands's anointed successor as its presiding spirit. He was also closely involved as an actor in the ambitious project, which Rylands masterminded, to record the complete Shakespeare canon with a mixture of Marlowe Society actors and professionals. Hall, on the other hand, played no part in this. Yet it is Hall, not Barton, who constantly invokes Cambridge inheritances when legislating about how Shakespeare should be performed.

Hall's persistent reverence for his *alma mater* is striking. In an extraordinary diary entry, he records how, when waiting to go onstage to receive a University of Liverpool honorary degree, he was seized with a conviction that the 'whole thing' was 'an unpardonable vanity'. Showing scant gratitude to his hosts, he reports that he 'would like a doctor's degree from Cambridge and that is about it' (*Diaries*, 108). (He finally achieved this distinction in 2003.) Visiting his daughter in 1978 while she was a student at Cambridge, he experiences a painful fit of nostalgia and confesses to his diary that 'I would like to return here', but then sadly notes that this can never happen:

I haven't a good enough degree. That's where my reassurances to Christopher [his elder son] break down. 'Never mind,' I say to him, 'Just do well enough to stay here the full time.' But I didn't do well enough to come back. I was too busy directing plays.   (*Diaries*, 341)

It is striking that regret about a desired return of this kind, forever impossible to achieve, should weigh so heavily, even if momentarily, on a man of such outstanding attainments as Hall.

Appointed Artistic Director of the Arts Theatre in London at the age of 25, he soon seized the opportunity to direct the English premiere of *Waiting for Godot*. At 29, he was appointed Artistic Director of the Shakespeare Memorial Theatre in Stratford-upon-Avon and immediately set about reshaping an annual festival into the modern Royal Shakespeare Company. By 1963 praise for the company's achievements was already recognizing it as a significant player on the world stage. As the second Artistic Director of the National Theatre, Hall secured the company's move onto the South Bank, despite the prevarications and obstructiveness of architects, builders and apparatchiks. Responsible for a host of iconic theatre productions, he has also been an indefatigable director of opera, with a repertoire extending from Cavalli and Monteverdi to Schoenberg and Tippett. Yet the thought of Cambridge University can still trigger in him a wounding conviction of lack of fulfilment.

Crucially, he also looks to Cambridge when seeking legitimation for his views on acting Shakespeare. He has repeatedly expressed his gratitude for all that he claims Rylands taught him and makes that inheritance avowedly the foundation for his own Shakespearian practice. What Rylands passed on was not, in Hall's account, the result of his own discoveries. He was, rather, the custodian of a precious tradition which he had, in his turn, inherited from honoured, non-academic forebears. Hall has offered variant accounts of the imputed chain of descent which eventually entrusted this wisdom to Cambridge's, and Rylands's, safe-keeping; but

---

[13] Abigail Rokison's helpful *Shakespearean Verse Speaking: Text and Theatre Practice* (Cambridge, 2009) makes telling points about contemporary theatrical theories on apt ways of handling Shakespearian verse. As far as my immediate subject is concerned, however, Rokison tends to discern little difference in approach between Hall and Barton, and is also inclined to accept at face value Hall's debatable account of the situation he confronted when he founded the RSC in 1960 (29).

the broad outline always remains the same. Speaking to a Cambridge audience in 2000, Hall traced it back to the Marlowe Society's foundation in 1907, 'inspired by the example of William Poel, the great Shakespearean revolutionary and scourge of Irving'. But Poel, too, allegedly had his mentors, 'the actors in Macready's company', who 'had been taught by Kean's actors, who had been taught by Garrick's, who had been taught by Betterton's'. So, by a series of implausibly gigantic chronological leaps, Hall contrives to reach back as far as 1660.

But then a problem arises. The tradition should ideally stretch back unbroken to, at least, Shakespeare's professional heyday, but Hall has to acknowledge that the enforced closure of the playhouses in 1642, and the eighteen-year hiatus in performance traditions which followed, 'destroyed' the direct line of descent (*Exposed*, 42). He does not pause to assess the potentially damaging implications of this admission. Even if the family tree he sketches were more persuasive, what claims to ultimate validity can it have, if it can only connect us to a post-Shakespearian moment of radical re-invention in English theatre, when new playhouse designs were being introduced, novel performance styles were being experimented with, and Shakespeare's plays were being radically rewritten to suit changing tastes?

That is not the only question Hall's genealogy provokes. Seeking to absorb Poel seamlessly into a playhouse laying-on of hands would not have pleased that 'great Shakespearean revolutionary', who relished asserting that key passages in *The Tempest*, for example, have probably 'never been spoken on the stage with the dramatic effect intended by the poet'.[14] Unlike Hall, this self-willed iconoclast felt the need of no-one's authority but his own to discern what he considered to be the true priorities for actors seeking to meet Shakespeare's performance demands.

In some versions of his treasured line of descent Hall accords Harley Granville-Barker a special place as the anointed one in the generation after Poel (for example, *Exposed*, 42–3), but Granville-Barker, too, confidently rejected precedent,

declaring that 'There is no Shakespearean tradition', and insisting that 'We have the text to guide us, half a dozen directions, and that is all'[15] – a prospect which caused him no nightmares. In contrast, Hall recurrently cites a crucial bequest of knowledge and skills, sanctified by the passage of time, as an indispensable authenticator of his own directorial strategies. He needs to be able to conceive of himself as part of a hallowed tradition. Delighted to be told by Peter Brook that 'it was up to [him] to hand on traditions', Hall proudly labelled himself 'militantly classic' (*Diaries*, 290 and 355).

Hall's roll-call of eminent predecessors never invokes specifics. All those named are asserted to have shared the same priorities as performers, and to have preached the same essential gospel as Rylands handed on to Hall, but, beyond that, he pays them no detailed attention. Exploring particular cases immediately exposes the frailty of his claims. I will later discuss in greater detail Hall's prohibition on mid-line pauses except in very special circumstances. For the moment, it is sufficient to note that Garrick was famous – to some, notorious – for his delight in inserting pauses between, for instance, adjective and noun, as in, for example, 'Oh that this too too solid – flesh would melt', a practice Hall would certainly wish to outlaw. Garrick's persistence in indulging this habit provoked contemporary controversy and inspired him to eloquent defences of his interpretative preferences.[16] The gap between those preferences and the gospel Hall preaches is palpable.

The theatre has traditionally been a fertile breeding-ground for stories about craft knowledge handed on from one acting generation to another, which serve to comfort current practitioners with

---

14 William Poel, *Monthly Letters* (London, 1929), p. 26. Rokison, *Shakespearean Verse Speaking*, p. 32, notes other ways in which Hall's priorities are in conflict with Poel's.

15 Eric Salmon, ed., *Granville Barker and His Correspondents: A Selection of Letters by Him and to Him* (Detroit, 1986), p. 528.

16 Peter Holland, 'Hearing the Dead: The Sound of David Garrick', in Michael Cordner and Peter Holland, eds., *Players, Playwrights, Playhouses: Investigating Performance, 1660–1800* (Basingstoke, 2007) pp. 262–3.

the reassurance that their efforts are supported by the wisdom of their predecessors. Such fables have rhetorical and sentimental force, but often will not withstand serious scrutiny. Hall's favourite narrative belongs in this category. But the tenacity with which he holds to it, and the role he accords it in authenticating the principles he proclaims, are remarkable. His tone in addressing such matters can display a hushed reverence. He reports, for instance, that he was taught the techniques which he in his turn teaches 'by others as part of a living tradition, which has been handed down willingly to my generation', and adds that 'Those who taught me believed that what they said was self-evident' (*Advice*, 14). Peter Holland has noted how Hall's language on this subject often borders on the religious and sacramental.[17] At such moments as this, he comes close to instructing his readers, in the style of Shakespeare's Paulina in *The Winter's Tale*: 'It is required / You do awake your faith.'

In comparison, Barton's discussions remain secular and present-tense. In *Playing Shakespeare* he scarcely ever invokes earlier performers; and when he mentions Granville Barker's pioneer work it is with respect, but also the judgement that 'Acting is built upon specifics, but Granville Barker is tantalisingly literary and vague.' Accordingly, modern 'actors do not respond to him' (*Playing*, 2). Barton is generous in his hope that the modern performance-turn in Shakespeare scholarship – his words date back to 1984 – might yet breed a more effective melding of specialist academic knowledge and practical application (*Playing*, 3). For the moment, however, actors and directors must manage as best they can, since no reservoir of reliable inherited lore exists on which they can depend. Barton shows, therefore, not the slightest trace of Hall's faith in the laying-on of hands. No apostolic succession for him.

That extends to his attitude to Rylands. The two men were able to work productively together, but that does not mean that Barton feels himself to be Rylands's acolyte. In Barton's account, Rylands as director 'stuck to expounding the sense (or non-sense) of the text', while the undergraduate cast 'fended for themselves in directing and staging,

and learned as they went'.[18] When the two men co-directed productions together, Rylands effectively ceded everything but the delivery of the language to his partner. Theresa Moore, Juliet in the Rylands–Barton 1952 Marlowe Society *Romeo and Juliet*, recalled Rylands 'with his eyes on the text, calling out instructions only when the rhythm of a line of poetry was at fault' (*Power*, 53) – an image echoed by Hall's own evocation of Rylands directing 'with his nose firmly in the text' (*Making*, 72). In contrast, Hall's memories of Barton during their Cambridge years are of a radical presence who 'with his rigorous demands . . . would have no truck with amateurism' (*Making*, 71) and accordingly set new standards for undergraduate performance on a range of fronts from scenic design to sword-fighting. Barton himself remembers his experimentation in these years, as regards the interpretation of the text (including its voicing), not as an imbibing and application of Rylands's doctrines, but as a gradual, experimental development of approaches which were to become distinctively his own. Whereas Hall seeks an authorizing inspiration beyond himself for his Shakespearian practice, Barton sketches an accumulative process of finding out, which certainly began in Cambridge but has continued throughout his professional career.[19]

Barton's predominantly optimistic rhetoric is, therefore, founded in his conviction that an open-minded commitment to the exploration of Shakespeare's scripts in rehearsals can generate valuable discoveries, which need not be inflected in any major way by the guidance of voices from the past, recent or ancestral. Hall's language, on the other hand, oscillates between the encouraging and the prophetically despairing. Entrusted, in his own

---

17 Peter Holland, 'Peter Hall', in Russell Brown, ed., *Directors' Theatre*, pp. 146, 153.

18 'Dadie and Cambridge Theatre (A Conversation with John Barton, October 1999)', in Peter Jones, ed., *George Humphrey Wolferstan Rylands 1902–99: Fellow, Dean, Steward, Assistant Bursar, Praelector, Director of Studies and University Lecturer in English: A Memoir* (Cambridge, 2000) pp. 20–1.

19 'Dadie and Cambridge Theatre', p. 21; Michael Greenwald, *Directions*, p. 21.

mind, with the custodianship of a hallowed inheritance, he worries at times that he may be living in that tradition's final days. In one interview he sighs, 'It's a dying art.'[20] At the present time, he testifies, there 'are some fifty actors who practice' this tradition-ratified 'technique in Britain', and only 'a handful of directors' (*Advice*, 13). This 'happy few', this 'band of brothers' (and some sisters), is fighting against an ocean of indifference. He regrets that, in universities, 'little attention [is] paid to the form of Shakespeare's verse'. 'With few exceptions', he notes, 'scholarship *reads* the text, it does not *hear* it' (*Advice*, 14). He laments that, in the professional theatre, apart from Barton's 'heroic' work, 'there is very little acceptance of a method of approaching verse', and most productions provide 'a symphony of mis-scansions and mis-emphases and seem unaware of the fact' (*Exposed*, 42). The swift mutation of the language, he grieves, also threatens a time, perhaps imminent, when Shakespeare will become incomprehensible to theatre audiences. While recapitulating dire scenarios of this kind, he congratulates himself on his good fortune in having 'lived at a time when an actor delivering a speech of Shakespeare's with intelligence can make an audience understand collectively what they would never have understood individually on one reading' (*Exposed*, 60). An element of the apocalyptic, therefore, lurks just beneath the surface in his thinking on this subject.

He also sometimes indulges golden age fantasies of a recent past when 'it was hardly necessary to train actors to speak verse', because they 'had – all of them – been marinated in so much Shakespeare during their early years in regional theatres or on classical tours that the rhythm came naturally to them' (*Advice*, 11). The unreality of this vision of 'marinated' actors is betrayed by that parenthetical 'all of them'. When can this magical moment have been, when every actor in the kingdom possessed this convenient gift, as if by birthright? In other moods, however, Hall is much more dismissive of the state of play in the theatre immediately before he launched his RSC initiative, claiming that, when he first directed at Stratford in 1956, 'there were basically three kinds of actor', all of

them misguided in their handling of Shakespeare's lines. He roots their various fallibilities in longer histories of error – for instance, 'the men of the '30s', who remained loyal to the 'studied nonchalance' apt to 'Maugham, Coward and Rattigan', but inimical to Shakespeare (*Advice*, 199). If this contradicts his sense of an erstwhile golden age, its sweeping condemnations also clash with his fervently expressed admiration for such actors as John Gielgud, Peggy Ashcroft, Harry Andrews, Edith Evans and Michael Redgrave, all key Stratford presences in the 1950s.

Similarly, he has a tendency to accord his own views an absolute fixity the record does not confirm. He now, for example, insists that actors must sustain forward momentum in delivering Shakespeare's text and eschew the multiple pauses in which performers habituated to naturalistic writing often indulge. A characteristic comment has him informing Judith Cook that his 1980s trilogy of late plays are

very quick, we get through a lot of text – we speak the speech 'trippingly on the tongue'. That's very important in Shakespeare. I cannot bear all the pauses in modern productions. I don't know what they're for.[21]

He now claims this as, from the start, a prime aim of his Stratford reforms and entertains rosy memories of what was achieved:

Plays became shorter because they were spoken more quickly. Audiences responded by understanding them better; and the theatre experience became keener and more lively. (*Advice*, 205)

Yet mid-1960s reports sometimes observe a lack of precisely this quality in his own work, as, for instance, in John Russell Brown's criticism of verse-speaking in the 1964 history play cycle, co-directed by Hall and Barton with Clifford Williams:

there is a lack of sustained line or rhythm, and a would-be impressive slowness. Long speeches are broken with

---

[20] Judith Cook, *Directors' Theatre: Sixteen Leading Directors on the State of Theatre in Britain Today* (London, 1989), p. 21.

[21] Cook, *Directors' Theatre*, p. 22.

pauses and far too frequently short speeches are prepared for with silent business, or followed by some such
invention.[22]

From a more sympathetic perspective, Ronald
Bryden described the same tendency when reviewing Hall's innovative 1965 *Hamlet*:

Above all, it's slow, badly lacking the headlong impetus
the plays [*sic*] needs to reveal its shape . . . But I don't see
how this could be otherwise. Thursday's was a first performance. Offering a radical and complex new reading
of the play, Hall has taken apart and reassembled each
line so that the audience can see how it's done. Pace can
come when actors and public have had time to get used
to the idea.[23]

By the 1970s, from the vantage point of the
National Theatre, however, Hall would be rebuking his RSC inheritors for the very qualities Russell Brown and Bryden had detected in his own
earlier work, but making it seem as if they were,
as a consequence, deviating from his own, long-
established, commitment to pace and form:

Again there was this slow, over-emphatic, line-breaking
delivery of the text. The actors are so busy telling us
the ambiguities and the resonances that there is little or
no sense of form. You cannot play Shakespeare without
a sense of line. RSC Shakespeare is getting slower and
slower.   (*Diaries*, 302)

Revisionism is at work here. In loyalty to his new
ruling passion, Hall, when directing *Coriolanus* at
the National Theatre, is recorded to have complained late in rehearsals that 'There are still hundreds of pauses in the show' and demanded that
'they must be cut'.[24]

Whatever inconsistencies between past practice
and currently professed principles may be dis-
cernible in the longer arc of his career, Hall's
pronouncements on how actors should perform
Shakespeare have maintained a remarkable, not to
say repetitive, consistency over the last two decades.
He has enunciated a few core principles again
and again, with similar or identical phrasings often
being repeated in different places. At the heart of
his creed is a faith in form and an insistence on the
actor's imperative need to be responsive to it. Hall

points out that all playscripts have formal properties
and that none achieves, or indeed aims to achieve,
a complete simulacrum of the interactions of daily
living. Accordingly, in one of his favourite formulations, 'the actor has to endorse the form of any
piece of drama' (*Exposed*, 36). In Shakespeare's case
the form's demands are arguably more taxing, more
intricate, than those of, say, naturalistic drama; but
the fundamental principle remains the same.

He further insists that, if we learn how to be
aptly attentive to the text's logics, then Shakespeare himself will start to guide us via the clear
instructions he has encoded within his handling of
verse-form. Commenting on a *Measure for Measure*
speech, for instance, he assures us that 'If Shakespeare's notation is followed, the variety of tempo
is assured' (*Advice*, 147). That imputed notation,
however, clearly requires unpacking. Listen to me,
and I will initiate you, is the clear invitation. The
acolyte of Rylands is preparing to pass on the wisdom he received.

Hall is explicit about the key element in his
inheritance from Rylands: 'What I was taught was
that Shakespeare wrote lines, not words.'[25] Rylands
published comparatively little; assessing exactly
what Hall may have derived directly from him,
and what may be his own subsequent embellishments or extrapolations, is accordingly sometimes a

---

22 John Russell Brown, *Shakespeare's Plays in Performance* (London, 1966), pp. 199–200.
23 Ronald Bryden, *The Unfinished Hero and Other Essays* (London, 1969), p. 64. This was despite the fact that Hall cut
almost one-fifth of the play (Stanley Wells, *Royal Shakespeare: Four Major Productions at Stratford-upon-Avon* (Manchester, 1977), pp. 25–6). Terry Hands has recently claimed that
he disliked the consequences of 1960s priorities in verse-
speaking at the RSC both for length of performances and
for the cutting of text and sought to pioneer more limber
ways of handling the text which meant 'we could play far
more Shakespeare than before'. See Carol Chillington Rutter, 'Becoming the RSC: Terry Hands in Conversation',
Shakespeare, 8 (2012), pp. 211–12.
24 Kristina Bedford, '*Coriolanus*' at the *National*:
'*Th'interpretation of the time*' (Selinsgrove, PA, 1992),
p. 330.
25 Richard Eyre, *Talking Theatre: Interviews with Theatre People*
(London, 2009), p. 38.

matter of surmise. But the emphasis on verse structure, and especially the logic of the line, is recognizably a Rylands obsession. Here he is, for example, in his only book-length critical work, expatiating on the properties of metre:

Metre . . . creates boundaries and limits, which are very useful. The poet may override them, when he so desires; but even in the blank verse of, say, Shirley, there remains the visual division, and the actor pauses imperceptibly at the end of the line.

So, the division into lines takes on almost numinous properties. It restrains and guides the performer, via a visual memory of lay-out, as s/he works to articulate a passage of verse in performance. This is a large claim, and one to which we will need to return. Rylands immediately proceeds to make another important assertion:

One advantage of these boundaries is that they enable the changes of style, noticed above, changes which are unnatural and almost impossible from sentence to sentence in prose . . . [26]

His book was celebrated in its time for 'its emphasis on the importance to a line of the weight, colour and overtones of every single word'. The enthusiast I am quoting said it 'brought' him 'down to the earth of craftsmanship and truth' from a 'more sentimental view of poetry'.[27] Rylands valued and savoured each individual word and its potential wider reverberations across a text. In his 1951 British Academy lecture, for example, he singled out the word 'honour' as 'the atom of poetic energy informing *Julius Caesar*'.[28] But he was also alert to the ways in which the telling juxtaposition of words and phrases can generate a power greater than any of them can achieve singly. The sharper focusing of such juxtapositions by their being rhythmically aligned with (and played off against) one another, within the formal discipline of a metrical line, deeply appealed to him. From this grew a conviction that performance should, above all, acknowledge and convey that resonant patterning. Hall relishes the memory of Rylands in rehearsals, 'more concerned with our line endings

and iambics than with whether we were bumping into each other' (*Making*, 72–3).

Hall inherits Rylands's obsession with the importance of the division marked by the end of the verse-line. As he informed Richard Eyre, 'the iambic pentameter . . . has a strong rhythm and needs marking as a line'.[29] So, its organizing pattern – ten syllables, with a set pattern of recurring heavier stresses – constantly completes itself at the line-ending, and the audience needs to be able to hear that pattern clearly, if gently, marked in an actor's performance.

Clarity of communication is, therefore, best served – indeed guaranteed – by ensuring that the actor's delivery carefully reflects the verse's formal properties. One characteristic pronouncement asserts that, despite the passage of the centuries, 'if Shakespeare's form is observed, an audience is still held; if it is not observed, the audience's attention strays and strays very quickly' (*Advice*, 11). Hall repeatedly asserts that the English language favours speech units of around ten syllables, from which derives, in his account, the dramatic potency of iambic pentameter verse. Its 'five beats' are 'just about as much as an audience' can 'take in without a sense break'. Accordingly, Hall's core conviction is that, if a verse-line 'is delivered with the five accents as written, and with a tiny sense break (*not a stop*) at the end of each line, communication with an audience is immediate' (*Advice*, 12). His respect for the line as the primary organizational unit of Shakespearian verse writing means that, in all but a tiny minority of cases, Hall's rule-book forbids mid-line pauses. Without this discipline, he insists, chaos impends, since

if the actor does not know the end of the line, he will have no control over breath, voice, emotion, or intent. To a greater or lesser degree, he will be incomprehensible . . . (*Exposed*, 55–6)

---

[26] George Rylands, *Words and Poetry* (London, 1928), p. 38.
[27] John Lehmann, *The Whispering Gallery: Autobiography, Volume I* (London, 1955), p. 140.
[28] George Rylands, 'Shakespeare's Poetic Energy', *Proceedings of the British Academy*, 37 (1951), 105.
[29] Richard Eyre, *Talking Theatre*, p. 38.

Hall's directorial work is often informed by the most recent scholarly research. For his 1988 National Theatre *Tempest*, for instance, he drew on Stephen Orgel's 1987 Oxford Shakespeare edition, which he judged 'the best thing he had ever read on the play'.[30] In thinking about the handling of Shakespeare's line-endings, however, the clock has effectively stopped for him. Nothing post-Rylands is taken into account. He does not even acknowledge in passing George T. Wright's magisterial work on Shakespeare's metrical art, and the latter's emphasis on what he terms 'the play of phrase and line' in Shakespeare's mature verse, whereby two countervailing principles are simultaneously at work – the metrical patterning which structures each line, and the phrasal logics which increasingly overflow the line-endings. It is the complex counterpoint between these two that, for Wright, enables the extraordinary experimentalism of Shakespeare's greatest dramatic writing. From *c.*1600 onwards, in his account,

> line and sentence appear to have achieved a comparable eminence, the sentence acknowledging the metrical authority of the line on its own ground but extending the flow of words beyond the single or double line . . .[31]

If this is accurate, is it then so certain that an actor's careful marking of the line patterning in his/her delivery is the best guarantor of clarity of communication? For Wright, the ultimate impetus of Shakespeare's development is towards a late style, where

> The verse that results is harder to follow, to hear as verse. Paradoxically, one may get a better sense of the meter from a printed text (if we can trust the early compositor or the later editor) than from a performance. In the theater enjambed blank verse sounds much like actual, improvised (if elevated) talk, and though Shakespeare's later language is as figurative as ever, its figures run less and less in harness with the meter but cut across the lines and obscure their common accentual patterns.[32]

Wright's analysis casts doubt on the logic of continuing to insist that the line-endings need still to be vocally policed, in this later writing, in the way Hall and Rylands advocate. From Wright's perspective,

such insistence looks like an obstinate denial of the direction Shakespeare's treatment of blank verse has taken. There is no necessity that Hall should accept what Wright proposes; but it is odd that the enthusiast for the latest Oxford re-editing of *The Tempest* should continue to ignore such substantive scholarly work, whose implications directly challenge his own emphatic preferences.

It is yet odder, given that Rylands had been challenged on precisely these grounds by one of the finest and most intelligent of twentieth-century English actors, whom he had directed as Edgar in *King Lear* while this actor was a Cambridge undergraduate. In his diary, Hall dubs Michael Redgrave 'one of my favourite actors in his prime' (*Diaries*, 416). Redgrave's talents were already vividly apparent during his Cambridge years. Rylands delighted in spending long sessions coaching his student players, but, sensing Redgrave's innate gifts and independence of mind, he 'left him fairly much alone'. In the event, his performance 'completely dominated the evening, surprising everyone (even Dadie [Rylands' nickname]) in performance by his authority and mature handling of the verse'.[33] Which makes it intriguing that Redgrave should in 1954 record his scepticism about the praise heaped by some on the Marlowe Society's achievements under Rylands. The Marlowe maintained, he granted, a 'standard, but a very specialized, small standard', and its 'verse-speaking (its chief pride) was distinctly below that which is nowadays attained by the better professional productions'. In the same essay he went on to dispute the argument that 'the end of each line should by

---

30 Roger Warren, *Staging Shakespeare's Late Plays* (Oxford, 1990), p. 2.

31 George T. Wright, *Shakespeare's Metrical Art* (Berkeley, 1988), p. 217. The phrase, 'the play of phrase and line', is taken from the title of Wright's Chapter 14, which, in an earlier form, had been published in *Shakespeare Quarterly*, 34 (1983), 147–58.

32 George T. Wright, *Hearing the Measures: Shakespearean and Other Inflections* (Madison, 2001), p. 245.

33 Alan Strachan, *Secret Dreams: The Biography of Michael Redgrave* (London, 2004), pp. 75–6.

some means be marked'. He conceded that this worked fine for the earlier plays, but in

some of the later plays, it becomes the rule rather than the exception that the lines should overrun and finally, in the last plays of all . . . it becomes almost impossible except for someone with an exceptionally strong photographic memory to memorise the lines in the shape in which they were written.[34]

So, in privileging loyalty to Rylands's dicta, Hall elides all recollection of the fundamental objections posed by a great actor whom he admires – and who experienced at first hand Rylands's principles – with core beliefs Hall proudly derives from the university mentor whom Redgrave challenged.

In policing the 'sanctity of the line' and outlawing, wherever possible, pauses within the line, Hall is driven by a wish to counter the modern actor's inclination 'to stop when he shouldn't', because the latter 'believes that pauses make a text sound spontaneous' (*Advice*, 24) – a technique which splinters verse writing into incoherence. But forbidding that practice does not necessarily entail going to the opposite extreme and prohibiting any pausing within the line except in very exceptional circumstances. Hall's devotion to the integrity of the line, however, leads him to do just that. Once again his language turns sacramental. The 'sanctity of the line is paramount', he asserts, and it must, therefore, 'be maintained wherever possible' (*Advice*, 28), with 'its iambic purity' preserved against violation (*Exposed*, 50). Similarly, he advises that a 'pause is always possible at the end of a line, but never, never in the middle of it', because a 'pause in the middle of the line destroys the line' (*Exposed*, 54). As he warms to his task, Hall becomes yet more prescriptive and starts to label certain practices 'mandatory' (*Advice*, 32). He also waxes ever more confident that he is exactly transcribing Shakespeare's intentions, and phrasings such as 'he [i.e. Shakespeare] requires the line-structure to be preserved' (*Advice*, 55) proliferate, without any evidence being advanced to warrant such incisive laying-down of the law.

In expounding his doctrines, he is repeatedly drawn to musical analogies. Thus, he tells us that 'Shakespeare's text is a complex score that demands to be read as a piece of music' (*Advice*, 18). He conducts rehearsals for his National Theatre *Coriolanus* in the conviction that the text is ordered like 'the orchestration of a symphony, with each instrument or voice coming in on cue with the proper phrasing and intonation'.[35] He recommends that a Shakespearian actor should study his script in the manner of a musician studying a demanding score – i.e. as a complex phenomenon with distinctive formal properties, which need to be mastered before interpretation can begin. As an opera singer, preparing to perform a Richard Strauss aria, needs to plot the apt breathing and absorb it, through practice, into her/his body, so too the Shakespearian actor. And it is, for actor as for singer, a blemish for the performer to break the flow of the vocal line by audibly snatching a breath at an unjustified point.

Which begs the question of how an actor is to discern, in an early modern playscript, which hesitations or pauses might or might not be justified. For Hall, this presents no problem, because – the musical analogy again – 'Shakespeare's text is scored precisely' (*Exposed*, 41). Better still, 'his notation is amazingly accurate' (*Advice*, 14), and so

Shakespeare's text tells an actor quite clearly when to go fast, when to go slow, when to pause, when to come in on cue. He indicates which word should be accented and which word should be thrown away. (*Exposed*, 41)

For all but the most fervent believers, this is likely to stretch faith close to breaking point. It attributes to dramatic notation qualities it has traditionally been taken to lack. Musical notation employs a variety of methods to signal relative lengths of notes, variations in levels of sound and differences of tempi between passages, for which drama has never possessed equivalents. In effect, Hall, the talented musician and distinguished opera-director, wishes us to accept that the formal properties of blank verse, as ingeniously orchestrated by a supremely

---

[34] Michael Redgrave, 'Shakespeare and the Actors', in John Garrett, ed., *Talking of Shakespeare* (Toronto, 1954), pp. 128, 142–3.

[35] Bedford, '*Coriolanus*', p. 245.

talented playwright, became a comparably precise notational system.

Like many before him, Hall looks to Hamlet's advice to the players for evidence to support his performance preferences. He fixes, in particular, upon the prince's reference to 'a temperance that may give it [i.e. an actor's performance] smoothness' and, assuming that Hamlet speaks for his creator, applies it to his favourite topic:

I think 'smoothness' must refer to the line of the iambic text. Its structure must be observed and its flow maintained. There must be no sudden *sforzandos* or mis-accents in the line. It must be smooth, so that it is capable of communicating the rough. The temperance makes it acceptable. (*Exposed*, 47)

The opening leap there – via '*I think* "smoothness" must refer . . . ' – lacks any ratification beyond his own desire that it should be so. Hamlet speaks only of 'my lines' and nowhere examines how an individual line should or should not be voiced. Equally, nothing in Hamlet's speech ratifies the claim that 'no sudden *sforzandos*' should erupt to blemish the 'smoothness' of expression with which a line is delivered. (Hamlet does, after all, counsel the players not to be 'too tame neither'.) And why, in any case, should '*sforzandos*' be outlawed? Musical notation includes them; why not dramatic practice? They can doubtless be indulged melodramatically and purposelessly by poor or miscalculating performers, whether actors or musicians; but what logic decrees that they can in no circumstances be used? And if the issue is the suddenness with which an individual '*sforzando*' is deployed, is that not a judgement specific to the demands of a particular dramatic moment? Why should we legislate, as a foundational principle, that a character's emotional impetus or tactical needs can never license the use of a sudden, strong emphasis in the midst of a sequence otherwise rendered in a quieter style of delivery? To a sceptical reader, it may appear that Hall's ban originates in a firm set of personal aesthetic loyalties, which seek confirmation from the *Hamlet* passage, but do not succeed in securing it.

Hall's fixation with 'smoothness' of expression inspires other debatable decrees, especially when it is yoked with his Rylands-derived investment in 'the sanctity of the line' (*Exposed*, 50). He becomes obsessed, for instance, with the need for swift, almost imperceptible transitions when a single verse-line is shared between two characters. These cues, he instructs his *Coriolanus* company, 'must be picked up immediately or the dynamic is lost'.[36] Alacrity of response at such moments is not his only desideratum. His stress on continuity of metrical pulse leads him to require that the two performers must be so exactly attuned to one another that, in addition, the moment of transition between speakers should entail no alteration in tempo or tone. For Hall, the aim has to be the maintenance of a 'line which has the same pace, dynamic, rhythm and volume' (*Advice*, 32) throughout its length. His key demand – 'Whatever else is jettisoned, the rhythm of the line must be preserved – kept smooth' (*Exposed*, 50) – is thus extended to determine the orchestration of elements beyond the purely rhythmical.

Ensuring that metrical patterns are sustainedly observed is one thing; but why should that require the second speaker to echo the first one's 'pace, dynamic . . . and volume'? Some of these mid-line interceptions mark moments of dissent, challenge, mockery, aggression, and/or interrogation, all of which, one might think, could be quite effectively registered through emphatic alterations of 'dynamic' and 'volume'. Hall's instructor, George Rylands, keenly admired the work of the American critic Stark Young.[37] One of Young's anathemas was what he considered to be the deadening monotony of utterance on the contemporary New York stage:

you will very commonly hear actor after actor take the tempo of his speech from the speech that has just been spoken. And so it happens sometimes that for a whole

---

[36] Bedford, '*Coriolanus*', p. 254.

[37] Tim Cribb, *Bloomsbury and British Theatre: The Marlowe Story* (Cambridge, 2007), p. 101.

scene the tempo of all the speeches have about the same measure.[38]

Hall's *ex cathedra* prioritizing of 'smoothness' over all else threatens to deprive his actors of legitimate resources and, if slavishly obeyed, would risk a return to the inert theatre which Young, with Rylands's approval, condemned.

And then there is the question of Hall's redefinition of the caesura. Without signalling that he is aware what he is doing, he reinvents the word's meaning and explains that a caesura occurs only when 'one sentence stops and another begins' in the middle of a line (*Exposed*, 47). He notes that such moments happen relatively rarely, but, even so, they must not be allowed to breach 'the sanctity of the whole line'. Accordingly, he legislates that, when a caesura (in Hall's definition of it) approaches, the actor must usually change 'pace at the end of the previous line so that the first half of the new line can be slowed up in order to earn the time for a full-stop' (*Exposed*, 58), while not disrupting the overall tempo of the line's delivery. The immediate inspiration for this remark is what Hall claims to be the first caesura in *Twelfth Night*, 1.1 – after 'Stealing and giving odour' in line 7 (*Advice*, 111). It is, however, Hall who limits the caesura's occurrence to moments when one sentence concludes, and another starts, in the middle of a verse-line. Normally, the term applies to the point of division in any line which is shaped into 'two distinct clusters of meaning', regardless of whether or not a sentence ends within it.[39] Caesuras occur, therefore, in the majority of verse-lines. Under this definition, the one in line 7 is merely the latest in an already plentiful series of them in this opening scene.

OED (*sb*, 2) defines the caesura as a 'pause or breathing-place', but there is no need in performance to mark it with a palpable pause, and in practice most experienced actors do not do so. After all, a host of other ways exist, in which the voice can distinguish between one cluster of meaning and another – by changes in relative tempi, alterations in intonation, inflection or expressivity, etc. The key usefulness of the idea of the caesura is, arguably, to alert readers and performers to the ways in which meaning is generated, varied and focused via the subtle use of changing groupings and kinds of phrasal shape from one line to another – a rich, potential source of acting energy, if it is aptly and responsively built upon in performance. It may be the traditional, but (as I argue) mistaken, association of the caesura with a 'pause or breathing-place' which makes Hall, in effect, silently obliterate its traditional meaning from his explorations in favour of his nonce-redefinition of it. His commitment to 'smoothness' makes him averse to acknowledging the internal differentiations within the line to which traditional prosody has given central emphasis. In the process, however, the self-avowed traditionalist reinvents core terminology to privilege his own aesthetic priorities.

He identifies the occurrence of his kind of caesura with the appearance of a 'full-stop in the middle of a line' (*Exposed*, 58). But to whose text is he referring here? As Hall explains, he now chooses to 'work from a specially prepared text for the actors which has sense punctuation and yet keeps as close as possible to the basic punctuation of the Folio' (*Exposed*, 45). His ultimate aim is 'a typescript stripped of everything but the essential full stops' (*Advice*, 24). So the answer is: a text created by Hall and his current academic collaborator. Hall delights in the precision of punctuation in the Pinter and Ayckbourn scripts he has directed, and he has always insisted that his casts in those productions observe such indications obediently and responsively. But in those cases he was dealing with authorial punctuation. However thoughtfully carried out, the punctuation in the 'specially prepared' Shakespeare scripts he uses for rehearsals is not authorial, but, rather, reflects how two modern minds hear, and interpret, the dialogue's syntactical organization (with some First Folio elements – themselves non-authorial, or at

[38] Stark Young, *The Flower in Drama: A Book of Papers on the Theatre* (New York, 1923), p. 106.
[39] Stephen Unwin, *So You Want To Be A Theatre Director* (London, 2004), p. 130.

least not demonstrably authorial – surviving in the mix). The briefest of comparisons with other modernized versions will illustrate that it is possible for others to reorder a script's punctuation in radically different, but often perfectly plausible, ways, including differing about which full stops are truly 'essential'. It may be sensible to prepare one's own scripts for rehearsals but the decisions which underpin that exercise need always to be seen as provisional. Throughout his writings on the subject, Hall effectively treats the punctuation in his rehearsal scripts as unimpeachably authoritative and draws large deductions for performance from it. In rehearsal too, he can be glimpsed requiring his actors to observe religiously the commas in the texts he has distributed to them.[40] Here, as so often, Hall, who claims to be the (almost impersonal) communicator of a precious tradition bequeathed to him, binds into his instructions a large admixture of personal preference dressed up as indisputable fact.

Hall's major pronouncements on this subject substantially postdate Barton's *Playing Shakespeare*. Earlier decades generated from him numerous public statements about verse-speaking; but it was from 2000 onwards that he published the kinds of detailed, prescriptive unpacking of rules of engagement for the Shakespearian actor I have been considering here. The books in which they appear evoke nostalgically the achievements of the RSC's first decade and closely align Hall with Barton, as two men with a single set of principles, who combined their strengths to make those achievements possible. Re-reading the two men's writings together, however, reveals the multiple ways in which their approaches diverge. Their views inevitably sometimes overlap. Barton expresses, for instance, similar views to Hall on the need for speed of pick-up in shared verse-lines, and shows a matching confidence that Shakespeare's intention can be readily discerned:

The second speaker is meant to pick up the cue at once, as surely as if Shakespeare had written in the stage-direction, 'don't pause here'. (*Playing*, 32)

But, tonally, they are frequently worlds apart.

In contrast to Hall's mandatory zeal, Barton stresses his aversion to laying down the law. Early in his explorations in the television series, flanked by leading RSC players, he offers this emphatic disclaimer:

There are few absolute rules about playing Shakespeare but many possibilities. We don't offer ourselves as high priests but as explorers or detectives. We want to test and to question. Particularly we want to show how Shakespeare's own text can help to solve the seeming problems in that text. Of course, much of it is instinct and guesswork. We will try to distinguish between what is clearly and objectively so and what is highly subjective. I hope that if I'm too dogmatic the actors will challenge me. (*Playing*, 7)

Instead of claiming that he is the mouthpiece for a body of impersonal wisdom inherited from a long line of theatrical descent, Barton stresses that his views reflect personal preference and experience:

Of course what we say is bound to be personal. We don't believe that there's only one way of tackling Shakespeare. That way madness lies. But out of the infinite numbers of questions which come up when we work on him we have picked the ones that seem to us the most important at this time. (*Playing*, 7)

So, his thinking is offered as rooted in a precise historical moment, and inevitably inflected by that moment. With that awareness comes a consciousness of likely evanescence, accepted as the common fate (no hint here of Hall's depression at the possibly imminent death of a valued tradition):

---

[40] Kristina Bedford, 'Coriolanus', p. 245. Cf. his biographer's account of Hall's developing thinking on this issue (*Power*, 246): 'Since Hall accepted without question that he could not alter a dot or comma in Harold Pinter's plays, why, then, should he do so in William Shakespeare's? This was the theory of directorial neutrality in its purest form.' But this argument could only gain traction if we had Shakespeare's own punctuation, which we do not. Despite this, Hall's instructions about the implications of the punctuation in the edited texts he has had a major hand in preparing can be meticulously precise, as when he tells his *Coriolanus* cast that a 'full stop means a gear change, a new beat, a shift in tone; it is the signal for variety in the coloration of a passage – a quality not shared by the semi-colon or comma' (Bedford, 'Coriolanus', p. 25).

these sessions will probably seem out-dated and odd before many years are past. That is the nature of the theatre. We can only speak about what we think and feel at this time. (*Playing*, 7)

He refuses to present his views as possessing special claims to primacy over those of other expert contemporaries:

Another actor or another director would rightly stress things differently or violently disagree with us or stress points which we shall leave out. (*Playing*, 7)

He also combines an admission that many of the views he is about to express will inevitably be approximate or sketchy with a confession that aspirations to absolute truth do not much concern him:

I must confess that I have never worried over-much about the precise accuracy of what I may say in the rehearsal room. The test there is not whether a given statement is objectively true but whether it helps, stimulates and releases an actor at a particular rehearsal. If it does so, then the advice is useful. If it does not, however true it may be, it has no practical use in that particular context. Dangerous words, I know, but I believe that, theatrically speaking, they are realistic. It is not enough for a director to speak true. He must reach and help the actors with whom he is working, and if he does not do so then he fails them. (*Playing*, 3)

It is impossible to imagine such pragmatic and relativistic words on Hall's lips. The general bent of Barton's rhetoric could hardly be more distinct from Hall's inclination to multiply laws and prohibitions. Are the differences between them as apparent when Barton is working with actors on specific sequences of text?

Let us take as an example his follow-up to the observation on end-stopped lines I quoted earlier. That leads into a performance by Sheila Hancock of Sonnet 29, which consists of a single, extended syntactical unit for its entire length. Barton proposes that the disposition of thoughts into lines helps the player comprehend, control and communicate that taxing arc of meaning. They then consider the transition from line 11 into 12 ('Like to the lark at break of day arising / From sullen earth, sings hymns at heaven's gate') – the only point in the

poem where, in Barton's interpretation, the phrasal unit overruns the line-ending.[41] How should the actor handle it?

Hall's answer would be unyielding. He would insist that performing Shakespearian verse 'as written' requires, in a phrase I have already quoted, 'a tiny sense break (*not* a stop) at the end of each line', and that, despite the enjambment, this line is no exception. Barton, in contrast, having expounded the assistance and support the division into lines can offer the actor, declines to legislate:

Should you run on the line or should you not? Ask yourself that question and simply decide which feels better. Shakespeare gives you a choice. If it's better for you to run the line on, run it on. But if the verse actually helps you to phrase the line then that's the right answer. Personally I think that if you lift the word 'arising' at the end of the first line, it is quite easy to take a small pause after it, perhaps a naturalistic pause for breath. (*Playing*, 35)

Barton's personal instincts here clearly make him sympathize with what would also be Hall's preference, but he refuses to proffer that option as the only correct version. In place of Hall's Shakespeare, who mandates in a host of detailed respects how his scripts must be performed, Barton's Shakespeare leaves most key decisions to his actors. Accordingly, Barton's responsibility is to alert them to the possibilities, but not to disenfranchise them or treat them as pupils to be commanded into conformity with 'general principles'. He also remains clear that his own preference is, in the end, a personal one, not a matter of an absolute rule.

Again and again, at moments where Hall's principles would lead him to decree mandatory solutions, Barton seeks to ensure that the nature of the technical issues, as he sees them, is clearly communicated, but then holds back from preaching the supremacy of one solution over others. The

---

[41] *Playing Shakespeare* predates John Barrell's argument (in *Poetry, Language and Politics* (Manchester, 1988), pp. 32–6) that construing the sonnet's organization in this way involves a misreading of its syntactical patterning and argument. Barrell's proposition has influenced the punctuation used at this point in numerous subsequent editions of the sonnets.

exchanges we have just been exploring, for example, end with this moralization:

We're talking about possibilities, not laws. Particularly with Shakespeare's late verse. All I'm saying is that you need to judge the question each time and then decide.

(*Playing*, 36)

He applies the same deeply engaged open-mindedness to an exploration with Judi Dench and Richard Pasco of the 2.5 encounter between Viola and Orsino in *Twelfth Night* – roles they had played for him in his acclaimed 1969 RSC staging.[42] The sequence they rehearse contains a series of lines divided between the two characters. Dench directly asks about these moments of decision: '*Can you make your own choice about it?*', and Barton replies:

Yes, you must. But first you've got to be aware that these things are happening in the text. Then you can choose. (*Playing*, 153)

At some moments he allows himself to be a little more interventionist than this and, in the process, sketches solutions which Hall would reject. One instance of this arises from the following exchange:

Orsino. What kind of woman is't?
Viola. Of your complexion.

Dench observes:

I feel I want to pause before 'Of your complexion'. Because she's caught out there, isn't she?

To which Barton replies:

There's always a third option about a pause. You can, as it were, pause *within* the words. When you say, 'Of your complexion', you could pick up the cue at once but then feel for the rest of the line: 'Of... (*pause*)... your complexion.'... Then you still follow Shakespeare's rhythm but you have your pause. (*Playing*, 155)

Dench's delighted reaction to this is logical, given that the suggestion is so apt to her own distinctive vocal style.[43] That delight, however, would not be echoed by Hall, since it breaches his prohibition against pauses within the line. But then Barton does not share Hall's obsession with the need to

sustain 'smoothness' at all costs. Indeed, he explicitly asserts as a prime imperative that the actor must urgently aim to avoid 'one note, one tone, and one tempo' (*Playing*, 51) – advice that would have earned Stark Young's energetic approval.

Both Barton and Hall acknowledge the difficulties many contemporary actors experience when confronting Shakespeare. Hall frames this within his recurrent sense of the hostility of the times to the values he endorses. 'In our post-Stanislavsky, screen-dominated age', he observes, 'actors often worry about disciplines that can constrict their individuality' (*Exposed*, 36) – a prejudice that must be overcome before they can be initiated in the Rylands-imparted mysteries of performing Shakespeare. And he recalls the moment of the RSC's foundation, similarly, as one when the 'discipline of verse was regarded as an unwarranted imposition; worse possibly than having to learn Standard English' (*Advice*, 201).

Barton's account of the same problem tends to be more empathetic. He identifies fear as 'the greatest obstacle an actor has to overcome with Shakespeare's verse' – a fear which is often rationalized by arguing that if the actor 'worries about the verse he will become unreal and unspontaneous'. Actors who are afflicted in this way often cite flawed performances by other actors, who, in Barton's view, are 'not unreal because of the verse but because they have fallen into the trap of playing qualities rather than intentions', or 'maybe [because] they are not very good actors'. Ever the optimist, he believes that

this kind of fear is less common than it used to be. It is certainly less overt, but it is apt to take the more insidious

---

42 Richard Pasco joined the cast after the untimely death of the original Orsino, Charles Thomas.

43 Much of the discussion in *Playing Shakespeare*, if not actually prescripted, clearly moves along agreed tracks. The *Twelfth Night* programme, however, revisits with two of its original cast a brilliantly successful production, and Barton's suggestion here is one which fully accords both with Dench's distinctive style of delivery and the hesitant tenderness with which she negotiated this scene in Barton's RSC staging.

form of an actor paying lip-service to the verse on the surface but being still inhibited by it internally.

(*Playing*, 104)

All the energy he has poured into teaching over the last half-century has been designed to overcome those inhibitions – a mission he still pursues, in his eighties, in his continuing involvement with the RSC, advising both actors and directors.

The central leitmotif of that work is his encouragement to the player to see that verse is 'above all a device to help the actor' (*Playing*, 25). Hall would echo that sentiment. The crucial difference between them is that Barton would never (as Hall is eager to do) wear with pride the label of 'iambic fundamentalist' (*Advice*, 209). Together they brought about, for a brief time, a marked transformation in the performance of Shakespeare within one company. Their writings, however, make it logical that Hall should have been the brilliant institutional strategist who enabled the creation of the RSC and the initiation of a training regime unprecedented in English theatre, but that it was Barton who principally delivered the training designed to convert the revolution they both desired into reality.

Some of the finest Shakespearian productions I have seen have been directed by Barton – including his 1969 *Twelfth Night*, his 1978 *Love's Labour's Lost*, and, above all, his 1968 *Troilus and Cressida*. Hall, too, has been responsible for some of the peaks of my Shakespearian theatre-going career – from his 1965 *Hamlet* to his 1987 *Antony and Cleopatra*. The outstanding directorial qualities which underpinned these achievements are never, however, fully reflected in what either man writes about performing Shakespeare.

Barton is explicit about his unease in thinking aloud about the subject outside the rehearsal-room:

I must confess that I feel very self-conscious expounding verse in the way I've just been doing. I'd feel much happier making specific points about it in the cut-and-thrust of rehearsal. Good verse-speaking is not really about general principles but comes from experience and practice. So although it's up to us to analyse the verse as well as we can, in the end we must treat it

intuitively. We must trust it and let it be organic rather than conscious.

(*Playing*, 46)

So, *Playing Shakespeare*, whether on screen or in print, is fated to afford, at best, only a shadow image of his real directorial gifts and insights. For a taste of him in action at the height of his powers, one must turn instead to Barbara Hodgdon's brilliantly illuminating report on, and analysis of, the 1978 *Love's Labour's Lost* rehearsals.[44]

Hall is less averse than Barton to pronouncing publicly on Shakespeare. It is inconceivable that Barton would ever have agreed to give the Clark Lectures, the prestigious annual lecture series sponsored by Trinity College, while it was in many ways a natural summation that Hall should return to Cambridge in 2000 for that purpose. He never, however, shows himself to best advantage in such forums, where the intransigently rule-giving side of his personality prevails. The Hall of the rehearsal room can, on occasion, value the presence in his casts of a 'contrary spirit' like the actor Basil Henson, ready to challenge 'all assumptions (including his own), never content to accept easy solutions', and also be prepared to concede to Geraldine James's vivid demonstration that Hall's conception of how a *Cymbeline* scene needed to be played was misguided.[45] His writing, however, affords scant evidence of even this degree of flexibility.

As one concluding example, let us take Hall's problematic account of Macbeth's 'Is this a dagger which I see before me' soliloquy. In his reading, this speech silently generates a multitude of commands to the player, who must, for instance, hesitate after 'Or art thou but', because otherwise he will not be able to 'invent what he fears – the image of '**a dagger of the mind**'' (*Advice*, 155). Assuming, for the purposes of argument, that we agree that the idea of 'the dagger of the mind' needs to be discovered in the moment in the way Hall favours, a skilled performer has at his command many other

---

44 Barbara Hodgdon, 'Rehearsal Process as Critical Practice: John Barton's 1978 *Love's Labour's Lost*', *Theatre History Studies*, 8 (1988), 11–34.

45 Roger Warren, *Staging Shakespeare's Late Plays*, pp. 109, 28–9.

ways of achieving this than by (invariably) using a brief pause to gather strength and focus before uttering the phrase in question. So, why *must* he pause there?

Some of what Hall insists on as mandatory, if treated instead as potentially helpful suggestions to be deployed as and when an actor finds them appropriate (in the manner Barton prefers), can often generate revelatory results. Greg Hicks, an actor who has often worked with Hall, but remains sceptical about the need invariably to observe line-endings, still found an unexpected yield in doing just that at a tricky point in an Aufidius speech in *Coriolanus*.[46] Similarly, Simon Russell Beale, for many the finest Shakespearean actor of his generation, had an identical experience, when, playing Leontes, he decided to observe, in the trial scene, a slight hesitation at the line ending in 'The daughter of a king, our wife and one / Of us too much belov'd'. In Russell Beale's words, 'Leontes is wondering how to phrase this. It was a tiny residual beat but it was there in the performance.' But he also stresses that such punctilious observation of a line-division remains very unusual for him. His decision was, in this instance, an entirely pragmatic one, not an obeisance to a general rule. In this situation, in this speech, at that moment, such a choice seemed resonant. Elsewhere, Russell Beale reserves the right to follow different logics. He also makes clear his fundamental scepticism about much that Hall holds dear:

I don't believe that it's an infallible rule that Shakespeare will always help you. I think that's a bit of a tease really. Sometimes he does, perhaps most of the time he does, but sometimes he doesn't, especially in the late plays. My job is to make it clear at first hearing if that's at all possible. *The Winter's Tale* is difficult enough as it is.[47]

Experienced actors, working with Hall, develop their own *modus vivendi*. An especially interesting example is furnished by Michael Pennington. In the 1970s, Pennington did brilliant work for Barton, including an outstanding Hamlet in 1980, as well as Berowne in Barton's classic 1978 *Love's Labour's Lost*. Describing his experience of rehearsing Hamlet, he gratefully recalls Barton's collaboration with him:

What was constant in John Barton's guidance of me was his encouragement always to use the language as a *necessary* funnel for the emotions in a scene. This may sound obvious, but in a part as emotionally turbulent as Hamlet the actor may sometimes allow a tide of feeling to distort highly-wrought areas of language and so make them obscure. In fact of course the feelings *require* those words, and only those words, to define them and make them communicable – it is all one thing, the feeling, the pressure, the need to speak, the image that defines. It can be like pressing a tornado through the eye of a needle, but a persistent attention to colour, texture, rhythm and characteristic music go beyond textual piety to become an emotional necessity.[48]

Fourteen years later, Pennington played Claudius for Hall. This was the first time they had tackled a major Shakespearian role together,[49] and it was an open question whether they would 'see eye to eye' on it. Pennington has, he recounts, his own devotion to 'the metrical disciplines of the verse', but with 'an occasional dash of libertarianism'. At the first rehearsal Hall took the initiative in a move Pennington dubs 'worthy of Claudius himself', by declaring 'to the company that his verse methods were non-negotiable' and turning to Pennington 'for a demonstration of them'. As a result, his 'colleagues young and old leaned forward to hear an exemplar of correct breathing and phrasing'. Put on the spot, Pennington improvised what he calls a 'Cheshire Cat performance', which, he hoped, 'allowed everyone to draw whatever moral they pleased'. Its key characteristic was speed, drawing 'on the dictum of an earlier director, Tyrone Guthrie, that you should be able to do half a dozen

---

[46] Kristina Bedford, '*Coriolanus*', p. 155.

[47] Mark Leipacher, *Catching the Light: Sam Mendes and Simon Russell Beale, A Working Partnership* (London, 2011), p. 128.

[48] Michael Pennington, '*Hamlet*', in Philip Brockbank, ed., *Players of Shakespeare: Essays in Shakespearean Performance by Twelve Players with the Royal Shakespeare Company* (Cambridge, 1985), pp. 121–2.

[49] Pennington had played Fortinbras in Hall's 1965 *Hamlet*, with David Warner in the title role.

lines of verse on a single breath'. The result was a 'serendipitous' moment of inspiration:

To my existing conviction that Claudius runs a Court so brazenly dazzling that you have to shade your eyes to see clearly, I now added the complete impossibility, in the face of his virtuosic fluency, of getting a word in edgeways even had etiquette allowed it. He literally silenced the opposition by starving them of the oxygen to speak. So a chance encounter that morning between directorial doctrine and actor's expediency had begun to create a character for me.[50]

Pennington's decades of acting experience enabled him to meet Hall's absolutism head-on and turn the encounter to creative advantage. In print, however, Hall's doctrinaire narrowness threatens to cabin, crib, confine performers who are much less knowledgeable than Pennington about the demands of this repertoire and who may, as a result, be only too eager to accept the apparent life-line offered by an instructor, who insists that mastery of a very few key principles, allegedly sanctified by generations of actors, will initiate them into its mysteries. Such dubious panaceas need to be firmly resisted. The challenges of Shakespeare's constant experimentalism require a matching responsiveness and exploratory flexibility in his interpreters. In Barton's formulation, 'Try to find what goes on in the text and ask yourselves if you can *use* it' (*Playing*, 209).

---

[50] Michael Pennington, 'Barnardine's Straw: The Devil in Shakespeare's Detail', *Proceedings of the British Academy*, 131 (2004), 210–11.

MAKING THE WORK OF PLAY

MICHAEL PAVELKA (IN CONVERSATION WITH CAROL CHILLINGTON RUTTER)

CCR: When Tony Harrison – northern working class lad, grammar school boy, poet, playwright – is having one of his regular anxiety attacks about how to maintain his working class street cred, he writes some 'Lines to My Grandfathers'. One of them was a fell farmer, another a railwayman. The third brewed beer. And Harrison, to keep company with these manual workers, borrows from Yeats phrases he wants to apply to the work of writing poetry: it's 'sedentary toil'; 'difficulty's our plough'.

Academics who engage themselves to 'Working With Shakespeare' would probably put their work in the category of 'sedentary toil'. Certainly, trying to match wits with Billy Big Boy, 'difficulty's our plough'. But as makers, academics are more like Harrison than his grandfathers. We're poets: the work is word work, taking Shakespeare's words and turning them into other words.

Michael Pavelka works differently with Shakespeare. He takes Shakespeare's words and turns them into objects: things for actors to use in performance, things for spectators to engage with in watching, things that set the world of the play and make the play work. He's a manual labourer collaborating with Shakespeare. He happens also to be a poet of the material imagination.

Pavelka is a theatre designer. With the director Ed Hall he is a founder of Propeller theatre company. Since the company was launched in 1997, he has been responsible for designing all but one of Propeller's productions: creating the signature 'look' of the company but also the actual built structures that allow the company to fulfil one of its defining aims, to apply 'a modern physical aesthetic' to performance. (He's also an academic, Reader in Theatre Design/Scenography at the University of the Arts, London. Based at Wimbledon College of Art, he led the 'Theatre: Design for Performance' BA pathway for fifteen years and, now, a new MA in Theatre Design.)

As a company, Propeller works to certain specifications, plays by certain rules, has certain attitudes, all of which pose challenges – or better said, opportunities – for the designer.

First, Propeller is a Shakespeare company. For them, that signals a commitment to honouring Shakespeare's writing, taking a self-imposed rigorous approach to the text. In the past fifteen years, Propeller has produced ten of Shakespeare's plays in eighteen productions, including a number of what they call 'pocket' productions for schools audiences, one-hour versions derived from the full, parent production that offer 'reduced' Shakespeare in terms only of duration, not acting or production values.

Second, it's an all-male company. This has nothing to do with historical authenticity – the fact that Shakespeare's company was all-male. Nor does it have to do with authenticity of impersonation. The company makes no attempt to disguise men as women. They're actors playing parts: the aesthetic is presentational and performative, lodged in the theatrical rather than the theoretical – beyond modern theorized constructions of gender, so you never read any cross-dressed performance as 'queer' or 'drag'; you read it as 'play'. In Propeller, as in the early modern playing company, there's no niche casting. Propeller actors are all available to play men *and* women and to cross genders as they continuously double roles inside a production.

Third: it's a genuine ensemble. It has a rehearsal policy that instils collaboration, the whole company called for every rehearsal, which has actors – as one of them says – throwing ideas at the wall like paint for director and designer to work on. It has a pay policy that is democratic. All actors are paid the same in an outfit that can afford (usually) fourteen actors, an administrative fact that itself conduces to ensemble. Propeller actors are constantly moving from 'Chorus' to 'named part' and back again, so they're on stage, or just off waiting to come on, all of the time, constantly doubling, always playing, which means a levelling between principals and so-called bit parts. Nobody sits in a dressing room waiting to be called for their cue. They're permanently 'cued up'. Then, too, Propeller has a casting policy that builds ensemble. It gives every member of the current company first refusal on the next project. Fresh blood comes in when vacancies appear, when an actor elects to sit the next tour out, but most Propeller actors are veterans. Continuity of this kind means that they have an understanding of a shared style that's physical and imaginative, that allows them to get 'stuck into' (as actors say) the work from the off. For the designer, continuity of this kind means working with known quantities and known bodies, even as new bodies keep turning up.

So: a Shakespeare company, an all-male acting company, an ensemble. Finally, Propeller is a touring company: in recent years, touring double bills (*A Midsummer Night's Dream* with *The Merchant of Venice*; *Richard III* with *The Comedy of Errors*; *Henry V* with *The Winter's Tale*). And touring not just up, down and across the UK but around the world – Europe, North America, China, Japan, Australia. Back in 1998 the company specifications that Ed Hall laid down for Propeller were an ability to travel light and to go anywhere: the actors, he said, would 'make all the music, do all the sound effects' and carry 'so little scenery' that it could 'go as excess baggage'.

He offered an example. The very necessary front door to Antipholus's house in Ephesus. All Propeller would need as a prop was 'a door knocker', because an 'actor would play the door'; Propeller, said Hall, would 'build the set with people'. Building the set with people is a technique that has endured.

So, Michael, given these company rules to play by, and given that so much of what actors do in performance and what spectators take away from performance is bound up in your work, the work of the designer, how do you do the work of designing – for Propeller, for Shakespeare? What's your journey?

MP: To begin with, I want to run through a fast forward of the journey. It's in the form of a Pecha Kucha [Illustration 10] twenty images coupled to twenty explanatory captions: a portfolio that works as a visual shorthand of what I do, how I and the Propeller team work, and what's imaginatively behind the work. Here goes.

1. Why do I want to work on Shakespeare? Because he presents an unstable, shifting world. I asked a student in a workshop once why he liked Shakespeare – he said, 'Shit happens; Shakespeare's just the best at saying *why*.' Everyone in a Shakespeare play has his own unique point of view about what life's dealt him. I, the designer, create a structure that allows for rapid narrative shifts and physical transformations – plastic worlds.

2. Our process starts with the text ... what else is there?! We remove editorial act and scene divisions to create a continuous narrative, that's also liable to change. We start by asking ourselves, 'Who is telling the story?' The script is my sketchbook – I use the blank page facing the text for drawing, so running in parallel to the speech is an emergent visual language.

3. One of our unwritten rules is to avoid referencing the work of other companies. We keep focused on our view of the text.

4. Films and popular culture are, however, a source of inspiration for Ed, me and the actors. It's a way of bonding with the audience through referencing common experience. An image from *L'Année dernière à Marienbad* was a reference point

10. A Pecha Kucha composed of twenty images in a portfolio that offers a visual shorthand of Pavelka's design work.

for *Twelfth Night* (2007, 2012); the little boy in *The Sixth Sense* helped us look for ways to frame *The Winter's Tale* (2005, 2011) through the point of view of Mamillius.

5. I went to a conference on theatre design. I got distracted – I spent most of the time drawing on my programme, coming up with early thoughts for *The Winter's Tale* set. Sketching was also a way to

131

purge the 'big design concept' from my thinking so I could later have a more open and detailed conversation with Ed.

6. This is the *Twelfth Night/Shrew* company (2007). They're my material. They're a known quantity. They're all men. They're in a space. They have something to tell you.

7. Here's a proscenium. A proscenium is a bridge. A gateway. An opening. An opportunity. A frontier to cross repeatedly. A mouthpiece. I don't think of it as an architectural structure. It's an idea: part of our language. We use it, playfully.

8. The venue – more material. The Watermill Theatre (shown in the top image) was the company's first home. There's no proscenium here. Our early productions were 'in the round'. The first, *Henry V*, started with the ensemble in the river that runs past the theatre. Coincidentally, our latest venue in Beijing (below) is surrounded by water. From Berkshire to Beijing, the company has 'come of age'. Each design has to expand and contract to account for radically varied spaces.

9. Practicalities now. I work speculatively in scale. All the three-dimensional ideas we develop are made twenty-five times smaller than reality. Using my scale rule (which *nobody* else touches), I translate the real world into a speculative virtual miniature: this allows me and the director to play practically, together, with the design.

10. This is a pair of computer-assisted drawings of a set. What they show is a panelled interior space for *Twelfth Night* where the characters were existentially suspended in a holding pattern – a purgatory. The two customary architectural views are shown: one looks down from above (a plan) and the other shows the side elevation (which gives what the actors see from the wings). Everyone in the company uses these drawings. They're our spatial blueprint for rehearsal.

11. This is a 3D model of the *Taming of the Shrew* set, generated from my technical drawing, and at the start of rehearsals, it is still very much a prototype. I 'built' this computer-aided model in virtual space so that I could fly through the set changes, move the furniture, and show the actors what it would be like not only to watch the show from any seat in the auditorium but also what it would feel like to be on the set looking out to their audience.

12. We think hard about the actors' bodies. We start by imagining them almost as so many physical blanks, then discovering a 'design signature' for the company, a costumed image that gives the ensemble a collective role or presence and that generates a collective voice. By giving the company a generic identity, particular to each play, we can dress actors up and down in full view of the audience to reflect their role, gender, status and so on. The ensemble's common outfit is often some sort of uniform. For example, in *Henry V* the troupe was a group of army squaddies in military kit, in *The Merchant of Venice* prison inmates in prison blues, in *Richard III* 'Orderlies' in white coats that made them look like workers in a hospital – or abattoir, perhaps.

13. These are parallel sets of costume designs from our 2011 double bill. In *Richard III* I used an Edwardian cut and silhouette for the costumes, with fitted tailcoats on the torsos for all the actors – but for the women characters, formal Edwardian skirts below the waist. *The Comedy of Errors* had a pop-culture aesthetic: football shirts, sombreros, smiley-face T-shirts, greased quiffs, leopard skin leggings for the carnivorous women, Dame Edna spectacles, Maggie Thatcher handbags. The two sets of costumes were designed to complement each other and support the versatility of the company, conceptually, technically and aesthetically. Propeller productions share a common visual language but apply the syntax to a full range of theatrical effects.

14. In the speculative phase of production, ideas are generated by a small group loosely called the 'creative team' – usually consisting of director and designers. We're like the 'all stars' in the headshots on the cover of this vintage programme: we've each got our 'corner'; we're individuals; the tag wrestling we do is pretty robust; but we're all working in the same creative ring. We're the ones who prepare to launch the project into the next phase, rehearsal, where ideas are developed by a much larger but equally creative collective that includes everyone working in the Propeller organization.

15. Here's the ensemble. They're a pack. Seemingly similar but each fulfilling a distinctive role. The actors are skilled at slipping effortlessly from ensemble to principal or secondary character and back again. Equally, they could 'unmask' and declare themselves to be as commonplace as the audience. I like the meerkats because they look like they might be wearing half masks. Propeller sometimes uses masks to homogenize: to turn individuals into a near-anonymous group or to mask their real-ness, to twist them into 'things'.

16. The Propeller rehearsal room is busy, but extremely focused and a lot of fun to be in. Everyone is entitled to suggest ideas and try them, but 'the play's the thing'. If an idea swerves off piste, everyone in the room shouts 'Story!!!' to bring the detour back on track.

17. This is a production photograph, taken from backstage, behind the scenery. It shows the performers' view looking on to their designed acting space, in this case, the set for *Rose Rage*, Propeller's two-part adaptation of Shakespeare's *Henry VI* trilogy. I use materials in set design that, when back-lit, allow the audience to see 'behind' and 'off'; and likewise that allow the actors, offstage, to see 'on', to see all the activity onstage. This empowers them and makes an easy transition from the open rehearsal room (where the actors are all always present and seeing everything) to the stage. Everything in a Propeller design looks 'declared' – though actually, it's not.

18. The business of constructing the set, particularly for the first time in situ, can be immensely complex – as you can see from this high-angle view of a theatrical get-in that's showing the stage crew erecting the set in an empty space. Propeller makes duplicates of everything scenic so that we can tour across continents, sending the set and props by sea or land in two opposite directions while the company flies from location to location with their costumes as luggage. Engineering has to be exact and the resulting environment robust to withstand the intense physicality of the actors over nine months.

19. This shows the production from 'out front', from the spectator's point of view. The design has absorbed ideas from Resnais's *L'Année dernière à Marienbad*. The box trees that edge this formal garden can be picked up, pushed around and thrown. Being tapered at the top, the topiary leaves plenty of visual space for the actors' gestures whilst maintaining the illusion that they're hidden. The actor who played Olivia here is playing a *statue* of Olivia. He's masked – to show that he's a 'thing', that he's not to be confused with the 'real' Olivia (though the joke is that this statue can move, can change poses). Ironically, the forged letter was 'concealed' on the statue. When our Malvolio spotted it, it was being held between the statue's fingers (making a dubious gesture).

20. Finally, the collaboration in a Propeller production directly and continually involves the audience: we don't have a production until the play meets the audience. We now know that the experience of a Propeller show can have a moving affect on spectators' lives beyond the walls of the theatre. This letter gives an account of how a production can change a working life. It documents impact.

CCR: So that's the whistle-stop tour. Now, Michael, can you take us back through the process in more detail, unpacking some of those images? Am I right to think that, starting right at the beginning of a project, you're juggling four elements, you're working simultaneously from four points of departure: one, your initial conversations with your director, your 'chat' with Ed Hall; two, the text, the Shakespeare play you're going to produce; three, the ensemble, the men in black, the meerkats (as you've shown them in the Pecha Kucha), all of them individuals, but a collective who are a gang supporting each other; four, your pencil, that rather old-fashioned, humble instrument of design?

MP: Yes – that's right. But let me go back one step, to remind you that when you asked me to suggest a title for this talk, something that responded to 'working with Shakespeare' and 'making a play work', I remembered a bit from *Henry IV*, and thought it could be our strap line. I've not designed *Henry IV*, but the line seemed to leap out at me,

11. The designer's primary material: the Propeller actor ensemble, 2006–7. From left to right, Jon Trenchard, Dominic Tighe, Dugald Bruce-Lockhart, Bob Barrett, Chris Myles, Tam Williams, Tony Bell, Simon Scardifield, Joe Flynn, Jack Tarlton, Alasdair Craig, Jason Baughan.

to address another question you put, about why I do the work of designing Shakespeare. Hal says, 'If all the year were playing holidays, to sport would be as tedious as to work.' I don't subscribe to that because I spend all my working life 'playing'; my 'work' is 'sport' and it's rarely tedious. Designing Shakespeare, I have such fun; we all have such fun. The work requires discipline, without a doubt, and a meshing of disciplines (it's trans-disciplinary), but nevertheless at Propeller we have a great time.

CCR: I like it! A 'strap line' that works by contradiction! So – where does your 'working holiday' start?

MP: Where do I start? I start here. These are the boys [Illustration 11]. The ensemble. An unashamedly masculine bunch that allows us to approach Shakespeare in an overtly physical way. In the rehearsal room, as the clothes here indicate, everybody has an equal voice.

We throw in ideas that are filtered by the company, and we keep a very close eye on the story line. We keep very close to the narrative thrust.

We're scrupulous about telling the story clearly and if anybody makes a suggestion, the response is 'Right, let's try it, let's actually do it physically; put it on its feet.' Sometimes I'll be there, and sometimes not, but if the idea looks like it's straying from Shakespeare's text into a self-indulgent world, into a conceptual world that's disconnected from the drive of the narrative, that's a detour, we have a tradition, now, that the company will shout 'STORY!' – as in 'What has this got to do with the story?' This reconnects us; putting us back on track.

CCR: This image of 'the boys': this is your raw material, this is the blank canvas you start with?

MP: Yup.

CCR: Because you have these specific bodies in mind when you start thinking about the relationship between body and text and the materials that you're going to be using as you design the sets and costumes?

MP: That's right, and I respect them hugely. I come from a performance background myself.

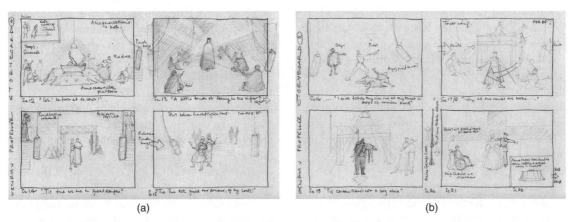

(a)   (b)

12. Designer's storyboard for *Henry V* (2011–12).

I got my Equity card performing, and I have a maxim in three parts: I respect the fears actors have when they're onstage, I respect and admire their ingenuity, both in the rehearsal room and onstage, and I also share in their respect for discipline. The interchange between us – between the actor and the designer – is very, very important. Our dialogue goes on all the time.

CCR: What do you – what does Propeller – mean by that word 'ensemble'?

MP: Here are four definitions that I've come across, some that have been said to me, some that have been written, some by my students. All of them apply to Propeller:

All the performers are on stage all the time.
The whole story is told by a chorus.
All the performers have an equal voice in the rehearsal process
– it's democratic.
It's a collective – all the actors are paid the same.

None of them quite clinches what 'ensemble' means as Propeller practises it, but this one probably comes closest:

The whole production is greater than the sum of its parts.

Having worked in both America and the UK, I think the North American take on the 'ensemble' comes closest to my view, to my politics: they extend the word beyond the acting company, to

other parts of the organization, to stage and company management, technicians, administrators. It's that extended understanding of 'ensemble' that we've brought home to Propeller. We try not only to wind it into our mission statement for the Arts Council, but to practise it.

Now, I draw quite a bit. I have this pencil. See: here it is. I'm not going to use it, but I sort of need it. It's a safety net, another limb. I use it in conversations, the ones right at the beginning of the process, with Ed. I use it to record what's going on and somehow to crystallize the discussion – so drawing is a form of notation, for me. Illustration 12 shows what I do with the pencil.

This is a storyboard of two sequences from *Henry V*. I put it together by running through a number of drawings, most of them first written into my script – which, if you recall, I use as a sketchbook. I take them out and I put them onto separate sheets of paper and then I assemble them into this storyboard – I call it a storyboard because that's the most familiar term for what is essentially a road map of moments, of events – events that we pitch at the company as a narrative tool-kit, a framework to work with. I'll also include in my notation relevant lines from the play. I will try to get a sense of where and who the audience are in relation to these events: where the interval comes is very important. What the storyboard gives us is a fluid way of seeing a prototype and, because the frames are done with this very, very crude and wonderful thing called a pencil, it means that they look provisional, disposable. They look plastic.

CCR: Provisional – because you always want to leave space in your design for the actor? Space so that the actors can see that this drawing isn't finished, that you haven't conceptualized everything for them, that there's a space for their creativity when they walk into the space and start working in it?

MP: Yes, that's right.

CCR: And the other thing is that you're always thinking about the audience and who they are and where they are and how they're going to be collaborating with the process. So this is a design that is very much organized for actors, but also one that's thinking about how spectators are going to respond and be part of that creative process?

MP: Absolutely. I've used arrows in the storyboard; not just because it's about Agincourt. There's an arrow in the drawing that's shooting through the proscenium, and that arrow is a 'note to self', a note to the company, a note for Ed. It indicates, 'This is where we'll assault the audience.'

CCR: 'Assaulting the audience' is dear to the heart of the Propeller aesthetic, isn't it?

MP: Yes – as you can see if you go on-line and look at any of the promotional trailers we've started producing for our shows.[1] They're film trailers, unashamedly in a film idiom – a paradox, perhaps, that I've been challenged on, and asked 'Why use film to promote live Shakespeare?' My answer is that the trailers capture our aesthetic; they simulate our style. Film works in close-up – like Propeller works on stage. A Propeller production always gets very close to the audience – hence the notion of an 'assault'.

You'll notice, too, that the storyboard drawing is a form of close-up; it's an iris. I shutter in or edit out distractions – and by 'distractions', I sort of mean the set. I'm becoming more and more convinced that I need to simplify my work and concentrate on pertinent objects, bodies and people, character and voice, and to present a platform for the voice and for the text through the voice. So these close-ups in the storyboard tend to ignore the fact that there is a

very expensive framework or skeleton surrounding and supporting the primary relationship that I'm interested in, between 'the boys', the audience and Shakespeare's words.

Storyboarding also gives us an opportunity to think about continuity: about how images from our previous productions link into the current production. In this case, I have in mind images across the Histories. Propeller is currently devising a big project – whose working title is *Bloodline*. We're aiming to put together into a cycle all of the history plays we've produced so far. Ed and I are now very conscious of images that bookend the plays, and how we might pick up the final image from the last history play at the beginning of the next. So, in the corner of the final frame in my storyboard at the bottom right you can see the coffin of Henry V, an image that will be taken up at the opening of the sequel to *Henry V*, *Rose Rage*.

Alongside the storyboarding, I'm building three-dimensional models [Illustration 13]. They're very time-consuming to make (I have assistants, thankfully). They're built to 1:25 scale. And they're really our pre-rehearsal rehearsal rooms. They're where Ed and I sit down, in my studio, and look at possibilities. Models offer a relatively cheap way of testing ideas. At this stage, if we want to scrap something or change something, we can. So we make some far-reaching decisions in my studio with the maquette.

CCR: The 3-D model is something like 24 × 24 × 24 inches [= 61 cm], the size of a doll's house?

MP: Yes. It's big enough to get our hands in, and their seductive impression is sometimes referred to as 'the doll's house factor'.

CCR: Looking at these models and the what they're showing about the parallel designs you created for productions of the two very different Shakespeare plays that Propeller toured back-to-back in 2011/12, *The Winters Tale* and *Henry V*, I can see how, in designing, you're creating structural components that are moveable, adaptable and multi-purpose. The look and feel of the two

---

[1] See http://propeller.org.uk/current-productions/henry-v-and-the-winters-tale/video

Henry V   The Winter's Tale

13. Three-dimensional 1:25 scale models of the *Henry V* and *The Winter's Tale* sets (2011–12).

designed worlds is completely different, *Henry V* with the gun boxes and military viewing platform, set in a red room lined with blood-red camouflage curtains, *The Winter's Tale* presided over by the grey moon in chilly, chaste, candle-lit Bohemia (where the music was made on a grand piano) while in Sicilia (where a drum kit and ear-splitting electric guitars accompanied the rave-up sheepshearing), a fantastic sunburst filled the sky. Looking at the models in close-up, I see the surfaces of the two productions as utterly distinct: the design is composed of eye-catching, poetically satisfying and *useful* visual details that work to tell the two stories. But if I look at the models (as it were) in long-shot, zooming out, I don't see the details of design. I can make out what's underneath, the built structure, the frame. In fact, the same skeleton, the same superstructure is holding up both productions.

MP: Exactly. What I'm now very aware of as a designer is how the material properties of

the set give a cue to the audience and to the performers: how, because of their material reality and believability and the audience's knowledge of what that material is, we believe we're all being told the story in the same room, even if a proscenium frame is spatially separating us from it. So at the moment I'm very interested in using recognizable materials in design, materials that convey the elemental properties of earth, air, fire and water, and materials that work like Shakespeare's verbal wit, to make ideas happen physically – like Mistress Quickly's wedding dress in *Henry V* – we made it from a recycled parachute.

Here's 'the body' (Illustration 14). In design terms, I've just been talking about 'the space'; now I'm moving on to 'the body'. This is a concept drawing. Once I'd drawn it I called it a 'concept drawing' because it struck me that it offered a way of approaching (or 'conceptualizing') the ensemble and the identity of the ensemble in one of our

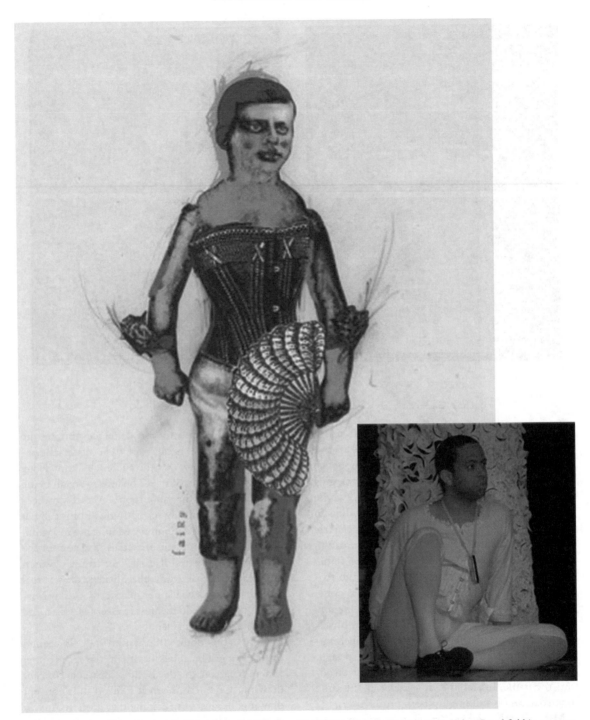

14. Concept drawing for the 'fairy basic' costume, *A Midsummer Night's Dream* (2008–09) with, inset, Kelsey Brookfield in costume.

productions. The design principle operating here is a kind of visual and structural duality: that is, in Propeller productions, characters are always both a *part* of the ensemble and a *product* of the ensemble; they melt into it; they emerge from it; they're 'chorus', they're 'characters'. To achieve this doubleness with integrity in terms of the context of the story, we have to give the ensemble a function and a corporate identity. This concept drawing came from work on *A Midsummer Night's Dream*. We started – as we always start – by asking ourselves 'Whose story is it? Who's telling the story?' In this case, taking a cue from Benjamin Britten, we decided to look at the play from the fairies' perspective, to see things from the spiritual side of the mortal/immortal divide that Shakespeare sets up in the play, and to look curiously from 'fairyland' back across that frontier into the mortals' world. So in this *Dream* the fairies would be telling the story.

What I attempted to do with the concept drawing was to show the company what their corporate 'uniform' would look like, how, as part of the 'fairy ensemble', they would present as androgynes, but then, emerging from the ensemble to play Theseus, Hermia, Bottom, Wall or whoever, they would put costumes on top of their 'uniform' that would turn them into other (gendered) parts. Making them androgynous I didn't aim to airbrush their sexuality, to make them sex-less. Rather, I wanted them to be male *and* female; to be a combination of genders; to have signifiers of both sexes. So in the design, we kept the male torso, the male bust, but then we dressed it in a corset. As you can see from my concept drawing, I'm very interested in the doll as an idea, as an idea for dressing up. Dressing up is fascinating; and it's also fascinating to an audience to watch dressing up, to observe it as a theatrical technique – layering story upon story upon the body – that produces narrative consequences. The main frame (in Illustration 14), then, could be titled 'Concept: Fairy'.

But in Illustration 14, there's a second image, one I've superimposed onto the drawing. It's a production shot that shows the concept translated into costume, and what it actually looked like in performance. We dyed all the company's hair brown (except Puck's, bleached blonde). We waxed their chests. We gave them schematic make-up – white faces, rouged cheeks, exaggerated red rosebud lips, heavily pencilled artificial eyebrows. This second image, then, is our 'Actual Fairy', in uniform – and from that 'blank canvas', we then 'layered up' characters by putting character costumes on top.

CCR: I'm told that the company called the *Dream* uniform 'fairy basics': they had white knee stockings, black dance pumps, white 3/4-length cotton flannel longjohns. They had their corsets worn over white long-sleeved pyjama tops that had tiny triangle 'wings' sewn on the cuffs and a band of lace around the neck. And over their longjohns, they wore a dance belt – which looked like a cross between an early modern codpiece and a modern cricket box. From the waist up, then, they were 'girls'; from below the belt, definitely 'boys'. 'Fairy basics' was the default costume, what everybody looked like until they started stepping out of the ensemble into the roles of principals. Then they started putting on more stuff – hats, capes, skirts – which they did in full view of the audience, dressing the scene while they were playing it. I take it that this is standard operating proceedure for Propeller, which means that you never stop for scene or costume changes. Design never stops the play. The performance runs continuously. And *that* means that a Propeller show is very, very fast-paced. Actors are moving into and out of character all the time, constantly doubling; but because they put on the doubles in front of your eyes, you're never confused about who's playing what and, most wonderfully, you're never unaware that *they are playing*, that what you're watching is a huge game, a play.

MP: Yes – and watching actors working with my designs is part of the satisfaction of being a designer. What you saw in Illustration 14 was me working conceptually. Illustration 15 gives an example of a different way of working. It shows how my designs can emerge from conversations with a particular actor, listening to an actor's ideas, which produces questions and further thoughts and in this case, a creative meeting of minds. Also

15. Collage of visual sources absorbed into design for Richard's costume in *Richard III* (2010–11).

how design operates by methodological collage. This is my design for actor Richard Clothier's Richard III. It developed from a conversation, a telephone conversation, actually, in advance of rehearsal. We all remember Antony Sher's 'spider' – the way Sher took the image of the 'bottled spider' that he found in Shakespeare's text and made it the key to his physical performance. But Clothier said, '*He's a crab. He's a fiddler crab.*' To which I replied, '*Okay . . . .?*' I was perplexed. '*Crab?*' But Clothier replied, '*No, no, no, no. Don't think "crab" as a kind of animal, or how scary crabs can be. Think "crab" as "structure", "asymmetry".*' I found a picture of a fiddler crab on the internet – and used it as a visual prompt to work with Richard's body to make it as asymmetrical as possible. Then other ideas went into the mix – like Murnau's Nosferatu, which I adore, and which you can see in the top corner. My

final design image was a combination of the fiddler crab and Nosferatu. Then Richard had this superb idea for his deformity: that instead of a withered left hand he'd have a sort of a mechanical stump into which he could fix a Captain Hook tool – and it could be interchangeable. So, one minute, it would be a sickle. Another minute it would be a knife. The next minute, he would pull a posy of flowers from it.

Illustration 16 shows the two sets of costume designs for the double bill we toured in 2010/11. On the left is the scheme for the whole *Richard III* wardrobe – so you can see how Richard's costume from illustration 15 fits in to the full scheme. The style is essentially Edwardian, not because we're interested in 'period' design as such but because, as we're thinking about building our *Bloodline* cycle of history plays, we need the design to key into

16. Two sets of costume designs for Propeller's double bill, *Richard III* and *The Comedy of Errors* (2010–11).

sequential periods of dress that we know audiences will instantly recognize and that will 'place' the play for them, and that will then locate it alongside the other eras we're proposing for the other history plays in the cycle. So it's inter-generational. The pair of lads in the middle – the ones carrying the head and the hacksaw and wearing the white gowns and the surgical masks over their faces: they're the 'ensemble'. That costume is this production's 'uniform'.

CCR: So if *A Midsummer Night's Dream* was a story told by fairies, *Richard III* –

MP: – was a story being told from inside Richard's head by this 'chorus of the faceless'.

CCR: So what the design contrived to do was to turn Richard inside out – to 'people' his mind, to make the inward outward and to externalize his brain, to act out his psyche in view of the audience?

MP: That's right – the ensemble were extrapolated from Richard's internal workings; they were *part* of Richard.

CCR: Who were they? What was their 'corporate identity'?

MP: Hospital 'Orderlies' – working in a kind of psychiatric unit. Colluding with him at the beginning. Then as the play's dynamic swings and Richard loses his mind, in this production he

literally lost it. The 'Orderlies' doubted his behaviour, started to rebel and finally carried him away.

CCR: 'Orderlies' who were responsible for choreographing mayhem! They were pretty terrifying – armed to the teeth with sharp tools and saws that you'd find in autopsy suites *and* abattoirs. (I thought they might double as meat packers in that 1906 tale of the Chicago stockyards, Upton Sinclair's *The Jungle*.) As it happened, the 'Orderlies' costume normalized the gallons of blood Propeller washed across the stage in this *Richard*. And the other characters shown in the costume drawing? Who are they?

MP: Standing to the right of the 'Orderlies' are the Murderers – the pair who assassinate Clarence. We saw them as a music hall double act – gallows humour – another Propeller trademark. The female characters below – Queen Elizabeth, Anne, Margaret – wear costumes that split and display gender – both the actors' (who are cross-dressing) and the characters' (who in this play are tough viragos, manly women). They have a formal masculine Edwardian upper half and a formal feminine Edwardian lower half.[2]

---

[2] See http://propeller.org.uk/archive/richard–iii/video

Richard III   The Comedy of Errors

17. Renderings of set designs for *Richard III* and *The Comedy of Errors* (2010–11).

CCR: And the other set of costume designs in Illustration 16 – they're for *The Comedy of Errors*, right? But they aren't drawings, are they? It looks like you're using a very different technique to come up with these images.

MP: I get very bored with my own methodologies – so I'm constantly re-thinking process, jettisoning the last procedure to think about how I might re-present design ideas and, in fact, how to *generate* design ideas. Costume ideas for *The Comedy of Errors* included a multicoloured antidote to the monochromatic *Richard III* : visually bold, and brash, and loud – developed as the result of a process of direct consultation with the performers. I hung plastic envelopes on the wall of the rehearsal room at the start of rehearsals and asked for their suggestions. They slipped them in. I scooped them up and made collages – which started (unlike the *Richard* drawings, which were produced before the final casting was done) with actors' faces and bodies. I knew who would be playing Luciana, the Dromios, the Courtesan. I stuck their photographs in the frame then started building their characters up from their input. We went out, shopped, and basically what you see in the design collage is what they got. It sounds easy – but in fact, it was tough to realize. My only schematic requirement for the costume collection was that somewhere along the bottom halves, all the costumes would include shades of blue. I'm always interested, as a designer, in how the characters contribute the scenic world, how the characters are themselves aspects of scenography. So in *Comedy*, there was a blue Aegean horizon that continually shifted throughout the play.

CCR: So you wanted the costumes to 'remember' the shifting horizon?

MP: Something like that . . . and you need to design the costumes into a specific space. So to complete my 'designer's journey' from 'body' to performance, I give you Illustration 17.

These are renderings for the sets. They aren't photographs of the built set – although they look like it. They're my antidote to model-making. I got fed up with building 3-D miniatures so I started making virtual models, on the computer, where I could produce much more vivid renderings of scenic ideas that I could pitch to the company. Importantly, what I was able to do on the first day of rehearsal was to project my virtual design large-scale. Normally, we'd all be peering into a little box and the guy at the front would get the best view and the guy at the back – well, '*hard cheese!*' What I have developed now is a way of presenting the design to make the occasion democratic and accessible, so the whole company are together at the 'off'. Very importantly, renderings allow us to see what the audience will see on stage roughly in the relationship that the audience will have to it.

CCR: Your rendering for *Richard* shows an NHS disaster zone – a ward trolley (that, cunningly, could be converted into a wheel chair – or throne), mobile privacy screens, a row of rickety metal staff lockers, the kind of thick PVC industrial slashed curtains you find in hospital corridors (and the back rooms of butcher shops), that gantry on wheels that could be curtained off with see-through plastic sheets for interiors – and executions. And the flag-pole – flying the Cross of St George: which puts in an appearance in every Propeller history play. The whole place grey, gloomy, derelict. A design that puts the 'winter of our discontent' squarely in view. And then alongside *Richard*, using the same metal super-structure, you've got *Comedy*!

MP: We set it on a holiday island – a terrible place where people can pretend to be other people, so the other central design condition that I put to Ed was that everything had to look fake.[3] Absolutely everything. So those high street shop shutters that have a rather attractive, transluscent surface, finally have a grungy grafittied reality – you just *know* that all the merchandise they sell inside is imitation tat. You can also see the characters that populate this holiday island crashing through them and from beyond them. The ubiquitous flagpole from the Histories has now become a sort of Vene-tian icon laced with '*fun-fun-fun*' lightbulbs. This world's link with *Richard* is that it, too, is morally and materially derelict.

CCR: So when, as a designer, is your job done? When's the holiday over? On press night? Or not until the last performance in the last tour date – the last get-out, when costumes, sets, props are packed up for the last time and sent home for breaking up or recycling?

MP: Certainly, one big leg of the journey is over when the production meets the audience. That's when we know something about the impact we're making – lasting impact is hugely significant to the whole company. So I want to end our conversa-tion by saying something about it, first quoting a lad, aged 13, in Kent, who'd just seen Propeller's *Pocket Dream* (2010). He wrote, 'Well, *that* was

certainly worth missing the football for!' (Of course he must be mistaken. *Nothing* is ever worth miss-ing the football for!) But that sort of comment is heartening. So is fan mail – like this letter the com-pany received a couple of weeks ago.[4] Of course everyone loves fan mail; it's flattering. But this let-ter from Derbyshire (and from a spectator who's seen our work across the years from *Henry V* and *Richard III* to *The Merchant of Venice*, *The Taming of the Shrew*, *A Midsummer Night's Dream*, *The Win-ter's Tale*, *The Comedy of Errors*) is more than that. First, it reviews highlights of Propeller's history in one paragraph, but then it goes on to articulate the impact that Shakespeare and our company has on people in grounded, important, perplexing, every-day life.

It reads:

Dear Propeller,
Most viscerally, it's the moments around the text that get me: begrudgingly trudging through the rain for a pair of brown eyes; the terror of Scroop as he waits for exe-cution; the suppressed fidgeting of Henry as he wades through Sallic swamps towards the "yes" he needs. Of course, the sheep, and the sparkler up the arse. Portia's lip licks; Nerissa's card tricks. The casual violence to tame the Shrew, and the slapstick gore of Richard's body bags. The faeries breathing in and out as one. Always, the music. But it is also the new-ness, the first-time-ness, that you-have-really-done-the-work-ness of the text. "For if you hide the crown even in your heart, there will he rake for it". I've never really heard that line before. Interest-ing. A line I would assume belongs to Coriolanus rather than Henry, who's a little bit chummy, a little bit prone to touching in the night whether you're Olivier's Henry, or Branagh's or Propeller's. To come away from each pro-duction with a new regard for the text is an extra gift. The other gift – a treasure, really – is to be allowed to know you as an ensemble, a troupe. I've spent happy hours rummaging in Shakespeare since adolescence, but it's only since discovering Propeller that I've really understood what it would have meant to go see The Chamberlain's Men, or The King's Men, or Kempe or

---

3   See: http://propeller.org.uk/archive/the-comedy-of-errors/ video

4   We're very grateful to Rebecca Widdowson for giving us permission to quote her letter in full.

Burbage or Tarleton. I love it when you are cast unexpectedly, and I love it that you're so versatile, and so profoundly good at doing your jobs, and that we're allowed to see all that. It's exciting how you re-create yourselves like a football team: your players move to Real Madrid, or China, and your fans fear it's the end. But, here you are next season, still Propeller, still winning the league but with a holding mid-fielder rather than a tricksy striker. (It is too odd, though, when you turn up in Northern Broadsides or *Swallows and Amazons*, and you're wearing the wrong kit.) This is a love-letter, but it's also a thank-you letter, from a Mummy, whose endless task of counting Roo's vests threatens to overwhelm all other facets of her self. Through going to your shows, I have recourse to the world I used to inhabit. I can know it will still be there when the vests are counted. I feel for you. Your work is to summon the rough magic, but to have to do it every bloody evening at 7.30, whether or not you have a cold, when you don't want to be in bloody Sheffield, and you just want to be at home and not have to bother for a while . . . it must be a monumental task, sometimes. Thank you for doing it, and giving of your selves. I hope you won't mind me presuming a non-existing intimacy, in order to thank you, honestly. Having Propeller is an illumination in the often dull manuscript of getting through the days. Thank you all for playing.

CCR: I started off this conversation calling you 'a manual labourer' working with Shakespeare who 'happens also to be a poet of the material imagination'. The writer from Derbyshire tells us why the 'making' you do as labourer and poet matters so much 'in the real world'. What I've found fascinating about the journey you've mapped is not just the ducks into the lay-bys that have given me a chance to stop and study what your creativity has produced. It's also the sense that we've been travelling in time: your battered scale rule at one end of your career, and still in use; the computer screen as draughtsman's table at the other end; drawing with your arm-extension pencil — and more recently with a mouse; work that reaches back to connect you with the kind of playhouse doodling we can see in Philip Henslowe's Elizabethan theatre account book and forward to the next generation of CGI, that spans the stubbornly real and the teasingly virtual but that's always interested in achieving a perspective. You make us look. And give us a place to look from, stuff to look at, so that we listen to Shakespeare. When you and Propeller do the work of the play, you make the play work. Thank you for talking about it.

'ON THE WRONG TRACK TO OURSELVES': ARMIN SENSER'S *SHAKESPEARE* AND THE ISSUE OF ARTISTIC CREATIVITY IN CONTEMPORARY GERMAN POETRY

TOBIAS DÖRING

Stratford-upon-Avon, November 1615, a grey and rainy day. An old man sitting by the fireplace, contemplating his adventurous life and brooding on the burning question where, at the many junctures of his journey, he went wrong. Talking partly to himself and partly to his daughter, prompted by her reproachful words, he tries to piece together an account of his existence and answer to her angry pleas – both dialogue and monologue, both self-defence and self-examination. But he is in ill health, in need of medical assistance, and eventually faints from the fatigue of recollection and remorse. When he comes round again, he can hardly remember who he is.

This is the setting and the speaking situation of Armin Senser's *Shakespeare*, a novel in verse published in 2011 by Carl Hanser, one of Germany's most prestigious literary presses.[1] The author is Swiss, born in 1964 in Biel and now living in Berlin, a prize-winning poet whose debut *Großes Erwachen* (Great awakening) came out in 1999, also with Hanser, followed by two other poetry collections over the next eight years. His books all attracted a fair amount of favourable attention from reviewers, brought him literary awards and established him among the leading German-writing poets of his generation. His *Shakespeare*, however, seems to mark a new departure in his work. Senser clearly ranks as a *poeta doctus*, a scholarly and serious poet steeped in the tradition of classic lyric forms such as the eclogue or the elegy, whose potentials he likes to revive and put to the test for contemporary concerns. In 2010, Senser published 'Die menschliche Komödie' (The human comedy), a

long poem dramatizing the encounter of a present-day reader with Dante, whom he happens to meet at a buffet reception and involves in an informal chat about literature and life. In this way, several of his earlier poems already include story-telling elements; yet the extended narrative of an entire novel in verse, with 62 chapters and some 8,000 lines, is certainly an innovation in his oeuvre and, in the entire literary scene of our time (not just in Germany), rather unusual. What is its point? Why does a contemporary poet invent such a persona, ventriloquizing Shakespeare's voice and words? What is he trying to pursue or produce when following his tracks – or rather, the tracks laid out by the biographers and mythographers of Shakespeare's afterlife? What are we as readers actually witnessing in Senser's text: an elegy perhaps on the masquerades of a theatrical life, set in the appropriate elegiac season of November, a poetic séance of lost causes, or a desire simply to speak with the dead?

Whatever it may be, Senser's *Shakespeare* merits interest as a very recent poetic work on Shakespeare and his legacies, a cultural exploration trying to determine present-day positions in the field of literature by reconnoitring this field with Shakespeare as a kind of compass. In Germany, as elsewhere, the main Shakespearian engagements take

I wish to thank all respondents to an earlier version of this paper presented at the International Shakespeare Conference, Stratford, in August 2012 for their generous comments.

[1] Armin Senser, *Shakespeare. Ein Roman in Versen* (München, 2011). Quotations from this book will be referenced in brackets with the abbreviation *Sh*.

place of course on the stage, not just in theatrical productions of the familiar plays but often also in their adaptations or rewritings by major literary figures like Heiner Müller, Botho Strauß, Albert Ostermaier or other well-known dramatists.[2] So what about Shakespeare's *poetic* work and its presence in contemporary German culture? And what, in particular, is different in the ways in which contemporary *poets*, as opposed to playwrights, draw on Shakespeare's texts? As regards the first question, the Sonnets no doubt must hold pride of place, surpassing in their popularity even many of the plays, especially in Germany where an incurable 'sonnetomania' has long been diagnosed.[3] The literary text most frequently translated into German, Shakespeare's Sonnets, also have a German stage life, with Robert Wilson's visually stunning version, premiered at the Berliner Ensemble in 2009, as the most prominent recent example.

As regards the second question, Neil Corcoran has recently explored the ways in which Shakespeare figures as a 'central, consuming, protean and permanent critical as well as creative concern'[4] in the work of major twentieth-century poets – Yeats, Eliot, Auden and Ted Hughes – and has established what particular challenge Shakespearian language legacies may hold for poets writing in English. In fact, Hughes himself once offered an incisive comment when comparing Shakespeare's function for dramatists with poetic projects of our time:

Modern British playwrights display in their work little filial regard for Shakespeare. Not surprising, considering how, for some three centuries, like Saturn, he devoured nearly all his dramatic inheritors alive. Toward poets, on the other hand, he seems to have proved less of a cannibal father, more of a nurturing mother. At least, that's how it has appeared to the poets.[5]

Writing in the foreword of a 1988 *Anthology of Poetry for Shakespeare*, Hughes here makes a claim not just for British poets when he sets up Shakespeare as their 'nurturing mother'. What he, in fact, claims is distance, or detachment, as the crucial condition of creation, so that poets *not* working in Shakespeare's own main medium of drama will find his model more inspiring and his legacy more liberating than playwrights who feel burdened or restricted through his overpowering presence. By the same logic of this Oedipal argument, German writers – or indeed, any non-English writers – should feel even more inspired when choosing Shakespeare as their muse, because for them the sense of cultural detachment is still greater and the sense of literary rivalry less nagging, not least by virtue of their different language. Translating Shakespeare into another verbal medium, thus appropriating his creative ancestry while also foreignizing and enriching their own language, German writers have indeed reworked Shakespearian figurations since the eighteenth century and often famously invented themselves on Shakespearian grounds.[6] In Hughes's terms, rather than let themselves be devoured by his paternal power, they have happily cannibalized his corpus and fed on it for the past 250 years – right up to the most recent German stage productions, which, crucially, also involve literary and poetic work because of their translation, often actually *new* translations and sometimes by

---

[2] Heiner Müller (1929–1995) wrote and produced rewritings of *Titus Andronicus* (*Anatomie Titus Fall of Rome: Ein Shakespearekommentar*, 1984), *Macbeth* (*Macbeth*, 1982) and *Hamlet* (*Die Hamletmaschine*, 1977); Botho Strauß (b. 1944) wrote contemporary versions of *A Midsummer Night's Dream* (*Der Park*, 1983) and *Titus Andronicus* (*Die Schändung*, 2005); Albert Ostermaier (b. 1967) wrote lyrics for a Vienna Burgtheater production of *Twelfth Night* (*zwei zimmer illyrien*, 2003); in 2012 his new version of *The Merchant of Venice* (*Ein Pfund Fleisch*) premiered at the Deutsches Schauspielhaus Hamburg, published together with other recent translations or adaptations in *Shakespeare Variationen*, ed. Uwe C. Carstensen, Stefanie von Lieven and Bettina Walther (Frankfurt a.M., 2012).

[3] Werner von Koppenfels, ' "*Dressing old words new*": William Shakespeare's Sonnets into German', in *William Shakespeare's Sonnets. For the First Time Globally Reprinted. A Quartercentenary Anthology 1609–2009*, ed. Manfred Pfister and Jürgen Gutsch (Dozwil, 2009), pp. 277–84 at 277.

[4] Neil Corcoran, *Shakespeare and the Modern Poet* (Cambridge, 2010), p. 25.

[5] Ted Hughes, 'Foreword', in *An Anthology of Poetry for Shakespeare*, ed. Charles Osborne (London, 1988), p. 5.

[6] This creative process of appropriation, or indeed annexation, has most recently been reviewed by Roger Paulin: 'Shakespeare and Germany', in *Shakespeare in the Eighteenth Century*, ed. Fiona Ritchie and Peter Sabor (Cambridge, 2012), pp. 314–30.

very well-known writers such as Peter Handke, Feridun Zaimoglu or Marius von Mayenburg.[7]

Senser's Shakespeare project clearly is in line with this tradition, specifically evoking, as I hope to suggest, the most enthusiastic and productive Shakespeare readings, or misreadings, by the German Romantics. As with all fictional inventions of a Shakespeare persona – a long-standing literary practice also in English,[8] producing often ludicrous results but with some diagnostic value for the cultural needs thus served – Senser's *Shakespeare* may perhaps come perilously close to what Peter Holland calls 'the most dangerous of all aims: to become Shakespeare in the act of writing about Shakespeare',[9] a danger to which English playwrights may indeed fall prey when they decide to dramatize their famous forebear and thereby inherit his authority. By contrast, as a German novel in verse, Senser's is a foreign, fictional and a poetic enterprise, working on the premise of this threefold distance while probing into cultural myths of authorship and creativity as well as recycling them. In fact, the text is anything but celebratory. Its mood is grey, its tone subdued and outlook rather bleak and quite depressed; the name *Stratford*, we are told at one point (*Sh* 205), rhymes with the German word *Selbstmord*, i.e. 'suicide'. And even the ending hardly offers any comfort: 'I have been more concerned with my phantasms than with real people', Senser's Shakespeare persona admits: 'I now wish I had done things differently and never written a line . . . Every line now seems like a crime to me, like a sin. A wrong track on which I have put people and will continue to put them. On the track to themselves.'[10]

These are his final words, less interesting as a sentimental confession of human failure than as a poetic palinode, i.e. a formal retraction of previous writing. Yet as such, it is a paradoxical speech act, the negation of the actual premise on which the very text we read proceeds, for, had Shakespeare never written a line, the present text entitled *Shakespeare* and retracing many of his well-known lines could never have been written either. Equally puzzling is the final point that Shakespeare has put us all on the wrong track (*Irrweg*), which

he says is the track to ourselves. This dire statement echoes Heiner Müller's famous diagnosis, made in his speech to the German Shakespeare Society in Weimar the year before the Berlin wall came down, that we have not arrived at ourselves as long as Shakespeare writes our plays.[11] It is against the background of these issues – debates on cultural authority and self-seeking along the German/Shakespeare force- and fault-lines – that I will now discuss Senser's text, paying attention to its strong engagement with poetic productivity: what are the cultural energies and models by which we can imagine writing to proceed? What uses, in particular, may Shakespeare's model have for contemporary German poetry? And *whose* Shakespeare

---

[7] Peter Handke (b. 1942) translated *The Winter's Tale* (1991) for Luc Bondy's production at the Schaubühne Berlin; the Turkish-German author Feridun Zaimoglu (b. 1964), in cooperation with Günther Senkel, wrote translations/adaptations of *Othello* (2003), *Romeo and Juliet* (2006) and *Hamlet* (2010) commissioned for Munich and Hamburg stage productions by the Belgian director Luk Perceval; Marius von Mayenburg (b. 1972) translated *Hamlet* (2008), *Othello* (2010) and *Measure for Measure* (2011) for productions at the Schaubühne Berlin, directed by Thomas Ostermeier.

[8] See, together with the ample literature they cite, Peter Holland, 'Dramatizing the Dramatist', *Shakespeare Survey 58* (Cambridge, 2005), pp. 137–47; Paul Franssen, 'Shakespeare's Afterlives: Raising and Laying the Ghost', *Critical Survey*, 21:3 (2009), 6–21; Paul Franssen, 'The Bard, the Bible, and the Desert Island', in *The Author as Character: Representing Historical Writers in Western Literature*, ed. P. Franssen and A. J. Hoenselaars (Madison, 1999), pp. 106–17; Maurice J. O'Sullivan, *Shakespeare's Other Lives: An Anthology of Fictional Depictions of the Bard* (Jefferson 1997).

[9] Holland, 'Dramatizing the Dramatist', p. 146.

[10] 'Ich habe mich mehr um meine Hirngespinste / gekümmert als um wirkliche Menschen. Und wünschte / mir, ich hätte es anders gemacht und nie eine Zeile / geschrieben. Keine einzige. Jede Zeile kommt / mir jetzt wie ein Verbrechen vor, wie eine Sünde. / Ein Irrweg, auf den ich die Menschen gebracht / habe und bringen werde. Auf den Weg zu sich selbst' (*Sh* 328).

[11] 'Shakespeare ist ein Spiegel durch die Zeiten, unsre Hoffnung eine Welt, die er nicht mehr reflektiert. Wir sind bei uns nicht angekommen, so lange Shakespeare unsere Stücke schreibt.' Heiner Müller, 'Shakespeare eine Differenz. Überarbeitete Fassung einer Rede bei den Shakespeare-Tagen in Weimar am 23. 4. 1988', in Heiner Müller, *Shakespeare Factory 2* (Berlin, 1989), pp. 227–30 at 228.

is at stake here? I would like to comment on these questions and their treatment in the text before, in a short final part, trying to place Senser's verse novel in a slightly broader framework of contemporary German culture.

* * *

'Dark is every beginning. / Whether in school or in writing.'[12] This is the opening of Chapter 5 and the first point at which Senser's text reflects on processes of writing, especially the mysterious origin whence writing springs. Over the course of the old man's musing, this Shakespeare touches many points, prominent among them his theatrical career, the uneasy oscillation between family life in Stratford and working life in London, many sexual affairs with both men and women, debates with Anne on infidelity, long conversations with his father on issues of religion in which Catholicism features largely but also, more surprisingly, Judaism and the Caballah turn out to play a major role. Family life, too, turns out to hold a few surprises: this Shakespeare discovers in old age that his first-born child, Susanna, was not fathered by himself but that Anne was sleeping around before marrying Will as a convenient match, a pattern repeating itself in the following generation when, we learn, Susanna marries John Hall while being pregnant by another man. Some of the biographical material reworked here can be traced to the usual suspects, while the rest derives from the main source to which, as Lois Potter has remarked, most Shakespeare biographers eventually confess: their own imagination.[13]

Imaginative scenes and parts are plentiful in this fictionalized version of the life. Much of the plot centres on Shakespeare's affairs in London, where he leads a stereotypically bohemian existence mingling the personal with the professional, stereotypically involving lots of sex and regularly finding inspiration for his writing from the accidents of living. He shares living quarters with a man and a woman, all three of them predictably soon sharing their beds – an experience of triangular desire and love-making which, equally predictably, soon makes it into various of his works, just as a subsequent girlfriend's death by drowning reappears as Ophelia in the brook. So far so familiar – Senser's *Shakespeare* takes the well-tried approach of biography to ransack Shakespearian texts for details of the personal life which extant documents give us so scantily. It is therefore not surprising that, among all his texts, the Sonnets again feature largely, serving to suggest the triangle of longing, loving and betrayal that the poet is said to have lived through – an unabashed revival, on Senser's part, of the well-worn Romantic notion that the Sonnets must have been the key by which the bard unlocked his heart. What is more, the Sonnets also form a main point of contention between Susanna and her father in the framing dialogue. Susanna is scandalized by their sexual revelations, so Shakespeare tells her that he never intended them for publication; the manuscript he says was stolen and given to Thorpe for unauthorized printing, with the aim of having their author compromised in public. It later turns out that the culprit of this crime was none other than Anne, the deserted Stratford wife who stole the secret Sonnets and had them published so as to revenge herself on her errant husband. On the level of its plot, then, Senser's *Shakespeare* novel strains our credulity, and indeed our patience, with its unabashed invention of a turbulent private life, full of crime, debaucheries and dissipations, as well as with its bold recycling of old myths. What are we to make of such blatantly imagined and imaginative elements? Are we seriously supposed, as twenty-first century readers, to take them for real?

My sense is that Senser's text is testing the poetic strategies of realization, i.e. of making real what has been imagined. In the context of this biographical fantasy about a writer's fictionalized life, a life turned fully into writing, imagination also marks the crucial point from which the project itself, as a novel in verse, springs. 'I am but the lines which

---

[12] 'Dunkel ist jeder Beginn. / Ob in der Schule oder beim Schreiben' (*Sh* 22).

[13] Lois Potter, 'Having our Will: Imagination in Recent Shakespeare Biographies', *Shakespeare Survey 58* (Cambridge 2005), pp. 1–8 at 1.

I have ever written',[14] this writer answers to the charges of his daughter, thus defending by defining himself as a poetic product, shaped and generated by the same faculty of imagination that is traditionally claimed to shape and generate all art. 'Loving is like writing a reaction.'[15] – 'Art can lead only to art'[16] – 'Life is what art is measured against'[17] – or 'Life is just the waste of art.'[18] These are just some of the many aphorisms which pervade this narrative throughout, self-conscious statements on the state of art or on poetic principles, by which the text establishes a meta-level of reflection, beyond the biographical tales and plots it also constantly unfolds. In all these ways, Senser's *Shakespeare* also revives a traditional idiom of artistic productivity in terms of personal experience and suffering, coupled with imaginative investments, a determined faith in the creative power of the imagination most familiar to us from Romantic texts.

'There are many arbitrary and invented characters who, when played with, become real':[19] this statement may sound like the maxim of many a biographer defending his or her invention of the Shakespearian persona they construct as an *imagined* character that eventually turns into a *real* character if only it is played with long enough – imagination realized through continued play (*Fortspielen*, in the German original). It is a statement which could serve as a maxim for the many fictional depictions of Shakespeare, from Walter Savage Landor to Anthony Burgess and beyond to Roland Emmerich, whose Shakespeare inventions eventually take on cultural life and value of their own. In fact, the statement comes from one such fiction, the Romantic novella entitled 'The Poet and his Friend' by Ludwig Tieck, published in 1829 as the third part to the trilogy of novellas in which Tieck, father of Dorothea and co-translator of the canonical German Shakespeare, summed up his life-long engagement with this poet. These three charming narratives each depict him at a different point of his career: one as the young Warwickshire lad of eleven, the next at the age of twenty-eight, just before his breakthrough on the London stage, the third as an established dramatist in the prime of life and at the climax of his fame as national bard; it

is at this point, according to Tieck's fiction, that Shakespeare talks to his close friend Southampton and explains to him his art of character, turning arbitrary and invented figures into real people ('There are many arbitrary and invented characters who, when played with, become real'). Thus the maxim, which I quoted from this conversation, serves not just as a commentary and defence of Tieck's own fictional project but also, I suggest, of Senser's.

In fact, I propose to read Armin Senser's contemporary Shakespeare fiction as a programmatic supplement to Tieck's Romantic Shakespeare fiction, adding old age as a fourth stage to Tieck's three ages of the poet and thus completing the Romantic series as well as countering its cultural agenda. For, significantly, in the nineteenth-century tradition of fictionalized Shakespeares, according to Peter Holland, the 'overwhelming emphasis' is always to portray the artist as a *young* man, a would-be writer and emerging dramatist, 'the genius waiting to be discovered, not created'.[20] By contrast, portraits of an old, withdrawn and resigned Shakespeare – as shown, for instance, also in Bond's *Bingo* (1973) – are rather rare for earlier writers and Romantic artists who like to project their own aesthetic aspirations onto this culturally hallowed figure. In contrast and in complement to this tradition, Senser's dramatist is embittered, dying and despairing, a one-time genius in retirement, embodying post-prodigy and the afterlife of creativity. That is to say, Senser's *Shakespeare* does not only revive but, at the same time, also reverses the Romantic Shakespeares. If the Romantic revival of the Sonnets was based, as

---

[14] 'Ich bin nur die Zeilen, die ich je geschrieben habe' (*Sh* 133).

[15] 'Liebe ist wie Schreiben eine Reaktion' (*Sh* 48).

[16] 'Kunst kann nur zu Kunst führen' (*Sh* 84).

[17] 'das Leben ist, woran man die Kunst misst' (*Sh* 139).

[18] 'das Leben ist nur der Abfall / der Kunst' (*Sh* 170).

[19] 'Es gibt viele willkürlich angenommene Charaktere, die durch Fortspielen zu wirklichen werden.' Ludwig Tieck, *Shakespeare-Novellen*, ed. Joachim Lindner (Berlin, 1981), p. 271.

[20] Holland, 'Dramatizing the Dramatist', p. 144.

Manfred Pfister argues,[21] on a threefold misreading – reading them as expressions of authentic feelings, reading them as a novel in verse, and reading them in terms of latter-day sexual notions – Senser's project is these misreadings writ large: his text insists on following their understanding on all three accounts, claiming what Romantic readers claimed, as if to argue that their wrong track is the only track by which poetic productivity may once have worked. Yet precisely by presenting Shakespeare to us in the figure of a pathetic old man, looking back on his life's work, Senser's text offers a retrospect on the old figure of genius, the Shakespeare of creative pathos whom we find hard to imagine today. Senser's imaginative portrait both posits and casts doubt on this Romantic poet; he seems to return to us here in the semblance of a ghost, like a father figure of tradition, calling out 'remember me!', as if testing our faith.

One way, then, to account for Senser's work with Shakespeare is to see it partly in connection with, partly in juxtaposition to, the Romantics and their cult of the imagination, as formulated in Tieck's Shakespeare novellas and their poetological debates. But we should also note another way in which we may see Senser's project, when we place it in relation to modernism and to W. H. Auden. In his debut collection twelve years earlier, Senser published a poem entitled 'Letter to W. H. Auden', which is relevant in our context. Here the persona of the present poet addresses Auden in the following terms: 'We have never been introduced / But verses like yours leave traces / when they awaken. . . . What we call muse / turns out to be just copulating words / or times. For every work needs for / subsistence the entire past.'[22] Senser's *Shakespeare*, in the sense suggested by these early lines, can be seen to subsist on Auden's Shakespeare project *The Sea and the Mirror*,[23] written and first published during World War Two, his powerful poetic sequence on *The Tempest*, a programmatic text that Auden liked to call his *ars poetica* in the same way he believed *The Tempest* to be Shakespeare's,[24] that is to say, a poetic artwork which self-consciously explores and reflects the principles and possibilities of art, hence of itself.

This, arguably, is also the case in Senser's *Shakespeare*. Just as *The Sea and the Mirror* imagines and poetically projects what might happen after the end of a *Tempest* performance, recasting Shakespeare's figures into their own roles and making them speak in defamiliarized voices, this poetic narrative makes Shakespeare himself the speaker of his own life, after its public performance has ended, so as to consider what remains when, like Prospero, he has renounced his potent art. For this version does not just imagine, invent or recycle scenes from a poet's life and work but also, crucially, explores the *conditions* of imagination, literary invention or, as a last resort, literary recycling, i.e. the conditions by which a present poet's life and work must always subsist and draw on past traditions, while also redrawing them. For as much as our literary present is shaped by the past, this very past turns out, as Senser's *Shakespeare* amply demonstrates, to be contingent on contemporary acts of shaping and reshaping, i.e. the past is also product of the present. Old verse leaves traces, Senser writes to Auden, and it is these traces, or tracks, in our present-day language and poetic diction which he follows when inventing himself as a poet by means of imagining his version of an earlier poet for himself. What is commonly called a poetic 'muse', he calls 'just copulating words' – a powerfully suggestive phrase to mark both sexual and linguistic acts, the *copula* also being the type of verb that connects the subject of a sentence to its complement. In such a sexual-linguistic double-sense, 'copulating' means both to produce discourse and to produce offspring.

---

21 Manfred Pfister, '"*Mein Lebenszins, er liegt in dieser Schrift*": Essay', in *Shakespeare: Die Sonette*. Bilingual edition, trans. Christa Schuenke (Munich, 1999), pp. 174–94 at 177.

22 'Wir wurden uns leider nie vorgestellt. / Jedoch Verse wie die Ihren hinterlassen, / wenn sie aufwachen, Spuren. [. . .] / Was wir dann Muse nennen, / entpuppt sich als kopulierende Worte – / oder Zeiten. Denn jedes Werk braucht für / seinen Unterhalt die ganze Vergangenheit.' Armin Senser, *Großes Erwachen: Gedichte* (Munich, 1999), p. 18.

23 W. H. Auden, *The Sea and the Mirror: A Commentary on Shakespeare's 'The Tempest'* [1944], ed. Arthur Kirsch (Princeton, 2003).

24 Auden, *The Sea and the Mirror*, p. vii.

The most powerful manifestation of this double-principle in Senser's *Shakespeare* comes in Chapter 40 when the poet, instead of sleeping with the girl he happens to find in his bed, reads to her a poem from *The Passionate Pilgrim*, a text familiar to us as Sonnet 144 – 'Two loves I have, of comfort and despair' – but rendered here in an alluring, unfamiliar version,[25] half-poetic translation, half-colloquial transformation, full of half-rhymes and half-prose: contemporary German words copulating with Shakespearian words so that the actual text we read, Senser's hybrid text, strictly forms the copula, i.e. the connecting verbal element between the present and the past. Thus, Sonnet 144, with its triangle of doubt and desire, the speaker situated between good angel and evil angel as in the traditional triangle of the moralities, here emerges as the key device by which the present poet triangulates contemporary relations to Shakespearian legacies, the key by which he does not seek to unlock anybody's *heart* but to understand his *art*, contemporary art in its double determination by inherited as well as by invented traditions.

In this perspective, Senser's plot of the pirated sonnets reads rather like a commentary on his own project and his own productive process through which he grafts a current idiom in German poetry on Shakespeare's purloined letters, in fact continuing and repeating previous acts of German poetry production which, since the later eighteenth century, have sought to found themselves on Shakespearian idioms. In Senser's case, this line of the literary tradition is less given than retraced and partly reproduced, as we have seen, in the narrative. 'Shakespeare' serves here as the name both of the biographical persona and of the literary text we read, the novel in verse entitled *Shakespeare*. For this reason, we may perhaps also read the Shakespeare figure's many sexual affairs with various men and women that we find in Senser's text as a commentary on its own intertextual process, engaging in creative intercourse and discourse with a considerable line of counterparts, in the linguistic double sense of 'copulation' established earlier. In fact, the discursive connection thus drawn between artistic production and sexual reproduction forms

a topos in the literary tradition, discussed at greater length by David Wellbery,[26] i.e. a traditional way of speaking about art and literature and of conceptualizing their origins through notions of begetting and conception, pregnancy and birth.[27] This topos, Wellbery argues, long established in Western philosophy and aesthetics, was especially powerful and often used in early nineteenth-century Germany, the time of the Romantics and their incipient Shakespeare projects.[28] What does this mean for poetry and art in our time?

* * *

In a short and final part, I would like to place our particular example into a somewhat broader frame and briefly refer to two other examples of working with Shakespeare in contemporary German culture, in particular working with the Sonnets and

---

[25] Zwei Beziehungen sind, als hätte man zwei Seelen,
   die einen gleichzeitig trösten und fertigmachen.
   Die eine männlich, schön und von Herzen
   gut, die weibliche dagegen nur durchtrieben.
   Weiblicher Charme, der, nicht von dieser Welt,
   alles hat, meine bessere Hälfte rumzukriegen.
   Und, was mir heilig ist, in was Schlechtes verwandelt.
   Und Überheblichkeit es überheblich aussehen
   lässt. Schlecht gemacht, was einem heilig ist,
   lässt einen besser davon schweigen.
   Schließlich sind beide einander, was du bist,
   was uns alle und dich nur zum Leiden
   bringt. Was weiß ich. Ich hoffe nicht.
   Solange die schlechte Hälfte Gutes verspricht.   (*Sh* 219)

[26] David E. Wellbery, 'Kunst – Zeugung – Geburt: Überlegungen zu einer anthropologischen Grundfrage', in *Kunst – Zeugung – Geburt: Theorien und Metaphern ästhetischer Produktion in der Neuzeit*, ed. Christian Begemann and David E. Wellbery (Freiburg, 2002), pp. 9–36.

[27] Wellbery shows that 'terms like "begetting" and "conception", "pregnancy" and "birth", "genealogy", "fatherhood" and "motherhood" have long marked out a discursive field for plotting theories of artistic or intellectual production and thus for negotiating the relationship between nature and culture'. 'Begriffe wie "Zeugung, Empfängnis und Konzeption, Schwangerschaft und Geburt, Genealogie, Vaterschaft und Mutterschaft" stecken ein diskursives Feld ab, auf dem Theorien der künstlerischen bzw. intellektuellen Hervorbringung entworfen werden und das Verhältnis von Natur und Kultur schlechthin zur Debatte steht' (Wellbery, 'Überlegungen', p. 10).

[28] Wellbery, 'Überlegungen', p. 16.

their sexual-textual doubling. These two examples appeared in 2000 and 2010, so they precede Senser's novel in verse and they offer, I think, relevant relations to his project which I would like to suggest without, however, suggesting actual influence. One of these examples is a translation of the Sonnets, the other a citation of the Sonnets and their staging in the medium of film.

In 2000, the poet and novelist Ulrike Draesner published *Twin Spin*, her German rendering of 17 sonnets in a version she calls 'radical translation', inspired by a recent scientific breakthrough in reproductive biology, the successful birth of the first mammal to be cloned from an adult somatic cell, the British sheep called Dolly. As Draesner explains in her afterword, she happened to be picking up her volume of Shakespeare Sonnets from the shelf in spring 1997 when all the media were full of stories about Dolly and cloning, so it occurred to her that the semantic texture of the Sonnets – 'From fairest creatures we desire increase' – might also be reproduced in such a way: 'these poems', she decided, 'speak of cloning'.[29] With this calculated reconsideration Draesner is also, in fact, risking a retrospect on the notorious German Sonnet readings of the 1930s when the procreation series was openly interpreted in terms of racist anthropology and eugenics and declared as evidence that Shakespeare would approve of Nazi ideology to ensure pure human breeding.[30] In this historical perspective, Draesner's bold literary engagement with cloning as a technique of asexual biological reproduction may be seen to redress such a racist legacy by reinterpreting its premise through contemporary science as well as contemporary language. Her resultant German Sonnet versions deliberately transgress the limits of translation, searching for non-established word meanings and unconventional effects, suffusing the familiar poems with scientific language and harsh, disturbing verbal contrasts, so that they rather sound like poetry by Gottfried Benn. Continuing the Sonnets' quibbling on the name of Will and its slippery semantics, the poet has described her own translational strategy as a '*will-ful misunderstanding*'[31] of Shakespeare, thus paying tribute to his verbal art while

defining her own art against his well-established verbal sense. In the terms suggested by Ted Hughes (as quoted on the outset) we might therefore say, Draesner has been cloning Shakespeare's poems in another and deliberately contemporary language so as not to be devoured by him as a writer. However, what is most relevant about her project, in view of Senser and his copulating words, is the connection she suggests between poetic production and asexual reproduction, writing and cloning – a figure perhaps for the problem of cultural creativity in our time. The woods of Arcady are dead, the days of genius are gone: what, then, is our working model for producing poetry and art? If the traditional topos, as discussed by Wellbery, that creation is like procreation, and writing like fathering, no longer works in our world of grey, could cloning be a viable alternative, or what sort of alternative may we imagine? Senser's Shakespeare novel, with its silly plot about uncertain fatherhood and bastard children, raises just these issues when we read this plot meta-poetically, that is, as an engagement with the contemporary possibilities of art.

This is relevant also for the other example, a recent film by German director Tom Tykwer, best known for his 1998 experimental urban drama *Lola*

---

[29] Ulrike Draesner, *to change the subject. Twin Spin. Sonette von Shakespeare. Radikalübersetzungen* (Göttingen, 2000), p. 30.

[30] At the Weimar Shakespeare conference in spring 1936, Hans Günther, who held a Chair of Racial Science (*Rassenkunde*) and was board member of the Deutsche Shakespeare-Gesellschaft, gave a lecture on 'Shakespeare's Girls and Women' in which he cited Sonnets 11 and 12 as evidence for Shakespeare's view that only the fittest and fairest should produce offspring in order to improve the quality of the race: 'Durch solche Stellen ist hinreichend belegt, daß Shakespeare auch in den Fragen der Aufartung angeführt werden darf. Kinderreichtum der Erblich-Tüchtigen und Kinderlosigkeit der Erblich-Untüchtigen sind auch bei ihm Vorbedingung für die Erhaltung und Steigerung des Wertes eines Volkes.' Hans F. K. Günther, 'Shakespeares Mädchen und Frauen', *Shakespeare Jahrbuch* 73 (Bochum, 1937), pp. 85–108 at 88; for a discussion of the intellectual and institutional context, see Ruth Freifrau von Ledebur, *Der Mythos vom deutschen Shakespeare. Die Deutsche Shakespeare-Gesellschaft zwischen Politik und Wissenschaft, 1918–1945* (Köln, 2002), pp. 201–4.

[31] Draesner, *to change the subject*, p. 32.

rennt, released under the English title *Run Lola Run*. In 2010, Tykwer released an arthouse movie entitled *Drei* (Three). It tells the story of a couple in which both partners enter into other relationships and both eventually start a sexual affair with the same man, without knowing of the other's infidelity. This bisexual man happens to be a biologist and stem cell researcher, so his scientific field, again, is cloning and in-vitro reproduction. With the story of three people, two men and a woman, who enter into mutual relations of sex, desire and betrayal, the film reproduces the triangular structure of the fair youth, the dark lady and the suffering poet from the Sonnets. And indeed, the affair begins with a chance encounter between the woman and the biologist, one night at the theatre, the Berliner Ensemble where Robert Wilson's stage production of the Sonnets is being performed, several scenes of which are featured in the film sequence. 'Why is my verse so barren of new pride?' – 'What is your substance, whereof are you made?' When these questions and Shakespearian words, spoken in translation by a German actress impersonating the figure of young Shakespeare in a Berlin stage production of the Sonnets by an American director, are now recited and reproduced in a contemporary German film about triangular relationships grafted on the triangle of Shakespeare's Sonnets – then this film, I think, must question its own substance and making, and so explore the way in which contemporary work with Shakespeare may necessarily be barren of *new* pride, but not of productivity. Like Draesner's and like Senser's project, then, Tykwer's film engages Shakespeare's poetry in a self-engagement with present-day conditions of art, i.e. artworks in the aftermath of unquestioned beliefs in genius and original creation. Which brings us, finally, back once more to Senser and his reminiscing poet on the grey and dull November day.

'It is late. You are alone. / . . . The fireplace is going. The maid has put on some more / wood. It is Sunday. There is an afterlife, just as there are dreams.'[32] In this setting, described in the opening stanza of Senser's novel in verse, the keyword is 'afterlife', *Nachleben* in the original.

The term echoes a keyword from Senser's Dante poem, which I mentioned and which says programmatically that 'after all, we too live in an afterworld', *Nachwelt*.[33] These German terms *Nachleben* and *Nachwelt* also chime in with *Nachreife*, literally 'after-ripening', the special maturing process of certain seeds or fruits when kept in storage after harvesting. In a transferred sense, *Nachleben* and *Nachreife* have come to serve a special purpose in the theory of language and translation, as proposed by Walter Benjamin in his much-cited 1923 essay 'The Task of the Translator'. Here he formulates the process by which translations age and change and so develop in accordance with the translator's own changing language over time, just as poetry when untranslated remains alive in the poet's living language. In Harry Zohn's translation, Benjamin says that translation 'is so far removed from being the sterile equation of two dead languages that of all literary forms it is the one charged with the special mission of watching over the maturing process of the original language and the birth pangs of its own'.[34] It is this maturing process of an old original, this *Nachreife des fremden Wortes*, literally the after-ripening of the foreign word, which I argue we can witness in Shakespeare's afterlife, or *Nachleben*, in contemporary German poetry: an afterlife in the enduring aftermath of understanding Shakespeare as original genius, i.e. the idea

---

32 'Es ist spät. Du bist allein. / . . . Das Feuer im Kamin brennt. Das Mädchen hat Holz / nachgelegt. Es ist Sonntag. Es gibt ein Nachleben wie es Träume gibt' (*Sh* 7).

33 'Schließlich leben auch wir in einer Nachwelt': Armin Senser, 'Die menschliche Komödie', in *Utopie und Apokalypse in der Moderne*, ed. Reto Sorg and Stefan Bodo Würffel (Munich, 2010), pp. 273–86 at 282.

34 Walter Benjamin, 'The Task of the Translator', translated by Harry Zohn, in *The Translation Studies Reader*, ed. Lawrence Venuti (London, 2000), pp. 75–85 at 78; in the German original: 'Soweit ist sie entfernt, von zwei verstorbenen Sprachen die taube Gleichung zu sein, daß gerade unter allen Formen ihr als Eigenstes es zufällt, auf jene Nachreife des fremden Wortes, auf die Wehen des eigenen zu merken.' Walter Benjamin, 'Die Aufgabe des Übersetzers' [1923], in *Illuminationen: Ausgewählte Schriften 1* (Frankfurt a. M., 1977), pp. 50–62 at 54.

which historically watched over his first translations into German. Today, by contrast, to aspire to Shakespearian genius is impossible and could only mean for poets in the afterworld, or *Nachwelt*, committing artistic suicide – which is why we are told, as mentioned, that *Stratford* rhymes with this particular German word: there is no place of living genius anymore, so that Senser's bold ventriloquy of the Romantic genius and his words must end with a poetic palinode, a formal recantation. Instead, contemporary poets like Armin Senser or Ulrike Draesner or indeed filmmakers like Tom Tykwer explore alternative approaches for our post-creative age, tracing the maturing process of Shakespeare's foreign language in contemporary culture while suffering the birth pangs of our own. This, in conclusion, may also be a reason why, as Heiner Müller said, we never quite arrive at ourselves as long as Shakespeare writes our plays and why, as Senser's Shakespeare says, it will always be the wrong track, i.e. the track of translating and foreignizing, that eventually leads us to ourselves.

'WHAT COUNTRY, FRIENDS, IS THIS?': CULTURAL IDENTITY AND THE WORLD SHAKESPEARE FESTIVAL

STEPHEN PURCELL

A banner on the publicity material for the Royal Shakespeare Company's 2012 'Shipwreck trilogy' bears the slogan 'WHAT COUNTRY FRIENDS IS THIS?' Upper case and, aside from the final question mark, unpunctuated, it is emblazoned across posters, flyers, programmes and websites, for the most part sharing its space with the logos of the World Shakespeare Festival, London 2012, and corporate sponsors BP (the irony of the association with maritime disaster being apparently lost on the latter's PR department). The question presents itself as an urgent and ubiquitous one, but one which is not without ambiguity: to which country, or countries, is the question referring? And who are the 'friends' to whom the question is addressed? In this article, I shall attempt to put this question, in various ways, to my own partial and incomplete experience as an audience member of the World Shakespeare Festival, and to Shakespeare's incorporation into the Olympics and Paralympics opening and closing ceremonies.[1]

WHAT *COUNTRY*, FRIENDS, IS THIS?

Viola's question at the beginning of *Twelfth Night* is given a fairly direct and unambiguous answer: 'This is Illyria, lady' (1.2.1). There was no such certainty, however, for the audiences of Gregory Doran's acclaimed production of *Julius Caesar*, which relocated Shakespeare's Rome to what the publicity told us was a modern African state, though it remained no more specific than that.

In many ways, the parallel works extremely well: one need not look too far back in that continent's history to find stories of republics sliding into dictatorship, of civil war, or of militaristic and dangerously charismatic leaders. Certainly Jeffery Kissoon's Caesar was loaded with references to recent historical figures: he wore Colonel Gaddafi's safari suit, carried Hastings Banda's flywhisk, and the gigantic bronze statue in his likeness which stood at the back of the stage toppled when he fell in a clear invocation of (the distinctly non-African) Saddam Hussein. Commentators in the press found themselves reminded of Idi Amin and of Robert Mugabe.[2] Jude Owusu's Cinna the Poet was trapped in a tyre and doused with petrol in a scene which referenced the gruesome practice of 'necklacing' common in apartheid-era South Africa. The characters' accents, meanwhile, were indeterminately 'African': hard to pinpoint geographically but emphatically not the actual British accents of most of the cast.

Ray Fearon's funeral oration as Mark Antony was the most rousing version of the speech I have seen. Wearing a plain grey T-shirt and standing

---

[1] This essay was developed from a shorter article, 'Circles, Centres, and the Globe to Globe Festival', for the *Year of Shakespeare* website, and a subsequent paper at the International Shakespeare Conference, Stratford-upon-Avon, August 2012.

[2] See Charles Spencer's review in *The Daily Telegraph*, 7 June 2012, and Christopher Gray's in the *Oxford Times*, 13 June 2012. Gregory Doran himself mentioned Amin and Mugabe in an interview with the *Daily Telegraph* (Serena Davies, '*Julius Caesar* with a little help from Idi Amin and Mugabe', 30 May 2012).

atop a concrete bunker, Fearon's Antony addressed an onstage crowd of around thirty in a playing of the scene which emphasized the character's masterful orchestration of his audience's responses. Many of the citizens' lines were cut and replaced with a more generalized hubbub; Antony's first two assertions that 'Brutus is an honourable man' were both answered with a loud and affirmative 'Yes!' from the whole group (3.2.83, 88). Antony's first few rhetorical questions, though – beginning with 'Did this in Caesar seem ambitious?' (3.2.91) – were met with silent pauses, all the quieter for their noisy context, and his next two references to Brutus's supposed honour were left hanging in a similar way (3.2.95, 100). The crowd's murmurs of dissent grew louder and louder as he brought up the subject of Caesar's will, and as his speech neared its climax, his questions were soliciting hearty answers:

ANTONY Will you be patient?
CROWD Yes!
ANTONY Will you stay awhile?
CROWD Yes!
. . .
ANTONY You will compel me, then, to read the will?
CROWD Yes!
ANTONY Then make a ring about the corpse of Caesar,
  And let me show you him that made the will.
  Shall I descend?
CROWD Yes!
ANTONY And will you give me leave?
CROWD Yes!   (3.2.150, 158–61)[3]

The crowd's gasps at the wounds of Caesar's corpse and their outrage at their leader's betrayal generated precisely the kind of thrilling momentum that made their subsequent descent into mindless violence horrifyingly plausible.

But there were, of course, two audiences watching Antony's speech. Lurking in the shadows around the periphery of the stage was a second, very different crowd: seated, silent, for the most part white, and presumably largely British. We, unlike our easily-led 'African' counterparts, were able to see precisely what Antony was doing, and

could only watch with a kind of detached fascination as he pulled it off. This split between a politically-savvy 'us' and a superstitious and manipulable 'them' was, I felt, a rather problematic one, given the production's refusal to tie the onstage crowd's cultural identity to anything more specific than a general 'African-ness': had the rest of the production not been as nuanced as it was, it might have been all too easy to reduce the entire continent to a stereotype of warring factions, power-hungry politicians and credulous masses, to rest assured that these were 'African' problems, not 'ours'. As it was, though, Paterson Joseph's performance as a questioning, introspective Brutus – alongside those of a magnificent ensemble cast – helped to make it clear that this production was interested primarily in exploring the complex psychologies of a small group of characters, over and above making generic and questionable statements about African politics.

An evident anxiety about the representation of a cultural 'other' lay at the heart of the RSC/Wooster Group collaboration, *Troilus and Cressida*. The two companies started rehearsals separately, the RSC playing the Greeks and the Wooster Group the Trojans. The latter described the collaboration in a letter to potential sponsors as 'the lodestone of British culture as manifest in the RSC versus the experimental aesthetic of our New York ensemble',[4] and their presentation of the Trojans evidently drew both on this perception of themselves as cultural outsiders and their existing oeuvre of work deconstructing American presentations of racial difference (white actress Kate Valk, for example, played the title role in their version of O'Neill's *The Emperor Jones* in blackface). The Wooster Group presented the world of Troy as a disintegrating cliché of Native American culture, patched together from Styrofoam, fancy dress, sporting equipment and fluorescent paint; their performances as the Trojans were copied,

---

[3] The crowd's responses are transcribed from the version televised by BBC Four on 24 June 2012.

[4] The Wooster Group, http://thewoostergroup.org/twg/twg.php?donate.

often gesture-for-gesture, from the various pieces of found footage which played on screens around the performance space,[5] while their vocal inflections, mediated through radio microphones, were derived from the sounds relayed to them through their earpieces. The resulting performances were of the irretrievably, incomprehensibly different, patched together from second-hand impressions, and any cross-cultural meanings the audience might have pieced together from them were self-evidently both arbitrary and culturally mediated.

That this was a *deconstruction* of presentations of cultural difference was missed by many of the production's critics in the British press. Michael Billington, for example, observed in *The Guardian* that

[p]olitically, there is something questionable about modern white Americans appropriating past tribal customs; and, however authentic the war cries and dances, the actors can't help resembling extras in a Bob Hope western.[6]

But surely the point of the Wooster Group's performance was to put precisely these sorts of re-uses of Native American culture under the microscope: to represent *representations*. Indeed, the Wooster Group's deliberately fragmented programme notes – themselves a patchwork of quotations – included references to Jean Baudrillard's comparison between Indian reservations and art galleries, and Philip J. Deloria's observation that 'whenever white Americans have confronted crises of identity, some of them have inevitably turned to Indians'.[7] This was a production which was problematizing its own presentations of cultural difference on every level – though we may wonder whether, in 2012, audiences really need reminding that media tropes about Native Americans are often politically dubious.

One might imagine that my title question was answered more easily by the productions which comprised the strongly intercultural Globe to Globe festival in London. An Afghan company set *The Comedy of Errors* in modern-day Kabul. A Māori adaptation of *Troilus and Cressida* relocated it to classical Aotearoa (pre-colonization

New Zealand). What country, friends, is this? Easy: it's Afghanistan; it's New Zealand. But in many cases, including both of these examples, the question of cultural identity was not quite so simply resolved. Both of these productions, for example, used archaic versions of their cultures' languages which were unfamiliar even to key members of their own creative teams.[8] The Afghan production, like many others in the festival, was directed by a foreigner, in this case the Paris-based Corinne Jaber – other examples included the British directors of the Kenyan *Merry Wives of Windsor*, the German director of the Zimbabwean *Two Gentlemen of Verona*, and the American director of the Macedonian *Henry VI Part 3*. Clearly this was not a simple showcase of the ways in which 'other cultures do Shakespeare', but rather a selection of truly international productions produced for a modern global theatre market. Some productions, such as the Zimbabwean and Afghan ones, had never actually been performed in the actors' homelands. In her account of the South African Isango Ensemble's preview performance of their *Venus and Adonis* in Cape Town, Colette Gordon notes that 'the ensemble's work is barely seen in South Africa', and describes the company's offstage attitude as 'tired, a little jaded, *putting on a show*, and not through any desire to deceive, but a need to please their "global" audience'. 'The international theatre circuit,' she explains, 'a rather profitable ghetto, allows Isango to survive, perhaps even thrive.'[9]

---

5 Most of these were clips from the 2001 film *Atanarjuat* (*The Fast Runner*), which depicts an ancient Inuit tribe. Others were of Warren Beatty and Natalie Wood in *Splendor in the Grass* (1961).

6 Michael Billington, 'Troilus and Cressida – review', *The Guardian*, 9 August 2012.

7 See Jean Baudrillard, *America* (London, 1989), p. 76, and Philip J. Deloria, *Playing Indian* (New Haven, 1998), p. 156.

8 See Harriet Shawcross, *Shakespeare From Kabul*, BBC HD, 21 July 2012 (broadcast again on BBC Four, 5 August), and Tim Masters, 'Globe to Globe: Maori *Troilus and Cressida* puts haka into Shakespeare', *BBC News*, 22 April 2012, www.bbc.co.uk/news/entertainment-arts-17769799.

9 Colette Gordon, 'Around the Globe and Back Again: A Moment to Reflect', *Year of Shakespeare*, 14 June 2012,

In fairness to the Globe, the festival was neither conceived nor advertised as an Olympian 'parade of nations', but rather as a festival of languages. Tom Bird, Globe to Globe's Festival Director, explained this priority in a talk at the 2012 International Shakespeare Conference:

It was really important to us that no group ever became like Olympic competitors. I didn't want any of these groups to be representative of nations or states, just for them to be examples of artists working in particular languages.... In our marketing we always described each show as coming from a city rather than from a country: *The Merchant of Venice* was from Tel Aviv, and so on.[10]

Many of the international companies involved, however, saw the festival as an opportunity to assert their cultural identities, often emphatically. Bird reports that the National Theatre of Albania and the Dhaka Theatre from Bangladesh both brought flags onto the stage during their curtain calls, since 'they felt they wanted to make the success of this performance a moment of national pride'.[11]

Some productions were co-opted into ongoing political projects. The official website for 'the Māori *Troilus and Cressida*', for example, describes the production as a chance 'to showcase Te Reo Māori [Māori language] and Te Ao Māori [Māori culture] to an international audience';[12] in her review, Catherine Silverstone discusses 'the production's contribution to cultural regeneration' in New Zealand and situates it as part of a wider project 'directed toward redressing the devastating effects of the British colonization'.[13] In similar terms, the British Council's Director of Arts described the British Council-funded *Comedy of Errors* as an opportunity to 'open the eyes of the British audience . . . to the rich culture of Afghanistan',[14] while one of the cast explained to the BBC that a central ambition was 'to show the world that Afghanistan is not what you think'.[15] That this affirmation of Afghan identity was directed outwards to a global audience, rather than inwards to an Afghan one, was perhaps emphasized in the production's liberal (even radical) incorporation of drinking, dancing, touching between genders, flirting and cross-dressing, all of

which would have been taboo in Afghanistan itself. Indeed, a recent BBC documentary showed the production's director Corinne Jaber having trouble persuading the actresses themselves to commit to some of these acts, and interviewed the actresses about the intimidation and persecution which they faced at home because of their choice of career.[16]

The formation of the South Sudanese Theatre Company for Globe to Globe's production of *Cymbeline* was in itself a strong assertion of cultural identity. Bird describes the company's initial proposal to participate in the festival as the 'most impressive' one he received:

It was a twenty-page letter from Joseph Abuk and Derik Alfred, which said things in it like 'We used to lie in the bush during our civil war, thinking about Shakespeare's plays to try and take our minds away from the killing that we knew would happen in the morning.' A letter like that is very difficult to say 'no' to, and a very strange thing to receive.[17]

Abuk and Alfred's project brought together a number of Sudanese theatre practitioners, from a variety of different areas and ethnic groups, to represent a country which was at that point only a few months old. Their performance at the Globe was presented as 'an offering to South Sudan', and it

http://bloggingshakespeare.com/year-of-shakespeare-around-the-globe-and-back-again.
10 Tom Bird, 'The Globe to Globe Festival', plenary talk at the International Shakespeare Conference, the Shakespeare Institute, Stratford-upon-Avon, 9 August 2012.
11 Bird, 'Globe to Globe'.
12 Ngakau Toa Company, '*Troilus and Cressida*: Brought to you by the Ngakau Toa Company', http://themaoritroilusandcressida.com/about/.
13 Catherine Silverstone, 'Ngākau Toa's *A Toroihi rāua ko Kāhiri*', http://blog.shakespearesglobe.com/ngakau-toas-a-toroihi-raua-ko-kahiri-troilus-and-cressida-by-catherine-silverstone/.
14 British Council, 'Shakespeare brings Afghan culture to the world stage', press release, 31 May 2012, www.britishcouncil.org/press/shakespeare-brings-afghan-culture-world-stage.
15 Harriet Shawcross & Tahir Qadiry, 'Shakespeare's Afghan journey to the Globe', *BBC News*, 27 February 2012, www.bbc.co.uk/news/world-asia-17159224.
16 Shawcross, *Shakespeare From Kabul*.
17 Bird, 'Globe to Globe'.

culminated in an impromptu musical party with the groundlings, in which some of them were pulled by the actors onto the stage itself. Alfred explained that a key aim was to create and celebrate a sense of South Sudanese national identity: 'It will make us have self-esteem and identity,' he told *The Guardian*, 'define who we are and what we want.'[18]

Sometimes national identity was placed, as it were, in quotation marks. At Globe to Globe, this was most evident in the Belarus Free Theatre's *King Lear*, in which Goneril, Regan and Cordelia competed for their father's affections in a parody of the Eurovision Song Contest. Wearing what appeared to be a pastiche of Belarusian traditional dress, each daughter danced and sang, accompanied on piano, before Lear passed his judgement upon her performance. For Tom Bird, the sequence was 'taking nationalism into irony', and 'clearly going for a critique of the current Belarusian regime'.[19] At the RSC, meanwhile, English nationalism was given a sideways look in Maria Aberg's irreverent *King John*, which opened with Pippa Nixon's Bastard leading the audience in a sing-along of *Land of Hope and Glory*. The tune then played over the speakers as Alex Waldmann's John, appearing at the top of a flight of steps, crowned himself. Following an anarchic first half in which England and France's 'anointed deputies of heaven' (3.1.62) behaved like petulant playboys, the opening sequence was then echoed at the beginning of the second half: only now, Nixon sang a ballad by the indie band Wye Oak and, as Waldmann's John crowned himself a second time, the stage erupted into a chaos of multicoloured balloons and ticker-tape. The release of the balloons revealed a neon sign across the back wall of the stage which bore the heavily ironic slogan 'For God and England'.

WHAT COUNTRY, *FRIENDS*, IS THIS?

Viola addresses the sailors as her 'friends', just as Antony repeatedly does the crowd in his funeral oration, Henry V his soldiers at the breach, and the dying Thisbe her audience at the end of the mechanicals' play. Puck is more tentative in his epilogue, requesting, rather than asserting, friendship: 'Give me your hands, if we be friends, / And Robin shall restore amends' (*Dream*, Epilogue, 15–16). Any public performance invites, asserts, or infers a particular group identity for its audience and a particular relationship with the stage, and, in many cases, the 'friendship' it requests the audience to enact has huge implications for the construction of cultural identity.

Writing in *The Spectator* on the first day of the Globe to Globe festival, Lloyd Evans described it as the 'most ambitious' and 'possibly the most futile' project of the whole Cultural Olympiad. 'How many play-goers,' he asked, 'are gagging to see *Troilus and Cressida* in Maori? Or *Cymbeline* in Juba Arabic, the dialect of Southern Sudan?'[20] A few weeks later, *The Independent*'s Christina Patterson found herself wondering 'why British audiences would want to see the work of the greatest poet who ever lived without actually hearing the words',[21] while the *Today* programme's James Naughtie questioned the festival's choice of 'obscure' languages.[22] What these commentators underestimated, though, was the sheer number of British play-goers, many of them presumably first- or subsequent-generation immigrants, who were fluent in the languages concerned. Contrary to Evans's expectations, both *Troilus and Cressida* and *Cymbeline* sold very well and, at all of the Globe to Globe performances I attended, there was evidently a substantial proportion of the audience – and in some cases, such as the Greek *Pericles*, an

---

[18] Alex Needham, 'Taking South Sudan to the Globe: Shakespeare from the Newest Nation', *Guardian Online*, 20 March 2012, www.guardian.co.uk/stage/2012/mar/20/south-sudan-globe-shakespeare-cymbeline.

[19] Bird, 'Globe to Globe'. Members of the Belarusian Free Theatre have been heavily persecuted in their homeland.

[20] Lloyd Evans, 'Playing with the Games', *The Spectator*, 21 April 2012.

[21] Christina Patterson, 'Lost in Translation: The Globe's Shakespeare Season Offers a Surprising Insight into Different Cultures', *The Independent*, 7 June 2012.

[22] *Today*, BBC Radio 4, 2 June 2012.

overwhelming majority – who heard and understood the words very clearly indeed.

Tom Bird revealed in his International Shakespeare Conference talk that he had begun the process of programming the festival by identifying what he called 'London languages':

By 'London language' I mean something like Bangla. About a mile away from the Globe, in the London borough of Tower Hamlets, there are 60,000 people, I think, who speak Bangla as their native language. So what we wanted to do was to bring the biggest theatre in Bangladesh – the Dhaka Theatre – and their *Tempest* over, and hope that that would appeal to that community.[23]

Each production, then, cast a spotlight on a different constituent part of London's own cultural make-up – often, those groups which are most frequently marginalized. Each performance showcased the language of a particular community and provided the occasion for some of its members to assert their collective identity within the crucible of the Globe.[24]

Those group identities were often powerfully expressed. At the start of the British Sign Language *Love's Labour's Lost*, countless members of London's deaf community could be seen signing enthusiastically to friends and acquaintances across the full breadth of the yard and, at the end, as the cast joined together to sign the 'Poem of Spring and Winter', hundreds of hands all around the auditorium waved in silent applause. At the Nigerian *Winter's Tale*, numerous Yoruba-speaking audience members availed themselves of the wide West African vocabulary of non-verbal interjections to express their shared disapproval of Leontes, their endorsement of Paulina and Hermione's defiance, or their delight at Florizel and Perdita's flirtation. The joyful cheering which greeted the family reunions at the end of the Afghan *Comedy of Errors* is a memory of audience collectivity which will stay with me for a long time.

Sometimes these group responses were tinged with the harsher experiences of particular expatriate communities. When *The Taming of the Shrew*'s Tranio boasted that he owned a British passport, an

audience which must have included a fair proportion of Pakistani emigrés laughed and applauded loudly. A character in *Pericles* joked about the precarious state of the euro to an audience which was audibly dominated by Greek-speakers, many of whom must have had friends and family in Greece; when Gower concluded the play with a tribute to endurance in the face of adversity, some of the people around me had tears in their eyes.

Perhaps the most politically loaded expressions of friendship – and of enmity – came in the reactions to the Israeli company Habima's production of *The Merchant of Venice*. Bird was sensitive to the potential controversy of Habima's invitation from the very earliest stages of programming:

We had a group from Israel, and we had a group from Palestine as well. The temptation to have neither was very strong – but as with everything at the Globe, we wanted to be bold and try and meet it head on, right at the programming stage, and to be provocative.[25]

But as Bird himself recognized, the problem was more specific than this. Habima's touring practices are extremely controversial: like many Israeli theatre companies, they have toured to the illegal settlements in the West Bank, in this case Ariel and Kiryat Arba. Keenly aware that Habima 'shouldn't be doing' this, Bird registered a dilemma:

As far as I understand, every single subsidized Israeli theatre, every single professional Israeli theatre, as part of their government funding, *has* to tour into those places. So it became a question of whether we would have a professional Israeli theatre in the festival, with

---

[23] Bird, 'Globe to Globe'.

[24] Bird noted, though, that a comprehensive representation of London's various communities was impossible in a festival of only 37 plays: 'In such a finite arts festival as this, there's no way you can include everyone. So we missed a show from Scandinavia completely; there was no show from Ghana, despite the huge Ghanaian community in London; no show from the Netherlands; no show at all from Southeast Asia. The festival would always have been richer, I think, for the presence of those cultures, but that was something we just didn't have space for.'

[25] Bird, 'Globe to Globe'.

a huge tradition of Shakespeare in Hebrew in that country – along with the Palestinian production from Ashtar – or whether we would somehow censor, somehow ban that production, that company, and almost that language, from being part of the festival.

Feeling that 'inclusion, dialogue and conversation' were preferable to 'exclusion and silencing', the Globe decided to go ahead with Habima's invitation.[26]

The production was generating controversy long before its performers arrived in London. The pressure group Boycott From Within had sent Shakespeare's Globe an open letter in January, calling upon them to withdraw the invitation. By inviting Habima to perform, they argued, Shakespeare's Globe was 'siding with its administrators in the debate on settlement performances', and 'taking a step against the conscientious Israeli actors and playwrights who have refused to perform in the settlements'.[27] The Globe responded with another open letter, describing the request for boycott as 'a profoundly problematic stance' and emphasizing the festival's role as a celebration of languages rather than 'of nations or states'.[28] Two months later, various luminaries of the British theatrical establishment repeated the debate in a series of open letters to *The Guardian*, with one group (which included the Globe's former Artistic Director, Mark Rylance) accusing the Globe of 'associating itself with policies of exclusion practised by the Israeli state',[29] and the other charging their opponents with 'seeking to delegitimise the state of Israel and its success'.[30] Despite the Globe's best efforts, the production had become central to a debate about much more than a straightforward celebration of languages; Habima's own General Manager Odelia Friedman, in fact, described the company's invitation as 'an honourable accomplishment for the State of Israel in general'.[31] Indeed, since the Gaza War of 2009, the Israeli Foreign Ministry has adopted a policy of sending its leading cultural figures overseas in what Arye Mekel, its deputy director-general for cultural affairs, described as an attempt to 'show Israel's prettier face, so we are not thought of purely in the context of war'.[32]

In this context, the very act of attending the production was, intended or otherwise, a political one.[33] The event itself was framed by a heavy police presence and airport-style security checks, while both pro- and anti-boycott protests were staged outside the theatre. The Globe's Artistic Director Dominic Dromgoole appeared onstage at the start of the evening to reassure the audience that anyone who disrupted the performance would be immediately evicted, and to request them to leave such action to the security staff. As it happened, there were a number of protests during the performance, many of them silent: some protestors unfurled banners and flags, while one group simply stood with masking tape over their mouths. During the trial scene, a protestor shouted out 'Hath not a Palestinian eyes?', and when he was subsequently escorted out by security, a fellow playgoer called out 'Piss off!' after him, to audience laughter. Peter Kirwan's thoughtful account of the performance draws a parallel between the jeering of these audience members and the behaviour of Gratiano in the scene they were watching.[34]

---

26 Bird, 'Globe to Globe'.

27 Boycott From Within, 'A Call to Shakespeare's Globe Theatre', http://boycottisrael.info/content/call-shakespeares-globe-theatre.

28 Shakespeare's Globe, 'Response to Letter from Boycott from Within', 6 January 2012, http://www.facebook.com/notes/shakespeares-globe-theatre/response-to-letter-from-boycott-from-within/10150479613843577.

29 David Aukin *et al.*, 'Dismay at Globe Invitation to Israeli Theatre', *The Guardian*, 29 March 2012.

30 Arnold Wesker *et al.*, 'We Welcome Israel's National Theatre', *The Guardian*, 10 April 2012.

31 Merav Yudilovitch, 'London Theater Urged to Boycott Habima', *Ynetnews*, 1 February 2012, www.ynetnews.com/articles/0,7340,L-4170210,00.html.

32 Ethan Bronner, 'After Gaza, Israel Grapples with Crisis of Isolation', *New York Times*, 18 March 2009.

33 I did not attend the production myself, so the account that follows is based on second-hand reports; I am especially indebted to Peter Kirwan's write-up on *The Bardathon* (see below).

34 Peter Kirwan, '*The Merchant of Venice* (Habima) @ Shakespeare's Globe. Part 1: Outer Frame', and 'Part 2: The Production', *The Bardathon*, http://blogs.

The effect of all this was, of course, to polarize the debate into something that equated to 'Either you are with us, or you are against us'. This antagonism was played out countless times on the online messageboards of reviews and blogs in the days following the event, in ways which overlooked almost entirely the nuances of the company's politics: that Yousef Sweid, for example, the Arab-Israeli actor who played Bassanio, had in fact boycotted Habima's West Bank performances himself.[35] In yet another letter to *The Guardian*, the playwright Howard Brenton pointed out that Habima's own staff were 'deeply divided' about their performances in the territories, and he called for Britain's theatre community to 'argue' rather than 'ban'.[36] In effect, of course, this is precisely what happened: no ban took place, but neither was the performance a successful 'rebranding' exercise for the Israeli government. Where the production's theatre audience might have seen a culturally affirming *Merchant of Venice*, the audience of the national media saw protest.

WHAT COUNTRY, FRIENDS, IS *THIS*?

A key purpose of the World Shakespeare Festival, according to its director Deborah Shaw and the RSC's Michael Boyd, was to celebrate 'Britain's greatest cultural export at a moment when the eyes of the world are on London and the UK'.[37] The festival was, of course, part of the wider Cultural Olympiad, itself an adjunct to the London 2012 games. Under the gaze of the rest of the world, it seems, this was a moment to assert, and perhaps to question, Britain's own cultural identity; a time to ask: 'What country, friends, is *this*?'

This was certainly the most widely expressed interpretation of July's Opening Ceremony. In her write-up for the *New York Times*, Sarah Lyall concluded that in it, 'Britain presented itself to the world . . . as something it has often struggled to express even to itself: a nation secure in its own post-empire identity, whatever that actually is.'[38] Lyall's hesitant phrasing here is telling:

Britain's post-imperial identity may be indeterminate, but paradoxically, it is also 'secure'. In the UK, commentators from across the political spectrum recognized that what was being offered in the multi-million-pound pageant was not an accurate portrait, but rather a 'myth' of Britishness: as Trevor Phillips put it in *The Observer*, director Danny Boyle had 'conjured a beguiling vision of the Britain that we could be – energetic, inventive, witty, profound, and delightful',[39] while Melanie Phillips identified it in *The Daily Mail* as 'the fantasy of an inclusive, generous, warm-hearted, joyful image' of the British people.[40]

Shakespeare was central to this myth-building, and though the Opening Ceremony was not an official part of the World Shakespeare Festival, its Shakespearian elements served to make the link between the festival and the Olympics explicit. At the start of the ceremony, Kenneth Branagh – dressed, rather incongruously, as Isambard Kingdom Brunel – stood upon a grassy replica of Glastonbury Tor and, to the accompaniment of 'Nimrod' from Elgar's *Enigma Variations*, recited the speech from *The Tempest* beginning 'Be not afeard. The isle is full of noises' (3.2.138–46). Branagh delivered the whole speech with a gigantic smile, combining a soothing timbre with a rousing climax as only Branagh can. For Melanie Phillips, it expressed the 'essentially benign nature of Britain'.[41]

---

nottingham.ac.uk/bardathon/2012/05/29/the-merchant-of-venice-habima-shakespeares-globe-part-1-outer-frame/ , and http://blogs.nottingham.ac.uk/bardathon/2012/05/29/the-merchant-of-venice-habima-shakespeares-globe-part-2-the-production/.

35 Donald Macintyre, 'Israeli Actors Refuse to Take the Stage in Settlement Theatre', *The Independent*, 30 August 2010.

36 Howard Brenton, 'Denounce, Don't Censor: Globe's Invitation to Habima Should Stand', *The Guardian*, 3 April 2012.

37 Introduction to Festival Guide.

38 Sarah Lyall, 'A Five-Ring Opening Circus, Weirdly and Unabashedly British', *New York Times*, 27 July 2012.

39 Ai Weiwei *et al.*, 'London 2012: Opening Ceremony – Reviews', *The Observer*, 29 July 2012.

40 Melanie Phillips, 'Oscars All Round for a Spectacular Feel-good Fantasy of Modern Britain', *Daily Mail*, 30 July 2012.

41 Phillips, 'Oscars All Round'.

It will not have escaped the attention of careful readers of *The Tempest* that 'essentially benign' is, to say the least, an odd description of Caliban's speech. At the point in the play that these words are spoken, Caliban is plotting with a pair of clowns to overthrow and murder the man who has colonized his island – hardly the emblem of 'a nation secure in its own post-empire identity'. Caliban's faith in the benevolence of the noises is misplaced: the music is being made by Ariel, who has been invisibly manipulating the conspirators in order to provoke division between them, and acting as the eyes and ears of the remote and powerful Prospero. Furthermore, the dreams that Caliban describes are so infinitely preferable to the poverty of his reality that, when he wakes, he cries 'to dream again'. If the Olympics Opening Ceremony was 'Caliban's Dream', as the title of the accompanying musical score suggests, this hardly bodes well for the awakening which awaits post-games Britain.

These incongruities, of course, may have occurred only to viewers who are familiar with *The Tempest*. It is possible that Shakespeare functioned here merely as a free-floating signifier of conservative Britishness; without careful listening, the speech may simply have invoked a comfortable and nostalgic patriotism with its chimes of 'isle', 'delight', 'riches' and 'dream'. Branagh delivered it in a style reminiscent of his 'St Crispin's Day' speech from his film of *Henry V*, intoned as it was on a grassy hill, to a swelling orchestral score. Perhaps, like that moment, it evoked glorious English victory even as the surrounding text seemed determined to resist.

But it is possible, I would argue, to read the quotation in more nuanced terms. Branagh's Brunel surveyed the onset of Britain's Industrial Revolution as both an awestruck Caliban and its Prospero-like architect, in a sequence of visual symbolism which was for me highly ambivalent: the destruction of the rural idyll for a gigantic, smoking furnace in which dehumanized workers forged the all-powerful Olympic rings evoked the dystopia of Tolkien's *Lord of the Rings*. The ceremony was certainly very Blakean, opening with a sung solo of the hymn 'Jerusalem', so it was almost too easy

to read the products of Brunel's wizardry as 'dark Satanic Mills'. That this new industrialized Britain was at least partly oppressive was highlighted by the ceremony's prominent inclusion of such figures as the suffragettes and the Jarrow marchers. The rest of the ceremony resonated with fragments of *The Tempest*, too, from the inventor Sir Tim Berners-Lee as the hidden, Prospero-like facilitator of the romance between 'Frankie and June', to the echo of Caliban in rapper Dizzee Rascal's *Bonkers*:

> I wake up everyday it's a daydream
> Everythin' in my life ain't what it seems
> I wake up just to go back to sleep

Boyle's vision of modern industrial Britain was, it seems, just as double-edged as Caliban's speech. I find myself wondering whether these resonances would have been even clearer had the Brunel/Caliban passage been delivered, as originally planned, by Mark Rylance: Rylance's most celebrated performance to date was as Johnny 'Rooster' Byron in Jez Butterworth's play *Jerusalem*, the climax to which featured Rylance's character frantically drumming in an attempt to invoke England's mythological past and hold back the tide of capitalism.[42]

The superficially jingoistic reading was the primary one reflected two weeks later in the Closing Ceremony's reincorporation of the Caliban speech, where it was delivered by Timothy Spall in character as Britain's quintessential wartime orator, Sir Winston Churchill, from the top of a model of the Big Ben clock tower.[43] The Closing Ceremony was littered with Shakespearian quotations – in some cases quite literally – as excerpts from

---

[42] This parallel was brought to my attention by Erik Simpson on his blog *Pages and Lights* (https://pagesandlights. wordpress.com/2012/07/28/calibans-dream-on-danny-boyles-london-opening-ceremonies/). For details of Rylance's planned involvement in the ceremony, and his subsequent departure, see Mark Brown, 'Mark Rylance Exits from Olympics Opening after Step-daughter's Death', *The Guardian*, 6 July 2012.

[43] Spall had previously played Churchill in the 2010 film *The King's Speech*.

English literature appeared as mocked-up newspaper headlines and articles all over the set and costumes. 'To be or not to be: That is the question' was perhaps the largest and most prominent of all, written in huge letters (the first six words especially) across the floor of the stage; 'We are such stuff as dreams are made on' was emblazoned across a truck (and was one of the first 'headlines' shown in close-up on the BBC's TV coverage), while 'The rest is silence', 'My mistress' eyes are nothing like the sun', and various snippets from *Richard III*'s opening soliloquy could also be spotted. These decontextualized fragments functioned more as empty signifiers of 'great English literature' than anything else but, once again, the use of the Caliban speech was double-edged: while Spall's Churchill seemed at first to want to celebrate the noisiness of his island, he lost patience when the noises became a rush-hour din, yelled 'Stop!', and silenced everyone in an impulsive flash reminiscent of Prospero's interruption of the masque.

Shakespeare was co-opted into a very different model of Britishness at the Paralympics Opening Ceremony in August. This ceremony was structured around a narrative in which Ian McKellen's Prospero sent disabled actress Nicola Miles-Wildin's Miranda on a literal journey of scientific discovery: McKellen, costumed in a starry blue gown, delivered a series of mostly non-Shakespearian lines in which he commanded Miranda to 'go out into the world' and 'shine [her] light on the beautiful diversity of humanity'. In a section titled 'Brave New World', six noted British Paralympians flew into the stadium on wires, in slow motion, towards a large central astrolabe. Miles-Wildin, looking up in wonder, delivered Miranda's famous lines: 'How beauteous mankind is! O brave new world / That has such people in't!' (5.1.186–7). But whereas in Shakespeare's play, Prospero's reply is cynical – ''Tis new to thee' – McKellen's Prospero instead instructed Miranda to 'Look to the light... and discover new worlds!' Miranda then sailed off in a giant upturned umbrella to explore 'the wonders of science and the universe', in a sequence of episodes titled 'Navigation', 'Gravity' and 'Collision'. This manifestation of Shakespeare may have been 'essentially benign', but it was by no means passive: the ceremony's climax featured both McKellen and Miles-Wildin waving placards for 'Equality' (in a clear nod to McKellen's activism as a gay rights campaigner) while Graeae Theatre Company played the song 'Spasticus Autisticus'. Prospero's exhortation to Miranda at the very end encouraged her to 'Look up and fly... Break that glass ceiling, and set us all free!' The symbolism was evocative of both Prospero's epilogue and his release of Ariel, and associated the character – perhaps somewhat against the grain of the Shakespearian source – with progressive politics and social optimism.

If Shakespeare functioned in the Olympic and Paralympic ceremonies both to assert and to question British cultural identity, this was a theme which ran through much of the accompanying World Shakespeare Festival. Globe to Globe did much to decentre dominant notions of 'Englishness', inviting London's marginalized communities, languages and cultures to take ownership of the Globe space and achieve a temporary centrality. Bird reports that 83 per cent of the festival's audience members were first-time Globe visitors, and infers from this that 'various different linguistic and cultural communities in London did want to come and join us'.[44] Indeed, both Shakespeare and the Globe were transformed at each performance by the cultures that appropriated them, from the dominant language of the pre-show chatter to the norms and patterns of audience response. Each show was also attended by large numbers of audience members who did *not* speak the language concerned and, for these playgoers, the sense of gentle displacement involved may well have been both surprising and liberating (as it certainly was for me). Bird describes some of the performances in which he experienced a similar effect:

There were some extraordinary nights – the Greek *Pericles* being one, the Bangla *Tempest* being another – where you found yourself just not getting a lot of in-jokes,

---

44 Bird, 'Globe to Globe'.

because there were so many members of those particular linguistic and cultural communities in the theatre, which is not something you see in every London theatre at all.[45]

Notions of Englishness and of London itself were open for inversion, reassessment and renegotiation.

Globe to Globe achieved another kind of decentring by commissioning London-based companies to work in minority languages: namely the BSL *Love's Labour's Lost* by Deafinitely Theatre, and the Shona *Two Gentlemen of Verona* by Two Gents Productions. Furthermore, the festival's first English-language contribution – despite its insistence that the language used was not English but 'Hip Hop' – was a pop-culture reworking of *Othello* by the Chicago-based Q Brothers. If these potentially radical programming choices went some way to challenge the hegemony of 'straight English' Shakespeare, though, this was somewhat undermined by the festival's conclusion – a traditional and patriotically English *Henry V* by the resident Globe company, in which the Scots, Irish and Welsh were either idiotic or incoherent, the downbeat epilogue was cut in favour of a more politically uncomplicated jig, and the audience really did cry 'God for Harry, England and Saint George!' *Henry V* was, moreover, separated from the rest of the festival by a gap of three days, and subject to none of the constraints imposed on the other festival productions regarding running time and resources.[46]

It is difficult to draw conclusions about the general character of the World Shakespeare Festival as a whole. The wider festival has, I think, failed to achieve the sense of a cohesive identity which was evident at Globe to Globe – no doubt partly because the Globe festival was confined to a very specific time and place, whereas the World Shakespeare Festival has been scattered across the whole country and spread out over several months.

The experiences of seeing Ninagawa's *Cymbeline* at the Barbican, for example, or dreamthinkspeak's *The Rest is Silence* at Riverside Studios, were, for me, framed in almost exactly the same way that they would have been had the productions not been part of the festival, with the presence of the festival logo on the productions' programmes the only clue as to their affiliation.

But perhaps the brand is the point. The World Shakespeare Festival logo shows us an image of the globe from a strange angle, somewhere above the North Pole; the British Isles are obscured by the writing, but by my estimation they must be somewhere between the 'O' and the 'R' of 'WORLD' and the central 'S' of 'SHAKESPEARE'. In the World Shakespeare Festival's official iconography, Britain is right at the centre of the world, in more ways than one; it is also right at the heart of that international symbol of humanity, 'Shakespeare'. The Olympics have been repeatedly portrayed in the media as an attempt to reinvigorate 'Brand Britain', asserting the country as a modern, caring, global nation. In the World Shakespeare Festival, Shakespeare – our 'greatest cultural export' – likewise becomes a touchstone in affirming, testing, and occasionally challenging ideas about Britain's 'post-empire identity'. Whatever it is that global cultures make 'Shakespeare' mean, Britain seems to be claiming that for itself.

---

[45] Bird, 'Globe to Globe'.

[46] While the programming of *Henry V* may, from a pan-festival perspective, have been a problematic 're-centring' of traditional Englishness, one might note with more optimism that it is likely to have made little impact on the more radical 'decentrings' experienced by audience members at individual shows. A cynic might argue that it was never really part of the festival at all, but simply the beginning of the Globe's summer season.

REDEFINING KNOWLEDGE: AN EPISTEMOLOGICAL SHIFT IN SHAKESPEARE STUDIES

PÉTER DÁVIDHÁZI

Changes in our critical vocabulary are always symptomatic, and nowadays they reveal an interesting shift in the rationale of our discipline. Reading almost any selection of representative works published around the year 2000 in Shakespeare scholarship one cannot help noticing a distinct change in intellectual climate, a methodological turn that seeks to redefine, consciously or otherwise, our criteria of relevant knowledge at the beginning of the new millennium. The first conspicuous sign of a new methodology is that the very words 'speculate' and 'speculation' shed their former pejorative connotation in Shakespeare studies and became almost as prestigious as 'describe' or 'description' used to be in the heyday of positivist scholarship. No longer the equivalent of looking at or musing about something without any useful result, and no longer the 'idle speculation' branded as dishonourable by the Constable of France (*King Henry V*, 4.2.31), speculation is back again, triumphantly rehabilitated even when empirical verification is out of the question. We have come a long way from the times when it was devastating to suggest that a group of scholars displayed a predilection 'for speculations that are quite indemonstrable', hence they indulged in 'pure mental gymnastics'.[1] Scholars today are aware of a speculative component in their own work. 'And, grounded as my claims are in what scholars have uncovered, a good deal of what I make of that information remains speculative', an unrepentent James Shapiro admits in his book *1599: A Year in the Life of William Shakespeare*, because now he can take it for granted that speculation is inevitable, differing only in degree, and in most

cases allowing a generalized statement covering the matter: 'Rather than awkwardly littering the pages that follow with one hedge after another – "perhaps", "maybe", "it's most likely", "probably", or the most desperate of them all, "surely" – I'd like to offer one global qualification here: this is necessarily my reconstruction of what happened to Shakespeare in the course of this year and when I do qualify a claim it signals that the evidence is inconclusive or the argument highly speculative.'[2] Yet in spite of the suggested difference between 'speculative' and 'highly speculative', a distinction nowadays symptomatically unexamined though rather problematic in itself, the main assumption implied here is that *to some extent* any reconstruction is *necessarily* speculative and, moreover, it is always *somebody's* speculation. Nevertheless, it is the best (and only) thing one can hope for in scholarship.

This new methodological insight is not confined to biographies, but recent biographies display ample evidence for a similar scholarly rehabilitation of the speculative. 'Even with this relative abundance of information, there are large gaps in knowledge that make any biographical study of Shakespeare an exercise in speculation.' This is Stephen Greenblatt's disarming admission at the beginning of his *Will in the World: How Shakespeare Became Shakespeare*, in a caveat

---

[1] C. Kerényi, *Prometheus: Archetypal Image of Human Existence*, transl. Ralph Manheim (London, 1963), pp. 64–5.
[2] James Shapiro, 'Preface', in *1599: A Year in the Life of William Shakespeare* (London, 2005), p. xxiii.

characteristically titled 'A Note to the Reader', adding that although the dating and ordering of the plays have reached a relatively stable consensus, it still 'is inevitably somewhat speculative', the scholars who fixed Shakespeare's birthday 'were engaged in speculation', and there are numerous details in Shakespeare's education about which, 'as in so much else from Shakespeare's life, there is no absolute certainty'.[3] Different as they are in methodology or theoretical affiliation, most of the leading authorities in present-day Shakespeare scholarship admit that they have to work with uncertain and alternative explanations and residual differences they cannot hope to resolve. Referring to *Hamlet* 3.2.8–13 in his *Shakespeare & Co.*, Stanley Wells meditates about the word 'groundlings', saying that it 'may have amused those who flocked to early performances of the play, but equally it may have offended them', and adding that 'Hamlet's term is a metaphor, chosen presumably because the groundlings gaped up at the actors on the platform above them like fish from the bottom of a stream'.[4] For Wells the same applies to distinctly biographical details, such as Shakespeare's acting career after having been listed as one of the principal comedians in Ben Jonson's *Sejanus*. 'How long after this he continued to combine acting with his other responsibilities to the company is anyone's guess. The fact that his name does not occur in the actor list for Johnson's *Volpone* in 1605 may indicate that his acting career had come to an end by then.'[5]

The gist of the new claim is that the tentative arguments and hypothetical conclusions built on inconclusive evidence are worth our while in scholarship. Scholars admittedly cannot verify what went on, say, in the spectators' mind four hundred years ago, yet they are willing, indeed eager, to speculate about it on the basis of indirect and insufficient evidence, and to display conclusions that are (admittedly) inconclusive by traditional standards. Characteristically, the repeated verb 'speculate' is less and less coupled with 'only' but, even when it is, it usually comes with the new implication that there are issues in Shakespeare scholarship *worth* speculating about. 'We can, of course, only

speculate whether Shakespeare . . . had this story at the back of his mind while writing Antonio's speech. The point of juxtaposing a play and a contemporary event, however, is not to suggest its influence on Shakespeare but to speculate about what kind of knowledge of the Illyrians . . . might have given rise to the ideas about their national traits and actions in the English poetic imagination.'[6] Characteristically, again, the term 'speculate' is redeemed in a footnote by Jonathan Bate when he argues that 'David Scott Kastan speculates interestingly on the Rudolfine context of *The Tempest* in his *Shakespeare after Theory*'.[7] Bate praises his American colleague by using the verb to refer to Kastan's exploration of possible or (at best) probable political contexts for the play. The abverb 'interestingly', appreciative as it undoubtedly is in Bate's footnote, clearly differs from (say) 'conclusively', and if we go back to Kastan's text[8] we find that his interpretation was meant to be no more than a possible or, at best, a probable alternative context for *The Tempest*, with relative merits when compared to rival interpretations. Kastan's argument is cited and used by Richard Wilson as well, backing up his hypothesis that probably it was Rudolf II's example that led to the formation of two other plays as well: 'Rudolf II's "mad, fantastical trick to steal from the state" and abandon Vienna in 1583 for a scholarly "beggary he was never born to" (*Measure for Measure* 3.1.358–60) may have prompted the dramatist in the Rudolfine strategy – aborted

---

[3] Stephen Greenblatt, *Will in the World: How Shakespeare Became Shakespeare* (New York, 2004), pp. 18–19.

[4] Stanley Wells, *Shakespeare & Co.: Christopher Marlowe, Thomas Dekker, Ben Jonson, Thomas Middleton, John Fletcher, and the Other Players in His Story* (London, 2006), pp. 8–9.

[5] Wells, *Shakespeare & Co.*, p. 28.

[6] Goran Stanivukovic, 'Illyria Revisited: Shakespeare and the Eastern Adriatic', in *Shakespeare and the Mediterranean: The Selected Proceedings of the International Shakespeare Association World Congress Valencia, 2001*, ed. Tom Clayton, Susan Brock and Vicente Forés (Newark, 2004), p. 409.

[7] Jonathan Bate, 'Shakespeare's Islands', in *Shakespeare and the Mediterranean*, p. 306.

[8] David Scott Kastan, *Shakespeare After Theory* (London, 1999), p. 193.

in *Two Gentlemen* but perfected with *Measure* – of having some "ghostly father" (4.3.46) shadow his plot.'[9] *May have prompted*, that is, we cannot exclude the possibility that it was something else that prompted Shakespeare's use of a ghostly father.

None of these arguments can exclude that it was something else that prompted Shakespeare's decisions, yet this kind of speculation is now considered a fully legitimate enterprise. To demonstrate the probability of an author's motive is considered a result worth knowing, something to be taken seriously even if no positivist evidence (answerable to the criterion of direct empirical verifiability) is available to confirm it beyond mere likelihood. Yet Bate's well-disciplined argument also reveals how tenaciously the best kind of positivist scruples about a lack of precision may survive into an age of alternative possibilities and (with some luck) may save us from any slackening of logic. *If* Shakespeare read Richard Knolles's *Generall Historie of the Turkes* 'all the way through', says Bate, *then* 'he would have learned' about how the Turks trained Christian children to become Janizzaries, and *then* it would make even more sense to consider Othello a Janizzary in reverse.[10] This 'if' plus 'would have' is a conditional that offers no more than a hypothetical possibility or (at best) a probability, and strictly speaking we don't know whether Shakespeare read the book through or not. Bate is convinced that Shakespeare knew Knolles's book. Talking about the sources of *Othello* he says that Shakespeare found the story in Giovanni Battista Cinthio's *Gli Hecatommithi*, and gave it local texture 'courtesy of such recently published books as . . . Knolles's 1603 Generall Historie of the Turkes'. Moreover, Bate claims that there is 'good evidence' (in *Othello*, 1.3.14–15) 'that Shakespeare read Knolles shortly before writing the play', so the question is precisely whether he read it 'all the way through', and Bate finds it important to warn us that there is no evidence for that. He is also aware of the dangerous habit of attributing absolute certainty to any assertion about the supposed causal connection between source and play. 'Knolles has been accepted as a source by most scholars for some time, but I don't think anyone has paused on the

significance of Piall Bassa . . . I suspect that it was the story of Piall that furnished Shakespeare with the idea of giving depth and historical specificity to Cinthio's tale of the Venetian Moor sent to defend Cyprus.'[11]

I suspect, says Bate, which reveals that to identify Knolles's book as a source of *Othello* and to have evidence that Shakespeare read (some parts of) Knolles shortly before writing his play is still not the same as being sure about the specific nature and extent, or even the sheer existence, of the causal connection. One can only suspect that a conjecture is right, but the new latent assumption shared by the interpretive community of Shakespeare scholars is that to reach an uncertain, inconclusive, hypothetical assertion indicating something which may or may not be the case is definitely worth the effort. 'When he [Hamlet] says, "there is nothing either good or bad, but thinking makes it so" (2.2.251–2),' as Robert Ellrodt argues, 'he is . . . not necessarily echoing the speculations of Montaigne in his essay, "That the taste of goods or evills doth greatly depend on the opinion we have of them".'[12] Not *necessarily*, that is; Shakespeare may or may not be echoing Montaigne, and we are implicitly urged to be content with this uncertain result, at least for the time being. We should be even more content with such results when a scholar manages to discredit false certainties cherished by his or her predecessors, as for example when Stephen Orgel contests the relevance of the Roderigo Lopez case to *The Merchant of Venice*, a relevance that Orgel finds both dubious and exaggerated even though it has appeared almost axiomatic for more than a century.[13]

Most scholars seem to have realized that any attempt to reconstruct something, whether the

---

[9] Richard Wilson, '"Every third thought": Shakespeare's Milan', in *Shakespeare and the Mediterranean*, p. 419.

[10] Bate, 'Shakespeare's Islands', p. 294.

[11] Bate, 'Shakespeare's Islands', pp. 291, 296–7.

[12] Robert Ellrodt, 'Self-Consistency in Montaigne and Shakespeare', in *Shakespeare and the Mediterranean*, pp. 144–5.

[13] Stephen Orgel, 'Shylock's Tribe', in *Shakespeare and the Mediterranean*, p. 41.

authorial text of a play or the original design of a playhouse, is *bound* to be speculative, it moves within the realm of the possible or (at best) the probable, and cannot warrant certainty. Our knowledge thus remains hypothetical, a well-informed guesswork containing an element of the imaginary, and there is no way to reduce an array of possible alternatives to one authentic solution tested and ascertained by historical research. 'Any attempt to recover Shakespeare's original inevitably depends upon a speculative reconstruction of the lost process by which Middleton in 1620 transformed what Shakespeare had written in 1604', says Gary Taylor about *Measure for Measure*, highlighting the fuzzy edges of our knowledge. 'It is certainly possible to identify elements of the 1623 text as the work of Middleton, but it will always be harder to reconstruct the process of transformation.'[14] This applies to all reconstructions based on analysis and interpretation, even to the material reconstruction of Shakespeare's Globe and the Spanish corral theatres. Franklin J. Hildy's essay 'The Corral de Comedias at Almagro and London's Reconstructed Globe' reveals the share of speculation in a methodology that combines the results of historical research with the (transhistorical but hopefully analogous) working experience of present-day actors.[15] So there is no way to know for sure, and all we may hope for is some degree of rightness: this is the predicament of modern Shakespeare scholarship.

Hildy offers a good example of both the new speculative reasoning and the new idiom of probability. His language clearly indicates that speculative reconstruction is inconclusive or leads to alternative hypothetical possibilities usually expressed (and subtly differentiated) by 'may have been', 'could have been', 'looks to have been', 'appears to have been', 'it seems that', or simply 'perhaps'. The final paragraph gives alternative conclusions, yet emphasizes that the knowledge thus attained is well worth the trouble for Shakespearians who can use it only as an analogy, and that the lurking possibility of erroneous reasoning does not make it less desirable. Hildy admits that some reconstructions turn out to be utterly fictitous or manifestly wrong, but

hastens to add that they might nevertheless serve the progress of learning, as the inauthentic brontosaurus did inspire further research.[16] The grammar of most papers today suggests parallel possibilities: whether a conjecture attributes high or low probability to a supposition, it does not exclude an alternative; typically, there is an *if* or *unless* to indicate the hypothetical status of the assertion. 'Unless evidence of some sort is produced that Shakespeare knew a Latin or a vernacular version [of Homer]', Yves Peyré argues cautiously, 'one can safely assume that he almost certainly never read the *Odyssey*.'[17] Moreover, scholars nowadays often feel that both (or all) possible ventures are bound to be wrong and probably there is no passage to the haven of truth. As far back as 1927 and 1933 T. S. Eliot warned critics that they can usefully correct their predecessors by replacing former errors with new ones: as they cannot really hope to be right about any author as great as Shakespeare, and cannot reach Truth or the real Shakespeare ('if there is one'), at least they should occasionally change their minds, that is, change their 'way of being wrong'.[18] Scholars today are compelled to realize that the alternative methods and vocabularies available to them are almost equally misleading, and they should opt for the lesser of two evils. Michael Neill argues that we cannot escape interpreting *Othello* in terms of race, yet we cannot but err if we do so; 'to talk about "race" in *Othello* is to fall into anachronism; yet not to talk about it is to ignore something fundamental to [the] play . . . it is probably impossible to

---

14 Gary Taylor, 'Shakespeare's Mediterranean *Measure for Measure*', in *Shakespeare and the Mediterranean*, p. 255.

15 Franklin J. Hildy, 'The Corral de Comedias at Almagro and London's Reconstructed Globe', in *Shakespeare and the Mediterranean*, p. 89.

16 Hildy, 'The Corral de Comedias', pp. 97, 101.

17 Yves Peyré, 'Shakespeare's *Odyssey*', in *Shakespeare and the Mediterranean*, pp. 231, 239.

18 T. S. Eliot, 'Matthew Arnold', in *The Use of Poetry and the Use of Criticism: Studies in the Relation of Criticism to Poetry in England* (London, 1975), p. 109; T. S. Eliot, 'Shakespeare and the Stoicism of Seneca', in *Selected Essays* (London, 1948), p. 126.

think our way back through this history [of racial thinking] to an undistorted reading of the protagonist's otherness'.[19]

To rehabilitate the probable, the likely, or the merely possible, to consider them as knowledge worth knowing, Shakespeare scholarship had to go one important step beyond positivism. Under the auspices of positivism and during its long aftermath, the general rule was to confine discourse to what was considered positive knowledge, i.e. to statements thought to be empirically verifiable. Scholars were not allowed to take seriously anything less than the verifiable; hence they referred to anything unverifiable as a mere figment of the imagination. They used to insist on a sharp dividing line between popular biographies, allowed and even assumed to be fictitous, and scholarly work, expected and even demanded to be factual and fully reliable. That clear-cut division has become theoretically untenable in Shakespeare scholarship; hence James Shapiro can safely voice an opinion that would have been considered outrageous for most of his predecessors. 'Conventional biographies of Shakespeare are necessary fictions that will always be with us – less for what they tell us about Shakespeare's life than for what they reveal about our fantasies of who we want Shakespeare to be.'[20] Explicitly or otherwise, this relocation of the main referential value of biographies acknowledges the self-serving motivation, almost like wishful thinking, of the imaginative contribution whereby any biographical narrative about Shakespeare can be made possible at all. When Stephen Greenblatt prefaces his scholarly book on Shakespeare's life with the warning that 'to understand how Shakespeare used his imagination to transform his life into his art, it is important to use our own imagination', he is paving the way for the surprisingly fictional opening gambit of his first chapter: 'Let us imagine that Shakespeare found himself from boyhood fascinated by language, obsessed with the magic of words . . . it is a very safe assumption that it began early, perhaps from the first moment his mother whispered a nursery rhyme in his ear.' After this opening we find a long series of qualified statements and conjectures, such as 'John Shakespeare

himself seems to have had at most only partial literacy' or 'Will almost certainly attended this school' or the school's method of making the boys perform ancient plays 'must have given Will pleasure' and 'Perhaps there was a time, a year or so before Will left school, when the teacher . . . decided to have the boys perform Plautus's frenetic farce about identical twins, *The Two Menaechmuses*.'[21] The language of these carefully guarded, yet uncertain, scholarly propositions is not far from the idiom of those more fictional biographies written outside the scholarly domain. Whatever the differences, Peter Ackroyd's *Shakespeare: The Biography* is teeming with auxiliaries such as *may have been*, or *must have been*, or *would have been*. Starting with the obvious case of Shakespeare's birthday 'supposed to have been' 23 April but 'may in fact have been 21 April or 22 April', we are offered a long series of similar guesses, whether about Shakespeare's family at his baptism ('John Shakespeare and his newborn son would have been accompanied by the godparents'), or about the feelings of his parents ('care devoted to their first-born son must have been close and intense'), or about the usual attire of the playwright himself ('There is no doubt he would have dressed well'),[22] and legions more.

The new turn in Shakespeare studies can be characterized as willingness to take very seriously the less-than-certain knowledge of something that might or could have taken place. This attitude is most conspicuous when scholars resort to thought experiments which are, by definition, unverifiable. Whenever they investigate what difference would have been made if something that did not happen had indeed happened, they come very near to what philosophers consider the basic function of 'counterfactual conditionals' or simply 'counterfactuals'.

---

[19] Michael Neill, '"His master's ass": Slavery, Service, and Subordination in *Othello*', in *Shakespeare and the Mediterranean*, pp. 215–16.

[20] Shapiro, 'Preface', in *1599*, p. xx.

[21] Greenblatt, *Will in the World*, pp. 14, 23, 24, 26–7.

[22] Peter Ackroyd, *Shakespeare: The Biography* (London, 2005), pp. 3, 4, 380.

According to a standard definition, 'the so-called "counterfactual conditionals" . . . state that if something which is not the case had been the case, then something else would have been true'.[23] When the examples philosophers cite are not timeless, like the classic 'If kangaroos had no tails, they would topple over',[24] they are historical in precisely the same way as in the proposition 'If Kennedy had been president in 1972, the Watergate scandal would not have occurred.'[25] Yet literary scholars, just like historians and philosophers, used to abstain from dealing with any kind of counterfactuals for fear of compromising their profession by being vague and unreliable. 'The endlessly attractive game of speculating on the might-have-beens of history can never take us far with sense or safety.' This stern view, spelled out by the prestigious historian G. M. Trevelyan in 1948, went unchallenged for a long time, and his argument, characteristic of the rear-guard of positivism, was accepted without close scrutiny. 'For if one thing had been different, everything would henceforth have been different – and in what way we cannot tell. . . . As serious students of history, all we can do is to watch and to investigate how in fact one thing led to another in the course actually taken.'[26] Until quite recently many philosophers were no less reluctant to take conditional or counterfactual statements seriously, considering their meaning too context-dependent and uncertain to convey any reliable knowledge about the world. However, in recent decades more and more philosophers came to realize that 'the context-dependence of philosophers does not, by itself, provide a reason to say . . . that counterfactuals lack determinate truth-conditions, or . . . that a correct scientific description of the world would not contain or imply counterfactuals'.[27] In Shakespeare scholarship, this reluctance is now over: scholars of our ever more virtual new world are willing to contemplate the hypothetical outcome of an unreal condition, imagined as real, and explicitly instigate their readers to follow suit.

As the imagined alternative is often a transformation of something that was fictional in the first place, maybe we could call this type of conditional (if I am allowed to coin a phrase by analogy

with 'counterfactual'), *counterfictional*. 'Consider the trial as a whole', says Stephen Orgel inviting us to contemplate the probable consequences of an alternative plot in *The Merchant of Venice*: 'Suppose Portia had stopped the proceedings at the point where Shylock has lost his case on technicalities: how would the play be changed if, after her close reading of the bond, Shylock were sent home unsatisfied, with Antonio's life intact, and only the return of his principal, or not even that, for comfort?'[28] The imperative of the verb *suppose* is closely, if implicitly, related to that of the verb *imagine*, and the parallel use of the latter is not far to seek: thought experiments may be conveniently heralded by an explicit appeal to the imagination. Asking us to imagine something counterfactual leads Marina Warner to a duly hypothetical question and an unverifiable answer; more importantly, she can safely rely on the widespread, if tacit, methodological assumption that acknowledges her procedure as a fully legitimate way of producing knowledge. 'So imagine a visitor from the New World to Shakespeare's England, with a twenty-first-century ethnographer's curiosity about other people's religions and beliefs: would such a tourist have been able to deduce from Shakespeare's plays much about Christianity as a faith or a moral system?' Marina Warner's answer to her own question: for this imaginary visitor Shakespeare's plays 'would have provided' more research material about pagan and Renaissance magic than about Christianity and divine redemption.[29]

Counterfactuals are sometimes invented for the sake of providing an imaginary counter-example

---

[23] John L. Pollock, *Subjunctive Reasoning* (Dordrecht and Boston, 1976), p. 1.

[24] David Lewis, *Counterfactuals* (Oxford, 1973), p. 1.

[25] Pollock, *Subjunctive Reasoning*, pp. 1–2.

[26] G. M. Trevelyan, 'Stray Thoughts on History', in *An Autobiography and Other Essays* (London, 1949), p. 91.

[27] Robert C. Stalnaker, *Inquiry* (Cambridge, MA, 1987), pp. 147–69.

[28] Stephen Orgel, 'Shylock's Tribe', p. 51.

[29] Marina Warner, 'Painted Devils and Aery Nothings: Metamorphoses and Magic Art' in *Shakespeare and the Mediterranean*, pp. 311–12.

to underpin a thesis. 'These explanations [for Shakespeare having changed the Bohemia of Robert Greene's *Pandosto* to the Sicilia of *The Winter's Tale*] are genre-dependent', says Jonathan Bate, 'They grow from a perception of the play as romance, myth, pastoral, tale. . . . Similar explanations would not have been forthcoming if Shakespeare had swapped England and Scotland in a history play.'[30] The fact that Shakespeare had *not* swapped those countries in a history play is neither weakening the argument nor making it less serious, as it would have done in the heyday of positivist strictures. Observing that it is Iago, not the Turk, who drives Othello back to barbarity, Jonathan Bate attempts to restore a faded (probable) meaning of the play by imaginatively re-enacting a contemporary act of indirect communication a performance was (might have been) meant to serve. 'If we want to read the play for a contemporary political "message", the newly-anointed King's Men might be saying to the new king, "It's not the stranger, the alien power, the Turk, who is now the threat – they have been defeated, as you reminded us in your poem on the battle of Lepanto; no, the danger is the cunning, self-serving politicker, the enemy within"'.' This is not far-fetched, of course, and sounds plausible enough, especially when supported by the impeccable logic of a further argument: 'One might even go so far as to identify that enemy with Catholicism and Spanish sympathy. Why does the Venetian Iago have a Spanish name, reminiscent of St Iago of Compostella, who was known as Matamoros, the Moor killer?'[31] Yet the verb 'might be saying', meant to reconstruct the probable message of the King's Men, is heralding something no less hypothetical than the 'one might go so far' formula referring to the scholar's own process of experimental thinking. Although the final question is rhetorical, suggesting (persuasively) that no other explanation is plausible, experiments like these offer a kind of knowledge transcending the limits of our evidence and relying, partly at least, on what we suppose and imagine. The best practicioners of this hypothetical reasoning are fully aware of the rules, assumptions and consequences of the twilight zone they are entering; they know the intricate logic that goes with the territory and make the most of it.

In order to make the most of it, however, Shakespearians have had to overturn the taboo that used to be called the intentional fallacy and to be free to ask, even answer, the outmoded yet irresistible question: what was (or might have been) in Shakespeare's mind? Not that they have become insensitive to the methodological problems implied in this question. 'Throughout I try to be especially cautious when advancing claims about how Shakespeare might have felt – knowing that, except through the distorting lens of what he expressed through his characters or the speakers of his sonnets, we have no access to his feelings.' Yet this dutiful recapitulation of the intentional fallacy (in James Shapiro's preface) is promptly followed by a defiant insistence on the project. 'Still, I hope to capture some of the unpredictable and contingent nature of daily life too often flattened out in historical and biographical works of greater sweep.'[32] Remembering the general caveat of the New Critics does not mean that we take heed of doing what they considered futile guesswork. In the 1940s Cleanth Brooks maintained that we know too little about poets' methods of composition to tell why an Elizabethan poet used a particular metaphor. 'In any case', added Brooks, 'we shall probably speculate to better advantage – if speculate we must – on the possible significant interrelations of image with image rather than on the possible amount of pen-biting which the interrelations may have cost the author.'[33] Nowadays there is a renewed interest in some kinds of pen-biting, especially in the process of thought that may have preceded authorial decisions.

Trying to ascertain where Shakespeare set *Measure for Measure* (before Middleton changed the setting to Vienna), Gary Taylor enumerates the

---

30 Bate, 'Shakespeare's Islands', p. 299.
31 Bate, 'Shakespeare's Islands', p. 295.
32 Shapiro, 'Preface', in *1599*, p. xx.
33 Cleanth Brooks, *The Well Wrought Urn: Studies in the Structure of Poetry* (New York, 1947), p. 24.

interpretations and adaptations of the play which have set the story in Italy, points to Italian names and motifs in the text, the church called Saint Luke's, the vineyards mentioned three separate times, the chastity belt associated with Italian lasciviousness and male jealousy, and concludes that 'Shakespeare, writing *Measure*, was thinking of Italy, not Germany.'[34] Such queries, once rejected as both impossible and irrelevant, are now considered indispensable, and the tentative answers may be offered as the final result of a scholar's work. A case in point is the conjecture at the end of Alexander Leggatt's paper on *A Midsummer Night's Dream* and *Timon of Athens*: 'It may be that when Shakespeare contemplated the walled cities of the Mediterranean world one conclusion he came to was that for all society's dependence on the barriers that divide and distinguish, true communities are made not when walls are built but when they are taken down.'[35] Well, 'it may be' that Shakespeare came to this conclusion 'when' (and *if*) he contemplated those walled Mediterranean cities, but we don't have (and most probably, shall never have) sufficient evidence to substantiate the conjecture and assert that he did or did not come to this conclusion, or that he did or did not contemplate those cities at all. The sentence is predicated on a fictitous, imaginary situation and asserts something unverifiable, and unfalsifiable. Yet, conjectures like this are accepted as depositories of knowledge, sufficient enough to justify the publication of a paper.

Such probings into Shakespeare's mind are often searching for the author's motivation behind a concrete textual move, and are leading to hypothetical results summed up in conditional sentences. Jonathan Bate uses the same kind of subjunctive reasoning to demonstrate that some hypotheses of authorial intention can be safely excluded in order to emphasize the probability of others. 'Shakespeare wrote all his later plays in the knowledge that the King's Men were required to give more command performances at court than any other theatre company. Would he not have paused for a moment to consider the diplomatic resonances of such names as Bohemia and Sicilia in *The Winter's Tale*, Milan and Naples in *The Tempest*? After all, he knew from his run-in with the descendants of Sir John Oldcastle a decade earlier that to attach the wrong associations to a particular name could easily offend.'[36] Such attempts at reconstructing a political situation in order to divine whether and to what extent Shakespeare took into consideration the court's sensitiveness when writing his play, and how his self-censorship worked, cannot yield certainty but, as the cited (eloquently inconclusive) rhetorical question suggests, can lead to some degree of probability. 'In these circumstances,' concludes Bate, 'it seems eminently plausible that on deciding to dramatize a story about the kings of Sicilia and Bohemia, and knowing that the play would at some point go into the court repertoire, Shakespeare thought it would be politic to make the monarch with Spanish, as opposed to Rudolfine, associations the one who is irrational, cruel, and blasphemous.'[37] To be eminently plausible is of course not the same as being certain, and after this statement it is reassuring to see Bate himself carefully weighing the alternative hypothetical consequences of whether or not his supposition is right.

But right or wrong, such suppositions have an important limitation in common: they can never infer the absolute causal necessity of a textual decision from a motive that may have prompted it. At this point we have to reconsider René Wellek's sobering thesis, formulated half a century ago, that '[c]ausal explanation, in an ultimate sense, is impossible in matters of mind: cause and effect are incommensurable, the effect of specific causes unpredictable'.[38] Wellek doubted that 'anybody has yet succeeded in proving that because of certain events either in history or in literature there must

---

34 Taylor, 'Shakespeare's Mediterranean *Measure for Measure*', pp. 250–1.

35 Alexander Leggatt, 'The Disappearing Wall: *A Midsummer Night's Dream* and *Timon of Athens*', in *Shakespeare and the Mediterranean*, p. 204.

36 Bate, 'Shakespeare's Islands', pp. 299–300.

37 Bate, 'Shakespeare's Islands', p. 300.

38 René Wellek, *A History of Modern Criticism: 1750–1950*, 8 vols. (New Haven, 1955–1992), vol. 1, p. 8.

have followed another specific event'.[39] Doubting that the creativity of an artist can be fully determined by circumstances, and tracing back the positivist vogue of influence-hunting to the scholars' inferiority complex vis-à-vis the scientists, Wellek denied the validity of at least some kinds of causal explanation in literary studies. 'Causal explanation as deterministic scientific explanation by deduction from a general law or demonstration of a necessary efficient cause fails if applied to literature.'[40] These sceptical reflections on causality are worth remembering at this new turn of Shakespeare scholarship, especially because later Wellek referred to well-known Shakespearian examples to demonstrate that we cannot tell in what way literary works would be different if others had not preceded them. 'We . . . can never argue even that works of art as closely related as the pre-Shakespearean *King Leir* and Shakespeare's *King Lear* or *Hamlet* and the German *Bestrafter Brudermord* are connected causally: we can only say that Shakespeare knew the earlier play and can describe the use he made of it and we can show that the German play is ultimately derived from *Hamlet*.' To illustrate that 'a work of art need not have caused another one' and that a work can be considered as 'the necessary condition of another one' but not as its (sufficient) cause, Wellek transposed the case of Shakespeare into the hypothetical realm of counterfactual reasoning: 'even if we knew the life of Shakespeare in the greatest detail, knew the social and theatrical history of the time better than we know it now, and studied all the sources, we still could not predict the peculiar shape and physiognomy of a play like *Hamlet* or *King Lear* if we did not know the text or imagine it would have been lost'.[41]

Recalling all these arguments for their new relevance is of course not the same as accepting them without any qualifications. Concerning the basic terms of the debate I would argue that whereas Wellek took the concept of causation in the strongest possible sense (that is, implying necessity, sufficiency and predictability), nowadays we need less demanding concepts of causation with more use for literary scholarship. On the other hand we need not accept Wellek's contention that the impossibility of causal explanations (in the strong sense) discredits literary history writing and leads to the fall of literary history as scholarly enterprise. Moreover, Wellek's argument is marred by a pervasive distrust in the worth of speculative reasoning. When he maintained that we 'can speculate rather futilely' on 'eventualities', like how different modern literature would be 'if there had not been an *Iliad* or an *Odyssey* or an *Aeneid* or a *Divine Comedy*',[42] he used the verb 'speculate' in precisely the same (pejorative) sense it was used by positivist scholarship. Yet, I think, Wellek was right in denying that the sufficient cause of a literary work can ever be established, hence our new rehabilitation of the undemonstrable should proceed in full awareness of our uncertainties. This awareness need not be disabling and a scholar need not be paralysed by recognizing 'the impossibility of . . . demonstrating causal connections between historical events, since these events are, by definition, unique and unrepeatable'.[43] Philosophers testify to their own technical difficulties in defining concepts of causality in relation to probability and subjunctive reasoning,[44] so Shakespeare scholars can be proud of their concerted effort to explore the issue in practical research.

All in all, the latest shift in Shakespeare studies has taken place differently from the way it was expected or envisaged. Firstly, it cannot be fully described in terms of *what* it is that scholars have come to study, whether something definable in itself, or a cultural construct. 'Not so long ago, it went without saying that Shakespeare's works should be studied for their intrinsic meaning', says Paul Franssen, adding that by now 'many scholars

---

[39] René Wellek, 'Recent Czech Literary History and Criticism', in *Essays on Czech Literature* (The Hague, 1963), p. 203.

[40] René Wellek, 'The Fall of Literary History', in *The Attack on Literature and Other Essays* (Chapel Hill, 1982), p. 73.

[41] Wellek, 'The Fall of Literary History', pp. 72–3.

[42] Wellek, 'The Fall of Literary History', p. 72.

[43] David Perkins, *Is Literary History Possible?* (Baltimore, 1992), p. 18.

[44] Pollock, *Subjunctive Reasoning*, pp. 1, 145.

have turned their attention to the way Shakespeare has been appropriated, *made* to mean something'.[45] This is undoubtedly true, and yet it is not the latest shift. Nor can we fully explain it in terms of warring methodologies, be they those of Post-Colonialism, New Historicism, Feminism and Cultural Materialism, or the traditional 'vertical' analyses of literary historians versus the new 'horizontal' cultural studies which Jean E. Howard's methodology seeks to reconcile.[46] The monographs and papers of the last two decades testify to yet another kind of novelty: a methodological coherence warranted by a new epistemological consensus. They demonstrate how much a scholarly community can accomplish by accepting a coherent set of assumptions and strategies to establish a distinct logic and language, indeed a whole new rationale of research instead of what Charles Marowitz branded as 'the traditional claptrap of Shakespeare criticism', or 'a kind of theatrical balancing act which juggles theories, hunches, insights, propositions, analyses, paradoxes, paradigms, aberrations, and delusions'.[47]

Prevailing over any diversity, we are witnessing the emergence of a remarkably unified new discourse, a distinct grammar (and latent philosophy) of subjunctive reasoning, with counterfactual and counterfictional conditionals. The new idiom rehabilitates the dignity of uncertain knowledge, allows us to speculate about the highly probable or the merely possible, and accepts inconclusive and alternative results as opposed to the former, basically still positivist, drive to confine scholarship to the (allegedly) pure description of the (allegedly) factual and verifiable. Before this new turn, generations of scholars had been unwittingly following the footsteps of Johann Gottfried Herder who, having read that the Academy of Sciences offered an award, in 1769, for a lucid and comprehensive hypothesis about the origin of language ('En supposant les hommes abandonnés à leurs facultés naturelles, sont-ils en état d'inventer le langage? . . . On demande une hypothèse qui explique la chose clairement et qui satisfait à toutes les difficultés'),[48] flatly rejected the terms of the Academy, criticized the inconclusiveness of any hypothesis,

and did his best to answer the great question by a thesis based on what he considered solid and reliable data instead.[49] We owe a lot to the long, chequered reign of that sentiment, and need not allow its latent theoretical problems to eclipse the wholesome influence it exerted on the humanities, but we can be no less pleased with the current reappraisal of the hypothetical. The subdisciplines involved in Shakespeare scholarship (ranging from biographical studies to theatre history, or from textual bibliography to cognitive studies) may or may not all benefit from the new methodological stance, and it remains to be seen whether the diverse branches can use it in an equal measure, or whether some of them should use it, if at all, in a wholly different way. Yet remembering that Cicero considered the patient search for probable knowledge the proper task of academics (as opposed to the cleric's duty to vindicate the unquestionable certainty of prescribed doctrines),[50] one may conclude that our return to the probable is no reason to lament. We shall need a clearer awareness of our philosophical assumptions, and occasionally a little more sophistication, but on the whole the incipient new idiom and rationale of Shakespeare scholarship seems to be eminently suitable for what has recently been called the 'far-reaching epistemological and ontological shift' caused by our age of virtual worlds and hyperreality.[51] At a time when

---

[45] Paul Franssen, 'From Shakespeare's Italy to Italy's Shakespeare: Biographical Fantasies of Love and Power', in *Shakespeare and the Mediterranean*, p. 332.

[46] Jean E. Howard, 'Gender on the Periphery', in *Shakespeare and the Mediterranean*, pp. 344–62.

[47] Charles Marowitz, 'Shakespeare's Outsiders', in *Shakespeare and the Mediterranean*, pp. 206–7.

[48] Johann Gottfried Herder, *Frühe Schriften 1764–1772*, ed. Ulrich Gaier (Frankfurt am Main, 1985), p. 1274.

[49] Johann Gottfried Herder, 'Abhandlung über den Ursprung der Sprache', in *Herders Werke*, I–V, ed. Wilhelm Dobbeck (Berlin, 1969), p. 190.

[50] Cicero, *Academica: Liber secundus: Lucullus, in De natura deorum; Academica*, trans. H. Rackham (Cambridge, MA, 1994; Loeb Classical Library), pp. 472–4.

[51] Philippa Berry and Margaret Tudeau-Clayton, 'Introduction', in *Textures of Renaissance Knowledge*, ed. Philippa Berry and Margaret Tudeau-Clayton (Manchester, 2003), p. 2.

the criteria and, indeed, the very concept of our knowledge are bound to be redefined, to bring together Cicero and cyberspace would be no small achievement. Working with a precise methodological rationale of the probable would suit our new age of the virtual far better than the old reliance on an allegedly exclusive certainty of the tangible.

SHAKESPEARE AS PRESENTIST

JOHN DRAKAKIS

I. NOW

Between Saturday 30 June 2012 and Saturday 21 July the BBC broadcast the second tetralogy of Shakespeare, borrowing its title from Sir Peter Hall's and John Barton's larger, politically nuanced 1960s project, *The Hollow Crown*. The cinematography of Rupert Goold's production of *Richard II*, broadcast at the opening of Wimbledon Fortnight was lavish, and some of the images were drawn from 'Art': the death of Richard, presented in the manner of painting of the death of St Sebastian by Pietro Perugino (*c.*1446–1523), signalled early in the production by having one of the 'caterpillars of the commonwealth', a knowingly self-conscious Bagot, transformed into a court 'artist', finishing a canvas depicting the death of St Sebastian. The emphasis in this production was on a masculine politics, and upon the androgynous Richard's failure to embody them. As if to reinforce this impression, details such as the dialogue between the Duchess of Gloucester and John of Gaunt (1.2), were cut, and the actor playing Richard 'an effete and distanced' Ben Wishaw, was modelled, according to the director, on the figure of the late Michael Jackson. The final play, *Henry* V, directed by Thea Sharrock and broadcast some five days before the opening of the Olympic Games in London, offered a similarly severely pared down version of the play, omitting Captains Jamie and Macmorris, seriously restraining Fluellen, omitting Henry's soliloquy at 4.1. beginning 'Upon the king', Fluellen's report of the French killing of the 'boys' guarding the luggage, and the dialogue between Pistol and Fluellen that concludes 5.1. The meticulous visual 'realism' of Sharrock's production departed from cinematic tradition that had begun by acknowledging the discrepancies between theatre and film (Olivier) and the artificial nature of the cinematographic image itself (Branagh), with the result that it served to render the appeals of the 'voice over' Chorus to 'piece out our imperfections with your thoughts' largely superfluous.

The larger multiform 'context' that provides a cultural envelope for this version of 'The Hollow Crown' comprises two heavily commercialized sporting occasions (Wimbledon and the Olympics), the Leveson enquiry into a series of shocking press violations of democratic process involving Rupert Murdoch and his curiously extended 'family', the banking scandal that has escalated from the irresponsible selling of stock-market derivatives to the unethical (and apparently illegal) manipulation of the Libor rate, and the scandal involving a private company's failure (G4S) to provide adequate security for the Olympic Games. If we add to that promised strikes by various trade unions, then we have available to us a range of meanings that we can invest in a 'reading' of these plays. The downplaying of Irish and Scottish tensions, the containment of the 'trade union' voice (Williams and Bates), the brief emphasis on the responsibilities of the CEO (Henry) and his urging of the efforts of his soldiers ('We're all in it together'), the dynastic marriage and the emphasis on aristocratic history, and the triumphalism at a time of financial austerity, authorized through 'Shakespeare' as honorary Olympian, all provide us with what we need to render these plays meaningful to a twenty-first-century popular audience. But they do require us to perform acts of 'reading' upon them, since they appear to fall short with regard to one of the major principles of the 'presentism' to which they ostensibly appeal. Nor, it must be emphasized, is this a question of an ideological caricaturing 'of Shakespearean energies' as that most recalcitrant and splenetic of ideologues, Harold Bloom, seems to have thought.[1]

The recent rule-of-thumb definition of 'presentism' outlined by Cary di Pietro and Hugh Grady as 'an approach to the past based on a self-conscious positioning of the perceiver in the present aware of historical difference but aware as well of the approachable but real epistemic barrier between ourselves and the past, and deliberately choosing to highlight our presentness',[2] might stand as something of a rebuke to the casual and partial suggestiveness (intended or inadvertent) of 'The Hollow Crown' in its twenty-first-century incarnation. On the other hand, it could equally help to tease out an investment in what Bruno Latour has identified as the 'factish': 'the robust certainty that allows practice to pass into action without the practitioner ever believing in the difference between construction and reality, immanence and transcendence',[3] hence the obsessively Bloomian emphasis upon 'character' as the ultimate source of 'action'.[4] As a transparent mirror of 'reality' *Richard II* foregrounds a ruler out of touch with his people – an allegation frequently levelled at the present Prime Minister, David Cameron. It addresses a kingdom in need of austerity but 'leased out like to a tenement or pelting farm', to incompetent privatized concerns, and it counsels against the political perils of taxing the rich. Add to that a 'teflon' Bolingbroke who knows just how to sacrifice any lackey feckless enough to 'interpret' his bidding, and a warning to future manipulators of the economy from a self-consciously contrite deposed chief executive who finally, and belatedly, discovers a moral compass to warn that: 'The time shall not be many hours of age / More than it is ere foul sin, gathering head, / Shall break into corruption' (5.1.57–9),

and we have something whose resonances extend far beyond the confines of 'character'. Moreover, at this stage it is important to recognize that to acknowledge such resonances is not to 'universalize' these plays, since it is we who are projecting our concerns onto them.

In the following two productions, of *1* and *2 Henry IV*, textual and political subtleties are dispensed with in order to emphasize a progressively degenerating, self-seeking, aristocrat Falstaff who at one point in *2 Henry IV* has a gratuitous sexual encounter with Doll Tearsheet and a gradual quasi-romantic evolution of Hal from 'innocence' to 'experience'. The trajectory of the tetralogy is given a suitably ponderous epigraph by the director, Thea Sharrock, who asserted naively a week before the broadcast of *Henry V* that 'Hal learns to become a king in front of our eyes' (8.7.12). Brecht would certainly have had something to say about that process and about the details themselves.

'Shakespeare in the present' to purloin the title of a Terence Hawkes book, is, self-evidently, the position from which we start to make Shakespearian texts 'speak'. A recent review of the new National Theatre production of *Timon of Athens* – not by a 'critic' but by BBC Newsnight's economics editor Paul Mason – provides a convenient support for this claim. Mason observes:

At the very moment that Leveson, Chilcott and the Tyrie committee are crawling over the reputations of those in power, the National Theatre's corporate sponsors – which include Goldman, JP Morgan and Accenture – get

---

[1] Harold Bloom, *Shakespeare: The Invention of the Human* (New York, 1998), p. 13.

[2] Cary di Pietro and Hugh Grady, 'Presentism, Anachronism and the Case of *Titus Andronicus*', *Shakespeare*, 8:1 (2012), 49. But they go on quickly to observe that 'Without historical consciousness, we are in danger of succumbing to a false universalism. But without a firm understanding that the meaning of the past is rooted in our reconstruction of it in the present, we are in danger of immersing ourselves in an empty search for facts and differences for their own sake.'

[3] Bruno Latour, *On the Cult of the Factish Gods* (Durham and London, 2010), p. 22.

[4] Bloom, *Shakespeare: Invention of the Human*, p. 16.

to watch it all played out as a Jacobean drama, and from the best seats in the house.[5]

The Guardian, the newspaper that inaugurated the investigation into the activities of the Murdoch press, published Mason's review, and the narrative 'used' Shakespeare, as Hawkes would put it, 'as a powerful element in specific ideological strategies'.[6] Corporate sponsors and media-bedazzled academics can, of course, assent glibly to the anti-intellectual platitude that 'The truth that Shakespeare spoke still speaks to us today',[7] while at the same time shrugging their shoulders like Webster's Vittoria Corombona (or her modern lookalike, Rebecca Brooks), and assert, in the face of the overwhelming allegations to the contrary, 'This character 'scapes me'. In a later observation, addressed initially to the role that critics adopt, but that also has a wider current application, Hawkes observes:

Reaching backwards they can't afford to examine the position in the present from which that manoeuvre is undertaken. As a result they discount the nature of the choosing and the omissions, the selections and suppressions that determine it. Yet to avoid the pitfall by taking one's present situation fully into account seems inevitably to compromise the project.[8]

This observation, redirected, describes accurately the antics of News International executives, a discredited government Secretary for Culture, Media and Sport, and disgraced CEOs of major banks, to name but a few, but it is also a clarion call for a different mode of reading, capable of distinguishing between, and putting to cultural and political use, different kinds of 'knowledge'. A failure to acknowledge what is at stake, or, even worse, to dismiss it out of hand, is to get caught in a Shakespearian imaginary of our own making, a hall of mirrors that collectively purport to 'hold the mirror up to nature'.[9]

2. ANACHRONISM AND UNIVERSALITY

Of course, in dealing with Shakespeare, or any other pre-twentieth-century writing, we

encounter these texts, as di Pietro and Grady correctly argue, 'outside their moment of origin, and they have meaning for us because their very otherness is a challenge to our own thinking, feeling and values'.[10] This formulation, however, raises three issues: firstly, there is the question of 'their moment of origin', and secondly, of the extent of their 'very otherness'. But it is also in danger of eliding both the text's own 'presentist' investments, and what we then make of them when *we* invest their particularities with *our* meanings. Linked to both these issues is a third, the question of a 'universal' knowledge that is sometimes claimed for a writer such as Shakespeare, and appealed to by unwary historians. This third issue is the most difficult to deal with because it requires us to separate out the elements of what Alain Badiou has identified as a combination of 'the appropriation of particularities with the immutability of principles',[11] where the issue of appropriation, and for what purpose, becomes crucial. Suffice it to say that what Badiou seeks to do, in a critical account of St Paul's gospels that has a much wider application, is to negotiate two seemingly opposed tendencies:

Whatever people's opinions and customs, once gripped by a truth's post-eventual work, their thought becomes capable of traversing and transcending those opinions

---

[5] Paul Mason, 'The Elite Debacle', *The Guardian Review* (Saturday, 21 July 2012), 12.
[6] Terence Hawkes, *Meaning by Shakespeare* (London and New York, 1992), p. 3.
[7] Justin Champion, broadcast on BBC4 on 8 July 2012.
[8] Terence Hawkes, *Shakespeare in the Present* (London, 2002), p. 2.
[9] Harold Bloom's utterly unselfconscious gaze into Shakespeare's 'mirror' simply adds to an ill-thought – through metaphor, one more layer of mystification: 'Shakespeare's is a mirror within a mirror, and both are mirrors with many voices' (Bloom, *Shakespeare: Invention of the Human*, p. 15). This is hardly surprising since the elitist Bloom has already identified himself with Hamlet: 'we (sic) more than ever regard Hamlet as *one of us*, somehow dropped into a role in a play, and the wrong play at that' (p. 13).
[10] Di Pietro and Grady, 'Presentism', p. 51.
[11] Alain Badiou, *Saint Paul: The Foundation of Universalism*, trans. Ray Brassier (Stanford, 2003), p. 99.

and customs *without having to give up the differences that allow them to recognise themselves in the world.* (my italics)

And he proceeds to insist that 'it is imperative that universality not present itself under the aspect of a particularity'.[12] Recognizing 'differences' but also 'traversing and transcending' them, completes the equation outlined by Grady and di Pietro. It is also worth emphasizing here that 'universality' is not a neutral or 'objective' form of knowledge since the process of generalization from particularities discloses a *political* commitment that informs the very process of interpretation itself. It is this that allows us to gauge the partisan nature, indeed, the intellectual thinness of a conservative position such as that proposed by defenders of traditional hierarchies, such as Harold Bloom. It is also precisely this that dissuades literary presentism from making premature claims about the 'universality' of Shakespearian texts, while at the same time acknowledging, in principle, a capacity to 'traverse' and 'transcend' 'those opinions and customs' that comprise the 'particularities' that facilitate recognition 'in the world'. Ernesto Laclau's carefully discriminating gloss on Gramsci's analysis of the production of universality makes this point, emphasizing that it is the powers that prevail in civil society that seek to engineer a '*hegemonic* universality' (original italics).

With Marx and against Hegel, Gramsci moves the centre of gravity of social analysis from state to civil society – any 'universal class' arises from the latter, not from a separate sphere constituted *above* civil society. But with Hegel against Marx, he will conceive this moment of universality as a *political* moment, and not as a reconciliation of society with its own essence. For Gramsci, however, the only universality that society can achieve is a *hegemonic* universality – a universality contaminated by particularity.[13]

An alternative to the social imaginary that this produces is a universality that is an accumulation of particularities articulated as absences that are both determinate and radically other, but that offer a glimpse of an emancipated future. This is not, it should be emphasized, the sort of 'universalism' that, according to Bloom, writing in 1998 and overwhelmed by a tide of 'theory', was, even then,

in the process of ebbing, 'not much in fashion' and that for him was no more than a synonym for globalization and multiculturalism.[14] Bloom's defence was to lionize a representative figure from the (English) past in the face of a serious challenge to its assumptions and prejudices from an allegedly 'foreign' (French) present that his own institution had already taken great pains to domesticate.

Return to the present

In his contribution to *Presentist Shakespeares* (2007) Kiernan Ryan has eloquently argued that *Troilus and Cressida* 'estranges the present, enabling us to perceive our time as history, as the superseded past of a terminal future'.[15] Although there are moments in Ryan's essay when it is difficult to determine the difference between his own and Shakespeare's 'reading' of particular areas of this problematical text, his injunction to presentist criticism to engage 'in a dialogue with futurity as open and dynamic as the dialogue it must engage in with the past' confirms what has been there in the writings of Terence Hawkes for some time: a political investment in this dialogue to ensure, not a collusion 'in the perpetuation of the present', but rather to bring to bear 'upon the present, through *its accounts of Shakespeare's plays*, the prospect of a radically transfigured future'.[16] In other words, Ryan urges an evaluation of the present, rather than a description of its contours, as the pathway towards an emancipated future, and his claim is that 'literature' in general, and *Troilus and Cressida* in particular, offers ways of pre-figuring it. The question that

---

[12] Badiou, *Saint Paul*, p. 99.

[13] Ernesto Laclau, 'Identity and Hegemony', in Judith Butler, Ernesto Laclau and Slavoj Žižek, *Contingency, Hegemony, Universality: Contemporary Dialogues on The Left* (London and New York, 2000), p. 51.

[14] Bloom, *Shakespeare: Invention of the Human*, p. 3. It is difficult to see how Bloom squares this crude definition of 'universalism' with the obviously feared spectre that he caricatures and demonizes as 'the anti-elitist swamp of Cultural Studies' (p. 17).

[15] Hugh Grady and Terence Hawkes, eds., *Presentist Shakespeares*, p. 182.

[16] Grady and Hawkes, *Presentist Shakespeares*, p. 183.

this formulation fails to resolve satisfactorily, however, is that it is in danger of eliding two entities: the contours of the text *in itself* and the mechanisms for deciding what they are, and the 'reading' that is then projected onto it by the critic.

The question of 'moment of origin' that this argument implies is not so much one of absolute but of relative *difference*, since in purely structural terms any 'present' is made up of dominant, residual and emergent strands. If we follow this logic through then the exemplary Shakespearian play text is an 'event' and not a source, a collocation of words and implied actions, that subjects representations of the 'past' to the demands of its own 'present'. Elsewhere Ryan has applauded the virtues of a historicism that has 'dealt a devastating, but by no means fatal, blow to the complacent conservative cliché that Shakespeare's drama depicts the abiding truths of the human predicament'.[17] To this extent presentism cannot be perceived as an alternative to historicism, rather, it proposes a different way of dealing with historical material that is itself dynamic, and within a context that challenges the too-hasty claims made for 'the radical otherness' of the past as something that is both incomprehensible and entirely inaccessible. Indeed, we see Shakespeare himself engaged in precisely this dialogue *particularly* in those plays that deal with tracts of 'history' that have either run their course (Roman history), or that culminate in, and inform, the Elizabethan 'present' (the history plays). History is neither an object nor an obstacle, but part of a multifaceted dialogue which the reader/critic is consciously and actively engaged in, bringing with them their own, frequently complex cultural perspectives that shape particular narratives. This, of course, also includes the reader's own political predisposition in the broadest sense of the term. Nonetheless, it is crucial to emphasize that the stimuli that produced at various times Shakespeare's excursions into Roman history were *clearly* different from those that lie behind our own excursions into 'history' in films such as Ridley Scott's *Gladiator* or the HBO *Spartacus: Blood and Sand* series, or indeed behind Shakespeare's own 'history' or 'Roman' plays, and hence the 'particularities' on

which they draw cannot but be different. All 'imaginative' excursions into 'history' do not escape from this process, whatever their disclaimers, and this is something to which the recent spate of popular literary biographies of Shakespeare, no matter how carefully they are crafted, or how sensitive they are to historical detail, amply testify.

In their account of *Titus Andronicus*, di Pietro and Grady draw attention to an 'anachronistic, fictionalised setting in a Gothic-Moorish Rome that never was' which, they argue, derives from Shakespeare's investment in this particular stage of Roman history. But they then go on to add a further layer to the principle of 'anachronism' in their conviction that '[t]he play stages for audiences in the early twenty-first century, our contemporary experiences of terrorism in mediated, aesthetic form'.[18] The processes of 'mediation' and 'aestheticization' are important but they should not be allowed to obscure the '*moment* of origin' as itself deeply implicated in these processes *at the point of origin*. The 'particularities' may have changed, the *differences* may have become sharper, but the 'otherness' is not radical but constitutive, and relative, and it is we who fashion coherent universal truths from these particularities. Our engagements with the past should not, unless we are overwhelmed by 'wonder', involve our being surprised when we hear our own voices. Perhaps we need to rethink the concept of 'anachronism', not as historical matter displaced from a linear temporal structure, or even as a stimulus to organic allegorical thinking, but as a necessary, self-conscious drawing together of disparate particularities in new constellations that extend and expand the moment of the text's own identifiably presentist origins. This is certainly what Ryan's account of *Troilus and Cressida* does. Nor should this enquiry be relegated to the formal realm of an originary 'aestheticization' since this is never quite what it seems in the context of modern media, and both impinge upon the wider political debate in our own present in which the

---

[17] Kiernan Ryan, 'Shakespeare's Universality', *The Difference of Shakespeare*, ed. Allesandra Marzola (Bergamo, 2008), p. 25.
[18] Di Pietro and Grady, 'Presentism', p. 45.

assault on the humanities in higher education takes the form of requiring them to justify their existence in *economic* and 'impact' terms. Shakespeare's theatre, the beginning of a new enterprise, from the evidence we can glean from texts such as *Henry V* and *Julius Caesar*, sought to justify its own cultural identity, and in a hostile environment replete with contradictions. The resurgence of interest in 'Shakespeare' as a popular phenomenon that asserts national identity through cultural heritage, selectively displacing portions of his texts into the arena of sporting excellence (underwritten by a corporate financial ethos that is shamefully anti-democratic) enacts a dystopia that, in its own day and in terms of its 'particularities', *Troilus and Cressida* can be *made* to address. But it does require us to rethink, to translate even, some of its historically specific terms. Even so, 'we' (and we need to be careful how we characterize that 'we') are the future that these plays address, at the same time that we have our own, rather less collegial, 'present' and an even more uncertain future to contend with.

3. SHAKESPEARE'S PRESENTISM

But what of Shakespeare's own 'presentism'? What can we legitimately speculate about motive and practice at a time well before the building of a cultural icon had got under way? Perhaps we can glean something of the process from the evidence of the furore surrounding the publication and reception of Dr John Hayward's *the First Part of the Reign of Henry IV* published in 1599, situated between the appearance of the first three plays of the second tetralogy and *Henry V* and very quickly read as an allegory of the fractious relationship between Elizabeth and Essex. In an 'Epistle Apologeticall' that was intended for the suppressed second edition, Hayward insisted:

I have purposely passed over many imputations, as some secrete sences, which the deepe searchers of our time have rather framed then found, partly upon the science of myne owne conscience, and partly seeing no reason wherefore they should be more applied to this booke, then to the original authors out of which it hath been gathered.[19]

He adopts a conservative stance of resisting the 'presentism' of some of his readers in an appeal to 'the science of myne owne conscience', although he blames his own presentism on his 'sources' (Tacitus, Machiavelli) that are open to the same allegations. The distinction seems to be between an allegorical reading that he disclaims responsibility for and a 'presentist' reading that includes his 'sources' as the origins of his 'history's' topicality.

Hayward's most recent editor, John J. Manning, has argued that, '[l]ike Shakespeare in the history plays' and 'in his analysis of particular characters or events, [Hayward] resists pointed political advocacy: his reference point is the human condition'.[20] This familiar foreshortening of the process obscures the view that, structurally, 'the human condition' at any one time is, as we have already implied, an amalgam of 'particularities', and a too easy or too swift appeal to universalism distorts what is really dynamic, relative and impermanent in its detail. Hayward's understandable attempt to divest himself of the responsibility for the particular implications of his text testifies to the seriousness of his own predicament, and he spent some time in prison as a consequence, but the political climate changed in 1603 and he was released. Even if he was at pains to project onto his 'sources' the responsibility for his own brand of historiography, Elizabeth's own administration had no hesitation in according an ontological privilege to the 'present' in its reception of texts like *Richard II*, or Hayward's *Life and Raigne of Henrie IIII*.

That the history tetralogies are steeped in a Tudor ideology that exposes the contradiction between a providential reading of history and a practical political pragmatism is a commonplace, but what is less emphasized in relation to the current debate is that throughout these 'histories' an ontological privilege is accorded to the Elizabethan present as the vantage point from which the past

---

[19] John J. Manning, ed., *The First and Second Parts of John Hayward's the Life and Raigne of King Henrie IIII* (London, 1991), p. 65.

[20] Manning, *The First and Second Parts*, p. 41.

can be reviewed. More importantly, that ontological privilege can have very serious political consequences and the wary writer would, doubtless, seek to negotiate them with care. Engagement with the past is far from naive, but the larger pragmatic context that mediates its reception traverses a range of surviving texts, many of them non-dramatic, that focus on matters of governance, anxieties surrounding moral, ethical, economic, religious and political concerns as well as the role of the theatre in Elizabethan and Jacobean society. These are just some of what Paul de Man would call a world 'seen as a configuration of entities that designate a plurality of distinct and isolated meanings' that allegory might, from time to time, coalesce into 'a configuration of symbols ultimately leading to a total, single, and universal meaning'.[21] However, even allegorical reading sometimes obscures the fact that, as de Man also observed, 'if there is to be allegory, then the allegorical sign refers to another sign that precedes it', although the two can never coincide because 'it is of the essence of this previous sign to be pure anteriority'.[22] This is precisely the anteriority that Hayward appealed to in his own defence, although a presentist and thoroughly pragmatic reading proved to be the more politically persuasive, supported, we might surmise, by exposing Hayward to some of the instruments of torture. But also, in another sense, that 'pure anteriority' directs the alert *reader* to the tensions that are either explicitly presented in the text *or* that are the product of a reading that brushes these particularities against the grain.

As far as we know, Shakespeare managed to avoid the experience of Hayward, although we can only speculate about what he 'thought' about it. The most cursory reading of *Richard II* shows Shakespeare to have been much more circumspect than the Marlowe of *Edward II* about the question of deposition, even though his clearly Machiavellian reading of the emergence of Hal as the 'perfect' king can never quite free itself from the fear that a pragmatic politics *might* incur a divine wrath. The second tetralogy is also haunted by questions of representation and performance, and the extent of their deep implication in the politics of the period. This is also true of Shakespeare's tetralogy of Roman plays that deal ostensibly with larger tracts of Roman history but in much more obviously opportunistic ways. *Coriolanus*, and the possible context of its inception, is a play that immediately comes to mind, and we can see how complex questions of republican rituals, governance and questions of leadership are dealt with not only in a Jacobean guise but also, recently, in a very modern guise through Ralph Fiennes's 'translation' of the play into film. If we compare Coriolanus with other Shakespearian military leaders then he emerges as an exemplary figure. He powerfully resurrects the figure of Titus Andronicus as a foundational force that sustains Rome, and he possesses the physical prowess that kings such as Richard II or Lear lack. He is clearly the figure to 'represent' his fellow Romans *except that* he resists the republican rituals that would legitimize his claim. Indeed, Coriolanus is a 'king' transplanted into a republic where his military prowess is needed but feared.

In *Coriolanus* the eponymous hero, who takes his name from a geographical location and a battle, is admirably transparent in an environment where that transparency is open to political manipulation by various vested interests. In perhaps the most reductively materialistic way possible Coriolanus *is* his body, but ironically, the actor is uncomfortable at the prospect of 'acting':

> What must I say?
> 'I pray, sir,' Plague upon't! I cannot bring
> My tongue to such a pace. 'Look, sir, my wounds.
> I got them in my country's service, when
> Some certain of your brethren roared and ran
> From th' noise of our own drums.'   (2.3.50–5)

After Coriolanus has gone through the motions of seeking support from the Citizens for his consulship, the Machiavellian tribunes Brutus and Sicinius begin to undermine his newly acquired political legitimacy. Brutus echoes Coriolanus's critique of his electorate, but renders it ironical

---

[21] Paul de Man, *Blindness and Insight: Essays in the Rhetoric of Contemporary Criticism*, 2nd edn (London, 1983), p. 188.
[22] de Man, *Blindness and Insight*, p. 207.

by casting doubts on the Citizens' own political naivety in failing to quiz the candidate in a sufficiently thorough manner:

> Did you perceive
> He did solicit you in free contempt
> When he did need your loves, and do you think
> That his contempt shall not be bruising to you
> When he hath power to crush? Why, had your bodies
> No heart among you? Or had you tongues to cry
> Against the rectorship of judgement?   (2.3.199–205)

At a time when alternative forms of political organization were being openly discussed *Coriolanus* raises some serious questions concerning issues of popular representation, authoritative government and the qualities that a good figurehead must possess, all against the background of an emerging parliament and a monarch insistent upon his own absolute rule. Nor can we disregard these 'particularities' since they point to Shakespeare's own 'presentist' investment in a series of issues that, on the evidence of the historical narratives available to him, had already been resolved, and in ways that absolute monarchy was committed to avoiding. Of course, the Caroline future brought absolute monarchy into direct conflict with its subjects, and for a while the unthinkable actually occurred.

But there is another link, between *Henry V*, *Julius Caesar* and possibly *Coriolanus*, over and above their common concern with these ostensibly political and thematic questions. The first two of these plays are candidates for the inaugural performances in 1599 at the new Globe theatre, and the third offers a sophisticated representation of the distinction between the display of credible rituals of power before a willing populace including the republican demands imposed upon it, compared to the manipulations to which it can lead through theatrical display. Coriolanus is a good leader (in a strictly Machiavellian sense) who is a bad actor, and in the UK we have recently been exposed to a modern avatar in the figure of Gordon Brown. To view Coriolanus, the dramatis persona, *and* the play without reference to current particular questions of political leadership or the nature of modern political violence in all its guises, is

to fall into the very pit of abstraction in which much traditional criticism has wallowed for some time. Indeed, already the contours of the debate about modern political leadership have moved on, in Britain and in the USA. The play will, as it is resurrected, continue to be measured against new political yardsticks all of which will graft their own particularistic investments onto a 'text' whose language and social predicaments are open to constant reinvention and translation.

In addition to this presentist concern, these plays are also parts of 'histories' that seek to establish analogies between past and present through a principle of 'repetition': that human societies repeat archetypal conflicts (universals) but in situations (particularities) of their own making. But even repetition, as Gilles Deleuze has observed, is no guarantee of 'universal truth'. In what begins as an interpolation of Marx's famous axiom, he notes that 'repetition is never an historical fact, but rather the historical condition under which something new is effectively produced'. He continues:

Repetition is a condition of action before it is a concept of reflection. We produce something new only on condition that we repeat – once in the mode which constitutes the past, and once more in the present of metamorphosis. Moreover, what is produced, the absolutely new itself, is in turn nothing but repetition: the third repetition, this time by excess, the repetition of the future as eternal return. For even though the doctrine of eternal return may be expounded as though it affected the whole series or the totality of time, the past and the present no less than the future, such an exposition remains purely introductory . . . Eternal return affects only the new, what is produced under the condition of default and by the intermediary of metamorphosis. However, it causes neither the *condition* nor the *agent* to return; on the contrary, it repudiates these and expels them with all its centrifugal force. It constitutes the autonomy of the product, the independence of the work. It is repetition by excess which leaves intact nothing of the default or the becoming-equal. It is itself the new, complete novelty.[23]

---

[23] Gilles Deleuze, *Difference and Repetition*, trans. Paul Patton (London, 1994), p. 90.

This account could apply to *Coriolanus* in its Jacobean guise just as it might apply to Ralph Fiennes's recent 'return' to the play as something 'new' that prevents both the 'agency' *and* the 'condition' from returning to the 'default or the becoming-equal' of the text of Shakespeare's play.

Similarly, in relation to the second tetralogy, the logic that informs Hayward's *The Life and Raigne of Henry IIII* is modelled on earlier 'histories' that Sir Francis Bacon recognized when he castigated Hayward for having taken 'most of the sentences of Cornelius Tacitus, and translated them into English, and put them into his text'.[24] It was, however, Elizabeth's attorney-general, Sir Edward Coke who in 1600 queried why Hayward had chosen 'a storie 200 yere olde, and publisheth it this last yere'.[25] In their eagerness to attribute to Elizabeth I a direct identification with Richard II, scholars may have obscured the *differences* between Shakespeare's careful theatrical representation of the act of deposition itself and the more risky enterprise of relegating the persona of the monarch to the status of a professional performance. This anxiety occasionally informs the Roman plays but also, and in a slightly different register, the entire second tetralogy.

To take the particular example of *1 Henry IV*, informed criticism no longer reads the emergence of Hal into the figure of the perfect king as a romantic passage from 'innocence' to 'experience', or indeed as the 'education' of a prince – of which the recent *Hollow Crown* series seems to have been entirely unaware. The antics of our own Prince Hal notwithstanding, we would miss the point if we were to interpret Hal's strategy in Shakespeare's play as nothing more than an excusable youthful exuberance. From the end of Act 1 scene 2 of *1 Henry IV* Hal's Machiavellianism is made clear; it is Shakespeare's anglicized version of Machiavelli's *Il Principe*, and it drives a wedge between a residual ideology of divine right that Henry IV himself has violated, and whose rhetoric he has rendered bankrupt, and a secular history that is a direct challenge to the prescriptions of the theory of divine right but that, paradoxically, makes regicide a contributary *cause* of the arrival of the 'perfect' king.

Richard's 'tragedy', like that of Coriolanus in the later play, is that he fails to understand the inefficacy of the very ideology upon which his power rests until it is too late. Meanwhile political governance is shown to be a messy and, at times, bloody business in desperate need of a discredited discourse to shore up and legitimize its subterfuges and its actions. Hal's deception allows him to holiday in an Eastcheap that is what Slavoj Žižek might have called 'the traumatic real' out of which 'the social is *constituted*',[26] and his articulation of that process affirms the complex dialectic that, according to one editor of the play, subverts its dramatic form altogether:[27]

> So when this loose behaviour I throw off
> And pay the debt I never promisèd,
> By how much better than my word I am,
> By so much shall I falsify men's hopes;
> And, like bright metal on a sullen ground,
> My reformation, glitt'ring o'er my fault,
> Shall show more goodly and attract more eyes
> Than that which hath no foil to set it off.
> I'll so offend to make offence a skill,
> Redeeming time when men think least I will.
>
> (1.2.205–14)

Machiavelli was one of the first to recognize a disjunction between political theology[28] and secular politics, and Shakespeare's second tetralogy explores the tensions that that recognition generated. Stephen Greenblatt has argued that this soliloquy is evidence of a much more deep-seated and persistent tendency that Hal possesses:

---

[24] John Manning, ed., *John Hayward's The Life and Raigne of King Henry IIII* (London, 1992), p. 2.

[25] Manning, *John Hayward's The Life and Raigne of King Henry IIII*, p. 3.

[26] 'Holding the Place', in Butler, Laclau and Žižek, *Contingency, Hegemony, Universality*, p. 311.

[27] See David Scott Kastan, ed., *1 Henry IV*, Arden Series 3 (London, 2002), pp. 34–5.

[28] The phrase is familiar from Ernst Kantorowicz, *The King's Two Bodies: A Study in Medieval Political Theology* (Princeton, 1957), pp. 193ff. But see also Carl Schmitt, *Political Theology II: The Myth of the Closure of any Political Theology*, trans., Michael Hoelzl and Graham Ward (Cambridge, 2008), pp. 38–45.

He is an anti-Midas: everything he touches turns to dross. And this devaluation is the source of his own sense of value, a value not intrinsic but contingent, dependent upon the circulation of counterfeit coin and the subtle manipulation of appearances.[29]

Greenblatt goes on to note that Hal's 'redemption' 'is not something toward which the action moves but something that is happening at every moment of the theatrical representation'.[30] In other words, from the point of view of an audience's experience, the teleology that informs this play, and the three subsequent plays in the tetralogy, is given an unusually frank articulation even before the action gets under way. The dynamics of everything that follows point up the extent to which an identifiable symbolic order is caught in the act of negotiating the refurbishment of its supporting rhetorics in the face of a subversive energy that it both fears and lives off. Indeed, the precarious refurbishment of a political rhetoric is shown in *Henry V* to proceed hand-in-hand with an appeal to the theatre audience to authorize the very representational materials of the theatre itself as an institution committed to the principle of mimesis. It would not be unreasonable to conjecture that this is *Shakespeare*'s reading of a 'history' whose own fissures appear through an artistic process of the displacement of contemporary fears, idealizations and hopes that gesture towards both a future for the newly inaugurated theatre *and* towards a wider, extra-theatrical Elizabethan present. Here we see the 'present' shuttling between 'past' and 'future', between a cultural knowledge rooted in the narrative formulations of a 'history', colliding with a present torn between theological and secular perspectives and gesturing towards a future that, in this case, can only be provisionally secured, and in the process exposing serious tensions between dramatic form and political content.

4. PRESENTISM AND FORM

One of the difficulties that presentism poses involves a shuttling between 'form' and 'content'. We may acknowledge an affinity between Shakespeare's texts and our own concerns at the level of theme. For example, in what has become over the last few decades a familiar formulation, David Kastan suggests that the Falstaff scenes in the *Henry IV* plays are 'not a generously humane alternative to the power-seeking impulses of aristocratic history, but, rather, their very justification, an antimasque, to switch dramatic metaphors, that is routed in the face of, and to prove, legitimate authority'.[31] We may interpret this alternating formal emphasis as the play's attempt to stave off the extreme effects of a Lacanian 'real' that can, by definition, only be approached metaphorically and that is, in effect, 'that traumatic "bone in the throat" that *contaminates* every ideality of the symbolic, rendering it contingent and inconsistent'.[32] In some respects, therefore these formal tensions are readily recognizable to later generations as 'continuities' that have a trans-historical value, allowing us to bridge the temporal divide between 'then' and 'now'. However, to universalize these details is to empty the text of its particularities, the very details that the play itself appeals to in order to negotiate its way through them. In a purely formal sense each step in that negotiation forms part of what we may recognize as the play's aesthetic structure. However, what we cannot do is move directly to some recognized modern equivalent that can guarantee a timeless universality. Ernesto Laclau makes this point forcefully in the distinction he makes between 'pure particularity' that he argues has 'no politics' and the demands to 'be made in terms of something transcending it'. He continues:

The chains of equivalence are always disturbed, interrupted by other hegemonic interventions that construct meanings and identities through different equivalent chains . . . There is an essential unfixity in the meaning attached to some contested signifiers as a result of the

---

[29] Stephen Greenblatt, *Shakespearean Negotiations: The Circulation of Social Energy in Renaissance England* (Oxford, 1988), p. 42.

[30] Greenblatt, *Shakespearean Negotiations*, p. 43.

[31] Kastan, ed., *1 Henry IV*, pp. 37–8.

[32] Slavoj Žižek, 'Holding The Place', in Bulter, Laclau and Žižek, *Contingency, Hegemony, Universality*, p. 310.

operation of a plurality of strategies in the same discursive space. If I have called the general equivalent unifying an undisturbed equivalential chain the *empty signifier*, I will call the one whose emptiness results from the unfixity introduced by a plurality of discourses interrupting each other the *floating signifier*.[33]

To this extent, the 'universality', whose contours Laclau seeks to sketch out and that transcends particularity, is predicated upon a lack, and a desire to transform the 'empty signifier' that is the space of a hitherto 'undisturbed equivalential chain'. In its preoccupation both with the present and with the future, 'presentism' reads its own 'plurality of discourses' into the text and makes of its 'undisturbed equivalential chain' a contemporary document invested with a distinctly contemporary politics.

But this is not without its difficulties, as can be illustrated by Kiernan Ryan's account of Ulysses's critical 'definition' of presentism in *Troilus and Cressida*, in terms of 'the present eye' praising 'the present object' (3.3.181). The play is, indeed, as Ryan tellingly observes, 'Shakespeare's *Iliade travestie*' and Ulysses's championing of 'hierarchy' as a means of diagnosing the malaise of the Greek camp in Act 1 scene 3 is articulated, not unexpectedly, in a distinctively negative register. The same is true of his strategy designed to provoke Achilles into action two acts later in which inactivity in the present is asserted to obliterate the past and mortgage the future. In both instances the extra-dramatic context is the fear of a particular formulation of the Lacanian 'real', anarchy, the 'empty signifier' that Shakespeare's play in its own presentist garb acknowledges, but at the same time lays open to question. However, because the argument is couched in generalities, the text lays itself – or the critic himself, lays the text – open to re-inscription as 'a grim prevision of life under late capitalism at its most predatory, alienating and destructive'.[34] 'Shakespeare's *Iliade travestie*' is, without question, a 'presentist dramatic practice', but surely it *does not* and *cannot* 'speak directly to us' except through the mediation of a 'presentist critical practice', that seeks to engage with it, on its own terms. Ryan is, of course, right to warn us against the dismissal of 'the wealth of archival labour and interpretive ingenuity invested in recent historicist accounts', or the 'petrifying' of the play 'by the Medusan gaze of historicist retrospection'. We may recognize, in terms that transcend the play's particularities, 'the ruthless imperatives of egotism, competition and acquisition in love and war alike' that characterize the ethos of *Troilus and Cressida*,[35] or any situation that shares its structural contours, but measured against the fruits of 'archival labour' these general terms reveal historical *differences* that help to sharpen critically our own sense of identity. The result is a rather different model of presentism from that implied in part of Ryan's conclusion: that 'Shakespeare's compelling illusion of a continuous, inconclusive present subjects us, too, to the despotism of "the extant moment" and the prospect of oblivion forged by the lack of an alternative future.'[36] For him the 'empty signifier' and the 'floating signifier' have been elided and in such a way that the historicism against which he correctly inveighs slides in by the back door, despite his inadvertent refusal to separate Shakespeare's 'presentism' from our own. We are, of course, only 'subjected' in Ryan's terms, if we assent to that identification, and what *we* do with the Shakespearian text, that is itself a collocation of its own presentist concerns – and indeed with the Humanities generally – will be crucial if we are to 'make' our own history *and* our own future.

---

33 Ernesto Laclau, 'Constructing Universality', in Butler, Laclau and Žižek, *Contingency, Hegemony, Universality*, p. 303.

34 Kiernan Ryan, '*Troilus and Cressida*: The Perils of Presentism', *Presentist Shakespeares*, ed. Hugh Grady and Terence Hawkes (London and New York, 2007), p. 174.

35 Ryan, '*Troilus*', p. 174.

36 Ryan, '*Troilus*', p. 181.

GREATER SHAKESPEARE: WORKING, PLAYING, AND MAKING WITH SHAKESPEARE

HESTER LEES-JEFFRIES

Es handelte sich darum, aus einem Gedicht ein Halstuch zu machen[1]

This is an article about literary and cultural appropriation, its limits, the various forms that it takes, and the ways in which it has been, and might be, interpreted and assessed. That this epigraph is taken not directly from Benjamin's letter but rather stolen from Juliet Fleming's *Graffiti and the Writing Arts in Early Modern England* emphasizes that the discussion which follows is in many respects synthetic, drawing on work done by others in the fields of early modern literature and material culture, social anthropology and cultural studies. But I am also interested and indeed implicated (I suspect more literally than Benjamin and Adorno ever could be) in the changing, or making, of poetry into scarves: specifically Shakespeare's poetry, broadly interpreted, and not just scarves, but postcards, posters, T-shirts, earrings, necklaces, bags, mugs and even tea-towels. This essay's working title was 'theorizing the tea-towel', and indeed I have had to make my peace with the fact that more people will own a tea towel with my name on it than will ever read a single word that I write.[2]

Work on 'the Shakespeare industry' is not new, but I have recently had occasion to consider my own involvement in it, partly as a result of completing a book for the Oxford Shakespeare Topics series on Shakespeare and memory. The epilogue, 'Remembering Shakespeare', briefly rounds off the previous chapters' exploration of classical, early modern and theatrical memory with ideas about literary memory, from the First Folio onwards, institutional memory, in the form of libraries, theatres and theatre companies, and popular memory, especially Shakespeare tourism and souvenirs. This last is the area in which I have some practical experience, as since 2005 I have been collaborating sporadically with my friend the designer Kit Grover on memorabilia for the Royal Shakespeare Company, specifically *Greater Shakespeare*, the 'Shakespeare Tube Map' (see Illustration 18), which was launched across a range of products in September 2007 and attracted considerable media attention from all over the world.[3] To date a range of products bearing the map are available from the RSC in their shops and online, and it remains one of their core, and most successful, product ranges in terms of both sales and awards.

As befits an article about more-or-less jokey mass-market souvenirs, the discussion that follows

---

[1] 'It is a question of changing a piece of poetry into a scarf.' Walter Benjamin, in a letter to Gretel Adorno, used as an epigraph by Juliet Fleming, *Graffiti and the Writing Arts in Early Modern England* (London, 2001), p. 9. Some of this article is based upon papers I gave at the Seminar in the History of Material Texts in Cambridge (February 2010) and at the inaugural conference of the Centre for Material Texts in Cambridge (April 2010); a much-abbreviated version appears in *Shakespeare and Memory* (Oxford, 2013).

[2] But then again, so far as I know, I'm the only member of the Cambridge English Faculty even to have my name on a tea towel. That's impact for you.

[3] One of the weirder conversations of my academic life involved trying to convince a Russian journalist, over the phone, that no, the London Underground stations were not being renamed after Shakespearian characters.

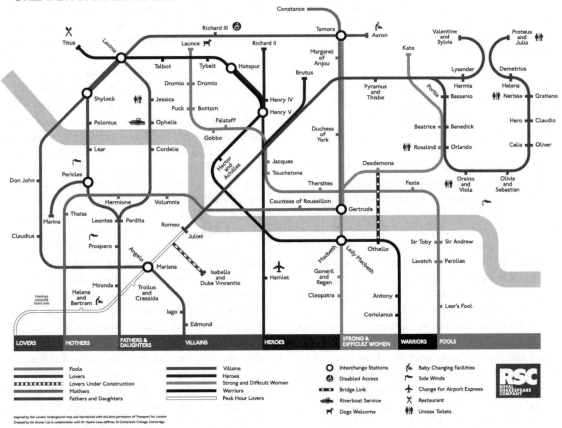

18. *Greater Shakespeare*, by Kit Grover.

here is open and playful. It is organized into three overlapping strands. The first concerns early modern ideas about the interactions between texts, images and objects, and in particular images and objects which are also texts. The second explores some of the work that has been done on souvenirs, and in particular on Shakespeare souvenirs; this part of the essay also discusses *Greater Shakespeare* in more detail. The third brings these two strands together, in order to suggest that what makes a good souvenir in the twenty-first century in particular is less its display or appropriation of pure text, but rather how it transforms the textual into a synthesis of form and content which is in some respects recognizably early modern in its appeal to the viewer or consumer's facility in interpretation, their delight in play, and in its wit.

Shakespeare souvenirs and other appropriations are an easy target. They are cheap fodder for the new historicist anecdote; cultural materialist fury directed towards Thatcherite arts, education and social policy in the 1980s had as one of its triggers the appearance, at that time, of Shakespeare's likeness on the £20 note and in holographic form on the Barclaycard bank card. Versions of Shakespeare's 'portrait', almost always derived from the First Folio Droeshout engraving, have long been applied to non-souvenir objects: Douglas Lanier mentions, almost in passing, 'beer, moving companies, cigars, and breath mints', and suggests that

Shakespeare's face offers an easy means for attaching commercially useful connotations to products, among them quality craftsmanship, *gravitas*, trustworthiness, Britishness, antiquity, cultural sophistication, intellectuality, and artsiness.[4]

Lanier's list of connotations, again, suggests the easy target that such appropriations can afford critics, ready to quibble iconoclastically (the term is telling) with such cultural naivety, if not simply to scoff.

Yet Shakespeare souvenirs, specifically, have a very long and diverse history, engagingly traced by Samuel Schoenbaum in *Shakespeare's Lives* (1970, 1991), Barbara Hodgdon in *The Shakespeare Trade: Performances and Appropriations* (1998), Graham Holderness and others in *The Shakespeare Myth* (1988). The New Place mulberry tree's apparently inexhaustible transformation into pipes and snuff boxes[5] has as its successors the fridge magnets and tea-towels, lavender bags and baseball caps that are the stuff of mid-range mass-market souvenir shops all over Stratford and beyond. Barbara Hodgdon notes that in the mid-1990s the Birthplace shop itself stocked 'framable notecard portraits – Titania as a squirrel, the Macbeths as weasels, Malvolio as a racoon, Portia and Hamlet as mice, Shylock as a fox, Desdemona as a white kitten' and suggests that 'With the purchase of a pair of Shakespearrings, one can take on attributes of his characters. Pearls signify most of Shakespeare's women – Hermione, Perdita, Portia, and Desdemona – as well as Hamlet . . . Cleopatra's profile appears on a silver coin-like disk, and Falstaff in his Dionysian guise, as a purple and emerald banana and bunch of grapes.'[6] The Shakespearrings at least were not in evidence in the summer of 2012, although there is clearly still a market for pictures of cats dressed as Shakespearian characters, and the Birthplace shop's window was filled with one of the current best-sellers, a yellow rubber duck sporting the 'iconic' hair, collar, and doublet of the First Folio portrait. (The Shakespeare duck was also on sale in the British Museum shop in 2012, where it was joined by Viking duck, Roman duck and – surely straining the limits of hybridity – Sphinx duck.)

As all these examples demonstrate (and many more would be possible, drawn from any decade) such objects and by implication (and more uneasily) those who purchase them are a soft target. It is very easy to turn a scholarly sneer upon such things, a sneer that is as much aesthetic and social as it is intellectual. Anecdotes are cheaper even than tea-towels. But what such objects also demonstrate is that as far as the souvenir market is concerned, Shakespeare's text and texts count for very little, for Shakespeare souvenirs above all display his signature, his 'likeness', and images relating to his biography, real or imagined. In the mid-1990s, according to Hodgdon, the best-selling souvenirs at the Birthplace shop in Stratford were the tea-towels printed with images of the Shakespeare properties. Best-selling in this context means that the tea-towels were being ordered for the shop wholesale in minimum lots of 240 *dozen*.[7] The connection between souvenirs and place is axiomatic, as I will explore more fully below, but here even the Shakespeare connection is almost incidental.

At other, earlier points in the history of the Shakespeare souvenir or related-object industry, it is scenes or characters from the plays that have dominated. One might think, for example, of Staffordshire and other pottery figures of both Shakespeare himself and prominent actors in character: the Victoria and Albert Museum collection includes William Macready as Shylock (1852), Edmund Kean as Richard III (1840) and John Philip Kemble as Hamlet (1852), as well as many other examples, and dozens of Shakespeares; many of these were based in turn on popular watercolours and engravings. They cannot be 'likenesses'

---

[4] Douglas Lanier, *Shakespeare and Modern Popular Culture* (Oxford, 2002), p. 112.

[5] A crab-tree near the village of Bidford, under which (according to 'tradition') the young Shakespeare slept off his youthful excesses and indiscretions, met the same souvenir end. See Samuel Schoenbaum, *Shakespeare's Lives* (Oxford, 1991), pp. 74, 109, 125.

[6] Barbara Hodgdon, *The Shakespeare Trade: Performances and Appropriations* (Philadelphia, 1998), p. 238.

[7] Hodgdon, *The Shakespeare Trade*, p. 234; the tea-towels are still available.

beyond the broadest of outlines, but the multiple associations, with actor, character and playwright, are what give the objects their significance and value. Some nineteenth-century paintings and engravings are still very familiar: the best-known example, John Everett Millais's *Ophelia* (1851–2), has become more or less detached from its Shakespearian origin. It is currently available in the Tate Britain shop as a fridge-magnet as well as a poster in two sizes, while an internet search turns up mugs, book-bags, key-rings, cushions, playing-cards, bathroom tiles, a babygro, and an iPhone cover. But the decline of the tradition of pictorial staging, and of the 'tales from Shakespeare' genre (although Charles and Mary Lamb's classic version remains in print, and other children's re-tellings appear regularly) has perhaps reduced the widespread familiarity of such scenes, outside a very small repertoire: Hamlet and the skull, Ophelia, the balcony scene, Othello and Desdemona perhaps, but probably not, for example, the nightmare scene in *Richard III*, in which David Garrick was portrayed by William Hogarth in a painting of 1745, which then became the model for, successively, an engraving and a popular Staffordshire figurine *c*.1840 (the V&A alone has at least eight examples). Today, even the Shakespeare Memorial by the Clopton Bridge in Stratford, which surrounds Shakespeare with figures from the plays (Hal trying on his father's crown, Falstaff, Hamlet, Lady Macbeth) needs decoding in a way that wasn't necessary when likenesses of Ellen Terry as Lady Macbeth were more widely known, for example. Now, she might as well be any old weasel in a frock.[8] Similarly, the recognizability of quotations from Shakespeare, if not their currency, is diminished. Most people don't know they are quoting Shakespeare, as Bernard Levin's much-reproduced squib, of which more below, informed them.

One of the challenges, therefore, of creating memorabilia is that familiarity with both the texts and the iconic 'moments' of Shakespeare's plays cannot be assumed. The audience at performances by the Royal Shakespeare Company are more self-selecting than those who dash from coach-park to open-top bus tour, but they don't necessarily know the texts of the plays very well; even though, if they have seen the same play in many different productions, they will probably have seen more varied interpretations of those iconic moments than a theatre or film-goer in the first half of the twentieth century. This challenge, however, presents an opportunity that can be met creatively by both designers and critics, and that is certainly what I have tried to help Kit Grover to do in his work for the RSC.

The genesis of *Greater Shakespeare* was roughly as follows. The RSC had been interested in developing a range of products with more 'content', for example, more engagement with the texts, plots and characters of the plays, than some of the earlier products that Kit had already very successfully produced for them (which had drawn on the RSC logo, on stylized patterns of 'Tudor' half-timbering, and on more general ideas relating to performance). One of the things that Kit had wondered about was a family tree of Shakespeare's characters, and, being a good early modernist with a garden history background, the first things that I thought of were heraldic family trees, which often used 'real' trees as frameworks, medieval Trees of Jesse, showing the genealogy of Jesus Christ as dreamed by his ancestor Jesse in Isaiah 1.1, and portraits of melancholy young men under trees, like the images of Henry Percy, Earl of Northumberland.[9]

The family tree idea kept returning, and it very much chimed with something that I was noticing in my teaching for the Shakespeare paper to first-year undergraduates in Cambridge, which was that

---

[8] As in Barbara Hodgdon's anecdote, quoted above.

[9] There is a fine sixteenth-century example of a heraldic family tree, in the form of a tree, at Charlecote Park in Warwickshire; the 'Lyte Pedigree', showing the descent of James I and presented to the King in 1610, similarly uses a framework of real branches. There are surviving examples of Trees of Jesse in the windows of York Minster and Canterbury Cathedral; the oldest known example is at Chartres. Henry Percy, ninth Earl of Northumberland, is portrayed in a miniature portrait attributed to Nicholas Hilliard and now in the Rijksmuseum; a smaller version is in the Fitzwilliam Museum, Cambridge.

I was increasingly favouring a broadly chronological (rather than, for example, a more genre-based) approach to Shakespeare's plays, starting with *Titus*, *Lucrece* and the first tetralogy, and working through in a rough sequence to *The Winter's Tale* and *The Tempest*. I had also become interested in the effects of chronology not only on the plays themselves, in terms of their echoes and other forms of intertextuality, but in the effects of chronology on both actors and audiences, in terms of memory. This can be seen very straightforwardly in the in-joke that Hamlet and Polonius share with the players: 'I did enact Julius Caesar. I was killed i' th' Capitol. Brutus killed me' (3.2.99–100). But something that has interested me more and more, particularly as I have thought more about the effects of doubling, ensemble casts and relatively stable repertory companies, like the Lord Chamberlain's / King's Men, was that (and to over-simplify) Shakespeare and Burbage both knew that Burbage could play Hamlet because he had already played Richard II, Brutus and Henry V (and indeed Richard III and Hal). Both actor and playwright, and their audiences, could bring those characters and performances to bear on the characters and performances that succeeded them (and, in a repertory system, were often revived alongside them).[10] These contexts suggested that sequence, in the sense of accumulation, rather than teleology, might be an interesting thing to try to represent in relation to Shakespeare's characters and plays for all sorts of reasons.

One of these was the role of character types, the aspect of the project which took it away from simply being a family tree, which is necessarily structured around proliferation and has a roughly pyramidal structure, to being a map. Kit still has the family trees that I drew; they proved a dead end in that particular form but were very much the genesis of the map as it now exists. The map uses character types not in any fixed or conventional sense, but a more playful one: its types include heroes and villains, fools, warriors, mothers and lovers, but also fathers and daughters and 'strong and difficult women' (all the way from Tamora to Cleopatra, joined by a branch line for Kate, Beatrice, Rosalind and Desdemona). Although the

now-familiar sense of 'lines' as applied to the words of an actor's part only emerges in the nineteenth century, and that of 'line of business', as applied to the type-casting of actors, in the eighteenth, actors, managers and audiences in the Restoration theatre were accustomed to thinking of actors as having 'lines' in the sense suggested by the latter:

Actors tended to develop stereotyped characters (sometimes called acting 'lines', sometimes called 'casts') that they always played. This limited the amount they had to learn, for their education only had to teach them how to perform certain types of role . . . Actors became known for their 'lines', which were associated with their personalities in the minds of the audience – and often in fact.[11]

Although Tiffany Stern does not explicitly discuss this terminology or practice in relation to the pre-Civil War theatre, given the many continuities of such techniques explored by John Astington and others between the acting companies of the early and late seventeenth century, it seems not unlikely that such a custom and expectation already existed in Shakespeare's theatre. The connection between these 'lines' and those of *Greater Shakespeare* is of course a happy coincidence, but also perhaps a suggestive one, and separating out these 'lines' of character types in broadly chronological terms, while considering their potential for intersection and proximity, was what took us to the Tube Map model.

One of the important things about the real London Tube Map, as it was conceived and designed by Harry Beck, is that it's 'topologically correct but

---

[10] There is an illuminating discussion of Burbage's roles (as well as those of other actors), especially in the context of revivals later in his career, by John Astington, *Actors and Acting in Shakespeare's Time: The Art of Stage Playing* (Cambridge, 2010), pp. 128–30. Astington suggests 'That Shakespeare wrote for him, as has often been asserted, we can believe, if we take that to mean that Shakespeare would have been quite aware of and familiar with Burbage's kinds of power on the stage, but that parts were precisely calculated to match Burbage's characteristics is not credible to me.'

[11] Tiffany Stern, *Rehearsal from Shakespeare to Sheridan* (Oxford, 2000), pp. 152–3.

topographically distorted';[12] it's schematic and relational, but not hierarchical or teleological. There may be a whole host of reasons why South Kensington is superior to Hammersmith, but its relatively greater proximity to Cockfosters is not one of them.[13] To translate this principle to *Greater Shakespeare*, all characters do not lead to Hamlet, although in trainspotter terms Hamlet may well be the Clapham Junction (or Grand Central Station) of the canon, at times both critically and in the popular imagination pulling all towards it. In fact we left Hamlet at the centre of the map, but although the characters are set out in roughly chronological 'order', with earlier works appearing at the top of the map and progressing down the line into later, the non-hierarchical map model means that it's the proximities and relationships that matter more than any sense of destination.

As Ken Garland engagingly traces in *Mr Beck's Underground Map* (1994),[14] Harry Beck refined his design over many years, making his first sketches in the early 1930s and continuing to update it into the mid 1960s; it has been a significant influence on most other maps of public transport systems around the world. The map (more properly a diagram) has almost since its inception been an icon of modern design as much as of cartography and informatics. Happily for a design icon, however, the colours, fonts and symbols of the Tube Map are not copyright, although the map itself is. There have been a number of responses or imitations, notably *The Great Bear*, the lithograph made in 1992 by Simon Patterson, in which the names of the London Tube lines are replaced with categories (ranging from 'Saints' to 'Sinologues') and station names with people (Cockfosters has become St Anselm); it is now part of the permanent collection at Tate Modern. More like the Tube Map itself than *The Great Bear*, however, *Greater Shakespeare* is largely content without text; its data is visual without necessarily being semantic. Its strong design element makes it immediately accessible, and attractive, to the non-specialist, that is non-Shakespearian, consumer. And this is Shakespeare as urban and contemporary: not a thatched cottage or doublet in sight. Some of the ideas, especially the jokes, are more obvious than others; the intention is that the others invite further investigation and, anecdotally, this certainly seems to be happening when the poster version appears on classroom walls. Macbeth may be familiar from GCSE, but who is this 'Coriolanus' who follows him? Why aren't all the kings on the same bit of the hero line? What's Desdemona doing over there? What's going on with the fathers and daughters at the end of the line? Disabled access for Richard III seems reasonable, as does the riverboat interchange for Ophelia, but Aaron, Helena and Bertram's baby-changing facilities, Titus's refreshments, and the generous provision of unisex toilets around the comedies perhaps need to be puzzled out more carefully. In my experience, the joke that has needed the most explanation has been Hamlet's 'change here for the airport express', because that requires textual knowledge, of the 'flights of angels'. Troilus and Cressida remain my favourite joke: on a branch line from the rest of the lovers, they, like Angelo and Mariana, remain 'evenings and peak hours only'.

It is particularly appropriate that *Greater Shakespeare* is a map. Souvenirs are intimately connected with journeys, and with the use of objects retroactively to locate memory, to construct narratives in space and time. In Graham Holderness's useful formulation,

---

[12] Elizabeth Baigent, 'Beck, Henry Charles (1902–1974)', *Oxford Dictionary of National Biography*, Oxford University Press, 2004; online edn, May 2007, www.oxforddnb.com/view/article/52164, accessed 12 December 2012.

[13] For our international readers: all three of these are stations on the (blue) Piccadilly Line of the London Underground. South Kensington is an affluent area of central London, home to the Victoria and Albert Museum and many embassies, and down the road from Harrods. Hammersmith is a commercial and retail area on the River Thames in west London, dominated by the A4 (a major traffic route out of London) and a major bridge over the Thames, and Cockfosters is the end of the line, in north London. Clapham Junction in south-west London is one of the busiest stations in Europe and a byword for complex interchanges; trainspotters will note that it is not in fact on the Underground network.

[14] Ken Garland, *Mr Beck's Underground Map* (Harrow Weald, 1994).

The symbolic function of a souvenir or photograph is partly acquisitive – you exhibit it to show that you've been there, done that place – but it also operates, like the medieval relic, as the embodiment of an experience: a trigger for memory, with a magical capacity to release recollection.[15]

In Stratford in particular, the popular narrative of Shakespeare's life is set out as a location-based chronology, from 'The Birthplace' to the monument in Holy Trinity Church: Hodgdon observes of the traditional 'Birthday' procession that 'this is Shakespeare's triumphalist text: following the traces of his body from cradle to grave, the Birthday procession's itinerary maps him onto Stratford, tying him to places and properties'.[16] It was interesting that when we were working on *Greater Shakespeare*, it was the addition of the river, implicitly the River Thames (as in the London Tube Map), that pulled the design together. By referring so explicitly to London, as much as in its contemporary, functional design aesthetic, it resists the open-top bus tour, Hodgdon's 'triumphalist text', the Stratford story of the Warwickshire lad whose biography is to be mapped on to a series of half-timbered houses and thatched cottages. *Greater Shakespeare* is not simply a souvenir of a life or a world elsewhere; it is mnemonic in ways other than those proposed by Holderness, ways that might in some respects be recognizably early modern. It shows not only the progressions and developments of character types, but Shakespeare's journey, and perhaps also actors' (and audiences') journeys and memories; in this respect it both builds on and calls into question the tendency for souvenir objects, and popular culture more generally, to privilege biography over texts (let alone performance), above all in the case of Shakespeare, the cultural paradigm of the (undead) author.[17]

In her discussion of souvenir tea-towels, Barbara Hodgdon suggests that

as an object with use value, the tea towel represents the ultimate triumph of Shakespeare consumer culture through its effective invasion of everyday life, which, in postmodern culture, can be composed of souvenirs of one's life elsewhere, evidence of another self who can, in one's own kitchen or sitting room, be reminded of the realities and authenticities of other worlds, other social fictions.[18]

There is a long tradition of the incorporation of ideological, religious or political content into items for domestic use, not least in early modern culture: Angela McShane notes the way in which embroideries, ceramics and other domestic objects, such as warming pans, could express Royalist loyalties and identities in the Civil War period, whereby national politics were integrated into the domestic economy (for example in images celebrating Charles I and Henrietta Maria as an icon of the faithful companionate marriage).[19] Such ideological or other, less specific content may be domesticated or otherwise translated through an object's form and functionality, but this does not necessarily diminish its capacity to signify, perhaps rather revivifying and amplifying it. Graham Holderness describes souvenirs more generally as 'mnemonic device[s] designed to preserve memory from the wastage of time'; the double process suggested here is important, in that the souvenir object both records or 'remembers' itself and enables the viewer, the consumer, to recall more than the object itself might directly embody or express.[20]

A successful souvenir, therefore, very often does not simply quote, but rather playfully alludes; its form, its status as a designed object, is very frequently also important. There is a difference between embroidering 'to be or not to be' on a pillowcase or printing it on a coffee mug and inscribing it on to a (2B) pencil ('2B or not 2B'), available

---

[15] Graham Holderness, *The Shakespeare Myth* (Manchester, 1988), p. 7.

[16] Hodgdon, *The Shakespeare Trade*, p. 193.

[17] On this tendency, see for example Lanier, *Shakespeare and Modern Popular Culture*, p. 114.

[18] Hodgdon, *The Shakespeare Trade*, pp. 234–5.

[19] Angela McShane, 'Subjects and Objects: Material Expressions of Love and Loyalty in Seventeenth-Century England', *Journal of British Studies*, 48:4 (2009), pp. 871–86.

[20] Holderness, *The Shakespeare Myth*, p. 7. Much of my own thinking about objects, in this essay and elsewhere, has been shaped by Arjun Appadurai's *The Social Life of Things: Commodities in Cultural Perspective* (Cambridge, 1986).

with matching pencil tin. One missing ingredient is wit, still encompassing issues of play, taste, and cultural and intellectual sophistication just as it did in the sixteenth century. A quotation, entirely alienated from any gesture towards its context, either original or reinvented, can become pallid or merely pretty; sometimes it becomes bathetic, occasioning that supercilious sneer. The columnist and essayist Bernard Levin's 'On quoting Shakespeare',

If you cannot understand my argument, and declare 'It's Greek to me', you are quoting Shakespeare; if you claim to be more sinned against than sinning, you are quoting Shakespeare; if you recall your salad days, you are quoting Shakespeare; if you act more in sorrow than in anger; if your wish is father to the thought; if your lost property has vanished into thin air, you are quoting Shakespeare . . . [21]

to my mind has a faintly admonitory tone: the unsaid follow-up to 'you are quoting Shakespeare' seems to be 'and you don't realize it, you ignorant peasant'. The *RSCycle* range, although it started from a similar point (the ubiquity of Shakespearian phrases in common speech) applied its quotations with understated wit to the new icon of early twenty-first century consumer culture, the cotton shopping bag. It was the wit in matching the form and function with the content that made the difference. Good design, and often functionality, is also important (there is a reason why souvenir tea-towels, fridge magnets, mugs and shopping bags endure): souvenirs do not have to be tacky or throwaway, even when they make jokes.

Near the beginning of her discussion of 'Pots' in *Graffiti and the Writing Arts in Early Modern England*, Juliet Fleming poses the question 'What if it could be demonstrated that there are works that have all the determinant characteristics of playfulness, discursivity, imagination and self-display that are not recognized as literature?'[22] I would be reluctant to make a case for *Greater Shakespeare* as literature. But I would certainly describe it as a work that is playful, imaginative and discursive and, moreover, as existing in a dynamic and quite close relationship to literary texts, in this case Shakespeare's plays. It displays, again in a playful and discursive way,

some ideas *about* those texts, not least in performance and in relation to each other, in graphic form. In functioning in this way, at least for some readers or consumers, it reflects ideas about the relationship between objects, images and texts that are akin to those, again explored by Fleming, set out by George Puttenham in *The arte of English poesie* (1589), in his discussion of 'devices'.

Puttenham describes the way in which visual, verbal and conceptual elements of a device (for example, an emblem or heraldic device) all work together:

[they] commonly containe but two or three words of wittie sentence or secrete conceit till they [are] unfolded or explained by some interpretation. For which cause they be commonly accompanied with a figure or purtraict of ocular representation, the words so aptly corresponding to the subtilitie of the figure, that aswel the eye is therwith recreated as the eare or the minde.[23]

Puttenham's own devices include shape-poems, with a head-note instructing the reader how to read the poem. Thus in order properly to interpret a poem praising Queen Elizabeth in the form of a 'Spire or Taper called Pyramis' (an obelisk, emblem of constancy and good government), the reader 'must begin beneath according to the nature of the deuice', that is, with the last line ('Like as this faire figure') which forms the base of the spire, rather than the first line ('Skie'), its pinnacle; the poem on the same page praising God as 'the fountaine of all good' must be 'reade downward', from 'God' to 'Sure hope of heauens blis'.[24] Here Puttenham shapes the reading process itself as it takes place in time and space; the 'beholder's' negotiation of *mise en page* is inseparable from his/her interpretation of both semantic content and the physical shape of

---

[21] The piece, which includes more than sixty common phrases 'quoting Shakespeare', appeared in Levin's collection *Enthusiasms* (London, 1985), pp. 167–8.

[22] Fleming, *Graffiti and the Writing Arts in Early Modern England*, p. 114.

[23] George Puttenham, *The Arte of English Poesie* (1589), N4v–*1. (A gathering of 4 leaves signed only with numbers is inserted between the N and O gatherings.)

[24] Ibid., N1v–N2.

the device on the page (the spire, the fountain). As Fleming puts it, quoting Puttenham,

Devices are concerned not to imitate the natural world, but to create new objects of thought, giving 'maruell to the beholder' by producing effects of pleasure, hope or dread in the mind that apprehends them. They are works of ingenuity, artificial things devised by art to distract or 'occupy' the mind by inviting it to supply the concepts to which they gesture.[25]

Early modern devices are often described as witty, curious, subtle or ingenious, adjectives which implicitly make the processes of reception and interpretation mirror those of creation. Levin's 'On quoting Shakespeare', even in the poster form in which it is still readily available, is not in the spirit of Puttenham's device; the RSCycle shopping bag, albeit fleetingly, is.[26]

Puttenham concludes that devices, whether they are heraldic or emblematic (he lists many examples of both, and also includes objects such as the Garter of the eponymous Order) have a single 'use and intent',

whether they rest in colour or figure or both, or in word or in muet shew, and that is to insinuat some secret, wittie, morall and braue purpose presented to the beholder, either to recreate his eye, or please his phantasie, or examine his iudgement, or occupie his braine or to manage his will either by hope or by dread, euery of which respectes be of no litle moment to the interest and ornament of the ciuill life.[27]

This conclusion makes clear that it is the way in which all the parts of the device work together that accounts for its success or failure, and that it is the reader or beholder, as much as the poet, who is responsible for fitting together and interpreting the component parts; it is the reader who constructs meaning and infers significance. Moreoever, the device should delight as much as it instructs; it may have a moral or intellectual purpose, but it should also be diverting and entertaining, and it should please the imagination even as it provides matter on which the intellect can work. A successful souvenir, it would appear, shares many features and qualities with early modern devices as

Puttenham describes them and Fleming interprets them. As Arjun Appadurai influentially speculated,

it may not be accurate to regard knowledge at the production locus of a commodity as exclusively technical or empirical and knowledge at the consumption end as exclusively evaluative or ideological. *Knowledge at both poles has technical, mythological, and evaluative components, and the two poles are susceptible to mutual and dialectical interaction.*[28]

I would argue that *Greater Shakespeare* invites forms of intellectual and imaginative participation akin to those of the device, and that its status as a commodity (and in the most literal sense, as a souvenir, a memento, an object for sale) in many respects also corresponds to Appadurai's formulation; its intellectual content is discursive and open, but at the same time the whole is playful and entertaining.

In the introduction to *Paraphernalia*, Steven Connor makes a connection between early modern emblems and what he terms 'magical objects', in his account the taken-for-granted, the every-day (his examples include bags, plugs and rubber bands) that at the same time 'are . . . not just docile things, but signs, showings, epiphanies'. As he puts it, in terms that recall Puttenham, 'they give us work to do as well as being merely available for us to work on. And yet, their power comes entirely from us.'[29] Connor points out that many objects have their capacity to signify bound up not simply in their form, function and material, but in their 'affordances', '[their] ways of proposing [themselves] for use', and that often the richer, more magical the object, the more indeterminate and varied its affordances:[30] again, it is the openness of the object,

---

[25] Fleming, *Graffiti and the Writing Arts in Early Modern England*, p. 119.

[26] The *2B or not 2B* stationery range and the *RSCycle* products (which included mugs, trays, and T-shirts as well as the shopping bag) were also created by Kit Grover for the RSC.

[27] Puttenham, *The Arte of English Poesie*, 3.

[28] Arjun Appadurai, 'Introduction: Commodities and the Politics of Value', in *The Social Life of Things*, pp. 3–63 at 41 (my emphasis).

[29] Steven Connor, *Paraphernalia: The Curious Lives of Magical Things* (London, 2011), p. 2.

[30] Connor, *Paraphernalia*, p. 3.

the combination of stimulus, invitation and room it leaves for viewer, consumer, user that accounts for much of its power. In an appropriately Shakespearian phrase, Connor describes 'magical objects' as 'such stuff as dreams are made on', as 'playthings' that 'invite a kind of practical *rêverie*, a kind of floating but intent circling through'.[31] These are large claims, perhaps, to make for a souvenir (or indeed an object) of any kind, let alone a *jeu d'esprit* that, no matter what its ambitions may be, is still a series of jokes emblazoned upon a mug, a poster or a tea-towel. Yet I hope that those who look at *Greater Shakespeare* treat it as they would a magical object; that they puzzle, ponder, make connections, infer meanings; that they in some respect construct a discursive text which is largely independent of the particularity of Shakespeare's words, but still dependent upon his plays, more or less as they were composed and performed. I hope that they find it witty and are delighted by it, in senses that Puttenham (and Philip Sidney) would understand. And of course I also hope that it will take them further into the plays. The way to find out why Titus has that knife and fork is to read or see the play, but I can't think of a single 'quotable quote' from the play that might have the same curiosity-piquing, appetite-whetting effect.

Jonathan Gil Harris's observation that 'the play is no longer the thing: the *thing* is the thing'[32] has become a commonplace of studies in early modern literature and material culture. In this essay, I have been suggesting that the relationship between play and thing, text and graphic, can be much more interesting, open and mobile than Gil Harris's aphorism suggests. The thing can sometimes be the way into the play, a small-scale act of appropriation by both designer and consumer that is capable of being more discursive, more open, more suggestive, and at once more serious and more fun, than any selection or compilation of quotable quotes. Literary critics are increasingly at ease with the fluid and indeterminately bounded nature of the material text, comfortable with the notion of paratext, with the demise of the imagined authorial text and the ideal text. Many critics are happy to incorporate (*inter alia*) graffiti, pots, textiles and monumental inscriptions – and indeed performance – into more 'traditional' work on printed books and manuscripts. Some of the objects I have been discussing, and in the creation of which I have been involved, both exist at and redefine the boundaries of the text. In their materiality, their openness to interpretation, their integration of form, content and even function, they recall early modern ideas about the text, in particular the device. They are largely non-textual artifacts that draw more or less obliquely on Shakespeare's plays but nevertheless share the characteristics of discursivity, imagination and self-display which can be discerned in many early modern texts, and indeed in objects and in performances. And yet, in the case of *Greater Shakespeare* in particular, I hope that the play is still very much the thing, even as the thing plays.

---

[31] Connor, *Paraphernalia*, p. 4.

[32] Jonathan Gil Harris, 'Shakespeare's Hair: Staging the Object of Material Culture', *Shakespeare Quarterly*, 52:4 (2001), pp. 479–91 at 479.

'A JOINT AND CORPORATE VOICE': RE-WORKING SHAKESPEARIAN SEMINARS

SCOTT L. NEWSTOK

The American Association of University Professors (AAUP) produces an annual survey of faculty salary trends. In 2007, faculty salaries outpaced inflation for the first time in three years. That was the good news. But the AAUP took note of another emerging pattern: increasing gaps in pay between *disciplines*. We might be momentarily flattered by the fact that in their attached table, they used English professors 'as the base to express other disciplines' salaries in comparison'. But that's only until one discovers that '[o]nly other arts and humanities professors earn less . . . while business professors are now earning twice as much'. To make the comparison more painfully close to home, Rosemary G. Feal, executive director of the MLA, 'said she wasn't surprised by the pay gap, but was worried by it . . . [Feal's words:] "We ought to be rewarding those who help us learn the lessons of Shakespeare's plays just as we reward those who can teach us the lessons of Enron".'[1]

It's easy to critique the opposition of Shakespeare vs. Enron. But Feal's comment more tellingly deploys the anaphoristic '*the lessons of* ____'; in this parallelism, Shakespeare and 'Enron' (meant to stand in more generally for [mis]management) come across as being opposed to one another, yet to some degree fungible: you can derive 'lessons' from either. The rhetoric of 'lessons', while conducive to sound-bite discourse, will make many literary scholars bristle, as they often pride themselves on making any such 'lessons' problematic through hermeneutic practices rather than takeaway morals ('Shakespeare says _____'), which seem to *lessen* Shakespeare, not to lesson him. The

early modern *quaestiones* tradition, which Shakespeare inherited and elaborated, itself sought to linger in this anti-doctrinal space.[2]

But beyond the Shakespeare vs. Enron dyad, we ought to be more unnnerved by the ways in which management consulting itself has found ways to rework Shakespeare in the corporate boardroom. 'The lessons of Shakespeare [taught by literary scholars] vs. the lessons of Enron [taught by management professors]' becomes 'The lessons of Shakespeare [taught *without* literary scholars to management]' – only the latest instance of the new class realizing that it no longer needs literary study as cultural capital, or at best requires only the merest image of its most canonical figure to confirm its extant practices.[3] The notion of 'Shakespeare as Management Consultant' became prevalent in the 1990s, when over a dozen titles related to this topic were published, with the greatest concentration appearing after 1998 as overt attempts to capitalize on the popularity of *Shakespeare in Love*.[4] These publications have been discussed by many

---

[1] Cited by Scott Jaschlik, 'Real Pay Increases for Professors', *Inside Higher Ed* (12 April 2007), www.insidehighered.com/news/2007/04/12/salaries.

[2] See Joel Altman's landmark study *The Tudor Play of Mind: Rhetorical Inquiry and the Development of Elizabethan Drama* (Berkeley, 1978), as well as Theodore Leinwand's more recent essay 'Shakespeare against Doctrine', *Literature Compass: Shakespeare* (March 2006).

[3] See John Guillory, *Cultural Capital: The Problem of Literary Canon Formation* (Chicago, 1993).

[4] Among many examples, see Norman Augustine and Kenneth Adelman, *Shakespeare in Charge: The Bard's Guide to Leading and Succeeding on the Business Stage* (New York, 1999);

198

Shakespeare scholars, including Marjorie Garber, Peter Holland, Douglas Lanier and Kate McLuskie; Donald Hedrick has gone so far as to examine them as a kind of genre.[5]

What's often overlooked about these volumes is that almost all of them were spun out of management consulting *seminars*, most of which are still ongoing endeavours. These include programmes directed by Laurence Olivier's son Richard, in England, as well as by the American Republican politico Ken Adelman. In such cases, the books serve as calling cards for the seminars as much as they are books unto themselves, making them part of a nexus of promotion rather than stand-alone guides. Such seminars provide a uniquely 'extramural' (that is, beyond the more conventional walls of either the school or the theatre) mode of Shakespearian programming.[6] While difficult to recapture, I seek here to elicit some of the dynamic of these 'seminars', and sketch a brief, preliminary map of their place in the (very recent) history of management as a field of enquiry[7] as well as in the longer arc of the seminar itself, in academia and beyond.

This article had its origin in response to the 'Shakespeare and the Civic' symposium hosted by Sharon O'Dair at the Hudson Strode Program in Renaissance Studies, University of Alabama-Tuscaloosa, 13–14 April 2007. While that event brought together a range of scholars (including O'Dair, McLuskie, Hedrick, Richard Burt and Amy Scott-Douglass), what I found most beguiling about the weekend was the seminar O'Dair had commissioned from England's 'Olivier Mythodrama' programme. While Richard Olivier did not himself attend, another British-trained actor and director, Nicholas Janni, led us through their programme's 'Influential Leadership' workshop on *Julius Caesar*. The Olivier Mythodrama organization is by far the most thoroughly conceived and administratively expansive of all the management consultants doing work with Shakespeare. In contrast to similar organizations (generally run by one or two people), Janni mentioned that they had two dozen employees – in other words, a staff larger than most typical English departments in US liberal arts colleges, and as large as some university programmes.

The sessions that Janni led were, counter to what they had announced themselves to be, not particularly Shakespearian. To be sure, he gave us a schematic plot summary of *Julius Caesar*, noting moments where 'leadership' was called upon. But he rarely shared with us words from the play itself to ground his statements. In fact, in conversation with the symposium speakers the night prior to the workshop, he acknowledged that Shakespeare wasn't necessary at all for the success of the programme. 'Mythodrama' is rather more based on a four-fold schema of primal psychological 'elements' (fire, water, earth, air), from which a leader/speaker is supposed to draw and balance. Janni insisted that the *words* don't matter; the *stories* do. And indeed any story would do: Shakespeare ultimately only provides a vehicle for the lessons.

---

5 Ric Charlesworth, *Shakespeare the Coach* (Sydney, 2004); Paul Corrigan, *Shakespeare on Management: Leadership Lessons for Today's Managers* (London, 1999); Jim Davies, John Simmons and Rob Williams, *Shakespeare's Role in Modern Business* (London, 2007); Richard Olivier, *Inspirational Leadership: Henry V and the Muse of Fire: Timeless Insights from Shakespeare's Greatest Leader* (London, 2002); Jay M. Shafritz, *Shakespeare on Management: Wise Counsel and Warnings from the Bard* (New York, 1992); John O. Whitney and Tina Packer, *Power Plays: Shakespeare's Lessons in Leadership and Management* (New York, 2000).

5 Garber, *Shakespeare and Modern Culture* (New York, 2008); Holland, 'Shakespeare's Two Bodies', in *A Companion to Shakespeare and Performance*, ed. Barbara Hodgdon and W. B. Worthen (Malden, MA, 2005): 36–56; Lanier, 'Shakescorp Noir', *Shakespeare Quarterly*, 53 (2002), 157–80; Hedrick, 'Bardguides of the New Universe: Niche Marketing and the Cultural Logic of Late Shakespeareanism', in *Shakespeare after Mass Media*, ed. Richard Burt (New York, 2002): 35–57; Hedrick, 'The Bard of Enron: From Shakespace to Noir Humanism', *College Literature*, 31:4 (Fall 2004), 19–43. In 2006, McLuskie was awarded an AHRC research grant for a project on 'Interrogating Cultural Value in the 21st Century: The Case of Shakespeare'.

6 See Denise Albanese, *Extramural Shakespeare* (New York, 2010).

7 Management theory itself has in the last two decades begun thinking critically back through its origins, sociologically as well as historically: see Christopher D. McKenna, *The World's Newest Profession: Management Consulting in the Twentieth Century* (Cambridge, 2006).

During the workshop, the only time Janni recited any extensive speech from the play was when he read Marc Antony's speech over Caesar's corpse. This recitation was remarkably restrained, to the point of being a-pathetic, as if he were deliberately denying us *pathos*. Such restraint seemed to contradict the stated purpose of the session:

Learn how to build and mobilise a successful coalition, identify the sources of power for and against you and how to best influence others. Participants will practice these skills in relevant exercises. Drawing lessons from Shakespeare's political masterpiece, *Julius Caesar*, this Master Class helps leaders operate more effectively within organisational power structures.[8]

As participants in this seminar, we were supposed to be drawing upon inner, Jungian resources to command authority. Yet here was a performer curiously pulling back from any sign of dramatic intensity.[9]

What I sensed at work was a familiar opposition between a scholarly approach to Shakespeare that insists upon being committed to close textual scrutiny (going back at least to Cleanth Brooks's 'heresy of paraphrase') and a popular approach that is oriented towards plot summary and character.[10] The latter impulse we seek to frustrate, complicate and develop in our own students. In the face of this apparently enduring opposition, might there be some way to retain, model and encourage our cherished close reading practices in this kind of a management setting? Might we, in other words, find ways in which to rework our own critical habits beyond our conventional classrooms? Or is our critical practice too fundamentally antithetical to the very thrust of such 'seminars'?

Hedrick helpfully places some of the major 'Shakespeare and Management' titles along a spectrum, from the least subtle to the most sophisticated in their deployment of Shakespeare. On one end of the spectrum you have books like Frederick Talbott's *Shakespeare on Leadership: Timeless Wisdom for Daily Challenges*.[11] This volume resembles a daily inspirational calendar: there is a single brief quotation on each page, topically clustered around themes, akin to Bartlett's mode of reference. The author, or rather compiler, doesn't quite

seem to trust that you'll appreciate the quotations on their own, brief as they are: every quotation is accompanied by a prose gloss, with the inspirational tone of a motivational poster. They serve as a kind of debased modern emblem, in which the Americanized platitude bears little resemblance to the early modern source. Here's one example: 'I am the feather for each wind that blows.' Strikingly, Talbott does not include the character's name for any such entry; not a single quotation is sourced with a voice. This exposes the mode of appropriation generally underway – the voice in 'Shakespeare, MBA' books is, predictably, that of the universal, contextless wisdom of 'the Bard'. There's little attending to individuated, and especially contradictory, voices within the plays themselves.

How does Talbott gloss this phrase?

'I am the feather for each wind that blows'
Be attuned to trends and changes.

If the Leontes quotation is coming back to you, you'll recognize how bastardized this translation is, as Leontes is contemplating the fantasy of murdering Mamillius on account of his possible illegitimacy:

I am a feather for each wind that blows:
Shall I live on to see this bastard kneel
And call me father?

Which of course means: *Be attuned to trends and changes*. The quotation has been orphaned from the text and made into the bastard whose brains 'with these my proper hands / Shall I dash out'. It feels a bit like Polonius quoting a compendium of

---

[8] Olivier Mythodrama, 'Introducing Influential Leadership Lessons from *Julius Caesar*', pamphlet from leadership seminar presented at Hudson Strode Program in Renaissance Studies, 13 April 2007.

[9] As Richard Halpern has detailed, this speech was specifically cited as a model for early twentieth-century studies of advertising and mass propaganda, making it telling that Kenneth Burke and Bertolt Brecht both turned to it in their attempts to critique demagoguery in the 1930s (Halpern, *Shakespeare Among the Moderns* (Ithaca, 1997)).

[10] Cleanth Brooks, *The Well Wrought Urn: Studies in the Structure of Poetry* (New York, 1947).

[11] (Nashville, 1994).

epigrammatic *sententiae* without a proper ground. One more from Talbott:

'Patience, I say. Your mind perhaps may change.'
Give decisions time.

This is Iago's disingenuous response to Othello's outburst 'O blood, blood, blood', following the elaborate verbal seduction he's made in Act 3. Immediately thereafter Othello vows never to 'give decisions time',

> Like to the Pontic Sea,
> Whose icy current and compulsive course
> Ne'er feels retiring ebb, but keeps due on
> To the Propontic and the Hellespont,
> Even so my bloody thoughts, with violent pace
> Shall ne'er look back, ne'er ebb to humble love,
> Till that a capable and wide revenge
> Swallow them up. Now, by yon marble heaven,
> In the due reverence of a sacred vow
> I here engage my words.

Talbott, formerly Associate Professor of English (Old Dominion University) and currently Clinical Professor of Management (Vanderbilt University), prefaces his volume with this plea for pardon: 'To scholars, I beg forgiveness for the out-of-context liberties. My goal is to share Shakespeare's messages to generate and promote positive leadership.' Here, in brief, is the dynamic of treating Shakespeare as holy writ and translating the supposed 'messages' of his words into business lingo. Most other volumes, as Hedrick demonstrates, exhibit considerably more sophistication in terms of intermingling summations of the plays with reflections on business strategy. In these more elaborated arguments, Hedrick finds 'the potential for something more rigorous and even progressive . . . [it] begins to take on a sort of self-critique we know from literary studies and literary theory'. I am rather less sanguine about this subversive potential; as Richard Burt suggests, 'Most instances of Shakespeare in mass media do not have sufficient hermeneutic density to qualify as politically transgressive.'[12] While I want to retain hope that the market for such studies points to a potentially inquisitive readership, I'm not convinced that the books

themselves genuinely enact this critique. They insistently return to a narrowly familiar canon, tellingly resembling that of the United States' secondary educational system: generally some major tragedies (*Julius Caesar*, *Macbeth*, occasionally *Hamlet*), the stray comedy or romance, and inevitably *Henry V*. These volumes serve as much as *invitations* to the corporate workshops as they stand as books – workshops that are now more lucrative than the books themselves. I don't know how much Olivier Mythodrama charges, but Kenneth Adelman's 'Movers & Shakespeares' had in 2005 a going rate of $25,000 for a day's session. It's difficult to capture the dynamic of the seminar from afar, but important to identify this as an idiosyncratic kind of space in which Shakespearian readings get *performed*.[13]

We have the convergence here of at least two strands of knowledge production: the field of management and the space of the seminar. Management studies has in recent years become increasingly sociologically aware of itself – at least within a small subfield, we are beginning to see Foucauldian analysis of organizational power,

---

[12] Richard Burt, 'To e- or not to e-? Disposing of Schlockspeare in the Age of Digital Media' in Burt, ed., *Shakespeare After Mass Media*, p. 8.

[13] Note that in addition to the aforementioned volumes, there have been scores of articles on Shakespeare and leadership written by business professors (e.g. William B. Stevenson, 'A Muse of Fire or a Winter of Discontent? Teaching Shakespeare in the Leadership Course', *Journal of Management Education*, 20:1 (1996), 39–47) and management consultants (Michael Lame, 'The Shakespearean Middle East', *Yale Israel Journal*, 10 (2007), 27–35), or even reporters interviewing a figure like Harold Bloom (see Diane L. Coutu, 'A Reading List for Bill Gates—and You: A Conversation with Literary Critic Harold Bloom', *Harvard Business Review*, 1 May 2001). Such essays most often follow the case study format, a pedagogical model first instituted at the Harvard Business School in the 1920s (see Katherine K. Merseth, 'The Early History of Case-Based Instruction: Insights for Teacher Education Today', *Journal of Teacher Education*, 42:4 (1991), 243–9). They are largely off the horizon of the *World Shakespeare Bibliography*, and hence remain under-represented in surveys of the phenomenon by Shakespearian scholars (and for the consultants themselves, who keep producing readings of the plays as if no one else has ever done so before).

Goffman-, Turner- and Burke-inspired readings of organizational dynamics, and historically self-reflective studies of the emergence of the field and its subsequent professionalization.[14] They are working to complicate what was too often found in 1960s textbooks: a handful of pages offering a putative pre-history of management, usually stopping for a moment with Moses and Machiavelli before launching the narrative of Taylor's late nineteenth-century studies and then subsequent elaborations of management technique by Mayo and others.[15]

Yet it is not yet the case that these 'Shakespeare, MBA' articles or books display this kind of critical self-awareness as being a part of any tradition. What the Shakespeare books give you is a doggedly under-theorized version of a post-1980s trend to look towards charismatic figures who will offer solutions which are not native to a field – in other words, *management consultants themselves*. As scholars have long pointed out, the paradox of management consulting is that is it somehow supposed to offer *generalizable* expertise. That is to say, such expertise is non-localized knowledge; if the expertise were specific enough, there would be a need to develop or hire internally, or risk losing trade secrets.[16] This challenge – of keeping counsel external but also somehow internalizing it, balancing secrecy with revelation – is captured in Francis Bacon's allegorization of Jupiter's eating the pregnant Metis, yet giving birth to Athena through his head:

Which monstrous fable containeth a secret of empire; how kings are to make use of their counsel of state. That first they ought to refer matters unto them, which is the first begetting or impregnation; but when they are elaborate, moulded, and shaped in the womb of their counsel, and grow ripe and ready to be brought forth, that then they suffer not their counsel to go through with the resolution and direction, as if it depended on them; but take the matter back into their own hands, and *make it appear to the world* that the decrees and final directions (which, because they come forth with prudence and power, are resembled to Pallas armed) proceeded from themselves; and not only from their authority, but (the more to add reputation to themselves) *from their head and device*.[17]

Bacon subsequently cites the aphorism 'optimi consiliarii mortui' (the best counselors are the dead): 'books will speak plain when counsellors blanch. Therefore it is good to be conversant in them, specially the books of *such as themselves have been actors upon the stage*' (even if Bacon is speaking of the *political* stage).

What's complicated about this field of Shakespeare and management is that there has often been a distinct reluctance to admit literary studies into the discipline of management – a kind of disavowal[18] – and even now when admitted, it's primarily as a source of *narrative*, rather than for any *methodology* of interpretation. I conclude by turning to one account of one such seminar, run by Kenneth Adelman. I was first made aware of Adelman's work when asked by a friend to fact-check a *Fortune* profile of his consulting firm 'Movers & Shakespeares'. One of their 'lessons' from Henry's victory at Agincourt was that good leaders leverage superior technology to defeat their enemies. Henry's troops used the longbow, which helped them overwhelm a vastly more numerous French force. This fact is, of course, historically true. But this technological 'fact' is one that Shakespeare deliberately omitted from his narrative of

---

[14] See David Knights, 'Writing Organizational Analysis into Foucault', *Organization*, 9:4 (2002), 575–93; Timothy Clark and Iain Mangham, 'From Dramaturgy to Theatre as Technology: The Case of Corporate Theatre', *Journal of Management Studies*, 41:1 (2004), 37–59; Michael W. Sedlak and Harold F. Williamson. *Evolution of Management Education: A History of the Northwestern University J.L. Kellogg Graduate School of Management, 1908–1983* (Urbana, 1983).

[15] See Stephen P. Waring, *Taylorism Transformed: Scientific Management Theory Since 1945* (Chapel Hill, 1994).

[16] Andrej A. Huczynski, *Management Gurus: What Makes Them and How to Become One* (London, 1993).

[17] 'Of Counsel', in *Francis Bacon: The Major Works*, ed. Brian Vickers (Oxford, 2008), p. 380 (my emphasis).

[18] Peter Drucker proposed that managing is itself a 'liberal art . . . draw[ing] on all the knowledge and insights of the humanities and the social sciences – on psychology and philosophy, on economics and history, on ethics – as well as on the physical sciences'. (Literary study is notably omitted from this otherwise capacious catalogue.) Management becomes the art of arts: 'The Icon Speaks: An Interview with Peter Drucker', *Information Outlook*, 6:2 (February 2002).

Henry's victory, in order to play up the valour of the English soldiers and the glory of God. Thus the Adelmans actually invert Shakespeare's own 'lesson' from this play in order to justify a particular business strategy.

Shakespeare has apparently been a side-passion for Adelman since graduate study in Africa, when he listened to recordings of the plays. After working in the Ford administration as an assistant to Secretary of Defense Donald Rumsfeld, Adelman began teaching Shakespeare part-time at George Washington University. In the 1980s he served as assistant to Jeanne Kirkpatrick at the UN, then was narrowly approved by the Senate to be the negotiator for US Arms Control, followed by stints at various right-wing think-tanks. In the first years of the Bush administration, he was a member of Rumsfeld's Defense Policy Board and a primary cheerleader for Iraq invasion – earning him the nickname 'Cakewalk'.[19]

I invited Adelman to speak at the 2006 annual meeting of the Shakespeare Association of America, as part of a roundtable session on Shakespeare and the military. In response to a query from Amy Scott-Douglass about his 2003 National Public Radio invocation of *Othello* in support of the Iraq invasion,[20] Adelman demarcated a line, insisting that 'we can talk about Shakespeare, or we can talk about politics'. This was a complicatedly disingenuous gesture for him to make, given that he, more than any other contemporary figure, uniquely bridges political advocacy and (supposedly non-political) Shakespeare consulting.[21] Who else can boast that in 1989 they argued with Cheney and Quayle about whether Branagh's *Henry V* was a pro-war film? Who else has gotten Rumsfeld to dress up in kingly garb to recite the St Cripsin's Day speech? Or has participated in a mock debate about the justification of Henry's invasion of France at the DC Shakespeare Theatre, which drew together Judi Dench, Christopher Hitchens, Chris Matthews, David Brooks, Christopher Buckley, Margaret Carlson, Arianna Huffington, Cynthia Lewis, and himself?[22] Or suggested to Dana Gioia that the National Endowment for the Arts and Department of Defense

co-sponsor a Shakespeare production for military bases?

Yet these two tracks – of political advocacy and supposedly non-political consulting – occasionally veer towards one another. Note an account of a 2005 seminar Adelman conducted with twenty Air Force officers, where Adelman opened the normally closed seminar doors to *New York Times* reporter Bruce Weber. Unlike the Olivier programme, Adelman does show clips from films, often contrasting two versions of the same speech, in this case from *Julius Caesar*. As Weber details:

[I]t did not escape the notice of those in the room that the conspirators' hasty act of revolt failed to consider its aftermath, the lesson being that thorough planning, for any leader, is paramount. Those who would depose Caesar had, in effect, no exit strategy.

'As we have heard,' said Roger Blanchard, the Air Force's assistant deputy chief of staff for personnel, paraphrasing a famous locution of his boss, Secretary Rumsfeld, 'we don't know what we don't know – there are unknown unknowns.'

This was about as close as the discussion ever got to current events, though at one point, a parallel between Brutus and the conspirators and the Bush administration was raised. If the conspirators were in the wrong for taking violent action without hard evidence but only on

---

[19] See Scott L. Newstrom, '"Step Aside, I'll Show Thee a President": George W as Henry V?' *AlterNet* (28 May 2003); www.alternet.org/story/16025/right_pitches_dubya_as_henry_v; Scott L. Newstok and Harry Berger, Jr, 'Harrying after VV', in *Shakespeare after 9/11: How a Social Trauma Reshapes Interpretation*, ed. Matthew Biberman and Julia Reinhard Lupton (Lewiston, NY, 2011), pp. 141–52.

[20] Ken Adelman, 'Commentary: Argument for a Military Strike on Iraq Using Shakespeare's *Othello*', *All Things Considered* (26 August 2002). www.npr.org/programs/atc/transcripts/2002/aug/020826.adelman.html.

[21] For an incisive critique of Adelman's opportunistic (mis)citation of *Othello*, see Anthony B. Dawson, 'Staging Evidence', in *From Script to Stage in Early Modern England*, ed. Peter Holland and Stephen Orgel (Basingstoke, 2004), pp. 89–108.

[22] This event was covered by Bob Thompson for the *Washington Post*, 'The King and We: Henry V's War Cabinet: Mock Debate at Shakespeare Theatre Has Familiar Ring' (17 May 2004), C01.

suspicion of the tyrant Caesar might become, in effect making a pre-emptive strike, couldn't the same argument be applied to the Bush administration's invasion of Iraq and the absence of weapons of mass destruction?

'The president had more evidence than Brutus did', replied Mr. Adelman, who had been an early advocate of the Iraq invasion.[23]

Although Adelman cuts off that line of discussion, I want to see in such moments the potential for a further exchange. One senses that 'Shakespeare' was in this instance providing a comparatively safe, distant space for discussing contemporary leadership quandaries, much in the same way that classical literature provided appropriately distant yet nonetheless pointed parallels ('mirrors') for early modern culture reflecting on its own political situation.[24] In fact, I'd suggest that the prevalence of these seminars, as reductive and frustrating as we find them to be, should alert us to a genuine desire to be engaging in these kinds of conversations. As Geoffrey Harpham has recently posited, a critically reflective seminar exploring the extra-mural potential of teaching *Henry V* could

consider leadership, not in a way that would encourage leaders or would-be leaders to think well of themselves, but in a way that awakened the larger, darker, and more complex questions of context and character that always haunt even the most pure-hearted exercises of power.[25]

We tend to associate the seminar with late-nineteenth-century graduate education in the sciences and later social sciences, or perhaps twentieth-century philosophical and psychoanalytic sessions of master-thinkers like Heidegger and Lacan. Yet the seminar, as a pedagogical forum, originated in the eighteenth century as a space for *philological* enquiry.[26] Isn't this our native venue? Might there be some way for us to offer some kind of critical, philological pedagogy of Shakespeare that would appeal to those seeking a re-engagement with the plays?

A model I would suggest, one that would help blend a rhetorical and performative approach, would be the first-person readings of Shakespearian speeches that Kenneth Burke brilliantly elaborated

in the 1930s, most notably with his ventriloquism of Marc Antony's speech over Caesar's corpse:

Instead of addressing the mob, as he is pictured in the third act of *Julius Caesar*, he turns to the audience. And instead of being a dramatic character *within* the play, he is here made to speak as a critical commentator *upon* the play, explaining its mechanism and its virtues. Thus we have a tale from Shakespeare, retold, not as a plot but from the standpoint of the rhetorician, who is concerned with a work's processes of appeal.[27]

This isn't mere role-playing recitation – it's something more dynamic than that, inviting a practice of reading that is aware of multiple audiences, aware of rhetorical modes of persuasion. Or what if we invited business leaders to work through Ulysses's speech on degree, giving them enough context about a Tillyard-esque Elizabethan world picture, but also the immediate dramaturgical complexity of this scene, so that they could begin to see it as a strategic statement about order and disorder not quite so hierarchical as it might at first appear?[28]

What seems to me perennially limited about most Shakespearian 'outreach' programmes – whether by a management consultant, a prison-based production, a theatrical company visiting

---

[23] 'Friends, Generals and Captains of Industry, Lend Me Your Ears', *New York Times* (25 January 2005).

[24] See Rebecca W. Bushnell, *A Culture of Teaching: Early Modern Humanism in Theory and Practice* (Ithaca, 1996); Mary Polito, '"Warriors for the Working Day": Shakespeare's Professionals', *Shakespeare*, 2:1 (2006), 1–23.

[25] *The Humanities and the Dream of America* (Chicago, 2011), p. 143.

[26] See Gert Schubring, 'The Rise and Decline of the Bonn Natural Sciences Seminar', *Osiris* 2nd series, 5 (1989), 56–93; David A. Gerber, 'Rethinking the Graduate Research Seminar in American History: The Search for a New Model', *Teaching History: A Journal of Methods*, 13:1 (1988), 8–17; William Clark, 'On the Dialectical Origins of the Research Seminar', *History of Science*, 27:2 (1989), 111–54.

[27] Kenneth Burke, 'Antony on Behalf of the Play', *Kenneth Burke on Shakespeare*, ed. Scott L. Newstok (Lafayette, IN, 2007), 38.

[28] R. S. White provides a perceptive reading in his essay 'Marx and Shakespeare', in *Shakespeare Survey* 45 (Cambridge, 1993), pp. 89–100.

high schools, nursing homes, etc. – is the self-determined market segmentation of their audiences. They are, to be sure, approaching more diverse audiences than their normal theatrical clientele. But even in reaching beyond their theatres, they maintain their new audiences in isolated, self-homogenous locales, restricted to their home institutions. The model is that of Shakespeare as the hub of a wheel, radiating spokes out to discrete groups. Just as I am aware that it is only a thought experiment to suggest that we might imagine the captains of industry parsing the phrase 'untune that string', let me close with another fantasy, namely of a truly civic Shakespeare, a Shakespeare spun off into a kind of civic space in which to congregate.

The model I have in mind relates to the various efforts over the last decade to develop modes of civic engagement via deliberative democracy in the United States.[29] For instance, the 'By the People' project is an ambitious programme sponsored by American public television.[30] Over one weekend of debating, it is designed to draw together as representative of a cross-section of the national US population as possible. In one case, such a group delib-

erated the 2003 build-up to the war in Iraq; in the other, the state of federal healthcare policy. These gatherings are modelled on the lottery of Athenian democracy (and the Council of 500). Participants are paid a nominal stipend to attend; they are given reading materials in advance and, on the weekend itself, the opportunity to discuss the topic under scrutiny with policy experts as well as small groups. Most participants report being significantly more engaged in current events long after the weekend concludes, and vastly more informed about political challenges. Might there be some analogous way to rework the seminar, making Shakespeare the site for a more pluralistic interpretive exchange?

---

[29] See Martha L. McCoy and Patrick L. Scully, 'Deliberative Dialogue to Expand Civic Engagement: What Kind of Talk Does Democracy Need?' *National Civic Review*, 91:2 (2002), 117–35; Amy Gutmann and Dennis Thompson, *Why Deliberative Democracy?* (Princeton, 2002); Dennis F. Thompson, 'Deliberative Democratic Theory and Empirical Political Science', *Annual Review of Political Science*, 11 (2008), 497–520.

[30] See 'What is By the People?' www.pbs.org/newshour/btp/partners.html.

SHAKESPEARE AND THE CULTURES OF TRANSLATION

TON HOENSELAARS

PART I

This article presents some reflections on Shakespeare and translation cultures by someone who is a 'foreigner' to these English shores but who, as a Shakespearian scholar, is no complete stranger to this country either. Inspired by the social and cultural events that have dominated the London scene and dwarfed much else in Britain for quite some time now, it explores a range of attitudes towards foreign languages and translation in the work of Shakespeare, and seeks to relate these to the present day situation in Britain. It seems a paradox that theatre productions in 2012 prove to become more multilingual than ever, at a time when the status of foreign languages and translation, both in academe and society at large, are being severely challenged.[1]

Olympics and Shakespeare

One specific context for this article is that of the 2012 Olympic Games to be held in London. There is a certain affinity between Shakespeare and the Games. A number of the sports that feature in this year's Olympic Games, also occur in the plays. We all remember the wrestling match in *As You Like It*, the swimming incident in *Julius Caesar*, as well as Prince Hal's reputed skill at indoor tennis. We may even agree that Douglas's ability to run 'a-horseback up a hill perpendicular' would still qualify him for this summer's equestrian eventing sessions.[2] Moreover, the affinity between Shakespeare and the Games has actually been expanded by the London Olympics since for the opening ceremony the organising committee has devised a

show entitled 'Isles of Wonder'. Directed by Danny Boyle at a cost of £27 m (a third of the entire budget for the opening and closing events of the Olympics and the Paralympics together), it will be a Shakespeare-inspired event of unparalleled proportions. The ceremony – which is to take place on 27 July 2012 – has been visualized around Caliban's 'Isle is full of noises' speech from *The Tempest*:

> Be not afeard. The isle is full of noises,
> Sounds, and sweet airs, that give delight and hurt not.
> Sometimes a thousand twangling instruments
> Will hum about mine ears, and sometime voices
> That if I then had waked after long sleep
> Will make me sleep again; and then in dreaming
> The clouds methought would open and show riches
> Ready to drop upon me, that when I waked
> I cried to dream again.   (*The Tempest*, 3.2.138–46)

These particular lines from what *The Guardian* rightly identified as one of the principal 'antagonists' of Shakespeare's late comedy, are now to be

[1] The article is a revised version of the Sam Wanamaker Lecture, given at Shakespeare's Globe, London, on 20 March 2012, prior to the summer's Olympic Games in London. I am grateful for the encouragement and advice of Sarah Stanton, Margaret Bartley, Farah Karim-Cooper, Alex Huang, Susan Bassnett, Liz Oakley-Brown, Amy Kenny and Bridget Escolme. The lecture could not have been written without the generous assistance of many people. Dirk Delabastita, the undisputed doyen of Shakespeare and Translation studies, has been unusually supportive.
[2] *1 Henry IV* in *The Oxford Shakespeare*, ed. Stanley Wells and Gary Taylor, 2nd edn (Oxford, 2005), 2.5.346–7. Further references to the works of Shakespeare will be to this edition, and are given after quotations in the text.

engraved on the largest bell ever cast in Britain.[3] In this way, Boyle may realize the ambition of which he spoke to the BBC earlier in 2012, when he said that he wanted people to hear it 'for hundreds of years'.[4] Long live Shakespeare.

In the same way the organizers of the greatest sports event in the world discovered and subsequently rallied around their Shakespeare in 2012, so did the cultural sites of London where Shakespeare is rehearsed *also* in years that see no Olympic Games at all. There is the 'World Shakespeare Festival 2012' produced by the Royal Shakespeare Company, and the major international spring and summer programme called 'Globe to Globe', which, in the words of artistic director Dominic Dromgoole, has to 'create an international Shakespeare community in the heart of London as a prelude to the internationalism' of the London Olympics.[5] In this spirit, a special project has been set up to celebrate the Games with an unprecedented 'multilingual' Shakespeare Festival, a festival that will confront the theatre makers and their projected audiences with that elusive phenomenon of 'translation'. In educational terms, moreover, the art of translating Shakespeare is to be explored in a series of Shakespeare *Found in Translation* lectures.

I reflect here on the last two of these initiatives in particular – the multilingual Shakespeare Festival, and the 'Found in Translation' lectures. These initiatives, in linguistic terms anyway, effectively make visible and draw attention to two major and rather closely related traditions that are, at the same time, also distinctly different. The first tradition concerns the Englishman's timeworn encounter with languages not his own, his attitude towards these, then and now. The second tradition concerns the Englishman's attitude to the phenomenon of translation, of seeking to bridge the non-symmetrical relationship between languages and cultures, a tradition that extends to the translation of Shakespeare in particular.

Precedents

This is not the first time in history that 'Shakespeare' draws attention to the multilingual merits of the plays' language and that of the audience, or that the language barrier and translation are an issue. We simply need to recall the fate of the early modern strolling players who left London for the continent of Europe, either because the plague closed the theatres in London or because there was a glut on the performance market. The 2012 'strolling players' who are to participate in the 'Globe to Globe' project and will play Shakespeare in their own language in London, closely resemble Shakespeare's colleagues as they confronted Continental audiences 400 years ago. We do not know very much about the experience of the strolling players, but we know for certain that, during the late sixteenth and the early decades of the seventeenth century, they performed the plays in their native English.

It is, of course, not an entirely new practice for these strolling players in the 'Globe to Globe' project to perform Shakespeare in their own language. A number of developments in recent years have all tended towards the Globe's cross-border and multilingual Olympic theatre project. Over the past two decades we have witnessed – though never quite on this scale – how 'foreign' elements nurtured the productions of English directors. (I only really understood *Hamlet* when Peter Brook's 'ghost' spoke Swahili to the uncomprehending Prince of Denmark.) Also, over the past two decades we have seen the visits to Britain by foreign theatre companies, non-English, European, Asian Shakespeare companies, companies that, more often than not, perform their Shakespeare here in their own native tongues. Yukio Ninagawa is already a classical example of the globalization of the English stage, aptly brought into focus by Peter Holland, between the twin poles of

---

[3] In the event, only the opening line of this speech was engraved on the bell.

[4] Danny Boyle at www.bbc.co.uk/news/uk-16744477 (25 November 2012).

[5] Caroline Bishop, 'Globe becomes international for Cultural Olympiad' (20 January 2012) at www.officiallondontheatre.co.uk/news/latest-news/article/item113781/Globe-becomes-international-for-Cultural-Olympiad/ (25 November 2012).

xenophobia and xenophilia.[6] And finally, we have seen projects jointly undertaken by British and non-British theatre makers.[7] This process of the internationalization of the English stage is a complex phenomenon that has been gaining momentum for some time now and my Washington DC colleague Alexander Huang and I have playfully chosen to give it the brand name: 'Boomerang Shakespeare'. Boomerang Shakespeare is the phenomenon of the Bard who no longer is a prime British export product, but a newly imported commodity. 'Boomerang Shakespeare' further suggests a certain 'global' reach – when studied from the English *omphalos*, that is, of course, not from its aboriginal Australian wilds. 'Boomerang Shakespeare' suggests exchange, moreover, exchange that is currently booming and that is booming business too.[8]

If the situation of the strolling players in Shakespeare's time shows a number of similarities with that of the companies on the London stage in 2012, there are also several differences. First of all, there is the difference in scope. A many times more essential difference, however, is that during the seventeenth century it was the players' native English playwright who was presented in a foreign setting. The 2012 season has really marked the return of our – but perhaps I, as a foreigner still, should say 'your' own – 'Conquering Hero', who has travelled the globe and has 'gone native', now paradoxically speaking the tongues of the regions he subdued, and capable of English no more. This essential difference brings with it some unique consequences that directly relate to the twin-theme of my Sam Wanamaker Lecture. It explains why I have chosen to look at 'foreign languages' and 'translation' and to juxtapose the historical early modern situation that Shakespeare worked in (and, as I will show, also worked on) to the situation in today's context in England.

PART II

Foreign languages on the London stage

'*Goeden dach, meester, end you, vro, auch*';
'*Ik weet niet wat yow seg; ick verstaw you niet.*'[9]

'*Diaboli virtus in lumbis est.*'[10]
'*Alla nostra casa ben venuto, molto onorato signor*
  mio Petruccio' (*The Taming of the Shrew*, 1.2.25–26).
'*Probo tibi*, pupil: *stultus non est animal rationale.*'[11]
'*Boskos thromuldo boskos*' – '*Boskos vauvado*'
  (*All's Well that Ends Well*, 4.1.69 and 4.1.75).
'*Je, quand suis le posseseur de France, et quand vous avez le*
  possession de moi . . . donc vôtre est France, et vous êtes
  mienne.' – 'I cannot speak your England'
                    (*Henry V*, 5.2.181–3 and 5.2.102–3).

These are some of the many strange sounds that the unsuspecting theatregoer is likely to have heard, visiting the Globe theatre on London's south bank around the turn of the sixteenth century. The London stage spoke many tongues.[12] In a sense, it is astonishing how similar those distant sounds of London are to what the twenty-first century Shakespeare lover is likely to experience during the 2012 marathon performance of no less than 37 plays, each translated into a different 'foreign',

---

[6] Peter Holland, *English Shakespeares: Shakespeare on the English Stage in the 1990s* (Cambridge, 1997), pp. 253–70.

[7] On this phenomenon, with illustrations from recent productions, see Alexander C. Y. Huang, ' "What country, friends, is this?": Touring Shakespeares, Agency, and Efficacy in Theatre Historiography', *Theatre Survey*, 54:1 (2013), 51–85.

[8] Alexander C. Y. Huang, 'Boomerang Shakespeare', *Cambridge World Shakespeare Encyclopedia*, ed. Bruce Smith *et al.*, 2 vols. (Cambridge, in preparation).

[9] Thomas Dekker, *The Shoemaker's Holiday in English Renaissance Drama*, gen. ed. David Bevington (New York, 2002), scene 5, lines 75–76 and 92–93 respectively.

[10] John Marston, *The Dutch Courtesan*, ed. Peter Davison (London, 1968), 2.1.88.

[11] Thomas Middleton, *A Chaste Maid in Cheapside* in *English Renaissance Drama*, 4.1.2.

[12] See Michael Neill, 'Broken English and Broken Irish: Nation, Language, and the Optics of Power in Shakespeare's Histories', *Shakespeare Quarterly*, 45 (1994), 1–32; Paula Blank, *Broken English: Dialects and the Politics of Language in Renaissance Writings* (London, 1996); Janette Dillon, *Language and Stage in Medieval and Renaissance England* (Cambridge, 1998); Marianne Montgomery, *Europe's Languages on England's Stages, 1590–1620* (Farnham, 2012). This is the tip of the iceberg. A special issue of *English Text Construction*, 6:2 (2013), co-edited by Dirk Delabastita and Ton Hoenselaars, will be entirely devoted to multilingualism in the drama of Shakespeare and his contemporaries.

meaning, of course, non-English, language. How similar in terms of multitude and variety, and yet how different in terms of the prevailing circumstances!

During the early modern period, the acoustic signs of the theatre responded to, mimicked and represented the very real anxieties that prevailed in an increasingly cosmopolitan metropolis. London was a city frequented by ambassadors, humanists, religious refugees, merchants and travellers from the European continent. They included Johannes de Witt from Utrecht, who drew the interior of the Swan, and the Swiss Thomas Platter who reported on seeing *Julius Caesar* here.

These international visitors were a considerable cause of anxiety, not because they meant to stay (although a number of them did), but because communication was difficult. In early modern London foreigners like De Witt and Platter are likely to have spoken their own foreign tongues, or to have communicated in a shared language, like Latin. Only rarely would the language shared with visitors from abroad have been English. The English language enjoyed no international status, and certainly did not function as the *lingua franca* that it is today. The Italian translator and language teacher John Florio, that truly astonishing contemporary of Shakespeare's, said about the English language: 'It is a language that wyl do you good in England, but passe Dover, it is worth nothing.'[13]

One option available to the Englishman to overcome this Babylonian curse was to study foreign languages, but his attitude to this particular remedy was notoriously complex. On the one hand, the drama of Shakespeare and his contemporaries repeatedly mentions the Englishman's poor foreign language aptitude. In Shakespeare's own *Merchant of Venice*, Portia and Nerissa deplore English Falconbridge's foreign language skills as follows:

Nerissa. What say you then to Falconbridge, the young baron of England?
Portia. You know I say nothing to him, for he understands not me, nor I him. He hath neither Latin,

French, nor Italian ... He is a proper man's picture, but alas, who can converse with a dumb show?

(1.2.63–70)

Such moments of embarrassment which the plays show or discuss are neatly flanked by instances where the Englishman's foreign-language learning is made to look entirely unnecessary. This is the case in *Henry V*, a play about the triumph of the English language. The ability to convince the French to learn English – the play demonstrates – eliminates the Englishman's need to learn French. There is a tendency to derive credit with the audience by apologizing for one's poor language skills: 'I will tell thee in French – which I am sure will hang upon my tongue like a new-married wife about her husband's neck, hardly to be shook off' (*Henry V*, 5.2.178–80).

However, the embarrassment at one's own weak foreign language record could also frequently be overcome by generating laughter against the gibble-gabble of broken-English-speaking foreigners. Only less frequently was this done by an apparent show of generosity: 'O fair Catherine, if you will love me soundly with your French heart, I will be glad to hear you confess it brokenly with your English tongue' (*Henry V*, 5.2.104–6). In any case, this strategy deftly deflected attention away from the Englishman's own foreign language illiteracy.

But Shakespeare does not only have his English monarch chauvinistically as well as a-historically keep at arm's length the language of the other. He also knows and shows the humility of those unversed in other tongues, and expects sympathy, as in the case of the common Soldier at the end of *Timon of Athens* who finds the tomb and on it a Latin epigraph:

What's on this tomb
I cannot read. The character I'll take with wax.
Our captain [=Alcibiades] hath in every figure skill,
An aged interpreter, though young in days.

(*Timon of Athens*, 5.4.3–6)

---

[13] John Florio, *Firste Fruites* (London, 1578), 50v.

And this reference to Alcibiades as 'an aged interpreter' conveniently introduces my second theme, that of translation.

Renaissance Translation

In an early modern climate such as this – with its great confluence of what we today, drawing a much firmer distinction, term regional (Welsh, Irish, Scottish) and national vernaculars and cultures, with the challenged native aptitude of the English, as well as the perhaps rather obvious patriotic preferences sharpened by religious and political differences – interlingual 'translation' played a pivotal role. It has therefore been aptly said that 'the study of Elizabethan translation is a study of the means by which the Renaissance came to England'.[14] And one certainly would not over-interpret the situation if one noted that the Renaissance – as it transformed the Classical heritage of Greece and Rome into a Christian tradition and produced, among other things, the Tyndale and King James bibles in the vernacular – was really about 'translation' at its very core, converting tradition into innovation.

Given the decisive role of 'translation' in Renaissance culture, however, and given the pervasive use that Shakespeare himself made of such canonical translations as Plutarch's *Parallel Lives of the Noble Grecians and Romans*, or Ovid's *Metamorphoses*, it is surprising that his attitude towards the traditional concept of 'translation' in the plays and poems is not more favourable – indeed it is on occasion remarkably unenthusiastic. In fact, the organizers of the 'World Shakespeare Festival 2012' and of 'Globe to Globe' may well have reason to wonder if Shakespeare was really the most suitable candidate to enhance the climate of 'internationalization' in the year of the London Olympics. This may be demonstrated with a number of instances where Shakespeare's characters, or 'the speaker' of the Sonnets, actually allude to the practice of 'translation'. Before doing so, however, it is worth observing that the terminology Shakespeare used to discuss the process of translation in verbal or linguistic terms was, on occasion, considerably different from ours, both in terms of vocabulary and

in terms of semantics, the meaning that words had then and have now.

'Translate'

Shakespeare used the word 'translate', of course, but the word's meaning was not as obvious as it may seem to us now. The primary meaning of the word 'translate' was 'to transform' or 'to change', as in the line spoken by Quince as he meets Bottom in the forest, Bottom who has changed into an ass: 'Bless thee, Bottom', Quince exclaims in horror, 'bless thee. Thou art translated' (3.1.113). Ironically, Quince's line, by far the most frequently quoted observation about Shakespeare and 'translation' worldwide, makes no reference to language in any way. Quince is really speaking of 'translation' in a metaphorical sense, whereas modern users quoting Quince tend to apply the word's current, literal meaning. It seems to me as if this misinterpretation–cum–application of the term by modern audiences contributes to what gets the laugh in the theatre, although one does not wish to minimize the general incongruity of the situation when Quince speaks (also involving a pun on 'ass'), the effect of dramatic irony (Bottom is blissfully ignorant of change), and the sexual innuendo (ass = well-endowed). Yet, what is important here is that the laughter is in part, at least, generated by applying what is now a word associated with the intellectual endeavour and the educated act of commuting between different languages, to an ass. So we have to be on our guard. Patricia Parker has demonstrated that we may stretch the term 'translation' to reveal multiple forms of contemporary cultural anxiety and exchange operative in the work of Shakespeare.[15] By inversion, the

---

[14] F. O. Mathiessen, *Translation: an Elizabethan Art* (Cambridge, MA, 1931), p. 3.

[15] Patricia Parker, *Shakespeare from the Margins: Language, Culture, Context* (Chicago, 1996). Chapter 4 on "Illegitimate Construction": Translation, Adultery, and Mechanical Reproduction in *The Merry Wives of Windsor*' (pp. 116–48) and Chapter 5, ' "Conveyors Are You All": Translation, Conveying, Representing, and Seconding in the Histories and *Hamlet*' (pp. 149–84) represent some of the finest writing on Shakespeare and 'translation' of the past two decades.

use of the word 'translation' itself in *A Midsummer Night's Dream* demonstrates that it does not always mean what we think it means to Shakespeare.

However, at the same time, this does not mean either that the notion of linguistic, verbal translation, the notion of textual transfer could not, on occasion, be part of the semantic association. One borderline case may be found in *Hamlet*, when King Claudius is anxious to know the reason for Gertrude's distress: 'There's matter in these sighs, these profound heaves; / You must translate [= 'explain it to me']. 'Tis fit we understand them' (*Hamlet*, 4.1.1–2).

Another instance may be found in *As You Like It*, where Touchstone tells his rival, the clown William, that he, Touchstone, will marry Audrey:

Therefore, you clown, abandon, – which is in the vulgar, leave – the society – which in the boorish is company – of this female – which in the common is woman; which together is, abandon the society of this female, or, clown, thou perishest; or, to thy better understanding, diest; or, to wit, I kill thee, make thee away, translate thy life into death, thy liberty into bondage.

(*As You Like It*, 5.1.46–52)

Touchstone's use of the term 'translation' is a borderline case, and there are many more in Shakespeare, where the poet's use of the word 'translate' or 'translation' betrays his engagement with or a subliminal awareness of the linguistic act of translation as we commonly think of it. In fact, the speech by Touchstone is a nice example of the paraphrastic kind of self-translation – not the practice of Vladimir Nabokov or Samuel Beckett who translated or supervised the translation of their own writings for new readers – whereby the speaker's choice of synonyms and near synonyms makes his point. Another of Shakespeare's paraphrase artists is Holofernes in *Love's Labour's Lost*:

The deer was, as you know – *sanguis* – in blood, ripe as the pomewater who now hangeth like a jewel in the ear of *caelo*, the sky, the welkin, the heaven, and anon falleth like a crab on the face of *terra*, the soil, the land, the earth. (*Love's Labour's Lost*, 4.2.3–7)

'Interpret'

We are on slightly firmer soil, land, earth, on firmer ground with Shakespeare's use of the verb 'interpret' and its variants, the nouns 'interpreter' and 'interpretation' which occur more frequently in Shakespeare than 'translate' and its variants, possibly because of their association with oral communication, like that between stage characters. Essentially 'interpretation' is an act of analysis and explanation, but in Shakespeare it can also mean 'translation' in our modern sense of the term (probably because 'translation' nearly automatically involves an act of analysis-and-explanation on the part of the translator). But it also means 'interpreting' in the modern sense of the word, where the emphasis lies on facilitating oral but also gestured communication between users of different languages.

In his description of the painting of Timon of Athens, the Poet in the play of that title refers to speech and silence, thus activating the semantic field of sign language:

How this grace
Speaks his own standing! What a mental power
This eye shoots forth! How big imagination
Moves in this *lip*! To th' *dumbness* of the *gesture*
One might *interpret*.

(*Timon of Athens*, 1.1.30–4. Italics added)

A similar kind of usage may be found in the first part of *Henry IV* where the Welsh Owen Glendower acts as interpreter between his daughter and her husband, the Earl of Mortimer. He must, in view of the Englishman's genuinely agonized observation:

This is the deadly spite that angers me:
My wife can speak no English, I no Welsh . . .
O, I am ignorance itself in this!

(1 *Henry IV*, 3.1.188–9, 208)

In *Henry V* we have Catherine's lady-in-waiting Alice, who interprets for Catherine as well as many in the audience. On the battlefield of Agincourt, it is the Boy who interprets for Pistol when he meets Monsieur Le Fer (and the situation suggests that the actors playing young Catherine and experienced Alice may well have doubled as the Boy and Le Fer respectively, because of their French language skills, and one adds 'unusual' French language skills). Finally, speaking of interpreters and interpreting, let us not forget the matter of life-and-death encounter in *All's Well that Ends Well*, when Paroles meets the 'Moscows regiment' and fears that he 'shall lose [his] life for want of language' (*All's Well*, 4.1.72). Of course, the interpreter is part of the plan to fool Paroles, that rare wonder of languages in Shakespeare, and there is more than a double meaning in that. The suggestion is that regardless of the number of languages you know, there will always be languages you do not know, and there is, nearly as a matter of course, the crucial issue of trust and the possible risk of the translator being unreliable.

'Traduce'

Not uncommon in Shakespeare is the word 'traduce' – which may mean 'to censure, to decry, to defame' as in *Hamlet*, where the Prince worries about the way in which the Danish nation may be 'traduced and taxed' of other nations (*Hamlet*, Additional Passages, p. 716, B. 2). Or, as in *Othello*, where the Moor recounts how he 'smote' a 'turbaned Turk [who] / Beat a Venetian and traduced the state' (*Othello*, 5.2.362–3). Interestingly, also in Shakespeare this term for 'slander' and destroyed reputations enters the field of what we call 'translation' today, particularly in those instances where explicit reference is made to the ways in which language, speech and literature may affect our lives.

Helen in *All's Well that Ends Well*, for example, tells the King of France that she is aware of the risk she runs as an unqualified GP, but also that she is prepared to be 'Traduced [or slandered] by odious ballads' (*All's Well that Ends Well*, 2.1.172). Along similar lines we read the response to Enobarbus who tells Cleopatra that Marc Antony in Rome is '[t]raduc'd for levity' (*Antony and Cleopatra*, 3.7.13). Cleopatra takes up the *linguistic* connotation of such slander, and exclaims: 'Sink Rome, and their tongues rot / That speak against us!' (*Antony and Cleopatra*, 3.7.15–16). Finally, in *Henry VIII*, Cardinal Wolsey notes that to be '[t]raduced by ignorant tongues' is really 'the fate of place,

and the rough brake [=predicament] / That virtue must go through' (*All is True*, 1.2.73–7). And as Wolsey continues to develop this motif further, he also introduces the more familiar sense of 'interpreting' or 'interpretation'. Wolsey: 'What we oft do best, / By sick interpreters [is communicated as] "Not ours or not allowed"' (*All is True*, 1.2.82–4).

'Translation' in Shakespeare

Let us – following this exploration of some of the most readily available semantic options – turn to a number of the examples of 'translation' at work in Shakespeare.[16] As we shall see, the playwright's attitude towards the traditional concept of 'translation' in the plays and poems is far from favourable or enthusiastic.

On a number of occasions, as in the second part of *Henry IV*, 'translation' is perceived as a process not of improvement or enhancement, but of depreciation, of devaluation, of falsification. What better example than the famous sequence at Gaultree Forest in the second part of *Henry IV*. Here, the Earl of Westmoreland expresses his surprise at the pro-war stance of the Archbishop of York. Westmoreland asks him why he does 'so ill translate [him]self / Out of the speech of peace that bears such grace / Into the harsh and boist'rous tongue of war, / Turning [his] books to graves, [his] ink to blood, / [His] pens to lances, and [his] tongue divine / To a loud trumpet and a point of war' (*2 Henry IV*, 4.1.47–52).

When Shakespeare writes of love and matters of the heart, 'translation' is often associated with deceit. In *Love's Labour's Lost*, the declarations of love that the Lord Dumaine has sent to the Princess of France's lady-in-waiting Catherine are described as, 'A huge translation of hypocrisy / Vilely compiled, profound simplicity' (5.2.51–2). Hypocrisy

---

16 Further research into this matter may yield much, extending the terms to include 'render', 'construe', 'convey', 'transpose', 'English' (noun and verb). However, writing such a 'poetics of translation' for Shakespeare and his contemporaries, one would ignore Patricia Parker's work – the vocabulary that she has defined and her approach – at one's own peril.

and deception are also associated with 'translation' in *The Sonnets*: just 'As on the finger of a throned queen / The basest jewel will be *well* esteemed', the speaker in Sonnet 96 says, 'So are those errors that in thee are seen / To truths translated and for true things deemed' (96.5–8). In the same sonnet, the speaker is even more explicit about the potentially deceptive quality of the beloved's beauty, when he uses the word 'translate' again – glossed as 'meta-morphose' also by Katherine Duncan-Jones in her Arden edition of the *Sonnets* and read as an Ovidian phenomenon – and exclaims: 'How many lambs might the stern wolf betray / If like a lamb he could his looks translate!' (96.9–10).[17] It is inter-esting to see how the notion of 'translation' here is not associated with a process of deterioration, but, conversely, with the practice of unreliable embel-lishment. Of course, they are essentially two vari-eties or versions of the same thing.

It is not difficult to extend the list. In *The Merry Wives of Windsor*, Falstaff speaks of seducing Mis-tress Ford in terms of an interpreter of the signs – the body language, so to speak – that she commu-nicates to him:

I do mean to make love to Ford's wife. I spy entertain-ment in her. She discourses, she carves, she gives the leer of invitation. I can construe the action of her famil-iar style; and the hardest voice of her behavior, to be Englished rightly, is, 'I am Sir John Falstaff's.'

(*Merry Wives*, 1.3.38–43)

Pistol takes up the translation metaphor that begins with 'Englished' and replies, quite rightly too, that 'He [Falstaff] hath studied [Mistress Ford] well, and translated her will: out of honesty, into English' (*Merry Wives*, 1.3.44–5).

The extreme instance of 'translation' in action no doubt occurs in the Latin lesson in *The Taming of the Shrew* (3.1), where Lucentio successfully seduces Bianca while seeming to translate Ovid's *Heroides*. The scene seems fully to endorse the proverbial allegation that there is more than just a similar-ity in terms of sound between the words *tradut-tore* and *traditore*, and that the translator can easily become a traitor. The name that Lucentio adopts to approach Bianca does not only mark his disguise

identity, but also reflects on his alleged profession as a language instructor: clearly 'Cambio' signifies 'change' in more ways than one: '"*Hic ibat*", as I told you before – "*Simois*", I am Lucentio – "*hic est*", son unto Vincentio . . .' (*The Taming of the Shrew*, 3.1.31–2). Admittedly, this example of trans-gressive translation is so blatant and so excessive that it can also be taken to imply a positive comment on the honesty and accuracy that play a role in real, humanist translation. This example, therefore, also aptly introduces instances where Shakespeare imagines 'translation' as a positive achievement, although such instances are rare, as in *As You Like It*, where Shakespeare has Amiens full-heartedly compliment the Duke on the way in which he has managed to change his predicament in the forest of Arden: 'Happy is your grace / That can translate the stubbornness of fortune / Into so quiet and so sweet a style' (*As You Like It*, 2.1.18–20). Signifi-cantly, the word 'style' in this context activates the connotations of the translation endeavour in verbal or linguistic terms.

The classical example of Shakespeare imag-ining 'translation' as beneficiary occurs in *Titus Andronicus*. There, Titus concerns himself with the raped and muted Lavinia, saying he can and will 'interpret all her martyred signs' (*Titus Andronicus*, 3.2.36). He adds:

Speechless complainer, I will learn thy thought.
In thy dumb action will I be as perfect
As begging hermits in their holy prayers.
Thou shalt not sigh, nor hold thy stumps to heaven,
Nor wink, nor nod, nor kneel, nor make a sign,
But I of these will wrest an alphabet,
And by still practice learn to know thy meaning.

(*Titus Andronicus*, 3.2.39–45)

The scene that follows – structured, like the earlier one from *The Taming of the Shrew* – around the Latin text of Ovid – has been analysed many times, impressively, I think, by Jonathan Bate, and, more recently, by Liz Oakley-Brown, who is this

---

[17] *Shakespeare's Sonnets*, ed. Katherine Duncan-Jones, The Arden Shakespeare (London, 1997), p. 302, note to lines 9–10.

country's current specialist in the translation – verbal as well as cultural – from Greek and Latin into the early modern English of Shakespeare and his contemporaries.[18]

Since these fine critics have paved the way for us all, I shall not even begin to analyse the scene again here, and this does enable me to reflect on a possible distinction between the often doubtful act of 'translation' as Shakespeare presents it, and his apparently more lenient and affirmative stance on 'interpretation', as in the case of *Titus Andronicus*. This is neither the time nor the place to discuss the topic exhaustively, so let me share it with you – as a so-called Research Opportunity.

When Shakespeare thinks of 'translation' and, as he often does, associates it with deterioration, it is frequently a change that the subject, the speaking self, experiences as a change away from that same self. When Bottom is 'translated', it is from his true self as a Weaver into the identity of an Ass. This is the fear of loss. In the case of 'interpreting' or 'interpretation', however, the process – perceived from the perspective of that same subject – seems to be reversed, and involves the transfer of a strange object, sign, word, or phrase nearer to that self, made more understandable to that self. In an attempt to translate the Shakespearian psychogram into more familiar terms, let me give you an analogy. 'Translation' in Shakespeare resembles the process, experienced from the perspective of the present-day Englishman, of translating English literature into another, foreign language. To present English literature 'at one remove', so to speak, from what it is supposed to be. 'Interpretation' in Shakespeare resembles the process, experienced from the perspective of the present-day Englishman, of translating non-English literature – be it Goethe or Proust – into English. To present that foreign literature as part of the Englishman's tongue.

In the case of 'Translation *out of* a historical variety of English', the English tend to be rather wary, certainly when that literature is Shakespeare. In the case of 'Translation *into* English', the English tacitly tend to agree that their language can absorb any other literature without significant loss.[19]

A closer look at the psychology behind the complex and certainly not always consistent interrelation between 'translation' and 'interpretation' in Shakespeare reveals a double standard for the 'self' and the 'other'. In some form, it sometimes seems to me, we may identify a comparable double standard still existing in our own time.

Given Shakespeare's rather general association of 'translation' (in the early modern sense of the term) with alienation, one is tempted to conclude – and dare I curse inside the church? – that for Shakespeare it was always more likely than not, to be lost in 'translation'.

'Translation' in Shakespeare is perceived as the creation of likeness, but it is nearly impossible to achieve: Hamlet tells Ophelia that 'the power of beauty will sooner *transform* honesty from what it is to a bawd than the force of honesty can *translate* beauty into his [=honesty's] likeness' (*Hamlet*, 3.1.113–15. Italics added). Deterioration is very likely, but preserving the identity of the original is not.

'Translation' does not only have the power to diminish; it is also essentially unreliable. The character of the Poet in *Timon of Athens* imagines how Timon with his 'grace' or 'graciousness' – and with Fortune as his champion – may 'translate' or 'convert' his 'rivals' into 'slaves and servants' (*Timon of Athens*, 1.1.71–3). But surely the play as a whole demonstrates that this is a slippery truth indeed: Fortune is fickle, the opportunist Poet speaking these words is a 'true' liar, and the translation he speaks of is misleading, is illusory.

Shakespeare does not possess the cheeky optimism and delight of the Argentine poet Jorge Luis Borges who claimed that his international fame

---

[18] Jonathan Bate, *Shakespeare's Ovid* (Oxford, 1994); *Titus Andronicus*, ed. Jonathan Bate, Arden Third Series (London, 1995); Liz Oakley-Brown, '*Titus Andronicus* and the Cultural Politics of Translation in the Early Modern Period', *Renaissance Studies*, 19 (2005), 325–47.

[19] Compare the predominantly optimistic attitude in *The Oxford Guide to Literature in English Translation*, ed. Peter France (Oxford, 2000) and the tendency (until the early 1990s) to frown on the reliability and use of Shakespeare translations into the other languages of the world.

was due to the fact that he had had such eminent translators. But then again, of course, Borges also firmly believed that a translation can improve its original, that contradictory renderings of the same 'work' may be equally valid, and that an original can be unfaithful to a translation.[20] In Shakespeare we look for such a vision in vain.

Metaphorical or metamorphic translation
Even with my perhaps disturbing observations about Shakespeare and his views of verbal and linguistic 'translation' and 'interpretation', I would be the last to suggest that Shakespeare was suspicious of 'translation' in 'metaphorical' terms, of 'translation' in terms of 'change' or a 'transformation' of the self also for the better.

Shakespeare presents the notions of felicitous 'change' and wretched 'inertia' in simple as well as in complex terms. In simple terms we find it in *Much Ado About Nothing*. Here, it is the melancholic and criminal Don John who demands: 'let me be that I am, and seek not to alter me' (*Much Ado*, 1.3.33–4). In the same play, it is the comic co-lead, Signor Benedick, who ceases to rail at love and lovers when he is infected by the delicious disease himself, and proves capable of acknowledging, 'Gallants, I am not as I have been' (*Much Ado*, 3.2.14) and will, to his own delight, never be the same again. This is also the metaphorical type of 'translation' that plays such a central role in *A Midsummer Night's Dream*, involving Bottom as much as the lovers. This is the metaphorical type of 'translation' around which Shakespeare constructs his comedies, with the formative 'other' world, often a curative or restorative green world, at the centre.

Shakespeare is certainly not suspicious of 'translation' in metaphorical terms. Shakespeare subscribes to the Humanist ideal of life as man's trajectory of learning. This Humanist ideal of change-as-learning derives from Classical materials that the Renaissance makes available in translation. And one of the key Classical texts translated during the sixteenth century, and arguably Shakespeare's most important 'source' was Ovid's *Metamorphoses*, a poem whose theme is the fluidity of nature, the insubstantiality of man, the hazard of too firm a belief in a fixed self-identity. For Shakespeare, beneficial translation can really only be imagined in *metaphorical* terms, and, given his Ovidian source, we could begin to see the Shakespearian notion of healthy translation in *metamorphic* terms. This form of translation is really beyond verbal, linguistic terms.

In the case of Shakespeare, as is the case with many others – contemporaries of his and contemporaries of ours – language itself, and here, the English language, really represents the final frontier. In the status of the English language itself – that is where the real anxiety begins for Shakespeare, and we may understand this, if we are prepared to see him in the context of an early modern Europe that is fashioning a form of language-based nationhood, a form of linguistic national self-identity that gradually came to be solidified during the early nineteenth century, and that we are now slowly seeking to shake off, as we experiment with larger, supranational, federal structures instead, and seek to give shape to a mode of governance we call the post-nation.

PART III

Modern attitudes to translation and foreign language
Having looked at some of Shakespeare's experiences and perceptions of foreign language and translation, let me now consider in greater detail the prevailing attitude to foreign language learning and translation in present-day England. Since the field is vast, I concentrate on just two issues, and mix in Shakespeare for good measure. I shall mainly devote attention to (a) the way in which intralingual translation remains a barrier and (b) how foreign language learning fares in Britain these days.

(a) *Intralingual translation.* One of the intriguing issues involved in the translation debate is that of the so-called intralingual translation of

---

[20] Efraín Kristal, *Invisible Work: Borges and Translation* (Nashville, TN, 2002), pp. 1–10.

Shakespeare, the translation of Shakespearian text from early modern English into modern English. This is another way of referring to the debate or controversy about 'modernizing' Shakespeare, which occupied critics particularly during the early years of this new millennium. Susan Bassnett of the Centre for Translation and Comparative Cultural Studies at the University of Warwick was one of the champions for such a strategy of translating Shakespeare into modern English, of furthering the plays' intelligibility. Tom Deveson, however, reasoned that if we broke the verbal links to the usages that we have inherited, we would lose contact with a vital dimension of ourselves.[21] David Crystal, too, entered the fray – although the word may have gone out of fashion – and argued that the problem was far less serious than Susan Bassnett believed, in terms both of vocabulary and of grammar. According to Crystal, 'Translation should only be employed after all other means of achieving comprehension had been explored. It was an invaluable last resort – but a last, not a first resort. And even then the need for updating would be precious little.'[22] This is neither the time nor the place to revive the debate as to whether Shakespeare in other words is not Shakespeare, or to note that David Crystal's exclusion of multiple meanings resonant in Shakespeare's words did undermine his argument somewhat. However, looking at the mutual volleys in the debate, which resurfaces on and off, one is struck by the fact that the contestants primarily look upon 'translation' as something 'remedial', as a means of making Shakespeare intelligible again where the tooth of time has nibbled away at the communicative potential of both grammar and diction. 'Translation' is seen as the latest medical treatment for the Alzheimer's of the Shakespeare text that can no longer speak of its own origins, its beginnings, its early modern youth or youthfulness.[23]

Also, the British doctors who crowd around the hospital bed of patient Shakespeare, combatting his decline by prescribing bitter pills, really fail to consider what his own contemporary, the French novelist François Rabelais argued, namely that joy and pleasure are the eftest way to nurse the patient back to health. There is too little awareness in the English debate of all the all too real pleasures that 'translation' may produce – be it inter-lingual, intra-lingual, or inter-semiotic translation. There is too little awareness of the fact that such intra-lingual Shakespeare – which may still be insular Shakespeare up to a point, but which is emphatically not 'Shakespeare for Dummies', nor 'Shakespeare Made Simple' – may provide a boost to the creativity of the English language. The way in which the early nineteenth-century Shakespeare translation by August Wilhelm Schlegel and Ludwig Tieck revealed the potential of the German language may not be the most felicitous example – because it eventually led to the belief that Shakespeare must have been German – but it does focus our attention on the power of translation and the lasting achievement such a confrontation may bring.

Finally, the debate over modernizing Shakespeare was and tends to be characterized by an extraordinary level of rigidity. None of the contestants, all in fact having dug their heels in the sand, seemed prepared to consider that the traditional Shakespeare text might safely exist alongside a tradition that furthers creativity, a tradition much like that seen in all those countries where Shakespeare does not speak the native tongue, but also in countries where other Englishes have sprung up.

To me, there seems to be no justification for such trepidation in England. With the bibliographical heritage so professionally looked after in places like the Shakespeare Institute, in many English Departments in London and around the country, and by the distinguished publishers who issue the Oxford,

---

[21] See the exchange between Susan Bassnett and Tom Deveson in *Around the Globe*, 20 (Winter 2001/2002), 32–3. For the background to the exchange, see 'Shakespeare's in Danger: We Have to Act Now to Avoid a Great Tragedy', *The Independent* (15 November 2001), 6–7.

[22] See David Crystal at www.penguinclassics.ca/nf/shared/WebDisplay/0,,62049_1_10,00.html (25 November 2012).

[23] For a more detailed discussion of this issue in the context of Shakespearian translation worldwide, see 'Introduction' to *Shakespeare and the Language of Translation*, ed. Ton Hoenselaars, revised edition (London, 2012), pp. 1–27.

the Cambridge and the Arden Shakespeare, there would seem to be ample space indeed for immense creativity rather than dour remedy, in writing or rewriting Shakespeare, not in the academy, but certainly in the theatre, on all the living stages of the nation.

It may sound utopian to imagine a Shakespeare play in English without any archaic 'thee-ing' or 'thou-ing', with regularized verb endings ('what thinkest thou' changed to 'what do you think', and 'thou liest' to 'you liar'), with Shakespeare's shaky spelling and also his now quaint, irregular grammar corrected. With patriarchal Prospero saying 'Twelve year since, Miranda, twelve year since . . .' (*The Tempest*, 1.2.53), would you have your child learn English from Shakespeare? At the same time, the inability to imagine such change also means the inability to appreciate the change that 99 per cent of all Shakespeare in the 'Globe to Globe' project will have undergone.

Once the English have grown accustomed to the idea that there is indeed a tantalizing and desirable virtue in translating Shakespeare's early modern English into modern English – not because they must but because they can – just think what wonderful things might happen. Once the English have grown accustomed to the merits of intra-lingual translation, one could – beyond the idea of Tom Stoppard brushing up the dusty bits of the Bard – imagine shamelessly attending a production of, say, *Twelfth Night* or *As You Like It* entirely translated into Modern English by Kazuo Ishiguro. People would also begin to queue for hours to 'see' or shall we say 'hear' Ian McEwan or Julian Barnes's rendering of the Roman plays. Alan Hollinghurst's *All's Well that Ends Well* would be the talk of the town, lauded for its Edwardian timbre. Audiences would be clamouring to hear David Lodge's *Love's Labour's Lost*. Alan Bennett would reveal unsuspected layers of complexity and delight in his new dialect translation of *Henry IV, Parts 1* and *2*. I assume that you are beginning to find this a delightful exercise in its own right! All I can say is: do not stop at mind games and try the real thing.[24]

Apparently, there is still a marked tendency in Britain to think of Shakespeare solely in terms of his 'own' language. On this topic, Alex Huang notes that when it comes to assessing foreign productions in Britain, 'Theatre reviews are sometimes informed by a sense of self-sufficiency', and he proceeds to quote one critic for the *Daily Telegraph* as saying: 'Although it is stimulating to be exposed to different views of Shakespeare, there is something coals-to-Newcastle-ish about importing foreign-language productions to England. . . . There we sit, following [the] surtitles while listening to the performers delivering the matchless poetry in an incomprehensible tongue.'[25]

(b) *Foreign language learning in Britain*. If the English attitude towards Shakespeare in Modern English remains problematic, so does the Englishman's engagement with languages other than English. The Blair government's decision – with Estelle Morris as the Angel of Death up front – to abolish the requirement for foreign languages at secondary level has not furthered the knowledge or the appreciation in this country for languages other than English. A catastrophic decline in language study was the immediate outcome. It takes no effort to predict that the rise in student fees – unparalleled worldwide – will only aggravate the problem. The British Academy has been able to

---

[24] When Susan Bassnett proposed the intralingual translation of Shakespeare around the turn of the millennium, the anxiety of the establishment deprived it of sense that there might be anything poetic to gain. Incidentally, the practice of Shakespeare subjected to intralingual translation is not entirely original. In the 1960s, Peter Brook produced his famous *King Lear*. As Kevin Jack Hagopian puts it: Brook 'began by bringing in poet Ted Hughes, and asking him to "translate" *King Lear* as if it had been written in a foreign language, to render it, not into a 1969 idiom, but into a language that suited the contemporary needs of poetic expression. Having done this, Brook returned to the original Shakespeare, convinced that this defamiliarization had helped him to tap the core of the play.' For further information, see www.albany.edu/writers-inst/webpages4/filmnotes/fns98n11.html (25 November 2012). I am grateful to Tony Howard (Warwick University) for bringing this to my attention.

[25] Charles Spencer, *Daily Telegraph* (1 November 1994). Quoted in Aleander C. Y. Huang, ' "What Country, friends, is this?" '.

achieve relatively little in expressing its worries about the low take-up of modern languages at GSCE following the Government's decision in 2003 to make language learning optional from the age of 14.[26] However hard the British Academy has tried to explain that the current language policy in Britain is affecting the health of the humanities and the social sciences, there seem to be few signs of real improvement. Press release upon press release, supported by alarming figures, creates the image of a nation where 'Research in all subjects is becoming increasingly insular in outlook, because PhD students do not have language skills, or the time to acquire them.'[27] It is a nation, where that special breed of 'Cosmopolitan Islanders' – as Richard J. Evans has called them – are becoming extinct, those British historians who, fortified with the necessary languages, would write the history of other nations.[28] Lord Acton wrote the history of the French Revolution in English, only to be translated for French consumption afterwards.[29] Thomas Carlyle, with a grand knowledge of German, wrote his history of *Frederick the Great* in English but it was a German translation of Carlyle's classic that Joseph Goebbels is alleged to have presented to Hitler in the Bunker, and from which he is alleged to have read passages to the Führer during the final days.[30]

Doesn't the image of the English nation where 'Research in all subjects is becoming increasingly insular in outlook, because PhD students do not have language skills, or the time to acquire them' ominously recall the image of Shakespeare's early modern London with which this article began? This impression is confirmed when we extend our gaze beyond foreign language skills, and direct our focus to translation. Although Translation Studies are strong in England, with nuclei in London, Manchester, Leicester, Leeds, Aston and Portsmouth, no-one in his right mind could remain cheerful at the news that the Centre for Translation and Comparative Cultural Studies at the University of Warwick – long one of the undisputed beacons in the international world of Translation Studies – should have

lost its high-profile, and have now been subsumed under English Studies.

CONCLUSION

In this article I have explored a number of connections between English, foreign languages and translation, both in the early modern theatre and in our own twenty-first century as it affects the reception of Shakespeare's plays, particularly in Britain today. The comparison between these two periods reveals a number of parallels, and these are far from unproblematic in our present cultural and/or academic climate. These problems pose a challenge for today's strolling players who bring us Boomerang Shakespeare, but they also emphasize the need for a sense of responsibility, particularly from those native English audiences with whom they seek to interact across the language divide.

It is far from certain how this year's Shakespearian contribution to the internationalization of culture will fare in the climate that I have sketched. Please note that it has not been my intention to paint a gloomy picture and create a mood of utter despondency. Rather, I would argue that there could not have been a better moment than the year of the London Olympics for the Globe's multilingual marathon.

Should we wax gloomy, there will always be Shakespeare with his true assessment of the Olympic Spirit – not arguing that it is not important to win, as long as you have participated in the Games, but going for victory only. To the young Renaissance Shakespeare, the honours to be gained at the Olympics were in a special category all their own. As George of Clarence tells Warwick as well

---

26 See www.britac.ac.uk/news/news.cfm/newsid/266 (25 November 2012).

27 See www.britac.ac.uk/policy/dearing-2006/response-02-07.cfm (25 November 2012).

28 Richard J. Evans, *Cosmopolitan Islanders: British Historians and the European Continent* (Cambridge, 2009).

29 Evans, *Cosmopolitan Islanders*, pp. 82–91.

30 Evans, *Cosmopolitan Islanders*, pp. 70–6.

as the sons of York before the battle of Towton in the third part of *Henry VI*:

> Yet let us all together to our troops,
> And give them leave to fly that will not stay;
> And call them pillars that will stand to us;
> And, if we thrive, promise them such rewards
> As victors wear at the Olympian games.
> This may plant courage in their quailing breasts,
> For yet is hope of life and victory.
>
> (3 *Henry VI*, 2.3.49–55)

And this is also my credo for foreign language studies and translation studies in this island to which I am – as I said earlier – a foreigner but not a stranger.

SHAKESPEARE'S INHUMANITY

KIERNAN RYAN

It might seem perverse to impute inhumanity to the dramatist credited by Harold Bloom with nothing less than 'the invention of the human, the inauguration of personality as we have come to recognize it'.[1] Many critics would baulk, of course, at Bloom's conclusion that 'When we are wholly human, and know ourselves, we become most like either Hamlet or Falstaff',[2] not least because they find Bloom's notion of what it means to be human objectionable. But few would be inclined to divorce Shakespeare's drama from the enlightened commitment to the cause of humanity that most critics, from Dryden's day onwards, have discerned in it. The prospect of a thriving school of criticism devoted to exposing Shakespeare's implacable hostility to his kind appears to be at best remote. That said, the last decade has seen the publication of books bent on showing how the concepts of humanity and the human are problematized in Shakespeare's plays and early modern literature at large.[3] The contention of these studies is that, by blurring or erasing the boundaries between the human and the non-human, Renaissance writers – with Shakespeare foremost amongst them – reveal the instability of the idea of 'humanity' at this embryonic stage in its modern evolution. As Stefan Herbrechter observes: 'As soon as some form of *humanitas* begins to characterize the species as a whole, non-human (un-, in-, pre- or posthuman) others start proliferating and the process of inclusion, exclusion and differentiation is set in motion.'[4] If we are prepared to credit the creator of Hamlet and Falstaff with 'the inauguration of personality as we have come to recognize it', we

must also be prepared to accept that 'Shakespeare's "invention of the human"', as Herbrechter argues in a direct riposte to Bloom, 'implies the invention of the inhuman'.[5]

What part Shakespeare played in shaping these concepts as they are understood today is a less intriguing question, however, than that posed by the imaginative and emotional appeal of inhumanity to Shakespeare: inhumanity not only as a feature of the plays – the acts of physical and mental

---

This article is a revised version of The Annual Shakespeare Lecture, University of Hull, 23 April 2013. I am grateful to the University of Hull, and to Professor Janet Clare in particular, for inviting me to deliver the lecture and for permission to publish it here.

[1] Harold Bloom, *Shakespeare: The Invention of the Human* (London, 1999), p. 4.

[2] Bloom, *Shakespeare*, p. 745.

[3] See especially *At the Borders of the Human: Beasts, Bodies and Natural Philosophy in the Early Modern Period*, ed. Erica Fudge, Ruth Gilbert and Susan Wiseman (Basingstoke, 2002); *Renaissance Beasts: Of Animals, Humans, and Other Wonderful Creatures*, ed. Erica Fudge (Urbana, 2004); Erica Fudge, *Brutal Reasoning: Animals, Rationality, and Humanity in Early Modern England* (Ithaca, 2006); Bruce Boehrer, *Animal Characters: Nonhuman Beings in Early Modern Literature* (Philadelphia, 2010); Andreas Höfele, *Stage, Stake and Scaffold: Humans and Animals in Shakespeare's Theatre* (Oxford, 2011); *Humankinds: The Renaissance and Its Anthropologies*, ed. Andreas Höfele and Stephan Laqué (Berlin, 2011); *Posthumanist Shakespeares*, ed. Stefan Herbrechter and Ivan Callus (Basingstoke, 2012).

[4] Stefan Herbrechter, '"A passion so strange, outrageous, and so variable": The Invention of the Inhuman in *The Merchant of Venice*', in *Posthumanist Shakespeares*, ed. Herbrechter and Callus, p. 41.

[5] Herbrechter, '"A passion so strange"', p. 46.

cruelty, the murders and atrocities that characters commit – but also as a disconcerting aspect of their dramatic vision. The inhuman is inextricably entwined with the human in Shakespeare's imagination, but in ways that reveal how profoundly at odds he was with his era. To take the measure of Shakespeare's inhumanity as a dramatist is to grasp the intractably anachronistic nature of his art, its utopian intolerance of what passed for life in his time. It is also to grasp why Shakespeare would have known what Apollinaire meant when he wrote, 'Above all, artists are men who desire to become inhuman. They are tireless in their search for signs of inhumanity.'[6]

Signs of inhumanity in Shakespeare's plays are certainly not far to seek. Deeds of unspeakable brutality, both onstage and offstage, abound throughout the canon. The prime instance of an act that qualifies unequivocally as inhuman is the gouging out of Gloucester's eyes in *King Lear*, which is still generally considered too horrific for spectators to tolerate. Most productions opt to shift the actual blinding offstage or to obscure the audience's view of it, leaving Gloucester's cries of agony to work upon the mind's eye. The inhumanity of the act lies not only in its gruesome nature – so palpably evoked by Cornwall's grisly ejaculation, 'Out, vile jelly, / Where is thy lustre now?' (3.7.82–3)[7] – but also in the sadistic gusto with which Cornwall and Regan perform it, spurred on rather than deterred by the excruciating pain they are inflicting on a helpless old man. On the evidence of this scene at least, taking pleasure in the gratuitous infliction of suffering or death, a pleasure predicated on absolute indifference to the victim, seems to be the hallmark of the inhuman. Indifference was undoubtedly its defining feature as far as George Bernard Shaw was concerned. In *The Devil's Disciple* Anderson assures Judith that she is not as wicked as she thinks to feel hatred for someone, because 'The worst sin towards our fellow creatures is not to hate them, but to be indifferent to them; that's the essence of inhumanity.'[8] Anything may be done to those who are regarded with indifference, because they are deemed weak or worthless and consequently do not count.

The fact that the chief function of Gloucester's blinding is to demonize Regan and Cornwall as irredeemably malign does not explain, however, why Shakespeare compels the audience to witness it. The hanging of Cordelia loses little of its horror by occurring in the offstage realm of the imagination, as her father enters howling like a wounded animal, cradling her corpse in his arms. It is hard to suppress the suspicion that Shakespeare is emotionally engaged in the savage act of mutilation he has staged for his audience's entertainment. The thought of his obtaining vicarious gratification from dramatizing such a scene may be unpalatable, but it seems less improbable when the cumulative impact of the cruelties to which the protagonists subject each other is taken into account. 'Why should a dog, a horse, a rat have life / And thou no breath at all?' (5.3.305–6), Lear demands of his daughter's dead body, baffled by nature's ruthless indifference to the rank or desert of human beings. But Shakespeare's violation of precedent and expectation at the end of the play, by which point all but three of its aristocratic protagonists have been killed off, betrays a hardness of heart that mirrors the ruthlessness of nature and shows no mercy to the hopes of the audience. 'There is a cruelty in the writing', concludes Frank Kermode, 'that echoes the cruelty of the story, a terrible calculatedness that puts one in mind of Cornwall's and Regan's.'[9] That the tragedy is at pains to elicit compassion for the anguish, terror, despair and death its principal characters are obliged to endure goes without saying. But the compassion is eclipsed by

---

[6] 'Avant tout, les artistes sont des hommes qui veulent devenir inhumains. Ils cherchent péniblement les traces de l'inhumanité' (*Oeuvres en prose complètes: Tome II*, ed. Pierre Cazergues and Michel Décaudin (Paris, 1991), p. 8). My translation.

[7] *King Lear*, ed. R.A. Foakes (Walton-on-Thames, 1997). All other textual references are to *William Shakespeare: The Complete Works*, 2nd edn, ed. Stanley Wells, Gary Taylor, John Jowett and William Montgomery (Oxford, 2005).

[8] George Bernard Shaw, *Three Plays for Puritans* (London, 1931), p. 30.

[9] Frank Kermode, *Shakespeare's Language* (London, 2000), p. 197.

the play's Olympian contempt for the dispensation on whose terms the characters are doomed to live and die. As far as Shakespeare is concerned, the time that Albany fears will come, when 'Humanity must perforce prey on itself, / Like monsters of the deep' (4.2.50–1), has already arrived, and the inhuman world it has spawned is dispatched in *King Lear* with the chilling 'authorial savagery'[10] it deserves.

To look afresh at the English and Roman history plays, and at some of the tragedies, that preceded and succeeded *King Lear* in light of this view of it is to be reminded that Shakespeare's Leviathan (as Lamb dubbed *Lear*)[11] is merely the most remorseless of the many plays he wrote – close to half his entire output – in which the nobility slaughter each other or are driven to suicide, and rulers are hounded, usurped and murdered for the audience's amusement and edification.

It is perhaps no accident that the play with which Shakespeare commenced, in all likelihood, his career as a tragedian was *Titus Andronicus*. Given their obvious family resemblances in point of plot – the derangement and destruction of a tyrannical patriarch, whose initial act of cruelty brings about the death of his beloved daughter – *Titus* has long been pegged as a precursor of *Lear*. But their circumstantial similarities are less striking than the callous zest with which both tragedies cut a swathe through the ranks of their casts. In *King Lear* the callousness is mitigated by the expressions of grief, remorse and empathy that key characters are allowed to voice and exchange. But the pathos wrung from the sight of Lavinia's mutilated body in the wake of her rape, and from Titus's unhinged desolation, is too formal and undeveloped to offset the grotesque farce the tragedy creates from its mounting tally of fatal stabbings, lopped-off limbs and cannibalized corpses. The distinction between Lear and 'The barbarous Scythian, / Or he that makes his generation messes / To gorge his appetite' (1.1.117–19) collapses as the barbarism latent in his own regime breaks out, and humanity preys upon itself like monsters of the deep. But long before *Lear* Shakespeare demolishes the same illusory distinction in *Titus Andronicus*: when the

Goth prince Chiron hears that Titus and his sons are resolved to immolate Chiron's brother, Alarbus, upon a pyre and 'hew his limbs till they be clean consumed', he responds in disbelief, 'Was never Scythia half so barbarous' (1.1.129, 131). His brother Demetrius immediately chides him for the comparison: 'Oppose not Scythia to ambitious Rome' (1.1.132). But within minutes Titus has slain his own son, too, without a flicker of remorse, and Shakespeare's scathing caricature of 'ambitious Rome' – that pinnacle and prototype of Western civilization – as an abattoir has begun.

If it is true that 'Tone is just as much a property of the written text as are grammar and figuration', and if it is in the tone of a text that 'the libidinal forces motivating utterance are most clearly revealed',[12] then the sardonic tone of *Titus* secretes an intense libidinal investment in defiling a culture which is fit to be defiled. That tone is focused in the voice of Aaron the Moor, the *spiritus rector* of the play, who embodies and articulates the attitude that governs it. The 'inhuman dog' (5.3.14) who casually kills the nurse of his own child with a vicious quip ('"Wheak, wheak" – so cries a pig prepared to the spit' (4.2.145)), and confesses to his captors that, after tricking Titus into having his hand chopped off, he 'almost broke [his] heart with extreme laughter' (5.1.113), remains unrepentant to the end. Superbly indifferent to his impending death and the threat of eternal damnation, he exults in the atrocities he has committed and nurses only one regret:

> . . . I have done a thousand dreadful things
> As willingly as one would kill a fly,
> And nothing grieves me heartily indeed
> But that I cannot do ten thousand more.
>
> (5.1.141–4)

It would be disingenuous to deny the pleasure Shakespeare plainly takes, and invites the audience

---

10 Kermode, *Shakespeare's Language*, p. 195.

11 'On the Tragedies of Shakespeare' (1811), in *The Prose Works of Charles Lamb*, 3 vols. (London, 1836), vol. 1, p. 122.

12 Henry Staten, *Nietzsche's Voice* (Ithaca and London, 1990), p. 5.

to share, in the glee with which the defiant Moor trumpets his crimes against humanity.

Although Shakespeare gives him a rougher ride than his immediate theatrical progenitor, Richard III meets his maker in the same defiant mood as Aaron, once he has put his traumatic nightmare on the eve of battle behind him: 'Let us to't, pell-mell – / If not to heaven, then hand in hand to hell' (5.6.42–3). Richard's infamous boast in *3 Henry VI*, 'Why, I can smile, and murder whiles I smile' (3.2.182), could also have been uttered just as readily by Aaron. Before the avenging ghosts spook him, however, he enjoys a downstage intimacy with the audience of which the treacherous Moor could only have dreamed. The licence that intimacy entails is secured by the extraordinary speech with which Richard opens the play – the only play in the canon to begin with the main protagonist addressing the audience directly. Richard exploits this unique privilege by taking the audience into his confidence and presuming upon their compliance with his homicidal schemes. With the dramatic deck stacked so brazenly in his favour from the start, it would take a more pious mind than most playgoers are blessed with to refuse Richard's invitation to join him in savouring his ingenuity as the body-count rises.

Richard's theatrical energy and eloquence prove sufficiently seductive to withstand the barrage of vilification to which he is incessantly subjected. His killing of Henry VI is denounced by Anne as 'inhuman and unnatural' (1.2.60), as the latter's corpse bleeds afresh beside her; Henry's widow, Margaret, reviles him as 'the son of hell', 'that bottled spider', 'this poisonous bunch-backed toad' (1.3.227, 240, 244); Queen Elizabeth calls the kingdom he rules 'this slaughterhouse' (4.1.43); his own mother blames her 'accursèd womb, the bed of death' for having hatched 'A cockatrice . . . to the world, / Whose unavoided eye is murderous' (4.1.53–5); and the liquidation of the princes is deplored by Tyrrell as 'this piece of ruthless butchery' (4.3.5). But all the vitriol poured upon him cannot stop the charismatic 'hell-hound' (4.4.48) from stealing the show from his Tudor nemesis, or disguise the fact that Shakespeare was as captivated by his

monstrous creation as generations of audiences across the globe have been, and that he took delight in letting him run riot.

That Shakespearian villains like Aaron and Richard cast a theatrical spell, which the moral reflexes of most spectators are powerless to resist, will come as critical news to no one. But there is more at stake in that paradoxical appeal than meets the eye. Precisely what is made clearer by Shylock, whom the Duke of Venice condemns before the trial has started as 'A stony adversary, an inhuman wretch / Uncapable of pity, void and empty / From any dram of mercy' (4.1.3–5). Although he lacks the self-delighting panache of Aaron and Richard, and is spared a similar fate by the grace of comedic convention, Shylock shares enough of their demonic glamour – as his critical and theatrical history attests – to make him more than their kissing cousin in the pantheon of Shakespearean fiends. But his penetrating moral intelligence puts him in a different league from them, allowing us to unlock the logic of the inhuman that drives such characters and explain the affinity Shakespeare feels for them.

Vilified like his precursors as a creature of infernal provenance, Shylock becomes synonymous with Satan – 'the very devil incarnation' (2.2.25) in the clown Gobbo's shrewdly garbled words – and thus an avatar of the original enemy of humanity. As such, however, he also commands our secret sympathy as the victim of a diabolical injustice, for which he seeks revenge in kind. Shylock's metamorphosis from anti-Semitic stereotype into satanic anti-hero pivots, of course, on the speech commonly acknowledged as one of the most compelling protests against prejudice ever penned:

Hath not a Jew eyes? Hath not a Jew hands, organs, dimensions, senses, affections, passions; fed with the same food, hurt with the same weapons, subject to the same diseases, healed by the same means, warmed and cooled by the same winter and summer as a Christian is? If you prick us do we not bleed? If you tickle us do we not laugh? If you poison us do we not die? And if you wrong us shall we not revenge? If we are like you in the rest, we will resemble you in that. If a Jew wrong a Christian, what is his humility? Revenge. If a Christian wrong a Jew, what should his sufferance be by Christian example? Why, revenge. The villainy you teach me I will execute, and it shall go hard but I will better the instruction. (3.1.54–68)

Shylock rebukes the Jew-baiting Christians on the grounds that they share the same physical constitution, needs and emotions, which make them equally vulnerable, equally mortal and equally prone to revenge themselves on those who have wronged them. The bitter irony is that Shylock is bent on vindicating the principle of innate human equality to which he appeals by violating it through his demand for a pound of Antonio's flesh. His aim is to dramatize his human identity with his tormentors by replicating their rejection of that identity and of the right it entails to be treated with equal regard. The last line of the speech makes plain Shylock's determination to teach them a lesson by aping their inhuman abuse of him.

If that lesson is lost on Shylock's persecutors, it should not be lost on the audience, especially as its mordant satirical thrust cuts deeper as the play develops. Nowhere does it cut deeper than in his speech justifying his rejection of the Duke's plea that he show Antonio mercy:

> You have among you many a purchased slave
> Which, like your asses and your dogs and mules,
> You use in abject and in slavish parts
> Because you bought them. Shall I say to you
> 'Let them be free, marry them to your heirs.
> Why sweat they under burdens? Let their beds
> Be made as soft as yours, and let their palates
> Be seasoned with such viands.' You will answer
> 'The slaves are ours.' So do I answer you.
> The pound of flesh which I demand of him
> Is dearly bought. 'Tis mine, and I will have it.
> If you deny me, fie upon your law:
> There is no force in the decrees of Venice.
> (4.1.89–101)

The Jew denounced before he opens his mouth as an 'inhuman wretch' demonstrates irrefutably that the conduct the Christians excoriate in him as 'wolvish, bloody, starved, and ravenous' (4.1.137) is the keystone of Venetian society, whose institutionalized inhumanity is legally sanctioned as 'justice' (4.1.200): 'Why, this bond is forfeit', Portia acknowledges, 'And lawfully by this the Jew may claim / A pound of flesh' (4.1.227–9). How could it be otherwise in a society whose citizens exercise the same legal right to buy and own pounds of human flesh in the shape of slaves? What, after all, is so outrageous about Shylock carving his due like a butcher from 'Nearest the merchant's heart' (4.1.230) in a world where 'A pound of man's flesh taken from a man / Is not so estimable, profitable neither, / As flesh of muttons, beeves, or goats' (1.3.164–6)? Moralistic bickering about the play's alleged anti-Semitism, and whether it inculpates the Christians and exculpates the Jew, or vice versa, misses the point. Through Shylock *The Merchant of Venice* exposes the covert barbarism of an ostensibly civilized culture, in which property and commodities take precedence over people, whose shared human interests are sacrificed to the pursuit of profit and power by those who own and rule.[13]

Therein lies the key to what Aaron, Richard and Shylock have in common, not only with each other, but also with *King Lear* and with a number of other characters too, most notably Iago and Macbeth. In this unholy trinity Shakespeare portrays not egregious aberrations from the moral norms of their societies, but monstrously magnified, distorted reflections of the real ethos of those societies, stripped of their self-deluding façades. The Rome of *Titus Andronicus*, the England of *Richard III* and the Venice epitomized by Antonio find themselves terrorized by their spitting images, by caustic burlesques of their own dehumanized behaviour, which they abhor in the Moor, the hump-backed cripple and the Jew, and refuse to recognize in themselves.

Aaron, Richard and Shylock serve, in other words, as both scapegoats and scourges. As scapegoats they must take the blame and pay the price for the endemic inhumanity they embody and expose, but their societies disavow; as scourges, however,

---

[13] For a fully developed reading of the play from this perspective, see '"The deed of kind": *The Merchant of Venice*', in Kiernan Ryan, *Shakespeare's Comedies* (Basingstoke, 2009), pp. 104–33.

their role is to exact retribution from the societies they mirror and mock by paying them back in their own cruel currency, and in this capacity they are licensed by Shakespeare to persecute, to maim and to kill. When Hamlet, having run his sword through Polonius in the belief that he was killing the king, says, 'heaven hath pleased it so / To punish me with this, and this with me, / That I must be their scourge and minister' (3.4.157–9), he displays his kinship with these ostracized, alienated figures, a kinship sealed by the gory spate of 'casual slaughters' (5.2.336) with which the tragedy concludes. The murder of Polonius also clinches Hamlet's propinquity to Brutus, linking him to the latter's butchering of 'Imperial Caesar' (5.1.208) on stage in cold blood, in the play Shakespeare probably wrote just before *Hamlet*. The link is forged by Hamlet's punning retort to Polonius's boast, 'I did enact Julius Caesar. I was killed i'th' Capitol. Brutus killed me': 'It was a brute part of him', quips Hamlet, 'to kill so capital a calf there' (3.2.102–5).

Any doubt that Iago belongs in this company of wolves should be dispelled by the fact of his sharing with Aaron the distinction of being dubbed an 'inhuman dog' (*Othello*, 5.1.64). The motive for his malignity may appear enigmatic, but the inhumanity of his actions is beyond question. Like his fellow Shakespearian fiends his diabolical nature is underscored, identifying him with the nemesis of mankind. The infernal inspiration of the plot he hatches against Othello is established at the start – 'Hell and night / Must bring this monstrous birth to the world's light' (1.3.395–6) – and at the end of the tragedy Othello looks down at Iago's feet, half-expecting to see the cloven hooves of Satan himself (5.2.292). But it is Iago who notoriously hogs the spotlight, upstaging the eponymous hero through the thrilling downstage complicity Shakespeare forges between the 'inhuman dog' and the audience. Iago revels like Richard III in the latitude this complicity affords him, milking his magnetism at every step as he stages, improvises and directs the tragedy like a dark double of Shakespeare himself. In so far as the audience finds itself as enthralled by Iago as his creator, it also finds itself like Shakespeare not just theatrically but morally implicated

in the destruction of Othello and Desdemona, and in the racism and misogyny that authorize it. Neither audience nor author can be let off the hook in a tragedy for which it would be unjust to blame the villain alone, when his villainy was cultivated by the society that surrounds him.

Hence the care Shakespeare takes to scramble the reasons Iago contrives for siring 'this monstrous birth' and make his malignity seem motiveless. For if revenge for one clear reason or another – being passed over for promotion or genuinely believing himself a cuckold – supplied a credible, satisfactory motive for Iago, the cause of the tragedy could be confined to him and explained away as safely as writing him off as a psychopath. But Shakespeare takes equal care to show that the assumptions and attitudes from which Iago weaves his web of deceit are ubiquitous in Venice rather than peculiar to him. For Iago the Moor, as he repeatedly refers to Othello, is 'an old black ram' (1.1.88), but Roderigo derides him too as 'the thick-lips' (1.1.66), while Brabantio, in his public confrontation with Othello, confesses himself mystified by his daughter's desiring to 'Run from her guardage to the sooty bosom / Of such a thing as thou' (1.3.71–2). So pervasive are such perceptions that Othello and Desdemona themselves cannot help internalizing them: 'I saw Othello's visage in his mind' (1.3.252), Desdemona declares to the Duke and Senators of Venice, oblivious to what that brave declaration concedes; 'my name', laments Othello, 'that was as fresh / As Dian's visage, is now begrimed, and black / As mine own face' (3.3.391–3).

Sexual jealousy is likewise revealed to be the cultural norm rather than the unfortunate affliction of a psychologically warped individual. Roderigo's infatuation with Desdemona makes him intensely jealous of both Othello and Cassio; the same emotion flares up in Bianca, when Cassio gives her Desdemona's handkerchief: 'you are jealous now', says Cassio, 'That this is from some mistress, some remembrance' (3.4.182–3); and Iago himself betrays the same toxic disposition, when he automatically fastens on sexual jealousy as the pretext for provoking it in Othello and revenging himself on Cassio: 'I do suspect the lusty Moor / Hath leapt into my seat, the thought whereof / Doth, like a poisonous mineral, gnaw my inwards'; 'I fear Cassio with my night-cap, too' (2.1.294–6, 306). Although none of them is as devoured by jealousy as Othello is, all these characters fall prey like him to 'the green-eyed monster' (3.3.170) that stalks any society in which the sexual desire of one human being is regarded as the property of another.

The really terrifying thing about Iago is his pathological normality. Iago differs from the rest of the Venetians only in the ferocity with which he espouses their values and the deranged extremes to which he resorts to vindicate them. His devious stratagem works so well because it works by reflecting his victims' own beliefs, by confirming their suspicions and fulfilling their expectations. When Emilia begs him to deny that he duped Othello into murdering Desdemona, Iago replies: 'I told him what I thought, and told no more / Than what he found himself was apt and true' (5.2.183–4); and when Othello asks Cassio to 'demand that demi-devil / Why he hath thus ensnared my soul and body', Iago replies with the same dispassionate sang-froid: 'Demand me nothing. What you know, you know. / From this time forth I never will speak word' (5.2.307–10). The demand for a reason is bounced straight back by Iago, because the explanation lies as much with them as with him: 'What you know, you know.' In Iago Venice beholds the virulent personification of its own mentality, unshackled and hell-bent on mayhem.

Like his counterparts in previous and later plays, Iago poses troubling questions about the guilty pleasures such pitiless malefactors afford both Shakespeare and his audiences then and now. The fascination they exert and the latitude they enjoy are clearly not the consequence of their iniquity being endorsed or excused by the dramatist. Their odious deeds are rightly condemned as abhorrent within the plays. But the perpetrators of those deeds are granted immunity from unequivocal condemnation by their embodiment of the ethos that condemns them. There is something reprehensibly gratifying, and all the more gratifying for being

reprehensible, about watching the incarnate essence of society at its worst unleashed to play hell with the world it epitomizes. The vicarious pleasure springs in part from the villain's dramatic warrant to create carnage, unfettered by conscience, fear or contrition. But a more profound satisfaction derives from sensing that the havoc the villain wreaks is what the world that made him has brought upon itself, however innocent or culpable his victims may be. As the scapegoats of a society whose inhumanity they exemplify, Shakespeare's miscreants merit all the execrations they incur, notwithstanding the amoral allure with which he invests them; but as the inhuman scourges of that society, they serve the same transcendent poetic justice as *King Lear*, in the name of humanity as it could and should be. Through these fallen avenging angels the humanity of the future passes judgement on the inhumanity of the past, to which the inhumanity of the present, too, will one day belong.

'The inhumanity of art must triumph over the inhumanity of the world for the sake of the humane.'[14] Adorno's aphorism might have been framed with this aspect of Shakespeare's dramatic art in mind. So might Walter Benjamin's thesis that 'There is no document of civilization which is not at the same time a document of barbarism.'[15] Shakespeare's drama has no qualms about admitting, and sometimes relishing, its inescapable complicity with the barbarism of the culture that engendered and financed it. But one of its most arresting and disquieting virtues is its keenness to enlist that complicity in the service of the truly civilized society that lies beyond the barbarism to which most of mankind remains in thrall. This astute dramatic ploy is perfectly encapsulated in the speech already quoted, in which Shylock is unwittingly conscripted as a spokesman for the ethical obligations that spring from the fact that we

---

[14] Theodor Adorno, *Philosophy of Modern Music*, trans. Anne Mitchell and Wesley Blomster (London and New York, 2004), p. 132.

[15] Walter Benjamin, 'Theses on the Philosophy of History', in *Illuminations*, trans. Harry Zohn (London, 1973), p. 258.

belong to the same species. As a character whose consciousness is defined by his vindictive obsession, Shylock invokes that fact to buttress the rationale of his revenge, not to commend an enlightened precept to the Christians goading him. But Shakespeare puts in Shylock's mouth an argument which has wider egalitarian implications than the Jew is aware of, as the speech's enduring impact attests. In so doing he creates a tension between the divisive viewpoint of an individual immured in the hierarchical culture of Shakespeare's day and the universal perspective implicit in the potential equality of all human beings.

That creative tension between historical reality and utopian possibility, between the fact of institutionalized inhumanity and the prospect of humanity's emancipation, is the driving force of Shakespeare's anachronistic art. The devil's deal his drama strikes with the inhuman is a crucial factor in securing its alienation from the age in which it was written, and a crucial reminder not to sentimentalize Shakespeare's utopianism by divorcing it from his ruthless realism.

According to Aubrey's brief life of Shakespeare, 'His father was a Butcher, and I have been told heretofore by some of the neighbours, that when he was a boy he exercised his father's Trade, but when he kill'd a calfe he would doe it in a high style, and make a Speech.'[16] The anecdote with which Aubrey seeks to anchor the origin of Shakespeare's career on the stage in his flamboyant pursuit of his father's trade may be apocryphal, as some scholars suspect, but then again it may not be. Either way, the frequency with which, and the contexts in which, Shakespeare not only evokes acts of butchery but specifically employs the word 'butcher' and its variants (leaving aside his numerous allusions to the leather trades that depend on butchers) are, at the very least, suggestive. Aubrey's anecdote harbours an echo, whether unconscious or not, of Hamlet's quip about Brutus killing so capital a calf as Caesar in the Capitol. And in *Julius Caesar* itself the discourse of butchery has a salient role in determining how the assassination of Caesar is perceived. 'Let's be sacrificers, but not butchers', Brutus cautions Cassius. 'Let's carve him as a dish fit for the

gods, / Not hew him as a carcass fit for hounds' (2.1.166, 173–4). But as he stands over Caesar's lacerated corpse, Antony has no doubt about what kind of men he is dealing with: 'O pardon me, thou bleeding piece of earth, / That I am meek and gentle with these butchers' (3.1.257–8).

The fact that the vast majority of instances in which the word is literally or figuratively used in some form occur in the English and Roman history plays, and chiefly in the former, is hardly fortuitous. Butchery for Shakespeare is a craft in which those who rule society are as proficient as butchers themselves. When they are not forcing their subjects, who are 'All of one nature, of one substance bred', to 'meet in the intestine shock / And furious close of civil butchery' (*1 Henry IV*, 1.1.111–13), they are either butchering whoever impedes their pursuit of power, butchering whoever threatens their retention of power, or being butchered in their turn for the same reasons. Hence, not surprisingly, the high concentration of occurrences in the first tetralogy. Tyrrell's denunciation of the princes' murder as 'ruthless butchery' is only one of eight instances in *Richard III*, the first of which crops up in Anne's command, 'Behold this pattern of thy butcheries' (1.2.54), as she addresses Richard over Henry's corpse; and the last in Richmond's reminder of a war-torn kingdom, in which 'The father rashly slaughtered his own son' and 'The son, compelled,' was 'butcher to the sire' (5.8.24–5). Of the dozen usages in the *Henry VI* plays, the most vivid is the sustained simile Henry employs to describe the arrest of Gloucester:

> And as the butcher takes away the calf,
> And binds the wretch, and beats it when it strains,
> Bearing it to the bloody slaughterhouse,
> Even so remorseless have they borne him hence . . .
> (*2 Henry VI*, 3.1.210–13)

But the most telling cluster round Jack Cade's closest confederate, who, like the rest of the rebels, is 'inspired with the spirit of putting down kings and princes' (*2 Henry VI*, 4.2.36–7). Cade's right-hand

---

[16] *Aubrey's Brief Lives*, ed. Oliver Lawson Dick (London, 1949), p. 275.

man, who utters the immortal line 'The first thing we do let's kill all the lawyers', and who insists that if they 'mean to thrive and do good', they must 'break open the jails and let out the prisoners' (4.2.78, 4.3.14–15), is Dick, the butcher of Ashford, whom Cade singles out for his prowess in the field against the aristocratic foe: 'They fell before thee like sheep and oxen, and thou behaved'st thyself as if thou hadst been in thine own slaughterhouse' (4.3.3–5).

A proper account of the imagery of the abattoir in Shakespeare would address the way it reaches beyond the battlefield and the corridors of power to infect the economic realm, the domestic sphere, and even the language of love in the comedies. Shylock's demonstration that in Venice 'A pound of man's flesh taken from a man' is literally worth less than 'flesh of muttons, beeves, or goats', has already been noted. But even in *As You Like It* we find Orlando saying of the home he is forced to flee, 'this house is but a butchery' (2.3.28), while Phoebe rebukes Rosalind for accusing her eyes of being 'tyrants, butchers, murderers' (3.5.14). And in *Love's Labour's Lost* Katherine concludes a protracted bout of repartee, which turns on her mocking Longueville as a 'calf' (i.e. a dolt), by capping his line, 'One word in private with you ere I die', with 'Bleat softly, then. The butcher hears you cry' (5.2.254–5). Such playful raids on the language of the shambles, cushioned though they are by comedy, illustrate the contagiousness of this gory lexicon, but they are far less frequent and overshadowed by their widespread use in deadly earnest in the history plays and tragedies.

The point need not be laboured: even if there is no truth whatsoever to Aubrey's claim that Shakespeare was the son of a butcher (rather than the son of a more genteel glover) and for a time plied his father's trade, his imaginative affinity, if not quite consanguinity, with that trade is as pronounced as his penchant for staging plays in which blue-blooded killers and fomenters of butchery wind up being slaughtered themselves. Given the aristocratic death toll of the histories and tragedies, Jack Cade's words to Dick the butcher of Ashford might be addressed no less aptly to their author:

'They fell before thee like sheep and oxen, and thou behaved'st thyself as if thou hadst been in thine own slaughterhouse.'[17]

The spirit that animates these plays is one that Brecht, whose drama owed so much to Shakespeare, would have had no difficulty understanding. In *The Measures Taken* (*Die Maßnahme*) he gives the Chorus these lines:

> With whom would the just man not sit down
> To help the cause of justice?
> What medicine would taste too bad
> To someone dying?
> What vile act would you not commit to
> Eradicate vileness?
> If you could change the world at last, why
> Would you be too good to change it?
> Who are you?
> Sink into the mire
> Embrace the butcher, but
> Change the world: it needs it![18]

No play of Shakespeare's is more powerfully animated by this spirit than *Macbeth*, whose protagonist, reviled by Malcolm in the closing speech as 'this dead butcher' (5.11.35), is embraced in Brecht's sense by Shakespeare from the start of the play. He is embraced because his tragedy dramatizes both the inhumanity of the world that fosters his inhuman crimes and the human potential to live by principles upon which a quite different kind of world might be founded. By revealing that

---

[17] Dover Wilson famously deemed it a 'scandal' that Shakespeare's depiction in the Folio's Droeshout engraving as a 'self-satisfied pork butcher' had obscured our image of 'the true Shakespeare' for three centuries (*The Essential Shakespeare* (Cambridge, 1943), p. 6.) Perhaps the portrait is truer to Shakespeare's spirit than Dover Wilson's snobbery could countenance, and the source of his butcher's look of satisfaction more scandalous than Dover Wilson could imagine.

[18] 'Mit wem säße der Rechtliche nicht zusammen / Dem Recht zu helfen? Welche Medizin schmeckte zu schlecht / Dem Sterbenden? / Welche Niedrigkeit begingest du nicht, um / Die Niedrigkeit auszutilgen? / Könntest du die Welt endlich verändern, wofür / Wärest du dir zu gut? / Wer bist du? / Versinke in Schmutz / Umarme den Schlächter, aber / Ändere die Welt: Sie braucht es!' (*Gesammelte Werke*, ed. Elisabeth Hauptmann and Werner Hecht (Frankfurt am Main, 1967), vol. I, pp. 651–2). My translation.

potential in the tormented black soul of a killer, Shakespeare shows not just how inextricable the human and the inhuman are, but how vital a tragic part inhumanity is fated to play in the liberation of humankind.

'Human' and 'kind' are, indeed, key words in *Macbeth*, as they are in *The Merchant of Venice*[19] and, for that matter, Shakespeare's drama generally. They distil the essence of his vision, the quality that keeps it out of step with his time and more than one step ahead of our time. In Robert Winder's recent novel *The Final Act of Mr Shakespeare*, Edward Alleyn explains to John Donne's daughter that Shakespeare 'marches to a different tune' and is 'not quite like the rest of us', because his drama is driven by one overriding idea: 'Shakespeare's idea is simply this: that worms will gnaw on kings and knaves alike. It is so simple that it is easy to forget it. Shakespeare's strength is that he *never* forgets it.'[20] To which it is tempting to add that the weakness of most Shakespearian criticism is that it has found Shakespeare's simple idea all too easy to forget, and left the revolutionary implications of his egalitarian vision undeveloped.

The core of that vision can be glimpsed in the speech in which Shylock invokes the physical foundations of our common humanity. It surfaces again when Hamlet explains to Claudius, step by levelling step, how 'a king may go a progress through the guts of a beggar' (4.3.30–1). It finds sustained expression in the graveyard scene, where Hamlet's class-bound plight as a Renaissance prince is placed in a transhistorical perspective, stretching back to the common origin of our kind in Adam, before class society and forward to Doomsday, when every human who ever lived, regardless of rank or riches, will have equal rights at last in the democracy of the dead. And it is brought home with harrowing force in *King Lear*, as a demented monarch bound upon a wheel of fire realizes that beneath his royal robes and a mad beggar's rags shivers the same 'poor, bare, forked animal', the same 'Unaccommodated man' (3.4.105–6) that survives as sheer potentiality within everyone, and thus is capable of binding us together as one species, in defiance of everything that divides us.

What is so startling and moving about *Macbeth* is that this radical utopian vision is vested in a blood-stained regicide, whose henchmen brutally murder a child on stage before his mother's and the audience's eyes. Shakespeare leaves the appalling cruelty of which his tragic hero is capable in no doubt, even as he compels the audience to empathize with the excruciating agonies of conscience he endures. The source of those agonies is identified at the outset by Lady Macbeth in a phrase that has passed into common parlance as a cliché and lost all its original potency as a consequence: 'Yet do I fear thy nature', she muses in her husband's absence, 'It is too full o'th' milk of human kindness / To catch the nearest way' (1.5.15–16). The word 'human' is spelled 'humane' here as elsewhere in the First Folio. In Shakespeare's day the term 'humane' had not yet split into two separate words with cognate but distinct meanings. So in its original form in Lady Macbeth's line it conflates the descriptive term 'human', meaning characteristic of the genus *homo*, and the prescriptive term 'humane', meaning compassionate. The implication that being human and being humane are inseparable is reinforced by the noun that the adjective 'human(e)' qualifies. 'Kindness' is fully charged here with its early modern import: it means sympathetic, benevolent conduct consistent with one's belonging to the same kind as the person to whom kindness is shown. By his own wife's reluctant admission, the future homicide Macbeth is 'too full' of all the qualities condensed in these two words.

No less remarkable is the fact that Macbeth's 'human kindness' is metaphorically described as 'milk'. For this links the phrase subliminally with the nourishing milk the infant sucks from its mother's breast, as Lady Macbeth confirms thirty lines later, when she prays to the forces of evil to be unsexed and filled 'from the crown to the toe top-full / Of direst cruelty': 'Come to my woman's breasts', she pleads, 'And take my

---

[19] See Ryan, '"The deed of kind"', especially pp. 109–15.

[20] Robert Winder, *The Final Act of Mr Shakespeare* (London, 2010), p. 91.

milk for gall, you murd'ring ministers' (1.5.40–2, 46–7). Two short scenes later, in her electrifying argument with Macbeth, she seizes on the same imagery as she strives to steel his nerves for murder:

> I have given suck, and know
> How tender 'tis to love the babe that milks me.
> I would, while it was smiling in my face,
> Have plucked my nipple from his boneless gums
> And dashed the brains out, had I so sworn
> As you have done to this.   (1.7.54–9)

Here the image of a breastfeeding baby implicit in the image of a mother's milk becomes graphically explicit. Lady Macbeth conjures up the most horrifying act she can imagine to persuade Macbeth to become as inhuman as she is resolved to become.

The reason why Shakespeare's evocation of helpless human infancy matters so much is made plain in the stunning soliloquy with which Macbeth opens the play's seventh scene. The speech displays the same tension as Shylock's speech rebuking his tormentors: the tension between the historically circumscribed mind of an individual shaped by a particular culture and a universal human perspective that reaches back through history from the future it foreshadows. Macbeth's fear that Duncan's assassination will incur retribution in 'the life to come' gives way to a review of the grounds for also fearing 'judgement here' (1.7.7–8): to murder Duncan would be to break the established laws he should obey and the ancient customs he should observe, as the kinsman, subject and host of a monarch, whose virtuous character provides no moral warrant for killing him. Up to this point, Macbeth's mind is confined within the known parameters of his class, culture and time. But none of the prevailing religious and secular imperatives he enumerates, or the prohibitions they entail, are sufficiently intimidating to deter him. The only thing that stops him in his tracks is his terror lest

> pity, like a naked new-born babe,
> Striding the blast, or heaven's cherubin, horsed
> Upon the sightless couriers of the air,

> Shall blow the horrid deed in every eye
> That tears shall drown the wind.   (1.7.21–5)

What lends 'a naked new-born babe' such apocalyptic power is not only its capacity to personify pity and inspire compassion for the victim of murder, because its own claim on the kindness of human beings is innate and incontestable. It is also the fact that it is the poor, bare, forked, human animal in its most unaccommodated form, not yet defined by gender, race or rank, not yet 'cabined, cribbed, confined, bound in' (3.4.23) by history and consigned to the destiny such factors dictate. It symbolizes nothing less than the pure, unconditioned potential of humankind to deliver itself from its own inhumanity.

In *The Inhuman*, his critique of 'The inhumanity of the system which is currently being consolidated under the name of development'[21] – the 'cyborgization' of the human that commenced in the early modern era[22] – Jean-François Lyotard locates the potential for resistance and transformation likewise in the native indeterminacy of childhood:

Shorn of speech, incapable of standing upright, hesitating over the objects of its interest, not able to calculate its advantages, not sensitive to common reason, the child is eminently the human because its distress heralds and promises things possible. Its initial delay in humanity, which makes it the hostage of the adult community, is also what manifests to the community the lack of humanity it is suffering from, and which calls on it to become more human.[23]

Writing four centuries earlier, Shakespeare enshrined this insight in the proleptic vision of 'a naked new-born babe', which flashes into the mind's eye of a medieval warlord on the brink of butchering his way to oblivion, despite being 'too full o'th' milk of human kindness'. Since then,

---

[21] Jean-François Lyotard, *The Inhuman: Reflections on Time*, trans. Geoffrey Bennington and Rachel Bowlby (Cambridge, 1991), p. 2.

[22] Herbrechter, '"A passion so strange, outrageous, and so variable", p. 46.

[23] Lyotard, *The Inhuman*, pp. 3–4.

SHAKESPEARE'S INHUMANITY

Shakespeare's drama has been tirelessly praised for its humanity, the quality widely credited with rendering it timeless and universal. But the moment may have come to give the devil in Shakespeare his due for revealing at the heart of inhumanity the prospect of a time when the dream of human equality has at last become a universal reality.

MAKING SOMETHING OUT OF 'NOTHING' IN SHAKESPEARE

R. S. WHITE

Shakespeare frequently links up the time-honoured, common word 'nothing' with ideas behind the new learning which entered mathematics in his lifetime with the reception of zero as part of the English number system in about the 1570s. The word 'nothing' itself dates back to Anglo-Saxon *náþing* and derives ultimately from the Latin *nihil*, but interestingly there is a marked 'spike' in frequency of occurrences in the sixteenth and seventeenth centuries, according to the *Oxford English Dictionary*. I believe this is explained by the topicality of zero at the time. Never one to ignore conceptual puzzles and paradoxes, Shakespeare proceeded to explore those surrounding 'zero' in diverse contexts which draw upon the semantic, conceptual, and arithmetical senses, and often to merge these in inextricable ways in the word 'nothing'. A couple of isolated instances in *King Lear* and *Henry V* have been noticed and examined by critics, which at least show some evidence Shakespeare did think about the intriguing links between the number zero and the philosophical idea behind the word 'nothing'. My broader suggestion is that because the word 'nothing' itself holds for us little resonance these days, we underestimate or even ignore the intriguing fulness it held for Shakespeare's generation, and as a consequence we neglect its thematic resonance in a range of different plays.

The process was happening during Shakespeare's schooldays when he was learning mathematics, and he was alert enough to make professional use of a contemporary debate. He was also clearly intrigued by the teasing philosophical implications of 'nothing' when it came to refer not only to 'no thing' (an absence) but to a 'nothing' (an existence called nothing) named zero. To take a fairly obvious example, he was to write 'much ado about "nothing"' in one play containing such 'strange' riddles as these:

Benedick. I do love nothing in the world so well as you. Is not that strange?
Beatrice. As strange as the thing I know not. It were as possible for me to say I loved nothing so well as you, but believe me not, and yet I lie not. I confess nothing nor I deny nothing. I am sorry for my cousin.
(*Much Ado About Nothing*, 4.1.266–71)[1]

To us there is little to notice here about number theory since we are desensitized by familiarity, but substitute 'zero' for 'nothing' and we find an almost impenetrable and certainly Shakespearian set of conundrums, turning on a love which was not in existence but has suddenly become a reality. It reflects the prior ambivalence of these bickering characters who now mysteriously and suddenly find themselves 'in love'. Yet we know that the reasons turn on a literal non-event, an overheard fiction without substance. The play traces two romantic attachments which are the product of such pure fictions or plots, or emanations from 'nothing' in any tangible sense. We have heard much ado about 'noting' (overhearing, construing), but there may still be more to be said about 'nothing'

---

[1] Quotations from the Norton Shakespeare, ed. Stephen Greenblatt *et al.* (New York, 1997).

itself in the play.[2] Such meditations were favourite territory for a dramatist who regularly refers to his dramatic personages as 'shadows' and 'ciphers' who somehow both exist and do not exist at the same time. More than this one play, however, his writing is full of such paradoxical meditations on 'nothing'.

Two widely known book-length studies of the number zero, Robert Kaplan's *The Nothing That Is* and Charles Seife's *Zero: The Biography of a Dangerous Idea*[3] suggested that 'nought' entered European thought only after considerable religious and intellectual resistance, based on beliefs that a void is equivalent to original chaos and that its continued existence is the devil's work, especially given the historical suspicion of the Arab world by England and its colonies. England, it is asserted, was one of the most reluctant and the last country to accept the number, during the time when Shakespeare was writing his plays. Brian Rotman in *Signifying Nothing: The Semiotics of Zero*, whose subtitle announces its contribution to the science of signs, includes an analysis of *King Lear* and credits the introduction into Europe of 'nought' with even larger cultural and economic movements to come:

The transition from Roman [to] Hindu numerals based on zero, and from the code of iconic art to perspectival art based on the vanishing point, is reflected in the field of economic activity by a fundamental shift in the structure of money signs that occurred in the passage from feudalism to mercantile capitalism.[4]

However, as I began to research the history of mathematics the vaunted danger and religious subversiveness of the subject began to recede, to be replaced by more sobering and less controversial facts. The moral may be not to trust 'popular science' books without investigation, although it is unfair to label such erudite and wide-ranging works as Kaplan's and Seife's in this way. Although they are certainly right that the introduction of the 'cipher' accompanied larger European paradigm shifts, the particular historical process was not considered particularly ungodly in itself. If zero was viewed with suspicion in medieval Europe, it seemed not to be because of its subversive danger

amongst an elite of the learned, but rather because of the natural conservativeness of practitioners in the world of trade and commerce who saw little reason to change habits of centuries. Double-entry book-keeping was apparently the main practical context in which the new number became familiar in England, almost certainly because of its sheer convenience and utility in this context.

There is little argument about the general point that the number indicated by 'zero' and 'nought' had been known since antiquity in India and Babylonia and was at least considered in ancient Greece although not accepted in full. The paradox of Zeno's arrow turns on it – 'almost nothing' can never quite become 'nothing', and Odysseus tricks the Cyclops Polyphemus by naming himself 'Nobody' thus creating conversation of the joking kind: 'Whose fault is it? Nobody's. Then don't bother us.' However, as a formal sign in mathematics the 'cipher' or 'cypher' was introduced into Europe in the tenth century, first in Spain and then gradually fanning northwards. The Italian Fibonacci or Leonardo of Pisa in 1202 credited himself with bringing the 'Hindu' sign of 0 into mainstream European mathematics. The origin of the symbol, a small circle or upright oval is conjectural (in Arabic itself a dot was and still is used), but by the time it entered England it was the established European form. The name evolved from the Greek for 'vacant', then Hindu for 'void' and Arabic *zephirum* also meaning 'void', and thence to zero, which in French became *chiffre* and in English 'cipher' but it was also known by the Latin *nihil* and therefore becoming entangled with 'nothing' and 'nought'.[5]

---

[2] I have not included in this article reference to *Much Ado About Nothing* itself, but Paul A. Jorgensen analyses some of the philosophical issues in '"Much Ado About Nothing"', *Shakespeare Quarterly*, 5 (1954), 287 – 95.

[3] Robert Kaplan, *The Nothing That Is* (New York, 1999) and Charles Seife, *Zero: The Biography of a Dangerous Idea* (New York, 2000).

[4] Brian Rotman, *Signifying Nothing: The Semiotics of Zero* (New York, 1987), p. 23.

[5] See David Eugene Smith and Louis Charles Karpinski, 'The Symbol Zero', in *The Hindu-Arabic Numerals* (Boston, 1911),

During the historical process the so-called Arabic or Hindu-Arabic system of counting beginning with zero (or more precisely ending with zero in the Arabic system of writing from right to left, namely 0, 9, 8, 7, 6, 5, 4, 3, 2, 1) coexisted beside the Roman set which had no zero but began with one (I or i) and proceeded in progression by ones to infinity. Because there was no number prior to I (and no negative numbers), there must have been some confusion akin to the kind these days surrounding 'ground' and 'first' floors of buildings, or in deciding whether to count a person's age from the actual birth date or the day one year after birth (thus apparently rendering a child 'nothing' or non-existent until a year after birth), and in speculations about whether midnight should be 12 or 0 on the clock. But these were no doubt considered, if at all, as philosophical rather than mathematical questions. However, there seems little evidence to suggest that, at least in the circles where mathematics were used, there was much talk of zero being somehow a blasphemous concept, although the more theologically minded may sometimes have questioned whether absolute nothingness could or did exist in a cosmology where everything was created by a deity who himself could not be described as 'nothing' without blasphemy. Even though the status of zero may have been one issue caught up in the European controversies of the Ptolemaic system of cosmology being overturned by the Copernican, it seems to have been considered a side issue, and for most dealing in some way professionally with mathematics the use of nought just made sense. Among the professionals were those in the navy and maritime occupations more generally, who had little more than basic knowledge: 'There was in fact for long a complete divorce between practice and theory: the seamen were ignorant of mathematics and the mathematicians had no practical experience.'[6] But they did know about 'zero latitude' through another legacy of Arabic learning introduced into Europe in the tenth century, the quadrant and the astrolabe, the latter known to Chaucer: 'Thus ben there 6 degres of the zodiak on that 00 side of the lyne and 6 degrees on that othir.'[7]

Admittedly, even judged as a number among others, zero has unique and strange qualities since it refers to something which is nothing. Is it a number or not a number, a sign indicating the lack of a number or a meta-sign or meta-number?[8] While all other numbers are either negative or positive, odd or even, prime or non-prime, natural or non-natural, whole or fractional, zero is none of these, just as its existence in the physical world refers neither to matter nor anti-matter, and in the religious to neither body nor soul, heaven or hell, but rather to what 'existed' before anything except God, the original state of 'chaos'. Nothing else in human experience replicates it, since as Hamlet points out, even death is not a state of complete nothingness since it provides earth to fill a bung-hole in a barrel. Sidney, however, likened it to the closest to original chaos as human beings come: 'God, to shewe us that he made all of nothing, hath left a certeyne inclination in his Creatures, whereby they tend naturally to nothing.'[9] It is simply an absence, a void or vacuum, and in mathematical terms it has no meaning except in contiguity with an actual number. But again, these were probably considered, if at all, as religious and philosophical rather than pragmatic considerations and they seem not to have placed impediments in the way of zero's usefulness in systems of counting. But Shakespeare saw a little deeper.

Knowledge of zero, if not its widespread usage, reached England much earlier than Shakespeare's time, first in the twelfth century through astronomical calculations as Chaucer attested, and more generally in the thirteenth century. Some of the sources for the reception of nought into England are laid out in the Introduction to a book which is far from

---

ch. 4, pp. 51–62. This book is available online at the Gutenberg Project's website.

[6] E. G. R. Taylor, *The Mathematical Practitioners of Tudor and Stuart England* (Cambridge, 1970), ch. 7.

[7] Chaucer, *A Treatise on the Astrolabe*, book 1, p. 21.

[8] Zero as meta-sign is explored by Rotman in *Signifying Nothing*, pp. 1–6 and 53–6.

[9] Sir Philip Sidney and Arthur Golding's translation of Philippe de Mornay, *Woorke Concerning the Trewnesse of the Christian Religion* (1587), ch. 2, p. 26.

popular, published in the rather forbidding series of the Early English Text Society (EETS) under the name *The Earliest Arithmetics in English*.[10] The introduction into England of a method of counting which includes zero came in about 1120 in a translation by Adelard of Bath into Latin from Arabic of a treatise by Al-Khowarazmi whose name gave us the word algorism or algorithm. By the thirteenth century in England the system of Arabic numeration and calculation co-existed beside Latin numbers, and had ousted the earlier methods of using the abacus and the ancient, universal 'digital' method using digits or fingers. The editor, Robert Steele writes:

The date of the introduction of the zero has been hotly debated, but it seems obvious that the twelfth-century Latin translators from the Arabic were perfectly well acquainted with the system they met in their Arabic text...

There is also no sign of particular controversy surrounding the innovation in England, and it was accepted without apology but probably gradually, simply because of its manifest convenience in everyday calculations. The use of the 'cifre' or 'cipher' (derived from the Arabic *sifr* meaning 'empty, nothing') as the symbol denoting zero – or more precisely the absence of a number – would take meaning from its position relative to the numbers before and after it (102, for example, indicating the absence of tens), thus making it unnecessary to indicate multiples of tens, hundreds or thousands in any other way: 'the practical performance of calculations is thus enormously facilitated', as Steele puts it. Additions of large numbers could be carried out simply by putting the numbers in a column under each other, which was not meaningful or helpful with Roman numerals. In the laborious words of a manuscript from the fourteenth century, *A Treatise on the Numeration of Algorism*:

To alle suche even nombrys the most have cifrys as to ten, twenty, thirty, an hundred, an thousand and suche other, but ye schal understonde that a cifre tokeneth nothinge but he maketh other the more significatyf that comith after hym. Also ye schal understonde that in nombrys composyt and in alle other nombrys that ben of diverse

figurys ye schal begynne in the ritht syde and to rekene backwards and so he schal be wryte as thus 1000, the sifre in the ritht side was first wryte and yit he tokeneth nothinge to the secunde nor the thridde but thei maken that figure of 1 the more signyficatyf that comith after hem by as moche as he born oute of his first place where he schuld yf he stode ther tokene but one. And there he stondith nowe in the ferye place he tokeneth a thousand as by this rewle. In the first place he tokeneth but hymself. In the secunde place he tokeneth ten times hymself. In the thridde place he tokeneth an hundred tymes himself...[11]

Words like these are repeated in the fifteenth century in works such as *The Crafte of Nombrying* and *The Art of Nombrying*, the latter basically a translation into English of John of Holywood's *De Arte Numerandi*. Even in about 1399 Langland was certainly aware of the mathematics of zero and could use it for poetical purposes: 'Than satte summe, as siphre doth in awgrym, That noteth a place, and no thing availith';[12] and Thomas Usk wrote in 1400 'Although a sipher in augrim [algorithm or algorism, the Hindu-Arabic numerals] have no might in signification of it selve, yet he yeveth power in signification to other.'[13] It crops up even in political contexts, as when in 1547 James Harrison in *An exhortacion to the Scottes to conforme themselfes to the ... union betweene ... Englande and Scotland* wrote, 'Our presidentes doo serue but as Cyphers in Algorisme, to fill the place.'[14] By the later sixteenth century, then, all this was quite commonplace and was spelled out in the 'standard' work written by Robert Recorde (or Record), first under the name *Grounde of Artes* (1551), and later many times republished in the sixteenth century under various different titles. Late sixteenth-century editions were enlarged by

---

[10] *The Earliest Arithmetics in English*, edited with an introduction by Robert Steele (Oxford, 1922).

[11] Steele, *The Earliest Arithmetics*, p. 70.

[12] Langland, *Richard the Redeles* (1399), ed. Skeat (EETS, 1867–85, 1886), IV, 53, cited in *OED*.

[13] Usk, *The Testament of Love* (cipher, *n.*, 1.a) cited in *OED*.

[14] *An exhortacion to the Scottes to conforme themselfes to the ... union betweene ... Englande and Scotland* (in Complaint of Scotland, EETS 1872), cited in *OED*.

others, one printed in 1594 being 'By Iohn Mellis of Southwark, scholemaster', and given the author's occupation it is possible that Recorde's work had some currency in schools either before or after the 1590s, not as a text for students since they were not issued with books, but perhaps in the hands of more enlightened teachers.[15] The French mathematician Simon Stevin in his *Arithmetique*, published in 1585, invented counting by decimal points, as a logical consequence of counting with zero, a ploy which opened up an infinity of numbers before one, just as after.

Recorde was certainly amongst the most important figures in mathematical education in England in the sixteenth century. Born in about 1512 he was an Oxford graduate of medicine and a don who later moved to Cambridge and then London.[16] He was to write a medical text *Urinal of Physick* (1547) and to become involved in his century's political and religious struggles in the early days of the Reformation. In a later appointment as comptroller of the British Mint, he was accused of treason for supporting the Protector Somerset and his own patron Richard Whalley, and was imprisoned for two years. Later he had equally responsible positions dealing with money, but accusations of incompetence, profiteering and failure to pay debts continued to follow him, though the motives were still apparently political. Essentially, however, judging from his publications, Recorde was first and foremost a scholar, and 'his contributions to mathematics education in England were enormous and seminal'.[17] At that time schooling was quite rare and the curriculum restricted to Latin grammar, authors and composition. Virtually no mathematics were taught because the subject did not fit within humanist educational policies. Some very elementary arithmetic was taught in petty schools and grammar schools, mainly targeted at vocational education for future tradesmen, but as the indefatigable T. W. Baldwin shows in transcribing educational documents for the period, it was accorded a lowly place.[18] Until the middle of the sixteenth century (and then only briefly) there was also little emphasis on mathematics at universities. Recorde realized the growing vocational

importance of mathematics and to answer the need he wrote *The Ground of Artes* (1542/3) and, although not the first of its kind (Tonstall's *De Arte Supputandi* (1522, reprinted through to 1699) preceded it, and there were others), Recorde's work was certainly the most important, being steadily reprinted in expanded editions. Recorde also published *The Pathway to Knowledge* (1574, 1602) on geometry, stressing the subject's practicality for 'navigators, surveyors, merchants and craftsmen'. *The Castle of Knowledge* (1556, 1596), dealt with astronomy and was also written to be useful to practitioners rather than theorists. His last book, *The Whetstone of Witte* (1557) dealt with both algebra and arithmetic. All his books were written for autodidacts rather than use in schools and the fact they were in English was a signal he wished his words, 'plainely set foorth', to move beyond academic circles, and they were presented in dialogue form of questions and answers by a master and apprentice. Taken as a whole, his influence was to give rigour and clarity to mathematics teaching in England and to lay foundations for a curriculum. John Dee in the 1570s was to be influential in advocating for raising the place of mathematics in schools, and he lightly re-edited Recorde's *Grounde*, and this was to be re-edited several times again, becoming at least commercially successful, if not widely adopted, in schools where mathematics continued to hold an insignificant place. Dee, like Recorde, was in the circle of the Earl of Leicester (as Shakespeare was to be in his theatrical career) and he was associated with the increasing importance of mathematics in England as was his friend Ramus in France.[19] He was guardian to Thomas

---

[15] I am grateful to Edel Lamb for this suggestion. For details and texts of revisions of Recorde's works, see Early English Books Online database.

[16] This account is indebted to the chapter on Recorde in Geoffrey Howson's *A History of Mathematics Education in England* (Cambridge, 1982), ch. 1.

[17] Howson, *History of Mathematics Education*, p. 8.

[18] T. W. Baldwin, *William Shakspere's Small Latine & Lesse Greeke*, 2 vols. (Urbana, 1944), vol. 1, pp. 105, 254–5, 290, 318, 324, 431, 539.

[19] See Taylor, *Mathematical Practitioners*, pp. 170–1 and 320.

Digges who kept alive the mathematical findings of his own father Leonard as well as making discoveries in astronomy in his own right, and was important in popularizing Copernican discoveries. He provided the cryptic gloss on Recorde's contribution, summing up with the words, 'The Ciphra augmenteth places, but of himselfe signifieth not.'[20] Descriptions to this effect rapidly became commonplaces in books towards the end of the sixteenth century.

Although the full pedagogical facts about teaching in England, let alone in Warwickshire specifically, are not clear, it is not entirely misleading to say that in the decade when Shakespeare was at school there was some movement towards a greater amount of maths in the syllabus and a new regard for its practical importance, mainly due to the pioneering efforts of Recorde, as well as Dee and Digges. Rotman may be right to suggest that Shakespeare and Jonson 'were in the first generation of children in England to have learned about zero from Robert Recorde's Arithmetica'[21] and to have based their calculations not on the abacus and Roman numerals alone but also in terms of the Arabic counting signs. By the middle of the seventeenth century the state of mathematical learning in England was historicized and consolidated in the works of John Wallis, who looked back not only to the reception of European learning through Bede (672–735) but even further, to the Babylonian and Hindu roots, which by now were well known at least to scholars. Wallis presented this history as a more or less continuous tradition down to his own day, giving credit to his countrymen for discoveries made in his own time.[22]

It is not at all clear what Shakespeare himself would have learned about mathematics at school. Some very basic arithmetic was taught in the petty schools but it was not until the seventeenth century that it became part of the syllabus in grammar schools. Charles II ordered some regular instruction of the subject at Christ's Hospital after the Restoration, though this seems to have been preceded by Charterhouse according to a reference in 1612 which decreed that scholars there should be taught 'to cipher and cast an accompt'.[23] The

scene in which the boy William is put through his Latin paces in *The Merry Wives of Windsor* is exemplary of the fact that the purpose of grammar schools in the humanist educational programme was mainly to teach verbal skills of oratory, using Latin grammar, writing, rhetoric, logic and some philosophy and history, rather than numeracy.[24] Number skills were assumed to be learned later 'on the job' by tradesmen, which explains Don Armado's contempt in a play that shows several examples of deficiencies in mathematical learning at the time: 'I am ill at reckoning; it fitteth the spirit of a tapster' (*Love's Labour's Lost*, 1.2.38), a comment taken by Moth (Mote) to prove his master is 'a cipher' (1.2.52). In *Othello* Cassio is described as 'a great arithmetician' which means that he was specialized in the arts of navigation using calculations by instruments and charts, and the fact that it is his professional rival Iago who says this suggests it is offered dismissively or even pejoratively, in the sense that his rival is a theoretician rather than a practical man of action:

> A fellow almost damn'd in a fair wife [wise?];
> That never set a squadron in the field,
> Nor the division of a battle knows
> More than a spinster – unless the bookish theoric,
> Wherein the togaed consuls can propose
> As masterly as he. Mere prattle, without practice
> Is all his soldiership.   (1.1.20–6)

Iago proceeds to scorn Cassio as 'debitor and creditor', a 'counter-caster' (our 'bean-counter') and little better than a mercenary tradesman. Overall, the evidence suggests that Shakespeare's interest in

---

[20] Thomas Digges, *Stratioticos* (1579).

[21] Rotman, *Signifying Nothing*, p. 78.

[22] See Jacqueline A. Stedall, *A Discourse Concerning Algebra: English Algebra to 1685* (Oxford, 2002), esp. pp. 8–36 which survey the earlier history.

[23] Nerida Ellevton and M. A. Clements, *Rewriting the History of School Mathematics in North America, 1607–1861: The Central Role of Cyphering Books* (Heidelberg, 2012), p. 24.

[24] For an interesting and detailed account of education in *Love's Labour's Lost*, see Ursula Potter, 'Pedagogy and Parenting in English Drama, 1560–1610' (unpublished PhD, University of Sydney, 2001), ch. 2, 'The schoolmaster as comic pedant: *The Lady of May* and *Love's Labour's Lost*'.

'nothing' and 'ciphers' often includes mathematical connotations but mostly with reference also to metaphorical and philosophical implications. In this particular case they are intertwined and indivisible. What is certain is that however he acquired his knowledge about the matter, Shakespeare did learn enough about the mathematical properties of zero to play with and pun upon them both in relation to the word 'nothing' and numerical value. As with most things he touched, he immeasurably complicates and enriches even 'nothing' itself:

> And as imagination bodies forth
> The forms of things unknown, the poet's pen
> Turns them to shapes and gives to *airy nothing*
> A local habitation and a name.
> (*A Midsummer Night's Dream*, 5.1.14–17; my italics.)

He turns a number into a set of philosophical and imaginative possibilities, so that a word denoting an absence of meaning or value comes to carry a weight of signification that is apparently infinite (another strange number in its own right).

Some of Shakespeare's references are undoubtedly mathematical and expressed in words virtually identical to those used by the authorities and text books of his day: 'like a cipher, Yet standing in rich place, I multiply / With one "We thank you", many thousands more / That go before it' (*The Winter's Tale*, 1. 2. 6–9). Simple addition from zero suggests growth of a sort: 'a most homely shepherd, a man, they say, that from very nothing . . . is grown into an unspeakable estate' (*The Winter's Tale*, 4. 2. 33–5). The Fool in *King Lear* knows the mathematical principle that zero takes its meaning from the numbers around it: 'Thou art an O without a figure, I am better than thou art now, I am a fool, thou art nothing' (*King Lear*, 1.4.176). More complicated still, that most famous reference of all, Lear's 'Nothing will come of nothing', arguably draws upon the aspect of zero which strikes every schoolchild today as peculiar, the fact that no matter what we multiply or divide it by, no matter how we square root it or how many times we 'empower' it, the answer is always zero. Nought will come of nought, nothing will come of nothing, or as the author of *The Crafte of Nombryinge*

wrote, 'A o is nought, And twyes noght is but nought.'[25]

Lear's splenetic outburst can also be seen to carry a commercial meaning which would have been striking in the early days of western capitalism, the notion that paying no money will result in no material goods – pay me nothing and you get nothing back – or investment in nothing will secure no monetary or material return. That most commercial of all plays, *The Merchant of Venice*, plays continually on a range of such financial senses. Shylock lends money only for 'interest' and never for 'nothing' (zero-ducats), and even when his loan is apparently interest-free it carries the actual return of sweet revenge, money for the interest of a life. In the courtroom Portia harps once again on a different commercial sense, this time of exclusion: 'He shall have nothing but the penalty . . . Thou shalt have nothing but the forfeiture . . .'. When Shylock hears that his daughter has given away a turquoise ring in return for a monkey, the thing that most appalls him seems to be the lack of business acumen in a bargain with such a trifling consideration: 'I would not have given it for a wilderness of monkeys.' In a moment of dramatic rhyming at the end of the court scene Portia asks only for Bassanio's ring, circular as the sign of a zero, as her recompense for saving his life: 'I will have nothing else but only this', which Bassanio gives, not comprehending it is 'worth' much more in its emotional significance of marital fidelity than its financial value carries. Other references in this play are equally commercial, dwelling on different ways of measuring worth and value: Salanio's comment 'And, in a word, but even now worth this, / And now worth nothing?' and Bassanio's

> Her name is Portia, nothing undervalued
> To Cato's daughter, Brutus' Portia;
> Nor is the wide world ignorant of her worth . . .
> (1.1.165–7)

Lancelot shows his bad maths by thinking 11 plus 9 equals 15, but in his own sense he is right that 0 plus 0 equals 0: 'Go to, here's a simple line of life: here's

---

[25] Steele, *The Earliest Arithmetics*, p. 20.

a small trifle of wives: alas, fifteen wives is nothing! Eleven widows and nine maids is a simple coming-in for one man' – in other words 11 dead wives plus 9 mistresses equals no wives.[26] At other times nought in Shakespeare has the quasi-mathematical meaning of something of no independent meaning or importance, something that can be dismissed: 'To hear my nothings monstered' (Coriolanus 2. 2. 73); 'Thus he his special nothing ever prologues' (All's Well that Ends Well, 2. 1. 90); and from here a nobody or an insignificant person, in our parlance 'a nobody': 'That harsh, churlish, noble, simple nothing, that Cloten' (Cymbeline, 3. 4. 133); and by extension to something of no significance at all, which 'signifies nothing': 'No hearing, no feeling, but my sir's song, and admiring the nothing of it' (The Winter's Tale, 4. 4. 598–9).

Zero, then, holds for Shakespeare the potential for being a powerful and adaptable paradox, in an age when paradox was a favourite mode of thinking and even a genre in its own right.[27] The familiar phrase in the Prologue to Henry V is not 'this wooden O' but 'this wooden o' or 'nought' which would not only provide a more specific sense to what comes after – 'O pardon: since a crooked figure may / Attest in little place a million, / And let us, ciphers to this great account / On your imaginary forces work' – but would also encapsulate the recurring way in which Shakespeare turns nothing into 'more than matter'. Eugene Ostashevsky, in an article which covers some of my preliminary ground here, concentrates on the Chorus's allusion to multiplication as the actors, 'ciphers to this great account' are notionally swelled tenfold and a hundredfold.[28] Though he does not explore the 'wooden o' any further, Ostashevsky pursues the specific example in the Chorus's words to explore the treatment of genealogical succession in Henry V. He also points out that the Chorus's metaphor in 'ciphers to this great account' (or 'accompt') comes from book-keeping (Henry later refers to a ledger-like comparison between the number of French dead and the number of English), as does the synonym elsewhere used in Henry V, that of 'reckoning', which, Ostashevsky points out, 'carries the same numerical and verbal connotations'.[29] The general point he makes is the one that is relevant here also: 'As I take it, the appearance of zero in the Prologue allows one to apply Renaissance ways of thinking about numbers to seemingly non-mathematical aspects of Henry V ... The act of operating with nothing as if it were something reproduces every conceivable nihil paradox' (207), a conclusion reached also by the editors of the book in their Introduction: 'numbers themselves – in the raw, as it were – undergo significant reconceptualization in the early modern engagement with quantifying thought' and 'just as numbers themselves engage emotions, mathematics has social effects far beyond its rational aspirations'.[30]

In many of the examples given here, it is impossible, however tempting to the modern mind, to say whether Shakespeare has in mind simply the word 'nothing' irrespective of its mathematical properties or, as is more likely in his age, whether he is consciously aware of the shared properties of zero in number theory and the general concept of nothing. Once we can take this mental leap, a range of possible larger meanings in his plays reveal themselves. Shakespeare was conscious of what he was doing in creating this version of paradox, since he repeats it time and again in different ways. I wonder, whimsically, whether the insult offered by the Dauphin to Henry of delivery of tennis balls is because being round they may symbolize zero and therefore 'nothings'. It is no less facetious an association than Henry's own imaginative equations as he proceeds to assign to the infamous tennis balls a

---

26. For other mathematical references in the play see David Bady, 'The Sum of Something: Arithmetic in The Merchant of Venice', Shakespeare Quarterly, 36 (1985), 10–30.

27. For example, Donne's Problems and Paradoxes. See more generally Rosalie Colie, Paradoxia Epidemica: The Renaissance Tradition of Paradox (Hamden, CT, 1966), and Peter G. Platt, Shakespeare and the Culture of Paradox (Farnham, 2009).

28. Eugene Ostashevsky, 'Crooked Figures: Zero and Hindu-Arabic Notation in Shakespeare's Henry V', in David Glimp and Michelle Warren, eds., Arts of Calculation: Quantifying Thought in Early Modern Europe (London, 2004), pp. 205–28, 205–7.

29. Ostashevsky, 'Crooked Figures', p. 219.

30. Glimp and Warren, Arts of Calculation, pp. xx, xxi.

set of symbolic meanings from sport which reminds him of his 'holiday' youthful activities, to cannon-balls and 'mocks' that France will come to regret. Perhaps the Dauphin's little joke played on *Henry V* with deadly consequences contained an obscure, concealed riddle too, since the score of zero in tennis is named 'love', and one theory suggests that it comes from the French *l'oeuf* for an egg. Less contentiously, the 'hollow crown' in the history plays becomes a visible symbol of an 'empty all' to be brooded upon by most of the temporary incumbents and especially Richard II, a vacuous (and vicious) circle which denotes both supreme power and human impotence. In dealing with married love in *The Phoenix and the Turtle* Shakespeare describes a constancy so pure ("'twixt division none') that it is simultaneously a visible something and an invisible nothing, while he characteristically riddles on this concept as he does on others in the *Sonnets*:

> Among a number one is reckoned none.
> Then in the number let me pass untold,
> Though in thy store's account I one must be;
> For nothing hold me, so it please thee hold
> That nothing me a something, sweet, to thee.

> (Sonnet 136)

So far my examples from Shakespeare's works indicating the importance of 'nothing as zero' have been specific images and lines, and these could indeed be multiplied to include references from every play. However, rather than attempting to enumerate, I shall now briefly examine three plays in which the subject seems especially close to their central preoccupations, and suggest some ways in which the issue can guide interpretation on a thematic level. My intention here is to open up thoughts on the central importance of the subject rather than to exhaust it, and I suggest the approach yields dividends for other plays, as well as being suggestive of multiple interpretations of even these three plays.

HAMLET

Early in *Hamlet* the status of the Ghost is raised as a problem when Bernardo reports 'I have seen nothing' and he, Marcellus and Horatio debate whether it is 'something' created by 'fantasy' or an 'illusion' or perhaps nothing at all. The problematical issue is raised again later:

Gertrude. To whom do you speak this?
Hamlet. Do you see nothing there?
Gertrude. Nothing at all, yet all that is I see.
Hamlet. Nor did you nothing hear?
Gertrude. No, nothing but ourselves.

> (3.4.122–4)

Such questions that 'puzzle the will' run through the play at a structural level. Not only is the Ghost a 'nothing' which is 'something' to Hamlet and the audience, playing again on the notion of actors as ciphers, but also young Hamlet is soon faced with the need to decide whether its advice about fratricide and regicide is true or false, something or nothing. Even the most celebrated 'question' ever raised – 'to be or not to be?' – boils down to a consideration of the ethics of 'being' and 'not being', existence and non-existence, living or committing suicide; whether to die and to sleep are analogies when sleep brings dreams that the dead cannot have; whether 'The undiscover'd country from whose bourn / No traveller returns' is somewhere or nowhere. Even the unillusioned Laertes must later concede a paradox when hearing his sister's disjointed speech: 'This nothing's more than matter', and the watching Gentleman is at least baffled that 'her speech is nothing' and yet 'Indeed would make one think there might be thought, / Though nothing sure'. Witnesses are drawn to make sense somehow of her disordered speech, to 'decipher' (de-'cipher') the secret meanings in that word's meaning of a disguised manner of writing. Ophelia, even before speaking bawdily herself in her madness, had played with ideas of such language being 'naught' (the derivation of 'naughty', as used for example by the Fool in *King Lear*):

Hamlet. Do you think I meant country matters?
Ophelia. I think nothing, my lord.
Hamlet. That's a fair thought to lie between maids' legs.
Ophelia. What is, my lord?
Hamlet. No thing.

> (3.2.105–9)

The exchange illustrates yet another use of 'nothing' in the bawdy sense referring to the vagina, and perhaps brings to mind the number 101, which is perfectly innocuous to us but must have struck a generation to whom zero was new as somehow strange, a numerical palindrome that circles around a void. It is hard to avoid the conclusion that when he was writing *Hamlet* Shakespeare was at some imaginative level pondering the implications of nought as non-existence, so often does the concept flow into and emerge from the play's vocabulary and most significant themes.[31]

MACBETH

In *Macbeth* 'nothing' is given different work to do but it is no less significant in both dramatic and philosophical terms. One application is in the realm of the temporal. Macbeth's main preoccupation, and one of the repeated problems in the play as a whole, is the relationship between the known present time and the unknown future. His more confident wife claims Macbeth's letters have 'transported' her 'beyond / This ignorant present' to 'feel now / The future in the instant' (1.5.54–5), which is the only occurrence of the word 'future' in the play despite its importance to the action, although we also get 'hereafter'), but Macbeth from the time the Witches present him with their prophecy is plagued by doubts and uncertainty about the hereafter, both in this world and the next. If only events could happen 'now' and have no consequences then the future would be secure:

> If it were done when 'tis done, then 'twere well
> It were done quickly. If th'assassination
> Could trammel up the consequence, and catch
> With his surcease success: that but this blow
> Might be the be-all and the end-all, here,
> But here upon this bank and shoal of time,
> We'd jump the life to come.   (1.7.1–7)

The phrase 'the be-all and end-all' entered popular usage from this source, and when we scrape away its numbing familiarity we find a kind of mathematical puzzle (which number contains both the largest numbers imaginable and yet also no number?) whose solution is zero. Trying to see – or prevent or change – the future is from the start and throughout the play Macbeth's obsession and upsets his certainty of what is and what is not:

> Present fears
> Are less than horrible imaginings.
> My thought, whose murder yet is but fantastical,
> Shakes so my single state of man that function
> Is smothered in surmise, and nothing is
> But what is not.   (1.3.136–41)

It constantly fuels his 'rapt' imagination, and leaves him open to hallucinations or imaginative projections, where 'no thing' becomes a 'something':

> Is this a dagger which I see before me,
> The handle toward my hand? Come, let me clutch thee.
> I have thee not, and yet I see thee still.
> Art thou not, fatal vision, sensible
> To feeling as to sight? Or art thou but
> A dagger of the mind, a false creation
> Proceeding from the heat-oppressèd brain?
> I see thee yet, in form as palpable
> As this which now I draw.
> Thou marshall'st me the way that I was going,
> And such an instrument I was to use.
> Mine eyes are made the fools o'th' other senses,
> Or else worth all the rest. I see thee still,
> And on thy blade and dudgeon gouts of blood,
> Which was not so before. There's no such thing.
> It is the bloody business which informs
> Thus to mine eyes.   (2.1.33–49)

His vision of Banquo at the banquet (surely no coincidence of words in the play) is another example. By the end of his life Macbeth feels betrayed by the very kind of fallible foreseeing faculty he has been exercising throughout. An apparent oracle provides the riddle of Macbeth not being vulnerable until the woods come to Dunsinane and he interprets the advice that he cannot be slain by one of woman born, only to find that both unlikely

---

[31] In a footnote to Carla Mazzio's interesting chapter, 'The Three-Dimensional Self: Geometry, Melancholy, Drama', in Glimp and Warren, *Arts of Calculation*, pp. 39–66, n17, Mazzio promises a 'sequel to this essay' in which she will 'address the mathematical melancholy of Hamlet'.

events happen and fanciful 'nothings' become realities. He is finally undone by the very effort and
futility of trying to foresee 'the hereafter', an obsessive mental state that has trapped him from the start
of the play. If 'everything' is uncertain and chimeric
in the future, then all, including existence itself, has
no meaning:

> She should have died hereafter.
> There would have been a time for such a word.
> Tomorrow, and tomorrow, and tomorrow,
> Creeps in this petty pace from day to day
> To the last syllable of recorded time,
> And all our yesterdays have lighted fools
> The way to dusty death. Out, out, brief candle.
> Life's but a walking shadow, a poor player
> That struts and frets his hour upon the stage
> And then is heard no more. It is a tale
> Told by an idiot, full of sound and fury,
> Signifying nothing.   (5.5.16–27)

Underlying even this resonant last phrase is a mathematical basis made evident in a sermon delivered
in 1593 by the Revd Henry Smith, using words
more prosaic but equally threatening to his sinful,
cowering parishioners: 'You are . . . like cyphers,
which supply a place, but signifie nothing.'[32] In
Macbeth apprehension of 'nothing' takes on metaphysical implications of a future which is a void,
and of a moral emptiness that 'Cannot be ill, cannot be good' but is simply vacuous. If the future
yields its secrets in such deceitful ways and if the
life to come is so ambiguous, then to such a man
as Macbeth the future told by little more than
an actor, a 'walking shadow' (just as Puck had
referred to actors as 'we shadows'), and a fiction
written by a whimsical author determined to play
tricks on hapless human agents, is a tale told by
an idiot whose aim is to entertain a theatre audience with the 'sound and fury' of his bombas-
tic rhetoric. From a man who 'saw' things where
nothing existed and who obsessively tried to imagine an unknown future, Macbeth has now reached
a point where even in substance he sees nothing of
value or meaning. Psychologically he has reached
a point of desolate nihilism where the search for
meaning is literally exhausted.

KING LEAR

An apt subtitle for *King Lear* might be *All or Nothing*, so insistently are these two words brought
into conjunction in ways that open up differences of concepts behind each. Each word is subject to negotiation that is not only linguistic but
also philosophical, political, mathematical and even
commercial. On the side of 'nothing' there is one
set of references undoubtedly taken from the world
of mathematics, those surrounding the Fool's 'now
thou art an O without a figure'. His admonition to
Lear likens his master to a 'cipher' without a supporting number to give the nought a meaning: 'ye
schal understonde that a cifre tokeneth nothinge
but he maketh other the more significatyf that
comith after hym'.[33] So precise is this allusion that
typesetters of the line should probably use o rather
than O and an actor could be justified in saying 'a
nought' rather than 'an o'. Meanwhile, Lear's use
of 'all' and 'everything' is often unconditional and
tantamount to 'infinity' while context places strict
limits around each occurrence: '*Lear.* I gave you all
– *Regan.* And in good time you gave it'; '. . . they
told me I was every thing; 'tis a lie, I am not ague-
proof'. He is opposed by two of his daughters who
reduce his 'all' to 'nothing', brutally shrinking his
retinue from one hundred knights to fifty, to 'five
and twenty' and eventually 'what need one?'

'Nothing' occurs 16 times in *Macbeth*, 26 in *Othello*, 32 in *Hamlet*, and 35 in *Lear* but in the last of
these plays the positioning of the word is usually
emphatic rather than casual, none more so than in
the precipitating exchange:

> *Lear.*   . . . Speak.
> *Cordelia.* Nothing, my lord.
> *Lear.* Nothing?
> *Cordelia.* Nothing.
> *Lear.* Nothing will come of nothing, speak again.
>   (1.1.85–9)

Obviously interpreters always alight on these lines
(repeated by Lear later in dialogue with the Fool

---

[32] Smith, *Sermons* (1593, pub. 1622), p. 310, cited *OED*, cipher,
1.a.
[33] Steele, *The Earliest Arithmetics*, p. 70.

and echoed late in the play when Lear decides himself 'I will say nothing') and fill 'nothing' with 'all' in an infinity of possible meanings and significances which are far too many to mention here. Brian Rotman points out that since Lear has unadvisedly framed his question in commercial terms – 'how much [does the commodity] cost?' – he is reducing love to a dehumanized contract regarding 'exchangeable commodities', 'the buying and selling of natural love',[34] making Cordelia's reference to her 'bond' quite appropriate and her 'nothing' a verbalization of a silence which is appropriate in her moral universe.[35] One very simple meaning, however, which perhaps has not gained much attention, is again the mathematical: nothing plus / minus / divided by nothing is always nothing. Or 'a cifre tokeneth nothinge but he maketh other the more significat yf that comith after hym'. Lear can at least do basic arithmetic. Cordelia has set up the nought in a number which now requires to be given integers before it in order to create meaning.

However, more profound problems emerge today in translating the word into a different language and culture. Yang Zouhan in an interesting article, 'King Lear Metamorphosed',[36] observes, 'It is a curious linguistic fact that while "all" is translated by yi-qie in modern Chinese, an essentially pictographic language with minimal connectives, there is no true equivalent for the English "nothing"' (260):

Now to render the meaning-charged word *nothing* into Chinese, the translator has to resort to a variety of strategies. One of them is to restrict the word to one facet only of its meaning so as to fall in with Chinese idiom and to be made intelligible to the Chinese reader. (261)

Usually the word can be translated only by taking it to indicate an unspecified negative to which a nominated content must be added in order to give meaning ('no-words', 'no land', 'no love'), a kind of verbal equivalent of the numerical cipher itself. This again enforces on the translator the need to specify a context or localize the idea in ways that obviously misrepresent the aura of inferred meaning playing about Shakespeare's bare 'nothing'. On the other hand, such a translating

necessity does paradoxically reinforce the mathematical meaning of 'nothing' in the Arabic system of counting, in that it takes its meaning from the signs surrounding it and on its own means – well – nothing. In ancient Chinese counting, perhaps more logically, there was no symbol for zero, though, since negative numbers were used, the concept of the void dividing negative from positive – our nought – did exist and was accepted as meaningful. The exigencies of representing Shakespeare's words in a different language with its different cultural meanings can highlight metaphysical dimensions in the original that simply cannot be accurately reproduced. When the Fool asks 'Can you make use of nothing, nuncle?', he appears to be echoing a question being asked throughout *King Lear* by the play's creator, whose answer is emphatically 'yes . . . I can make *all* of nothing'.

King Lear teeters on the precipice of the last plays or romances by Shakespeare and, although these late plays are usually seen as reviving a particularly optimistic and even naive literary genre, yet, as Stephen Greenblatt has recently argued, they also demonstrate a dramatist who is in some ways rethinking his own younger idealism and applying to it an undermining scepticism.[37] 'Nothing' plays its part in this process too, and to mention just two of the more memorable occasions, we have first a king in *The Winter's Tale* who is in a state of denial even more pronounced than the mad Lear's:

> Is whispering nothing?
> . . . Is this nothing?
> Why then the world and all that's in't is nothing,
> The covering sky is nothing, Bohemia nothing,
> My wife is nothing, nor nothing have these nothings
> If this be nothing. (1.2.286, 294–8)

The factual answer to each of Leontes's repeated questions which he thinks are rhetorical ones, is 'yes' rather than the 'no' he expects, and here,

---

[34] Rotman, *Signifying Nothing*, p. 81.

[35] Rotman, *Signifying Nothing*, pp. 80–1.

[36] Yang Zhouhan, 'King Lear Metamorphosed', *Comparative Literature*, 39 (1987), 256–63.

[37] Stephen Greenblatt, *Shakespeare's Freedom* (Chicago, 2010), ch. 5, 'Shakespearean Autonomy'.

Shakespeare suggests, 'nothing' lies in the eye of the beholder just as 'something' is created by the act of perception. And secondly, Prospero as the final benevolent ruler in the corpus, who is also a reader, writer and dramaturg, expresses deep doubt about the truth-value of drama itself:

> Our revels now are ended. These our actors,
> As I foretold you, were all spirits, and
> Are melted into air, into thin air;
> And like the baseless fabric of this vision,
> The cloud-capped towers, the gorgeous palaces,
> The solemn temples, the great globe itself,
> Yea, all which it inherit, shall dissolve;
> And, like this insubstantial pageant faded,
> Leave not a rack behind. We are such stuff
> As dreams are made on, and our little life
> Is rounded with a sleep.   (4.1.148–58)

Borges in a brief essay entitled 'Everything and Nothing' in which he describes Shakespeare's creativity as a 'controlled hallucination', finds a similarly nihilist vision in the final phase of plays: 'there was no one in him; behind his face . . . and his words, which were copious, fantastic and stormy, there was only a bit of coldness, a dream dreamt by no one'.[38] Borges ends with a parable in which God says to the dramatist: 'Neither am I anyone; I have dreamt the world as you dreamt your work, my Shakespeare, and among the forms in my dream are you, who like myself are many and no one.' 'Nothing', like the Bible's void of original chaos or the Zen Buddhist's full emptiness continues throughout Shakespeare's career as a method of thinking with apparently infinite applicability. If he was taught the existence of zero as a boy in the classroom then his teacher gave him a precious gift.

* * *

'Nothing' continued to puzzle the minds of major poets in the seventeenth century. John Donne, aware that 'new philosophy calls all in doubt', muses in his sermons upon the nature of 'absolutely nothing'.[39] He contemplates in his poem 'Air and Angels' the neoplatonic notion that love is divine rather than fleshly, and the more recognizably modern emotion by which love can make

us feel we already know somebody when we first meet them, paradoxes generated from feeling that he has loved a woman even before he sees her face or knows her name – 'some lovely glorious nothing did I see'. This 'nothing' is supplied with a body, but given the corporeal multifacetedness of counting 'every hair', there is 'much too much for love to work upon' just as the prior 'nothing' is too little, requiring a finer definition of love:

> For, nor in nothing, nor in things
> Extreme, and scattering bright, can love inhere.

The metaphor found by the persona of this poem is that the mutual love between man and woman who are separate and yet 'at one' is like an angel – not quite 'nothing' since its appearance is constituted 'Of air, not pure as it, yet doth wear' and air was regarded as the purest thing in existence, but still not as pure as spirit:

> Just such disparity
> As is 'twixt air's and angels' purity,
> 'Twixt women's love, and men's, will ever be.[40]

Milton in *Paradise Lost*, perhaps knowing Donne's poem or a common source, also ponders the angel as a 'something' that is also 'nothing', an appearance without substance, and he famously hypothesizes that such beings can have sexual relations and they can blush 'rosy red, love's proper hue' to think of such pleasure without any 'exclusive bars' 'Of membrane, joint, or limb':

> Easier than air with air, if Spirits embrace,
> Total they mix, union of pure with pure
> Desiring; nor restrained conveyance need
> As flesh to mix with flesh, or soul with soul.
> *Paradise Lost*, 1674, VIII, 626–9[41]

---

38 Jorge Luis Borges, *Labyrinths: Selected Stories and Other Writings*, ed. Donald A. Yates and James E. Irby (Norfolk, CT, 1962), p. 284.

39 *Donne at Sermons*, ed. Gale H. Carrithers Jr (Albany, 1972), p. 41 and elsewhere. Some occurrences are quoted by Kaplan, *The Nothing That Is*, pp. 34–5, 99, 191–2.

40 John Donne, *The Complete English Poems*, ed. A. J. Smith (Harmondsworth, 1973), p. 41.

41 *Milton: Poetical Works*, ed. Douglas Bush (Oxford, 1966), p. 369.

He too plays on the inner riddle that makes nought into a nothing which yet confers great value, writing in *The Readie and Easie Way to Establish a Free Commonwealth* (1664), 'like a great Cypher set to no purpose before a long row of other significant Figures' (429). About the same time (sometime before 1678), the libertine John Wilmot, Earl of Rochester explores in 'Upon Nothing: A Poem' the paradox *ex nihilo omnis sit* that had often been mined, from the time of a Latin poem written in 1587 by Jean Passerat, '*Nihil*', through to a 'crude broadside ballad in black letter, *Much Ado About Nothing* (1660)'[42] whose title no doubt draws consciously on the much more famous work. Rochester uses the poem to create a genealogy for Nothing that shows Everything evolving from it – 'Time and Place', 'Form and Matter', Light, Body – and he plays wittily upon various aspects of the trope, showing how Nothing dwells with princes and fools alike.

Even if we have found that the introduction of zero into England was not so tardy and so enshrouded with a mystique of danger as has been surmised, yet for such an insignificant cipher it has certainly created a wealth of literary meaning in the Renaissance. The unknown schoolmaster who taught arithmetic to the boy Shakespeare has indeed bequeathed us much to 'reckon' with.

---

[42] Frank H. Ellis, ed., *John Wilmot: Earl of Rochester* (Harmondsworth, 1994), pp. 402–3.

'A BOOK WHERE ONE MAY READ STRANGE MATTERS': EN-VISAGING CHARACTER AND EMOTION ON THE SHAKESPEARIAN STAGE

MICHAEL NEILL

'Birds don't have faces,' says his mother, 'fish don't have faces, why should cats have faces? The only creatures with proper faces are human beings. Our faces are what prove us human . . . We are not even born with faces. A face has to be coaxed out of us as a fire is coaxed out of coals . . . Animals don't have characters in just the same way they don't have faces.'

J. M. Coetzee, 'The Old Woman and the Cats'

The human body is the best picture of the human soul . . . The face is the soul of the body.

Ludwig Wittgenstein, *Philosophical Investigations*

One of the distinguishing characteristics of early modern culture, we have learned to think, was its discovery of new ways of understanding the self; and it was the peculiar achievement of Shakespearian dramaturgy to translate this understanding to the stage, creating an illusion of unique access to the mysterious labyrinth of interiority – 'that within which passeth show' (*Hamlet*, 1.2.85). Yet it is difficult to talk about these matters without falling into anachronism: we may think of Shakespeare as unsurpassed in the invention of character and in his exploration of the perplexities of emotion – but neither of these terms was available to him in anything like its modern sense. 'Character' – though the vogue for books of Theophrastan 'characters' was beginning to shift the meaning of the word – had barely begun to develop its psychological reference. Instead, a person's 'character' was conceived as a set of external attributes: deriving from Greek χαρακτήρ through Latin *charactēr*, the word originally signified an engraving tool or stamp, before coming to describe the marks

made by such instruments; from there it was readily transferred to the marks or signs inscribed on an individual's face, whether these resulted from the shaping force of temperament or from the pressure of external events. To speak, as Shakespeare does, of inherent qualities being 'charactered' upon a person was more than simply metaphorical, since inward feelings were capable of etching physical 'impressions' upon the visage – as they have in *The Rape of Lucrece*, where the heroine's face is imagined as a 'map which deep impression bears / Of hard misfortune, carved in it with tears' (lines 1712–13)', or in Sonnet 112 where the poet's brow bears an 'impression . . . stamp'd' upon it by the painful effects of 'vulgar scandal' (1–2). Properly inspected, the arrangement of a face, as Sir Thomas Browne insists, contains a lucid script, in which the truths of the inner self are always available for decipherment:

there are mystically in our faces certain Characters which carry in them the motto of our Souls, wherein he that cannot read A.B.C. may read our natures . . . The Finger of God hath left an Inscription upon all His works, not graphical or composed of Letters, but of their several forms, constitutions, parts and operations, which, aptly

I am grateful to Tiffany Stern, Andrew Gurr, and Benedict Robinson for advice on this essay – and also to the audiences at the University of Auckland, at the 9th World Shakespeare Congress in Prague (2011), at the University of Otago's 2012 colloquium on Practical Knowledge and Skill in Early Modern England, and at the 2012 ANZSA conference on the History of the Emotions in Perth, all of whom responded helpfully to its various drafts.

joined together, do make one word that doth express their natures.[1]

The notion of 'inscription' or 'impression' extended beyond the God-given signatures of essential 'nature', to reflect the way in which inward feelings – what we nowadays call 'emotions' – might put their marks upon the outward person. Like 'character', 'emotion' seems not to have established anything like its current sense until the latter half of the seventeenth century (*OED n.* 4). To Shakespeare's contemporaries – though he himself nowhere uses the word – it would have carried its literal signification: a 'moving out' or 'migration', perhaps extending to the quasi-metaphorical sense of 'popular disturbance' or 'tumult' (*OED n.* 1, 3). The nearest equivalent to the modern term would have been simply 'motion' – a word that insists upon the physiological basis of 'passions' and 'affections' as they were described by humoral science. The polyglot John Florio occasionally speaks of 'emotion' in a way that suggests the influence of French *esmotion*[2] – a word which had already developed something like its modern English meaning; but Randle Cotgrave's 1611 French–English Dictionary is at pains to separate its psychological from its senses, glossing it either as 'An emotion, commotion, sudden, or turbulent stirring' or as 'an agitation of the spirit, violent motion of the thoughts, vehement inclination of the mind.'[3] For Cotgrave it is 'motion' that agitates the spirit, as it is for Brabantio when he recalls how his chaste daughter's 'motion / Blushed at herself' (1.3.95–6): Desdemona's blush and the emotion it both advertises and reflexively arouses are understood as part of a single physiological process – a movement that is at once internal and external. On occasions, of course, Shakespeare writes of 'inward motion' (*King John*, 1.1.212), or thinks of love as either a 'motion of [the] heart' (*Dream*, 1.1.193) or a 'motion of the liver' (*Twelfth Night*, 2.4.97); but at other times it is hard to know whether the word is intended to denote a muscular movement, or an emotional state, or some combination of the two – as when Leontes remarks of Hermione's statue 'The fixture of her eye has motion in't' (*Winter's*

Tale, 5.3.67), or when Lady Percy observes 'strange motions' in Hotspur's face (*1 Henry IV*, 2.3.60). The emotional paralysis that seizes Cordelia in the opening scene of *King Lear* is imagined as precisely as a suspension of motion; 'I cannot heave / My heart into my mouth' (1.1.91–2). The gradual substitution of 'emotion' for the original word began when, with the decline of humoral doctrine, it became necessary to draw a firmer line between psychology and physiology; yet the etymology of the new term indicates that it must initially have retained some of the physical suggestiveness that belonged to the earlier term; and it is the kinetic power attributed to the 'motions' that informs Shakespeare's language when his dramaturgy (as it so often does) draws attention to the actor's countenance as an instrument of theatrical meaning.

I. READING THE VISAGE

Doth he study physiognomy?
There's no more credit to be given to th'face
Than to a sick man's urine, which some call
The physician's whore because she cozens him.
John Webster, *The Duchess of Malfi*

In dealing with people, I, like most people, believe that reading someone's face gives me the important information in making a decision. The burqa denies me this . . . There are places we expect everyone to show their face, there should be no exceptions.
'DJ' in *The Age* blog (Melbourne, 27 August 2010)

There are, of course, good evolutionary reasons why human beings pay particularly close attention to faces, both as indexes of feeling, attitude

---

[1] Sir Thomas Browne, *Religio Medici*, intro. M. R. Ridley (London, 1965), pp. 67–8.

[2] See, for example, Book 3, Chapter II, 'Of Repenting': 'the Latine tongue is to me in a manner naturall . . . but it is now fortie yeares, I have not made use of it to speake, nor much to write; yet in some extreame emotions and suddaine passions . . . I have ever, even from my very hart uttered my first words in latine', cited from *Montaigne's Essays*, trans. John Florio (London: Dent, 1965), vol. 3, p. 30.

[3] Randle Cotgrave, *A Dictionarie of the French and English Tongues* (1611), Sig. Llv.

and intention, and as presumed registers of character. The face is typically imagined as something to be 'read': an open book, or map of the inner self; no wonder, then, that something called 'Facebook' should have emerged as the most astonishingly successful enterprise in the ascendant social media, or that the *burqa* should have become the focus of our most paranoid anxieties about the veiled intentions of the Other. When we look into a person's face we think we know what we see. This conviction is founded on two widespread assumptions: the first is the largely unsubstantiated conviction that the lineaments of the face are in some profound way a register of the essential self – by the time they are forty, the saying goes, everyone has the face they deserve; the second is the better grounded, but still imperfectly reliable, belief that facial expression (etymologically speaking, something pushed out from within) constitutes a perfectly legible index to feeling, attitude, and intention; so that the eyes, in particular, offer a pellucid window to the soul.

Needless to say, there is also a small store of folk wisdom that calls in question the dependability of the impressions that we derive from the faces of others: we are warned not to judge a book by its cover, just as we are made aware that 'face' is something that can be 'kept' or 'lost', and that one may be 'put out of countenance' like Holofernes in *Love's Labour's Lost*, because he '[has] no face' (5.2.602–3). 'Visage', we may remember, shares with 'visor' and 'vizard' a common root in Latin *visus* ('face'); and this, after all, is the basis of the joke in *2 Henry IV* when Davy begs Justice Shallow to 'countenance William *Visor* . . . I grant your worship that he is a knave, sir; but yet God forbid, sir, that a knave should have some *countenance* at his friend's request' (5.1.31–48, emphasis added). Such awareness, however, does relatively little to modulate reactions that are so fundamental to human behaviour that they appear inborn and natural: error typically leads only to the assumption of accidental misreading – all we really needed to do was to look harder, and therefore (so we persuade ourselves) deeper.

Aficionados of the comedy series *Curb Your Enthusiasm* will be familiar with the silent ferocity of the Larry David stare and the protracted face-to-face confrontations through which the protagonist attempts to penetrate the treacherously hidden motives of his luckless friends and acquaintance. At a more scientific level, the work of the neo-Darwinian, Paul Ekman, has highlighted the tell-tale significance of those minute and fleeting adjustments to the musculature of the face that he dubs 'micro-expressions'. Ekman's research has led to the development of the now widely deployed 'Facial Action Coding System', which provides the basis for an entire industry of facial surveillance, carried out by the 3,000 Transport Security Administration officers trained in SPOT (Screening Passengers by Observation Technique) who work at airports throughout the United States, and by their counterparts in Britain and Europe.[4] It was this phenomenon that provided the inspiration for a popular television series, *Lie to Me*, in which Tim Roth's Dr Cal Lightman (reputedly modelled on Ekman himself) uses his exceptional sensitivity to micro-expressions to unmask (or perhaps, as his name suggests, illuminate) the plausible deceits of a whole gallery of fraudsters, killers and terrorist fanatics.

Whatever the scientific validity of such techniques, they provide a particularly striking illustration of how, in important respects, human interaction continues to be governed by the same assumptions that underlie the pseudo-science of physiognomy as it was understood by early moderns: thus we often act as if a person's nature were something permanently etched upon the features, as readily available to interpretation as are the painted images of Ajax and Ulysses in *The Rape of Lucrece*, where 'The face of either cipher'd either's heart' (line 1396). Told of a soothsayer's warnings about the Ides of March, Shakespeare's Julius Caesar insists upon confronting the impertinent prophet: 'Set him before me; let me see his face' (*Caesar*, 1.2.20) – sure enough, one glance will be enough

---

4 See Evgeny Morozov, 'In Your Face', review of Kelly Gates, *Our Biometric Future: Facial Recognition Technology and the Culture of Surveillance* (New York, 2011), in *London Review of Books*, 34: 7 (5 April 2012), 25–7 at 26.

to convince him of the seer's unreliability: 'He is a dreamer, let us leave him' (26). In the same way Othello takes it for granted that, properly scrutinized, Desdemona's face will immediately reveal the veracity of his suspicions: 'Let me see your eyes – / Look in my face' (*Othello*, 4.2.26–7). For Lear, Regan's 'warp'd looks' infallibly 'proclaim / What store her heart is made on' (3.6.53–4).[5] It was partly for this reason that moralists like Thomas Tuke inveighed so furiously against cosmetics, for the painting of faces amounts to a species of visual hypocrisy: 'a painted face,' declared Tuke, 'is a false face, a true falsehood, not a true face . . . *paintings, tinctures, and affected dressings do signifie, that the soule is sicke within* . . . And what is a woman painted, but a certain kinde of hypocrite, resembling that in shew, which she is not truly . . . And what is this *artificial facing*, but a true deceit or deceitfull truth.'[6]

From the beginning, Elizabethan theatre had exhibited an active interest in the expressive power of the actor's face; and the early work of Christopher Marlowe is especially rich in examples of physiognomical reading, where character is perfectly inscribed upon the countenance. If the prologue to Marlowe's first great popular success promises the audience that they will '*hear* the Scythian Tamburlaine / Threat'ning the world with high astounding terms', he then urges them to concentrate their attention upon his visual magnificence: '*view* but his picture in this tragic glass, / And *then* applaud his fortunes as you please' (5–8, emphasis added).[7] We might take this glass to be purely metaphorical, were it not for the fact that *Tamburlaine* so repeatedly puts faces on display. In no other play, perhaps, is a character's countenance credited with such energetic power. On Tamburlaine's first appearance, Techelles marvels at the overwhelming force of personality that informs the hero's gaze: 'Methinks, I see kings kneeling at his feet, / And he with frowning brows and fiery looks / Spurning their crowns from off their captive heads' (1.2.55–7) – an impression immediately confirmed by the reaction of Tamburlaine's awestruck opponent, the Persian general, Theridamas –

His looks do menace heaven and dare the gods;
His fiery eyes are fixed upon the earth
As if he . . . meant to pierce Avernus' darksome vaults
To pull the triple-headed dog from hell . . .
Won with thy words, and conquer'd with thy looks
I yield myself, my men and horse to thee.

(Pt 1, 1.2.157–161, 228–9)

Theridamas may be 'won' by Tamburlaine's words, but it is his looks that 'conquer'; and they appear equally daunting to the Persian emissary, Menaphon:

'twixt his manly pitch
A pearl more worth than all the world is plac'd,
Wherein by curious sovereignty of art
Are fixed his piercing instruments of sight,
Whose fiery circles bear encompassed
A heaven of heavenly bodies in their spheres . . .
Pale of complexion, wrought in him with passion,
Thirsting with sovereignty, with love of arms;
His lofty brows in folds do figure death,
And in their smoothness amity and life.

(Pt 1, 2.1.11–22)

The optical theory that explained sight as a function of beams of light emanating from the eyes meant that, as Bruce Smith has reminded us, their 'force [was] not just metaphorical but physical';[8]

---

5 For convenience, *King Lear* is cited from R. A. Foakes's Arden edition (Thomas Nelson; London, 1997), which combines the Quarto and Folio texts of the play.

6 Thomas Tuke, *A Treatise against Painting and Tincturing of Men and Women* (London, 1606), C1v, C3v, C4. 'Doubtlesse', Tuke declares, 'falshood is in his or her heart, whose face or haire is falsified to deceit. Falshood vttered in the face, or haire, is first conceiued and coined in the heart', since 'the condition of the mind is discerned in the state and behauiour of the body' (D4). Thus, in a strange way, the painted face reveals by its very intention to conceal: 'How can they begge pardon, when their sinne cleaues vnto their faces, and when they are not able for to blush' (E1v).

7 All citations are from Roma Gill, ed., *The Plays of Christopher Marlowe* (London, 1971).

8 Bruce R. Smith, 'Eyeing and Wording in *Cymbeline*', in Lowell Gallagher and Shankar Raman, eds., *Knowing Shakespeare: Senses, Embodiment and Cognition* (Basingstoke, 2010), p. 57. Smith further cites Joseph Roach on how such eyeing was part of the actor's stock-in-trade: 'His passions, irradiating the bodies of spectators through their eyes . . . could literally transfer the contents of his heart to theirs, altering their moral

so the Scythian's ferocious stare is quite literally 'piercing' and powerful enough to produce the fearful motions that can drive a hapless victim to suicide: confronted by an ominously silent Tamburlaine, who enters '*looking wrathfully on [him]*', Agydas feels himself

> Threaten'd with frowning wrath and jealousy . . .
> To see his choler shut in secret thoughts,
> And wrapped in silence of his angry soul.
> Upon his brows was portray'd ugly death
> And in his eyes the fury of his heart,
> That shine as comets, menacing revenge,
> And cast a pale complexion on his cheeks.
>
> (Pt 1, 3.2.66–75)

The naked dagger presented to Agydas by Techelles appears as a mere extension of Tamburlaine's 'killing frowns of jealousy and love' (lines 90–1). No wonder that 'his foes like flocks of fearful roes / Pursu'd by hunters, fear his angry looks' (Pt 1, 3.3.192–3), or that his 'imperious eyes' and 'frowning looks' should remind the Soldan of Egypt of the Gorgon's deadly stare (Pt 1, 4.1.12–18). Even Tamburlaine's humble captains and common soldiers are said to 'look / As if they meant to conquer Africa' (Pt 1, 3.2.9–10), while Theridamas is credited with 'looks [that] conquer . . . all thy foes' (Pt 1, 1.1.75), praised for the 'majesty' with which 'he rears his looks', and admired for the martial authority revealed by 'characters graven in thy brow' (Pt 1, 1.2.165–71). But none amongst his followers, let alone his enemies, can match the conquering power of Tamburlaine's own gaze which is stressed again and again through the two parts of the play (Pt. 1, 4.2.36–40, 5.1.57–9; Pt 2, 1.3.139; 3.4.46–53; 3.5.156–7) until even King Death himself seems to quail 'at every glance I give' (Pt 2, 5.3.70).

The only countenance whose fiery energy can begin to challenge Tamburlaine's is that of his beloved Zenocrate, 'Whose eyes are brighter than the lamps of heaven' (Pt 1, 3.3.120). But hers is a softening feminine power whose 'looks can . . . clear the darken'd sky, / And calm the rage of thundering Jupiter' (Pt 1, 3.3.122–3). She is a kind of second sun, 'the world's fair eye, /

Whose beams illuminate the lamps of heaven, / Whose cheerful looks do clear the cloudy air / And clothe it in a crystal livery (Pt. 2 1.3.1–4). Tamburlaine seeks to make of her overwhelming beauty an emblem for his own success

> As Juno, when the giants were suppress'd,
> That darted mountains at her brother Jove,
> So looks my love, shadowing in her brows
> Triumphs and trophies for my victories.
>
> (Pt. 1, 5.1.508–11)

But if Zenocrate's eyes 'shoot fire', like his own, their erotic energy works in an opposite fashion, serving to 'temper . . . every soul with lively heat' (Pt 2, 2.4.9–10): indeed, surveying the countenances of his sons, Tamburlaine fears they have been effeminated by 'look[ing] on their mother's face . . . their looks are amorous, / Not martial as the sons of Tamburlaine' (Pt 2, 1.3.20–2); and though Zenocrate insists that if 'they have their mother's looks', they nevertheless 'have their father's conquering heart' (34–5), the example of Calyphas suggests otherwise – so that, in his dying speech, Tamburlaine is constrained to warn his heir, Amyras, that he must 'learn with awful eye / To sway a throne as dangerous as his' (5.3.234–5). It is only in death that Zenocrate's looks can be turned to serve a properly martial purpose, 'shed[ding] such an influence in my camp / As if Bellona, goddess of the war, / Threw naked swords and sulphur-balls of fire / Upon the heads of all our enemies' (Pt 2, 39–42).

Characters in *Tamburlaine* are credited with extraordinary visual eloquence and power; but the force of their personalities is inseparable from the static, mask-like quality of their countenances: essentially unchanging, they epitomize the fundamental assumption of early modern physiognomy that 'character' is permanently engraved upon the

---

natures' (pp. 62–3). Alternatively, as Richard Sugg explains, vision could be thought of as a function of 'spirits' entering or leaving the eye, thereby transmitting objects to the brain, so that when 'dangerous spirits entered [a] victim's eyes' they might transmit disease or even the malice of a witch's gaze with mortal consequences – see Richard Sugg, *Mummies, Cannibals and Vampires* (Abingdon, 2011), p. 175.

face. Tamburlaine (like those who surround him) is conceived not as a fully rounded human personality, but simply as the embodiment of a certain kind of nature – resembling those carefully delineated types who populate Theophrastan character books like Sir Thomas Overbury's *Wife*. To that extent, despite the ferocious concentration on their facial characteristics, there is surprisingly little difference between Marlowe's characters and the figures of medieval religious drama, whose faces scarcely require any description at all, because their characters are, after all, a given, pre-scribed by the word of God. In *Tamburlaine* there can be no disjunction between inner and outer selves: the hero is endowed with a face that precisely traces the lineaments of his martial soul.

In Shakespeare's early work, there are instances where a face is given some of Tamburlaine's iconic fixity: the countenance of the inflexibly vindictive Queen Margaret in *3 Henry VI*, for example, is 'vizard[visor]-like, unchanging' (1.4.117); but here the effect is a little different, for hers is explicitly a face 'made impudent with use of evil deeds', a self-fashioned mask that has served to protect her from the empathic claims of 'young Rutland's looks', whose 'face ... the hungry cannibals / Would not have touch'd' (*3 Henry VI*, 1.4.118; 153–4). More stiffly archaic are the moments when the young Henry VI discovers in good Duke Humphrey's face 'The map of honour, truth and loyalty' (*2 Henry VI*, 3.1.203), or when he recognizes in his wife's lover the appallingly fixed gaze of the 'basilisk' (3.2.52):

> out of my sight!
> Upon thine eyeballs murderous tyranny
> Sits in grim majesty, to fright the world.
> Look not upon me, for thine eyes are wounding.
> (*2 Henry VI*, 3.2.48–51)

But that way of envisaging character is formally deconstructed in the deposition scene of *Richard II* when the king confronts his own image in a glass: significantly perhaps, his speech begins with a deliberate echo of Marlowe's celebrated paean to the overwhelming power of an iconic visage ('Was this the face that launch'd a thousand ships ...?', *Dr Faustus*, xviii.99):

> Was this the face
> That, like the sun, did make beholders wink?
> Is this the face which faced so many follies,
> And was at last outfaced by Bollingbroke?
> A brittle glory shineth in this face,
> As brittle as the glory is the face,
> For there it is, crack'd in an hundred shivers.
> (*Richard II*, 4.1.283–9)

And Richard's gesture is significantly followed by a speech in which he implicitly problematizes the relationship between outward expressions of feeling and the inner 'substance' of emotion, in a way that invites immediate visual scrutiny of his facial performance by the audience:

> my grief lies all within,
> And these external manners of laments
> Are merely shadows to the unseen grief
> That swells with silence in the tortur'd soul.
> (4.1.285–8)

Like Hamlet's 'dejected haviour of the visage', Richard's passion is merely a theatrical 'shadow', part of the self-consciously arranged 'trappings ... of woe' (*Hamlet*, 1.2.81, 86) that bear no necessary relation to the 'swelling' motion within. Later, in *Coriolanus*, Menenius will hold up to mockery the very idea of the face as offering anything like the cartographic record of character imagined by Henry VI: addressing the mob he declares

> they lie deadly that tell you have good faces. If you see this in the map of my microcosm, follows it that I am known well enough too? What harm can your ... conspecuities glean out of this character, if I be known well enough too? (2.1.60–4)

If Shakespeare repeatedly draws the audience's attention to faces, it is less often to register the fixed inscriptions of character, than to invite scrutiny of the actor's changing expressions and to register in that process the potential disparities between outward persona and inward personality. His dramaturgy turns the theatre into an arena where the art of physiognomy is put to the test.

2. 'INWARD MOTIONS': READING THE COUNTENANCE

In *Romeo and Juliet*, Lady Capulet seeks to persuade her daughter that all she needs to know of her prospective husband is written upon his visage:

> Read o'er the volume of young Paris' face,
> And find delight writ there with beauty's pen...
> And what obscur'd in this fair volume lies
> Find written in the margin of his eyes.   (1.3.83–8)

But if 'character' resembles a fundamental signature of the self, unalterably etched upon the face, there are more ephemeral writings, signs of passing emotions, attitudes and intentions, that we can also learn to read – the expressive marks that are sometimes said to distinguish the changing 'countenance' from the unchanging visage.[9] These too are the province of the physiognomist. In his psycho-physiological treatise, *The Passions of the Minde in Generall*, Thomas Wright maintains that because 'The heart of a man changeth his countenance... wise men often, thorowe the windowes of the face, behold the secrets of the heart.'[10] So Macbeth's failure to manage the emotions of his countenance reduces his face, in the eyes of his anxious wife, to an all-too-legible 'book where / Men may read strange matters' (1.5.61–2). The truth of even a 'false heart's history' can be discerned 'in moods and frowns and wrinkles strange', as Sonnet 93 has it (lines 7–8); for the physiological basis of early modern humoral psychology[11] ensures that inward motions will make their way to the expressive surface precisely as Falstaff's sherris sack 'makes its course from the inwards to the parts' extremes [and] illuminateth the face' (*2 Henry IV*, 4.2.103–4). Thus, in *The Rape of Lucrece*, the countenance of the violated woman appears as an open book, in which even the most unlettered critic can read the history of her shame:

> Make me not object to the tell-tale day:
> The light will show charactered in my brow
> The story of sweet chastity's decay,
> The impious breach of holy wedlock vow.
> Yea, the illiterate, that know not how

> To cipher what is writ in learnèd books
> Will quote my loathsome trespass in my looks.
>
> (806–12)

What are here 'charactered' upon the features of the dishonoured woman, are not the unchanging fundamentals of her essential nature, but more ephemeral 'looks' that expose the narrative of her rape. Of course, the countenance is not always so readily deciphered as it is in the case of the guileless Lucrece; but the repertory of facial expression, if properly studied, constitutes a lexicon that should render any person transparent to a trained eye – as Marin Cureau de la Chambre declares in his *L'Art de Connoistre les Hommes* (1660):[12]

[Nature] hath not only bestow'd on Man voice and tongue, to be the interpreters of his thoughts; But out of a certain distrust she conceiv'd, that he might abuse them, she hath contriv'd a language in his forehead and eyes, to give the others the Lye, in case they should not prove faithful. In a word, she hath expos'd his soul, to be observ'd on the out-side, so that there is no necessity of any window, to see his Motions, Inclinations and Habits, since they are apparent in his face, and are there written in such visible and manifest characters.[13]

---

9 For this distinction, see Sibylle Baumbach, *Shakespeare and the Art of Physiognomy* (Penrith, CA, 2008), pp. 68–70.

10 Thomas Wright, *The Passions of the Minde in Generall* (London, 1604), p. 27. For discussion of the evidential value attributed to faces, see Subha Mukherji, *Law and Representation in Early Modern Drama* (Cambridge, 2006), ch. 4, '"Painted Devils": Image-making and Evidence in *The White Devil*'.

11 See Gail Paster, *Humoring the Body: Emotions and the Shakespearean Stage* (Chicago, 2004).

12 Cureau's treatise – translated by John Davies of Kidwelly as *The Art How to know Men* (London, 1670) – provides an elaborate compendium of available ideas about reading the various surfaces of the human body, especially faces and hands, nearly all of which would have been thoroughly familiar to informed observers of humankind half a century earlier. All citations are from Davies's translation.

13 Cureau, B1v. The physiognomist's gaze could claim particular authority partly because Renaissance psycho-physiology regarded eyesight as the loftiest of the senses: the eyes, as the physician and anatomical theorist Helkiah Crooke declared, 'are situated in the head in the highest and best defensed body, immediately under the forehead as Scoutwatches... to foresee and give warning of any danger that may be toward us', *Microcosmographia* (1616), p. 536, cited

Cureau's is a science able to pierce the most hardened surfaces, exposing 'their most secret Inclinations, the Motions of their Souls, their Vertues and their Vices',[14] an art that

teaches the way to discover secret designs, private actions, and the unknown Authors of known actions. In a word, there is no dissimulation so deep into which it does not penetrate, and which, in all likelihood, it will not deprive of the best part of those veils, under which it lurks.[15]

For all the enthusiasm of its partisans, however, the reliability of physiognomical reading was not beyond question: in his essay on the subject, Montaigne writes of 'favourable Physiognomies' to which one may be instinctively drawn, though 'not properly by the consideration of beauty... And I think, there is some Art to distinguish gently-milde faces, from nyæs and simple, the severe from the rude; the malicious from the froward; the disdainefull from the melancholike and other neighbouring qualities', yet he also cites the instance of Socrates's notorious ugliness to call in question the platonic assumption that outward beauty is the proper sign of inner goodness; after all, he observes, the truth of our natures is unavailable to outward inspection, since

[o]thers see you not, but ghesse you by uncertaine conjectures. They see not so much your nature as your arte. ... Every one may play the juggler, and represent an honest man upon the stage; but within, and in bosome ... all is concealed.[16]

Francis Bacon, while he acknowledges a frequent correspondence between face and character, nevertheless insists that physical appearance is likely to be a cause rather than a consequence of one's inward condition: 'Certainly, there is a consent between the body and the mind. But... it is good to consider deformity, not as a sign, which is more deceivable, but as a cause, which seldom faileth of the effect.'[17] Even Thomas Wright, convinced though he is that character must write itself upon the face, counsels caution, admitting that the most skilled practitioners of physiognomy must sometimes depend upon conjecture, since they can never

exactly understand the heartes which bee inscrutable, and onely open vnto God, but... by coniectures they may aime well at them: for he which beholdeth his face in the water, doth not discerne it exactly, but rather a shadowe, than a face; even so he, that by externall phisiognomy and operations, will divine what lyeth hidden in the heart, may rather conceive an image of that affection that doth raigne in the minde, than a perfite and resolute knowledge.[18]

For Pierre Charron, exterior signs are an even less dependable guide: to know the truth of a man, he maintains

---

in Shankar Raman, 'Hamlet in Motion', in Gallagher and Raman, *Knowing Shakespeare*, pp. 116–36 at 117.

[14] John Davies, 'The Dedicatory', in *The Art How to know Men*, A4. On early modern ideas of the face as the 'window' or 'mirror' of the soul, see Jean-Jacques Courtine and Claudine Haroche, *Histoire du Visage; Exprimer et Taire ses emotions (du XVIe au XIXe siècle)* (Paris, 1988), pp. 50–2.

[15] Cureau, B7v. According to Cureau's translator, John Davies, it was the ability of physiognomy to lay bare the 'secret... motions' of the inner self that would make it especially valuable to 'persons entrusted with the management of Embassies, and the most important Transactions of Crowns and Scepters, and consequently obliged to treat with People of different Tempers and Climates' since 'In these last it suffices not, to be guided by those common observations and characters of men, which are obvious to the Populace, and commonly mask'd and disguiz'd; but the grand secret is, to penetrate into the Closets, and insinuate into the very bosomes, of Princes and Favourites' (Av–A4v). Indeed it was Cureau's own travel experiences, in 'a Negotiation, which led, from the most, to the least civiliz'd extremities of Christendom' (A5), that made him especially well equipped to read the most alien and enigmatic of countenances. For discussion of Cureau and the politics of physiognomy as an instrument of 'civil government'; see Courtine and Haroche, *Histoire des Visage*, pp. 25–8.

[16] Montaigne, Book 3, Chapter XII, 'Of Phisiognomy', and Chapter 2, 'Of Repenting', in *Essays*, pp. 314, 316, 26–7.

[17] Francis Bacon, Essay XLIV, 'Of Deformity', in *Essays*, ed. Oliphant Smeaton (London, 1962), p. 131. Cf. also Essay XLIII, 'Of Beauty', pp. 129–30.

[18] Wright, *Passions of the Minde*, p. 27. Wright's phrasing here resonates intriguingly with Horatio's and Gertrude's account of the hearers' response to the mad Ophelia in *Hamlet*: 'They *aim at it* / And botch the words up fit to their own thoughts, / Which as her winks and nods and gestures yield them, / Indeed would make one think there might be thought... 'Twere good she were spoken with, for she may strew / Dangerous *conjectures* in ill-breeding minds' (4.4.9–15, my italics).

We must look into his inward part, his privy chamber... beholding him with all visages, feeling his pulse, sounding him to the quick, entering into him with a candle and snuffer, searching and creeping into every hole, corner, turning, closet, and secret place. For this is the most subtle and hypocritical, covert and counterfeit of all the rest, and almost not to be known.[19]

Marlowe's Tamburlaine may have a countenance whose power depends on the precise correspondences between character, intention and action. But it is, of course, quite otherwise with his satiric counterpart, Barabas, who boasts to Ithamore of how 'We Jews can fawn like spaniels when we please; / And when we grin we bite; yet are our looks / As innocent and harmless as a lamb's' (*Jew of Malta*, 2.3.20–2); and in the Machiavellian world of *The Spanish Tragedy*, written by Marlowe's roommate, Thomas Kyd, the face proves equally unreliable as index to the 'heart'. For Hieronimo, the tormented countenance of a bereaved old man may serve as a 'lively image of my grief':

Within thy face my sorrows I may see.
Thy eyes are gummed with tears, thy cheeks are wan,
Thy forehead troubled, and thy muttering lips
Murmur sad words abruptly broken off
By force of windy sighs thy spirit breathes.

(3.14.162–7)

But the First Nobleman, contemplating the alleged treachery of Alexandro, is there to warn us that 'there's no credit in the countenance' (3.1.18) – a mosreflection that might better be applied to Alexandro's traducer, the plausible Villuppo, who hastens to persuade the Viceroy of his vulnerability to the 'feigned love... colour'd in [Alexandro's] looks' (20).

In Shakespeare, both Julius Caesar and Othello are undone by what they think they see in others' countenances, apparently confirming Duncan's conviction that 'There's no art / To find the mind's construction in the face' (*Macbeth*, 1.4.11–12).[20] Caesar may indeed be right about the menace of Cassius's 'lean and hungry look' – the sign, he believes, of a malcontent who 'thinks too much' (*Caesar*, 1.2.195–6), but Brutus's capacity

for betrayal remains impenetrable to him. Elsewhere even the most spontaneous expressions are liable to misconstruction through either incompetence or sheer bias, as Worcester reminds his fellow rebels in *1 Henry IV*: 'Interpretation will misquote our looks' (5.2.13); or they may remain frustratingly enigmatic, as when Imogen confronts Pisanio's distracted 'stare' in *Cymbeline*, recognizing it, like his sigh, as the expression of an 'inward' torment, whose precise nature nevertheless remains indecipherable: 'One but painted thus / Would be interpreted a thing perplexed / Beyond self-explication' (3.4.5–8).

What appears to be the spontaneous expression of inward motion may, after all, be merely *sur-face* (or *super-facies*), something placed upon or over the face, a wholly unreliable covering. As Charron's emphasis on counterfeiting and hypocrisy acknowledges, the problem with physiognomical scripture is precisely that it can be consciously arranged and, when necessary, devoted to deliberate deception. Indeed, according to Castiglione's influential manual of courtly conduct, *The Courtier*, this is precisely how the countenance ought to be managed. Castiglione accepts the Platonic assumptions that underlie physiognomy's insistence upon the correspondence of inner self and outward appearance:

very seldom [doth] an ill soul dwell in a beautifull bodie. And therefore is outward beautie a true signe of the inwarde goodnesse, and in bodies this comeliness is imprinted... for a marke of the soule, whereby she is outwardly knowne... Judge you how plainely in the face of a Lyon, a horse, and an Eagle, a man shall discerne anger, fiercenesse, and stoutnesse: in lambes and

---

[19] Pierre Charron, *Of Wisedome*, trans. Samson Lennard, 2nd edn (London, 1630), pp. 6–7.

[20] Compare the complaint of Roxano in Middleton and Dekker's *The Bloody Banquet*: 'I have some skill in faces – and yet they never were more deceitfull. A man can scarce know a bawd from a midwife by the face, an hypocritical puritan from a devout Christian, if you go by the face' (1.4.114–17), cited from Gary Taylor and John Lavagnino, eds., *The Collected Works of Thomas Middleton* (Oxford, 2007), p. 648.

doves simplenesse and verie innocencie: the craftie sub-
teltie in foxes and wolves, and the like . . . in all other
living creatures.[21]

Yet he not only advises his courtiers how to frame
their countenance in order to maximize 'the grace
and beautie of phisnomy', but also urges a kind
of seemly 'counterfeiting' that will 'frame our gestures after a certain manner, that who so heareth
and seeth us, may by our words and countenances
imagine much more than he seeth and heareth';
insisting that 'in the conditions of men . . . that
you see outwardly is the least parte', he advises
his reader 'never to put [his] trust in any person
in the world . . . because there are in our minds
so many dennes and corners, that it is unpossi-
ble for the wit of man to know the dissimulations
that lye lurking in them'.[22] So it is in Cymbeline's
palace, following Imogen's marriage to Posthumus,
where 'not a courtier – / Although they wear their
faces to the bent – / Of the King's looks, hath a
heart that is not / Glad at the thing they scowl at'
(1.1.12–15); or in Macbeth's court, where 'False
face must hide what the false heart doth know'
(1.7.82), and where all must learn, like the protagonist himself, to 'make our faces vizards[visors] to
our hearts, / Disguising what they are' (3.2.35–6).[23]
As Shakespeare's own sonnets repeatedly insist, the
most expressive-seeming countenance may simply
be part of a deceitful masquerade – an example
of what Sonnet 127 punningly calls 'art's [heart's]
false borrowed face' (6), so that, as Sonnet 93 has it,
'Thy look[']s with me, thy heart in other place' (4).

Katharine Maus has eloquently described the
way in which, as a result of such conflicting
notions, English Renaissance culture was possessed
by 'two fantasies: one, that selves are obscure, hidden, ineffable; the other that they are fully manifest or capable of being made fully manifest. These
seem to be contradictory notions, but again and
again they are voiced together, so that they seem
less self-cancelling than symbiotically related or
mutually constitutive';[24] and Maus further observes
the ways in which the theatre learned to exploit
this symbiosis of opposites, deliberately 'foster[ing]'
theatregoers' capacity to use partial and limited

presentations as a basis for conjecture about what
is undisplayed or undisplayable', and playing on
their fascination with inwardness, while all the time
reminding them that 'inwardness . . . in the theatre
is always perforce inwardness displayed' – rendered
outward, and therefore not to be trusted'.[25]

Of course the contradictions that Maus examines are ultimately not so very different from those
that are exploited in the crucial confrontations of
Lie to Me, whose effectiveness depends on the
audience's believing that the faces of Lightman's
interviewees are carefully arranged and inscrutable
masks – surfaces that are nevertheless miraculously
open to the scrutiny of this penetrating observer. In
exploiting the tension between these two beliefs,
Lie to Me makes elaborate use of the same device
that gives a sharply comic edge to the face-to-
face confrontations of *Curb Your Enthusiasm* – the
cinematic close-up, with its associated techniques
of 'face-acting', through which audiences, as their
attention is fixed upon the countenance of a performer, are invited to discover, in the twitch of an
eyebrow or a tremble of the lip, a revealing glimpse
of the character's inner life.

---

[21] Baldassare Castiglione, *The Book of the Courtier*, trans. Sir
Thomas Hoby, intro. W. H. D. Rouse (London, 1966), Book
4, p. 309.

[22] *The Courtier*, Book 1, p. 38, Book 2, pp. 142, 124, 119.

[23] In a passage that resonates uncannily with *Macbeth*'s suspicion of both false faces and Jesuit equivocation, Thomas
Tuke avers that face-painting is licensed by 'the great Masters of lying, equiuocation, and mentall reseruation [the
Iesuites] . . . And therefore this old Romish *Iesabel*, as she
hath painted her owne face with the faire shew of many
goodlie ceremonies . . . thereby to set the world at a gaze,
so in this particular also she doth tolerate the abuses of her
children' (*Treatise*, H1v).

For further discussion of physical perception in *Macbeth*, see Sean H. McDowell, '*Macbeth* and the Perils of
Conjecture', in Gallagher and Raman, *Knowing Shakespeare*,
pp. 30–49; for an essay that places such passages in the context
of the play's 'politics of vision' and its play with the unreliability of apparitions and appearances, see Stuart Clark,
'Sights: King Saul and King Macbeth', in *Vanities of the Eye:
Vision in Early Modern European Culture* (Oxford, 2007), pp.
236–65.

[24] Katharine Maus, *Inwardness and Theater in the English Renaissance* (Chicago, 1995), pp. 28–9.

[25] Maus, *Inwardness*, p. 32.

The success of *Lie to Me*, despite its often unimaginative and formulaic scripts, has much to do with this use of close-up – the very technique that must have helped stimulate Ekman's original research. The game here is to tease audiences into testing their own ability to read looks against the uncanny expertise of Lightman and his associates; but a tricky sleight of hand is involved: since micro-expressions are normally involuntary, they are almost impossible for an actor to fake; yet for the fiction to succeed we must be persuaded that the countenance we have so carefully scanned did indeed register two levels of facial coding – one a mere surface, an effect consciously arranged by the character; the other seemingly spontaneous, a revelatory glimpse of the occluded inner self. It is Roth's job to talk us into the belief that this is what we have seen.

Needless to say, the stage offers no obvious equivalent to this device; yet Shakespeare's work displays its own intense fascination with the semiotics of the face, developing in the process a technique of rhetorically managed close-up in which the apparent limitations of the stage are turned to practical advantage. I have explored elsewhere *Othello*'s peculiar obsession with looks, faces, and the physiognomic registers of character.[26] I now want to examine more broadly this aspect of Shakespeare's histrionic practice, to consider how far it may have been shaped by his own experience as an actor, and to explore the ways in which that experience might have affected his approach to the vexed relationship between outward person and inward nature.

3. LOOKS AND LOOKERS-ON

Because the body is *the* text that we read throughout our evolution as a social species, we are now stuck, for better or worse, with cognitive adaptations that forcefully focus our attention on that particular text . . . Because we are drawn to each other's bodies in our quest to figure out each other's thought and intentions, we end up *performing* our bodies (not always consciously or successfully) so as to shape other people's perceptions of our mental states . . . Because ours is a mind-reading and hence

endlessly performative species, there is no lasting, reliable escape from the double perspective on the body.

(Lisa Zunshine)[27]

Actors, of course, are the ultimate liars. They are the lords of the facial nerve and we reward them magnificently for it.

(Daniel McNeill)[28]

It is surely telling that, in one of the rare first-hand accounts of theatrical experience from Shakespeare's lifetime, it was the emotion registered on a boy-actor's face, rather than the power of his impassioned language, that seemed to have lodged itself most forcefully in the imagination of the playgoer: describing the murderous denouement of *Othello* in the performance he had witnessed at Oxford in 1610, Henry Jackson famously remembered that it was the tormented countenance of the murdered Desdemona, as it 'implored the pity of the spectators', rather than the eloquence with which she had pleaded her cause, that especially moved him (*quanquam optime semper causam egit, interfecta tamen magis movebat, cum in lecto discumbens spectantium misericordiam ipso vultu imploraret*).[29] It is impossible to be sure how much of the boy-actor's face was actually visible to Jackson in the Oxford inn-yard, where the King's Men performed; but there can be no doubt as to what he *believed* he had seen;[30] and the

---

26 Michael Neill, 'The Look of Othello', *Shakespeare Survey 62* (Cambridge, 2009) pp. 104–22.

27 'Lying Bodies of the Englightenment: Theory of Mind and Cultural Historicism', in Lisa Zunshine, ed., Introduction to Cognitive Cultural Studies (Baltimore, 2010), pp. 115–33 at 120–1.

28 Daniel McNeill, *The Face* (New York, 1998), p. 240.

29 Originally cited in Geoffrey Tillotson, '*Othello* and *The Alchemist* at Oxford in 1610', *TLS* (20 July 1933), 494. Commenting on this scene in a private communication, Andrew Gurr, assuming that the performance would have been 'in a hall dining room, probably at the high table end, most likely at night', concludes that it 'would only have been the folk closest to the stage who would have seen the face.'

30 A famous instance of the power of language to persuade the eye occurs in the account of a performance of *Macbeth* at the Globe on 20 April 1610, by the doctor-magician, Simon Forman: 'And when Macbeth had murdered the king, the blood on his hands could not be washed off by any means, nor from his wives hands, which handed the bloody daggers in hiding them, which by means they became both much

intensity with which he remembered the episode may have had less to do with what Desdemona's mien could be seen to express, than with the way in which the play had schooled him to envisage her, in the moment when Othello is made to direct the audience's gaze upon the pitiable countenance of his dead wife:

Now, how dost thou *look* now? O ill-starred wench,
Pale as thy smock, when we shall meet at count,
This *look* of thine will hurl my soul from heaven . . .
            Whip me, ye devils,
From the possession of this heavenly *sight*.
                    (5.2.279–85, emphasis added)

How much of Desdemona's expression was actually visible to Jackson and his fellow-playgoers, and how much was conjured into his mind by Othello's agonized language, is less important than the way in which performance and description worked together to produce a single powerful impression on the viewer.[31] Of course this is by no means the only such moment in the play, or even in this scene. Only a few lines earlier, it is Desdemona who draws attention to the wildness of her husband's expression: 'And yet I fear you, for you're fatal then / When your eyes roll so' (5.2.39–40). What is created here, and in innumerable other episodes throughout the drama of the period, is what we might describe as a kind of virtual close-up, in which the dialogue is used to school the audience's sense of what their eyes are actually seeing.[32]

Since the theatre's liberation from the constraints of nineteenth-century illusionism, criticism has learned to emphasize the pre-eminence of sound over sight on the relatively bare stage of the Shakespearian playhouse: in the words of Andrew Gurr – who has probably done more than any other theatre historian to entrench this view – theatres like the Globe were designed 'not for people to see, but to hear'.[33] 'It is now a cliché', he writes, 'that Elizabethan audiences were hearers before they were spectators', a crowd of 'auditors' whose 'alertness [was] to the oral [rather] than visual features', who were more likely to speak of 'hearing' a play rather than of 'seeing' it.[34] Early modern theatres were

intended, Gurr argues, for 'three-dimensional' performance in the round, and they were built this way because 'proximity to the source of . . . sound [was their] highest priority'.[35] Our own ideas of staging, he suggests, are unavoidably shaped by our experience of theatres constructed for front-on viewing, in which lighting enforces the audience's attention to what the director thinks important, thereby ensuring 'priority to the eye over the ear'.[36] Shakespeare's priorities, according to Gurr, were opposite ones; and insofar as a late Shakespeare play like *The Winter's Tale* – whose climactic discovery scene requires intense visual concentration from the audience – represents the start of a slow shift towards 'a more two-dimensional way of thinking

---

amazed and affronted', see www.shakespeare-online.com/plays/simonforman.html. Here Forman appears to remember seeing a piece of action that the play evokes, but never shows on stage.

31 In *Narrating the Visual in Shakespeare* (Farnham, 2009), Richard Meek offers an extended exploration of Shakespeare's fascination with the way in which language can 'make us see'. As his title suggests, however, Meek's primary interest, is in the imaginative power of *ecphrasis* and other narrative devices, rather than in more strictly theatrical effects of such verbal conjuring.

32 For a more detailed discussion of facial evidence in this play, see Neill, 'The Look of Othello', pp. 104–22. In ' "Ocular Proof" and the Dangers of Perceptual Faith', ch. 6 in *Image Ethics in Shakespeare and Spenser* (New York, 2011), pp. 143–160, James A. Knapp discusses *Othello* as a tragedy exploring 'the relationship of ethics and vision', one which 'specifically foregrounds the early modern struggle over the contradictory nature of vision as both the direct conduit to the world as it is and the sense most susceptible to illusion and misinterpretation' (p. 143).

33 Andrew Gurr, 'Why Was the Globe Round?', in Laury Magnus and Walter Cannon, eds., *Who Hears in Shakespeare?* (Plymouth, 2011), p. 3. Cf. also John Orrell's claim that the Globe was 'an acoustical auditorium, tended to serve the word and the ear more fully than the image and the eye' in *The Quest for Shakespeare's Globe* (Cambridge, 1983), p. 140, and Bruce Smith's assertion that early modern amphitheatres were primarily 'instruments for producing, shaping, and propagating sound', in *The Acoustic World of Early Modern England: Attending to the O-factor* (Chicago, 1999), p. 206.

34 Andrew Gurr, *The Shakespeare Company, 1594–1642* (Cambridge, 2004), pp. 47, 49.

35 Gurr, 'Why Was the Globe Round', p. 4.

36 Gurr, 'Why Was the Globe Round', p. 10.

about staging... that began to [privilege] visual over aural effects', this was an accidental function of stage architecture – in particular the dominance of the *frons scenae* with its flanking doors and central opening.[37] The argument is a powerful one, and provides an essential corrective to anachronistic assumptions shaped by our own culture's preoccupation with the visual; but, as a decisive article by Gabriel Egan has shown, Gurr's insistence upon the primacy of aural experience is significantly overstated.[38] Where Gurr maintains that sixteenth- and seventeenth-century playgoers were more likely to speak of 'hearing' than of 'seeing' a play, Egan's word-search of the Chadwyck-Healey Literature Online database shows that the opposite was almost certainly the case. Overwhelmingly, the texts in LION refer to 'seeing' a play (95 instances), rather than to 'hearing' it (8 instances). No wonder that when James Burbage christened London's first permanent playhouse 'The Theatre' he chose a name whose root lay in the Greek verb 'to see'.

That said, there are reasons for thinking that the debate is – to some extent at least – grounded in a false dichotomy. It is true that Shakespeare, as a poet who lavished particular care on the verbal texture of his plays, often seems to have privileged the auditory experience: although he refers to playgoers as 'spectators' as well as 'auditors', three of the eight references to 'hearing' a play are his, and he nowhere speaks of 'seeing' one. But Shakespeare was an actor as well as a poet; and Hamlet's instructions to the players are as attentive to the 'action' as they are to the 'word'. Of course the Chorus to *Henry V* famously celebrates the power of dramatic verse to compensate for the deficiencies of visual representation by dazzling the inner eye with the imaginary splendour of a (rhetorically) 'swelling scene': '*Think*, when we *talk* of horses, that you *see* them, / Printing their proud hoofs i'th' receiving earth' (Prologue, 26–7, emphasis added). But it would be a mistake to take this somewhat disingenuous parade of self-deprecation too literally: taken together, the choric speeches that introduce the play's successive acts can begin to seem like an elaborate exercise in *occupatio*, boasting of the very magic that the Chorus pretends

his modest playhouse cannot offer; and while the relative paucity of scenic spectacle in Shakespeare's theatre may seem to have privileged *poesis* over *pictura*, it also gave peculiar visual prominence to the actor's body – to the elaborate rhetoric of gesture at his command, and above all to the expressive power of the face, to whose communicative subtleties the language of the plays repeatedly draws our attention.[39]

Needless to say, in a large arena like the Globe – or even in smaller indoor houses, such as the Blackfriars, with their appreciably dimmer lighting – there were limits to how much facial detail most onlookers could be expected to discern, especially given the problematic sightlines for those seated beside the stage, or in the gallery behind it.[40] Thus Sibylle Baumbach, in her useful study of Shakespeare's involvement with physiognomical ideas, draws attention to the frequency with which viewers are implicitly encouraged to measure their own

---

37 Gurr, 'Why Was the Globe Round', pp. 7–8.

38 Gabriel Egan, 'Hearing or Seeing a Play? Evidence of Early Modern Theatrical Terminology', *Ben Jonson Journal*, 8 (2001), 327–47.

39 See Michael Neill, 'Amphitheatres in the Body: Playing with Hands on the Shakespearian Stage', in *Shakespeare Survey 48* (Cambridge, 1995), pp. 23–50.

40 That said, early modern theatres, where the maximum distance between players and audience seems to have been approximately 90 feet, were clearly better adapted to the observation of facial expression than the large proscenium arch structures which evolved from the late eighteenth century, and which, for that very reason attracted the hostile attention of the Scottish playwright Joanna Baillie in *Plays on the Passions* (1798). For an account of Baillie's proposals for a new, more intimate type of theatre, specifically adapted to the accurate reading of emotional expression, and partly drawing on her brother Matthew's scientific interest in the neurophysiological basis of the 'natural language' of the face, see Alan Richardson, 'Facial Expression Theory from Romanticism to the Present', in Zunshine, *Introduction to Cognitive Cultural Studies*, pp. 65–83 at 72–4. For the distances from which basic expressions, such as the smile, can be read, see McNeill, *The Face*, p. 204. Gurr (private communication) notes that 'if you had the... audience sitting all round, as at the Blackfriars, then facial expressions would have been primary, but... [never] the key or sole way of expressing... emotions [since they would necessarily have remained invisible to some].'

interpretation of actors' faces against the descriptions offered by other characters;[41] but she is forced to recognize the practical inaccessibility of some facial signs and signatures to many in the audience: 'expressions of . . . the eyes', for example – though considered particularly revealing – would have been largely invisible,[42] while involuntary registers of emotion, such as blushing and pallor, are always difficult to simulate. For these reasons Baumbach concludes that although 'it seems plausible that actors did their best to provide the visual text to descriptions imposed on them', such descriptions 'should be regarded first and foremost as verbal scenery', designed to draw attention as much to 'the person who . . . performs the act of physiognomic reading' as to the supposed object of their scrutiny.[43] To speak of such descriptions as being simply 'imposed' on actors, however, is not only to downplay the importance of their own agency in interpreting such implied stage directions; it also discounts the readiness of a viewer's imagination to take instruction – its willingness to see what it is told to see, and to read accordingly.

Unfortunately we know very little about the kinds of training to which professional actors were exposed in Shakespeare's day; but we can probably assume a significant degree of continuity between the informal practices of the Globe players, and the techniques advocated by the eighteenth-century playwright Aaron Hill in his *Art of Acting* (1746): Hill lays out instructions for managing a repertoire of no fewer than ten expressions, designed to convey the emotions of joy, wonder, love, pity, jealousy, fear, grief, anger, scorn and hatred, while David Garrick was famous for his ability 'to quickly cycle his face through nine feelings, joy, tranquillity, surprise, astonishment, sadness, despondency, fear, horror, despair, and back to joy'.[44] ' Such expressions, as we can gauge from contemporary illustrations, were necessarily of a stylized and exaggerated kind; and Hamlet's testy response to the spectacle of Lucianus preparing for the poisoning of Gonzago – 'Begin, murderer. Pox, leave thy damnable faces and begin' (*Hamlet*, 3.2.240–1) – is reminder of the extent to which

a form of conspicuous face-acting, deriving from the mime-techniques of dumb-show, formed a significant part of the Elizabethan actor's repertory. It is not accidental that Lucianus's display should immediately follow his entry, since Shakespeare's scripts offer numerous instances where virtual close-ups of this sort are used to draw attention to the dramatic importance of a character's entrance: 'Here comes the queen, whose looks bewray her anger', Exeter announces in the opening scene of *3 Henry VI* (1.1.212); a few scenes later, Richard of Gloucester greets the arrival of a messenger in similar terms: 'But what art thou, whose heavy looks foretell / Some dreadful story hanging on thy tongue' (2.1.43–4); in the climactic final scene of *Much Ado About Nothing*, Don Pedro confronts a coldly furious Benedick: 'Why, what's the matter, / That you have such a February face, / So full of frost, of storm and cloudiness?' (5.4.40–2); while in *Macbeth* Lennox greets the battle-weary Thane of Rosse: 'What a haste looks through his eyes! So should he look / That seems to speak things strange' (1.2.46–7). These, of course, are cue-lines that will often have been included in the manuscript 'part' supplied to the actors here making their entrances, instructing them how to compose their features:[45] but they are also designed to ensure that the audience, however distant they may be from the stage, register the cast of a particular countenance precisely as the onstage characters are supposed to do. Thus in the anonymous *True Chronicle Historie of King Leir* (1594), where according to the stage direction Ragan, as she reads Gonorill's letter, '*frownes and stamps*', the Messenger is made to school the audience in a more detailed reading of her expressions:

---

[41] Baumbach, *Art of Physiognomy*, p. 74.

[42] Baumbach, *Art of Physiognomy*.

[43] Baumbach, *Art of Physiognomy*, p. 99.

[44] McNeill, *The Face*, pp. 256, 180.

[45] For full discussion of the practical consequences of working from discrete 'parts', see Simon Palfrey and Tiffany Stern, *Shakespeare in Parts* (Oxford, 2007).

See how her colour comes and goes agayne,
Now red as scarlet, now pale as ash:
See how she knits her brow, and bytes her lips,
And stamps, and makes a dumbe shew of disdayne,
Mixt with revenge and violent extreames.

(16. 1173–7)[46]

Similarly, in Shakespeare and Fletcher's *Henry VIII*, Patience is made to prepare the audience of Katherine's death by instructing them how to read her countenance:

Do you note
How much her Grace is altered on the sudden?
How long her face is drawn? How pale she looks,
And of an earthly cold? Mark her eyes!   (4.2.96–9)

A particularly striking example of this technique occurs in the second scene of *Julius Caesar* at the dramatic moment when Caesar and his party return from the games at which he has failed in his bid for coronation:

Brutus.   But look you, Cassius,
The angry spot doth glow on Caesar's brow,
And all the rest look like a chidden train:
Calpurnia's cheek is pale, and Cicero
Looks with such ferret and such fiery eyes
As we have seen him in the Capitol

(1.2.183–8)

Here the audience's gaze is made to pan from one close-up to another, scrutinizing the characters' face for clues as to what may have happened off-stage.

In most episodes of this kind, the facial detailing is straightforwardly descriptive; but in other cases, where characters are engaged in conscious efforts to interpret the expressions of others, the effect becomes dramaturgically more ambiguous – as when Hotspur's wife struggles to translate the 'portents' she discerns in the 'strange motions' of her husband's face (*1 Henry IV*, 2.4.60–2); or when Humphrey of Gloucester offers his curiously equivocal response to the Chief Justice's grief over the king's death in *2 Henry IV*: 'I dare swear you borrow not that face / Of seeming sorrow – it is sure your own' (5.2.28–9).

More complex in its effect is a tensely comic episode in Act 2, scene 6 of *Antony and Cleopatra.*

After the initial reconciliation between Pompey and the triumvirs, the cynical Enobarbus and Menas are left to size one another up. Enobarbus offers his hand, characteristically ironizing this gesture of amity even as he does so: 'If our eyes had authority, here they might take two thieves kissing'; Menas responds in kind: 'All men's faces are true, whatsome'er their hands are' (97–100). The joke here is a complex one: the clasping of hands is a plighting of troth, but since these are thieves' hands, they are (albeit necessarily inscribed with the chiromantic signs of character)[47] by definition false: so verification must be sought in faces; but the truth that faces reveal may prove to be only the disconcerting evidence of falsehood. The implied stage direction, requiring the two characters to scrutinize one another's faces for proof of intention, serves to highlight the way in which the ensuing dialogue – with its gestures of male-bonding in the characters' misogynist joking about the treachery of women's faces and its sarcastic probing of their superiors' motives and intentions – is a kind of fencing between two men who know that fast friendship and mortal enmity are merely the alternative faces of interest: it is with them precisely as they know it to be with Caesar and Antony (and Pompey and Lepidus): 'you shall find the very band that seems to tie their friendship together will be the very strangler of their amity' (120–2). 'Strangler' here is beautifully placed – like 'throats' in the carouser's jest with which Enobarbus ends the scene: for Menas, after all, is the man who, only 70 lines into the following scene, will advise his master to cut their guests' throats. But for the moment neither he nor his interlocutor can be quite certain of the other's intention; and their probing stares will be matched by the equally interrogative gaze of the audience.

---

[46] Cited from the edition in Geoffrey Bullough, *Narrative and Dramatic Sources of Shakespeare*, 8 vols. (London, 1957–75), vol. 7.

[47] Cureau's treatise (note 9 above) contains a lengthy section (pp. 224 ff.) on the usefulness of palm-reading as part of the art 'how to know men'.

In *Othello* Shakespeare contrives a witty metatheatrical play on the use of virtual close-up to instruct the audience on how they are supposed to read a character's countenance: famously, in the eavesdropping scene of *Othello*, Iago instructs the Moor to 'mark the fleers, the gibes, and notable scorns, / That dwell in every region of [Cassio's] face', only to remind the audience that this will amount to nothing more than a theatrical sleight-of-hand designed to ensure that his victim 'must conster / Poor Cassio's smiles, gestures, and light behaviours / Quite in the wrong' (4.1.81–2, 100–2). A different kind of ambiguity is created in the crucial scene of Wolsey's downfall from *Henry VIII*, when the expressions and gestures intended to accompany the cardinal's apprehensive asides are, in effect, choreographed by Norfolk's subsequent report to the king:

> My lord, we have
> Stood here observing him. Some strange commotion
> Is in his brain. He bites his lip, and starts,
> Stops on a sudden, looks upon the ground,
> Then lays his finger on his temple; straight
> Springs into a fast gait, then stops again.
> Strikes his breast hard, and anon he casts
> His eye against the moon. In most strange postures
> We have seen him set himself.   (3.2.112–20)

The meaning of this display is transparent enough – but the theatricality of Wolsey's exhibition of 'commotion', as he 'sets' himself in 'postures' that could almost come from a handbook of gestural rhetoric like Bulwer's *Chirologia*, might cause us to question to what extent this is a calculated display, designed to manipulate the response of the courtiers who so studiously observe his 'countenance' (81). Episodes of this sort, furthermore, exemplify the way in which an audience's silent inquisition is liable to be complicated by the metatheatrical awareness that characters are, after all, merely histrionic artifacts – that there is, in that sense, no 'true' intention to be discovered behind their carefully managed countenances.

Richard III, centring as it does on the virtuoso triumphs of an actor-hypocrite, treats the potential disparity between face and intention with particular relish, playing (as Katharine Maus

points out) with cruelly ironic knowingness on the uncertain significance of physical appearance, so that although 'Richard's external distortion bodies forth moral deformity . . . the theoretical separability of the inside from the outside means that the equivalence can never be made with any certainty.'[48] This gap repeatedly allows the play to exploit the dramatic ironies of flattering misinterpretation – as when, for example, the doomed Clarence, professing to spy 'some pity' in the 'looks' of the Second Murderer (1.4.254), imagines he may escape his fate; or when, the guileless Hastings, observing that Richard 'looks cheerfully and smooth this morning', disastrously misconstrues this symptom of vindictive glee (3.4.48). Hastings is convinced that Richard's is a supremely legible countenance ('For by his face straight shall you know his heart' (53)); and in one sense he reads his enemy's expression correctly, but he is nevertheless misled by it, since the 'conceit' that so pleases his nemesis (as the audience well knows) is nothing less than a plan to indict Hastings himself for treasonable 'witchcraft' (68–75). The irony here is underlined in advance by Buckingham's warning, 'We know each other's faces. For of our hearts, / He knows more of mine than I of yours, / Or I of his, my lord, than you of mine' (10–12), as well as by the metatheatrical innuendo with which the Duke greets Richard's entry: 'Had you not come upon your cue, my lord, / William Lord Hastings had pronounced your part' (26–7).

As the histrionic resonances of 'cue' and 'part' are designed to remind us, Buckingham, like his

---

48 Maus, *Inwardness*, p. 51. For a more detailed examination of the play's exploitation of the ultimate unreliability of physiognomical signs, see Michael Torrey, ' "The plain devil and dissembling looks": Ambivalent Physiognomy and Shakespeare's *Richard III*', *ELR*, 30 (2000), 123–53: 'by making Richard deformed', Torrey writes, 'Shakespeare optimistically suggests that Richard's self was fully manifest, that his evil was easily known; but by making him a dissembler, Shakespeare pessimistically admits that Richard's self may actually have been obscure and his evil hidden . . . [Richard] can refashion his deformity into a sign of anything but the inward truth about him that it supposedly represents' (141, 147).

master Richard, is a character for whom theatrical self-fashioning is a necessary constant of behaviour:

> *Richard.* Come, cousin, canst thou quake and change thy colour?
> Murder thy breath in middle of a word . . .
> As if thou wert distraught and mad with terror?
>
> *Buckingham.* Tut, I can counterfeit the deep tragedian,
> Tremble and start at wagging of a straw,
> Speak and look back, and pry on every side,
> Intending deep suspicion: ghastly looks
> Are at my service, like enforcèd smiles,
> And both are ready in their offices
> At any time to grace my stratagems.
>
> (*Richard III*, 3.5.1–11)

This exchange is one that clearly requires from the actors' faces and bodies a self-conscious exhibition of actorly virtuosity – one that ironically seems to justify the charge made by the stage's Puritan enemies that acting itself was nothing less than a form of viciously systematized hypocrisy, closely akin – as that scourge of playing, William Prynne, complained – to 'the common *accursed art of face-painting*': 'the mere acting of the persons, parts, gestures . . . passions; especially . . . Anger, Furie, Love, Revenge and Villanies of other men . . . is hypocrisie . . . for what else is an *hypocrite in his true etymologie, but a Stage-player or one who acts anothers part*'.[49] Buckingham delights in his own deliberate hypocrisy, relishing its shallowness as a mere burlesque counterfeit of the proper counterfeiting exemplified in tragic performance. For Prynne, however the deep tragedian's masquerade was even more treacherous than such openly histrionic display, because of the way in which its fabricated motions might actually infect the inner self, since 'as it transformes the Actors into what they are not, *so it infuseth falsehood into every part of soule and body*' (p. 159; sig. x4).

The question that Prynne raises of how a studied physical display may actually succeed, by a kind of psychological back-formation, in creating the emotions it pretends to express,[50] is one that, sooner or later, most performers in a theatre of affect must confront. This is what we might call

the *im*-pression as opposed to the expression of theatrical emotion;[51] and just as Shakespeare's experience as an actor is reflected in his careful attention to the movements of the countenance, so it also seems to have produced in him a peculiar sensitivity to the psychological impressions of performance. Nowhere is this more apparent than in *Hamlet*, a drama of unmasking in which the scrutiny of faces plays a peculiarly crucial role, beginning with Hamlet's anxious questioning of Horatio about the Ghost's appearance:

> *Hamlet.*   . . . saw you not his face?
> *Horatio.* O yes, my lord, he wore his beaver up.
> *Hamlet.* What, looked he frowningly?
> *Horatio.*   A countenance more
>   In sorrow than in anger.
> *Hamlet.*   Pale or red?
> *Horatio.* Nay, very pale.
> *Hamlet.*   And fixed his eyes upon you?
> *Horatio.* Most constantly.   (1.2.227–32)

The play's preoccupation with the scrutiny of faces is most conspicuous, of course, in the play scene, where the Prince's irritation with the player's 'damnable faces' is set against his fierce attention to the king's countenance:

> Give him heedful note;
> For I mine eyes will rivet to his face,
> And after, we will both our judgments join
> To censure of his seeming.   (3.2.83–5)

For Hamlet to 'observe [Claudius's] looks' will be to probe the king's inner life, to 'tent him to the quick' (2.2.596–8), precisely as Ophelia describes him seeking, in his silent inquisition, to 'draw' her inward secrets from her face (2.1.81–2). In the performance of the 'Mousetrap', the audience

---

49 William Prynne, *Histrio-mastix* (1633), pp. 157–8 (sig. X3–X3v).

50 The existence of such a process is confirmed by contemporary cognitive research: see, for example, Bruce Hood, *The Self Illusion* (London, 2012), pp. 29, 108.

51 This is, I think, the kind of physical impact on the feeling self that William Lathum had in mind when he wrote of how his readers' 'tender hearts can entertaine / A quicke *impression* of another's paine' – see William Lathum, *Phyala lachrymarum* (London, 1634), 'Elegia Introductoria', A6v.

themselves are meant to become involved in the interrogatory 'censure' of Claudius's seeming – just as later, in the closet scene, they will find themselves, under the tutelage of the Ghost, forced to probe the significance of the shock that registers on Gertrude's face, questioning what it may reveal about the causes of the torment in her 'fighting soul': 'But look, amazement on thy mother sits . . . Conceit in weakest bodies strongest works' (3.4.112–14). But in the case of the 'Mousetrap' scene, the complex interplay of looks, in which theatrical onlookers become the looked-on, while their lookers-on in turn are overlooked by a larger audience, famously serves as a metatheatrical reminder of the intimate relationship between histrionism and hypocrisy.

Shakespeare's Denmark is a world for which Hamlet's sneer at Ophelia might stand as a motto: 'God hath given you one face, and you make yourselves another' (3.1.143–4) – a world where the court's display of histrionic grief for Old Hamlet is perfectly described in Claudius's jibe to Laertes when he sees him as 'like the painting of a sorrow, / A face without a heart' (4.7.108–9). In a world of carefully manipulated illusion, it is, paradoxically enough, the existentially 'questionable' Ghost, itself addressed by Horatio as 'illusion', whose look seems to Hamlet to represent a perfect conjuncture of inward and outward. 'Whereon do you look?' the Queen demands of her son in the closet scene, as she stares into seeming vacancy:

On him, on him. [he replies] Look you how pale he
    glares!
His form and cause conjoined, preaching to stones
Would make them capable. – Do not look upon me
Lest with this piteous action you convert
My stern effects . . .
Why look you there. Look how it steals away!
My father, in his habit as he lived!
Look where he goes.   (3.4.116–27)

Even here, however, the still-oscillating pronouns that have confused the ghost's identity from the opening scene ('he . . . it . . . he') are bound to trigger the histrionic connotations of 'piteous action', returning the audience to Hamlet's tormented

ruminations on the doubleness of the verb 'to act', and prompting them to further questions about what it is they think they see.

Inevitably it is in the scenes involving the players that the vexed business of looking and the credit to be given to faces is exposed to the most intense dramatic pressure. It is Polonius who first draws attention to the astonishingly vivid physical expressions of the First Player's grief for Hecuba: 'Look whe'er he has not turned his colour, and has tears in's eyes. Prithee no more' (2.1.521–2); but it is Hamlet whose reflections on the conundrum of theatrically exhibited emotion and its inward impression create the play's most notorious *mise en abyme*:

> Is it not monstrous that this player here,
> But in a fiction or a dream of passion,
> Could force his soul so to his own conceit
> That from her working all his visage wanned,
> Tears in his eyes, distraction in 's aspect,
> A broken voice, and his whole function suiting,
> With forms to his conceit? And all for nothing.
>   (2.2.578–84)

What is immediately striking about this passage is the way in which its effect depends upon virtual close-up – the imaginary framing of a countenance in turmoil: although Hamlet's outburst recognizes the persuasive power of 'horrid speech', invoking the evidence of 'ears' as well as 'eyes' (567), its rhetorical emphasis is overwhelmingly upon the visible signs of feeling, especially those that mark the player's 'visage' or 'aspect', which are offered as proofs of an inward condition – signs so infallible that they can only issue from a 'soul' that has itself been mysteriously transformed by the performer's 'conceit', converting the palpable fiction of 'actions that a man might play' (1.2.84) into the truth of felt emotion. Anyone who has ever found themselves upon a stage, responding with unaccountable feeling to another actor's emotional display, will recognize this moment of perplexity. It is both crucial to the effect of this scene – and yet ultimately insignificant – that the lines are themselves being spoken by an actor, himself engaged in the deliberate fabrication of affect – insignificant because, for an instant at least, the audience is invited to share the actor's perspective, and to recognize in the generation of pathos and in the consequent impression of deep feeling a kind of mystery.[52]

But the Player's is not, I think, the most mysterious look in Shakespeare: that is reserved for the closing moments of the Folio version of *King Lear*. This, after all, is a play in which confidently asserted claims to recognition ('I know thee')[53] repeatedly alternate with various forms of the challenge 'Dost thou know . . . ?',[54] whilst being conspicuously problematized by the motifs of blindness on the one hand and disguise on the other: again and again we see that faces are placed under more than usually intense scrutiny; but the play ends with a virtual close-up that exploits the audience's half-sublimated awareness of the emptiness of theatrical illusion to insist on the final unreadability of the human countenance, in which the fearful unknowability of others – 'Let them anatomize Regan; *see* what breeds about her heart' (3.6.73–4, my emphasis) – is confirmed by the motionless blank of death. A drama whose principal action is triggered by Cordelia's determination to say 'nothing', ends by reiterating the father's initial question, 'What can you say . . . ? (1.1.85): 'What is't thou say'st?' (5.3.270), and then by directing our gaze upon lips that truly can say nothing at all. This crisis is orchestrated through a self-consciously formal speech from the Duke of Albany, in which he seeks to restore order to the ruined kingdom by meting out the wages of virtue and vice to their deservers; just as he reaches the confident climax of his oration, Albany's attention is caught by a sight that confounds his talk of 'rights' and 'merit': 'O see, see!' he cries, directing all eyes upon the distraught king. Lear is gazing at his daughter's corpse, overcome by the recognition of what 'nothing' really means: 'Never, never, never, never, never' (l. 307). As the audience share his horrified stare, they are forced to envisage the detail of Cordelia's face:

> Do you see this? Look on her! Look her lips,
> Look there, look there!   *He dies*
>   (5.3.309–10)

This, surely, is the equivalent of that moment in the final scene of *Othello* where 'the pity of the spectators' is compelled by the protagonist's horrified response to his dead wife's accusatory 'look'. But here, at the end of a play that has insisted so remorselessly upon the need for clarity of vision, they are not allowed to know what Lear thinks he sees, how Cordelia looks to him, or what that look might mean, for the text refuses to explain. It is no wonder that commentators remain so divided about the significance of Lear's final lines – whether, like Gloucester, he 'dies smilingly', convinced that Cordelia breathes, or whether what he sees merely confirms his despair. The convention of virtual close-up requires that speakers gloss the significance of the countenances to which they draw attention; but Lear dies before he can tell us how to envisage her. 'Look up, my lord,' begs Edgar, as though to gaze in the king's face might provide him with some answer to the bafflement of this moment. It is as if he wanted (in the language of Kent's reproof) to stretch the old man further upon the rack of ocular inquisition. But the scene will end in surrender to a weary nescience, in lines that, among other things, imply an acceptance of what cannot now be seen and therefore lies beyond any knowing: 'We that are young / Shall never see so much, nor live so long' (301–2).

---

[52] Here I take issue with Zunshine who contrasts the feelings visible on the countenance of an engaged (but naive) audience member with those registered on the faces of the actors they observe: while recognizing that the former do not correspond to the depth of emotion that they would express in real life, she nevertheless argues that they 'reflect his state of mind more accurately than the body language of the performers reflects their state of mind' ('Lying Bodies', p. 129). I think this is to underestimate the mysterious emotional feedback loop involved in performance, and hence what is involved in the effort to 'fake the feeling' (p. 130).

[53] See e.g. 1.1.271; 1.4.27–8; 1.4.243; 1.4.324; 2.2.11–12, 28–9; 3.1.3; 4.6.95, 132, 73, 247; 4.7.50, 63, 69–70; 5.3.284–5.

[54] See e.g. 1.1.23; 1.4.26; 1.4.217–21; 2.2.13; 2.2.25–8; 4.6.131, 255; 4.7.10, 49; 5.3.119, 151; 5.3.276–7.

'HEAR THE AMBASSADORS!': MARKING SHAKESPEARE'S VENICE CONNECTION

CAROL CHILLINGTON RUTTER

To locate the 'ambassadorial moment' in Shakespeare, to ask how that 'moment' is inflected on Shakespeare's stage, and to connect his fictions to performances beyond the theatre, to the actual practice of early modern diplomacy, I begin with two sequences from *Antony and Cleopatra*. After Actium, after defeat, Antony sends to make terms with Octavius. He wants to live. He knows he must 'dodge / And palter' with 'the young man', must adopt 'the shifts of lowness'.[1] He 'Requires to live in Egypt' but, if that is not granted, he sues to 'breathe between the heavens and earth, / A private man in Athens'. Antony dispatches his messenger. The Folio stage direction calls him '*Ambassador*'. Antony says he's 'our schoolmaster'. This figure, introducing himself ('Such as I am') and his office ('I come from Antony'), places himself in the story with a fleeting reflection, an analogy between the mighty and the menial. 'Of late', he says, he was 'as petty to [Antony's] ends / As is the morn-dew on the myrtle leaf / To his grand sea.'

In Michael Boyd's RSC *Antony and Cleopatra* (2010), when John Mackay's Octavius, a strangle-voiced hysteric in a grey Armani suit (the dress uniform of all the non-combatant kill-joy Romans in that production) ordered 'Let him appear that's come from Antony' and turned to his aide to ask 'Know you him?', Dolabella sniggered, 'Caesar, 'tis his *schoolmaster*'. Peter Shorey, balding, bewildered, stumbled into their presence – a comically diffident schoolmaster-turned-ambassador. He blinked owlishly through wire-rim spectacles as though not used to the glare of day, as though plucked from some dim-lit mobile library

attached to Antony's military operations to appear before Caesar's celebrity. He delivered his message. He received his answers (one request denied, the other made perversely conditional). Then, dismissed with safe-guards ('Bring him through the bands'), he made a sudden, staggering move that told spectators everything they needed to know about Antony's future. He threw himself on his knees in the young man's path, grabbed one of the fists Octavius had instinctively balled, and fervently kissed it. (As Enobarbus would shortly observe of 'leaky' Antony, he's ripe for 'sinking' when 'Thy dearest quit thee'.)

Watching the Schoolmaster depart, Caesar instructs a reciprocal embassy – to the Egyptian queen. 'Dispatch', he commands his lieutenant, Thidias. 'Try thy eloquence now.' 'From Antony win Cleopatra'; 'promise / And in our name, what she requires'. And not just bare requirements: 'add more, / From thine invention, offers'. His contemptuous – empirical? – view of women sets the terms of the diplomatic interview: 'Women are not / In their best fortunes strong, but want will perjure / The ne'er-touch'd vestal.' So: 'Try thy cunning Thidias'. This sequence, in a modern dress student production that played just months after the Boyd *Antony and Cleopatra* at Warwick University where undergraduates had to live on their theatrical wits to cast Shakespeare's huge play from a limited availability of actors, put on

---

[1] Quotations are from the Arden 3rd series edition of *Antony and Cleopatra*, edited by John Wilders (London, 1995).

stage a cross-cast Thidias.[2] The flogging s/he was dragged off to at Antony's bellowed orders – 'Take hence the jack and whip him!' – was all the more brutal for that. Later, another young Roman – another cross-casting – stepped forward to take charge from over-officious Proculeius of the grief-demented, death-seeking Cleopatra ('Where art thou Death? / Come hither . . . ! . . . take a queen / Worth many babes and beggars!'). Quietly, the soldier cut through the woman's keening to ask, 'Most noble empress, you have heard of me?' Daffed aside ('I cannot tell'), the squaddie tried again. 'Assuredly you know me' – and turned his profile. To show across his face the disfigurement of still-bloody welts: Thidias was morphed into Dolabella, Caesar's latest ambassador to Cleopatra, assigned another message to the lethal queen. Knowing what Cleopatra had already cost this young Roman made what Dolabella did next all the more breathtaking. Listening to Cleopatra's *non sequitur*, her mesmerizing dream of an emperor Antony, this Dolabella got tangled up in the same 'strong toils' of 'grace' that had fascinated his superior. Was seduced. Seduced, capitulated to Alexandria, betrayed the imperial mission ('Know you what Caesar means to do with me?'), gave away the master's diplomatic secrets ('He'll lead me, then, in triumph'), produced the intelligence to inform Cleopatra's preparations and spoil Caesar's ('I tell you this . . . / Make your best use of this'). Dolabella turned coat ('sworn by your command') to become 'your' – Cleopatra's, not Caesar's – 'servant'.

Thidias, Dolabella and the Schoolmaster are not career diplomats. They're plucked from other occupations to have diplomacy thrust upon them, to be assigned what contemporary theorists of statecraft would call 'extraordinary' embassies, '*Ambassadors* [who] returne assone as [their] affaire is dispatched'.[3] The business they represent frames *Antony and Cleopatra*. Indeed, it expresses the political crisis of failed communication that leads to Actium – and after, to Cleopatra's 'immortal longings', her staged return to Cydnus. Ambassadors are there at the beginning. Hotfoot from Rome, they are the ones who are being made to cool their heels

waiting for an audience with the general whose 'dotage' is delinquency, whose eyes have turned 'The office and devotion of their view / Upon a tawny front'; the ones tauntingly summoned by Cleopatra ('Hear the ambassadors') to be brushed off by Antony ('Speak not to us'). They are there at the end, too, in Dolabella. Coming with perhaps deliberate foot-dragging diplomatic tardiness behind the 'Too slow a messenger' whom Caesar has sent to prevent her suicide, the compromised ambassador is the last to gaze on Cleopatra dead. He is the state agent whom Caesar, still supposing him faithful to Rome, still not realizing that he's been 'Unpolicied', 'beguiled', made an 'ass', names in the last line of the play to arrange her funeral ('Come, Dolabella, see / High order in this great solemnity').

PERFORMING DIPLOMACY

If Thidias, Dolabella and the Schoolmaster are placeholders for the ubiquitous ambassadorial business *Antony and Cleopatra* performs, they can also stand as front men to the dozens of legates, nuncios, ambassadors and liegers who cross Shakespeare's stage from official state agents like the French ambassador who brings on tennis balls at the beginning of *Henry V*, the English ambassadors who arrive with news 'That Rosencrantz and Guildenstern are dead' at the end of *Hamlet*, and Pandolph, the Pope's legate who crisscrosses the middle of *King John* playing diplomatic cat's cradle with national interests, to 'extraordinaries' like Thersites, made Achilles's ambassador to Ajax (as Ulysses, less improbably, the Greeks' to Troy); Cesario, Orsino's 'nuntio' to Olivia; Claudio, Angelo's 'everlasting lieger' to conduct his 'affairs to heaven'; Benedict, volunteered for an 'embassage to the pigmies'; Cloten, his decapitated head, thrown into a Welsh river, sent 'down the stream in embassy to his mother'; the female

[2] Directed by Claire Byrne and Joshua Elliott; Rio West played Thidias/Dolabella.

[3] Jean Hotman, *The Ambassador* (London, 1603), sig. B2v. Further internal citation, by signature, is to this edition.

triumvirate of Rome, Volumnia leading it, sent in delegation to Coriolanus.

This diplomatic traffic prompts a series of questions. What is the ambassador's status, what cultural and political assumptions does he carry, and how does his work differ from that of a messenger? When Cleopatra calls Rome's envoys not just 'messengers' but 'ambassadors' what surplus of signification is she adding? If Timothy Hampton, in *Fictions of Embassy* is right, that by the middle of the sixteenth century new forms of diplomatic practice had emerged across Europe, forms that installed new techniques and structures of representation, and that this diplomatic practice had become the subject of 'plays, poems, and essays', 'Diplomacy and its rituals' offering 'a storehouse of stock figures, scenarios, and problems' that were 'appropriated by influential writers' – among them, William Shakespeare – how did the knowledge transfer occur?[4] What could the playwright have known about diplomacy? How could he have known it?

To address one set of questions I return to the two sequences from *Antony and Cleopatra* to read against them early modern theorizations of diplomacy that help me unpack what they're doing politically and theatrically. To think further about Hampton's points, and what for me emerges from them – that is, the specific issue of knowledge transfer – I want to shift my ground from fictions to 'real' political life, from embassies staged to embassies enacted between London and Venice, to trace a possible affiliation, to ask not 'what' the playwright knew, but 'who'.[5]

THEORIZING DIPLOMACY

When Shakespeare began work on *Antony and Cleopatra* around 1605, two books on the subject of the ambassador were in print in England, both written by jurists who were resident foreigners in England and Protestant asylum seekers. Both authors were of an age, born in 1552 and incorporated – that is, their degrees awarded by foreign universities recognized by the Oxford colleges that admitted them as scholars –

on the same day in 1581; both were consulted by the Privy Council on the Mendoza affair, 1584, when the Spanish ambassador caused an international diplomatic crisis, being found implicated in an assassination plot against Elizabeth; and both of them, theorizing diplomacy, consulted history, pondering Roman Antony's treatment of Caesar's ambassador (citing it three times to different ends, to illustrate that 'how absolute soeuer the Prince . . . the respect and ciuilitie which [the ambassador] looketh for, is reciprocall on his part', to reflect that civil war puts particular pressure on diplomatic conventions, and to discriminate between permissible 'liberty of speech' and punishable 'insult'[6]).

The Italian, Alberico Gentili published *De Legationibus Libri Tres* in 1585, a book emerging directly out of the theoretical problems posed by Mendoza's case, that went into several editions, but not into English. The Frenchman Jean Hotman's *The Ambassador* appeared in 1603. Gentili's was 'the first systematic work' to investigate the 'special field of the Law of Nations';[7] Hotman's, by his own claim, 'the first' to speak 'of the duty of the ambassador in your language' – that is, English.[8]

Interested in describing the 'pattern of the excellent ambassador' (201) and aiming their treatises at 'such as . . . might be called to the great affaires of the common wealth' (sig. A4), both writers began with histories and definitions that established the antiquity of the institution and the weight of its charge. 'There never has been a sovereign', wrote

---

4 Timothy Hampton, *Fictions of Embassy: Literature and Diplomacy in Early Modern Europe* (London, 2009), pp. 1–2.

5 On the uses (and limits) of speculation in current Shakespeare studies, see Péter Dávidházi's 'Redefining Knowledge' in this *Survey*. I'm grateful to him for reading and commenting on this article; and also to Barbara Hodgdon, Peter Mack, William Ingram and Thomas Docherty for shrewd, sensitive and informed responses.

6 See Hotman, sigs. F6, F6v; Alberico Gentili, *De Legationibus Libri Tres*, translated by Gordon J. Laing (London, 1964), pp. 82, 120. Further internal citation, by page number, is to this translation.

7 Gentili, 'Introduction', p. 22a.

8 Quoted, Gentili, 'Introduction', p. 22a.

Gentili, 'or ever can be one, who is able to rule an empire without assistants'; it was because 'the policies of councillors' were 'so closely connected with the policy of the sovereign that the Roman emperors held that their councillors were part of their own person, and asserted that any injury done to them was violence done to themselves' (iv, v). In this formulation, we begin to see the ambassador as stand-in, or deputy, for the sovereign, 'my other self', and his role as, like an actor's, an impersonation, performative, with, as we will see, the conditions of his instructions opening up a space of improvisation, of 'free play'.

It was, according to Gentili borrowing an idea from Josephus, 'God who . . . made angels' the first ambassadors, to treat between heaven and earth: a scenario we see played out between Gabriel and the Virgin in hundreds of *Annunciations* (51). But he might have derived it from another contemporary core text on the subject, *Il Messaggiero*. For Torquato Tasso, the angel mediated between heaven and earth right enough; but his human counterpart, the ambassador, was 'il ruffiano', the pimp, a procurer, like a bawd, who brings people together.[9] It will be well to keep this split functionality in mind.

Producing etymologies, Gentili offered 'legate' and 'orator' as 'broader titles' for the ambassador: the first 'means one who has been sent', being derived from *legare*, 'to send'; while *orare* is 'to speak' or 'take someone's part' (5). An ambassador is a specialist in each area, being the state's legate and orator: 'The Ambassador', wrote Hotman, 'makes the Prince to speake' (sig. E5v). He 'is a statesman and is invested with the personality of his prince' (158), 'sent not only by the state, but also in the name of the state, and as the representative of the state' – but 'without the right of supreme command' (7). That is, he never speaks for himself; he is never, according to Gentili, permitted 'to think beyond his instructions' (17). His brief is weightier than a messenger's, who carries 'barely some word of mouth or letter, without authoritie to treate of any matter' (sig. B3v). He acts 'vnder the assurance of the publike faith, authorized by the law of nations', 'to negociate with forraine Princes or Commonwealths', 'and with dignitie to represent' his master's 'greatnesse during their Ambassage' (sig. B2).

That idea of the princely mouthpiece protected 'infallibly within the sanctuarie of the Lawe of Nations' (14), that is, the *ius gentium*, is fundamental. It establishes ambassadorial immunity, the inviolable safety of the person, registered absolutely in natural and immutable law. 'The right of embassy', wrote Gentili quoting Cicero, 'is defended by a rampart of human and divine authority' (58). And Hotman: 'Euery man knoweth, that by the laws of God & man, euen amongst barbarous nations, and in the middest of the armes and armies of enemies, the person of an Ambassador hath in all ages beene adjudged holy, sacred, and inuiolable' (sig. H2). Any who 'does violence to an ambassador violates the good faith of the state and the prince', commits 'an attack on the state' (96). The very 'person of the Prince seemeth to be violated in the person of the Ambassador' (sig. G5v). For this reason, 'the punishments of those that haue done violence vnto them, haue in all times beene very rigorous: this lawe being growne into a prouerbe: *Legatus neque caeditor neque violatur*' (sig. H2v).

Doubtless, immunity is right for the 'angel'. But what about the 'pimp'? What about the ambassador sent undercover as a spy, 'or for the sole purpose of hindering, baffling, and deceiving the person to whom he has been sent?' (67). The jurists were very clear on this. Since 'the whole grace' and 'the fruite' of an embassy 'hath no other end than *Honour*' (sig. D5), dishonourable embassies are oxymorons. The 'respect, freedome and assurance which [ambassadors] haue for their Maisters sakes, giueth them no libertie to doe euill' and 'a colourable Ambassage is so much the more to be punished, because oftentimes it concerneth the ruine of an Estate [i.e. State]' (sig. H4v). 'To lie, deceiue, betray . . . is directly against the Commaundement of God, against the Lawes of Nature, and of Nations'; more heinously, it is a violating

---

9 I am indebted to Hampton for this idea, *Fictions of Embassy*, p. 5.

of 'the publike faith, without which, humane societie, and finally the frame of the world would be dissoluled': the end of civilization as we know it (sig. H7). Further, 'all laws ordaine, that hee which abuseth his priuiledge, maketh himself vnworthy therof, and looseth it' (sig. H4v): 'in vaine, hee putteth himself vnder the sauegard of nations which violateth the lawe of nations' (sig. H5). Suppose, then, that a sovereign 'should order his ambassador to lie, break his word, or commit any disgraceful act of similar character' – such as corrupting a woman – what should he do? Fidelity, says Gentili, is the highest virtue in the ambassador (162); 'We owe to our sovereign fortune and life itself, and the ambassador will gladly give up both to prove his loyalty to his master.' But he should never 'abandon religion or virtue'. Nor can he claim immunity if he does. Perfidious ambassadors 'betray international law' (174). (Of course they both knew they were setting out the ideal, that, in actuality, 'there is not almost any publike charge, wherein there is more lying, and sometimes by the Masters commaundement, and for the good of his seruice' than diplomacy (sig. E6); that indeed, 'some call' ambassadors 'honourable Spies' (sig. I4).)

To avoid falling foul of ambiguity or a sovereign who changes his mind, before he sets out the ambassador should get his instructions to the letter, preferably in writing. But if he is given 'free instructions', '*de libero mandato*' to 'do what shall seem best to him', with 'full libertie to treate, doe, and conclude' what is 'iudged to be profitable for the seruice' of the 'Soueraigne' (178, sig. F3) – like the (otherwise anonymous) French ambassador who went into negotiations 'armed with . . . a blank sheet of paper' (178) – he should pay 'strict attention to the appointment' and exhibit the 'greatest prudence' (179). These are the trickiest assignments, the ones most likely to trap the ambassador in a 'laborinth' (sig. I1).

So, given that 'some affaires' he is charged with will be 'so secret, so important, so urgent, so desperate, that it is expedient to commit all to the wisedome of the Ambassador' 'without binding his tongue and hands' (sigs. F3v, F5) what sort of man is right for the job? Gentili and Hotman both provide full personal briefs – the 'compleat' ambassador being epitomized for the Italian in that nonpareil of Elizabethan courtiers, a young man who had already represented his monarch abroad, and the dedicatee of Gentili's treatise, Philip Sidney. But besides wanting him to know history, rhetoric, moral and political philosophy, and three languages, to have travelled, to be eloquent, stuffed with virtues, well-bred, and 'favored by fortune' (both of them citing as 'shameful' that 'Louis XI of France stooped to . . . employing a barber as ambassador'), they agreed that even the most unlikely men had succeeded as ambassadors, men whose study was literature, men 'summoned from their schools, although they had never participated in any kind of public life' – and 'even women' (159). Menenius Agrippa was sent 'to the people as ambassador . . . because he himself was of plebeian origin' (143). Only the 'embassy of women . . . obtained from [Coriolanus] what was wanted'. They conclude: 'Great indeed, great is the power that rests in the personality of the ambassador' (144).

STAGING THEORY

How then might we apply the jurists' theories, see them in conversation with diplomatic practice as Shakespeare portrays it in *Antony and Cleopatra*? They make an interesting fit. Sending his Schoolmaster ambassador to Caesar in 3.12 Antony is not like Louis 'employing a barber' but rather like him 'that appoynteth an Ambassador' who looks well 'to the disposition of him to whome hee is sent (sig. B6v) by nicely balancing in his 'other self' antithetical attitudes of humility and authority. In his ambassador Antony displays both: the man who is 'dew' on the 'myrtle leaf' is humble enough; the orator-mouthpiece who frames that analogy displays rhetorical power. The Schoolmaster's performance, then, potentially undoes Dolabella's 'argument' that Antony's 'plucked' when hither / He sends so poor a pinion of his wing'. Framing this as an ambassadorial moment, not just as a messaging service, Shakespeare mobilizes all of the established protocols of audience and immunity. Clearly, the Schoolmaster has been given limited instructions with 'authoritie to treate' with Caesar: he starts with courtesies that speak the political reality ('Lord of his fortunes') and the principal demand (Antony 'Requires to live in Egypt'). Then evidently alert to a reaction in Caesar, mid-line, modifies 'requires' to 'requests', and 'lessens' the suit, to Caesar's allowance simply 'To let him breathe . . . / A private man in Athens'. Here is an ambassador who is picking up signals and reading the political moment acutely. 'Next', he communicates what Cleopatra 'craves', positioning her, like Antony, as submissive to Caesar's 'greatness', but not abject: she claims her crown – impudent, given the circumstances. The ambassador, however, neatly turns her bluster, mediates it in the delivery with hard political truth that itself is instantly mediated. Her crown isn't hers; it's 'hazarded' – but (a diplomatic grace note) hazarded to Caesar's 'grace'.

The speech is a perfect textbook display of ambassadorial competence: 'graue, briefe, and significant' (sig. C3). He doesn't even need the last full iambic line to finish his message. He's properly impassive. He makes no answer to Caesar's diplomatic blanking of his master ('I have no ears to his request') nor to the treacherous bargain he conditionally proposes as Cleopatra's ransom, assassination the price of her (hypothetical) safety: 'if' she 'From Egypt' will 'drive her all-disgraced friend / Or take his life there . . . / She shall not sue unheard'. Escorted safely 'through the bands', he completes his mission in 3.13 by reporting Caesar's message back to Antony, making clear its terms: 'Is that his answer?' asks Antony. 'The Queen shall then have courtesy, so she / Will yield us up.' The ambassador is monosyllabic: 'He says so.' So is Antony: 'Let her know't.'

Had this scene been turned over to Shakespeare's lawyer contemporaries in one of the Inns of Court, it might have kept benchers in arguments for years. The monstrous ransom: does it, or not, violate the law of nations? Of course, the joke transaction it turns upon is one Shakespeare has used before: Cleopatra can keep her crown if she hands over her lover's – Antony's 'crown' troped in his 'grizzled head'.

Be that as it may, as I'm reading him, Antony's Schoolmaster-turned-ambassador has acted the angel, setting the pattern for appropriate diplomatic service. Something very different happens in the reciprocal mission. Authorizing Thidias 'in our name' to 'promise' 'what [Cleopatra] requires', Caesar in 3.12 issues him with 'free instructions', 'to add more, / From thine invention, offers'. So Thidias will have, in Hotman's terms, 'full libertie to treate, doe, and conclude' what is 'profitable for the seruice of his Soueraigne' [sig. F3]. And what is 'profitable'? What Caesar is instructing is that his ambassador corrupt the Prince he's meeting, the 'offers' he intends suggestively elaborated in his next sentence, where 'want' is tied to 'perjure'. Thidias is to be 'cunning'; to be active ('Try'). To 'win Cleopatra', he is to invent whatever conditions he likes, regardless of their lawfulness ('Make thine own edict for thy pains'). Caesar – like some anarchic imperial pre-vision of Jack Cade making 'the laws of England' out of 'my mouth' (2 Henry VI, 4.7.5, 12) – 'Will answer' these 'as a law'.[10] Given this set-up, it's hardly likely that Caesar's further charge, telling Thidias to 'Observe how Antony becomes his flaw', is simply instructing neutral witness. It's politically voyeuristic. He wants Thidias to spy, to report what 'thou think'st his very action speaks'.

Thidias, then, is to play the pimp. It's a performance Enobarbus watches in 3.13 where, as one ambassador exits at line 28 – Shakespeare's stagecraft here is brilliant – the other is announced at line 37, first attempting to turn state audience ('Caesar's will?') to private conference ('Hear it apart'); then, when that fails, opening with a gambit, a shrewdly turned diplomatic phrase, that will allow Cleopatra to treat Caesar as a liberator, herself as the victim-kept-captive: 'He knows that you embrace not Antony / As you did love, but as you feared him.' Thidias offers Cleopatra a diplomatic escape route – and she appears to take it ('He . . . is most right'). Enobarbus, 'To be sure of that', exits to 'ask

---

10 Understanding this line as referring to ambassadorial protocol, I gloss it differently from the Arden editor's 'Decide for yourself how much you should be paid for your trouble.'

Antony'. There follows a shift in register (Thidias politically representing Caesar as the beggar, the prop to Cleopatra's weakness, the 'shroud' – nicely ambiguous – to cover her metaphoric nakedness); tone ('What's your name?', asks Cleopatra, seeming to cosy up to the proxy-Caesar); and intimacy (Cleopatra, sending by the deputy a metaphoric 'kiss' for Caesar's 'conqu'ring hand', permits the deputy to reverse 'duty' and (literally) kiss hers).

So far Thidias's audience has been going well. The ambassador's rhetorical flourishes have been elegant, the metaphors, enabling ('begs'/'give'; 'staff'/'lean'; 'warm'/'shroud'). But then, does Thidias miscalculate? Count on his ambassadorial 'cover' too securely? 'Think beyond his instructions' in moving from words to actions? Antony enters, sees the kiss, roars, 'Favours?' Thidias outfaces him. Enobarbus predicts 'You will be whipped.' Thidias protests. But 'I-am-Antony-yet' ignores him: 'Tug him away!'; 'Whip him . . . . / Till like a boy you see him cringe his face / And whine aloud for mercy.'

Thidias's protest is right. He's safeguarded by diplomatic immunity. Everyone knows that 'the person of an Ambassador' 'euen amongst barbarous nations' 'in all ages' has been judged 'inuiolable'. In sending Thidias to be flogged, and 'boyed', Antony is not simply Hercules-in-love hyperbolically maddened by jealousy, by some 'fellow' being 'familiar' with his 'playfellow', Cleopatra's hand, and needing to humiliate him. Antony is violating the law of nations, committing an 'attack' upon the 'person of the Prince' whom Thidias stands in for, making war by other means. He's 'boying' the 'boy' Caesar. The violence is political and, ironically, a proxy for the one-on-one combat ('sword against sword') that Antony, before Enobarbus interrupted him, was in another room, writing in a letter – a dare that Caesar will shrilly decline ('Let the old ruffian know / I have many other ways to die' (4.1.4–5)). What Caesar dodges, Thidias – his 'other self' – suffers. But to appreciate the enormity of Antony's transgression, we must appreciate the scale of what he's violating. Such outrage upon an ambassador tropes another fall of man 'againe', wrote

Hotman, 'into that first Chaos, and confusion of things' (sig. H2v).

Or maybe Thidias isn't right. Maybe Antony's right. 'What', we remember Gentili asking, of the ambassador sent 'for the sole purpose of hindering, baffling, and deceiving the person to whom he has been sent?' (67). Doesn't perfidy justify 'inflicting . . . a punishment more drastic than dismissal'? Isn't 'pimping' Cleopatra what Caesar instructed? Hasn't Enobarbus seen her corrupted, heard her claim her 'honour was not yielded / But conquered merely'? Isn't that the information he takes to Antony? If Caesar objects to his ambassador's treatment, Hotman answers him: 'in vaine, hee putteth himself vnder the sauegard of nations which violateth the lawe of nations' (sig. H5).

Or maybe neither is right. Maybe pretending the angel to play the pimp, Thidias doesn't know whose comedy he's in, and maybe Enobarbus leaves the scene too soon – and with the wrong 'notice' of performance. For who is 'baffling' whom in 3.13's theatre of diplomatic exchange? Certainly, Thidias is playing a part, one cued by that misogynist premise so thoroughly absorbed into cultural performance that no man pauses to check it, because it's what 'everybody knows', that 'Women are not / In their best fortunes strong'. But what if Cleopatra, too, is playing a part? Not deceived, but deceiving? In the Folio, her reply to Thidias's opening offer is a single word – or sound: 'O'. How is 'O' performed? What does 'O' mean? Capitulation? Recognition? Or is 'O' a kind of actorly measuring of swords: 'O – this is the game'; 'this is the way we're going to play this "scene of excellent dissembling"'? 'O' then might mark Cleopatra's shift from 'self' to 'role' – a shift she later reverses when (brazen? incredulous? weary?) she faces off Antony (who like Thidias and Enobarbus has been taken in by the performance) with 'Not know me yet?' Jean Hotman insists that 'An Ambassage and a Comedie are different things; A man cannot therein play diuerse partes vnder diuers garments' (sig. F7v). But maybe he's wrong. England's future ambassador to Venice, Henry Wotton, will constantly see his 'ambassage' as 'a comedie' and will put himself either on the stage – or in the audience.

Given such ambiguities, it is perhaps theatrically satisfying that the angel Dolabella turns out, at the end of Shakespeare's play, to be 'il ruffiano', the ambassador from Caesar who deceives Caesar – a nice riposte to Peter Shorey's Schoolmaster from 2010, the 'ruffiano' 'master-leaver' whom Mark Antony supposed his good angel.

DIPLOMACY IN ACTION: LONDON, 1603

I turn now to my question about knowledge transfer, about how the playwright knew what he knew. Shakespeare might have read Gentili or Hotman (the latter, hot off the press in 1603). A couple of years earlier, he might have observed ambassadors first-hand (and the scandalized discourse around them), attending as other Londoners did to the spectacular (uninvited) embassy of the Moorish ambassadors from Muly Hamet who arrived in September 1600 and (inconveniently) hung around through the end of the year (while the Court was otherwise occupied on a daily basis with the festering problem of disgraced Essex, under house arrest: ironic, really, since the Moors were in London on account of Essex, emboldened by his Cadiz raid in 1597 now to propose – this, their mission to Elizabeth – 'the total conquest of Spain').[11] Then, too, a couple of years later, around the time he was writing about a 'Moor of Venice', during the post-Christmas holiday weeks when the playing companies were performing at Court (and picking up Court gossip?), Shakespeare may have heard significant news from Venice, news that would lead to personal contact with one Venetian diplomat. It's this thread, leading to 'who', not 'what', that I want to follow.

'BEN VENUTO IN INGHILTERRA, SIGNOR SEGRETARIO'

By 1603, there had been no official representation of the Venetian Republic in England for some forty-three years, since the Papal Bull of 1570 excommunicated Elizabeth, absolving her subjects of allegiance to her laws. Now, however, English piracy in the Mediterranean had grown so brass-necked ('there is not a sailor of that nation but is a pirate,' wrote the Governor of Zante[12]) and costly to the Venetians that the Republic determined to send an agent – without ambassadorial title, pay or suite, functioning as legate and orator – to make complaint to the Queen. Giovanni Carlo Scaramelli, Secretary to the Signoria, was appointed at the end of December 1602, instructed (ambassador-wise) to 'start at once', 'make all speed possible', 'commend to her Majesty's attention the business committed to him', 'stay in England as long as may be necessary', and 'if any thing worthy of notice occurs' to 'report' it (CSPV.9.1113). One of the Republic's 'ablest instruments',[13] Scaramelli, a self-described 'old man', said he'd left Venice 'in such a hurry . . . almost flying one might say' firmly 'in the belief' that his 'mission would last a few days only' that he packed only 'one trunk' (CSPV.10.69, 78). He avoided shipwreck crossing to Dover from Calais, arriving in London on 28 January[14] to learn from Robert Cecil, Elizabeth's Secretary of State (through whose 'hands', wrote Scaramelli, 'pass all the affairs of the Government'), that the Queen was at Richmond. The Venetian attended her there on 9 February. This audience produced in Scaramelli's detailed dispatch our last long look at England's aged queen, which begins:

---

[11] Bernard Harris, 'A Portrait of a Moor', in *Shakespeare Survey* 11 (Cambridge, 1958), pp. 89–97. In October, John Chamberlain knew about the 'Barbarians'. See Norman Egbert McClure, ed., *The Letters of John Chamberlain* (Philadelphia, 1939), vol. I, p. 107.

[12] Horatio Brown, ed., *Calendar of State Papers Venetian*, vol. 10, (London, 1900). Further citations use a compressed form, giving the volume and entry numbers; here, CSPV.10.27.

[13] Henry Wotton to Robert Cecil, National Archive SP99.2, f.167.

[14] We must keep in mind, dating these moves, that the Venetians (and most of the rest of Europe) used the 'stilo nuovo', the Gregorian calendar, while the English retained the 'OS' – old style – Julian system. The English calendar, then, was ten days 'behind' the Venetian, 1 January in England being 11 January in Venice. I give dates by the English calendar.

Era la regina in quel giorno vestita di tabì d'argento e bianco fregiato d'oro, con abito aperto alquanto davanti sì che mostrava la gola, cinta di perle e di rubini fino a mezzo il petto...La testa avea di capelli di un color chiaro che non lo può far la natura.[15]

But what occupied him more nearly was her (dry? wry? teasing?) opening greeting, spoken in Italian, 'Sia ben venuto in Inghilterra il segretario. È ben ora che la Repubblica mandi a vedere una regina che l'ha tanto onorata in tutte le occasioni.'[16] 'Ben ora' indeed. She'd only been waiting, she said, '44 anni' for the Republic to recognize her, and wondered (a thought worthy of Cleopatra) whether it was 'mio sesso' – 'my sex' – that was the problem. But how could that be, when she was recognized by other Princes – ones to whom the Republic *did* send ambassadors? Scaramelli finessed whatever tartness he may have heard, replied that since she had reigned so magisterially for such a long time he knew she was no novice to the ways of the world ('nuova nelle cose del mondo') but understood that 'tutti i principi si governano secondo gli accidenti' – leaving those 'accidenti' diplomatically unspecified. Saying only, further, that the Venetian Republic made up her own political mind, taking instruction from no one, either secular or ecclesiastic. (So much for the Papal Bull.) This answer satisfied Elizabeth, and the ambassador achieved his diplomatic object, Elizabeth agreeing to appoint Commissioners to examine the piracy of the 'Speranza', and to do it 'senza dilazione', without delay. Before giving him her hand to kiss (a second time in this audience) and licence to depart, she added her own grace note: 'non so se avrò ben parlato in questa lingua italiana, pur perchè io la imparai da fanciulla credo che sì di non avermela scordata'.[17] So not only were formal relations reopened; they were reopened in Italian. The Queen spoke the language she'd learned as a child. Scaramelli may have been grateful. He evidently had no English. (Why would he? According to one contemporary teach-yourself-Italian textbook, English was 'a language what wyl do you good in England, but passe Douer, it is woorth nothing.'[18]) Communicating in Italian, they needed no interpreters.

Elizabeth was as good as her word. The following day, the three Commissioners were named, one of them, Edward Wotton, Comptroller of Her Majesty's Household. Swift satisfaction looked to be on the cards. A cheerful Secretary wrote of his hopeful result 'upon the first of the missions imposed on me' (CSVP.9.1143). By 17 February, however, he was back to diplomatic square one. He'd received reports from home of another notorious piracy, the galleon 'Veniera', looted of rich Venetian cargo. Worse, some of the loot belonged to the Venetian consul on board. Diplomatic outrage, then, compounded commercial injury.

For the next three weeks, Scaramelli waited on the Commissioners. He occupied himself with writing home once, sometimes twice a week, long 'state of England' dispatches, one of them profiling the various claimants to the English throne, their historic rights ('White Rose' v. 'Red Rose') and likelihood of succeeding. Some information he felt was sensitive enough to require encoding, like the description of 'Secretary Cecil' as 'omnipotent in all the affairs of State', and the determination of the Privy Council 'not to be governed by a woman again, but to give the Crown to the King of Scotland' (CSPV.9.1143). On 10 March, he 'sought an audience of the Queen in order to conclude the business entrusted to me so that I might return to [Venice and] the feet of your Serenity.' She replied that she 'desired to discuss

---

[15] CSPV.10.1135. 'The Queen that day was dressed in silver and white taffeta, decorated with gold, open at the front, showing her throat, circled with pearls and rubies reaching down her breast...The hair on her head was a light colour that nature can't make.' I'm grateful to Giorgio Bertellini for checking my translations.

[16] 'The Secretary is welcome to England. It's a good time for the Republic to send someone [or: it's about time that the Republic sent someone] to see a queen who has honoured her so highly on all occasions.'

[17] 'I do not know whether I have spoken Italian well, but because I learned it as a girl, I believe, indeed, that I haven't forgotten it.'

[18] John Florio's *First Fruits* (1578), Dialogue 15; quoted in Frances Yates, *John Florio: The Life of an Italian in Shakespeare's England* (Cambridge, 1934), p. 32.

pleasant topics only', not business, which could wait, the Commissioners' meeting having been delayed by the death of Elizabeth's cousin and dearest female courtier, Kate Carey Howard, Countess of Nottingham, wife of the Lord Admiral, one of the Commissioners. 'The Queen', Scaramelli reported, 'for many days has never left her chamber', though whether it was grief for Kate or anxiety about subjects' manoeuvrings for succession that was on her mind he couldn't say. She was 'suddenly withdrawn into herself'. Scaramelli was doing his best to 'prevent ... public affairs from interfering with the despatch of my particular business'; he wanted to get home; he had 'no desire to be a witness of what may shortly happen here' (CSPV.9.1159).

And then he was that witness. On 17 March he wrote in code of the Queen's last illness, her 'mind ... overwhelmed by a grief greater than she could bear'. Only the day before, she had at last granted the Irish rebel, Tyrone, a pardon, which had made her reflect that she'd been wrong about Essex, that 'he might have been quite innocent after all' when, 'each on horseback on different sides of a river' he'd concluded the truce with Tyrone in September 1599 that had led to his disgrace, rebellion and death. Now, the Privy Council 'was convened in perpetual session at Richmond'. The City of London, which, 'incredibly', is 'unprotected by walls', was taking steps against the 'universal dread of dangerous uprisings'. On 25 March, 'Her Majesty's life' was 'absolutely despaired of'. A postscript added: the 'Queen's death ... took place last evening' (CSPV.9.1166).

Now Secretary Scaramelli and his one trunk were stuck. Diplomatically marooned. He needed instructions. But his dispatch would take twenty-two days to reach Venice; the Senate's reply twenty-two days to reach him (CSPV.10.261). Meanwhile, he waited, observed, conducted the business he could (the 'Veniera' case dragged on); he wrote – both gossip and hard information. In March, he sent an extensive character of the Queen and a translation of James's accession proclamation; in April, notice that the new king 'resolved to maintain the heresy' – that is, reformed religion in England – which would 'cut all the Catholic princes to the heart'. While James was en route from Scotland via Berwick, sending before him a reputation for being 'a man of letters and of business' (an opinion that would shortly be revised), 'fond of the chase and of riding', speaking 'Latin and French perfectly', and understanding 'Italian quite well', the dead queen was 'lying in the palace of Westminster' where 'the Council waits on her continually with the same ceremony, the same expenditure, down to her very household and table service as though she were not wrapped in many a fold of cere-cloth ... but was walking as she used to do ... about ... her gardens' (CSPV.10.6). Scaramelli did not attend the funeral, to avoid 'entering the church and attending heretic services', but he observed the rehabilitation of those out-of-favour courtiers who had survived the Queen's displeasure: Southampton, released from the Tower, and Devereux's son, the little Earl of Essex, made 'eternal companion' to James's son, the boy-Prince of Wales. For Catholics, though, there were signs that their expectations for toleration in the new regime (nurtured while Scots James was English-king-in-waiting) would be disappointed. Every pulpit in the land was instructed to announce the King's policy: 'only one God in heaven, one King and one Christian religion only in England' (CSPV.10.40).

On 10 May, Scaramelli finally received cheering news: two ambassadors were coming, an 'extraordinary', to congratulate the new king, an 'ordinary', Nicolò Molino, to reside (CSPV.10.43). Of course, they wouldn't arrive for months. Meanwhile, Secretary Scaramelli had to stay put. 'I have been here', he wrote on 9 June, 'months, and will have to stay on six or seven more at the least ...', required 'to maintain a decent state'. But on his 'poor pay' that was impossible, not least because the currency exchange rate between London and Venice was 18 per cent to which was added a 4 per cent bank charge (CSPV.10.78). The Signory read his mind, on 15 June providing Scaramelli's maintenance 'at the public cost and a salary of 120 crowns a month' (this, against Molino's ambassadorial pay of 200 ducats per month (CSPV.10.79)[19].

Across these weeks the ambassador assiduously posted information, news, comment-as-analysis: the big topics, a Catholic assassination plot against the King (CSPV.10.40), the coronation set for July (CSPV.10.40), crowds flooding into London (CSPV.10.55), knighthoods – 700 in two months – proliferating (CSPV.10.106), and the sudden outbreak of plague. Scaramelli reported fourteen deaths in six infected parishes one week in May, a mortality he'd report rising relentlessly, horrifically to 4,000 a week by September (CSPV.10.55, 132). The new government was arousing plenty of animosity as 'every day posts' were 'taken from the English and given to the Scotch', resentment exacerbated by James's 'Great Britain project', his determination 'to extinguish both names', and to put 'both people . . . under the common name of Britons' (CSPV.10.69, 132).

Personally, Scaramelli had little to complain of. Arriving in London, 'The King had not been two hours in [his royal apartments in] the Tower of London – in sight of which, and hard by, I have my lodging in a house in the borough, quite new, with a great Italian garden, belonging to a merchant of Lucca – when his Majesty sent one of his gentlemen' to invite him to an audience (CSPV.10.56). At Greenwich on 18 May, the Secretary pushed through 'such a crowd that I never saw the like', 'upwards of ten or twelve thousand persons' to reach the King who, 'from his dress . . . would have been taken for the meanest among the courtiers, a modesty he affects, had it not been for a chain of diamonds around his neck' (CSPV.10.66). The Venetian's 'discourse was brief', James replying, 'I know that you speak French, and so I will employ that language so as to dispense with an interpreter, for I cannot speak Italian as I could wish.' Their future audiences would be conducted in French (see also CSPV.10.102, 142).

But for the rest, Scaramelli seemed to be watching a monarchy unravelling: a king who'd set himself up as 'the real arbiter of peace' principally because he desired 'to have no bother with other people's affairs and little with his own', wanting

'to dedicate himself to his books and to the chase' (CSPV.10.73).

By July, Scaramelli was having to trail around the country (Richmond, Oatlands, Windsor, Sunbury, Salisbury) behind the king's hunting party (the king, at one point, helpfully giving him a route-map so he would know where to look for him), behind the Court, trying to keep distance between it and the plague, writing of a king who seemed to have abdicated his government; who'd turned his state business over to Secretary Cecil, seeming 'to have forgotten that he is a king except in his kingly pursuit of stags, to which he is quite foolishly devoted' (CSPV.10.101). Scaramelli reported on St James's Day the gorgeous but limited spectacle of the coronation. Londoners were told to stay home because, by this day in July, 1,000 of them a week were dying of plague (CSPV.10.105). 'Upwards of two hundred thousand persons have fled' the city, wrote Scaramelli. 'The terror is all the greater, for they still bury the dead to the sound of the parish bells'; 'no steps are taken about the sick, except to close the infected houses and commend them to the mercy of God' (CSPV.10.118).

More happily for Scaramelli, by mid-August he was planning his diplomatic handover (CSPV.10.117). He'd established with Cecil that, in terms of religious observance, Ambassador Molino 'would be allowed to exercise the Roman rite in his house [that is, in private, in the space of diplomatic immunity] for the benefit of his suite of those Venetian and Italians' living in London. Cecil countered that when an English Ambassador was 'sent to reside in Venice' he 'should enjoy a similar privilege'. Scaramelli argued that the cases were not comparable, for 'at the present moment there were no Venetians in London, except the two brothers Federici . . . and only six or seven other Italians', who would hardly be noticed attending the ambassador's house for Catholic mass, 'whereas in Venice there were thousands of English', so many that a

---

19 That is, £30 vs. £93 15s, there being four crowns to the pound and 9 shillings and 4 pence to the ducat, also called 'zecchino' from the Venetian 'zecca' ('mint'), Englished 'chequin'.

specialist 'English lodging-house' catered for them (CSPV.10.165). Offering Protestant communion, the English Ambassador 'might draw such a number of people as would certainly cause a scandal and might invite reprisals'.[20] He suggested – mischievously? straight-faced? – to Cecil that since 'there were about the Court many able men, openly declared Catholics, and still more living in retirement, his Majesty might choose one of these for the post of Ambassador' to Venice. And he further suggested to one of those Catholics, Lord Crichton of Sanquhar, that he should apply for the job. Sanquhar did; and was promised it. A Catholic ambassador, wrote Scaramelli home with diplomatic understatement, would 'free your Serenity of many anxieties' (CSPV.10.118).

But the bad news at the end of August was that the king seemed 'to have sunk into a lethargy of pleasures', would 'not take any heed of matters of state', 'remits everything to his Council' (CSPV.10.125). By September, the poor Flemish ambassador had waited forty days for an audience; the Spanish, nearly as long (CSPV.10.136). In mid-October it was clear to Scaramelli that the Great Britain project was dead in the water. Who cared, when 'all public and private affairs' were 'in absolute confusion', 'forty thousand persons' in 'the City of London alone, in seven months' having been 'carried off' by plague, and 'still dying at the rate of 1,500 a week'? 'No one will pay his debts, as he thinks his creditor must die one day or another. All orders on merchants have been recalled, all trade is at a standstill. Taxes, duties, customs bring in not a ducat in the whole city... the Treasury is in confusion, and without a penny in it... exchange from London to Venice is at 28%, and falling still' (CSPV.10.147).

Still, in that same dispatch he thought 'the illustrious Ambassadors must be... at Calais'; in 'two days' he'd be 'on [his] way to Dover'. It wasn't until the end of November that his English mission was completed: Molino had his first audience with James on 20 November (CSPV.10.164), and two weeks later, private audiences and lunches with the King and the Prince of Wales. The man who'd fronted Venetian relations until now,

talking directly with the principals, was returned to secretarial duties, fetching and carrying, briefing – and dining in another room (CSPV.10.166–170). On 15 December Molino wrote, from London, that 'No one ever mentions the plague, no more than if it had never been.' And: 'Tomorrow Scaramelli leaves for Holland' and home (CSPV.10.175), exactly a year after he'd crossed La Serenissima's lagoon on the mission he thought 'would last a few days only' – he, and his 'one trunk'.

Scaramelli was the 'compleat' civil servant. Except for his little moan about money, he never complained. Plucked from secretarial duties in the Signoria, assigned a quick mission to London, virtually Antony's 'extraordinary' Schoolmaster, he was accidentally made 'resident', unwillingly 'witness', the eyes of the Republic. Watching day-to-day the fraught business of England's transition of power, the reconstitution of the central government, he represented to the Signoria the view of England-under-James that would frame Anglo-Venetian politics over the course of years, not least, during the international 'Interdict crisis' that was even now shaping up for Venice, which would have Venice defensively dependent on England, and on a king 'kingly' only in his 'pursuit of stags'.

Venice knew England by what Scaramelli wrote of England. How was he prepared for this turn of events that made him inter-governmental reporter: information gatherer and communicator? What Venetian training did he have, equipping a mentality for this business? And what framework of assumptions about information gathering and reportage was in place governing the circulation of political communication, the Venetian end of which Filippo de Vivo has so brilliantly explored?[21]

---

[20] He probably wasn't miscalculating. A count of Italians living in London in 1580 put the number at 116 – a drop from 140 in 1567 (see G. K. Hunter, *Dramatic Identities and Cultural Tradition* (Liverpool, 1978), p. 21). What he didn't admit was the claim the English ambassador would later make, that most of the Englishmen resident in Venice were Catholic ex-pats (CSPV.10.282).

[21] de Vivo's seminal work is *Information and Communication in Venice: Rethinking Early Modern Politics* (Oxford, 2007).

Not speaking English, how did he pick up the news and gossip he relayed (so much of which can be read against the letters of that thoroughly English, indefatigable news-writer, John Chamberlain)? Who were his sources? Was he isolated – coming without the kind of personal suite that would have attended an ambassador, allegedly one of only three Venetians in London, lodging in the merchant's house of Lucca? Did he circulate among the Italian-speaking English intelligentsia? (Certainly, court business would have brought him in contact with Edward Wotton, an Italian-speaker.) Or was the French connection his network – via, for one, Robert Cecil? Was he bored? How did he occupy himself during those long waits – we remember the Flemish ambassador's 40-day frustration – for audience? Answers to these questions await further research. But what is certain is what seems never to have been noticed before, that by April 1603 Scaramelli had one English-born Italian to talk to: John Florio, author of the Italian-English dialogue books, the *First* (and *Second*) *Fruits* (1578, 1591), the Italian/English dictionary, *Worlde of Wordes* (1598) and, most famously, the book that would come out this year (whose 'first begetter' was his benefactor, Edward Wotton), the translation of Montaigne's *Essayes* (1603).[22]

Seeing a friendship with Florio opens up Scaramelli's access to extended networks – and theirs to him. He might have been introduced to old friends like Gentili, and to the illustrious, like the Countesses Bedford and Rutland, Penelope Rich (Essex's sister), all dedicatees of the Montaigne, to Southampton, newly released from the Tower (like Rutland, once Florio's tutee; latterly, Florio's patron and, like Rutland, dedicatee of the 1598 *Wordes*), to William Herbert, Earl of Pembroke, another tutee, the 'handsome youth . . . always with the King, always joking with him' (CSPV.10.105) who quite possibly was responsible for rushing through, in the opening days of the new reign, the patent for Shakespeare's company that elevated them from Chamberlain's to King's Men.[23] Through Florio, Scaramelli could have met the writers Lady Bedford patronized: Jonson (who owned a copy of the *Essayes*), Donne,

Drayton, Chapman, three of them out-of-work playwrights in that plague year, one of them, a couple of years hence, a theatre writer of Venice (who'd inscribe his debt to Florio on the flyleaf of a copy of his *Volpone*).[24]

If he met Jonson through Florio, might Scaramelli also have met through him another writer patronized by Southampton and Pembroke, William Shakespeare? Given their shared circle, it seems unlikely that Shakespeare didn't know personally the man he'd gently lampooned as Holofernes in *Love's Labour's Lost* (1594–5), putting into Holofernes's mouth Florio's version of the proverb 'Venetia, Venetia, chi non ti vede non ti pretia'. Shakespeare's interest in the 'matter' of Venice was evident: he'd treated it in *The Merchant of Venice* (1596–7). Now, throughout 1603, he'd occupy himself with his most ambitious Venetian project to date: *Othello, The Moor of Venice*, a play King James, some months hence, would settle down to watch at Whitehall even as his envoy, the first English ambassador to the Republic in near fifty years, was making his way across Europe to Venice. Did Florio give the playwright access to the Venetian secretary, to one who would certainly 'know our country disposition well'?

Three letters in the National Archive (London), dated April and September 1603, testify to Scaramelli's friendship with Florio. The final one (Illustration 19), posted from Sunbury, where Scaramelli was lodged, waiting for a break in the King's hunting routine that might permit an audience, refers, opaquely, diplomatically but with some irritation, to frustrations and, it appears, business left hanging, framed as unfulfilled 'desire':

---

22 Neither DNB nor Yates in *John Florio* makes the identification; for the Wotton connection, see Yates, *John Florio*, p. 220.

23 See Yates, *John Florio*, pp. 284, 299; Florio later bequeathed Pembroke his library. For Pembroke's role in securing the exceptional patent, see J. Leeds Barroll, *Politics, Plague, and Shakespeare's Theatre* (London, 1991), pp. 38–42. I am grateful to R. A. Foakes for sending me to Barroll and for reading and commenting on this essay.

24 Yates, *John Florio*, pp. 191, 241, 277–8.

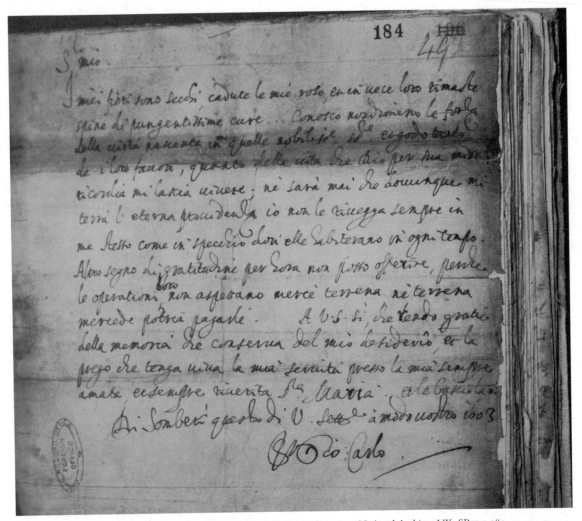

19. Giovanni Carlo Scaramelli to John Florio, 5 September 1603. National Archives UK, SP99.2.184.

Signore mio I miei fiori sono secchi, cadute le mie rose, et in vece loro rimaste spine di pungentissime cure. Conosco nondimeno la forza della virtù nascente in quelle nobilissime Signorie et godo tanto de i loro favori, quanto della vita che Dio per sua misericordia mi lascia vivere; né sarà mai che dovunque mi terrà l'eterna providenza io non le rivegga sempre in me stesso come in specchio dov'elle habiterano in ogni tempo. Altro segno di gratitudine per hora non posso offerire, perché le operationi [interlined: <loro>] non aspettano merce terrena nè terrena mercede potria pagarle. A Vostra Signoria sì, che rendo gratie della memoria che conserva del mio desiderio, et la prego che tenga viva la mia

servitù presso la mia sempre amata, et sempre riverita Signora Maria: et le bascio la mano. Di Somberi questo di V Settembre à modo vostro 1603.

S[flourish] Gio: Carlo[25]

---

[25] NA SP99.2.184. See also SP99.2.157 and SP99.2.183. I'm grateful to Eugenio Refini for correcting my transcription of this letter and Irene Musumeci for checking this translation.

My Lord,

My flowers are dry, my roses fallen, and in their place remain thorns of the most stinging cares. I nevertheless know the force of the virtue budding in those most noble

I will return to this manuscript shortly, when what will interest me is not the letter's contents but its handwriting.

A PARALLEL LIFE

Meanwhile, an English life was taking shape in parallel to the Italian's: Henry Wotton's. He, not Crichton of Sanquhar, would be appointed Venetian ambassador in 1604, coming to the post by education, training and strategic intervention, but also, by anybody's reckoning, accident most strange. So the Venetians finally got not a Catholic, but an ardent Protestant. They got a linguist fluent in Italian, a scholar, a non-risk-averse adventurer, rhetorically expert but not seeming to have outgrown a certain schoolboy habit of wit, equipped with an instinct for the theatrical – whose left foot seemed permanently planted on a banana skin. It's this parallel life I need briefly to trace before seeing two lives converging.

Harry was the younger half-brother of Edward (twenty years his elder), Privy Councillor and King James's Master of the Household, a post he'd retained from Elizabeth, appointed in 1602.[26] As a younger brother, born in 1568, Harry's business from childhood was to make his way in the world. He went to Winchester, getting the same kind of grammar school training William Shakespeare acquired at 'the Kyng's newe Scole of Stratford upon Avon', then to New College, Oxford. He studied civil law under – indeed, was taken into 'a bosom friendship with'– the ex-pat Italian who was then theorizing diplomacy, Alberico Gentili, who also taught him Italian. *De Legationibus Libri Tres* was just published; perhaps it was on Wotton's syllabus. Awarded his BA in 1588, he embarked the following year on 'finishing school', travel across Europe to pick up the kind of contacts and knowledge of foreign courts that would equip him to be useful in Francis Walsingham's new model civil service as a secretary - or ambassador. Not infrequently, arriving somewhere, he would 'find [him]self the only Englishman in this town'.[27] Aiming to further his education in law, he wanted to 'procure by all

possible meanes Franciscus...Hotomanus...to be my master in [tha]t studdye'. To that end, from Heidelberg, Henry wrote his brother a begging letter to secure him an introduction, having 'learned' that 'Hotoman hath a sonne [the very Jean of *The Ambassador*] 'about the Courte in Englande some tyme secretary to the Erle of Lecester's'.[28] When study with Hotman fell through owing to his death, Harry attended law lectures in Vienna, then in August 1591 crossed the Alps into Italy.

The territory, for a Protestant, was dangerous. He wrote of himself 'in continual motion' (Smith, I:271): taking in Pisa, Lucca, Siena, Venice, Padua, Naples, Florence. He rode into Rome theatrically incognito under 'a mighty blue feather in a black hat' – ostentation designed, by the very fact of calling gawpers' attention to himself, to 'prove' he was 'no English'. Equally dramatic was his exit from Rome. Ten days later, he ducked out from dinner leaving the salad course ('our first dish') uneaten when he recognized someone coming in

---

of Ladies whose favours I enjoy as much as the life that God by his mercy allows me to live; wherever Providence may keep me, it shall never be that I will cease to see them within myself as in a mirror where they shall live forever. For now, I cannot offer any other sign of gratitude, because their deeds do not expect [to be repaid by] earthly goods, nor could earthly goods repay them. To Your Lordship indeed I give thanks for the memory you preserve of my desire, and I pray to my always beloved, and always revered Lady Mary, that you maintain my suit alive: and I kiss your hand.

From Sunbury this 5th of September your style 1603

26 Edward Wotton, it seems, was responsible for the great gaiety at Court in the last months of Elizabeth's reign and the splendour Scaramelli encountered in his first audience at Richmond. The Christmas just past, wrote John Chamberlain (in McClure, *Chamberlain*, vol. I, p. 180), 'the court' had 'flourisht more than ordinarie', 'the new controller' having 'put new life into yt by his example, being allwayes freshly attired and for the most part all in white, *cap a pied* '.

27 Logan Pearsall Smith, ed., *The Life and Letters of Sir Henry Wotton* (Oxford, 1907), vol. I, p. 235. Further citation is given internally by volume and page number.

28 BL Stowe MS.697/154, 8 January 1590.

who could have blown his cover. He scarpered at dawn. Throughout 1592 he was in Florence; the following year, in Geneva, lodging with Isaac Casaubon, reading Greek. By now, he spoke German like a native, Italian fluently and French proficiently (as well as reading and writing Latin). As can be seen from the letters that let us track him across these years, he'd also picked up the kind of skills in shrewd observation, conversational entrapment and detailed reportage that would make him valuable to England's intelligence network. To say nothing of what else he'd gathered: a long list of contacts.

When he returned to England in late 1594 Walsingham was dead but, by then, his son-in-law, Robert Devereux, Earl of Essex, had set up a rival intelligence service, in competition with the secretariat attached to the Cecils. He took Wotton on as one of two principal private secretaries, Henry Cuffe the other.[29] Wotton went with Essex to Cadiz, the Azores, and (perhaps to help Essex repair his credit after that last misadventure) on information-gathering trips to Germany. Then in April 1599, surviving gales that swamped one of the expedition's ships and made the Irish Sea crossing a hellish four-day endurance test, but inspired by 'a good cause, and the worthiest gentleman of the world to lead it', he sailed with Essex to Dublin (Smith, I:310). Within months, he would be caught red-handed by the evidence of Essex himself in the rapidly deteriorating operations of that frustrated mission: it was Wotton who, in September 1599, wrote out the treaty Essex had negotiated with Tyrone when the two earls met, their horses standing belly-deep in Bellaclynthe ford – the treaty Scaramelli knew about in 1603. As Essex reported to the Privy Council, 'H. Wotton hath both the articles of cessation, signed by Tyrone, and the Instructions I gave to treat, and is best able to deliver all circumstances, the whole business being chiefly left. . . . to him'.[30] Days later Wotton was with Essex on that deeply miscalculated dash back to London that had the earl, 'stain'd with the variation of each soil' between Dublin and Nonsuch, thrusting himself into the royal apartments – and the Queen's unready presence.

Over the next fifteen months, while his enemies manoeuvred on the Privy Council and disgraced Essex went from house arrest to banishment from Court, his adherents split. The diehards, Southampton and Henry Cuffe, pushed for action. The moderates councilled patience – advice that looked doomed when in October Elizabeth refused to renew Essex's lease on the import of sweet wines, effectively bankrupting him. In November, Wotton left England for France. Was he sent by Essex – a bid to show himself still necessary to Elizabeth?[31] Was he sent by his big brother – party to the Privy Council's deliberations, watching the way Essex House was growing dangerous, a magnet to 'discontented persons, adventurers of all sorts, and soldiers out of employ' preached at 'daily' by 'Puritan divines', wanting to get his little brother out of the way?[32] Or did Harry run – because, as his contemporary biographer, Izaac Walton, delicately put it, 'he thought prevention by absence out of England, a better security than to stay in it, and there plead his innocency in Prison'?[33] In February 1601, when Cuffe dined with Charles Percy, Gelly Meyrick and Christopher Blount (leaving them later when they crossed the Thames to see a play at the Globe),[34] when the half-baked rebellion ran its fizzled 12-hour course, when the treason trial reached its foregone verdict, and when execution came, Harry was three months gone. His self-imposed exile would last two years and take him back to Venice, via Florence.

---

[29] Essex also employed as secretaries Thomas Smith, William Temple and Edward Reynoldes. See Paul Hammer's excellent account of these men, their work and rivalries in 'The Uses of Scholarship: The Secretariat of Robert Devereux, Second Early of Essex, c. 1585–1601', *English Historical Review*, 109 (1940), 26–51.

[30] Ernest George Atkinson, ed., *Calendar of State Papers Ireland* (London, 1903) 8.181.

[31] That is Hammer's opinion in 'Scholarship', p. 42.

[32] Walter Bourchier Devereux, *Lives and Letters of the Devereux Earls of Essex* (London, 2005), vol. II, p. 134.

[33] Walton, 'The Life of Sir Henry Wotton' in *Reliquiae Wottonianae* (1685), sig. B8.

[34] See Paul E.J. Hammer, 'Shakespeare's *Richard II*, the Play of 7 February 1601, and the Essex Rising', *Shakespeare Quarterly*, 59 (2008), 25.

It was in Florence in 1602 that he met the accident – almost the farcical cloak-and-dagger stuff of, say, the first four acts of *Arden of Faversham* – that would set the course of his life. Receiving intelligence that Protestant James of Scotland (Elizabeth's likeliest successor) was to be poisoned to keep the English throne clear for a Catholic succession, the Grand Duke of Tuscany needed some likely lad to undertake a cross-European race against treachery to Holyrood. His secretary knew just the man. Entrusted with a box of 'such Italian Antidotes against poyson, as the Scots till then had been strangers to' (probably the secret-formula Venetian wonder-drug, triaca), Harry Wotton set off in disguise as one 'Ottavio Baldi', posting through Norway 'to avoid the line of English intelligence and danger' that was still looking out for Essexmen (Walton, sig. B8). As 'Baldi' he was admitted to the king's presence, as 'Baldi' he delivered his message in Italian, and as 'Baldi' he then stepped forward and whispered in the king's ear 'in his own Language, that he was an English man' and desired secret conference. James was delighted with the ruse, allowed Wotton to remain three months in his court under cover and depart 'as true an Italian as he came thither' (sigs. B8v, C).

James, then, had prior knowledge when, a year later, now King of England, he asked an amazed Edward Wotton 'If he knew one Henry . . . ?' and instructed him to send into Italy for his brother who, when James re-greeted him in London, he called 'the most honest, and therefore the best Dissembler that ever he met with', qualified (also, or thereby?) 'to manage an Ambassage' (Walton, sig. C1v). Within months, Harry, the 'honest' 'Dissembler', would be named ambassador to Venice.

As it happened, when his summons came in May 1603, Harry was in Venice. Clearly, his brother had instructed him to pave his way home with a grace-seeking letter to Robert Cecil (now, not the power behind, but *instead* of the throne) apologizing for being mixed up in 'that unfortunate family' of Essex, which he did, in his best school-boy handwriting, a letter tongue-tied with parentheticals. His faltering fell away though when he turned, secretary-wise, to 'a short accompt' of Venice as

he was leaving it. He named the newly nominated ambassadors to England and said they'd be coming 'with divers young Clarissimi: who (since the introduction of horsemanship into this citie) are more subiect then they were to noveltie and motion'. And he reported that 'Carolo Scaravella must return home for want of nothing but nobilitie, being otherwise esteemed one of theire ablest instruments'.[35]

'Scaravella' for 'Scaramelli': a slip of the pen? Or indication that Wotton was not yet acquainted with 'il Signor Segretario'? Did they just miss each other, in transit in opposite directions, in December, or did their paths cross? On the 15th, Molino learned that Wotton, then in Paris, had been appointed to Venice; Scaramelli, he reported, would leave London for Venice on the 26th (CSPV.10.172, 175). The dates make a meeting in London possible.[36]

That said, when Wotton – now Sir Henry – arrived back in Venice as Ambassador in September 1604, it was Scaramelli he wanted to contact because, he said, although he'd spent time in Venice as a traveller, he had no official acquaintance with a 'public person' other than Scaramelli ('non conoscendo egli qui con tutto ciò altra persona publica'), and he wanted briefing (CSPV.10.282). He aimed to remain incognito in the city five or six days, time to get his house in order and to take physic, but also to be prepped about the daunting official ceremonial entrance he would be making a week or so hence across the lagoon, in full ambassadorial costume, accompanied by a flotilla of gondolas, to meet at San Marco the massed Senate headed by the Doge, Marino Grimani, all in preparation for his first audience in the Collegio. His request stretched protocol. As Filippo de Vivo writes, the Republic aimed to 'limit all unofficial contact between the power's inner sphere and the outside world', not just by channelling all diplomatic communication through formal audiences in the Collegio but by forbidding patricians (and after 1542, all nobles) 'to entertain any contact (however

---

[35] NA SP99.2.168.

[36] Hammer, *DNB*, writes that Wotton did not reach London until April, 1604, a date I have yet to verify.

occasional) with foreign diplomats'.[37] (As Wotton's successor would put it, ambassadors were forbidden to exchange 'almost a word with any man of merit unless it be with a public minister (whose conversation consists only of compliments) or a straggling traveller'.[38]) To talk with Wotton, Scaramelli had first to obtain the permission – 'la licentia' – of the Consiglio di Dieci (the 'Ten'). Afterwards, he had to submit to the Collegio a full report of his visit to Wotton's residence, including a transcript of the substance of their conversation (CSPV.10.282 and Illustrations 20 and 21).[39]

The formal entry went to plan. Wotton gave his first audience in the Collegio on 1 October 1604 ('stilo nuovo', CSPV.10.275),[40] launching his business as ambassador (Illustration 22) that would have him not just speaking in Venice but sending regular dispatches home that would speak Venice in London, disseminating information to policy-makers and, as information leaked into the public domain (Chamberlain's letters clearly demonstrating it did), to a wide readership – including, potentially, playwrights.[41] Wotton would spend the inaugural year of a posting that would keep him in Venice until December, 1610 (sometimes acting like Antony's angelic Schoolmaster, sometimes, quasi-Thidias) dealing with cases of piracy, negotiating customs charges, nit-picking protocols for recognizing friendly sails on the open sea, defending indefensible scape-grace English (and Italian) lads arrested by the Signoria, pursuing justice for the murder of an English merchant, and, right at the end of this first year, having to declare news from London that clearly rocked him to the core, the gunpowder treason of November 1605.

All of his audiences were oral performances, delivered in the designed-to-impress wood-panelled ante-chamber whose door opened onto the Sala del Maggior Consiglio, decorated with Veronese canvases and a 24-hour clock that told the time anti-clockwise, where the twenty-five or so members of the Collegio, presided over by the Doge, met daily to screen all the business that would be passed on to the Senate, being, as de Vivo describes it, 'the central mechanism in the transmission of information inside the political

system'.[42] The Collegio had responsibility for dealing with foreign diplomats, for listening to ambassadors, a scene captured in a painting by Odoardo Fialetti showing Wotton speaking from his

---

[37] de Vivo, *Information*, p. 70.

[38] Quoted de Vivo, *Information*, p. 71.

[39] The report begins: 'à 28 Ottobre 1604. Havendo il Signor Ambasciator d'Inghilterra fatto sapere à me Giovanni Carlo Scaramelli secretario et servitor humilissimo della Serenità Vostra che era giunto in questa Città a 23 de'l passato dove desiderava star senza saputo di niuno cinque o sei giorni, non solo per veder la sua casa accommodata prima che ammetter visite, ma anco per pigliar un poco di purga in questa stagione, et che se ben è stato altre volte in Venetia non conoscendo egli qui con tutto ciò altra persona publica che me, mi pregava di volermi trovar seco, per poter concertar con volontà della Serenità Vostra le cerimonie della sua publica entrata in Venetia, et della sua prima publica audientia, et havendo io fatto saper riverentemente questo tanto alli Eccellentissimi Signori Savij che in risposta mi ordinorono di prender la licentia, dalli Eccellentissimi Signori Capi del Consiglio de X [Dieci], et poi di andarvi come ho fatto à 27 secondo l'hora assignatami, mi disse il Signor Ambasciator dopo premesse alcune parole di ufficio, che egli haveva desiderato di abboccarsi meco per poter saper quando, et come doverà esser la sua venuta à Vostra Serenità . . .' And ends: 'che se sua Serenità mi convitasse mai alli suoi publici conviti, non lo farebbe se non quando dovessi esser solo, et senza contesa, il che però credo che non potrà esser quasi mai, et havendosi dimostrato cauto, et eloquente assai, mi ricercò di basciar à Vostra Serenità et all' Eccellenze Vostre à suo nome le mani. et dicendomi che mi aspetteria con la risposta per apuntamento dell'audientia, mi licentiai.' I am grateful to Isabella Cecchini for checking my transcriptions of Archivio documents quoted here and to Micky White for photographing them.

[40] It begins: 1604 a primo ottobre

Letta in pregadi à
.2.ottobre 1604

Venuto questa mattina nell' Eccellentissimo Collegio in publica audientia il Signor Ambasciator d'Inghilterra, accompagnato dell' Illustrissimo Signor cavalier Vendramin, et da numero di senatori secondo l'ordinario, recevuta da sua Serenità con termine di honore et di affettione, seduto che fù, disse bassamente, che si rallegrava di ritrovar sua Serenità nella buona salute et prosperità che la vedeva et apresentò una lettera la qual fù letta, et questa è la traduttione.

[41] I am grateful to Filippo de Vivo for personal correspondence on these matters.

[42] de Vivo, *Information*, 37.

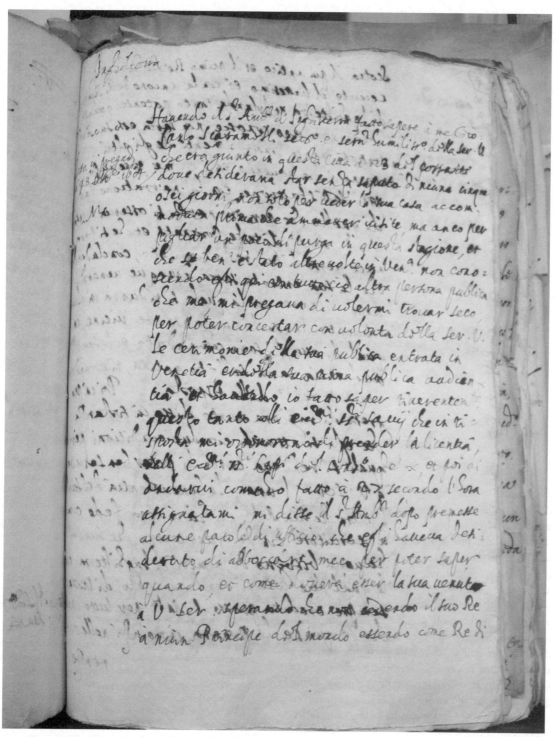

20. Scaramelli's report to the Collegio, 28 October 1604 (opening). Collegio, Esposizioni Principi filza 14.

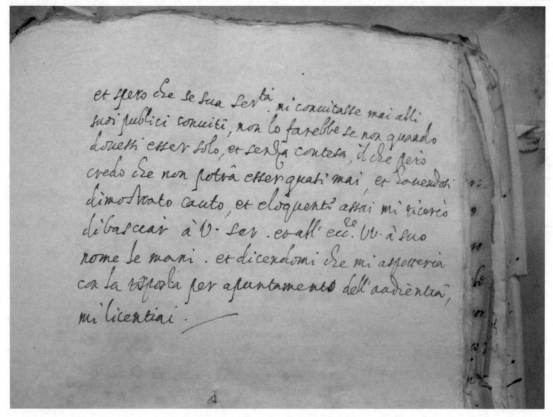

21. Scaramelli's report to the Collegio, 28 October 1604 (closing). Collegio, Esposizioni Principi filza 14.

accustomed place, on the Doge's right hand.[43] All of Wotton's audiences were recorded verbatim: taken down by a scribe. (In the Prado Museum's so-called 'Bedmar Portrait' – a near copy of Fialetti – scribes are shown clustered, standing, around two desks in the foreground, pens in hands, ink pots at the ready, scribbling.[44]) A day or so later, the scribe read the ambassador's 'exposition' to the full Senate. So if the Collegio was a listening place, a place to 'hear the ambassadors', the Senate was the place of deliberation and decision making, a place to frame responses. Delivering his writing to the Senate by restoring it to orality, ventriloquizing the ambassador, the scribe was not just recorder but reporter: the ambassador's ambassador, his mouthpiece and 'other self'.[45]

Thereafter, the individual manuscript was filed. The method was to thrust the day's papers down onto a metal clerk's spike. When the accumulated pile got thick enough, the papers were un-spiked and bound into a '*filza*'.[46] The surviving documents, then, each have a hole mid-page. This

---

[43] In the royal collection at Hampton Court but currently in storage, *Doge Leonardo Donato Giving an Audience to Sir Henry Wotton* can be viewed online at www.bridgemanart.com/asset/452128/Fialetti-Odoardo-1573-1638/Doge-Leonardo-Donato-giving-an-audiece-to-Sir-Hen

[44] By Pietro Malombra, representing Don Alonso de la Cueva, Spanish Ambassador in Venice from 1604, this painting can be viewed on the Prado Museum website. I am grateful to Isabella Cecchini for pointing me to it.

[45] On this process, see de Vivo, 'Ordering the Archive in Early Modern Venice, 1400–1650', *Archival Science*, 10 (2010), 231–48.

[46] i.e., 'thread': sharing the same latin root as 'filum', from which English derives 'file', meaning 'to string upon a thread', *OED*1.

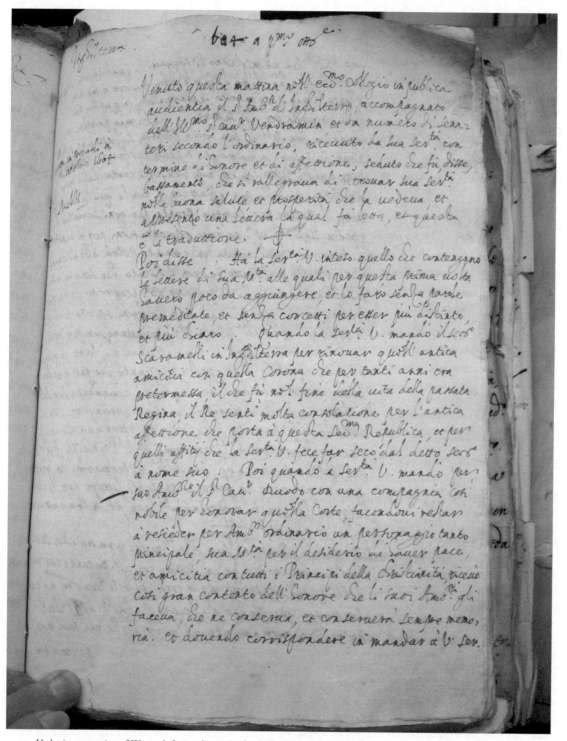

Venuto questa mattina nell' ecc.mo Collegio in publica
audientia il S.r Amb.r d'Inghilterra, accompagnato
dall' Ill.mo S.r Cav.r Vendramin et da numero di Senar-
tori secondo l'ordinario, riceuuto da Sua Ser.tà con
termine di honore et di affettione, seduto che fù, disse,
passamenti, che si rallegraua di ritrouar Sua Ser.tà
nella buona salute et prosperità che la vedeua, et
appresentò una lettera, la qual fù letta, et questa
è la traduttione.

Poi disse. Ha' la Ser.tà V. inteso quello che contengano
le lettere di Sua M.tà alle quali per questa prima uolta
haurò poco da aggiungere, et lo farò senza parole
premeditate, et senza concetti per esser più distinto,
et più chiaro. Quando la Ser.tà V. mandò il secr.o
Scaramelli in Inghilterra per rinouar quell'antica
amicitia con questa Corona che per tanti anni era
pretermessa, il che fù nel fine della vita della passata
Regina, il Re senti molta consolatione per l'antica
affettione che porta à questa Ser.ma Republica, et per
quelli uffitij che la Ser.tà V. fece far seco dal detto secr.o
à nome suo. Poi quando la Ser.tà V. mandò per
suo Amb.r il S.r Cav.r Duodo con una compagnia così
nobile per honorar questa Corte, facendoui restar
à risieder per Amb.r ordinario un personaggio tanto
principale, sua M.tà per il desiderio di hauer pace,
et amicitia con tutti i Principi della Christianità, riceue
con gran contento dell' honore che li suoi Amb.ri gli
faceua, che ne conserua, et conseruerà sempre memoria. et douendo corrispondere in mandar à V. Ser.

near-foolproof filing system meant that the oldest papers were on the bottom of the *filza*, the most recent on top (so the bound *filze* have to be read back to front for chronological sequence). The system also made for a dizzying sense of international traffic, documenting the Collegio as a kind of diplomatic revolving door: the Spanish ambassador's business (presented on, say, Monday) sat next to the French ambassador's (on Tuesday), who preceded the English ambassador on Wednesday, who was followed by the Papal nuncio on Thursday. Far from effecting an early modern communications mash-up, however, the Collegio's processes literally in-scribed national distinction because, while the scribes were anonymous servant-secretaries who didn't sign their transcriptions, it's clear that they were individually attached, long-term, to one ambassador or another. The handwriting across the *filze* indicates as much. Spain was recorded by one distinct hand. France by another. The same nameless scribe who recorded Wotton's first audience in October 1604 continued writing his oral reports into the record until February 1606.

What do we know about the Collegio's scribes, the men I'm calling the 'ambassador's ambassador', who appear paradoxically to English eyes one half in the thankless role of copyist-drudge (some of Wotton's 'expositions' run to thirty manuscript pages), the other half as powerful political ventriloquist? Almost, says de Vivo, nothing. Many of them were 'drawn from the second-class elite of the *cittadini*', permitted by that birth 'to serve in the administration of the state', the rule of which was the prerogative of a patrician 'caste defined by birth' that 'allowed for no power sharing with others' or 'scrutiny from outsiders'. Such *cittadini* 'were trained to become chancery servants' in public schools like the ones governmentally funded from 1551 in each Venetian sestiere where they were taught 'grammaticam, rethoricam et alias scientias' and, the basis for the rest, eloquence, which was seen as an arm of politics, speaking well being a 'mark of freedom'.[47] So a curriculum not unlike the one set in Elizabethan English grammar schools.

Now, however, I can add a little to our knowledge (and pose, for the future, some questions about what it might mean) by bringing together documents from the National Archive in London and the Archivio di Stato in Venice, that have never before been placed side-by-side.

Wotton's scribe was Giovanni Carlo Scaramelli. Palaeographic comparison of the handwriting in Illustrations 19–22 demonstrates as much. It shows Scaramelli in England writing privately to Florio, then in Venice reporting in the first person – 'io' – his exceptional meeting with Wotton, before disappearing into the daily business of the Collegio, anonymously taking dictation. The man who'd served as ambassador in all but name to England the previous year, the man Wotton said Venice 'esteemed one of theire ablest instruments', his 'want of... nobilitie', however, barring him a patrician's appointment to ambassadorial office, was now the English ambassador's word-taker and spokesman. Was such service a come-down? Or did it display the Venetian political system's intricate, secretive workings at their politic best, appointing the Venetian who knew most at first-hand about England to record England-in-Venice, to offer distant surveillance, perhaps, of someone, an ardent Protestant, who'd particularly need watching, and to supply interpretation of what England might mean, speaking in Venice? If Scaramelli was meant somehow to monitor, to control Wotton, Wotton regularly eluded his minder, blundering his way past Venetian protocols, managing (hair-raisingly for his Republican hosts) to stretch the limits of diplomacy to reframe Anglo-Venetian communication along more English lines.

The story of their diplomatic partnership – 'ablest instrument' yoked to loose cannon – awaits further telling. For now, my *filza* stretches from London to Venice, marks some connections, snagging in its tangles Scaramelli, a brace of Wottons, Florio, and possibly a cry of playwrights – among them, perhaps, Shakespeare.

---

[47] de Vivo, *Information*, pp. 4, 21.

'O, WHAT A SYMPATHY OF WOE IS THIS': PASSIONATE SYMPATHY IN *TITUS ANDRONICUS*

RICHARD MEEK

In 3.2 of *Titus Andronicus*, Titus describes to Marcus the difficulties that he and Lavinia face in expressing their sorrows: 'Thy niece and I, poor creatures, want our hands / And cannot passionate our tenfold grief / With folded arms' (3.2.5–7). This moment addresses some of the central concerns of the play: how do you communicate extreme grief, and make others understand or feel your pain? What is the relationship between the experience of emotions (Titus's 'tenfold grief') and the words and gestures ('folded arms') that might be used to express them?[1] Shakespeare's use of the word *passionate* also raises some larger methodological questions for critics interested in the history of emotion. The primary meaning of the word in this period was 'susceptible to or readily swayed by passions or emotions; easily moved to strong feeling; of changeable mood, volatile' (*OED*, 1; first cited usage 1425). Shakespeare uses the word in a narrower sense to describe characters affected by anger ('I am amazed at your passionate words' (*Dream*, 3.2.221)), sadness ('She is sad and passionate at your highness' tent' (*King John*, 2.1.545)), and love ('Warble, child; make passionate my sense of hearing' (*Love's Labour's Lost* 3.1.1)). By the 1580s the word could also mean 'Inclined to pity, compassionate' (*OED*, 5c). This latter usage occurs in *Richard III*, when one of Clarence's murderers has second thoughts about his grim assignment: 'Nay, I pray thee. Stay a little. I hope this passionate humour of mine will change' (1.4.114–15). Several of these examples might seem to confirm the notion that passions were things that happened *to* people in the Renaissance; the Second

Murderer's passionate mood in particular is described as something bodily, unstable and outside his control. But in the passage from *Titus* quoted above *passionate* is used in an innovative way as a verb ('To express or perform with passion' (*OED*, *v.*, 2; first cited usage 1567)). Titus uses the word to describe his attempts to *perform* his grief, suggesting that passions can be things that individuals do, as well as being forces that act upon them.

Several recent critics have argued that the primary contextual and critical framework for understanding the passionate expressions of Shakespeare's characters is Galenic humoral theory. In *Humoring the Body* (2004), Gail Kern Paster argues that early modern texts point to a 'psychophysiological reciprocity between the experiencing subject and his or her relation to the world'. She writes that the humoral body is 'characterized not only by its physical openness but also by its emotional instability and volatility, by an internal microclimate knowable, like climates in the outer world,

An earlier version of this essay was prepared for Katharine A. Craik's seminar on 'Passionate Shakespeare' at the International Shakespeare Conference at Stratford-upon-Avon in 2012. I am grateful to Katharine Craik and the participants in the seminar for their comments and encouragement. Thanks also to Erin Sullivan and, as ever, Jane Rickard for their comments on earlier drafts.

[1] Quotations from *Titus Andronicus* are taken from Jonathan Bate's Arden 3 edition (London, 1995). On folded arms as a signifier of sad or melancholy thought see, for example, William Carroll's Arden 3 edition of *The Two Gentlemen of Verona* (London, 2004), note to 2.1.18.

more for changeability than for stasis'.[2] Paster's conception of emotion in the Renaissance thus resembles that of the Second Murderer in *Richard III*: feeling was something that happened to the body of the passive, receptive subject, who either gave way to these bodily impulses or attempted to resist them through stoical self-control. But while the Second Murderer's passionate humour might be usefully diagnosed via Galenic medicine, Titus's comments about his attempts to 'passionate' his grief are less easily accommodated within this framework. Indeed, some critics have begun to question the medical-humoral model as a way of exploring – or 'explaining' – Shakespeare's representations of emotion. Richard Strier has suggested that 'the problem of what is literal and what is metaphoric in early modern humors discourse is extremely tricky'. He continues: 'To think that people, then or now, directly experience (or experienced) their emotions in terms of scientific theories about the physiological bases of emotions seems to me a category mistake of a rather major kind.'[3] And, more recently, Lynn Enterline has argued that critics should broaden their attention to include other cultural influences, such as Shakespeare's rhetorical training at the grammar school, and the ways in which 'his reflections on the passions involve meta-theatrical or meta-rhetorical reflections on classical figures, texts, and traditions'.[4]

The present article is a contribution to these recent attempts to complicate (rather than replace) the humoral or bodily conception of early modern emotions. It explores the representation of sympathy in *Titus Andronicus*, and the various terms that Shakespeare uses to describe emotional correspondence: not only *passion* and *passionate* but also *compassion*, *commiseration*, *pity*, *mercy*, *rue* and *sympathy* itself.[5] As we shall see, the play employs the word *sympathy* in an innovative way that associates it with ideas of cognition, projection and imagination, and thus points the word in the direction of our own understanding. This important act of redefining sympathy as an imaginative activity, rather than an occult phenomenon, corresponds with the play's interest in turning emotion

words – such as *passionate* – into verbs. Michael Schoenfeldt has argued that the Renaissance was a period 'when the "scientific" language of analysis had not yet been separated from the sensory language of experience'.[6] And yet *Titus*'s exploration of the unstable relationship between literal and figurative language complicates the attempts of 'new humoralist' critics to interpret Shakespeare's descriptions of bodily passions literally.[7] Certainly we can detect the influence of humoral theory and

[2] Gail Kern Paster, *Humoring the Body: Emotions and the Shakespearean Stage* (Chicago and London, 2004), p. 19. See also Michael C. Schoenfeldt, *Bodies and Selves in Early Modern England: Physiology and Inwardness in Spenser, Shakespeare, Herbert, and Milton* (Cambridge, 1999), and Gail Kern Paster, Katherine Rowe and Mary Floyd-Wilson, eds., *Reading the Early Modern Passions: Essays in the Cultural History of Emotion* (Philadelphia, 2004). Other critics influenced by the humoral model include Matthew Steggle, *Laughing and Weeping in Early Modern Theatres* (Aldershot, 2007), and David Houston Wood, *Time, Narrative, and Emotion in Early Modern England* (Farnham, 2009).

[3] Richard Strier and Carla Mazzio, 'Two Responses to "Shakespeare and Embodiment: An E-Conversation"', *Literature Compass*, 3 (2006), 15–31 at 16–17. In *The Unrepentant Renaissance: From Petrarch to Shakespeare to Milton* (Chicago, 2011) Strier has argued that the 'new humoralists' are akin to the new historicists in their questioning of individual agency, and that humoral theory is one of several tools used by scholars to characterize the period 'in dark and dour terms'. He writes that the focus of the new humoralists 'might be said to be on selves in the period as physiocultural rather than sociocultural formations' (p. 17).

[4] Lynn Enterline, *Shakespeare's Schoolroom: Rhetoric, Discipline, Emotion* (Philadelphia, 2012), pp. 26–7.

[5] For a valuable essay that explores some of these concepts in Shakespeare's works from a Virgilian perspective, see Heather James, 'Dido's Ear: Tragedy and the Politics of Response', *Shakespeare Quarterly*, 52 (2001), 360–82. R. S. White offers a wide-ranging discussion of Shakespeare's use of the term *passion* in '"False Friends": Affective Semantics in Shakespeare', *Shakespeare*, 8:3 (2012), 286–99.

[6] Schoenfeldt, *Bodies and Selves*, p. 8.

[7] For two important discussions of language and metaphor in the play, see Albert H. Tricomi, 'The Aesthetics of Mutilation in *Titus Andronicus*', *Shakespeare Survey 27* (Cambridge, 1974), pp. 11–19, and Gillian Murray Kendall, '"Lend me thy hand": Metaphor and Mayhem in *Titus Andronicus*', *Shakespeare Quarterly*, 40 (1989), 299–316. Such critics tend to focus on the ways in which the play literalizes its metaphors; in contrast, the present article explores the ways in which

quasi-scientific conceptions of affinity and correspondence in *Titus*; however, such paradigms are self-consciously evoked in ways that metaphorize certain aspects of emotional experience. In this way, Shakespeare implicitly questions the authority of medical-humoral theory as the sole framework for understanding the early modern passions. The characters in *Titus Andronicus* are not simply presented as passive bodies, affected by external climates or analogical forces, but rather as thinking and feeling human beings, capable of putting themselves imaginatively into the positions of others.

I

The term *sympathy* is particularly suggestive, not least because it had multiple and shifting meanings during Shakespeare's lifetime. In the late sixteenth and early seventeenth centuries, the word was primarily understood to mean a kind of correspondence or harmony between different objects in the cosmos, people or even musical vibrations. In this pre-social conception of sympathy, which appears in the works of classical writers such as Aristotle, Pliny and Plutarch, one is moved not so much by fellow-feeling for others as by physical and physiological processes.[8] In Philemon Holland's 1603 translation of *Plutarch's Morals*, for example, *sympathy* is included in the list of 'certeine obscure words' that are helpfully glossed at the back of the volume: 'Sympathie, that is to say, A fellow feeling, as is betweene the head and stomacke in our bodies: also the agreement and naturall amitie in divers senslesse things, as between iron and the load-stone'.[9] As this definition suggests, objects in the natural world were believed to have magical affinities that made them respond to each other.

In *The Passions of the Minde in Generall* (1604), Thomas Wright refers to the passions in this context, and likens the process of moving others to notions of physical transference and induction: 'If my hand be hot for the fire, the fire must bee more hot it selfe: if my chamber be lightsome for the beames of the sunne, the sunne it selfe must

be more lightsome: If I must bee moved by thy perswasions, first thou must shew me by passion, they perswaded thy selfe.'[10] Wright conceives of emotional transference in the same way that he regards the transference of heat and light between physical bodies or spaces. Similarly, in *A Late Discourse . . . Touching the Cure of Wounds by Sympathy* (1658), Kenelm Digby describes his famous 'powder of sympathy' – which could cure wounds without touching them – and suggests that laughing and sadness are also transmitted by an automatic process:

Now lets consider how the strong imagination of one man doth marvailously act upon another man who hath it more feeble and passive . . . If one come perchance to converse with persons that are subject to excesse of laughter, one can hardly forbear laughing, although one doth not know the cause why they laugh. If one should enter into a house, where all the World is sad, he becomes melancholy, for as one said, *Si vis me flere dolendum est primum ipsi tibi.*[11]

---

descriptions of physical and physiological phenomena are self-consciously metaphorized in the play.

[8] Neil Rhodes discusses the earlier physiological theory of sympathy in 'The Science of the Heart: Shakespeare, Kames and the Eighteenth-Century Invention of the Human', in *Posthumanist Shakespeares*, ed. Stefan Herbrechter and Ivan Callus (Basingstoke, 2012), pp. 23–40 (esp. pp. 26–7). See also Michel Foucault's description of sympathy in *The Order of Things: An Archaeology of the Human Sciences* (1970; repr. London, 2002): 'Sympathy is an instance of the *Same* so strong and so insistent that it will not rest content to be merely one of the forms of likeness; it has the dangerous power of *assimilating*, of rendering things identical to one another, of mingling them, of causing their individuality to disappear' (p. 26).

[9] Plutarch, *The Philosophie, Commonlie Called the Morals*, trans. Philemon Holland (London, 1603), sig. 6A1v.

[10] Thomas Wright, *The passions of the minde in generall. Corrected, enlarged, and with sundry new discourses augmented* (London, 1604), p. 173.

[11] Sir Kenelm Digby, *A Late Discourse Made in a Solemne Assembly of Nobles and Learned Men at Montpellier in France, Touching the Cure of Wounds by Sympathy, With Instructions how to make the said Power; whereby many other Secrets of Nature are unfolded* (London, 1658), p. 93. See Steggle, *Laughing and Weeping*, pp. 5–6; and Seth Lobis, 'Sir Kenelm Digby and the Powder of Sympathy', *Huntington Library Quarterly*, 74 (2011), 243–60 (at 252–3).

Here Digby refers to Horace's often-cited Latin tag 'si vis me flere' – the rhetorical ideal that in order to move others you have to be moved yourself. As Horace puts it in *The Art of Poetry*, 'The human face smiles in sympathy with smilers and comes to the help of those that weep. If you want me to cry, mourn first yourself; *then* your misfortunes will hurt me.'[12] Digby invokes this familiar rhetorical trope but suggests that such emotional transference has a physiological basis, continuing with the reflection that 'Women and Children being very moist and passive, are most susceptible of this unpleasing contagion of the imagination' (p. 93). Using language that recalls Renaissance antitheatricalists, Digby proposes that the transmission of sorrow is a form of contagion that affects weak and passive individuals.[13] Such examples offer a compelling picture of sympathy in the sixteenth and seventeenth centuries: the term, it would seem, described the process by which two things influenced each other or were attracted to one another.

This picture of early modern conceptions of sympathy – as a predominantly physical and physiological phenomenon – corresponds with the history of the word *sympathy* that we find in the *OED*. The idea of sympathy as 'The quality or state of being thus affected by the suffering or sorrow of another; a feeling of compassion or commiseration' (*OED*, 3c) does not, we are told, appear until 1600, while the more complex idea of sympathy as 'the fact or capacity of entering into or sharing the feelings of another or others; fellow-feeling' (*OED*, 3b) only appears in 1662. The *OED*'s account of the word's development might thus confirm the view that the modern understanding of sympathy – as a complex, imaginative engagement with the other – only emerges fully in the eighteenth century with the philosophical writings of David Hume and Adam Smith.[14] And yet when we turn to literary texts from the late sixteenth and early seventeenth centuries we can see the gradual emergence of the more 'modern' usages of the term considerably earlier than the *OED* suggests. This more complex usage of *sympathy* grows out of, and extends, an early modern fascination with ideas of

pity and compassion; and even before the term is used in this sense, dramatic and poetic representations of fellow-feeling from this period point to a complex imaginative and cognitive engagement with the other.

As critics have begun to recognize, *Titus Andronicus* reflects this early modern interest in pity and fellow-feeling. In a recent essay Joseph M. Ortiz has suggested that the play invokes Ovid as a way of 'exploring the possibility of sympathy in art'. Focusing on the idea of musical sympathy, he argues that *Titus Andronicus* 'raises serious doubts about music's ability to impart understanding – or, more generally, to mean anything at all'.[15] Ortiz's view of sympathy in the play is thus rather pessimistic, and he argues that Shakespeare's treatment of Lavinia 'undercuts any sense of true sympathy or expressiveness' (p. 70). It seems to me, however, that Shakespeare's treatment of sympathy in the play is more complex – and indeed more optimistic – than Ortiz suggests. I agree that Shakespeare is questioning the earlier occult conception of sympathy, but not that he is rejecting the possibility of sympathy altogether. As we shall see below, Shakespeare uses the term *sympathy* to mean

---

[12] Horace, *The Art of Poetry*, in D. A. Russell and M. Winterbottom, eds., *Classical Literary Criticism* (Oxford, 1989), pp. 98–110 at 100. See also Joseph R. Roach, *The Player's Passion: Studies in the Science of Acting* (Newark, 1985) and Robert Cockcroft, *Rhetorical Affect in Early Modern Writing* (Basingstoke, 2003).

[13] On the relationship between fellow-feeling and theatrical contagion, see James, 'Dido's Ear', pp. 361–4.

[14] In *The Theory of Moral Sentiments* (1759), Adam Smith writes that 'By the imagination we place ourselves in [the sufferer's] situation, we conceive ourselves enduring all the same torments, we enter as it were into his body, and become in some measure the same person with him . . . by changing places in fancy with the sufferer . . . we come either to conceive or to be affected by what he feels' (Smith, *The Theory of Moral Sentiments*, ed. Knud Haakonssen (Cambridge, 2002), p. 12).

[15] Joseph M. Ortiz, '"Martyred Signs": *Titus Andronicus* and the Production of Musical Sympathy', *Shakespeare*, 1 (June/December 2005), 53–74 at 54. The influence of Ovid on the emotional world of *Titus* is also considered by Cora Fox in 'Grief and the Ovidian Politics of Revenge in *Titus Andronicus*', in *Ovid and the Politics of Emotion* (Basingstoke, 2009), pp. 105–24.

emotional correspondence and throughout *Titus* he explores the extent to which pity and compassion are bound up with language, narrative and the imagination.

There are certainly moments in the play that allude to the idea of sympathy as a physical or occult process. In 3.1, for example, Titus pleads for the lives of Quintus and Martius by attempting to elicit pity from the tribunes. He claims that he has 'never wept before' (3.1.25), because in the past his other sons have been killed in battle, and thus died a noble death. When Lucius points out that no one is listening, Titus states that he has to go on talking, even if only the stones at his feet can hear him:

Why 'tis no matter man, if they did hear,
They would not mark me, or if they did mark,
They would not pity me; yet plead I must,
And bootless unto them.
Therefore I tell my sorrows to the stones,
Who, though they cannot answer my distress,
Yet in some sort they are better then the tribunes
For that they will not intercept my tale.
When I do weep, they humbly at my feet
Receive my tears and seem to weep with me,
And were they but attired in grave weeds
Rome could afford no tribunes like to these.
A stone is soft as wax, tribunes more hard than stones;
A stone is silent and offendeth not,
And tribunes with their tongues doom men to death.
(3.1.33–47)

Titus suggests that the stones are a better audience than the Tribunes, as they will not 'intercept' – that is, interrupt – his tale. The senseless stones '[r]eceive' his tears and thus appear to weep with him. Ortiz reads this moment in relation to the double meaning of the word 'moving' in Ovid's *Metamorphoses*. For Ortiz, the Ovidian sense of *movere* – which could refer to the literal moving of inanimate objects such as stones and musical strings – corresponds with the early modern occult notion of sympathy. However he argues that the occult model is being ironized here: 'Titus's confusion of the literal and metaphorical senses of "move" . . . invokes the doctrine of sympathy in a way which appears ridiculous.' For Ortiz, occult

sympathy 'is merely an empty conceit in the universe of the play'.[16] But perhaps Titus is not quite as confused as Ortiz suggests. Titus's desire to move the stones can be read as a metaphorical expression of his desire to move others: as Titus himself notes, the stones only 'seem' to weep with him.[17] The image of weeping stones is a way for Titus to express his disdain for the unsympathetic tribunes, and his desire for a more sympathetic hearing. Shakespeare does not simply offer a critique of occult sympathy, but rather has Titus use it as a powerful metaphor for the emotional receptivity he seeks.

Titus's ability to express his grief is tested even further later in the scene when his daughter is brought on with her tongue cut out and her hands removed. Titus's hand is then cut off by Aaron in what turns out to be a futile gesture to save the life of his sons. Titus asks the heavens to pity him: 'If any power pities wretched tears, / To that I call' (3.1.209–10). His language becomes increasingly metaphorical, as he describes how his sighs will 'breathe the welkin dim / And stain the sun with fog' (212–13). The stoical Marcus tries to get Titus to tone down these outlandish images, and to temper his passions with reason: 'do not break into these deep extremes' (216). Yet Titus suggests that, because his sorrows are bottomless, his 'passions' should be likewise (218), using the word in the relatively new, but now obsolete, sense of 'A literary composition or passage marked by deep or strong emotion; a passionate speech or outburst' (*OED*, 'passion', 6b). Titus allows himself another

---

[16] Ortiz, '"Martyred Signs"', p. 69.

[17] This recalls the moment in *Venus and Adonis* when Venus comes across Adonis's dead body after he has been killed by the boar. She sees the 'wide wound' made by the boar's tusk, and the blood on the landscape around Adonis: 'No flower was nigh, no grass, herb, leaf, or weed, / But stole his blood, and seemed with him to bleed' (1055–6). Here the landscape *seems* to be capable of appropriating Adonis's blood, and indeed human passions. The narrator describes this phenomenon as 'solemn sympathy' (1057). It is not clear, however, whether this is supposed to be an example of occult sympathy, in which the landscape magically bleeds in response to Adonis's injury, or whether his blood has simply dripped onto the flowers.

passionate outburst in which he compares the exchange of grief between himself and Lavinia to the processes of the natural world:

When heaven doth weep, doth not the earth o'erflow?
If the winds rage, doth not the sea wax mad,
Threatening the welkin with his big-swollen face?
And wilt thou have a reason for this coil?
I am the sea. Hark how her sighs doth blow.
She is the weeping welkin, I the earth.
Then must my sea be moved with her sighs,
Then must my earth with her continual tears
Become a deluge, overflowed and drowned,
For why my bowels cannot hide her woes,
But like a drunkard must I vomit them.   (3.1.222–32)

In this complex metaphorical schema, Titus is both the earth and the sea, while Lavinia is the sky, acting upon him. The metaphor develops into a description of the physiological nature of his emotions. The bowels were seen as the seat of the tender and sympathetic passions, and could actually mean 'Pity, compassion, feeling, "heart"' (OED, 'bowels', 3a). In addition, the 'her' in line 231 is ambiguous, and could refer to the woes of Titus's bowels, or to Lavinia's woes, further blurring the distinction between Titus's body and Lavinia's grief. This speech might thus be seen as evidence that 'the passions of the early modern subject have an elemental character more literal than metaphoric in force'.[18] Indeed Titus's comments recall Paster's description of the humoral body being 'like climates in the outer world', and suggest its open and porous nature.[19] Titus's woes have a physiological basis and have to be literally vomited out. But perhaps using the term 'literally' in the context of an explicitly poetical speech about the passions is problematic. Should we regard this speech, rather, as a metaphorical evocation of feeling, rather than an attempt to offer an accurate or quasi-scientific description of Titus's emotions?

The idea of bodily or automatic sympathy is further complicated in the play by its juxtaposition with what we might term a cognitive and imaginative conception of emotional correspondence. Immediately after Titus's meteorological speech we have a Messenger who feels the woes of Titus and his family, but not due to any kind of automatic sympathy:

Worthy Andronicus, ill art thou repaid
For that good hand thou sent'st the emperor.
Here are the heads of thy two noble sons,
And here's thy hand in scorn to thee sent back:
Thy grief their sports, thy resolution mocked,
That woe is me to think upon thy woes
More than remembrance of my father's death.   (235–41)

The Messenger remembers his father's death as he 'think[s] upon' Titus's woes: his pity for Titus is thus bound up with his own emotional experiences. Here emotional correspondence is the product of thought and memory, rather than a process of bodily contagion or straightforward 'identification'. Indeed the Messenger suggests that Titus's grief is actually worse than his own grief, but nonetheless invokes his father's death as he attempts to express and conceptualize his response to Titus's predicament. One might also suggest that the Messenger's speech implicitly reflects upon the audience's responses as well: Titus's losses will, one hopes, be far more violent and extreme than anything that members of the audience will have experienced; yet they may nevertheless recall their own losses as they too 'think upon [Titus's] woes'. In this way the Messenger can be seen as an example of what Alastair Fowler has called an 'involved spectator'. Fowler notes the 'intense participation' of such spectator figures in Renaissance art and literature, and suggests that they 'illustrate how far the Renaissance viewer's role was from passive observation'.[20] As the Messenger compares his woes to those of Titus, the audience may, in turn, compare their responses to those of the Messenger. This speech thus highlights the extent to which there is often a comparative aspect to our sorrows, or perhaps to all our emotional responses.

---

[18] Paster, *Humoring the Body*, p. 19.
[19] Paster, *Humoring the Body*, p. 19.
[20] See Alastair Fowler, *Renaissance Realism: Narrative Images in Literature and Art* (Oxford, 2003), pp. 66–84 (quotation on p. 76).

II

The play's treatment of sympathy is even more complex, however, because Shakespeare also demonstrates that such comparisons do not always elicit pity or compassion. In the opening scene Tamora offers a passionate plea for the life of her son Alarbus. Tamora asks Titus to imagine what he would feel if one of his own sons were executed:

> Stay, Roman brethren, gracious conqueror,
> Victorious Titus, rue the tears I shed,
> A mother's tears in passion for her son!
> And if thy sons were ever dear to thee,
> O, think my son to be as dear to me.
>
> (1.1.107–11)

Tamora invites Titus to 'rue' her tears and to imagine her feelings for her son. She asks him to be merciful, like the gods: 'Wilt thou draw near the nature of the gods? / Draw near them then in being merciful. / Sweet mercy is nobility's true badge' (1.1.120–2). As Tamora suggests, *mercy* was a quality associated with nobility, and implied a power structure in which the merciful individual was positioned above the poor wretch asking for pity.[21] In *A Table of Humane Passions* (1621), Nicholas Coeffeteau writes that '*Mercy is a Griefe or feeling which we have of another mans miseries, who we hold worthy of a better fortune.*' He continues: 'it is most certaine that such as feele their hearts toucht with pitty, must bee in that estate as they thinke that either themselves or their friends may fall into the like accident, and runne into the same misfortune that he hath done, whose misery doth move them to this commiseration'.[22] Yet Tamora's attempts to make Titus imagine experiencing the same losses, and thus move him to commiseration, are ineffective. Titus suggests – in a mathematical, business-like way – that Alarbus needs to be killed in order to pay for the deaths of others.

In 2.2, however, Tamora faces the piteous pleas of another woman: Lavinia. Demetrius enjoins his mother not to feel pity: 'let it be your glory / To see her tears, but be your heart to them / As unrelenting flint to drops of rain' (2.2.139–41).

Stones, flint and steel could all serve as metaphors denoting a lack of compassion, as we have already seen in Titus's description of the senseless stones in 3.1; we might also think of Lear's comments in the final scene of *The Tragedy of King Lear*, 'O, you are men of stones' (5.3.232). At the same time, however, hard substances were said to be worn away by water, as in Lucrece's comments to Tarquin in *The Rape of Lucrece*: 'O, if no harder than a stone thou art, / Melt at my tears, and be compassionate. / Soft pity enters at an iron gate' (593–5).[23] As these examples suggest, metaphors relating to compassion had a gendered dimension, with women often figured as water or tears, and men often figured as stone or flint. However, *Titus Andronicus* reminds us that this seductive set of metaphors does not describe intrinsic differences between men and women. Lavinia attempts to invoke the stereotypical idea of compassionate femininity and asks Chiron to entreat his mother to 'show a woman's pity' (2.2.147). Lavinia hopes that, even if her sons may be pitiless, Tamora may nonetheless show mercy:

> 'Tis true, the raven doth not hatch a lark.
> Yet I have heard – O, could I find it now –
> The lion, moved with pity, did endure
> To have his princely paws pared all away.
> Some say that ravens foster forlorn children
> The whilst their own birds famish in their nests.
> O be to me, though thy hard heart say no,
> Nothing so kind, but something pitiful.   (149–56)

Lavinia uses a proverbial fable as a kind of exemplary narrative to encourage Tamora to show pity.[24] Yet Tamora states that she will remain

---

[21] For a valuable account of the ways in which mercy was discussed in the period – as a virtuous act or a kind of 'contagion' – see John Staines, 'Compassion in the Public Sphere of Milton and King Charles', in Paster *et al.*, eds., *Reading the Early Modern Passions*, pp. 89–110 (esp. pp. 99–100).

[22] Nicolas Coeffeteau, *A Table of Humane Passions. With their Causes and Effects*, trans. Edward Grimeston (London, 1621), pp. 357–8.

[23] See R. W. Dent, *Shakespeare's Proverbial Language: An Index* (Berkeley, 1981), H311 and D618.

[24] See Bate's note to 2.2.151–2 and his 'Introduction', p. 93.

'pitiless' in imitation of Lavinia's father: 'Remember, boys, I poured forth tears in vain / To save your brother from the sacrifice, / But fierce Andronicus would not relent' (162–5). Tamora's description of Titus recalls the 'unrelenting' flint invoked by Demetrius, and she thus resists the stereotype of soft or passive female compassion. Tamora's emotional state is presented as a deliberate choice in which she imitates Titus's lack of feeling rather than Lavinia's passions.

The absence of pity or compassion is a key feature of the play, and part of its insistence that passions involve a considerable degree of choice, thought and judgement. Marcus's address to the heavens at the end of 4.1 also bemoans a lack of pity, but here amongst the gods: 'O heavens, can you hear a good man groan / And not relent or not compassion him' (4.1.123–4). This striking and unusual use of *compassion* as a verb – which corresponds with Titus's use of *passionate* quoted above – again implies that passions are active processes.[25] The play's interest in presenting emotions as things that individuals do illuminates Steven Mullaney's claims about the changes taking place in the emotional landscape of early modern England. Mullaney suggests that Elizabethan plays in particular 'demanded and produced new powers of identification, projection, and apprehension in their audiences, altering the threshold not only of dramatic representation but also of self-representation, not only the fictional construction of character but also of the social construction of the self'.[26] Mullaney's argument about the role played by dramatic texts in shaping early modern emotion is compelling, if broad; *Titus* gives us a specific example of an Elizabethan play that explores social processes of identification, projection and apprehension, not only through its complex exploration of pity but also through its use of the word *sympathy*. The appearance of this word in the play highlights a shift in the understanding of the concept from a quasi-scientific phenomenon to a process of imaginative engagement.

Towards the start of 3.1 Marcus offers to dry Titus's eyes, but Titus suggests that Marcus's napkin has lost its absorbency as it is already 'drowned' (3.1.142) with Marcus's tears. Lucius then offers to dry Lavinia's cheeks, and Titus suggests that he might have the same problem. There is thus a curious double-mirroring here: Marcus's grief matches that of Titus, while Lucius's grief matches that of Lavinia. In other words, there is a correspondence between these two examples of matching grief. And when Lavinia makes a non-verbal attempt to communicate, Titus attempts to imagine her thoughts and what Lavinia would say if she still had the facility of speech:

> Mark, Marcus, mark! I understand her signs:
> Had she a tongue to speak, now would she say
> That to her brother which I said to thee.
> His napkin with his true tears all bewet
> Can do no service on her sorrowful cheeks.
> O, what a sympathy of woe is this;
> As far from help as limbo is from bliss.
>
> (3.1.144–50)

Intriguingly, Titus employs the term *sympathy* to describe this correspondence of woe. The word is not glossed in Bate's Arden 3 edition, while the *Riverside* simply has 'sharing'.[27] Alan Hughes suggests 'likeness in suffering' in his New Cambridge edition.[28] The word does appear in several of Shakespeare's other early dramatic works in its earlier sense of correspondence and agreement. In *2 Henry VI*, for example, which was probably written in 1590–1, King Henry uses the term as he welcomes Margaret to the court: 'Thou hast given me in this beauteous face / A world of earthly blessings to my soul, / If sympathy of love unite our thoughts' (1.1.21–3). There is a similar usage in

---

25 The *OED* cites this passage as one of the few examples of *compassion* used as a verb, and notes that this usage was short-lived: 'To have compassion on, to pity. ("A word scarcely used", Johnson.)'.

26 Steven Mullaney, 'Affective Technologies: Toward an Emotional Logic of the Elizabethan Stage', in Mary Floyd-Wilson and Garrett A. Sullivan, Jr, eds., *Environment and Embodiment in Early Modern England* (Basingstoke, 2007), pp. 71–89 at 81.

27 *The Riverside Shakespeare*, ed. G. Blakemore Evans, 2nd edn (Boston, 1997), note to 3.1.148.

28 Alan Hughes, ed., *Titus Andronicus*, updated edition (Cambridge, 2006), note to 3.1.148.

A Midsummer Night's Dream, when Lysander comments on the various scenarios in which love has failed to run smoothly: 'Or if there were a sympathy in choice, / War, death, or sickness did lay siege to it' (1.1.141–2). But in *Romeo and Juliet*, which is roughly contemporaneous with *Titus*, the Nurse uses the word to describe the similarity between the emotions of the two protagonists: 'O, he is even in my mistress' case, / Just in her case! O woeful sympathy, / Piteous predicament!' (3.3.84–6). In this example Shakespeare again uses *sympathy* to mean correspondence, but uses it specifically to describe a likeness of grief. In the case of *Titus*, however, the word is not only used in conjunction with woe but also associated with communication, understanding and the imagination: Titus imagines what Lavinia would say and tries to communicate what she feels. It is striking that the word *sympathy* is used in this context and not in the passage later in 3.1 in which Titus employs a set of meteorological metaphors to describe his bodily passions. Titus's speech about a 'sympathy of woe' thus represents an important moment in the history of the word *sympathy* and highlights the ways in which Shakespeare's early dramatic and poetic works played an important role in refining and modifying the meaning of the term.

III

In the remainder of this article I want to discuss the ways in which the concept of sympathy relates to the emotional responses of the play's audiences and readers. *Titus's* fascination with the relativity or comparability of sorrows is also apparent in 3.2 – the so-called fly scene, first printed in the Folio – and here Shakespeare raises further questions about the ways in which grief might impede our ability to tell the difference between representation and reality. The Boy asks Titus to break off his sorrowful speech and instead to make Lavinia merry 'with some pleasing tale' (3.2.47). Marcus notes the extent to which the Boy is moved by Titus's pain: 'Alas, the tender boy in passion moved / Doth weep to see his grandsire's heaviness' (48–9). Yet their discussion of the Boy's passion is broken off

when Marcus stabs at a fly with his knife. Titus berates Marcus for his murderous act, and when Marcus responds that he has 'but killed a fly' (59), Titus invites him to consider the grieving parents the fly has left behind:

'But'?
How if that fly had a father and a mother?
How would he hang his slender gilded wings
And buzz lamenting doings in the air.
Poor harmless fly,
That with his pretty buzzing melody
Came here to make us merry, and thou hast killed him.
(3.2.60–6)

Here Titus's powers of sympathy are extended as he projects his own paternal grief for Lavinia's plight onto the newly deceased fly. Yet the scene also suggests that Titus's sympathy for the fly is excessive, or even arbitrary. Indeed the instability of Titus's interpretation of the fly is revealed when Marcus states that he killed the 'black ill-favoured fly' (67) because it reminded him of Aaron the Moor. Titus immediately accepts Marcus's suggestion that the fly is a figure for Aaron, and he asks Marcus's forgiveness, repeatedly stabbing the fly with Marcus's knife. It is at this point that Marcus points to the fragility of Titus's mind, in terms that are particularly germane to the present discussion: 'Alas, poor man! Grief has so wrought on him / He takes false shadows for true substances' (80–1). On one level, this comment suggests that Titus has lost the ability to tell the difference between fantasy and reality. For Bate the scene represents 'a glorious comic parody of tragic empathy'.[29] But rather than simply being a parody, we might also see Marcus's comment as reflecting upon the audience's engagement with the fictional world of *Titus Andronicus*. After all, the word *shadow*

---

[29] Bate, 'Introduction' p. 121. Charlotte Scott has also written about this scene in 'Still Life? Anthropocentrism and the Fly in *Titus Andronicus* and *Volpone*', *Shakespeare Survey 61* (Cambridge, 2008), pp. 256–68. Scott writes that 'This scene uses shadow to find its way to substance . . . the shadow or flattery of distraction leads Titus into action' (p. 264), but she does not tease out fully the metadramatic implications of Titus's comment.

is often used by Shakespeare to refer to actors, or to artistic representation more generally.[30] Most strikingly, perhaps, the word is used to describe a painted representation of the tragic Hecuba in *The Rape of Lucrece*, in the context of Lucrece's passionate reaction to her plight: 'On this sad shadow Lucrece spends her eyes, / And shapes her sorrow to the beldame's woes' (1457–8). These passages from *Titus* and *Lucrece* implicitly explore the ways in which audiences and readers might respond to 'false shadows' – the fictional personages who inhabit Shakespeare's plays and poems – as though they were 'true substances'. Both texts suggest that powerful representations of grief can work to blur any simple dichotomy between 'real' and 'imagined' emotions.

Certainly *Titus Andronicus* is interested in the ability of fictional narratives – including, implicitly, the play itself – to elicit an emotional reaction amongst readers and spectators. This concern with the complex interplay between life and art is made more explicit at the end of the fly-scene. We find that Titus is still attempting to make sense of unspeakable events by returning to other texts. He seems to want to replace emotion with narrative, and proposes a retreat to Lavinia's closet in order to read sorrowful tales:

> Come, take away. Lavinia, go with me;
> I'll to thy closet and go read with thee
> Sad stories chanced in the times of old.
> Come, boy, and go with me; thy sight is young,
> And thou shalt read when mine begin to dazzle.
>
> (3.2.82–6)

On one level, this recourse to other sad stories could be seen as a denial of reality. Yet Titus's remarks also point to the consolations that such tales can offer. In the following scene Titus suggests further ways in which fictional narratives can offer a welcome distraction from suffering: 'Come and take choice of all my library, / And so beguile thy sorrow till the heavens / Reveal the damned contriver of this deed' (4.1.34–6). For Cora Fox, this is a problematic moment for Titus, in the sense that he is deluded about the ability of literature to make sense of one's sorrows: 'Titus tries to instruct

Lavinia about literature's place in social life – that it can entertain her, or distract her from the "real" sorrows occurring around her – but literature in this play, and especially Ovid's poetry, does not function in the way Titus describes.' Fox goes on to suggest that 'Titus appears to be spouting a useless and escapist aesthetic theory.'[31] Yet the fact that Titus encourages Lavinia to compare her sorrows to those described within other texts does not necessarily suggest that Titus's aesthetic theory is useless: the play suggests, rather, that we need narratives to make sense of our lives, and to contemplate others' suffering. This is perhaps analogous to the way in which Titus uses the concept of occult sympathies as a way of expressing and making sense of his passions, despite his apparent awareness that the concept may be more fanciful than real.

The use of fictional or mythical narratives as a way of articulating extreme passions is also a focus of the play's final scene. The Roman Lord seeks an explanation for why the body of Rome – in a metaphorical sense – has been dismembered like Lavinia's body:

> Speak, Rome's dear friend, as erst our ancestor
> When with his solemn tongue he did discourse
> To lovesick Dido's sad-attending ear
> The story of that baleful burning night
> When subtle Greeks surprised King Priam's Troy.
> Tell us what Sinon hath bewitched our ears,
> Or who hath brought the fatal engine in
> That gives our Troy, our Rome, the civil wound.
>
> (5.3.79–86)

The Roman Lord here attempts to pre-empt the story he is about to hear by placing it in the context of other sad stories. He explicitly alludes to Aeneas's tale to Dido, one of the archetypal

---

[30] See the *OED*'s definition of *shadow*: 'Applied rhetorically to a portrait as contrasted with the original; also to an actor or a play in contrast with the reality represented' (*OED*, 6b). Cf. Theseus's comments in *A Midsummer Night's Dream*: 'The best in this kind are but shadows, and the worst are no worse if imagination amend them' (5.1.210–11).

[31] Fox, *Ovid and the Politics of Emotion*, pp. 113–14.

tragic narratives in the period.[32] And yet what has occurred is so dreadful that Marcus struggles to put it into words or translate it into a story. Nonetheless he is able to say that he cannot speak, and he tells us (rhetorically) what the effects of his narrative would have been:

> My heart is not compact of flint nor steel,
> Nor can I utter all our bitter grief,
> But floods of tears will drown my oratory
> And break my utterance even in the time
> When it should move ye to attend me most,
> And force you to commiseration.   (87–92)

Again, the audience's response is anticipated, but in a highly self-conscious manner. Marcus claims that he does not conform to the conventional male stereotype – which we considered earlier – of being flint-hearted, and is thus incapable of articulating his grief without being overwhelmed by tears. Yet he goes on to suggest the emotional power that such a speech would have, echoing Philip Sidney's claims that tragedy 'stir[s] the affects of admiration and commiseration'.[33] On the one hand, then, this passage seems to confirm the idea – described by Horace, Quintilian and many Renaissance commentators on acting and oratory – that an actor's tears could provoke spontaneous tears in their audience, and 'force [us] to commiseration'. On the other hand, however, it is worth emphasizing that this is a description of Marcus's story, rather than the thing itself. It is Lucius who offers a partial account of the play's events, after which Marcus finally begins his own narrative. The passage cited above invites the audience to *imagine* a scene of tragic storytelling, and perhaps it is all the more powerful for the fact that Marcus's tale is temporarily withheld from us. Marcus invokes the idea of emotional contagion and spontaneous sympathy, but it features here primarily as a rhetorical trope. This moment further highlights the extent to which sympathy in the play is often relational, comparative and intertextual – and bound up with the audience's imagination.

Perhaps, then, what is most striking about the emotional landscape of *Titus Andronicus* is that various early modern conceptions of the passions – such as occult sympathies and correspondence, humoral theory and rhetorical affect – are employed in ways that highlight their metaphorical or imaginary status. The play suggests that conceptions of emotional correspondence in the period involved a degree of imagination, projection and self-recognition, long before the supposed emergence of 'modern' notions of sympathy in the eighteenth century. This is not to say that the play is incapable of producing spontaneous tears in its audiences, nor that Shakespeare is dismissing Galenic humoral theory in any simple sense, but rather to suggest that *Titus* reflects upon the multiple and complex ways in which early moderns understood and experienced the grief of others. Along with several other early Shakespearian works the play dramatizes – and thereby facilitates – the redeployment of *sympathy* as a new term for expressing a highly complex emotional and cognitive process. The representation of sympathy in *Titus Andronicus* thus allows us to question certain critical conceptions of early modern emotion and reminds us that Shakespeare's works present us with a range of frameworks and models for thinking about the attempts of his characters – and perhaps his audiences and readers – to 'passionate' their grief.

---

[32] See James, 'Dido's Ear', pp. 366–8.

[33] Philip Sidney, *The Defence of Poesy in The Oxford Authors: Sir Philip Sidney*, ed. Katherine Duncan-Jones (Oxford, 1989), pp. 212–50 at 230. See Bate's note to 5.3.92.

WHO DREW THE JEW THAT SHAKESPEARE KNEW? MISERICORDS AND MEDIEVAL JEWS IN *THE MERCHANT OF VENICE*

M. LINDSAY KAPLAN

The question of what Shakespeare knew about Jews is necessarily a speculative one; for those of us who have offered suggestions, most have focused on written evidence contained in manuscripts and printed books produced and circulated in the early modern period. In this article I would like to propose considering the influence of persisting medieval visual representations of Jews in early modern English culture. In his book, *A Year in the Life of William Shakespeare*, James Shapiro imagines the 'aesthetic monotony' of early modern Stratford-upon-Avon, 'broken only by painted cloths that adorned interiors' and lamenting the post-Reformation loss of Holy Trinity's vivid paintings of religious scenes.[1] Although many religious images created for churches and cathedrals in medieval England were destroyed during the Reformation, a less colourful, virtually overlooked form of medieval art endures at Stratford to the present day: the twenty-six misericord carvings in the chancel of Holy Trinity Church. Crafted in the first half of the fifteenth century, these images represent a range of subjects, including real and fantastical animals, human figures and faces, foliage and heraldic emblems.[2] These depictions, many of which may have been inspired by illuminated manuscripts or book illustrations, suggest the continuing influence of medieval visual representations on early modern culture. A considerable number of these illuminated manuscripts and wood carvings survive in libraries and churches today. While we need to learn more about the accessibility and circulation of medieval graphic and plastic arts in the early modern period, we can assume that at

least as many if not more of these images persisted in Shakespeare's time.

In this article, I focus on one of the Stratford misericord carvings: an image of a devil framed on either side by two human faces rendered in profile. I demonstrate, using evidence from depictions in medieval visual representations, that the two men in the image represent Jews. However, an examination of visual and verbal portrayals of the demonic in the medieval period reveals, in addition to the convention for linking Jews to the devil noted by Joshua Trachtenberg, a more widespread association of the diabolic with heretics and sinful Christians, both clerical and lay. The correlation between Satan, or his earthly representative, Antichrist, and Christians becomes even more emphatic in post-Reformation England in polemical theological debates. While Jews still figure in early modern views of the diabolical, their importance is minimized in relation to what is perceived to be the larger threat posed by Catholicism or, depending on one's profession, varying iterations of Protestantism. Strikingly, *The Merchant of Venice* emphasizes the earlier association of Jews and the devil expressed in medieval exempla, other religious texts and visual art, including the Stratford misericord. While the play also links Christians, as

---

[1] James S. Shapiro, *A Year in the Life of William Shakespeare, 1599* (New York, 2005), p. 25.

[2] Russell Fraser describes the Stratford misericords in passing, noting only that they are 'not easily parsed'. Russell Fraser, *Shakespeare: A Life in Art* (New Brunswick, 2008), pp. 35–6.

well as Muslims, to the demonic, it overwhelmingly insists on a primary relation of Jews to the devil. In this regard, its representation of Shylock and Tubal perpetuates a particularly negative strand of medieval depictions of Jews that has become largely superseded in post-Reformation England. Shakespeare's linking of Jewish men to the devil anomalously continues a Catholic tradition preserved in the Holy Trinity misericords. While I cannot definitively prove this carving's influence on the author, I argue that it, like the play, represents an archaic, antagonistic view of Jews that had gradually receded in other contemporary discourses.

MISERICORDS

Misericords are wood carvings that make up part of the choir stall, the area in which monks would stand to chant the Divine Office, prayers recited in praise of God throughout the day and night. Because these prayers were lengthy, the stalls were fitted with hinged seats with a ledge on the underside; when closed, these ledges provided a little support to clerical posteriors, enabling chanters to rest a bit while still standing in prayer. Hence their name, from the Latin *misericordia*, 'compassion'; their placement lessened the rigours of the monks' duties.[3] The artisans who carved these stalls exercised their creative licence in fashioning a variety of embellishments on the undersides of the seats. Scholars continue to debate why these carvings escaped iconoclastic destruction but, whatever the reason, approximately 3,300 misericords exist today in 255 cathedrals and churches in England.[4] The Holy Trinity choir stall is carved out of a solid piece of black oak and dates, in all likelihood, from the second quarter of the fifteenth century.[5] Traditionally, misericord carvings cover a wide range of topics, including 'ancient fable traditions, early Christian literature and liturgy, scenes from everyday life, heraldry, popular romances and legends'.[6] Many misericord carvings seem to have been inspired by illuminated manuscript or book illustrations, and there is evidence that some have been taken from specific images in illustrated bibles

or bestiaries, revealing a link between the pictorial and plastic arts.[7]

That Shakespeare would have seen the Stratford carvings is practically without question. While the choir stall and misericords would originally have been hidden from public view, after the Reformation the rood screen that stood at the entrance to the chancel was torn down. Anyone living in Stratford in the second half of the sixteenth century would have had the opportunity to familiarize him or herself with this section of the church. Furthermore, evidence from the early seventeenth century indicates that Shakespeare assumed certain financial responsibilities associated with Holy Trinity that relate to this particular area of the church. In July 1605, he paid the hefty price of £440 to acquire an interest in the tithes from Stratford parish. The income from these tithes was accompanied by the duty to employ a priest and cover the costs of maintaining the chancel, where the misericords are located. These privileges also secured Shakespeare the right to be buried in the sanctuary, within a stone's throw of the misericords. Even though his acquisition of duties and benefits, as well as his choice to locate his tomb here, postdate the composition of the play, they may suggest a longstanding connection to and familiarity with this area of the church.[8]

The carving of interest to me in relation to *The Merchant of Venice* is a crude, homely image of a devil with large ears and four horns, somewhat damaged, and the profiles of two men, one of whom might be bearded, depicted with hoods, exaggeratedly large eyes, noses and lips

---

[3] Juanita Wood, *Wooden Images: Misericords and Medieval England* (Madison, 1999), pp. 16–17.

[4] Wood, *Wooden Images*, p. 19.

[5] Mary Frances White, *Fifteenth-Century Misericords in the Collegiate Church of Holy Trinity, Stratford-upon-Avon* (Stratford-upon-Avon, 1974, repr. 1991), p. 2.

[6] White, *Misericords*, p. 3.

[7] John Colin Dinsdale Smith, *A Guide to Church Woodcarvings: Misericords and Bench-ends* (Newton Abbot, 1974), p. 19.

[8] www.stratford-upon-avon.org/tour.html; Shakespeare Birthplace Trust Records Office, MS. ER 27/2; Misc. Doc. II, 3.

23. Devil and profiles of two Jews, # 18, Holy Trinity Church, Stratford-upon-Avon.

(Illustration 23). In her pamphlet on the Holy Trinity misericords, Mary White identifies these images as 'A satanic mask with four horns. A comic mask on each side'.[9] White tends to identify a number of the visages depicted in Holy Trinity's misericord as masks, but it seems to me that these are faces here; they sport head coverings and have necks, suggesting they represent human heads, not masks. Furthermore, they are represented in profile, with full-sided faces that extend to the back of the head, rather than flat forms with edges that would indicate a mask.

Even granting the likelihood that these images depict people and not masks, I still need to support my claim that the human faces in this carving represent Jews.[10] A consideration of Western conventions for the visual portrayal of Jews in the later medieval period helps to provide some of the necessary evidence. Ruth Mellinkoff's work on visual representations of social outsiders focuses a good deal of attention on the depiction of Jews. Because the subject is the outcast, many of the images of Jews that she considers are hostile and derogatory. One traditional means of denigratory representation was the portrayal in profile.

9 White, *Misericords*, p. 18.
10 Sylvia Tomasch, 'Postcolonial Chaucer and the Virtual Jew', in *The Postcolonial Middle Ages*, ed. Jeffrey Jerome Cohen (New York, 2000), pp. 243–60, and Elisa Narin Van Court, 'Socially Marginal, Culturally Central: Representing Jews in Late Medieval English Literature', *Exemplaria*, 12:2 (2000), 293–326, have demonstrated the continued and varied representation of Jews in England after the 1290 expulsion.

In Byzantine art, a sacred figure could not receive the beholder's veneration unless it was portrayed in a frontal or three-quarter position, for the strict profile was regarded as averted and was 'used only for figures who represented evil forces, such as Satan at the Temptation, Judas at the Last Supper and the Betrayal'. Although the significance of profile and back views in Western art is not as rigidly applicable as it appears to be in Byzantine art, nonfrontal views often have similar connotations. Strict profile and dorsal positions were frequently portrayed for enemies of the faith, and mockers, flagellators, and executioners, who, as we have seen, were depicted with many and varied deprecating attributes... The profile position was a favorite choice for the portrayal of Jews because it provided an opportunity to create stereotyped hooked noses for evil men.[11]

The portrayal in profile forged a link between the devil and the Jews, especially as the latter were almost exclusively used to represent enemies of the faith.[12] Of all the carvings that focus on the human head in the Trinity misericords, only these two faces are presented in profile.

The exaggeration and contorted representation of facial features provided another convention by which Jewishness could be indicated and degraded:

Distorted, and deformed... eyes were widely used as negative attributes. Excessively large eyes, for example, were considered ugly... From at least the thirteenth century, artists distorted noses, eyes, and mouths to produce Jewish caricatures. Typical distortions associated with Jews – enlarged eyes, hooked noses, enlarged mouths, and fleshy lips – became so common that the only differences we see are usually difference of degree, that is more or less exaggeration.[13]

While Jewish noses are frequently represented as hooked, they are not exclusively so. Large and/or deformed noses are also used in depictions of Jews. As Mellinkoff comments, 'Disparagement of the Jews in the visual arts by means of distortions and deformities is virtually endless... We would not expect to see a bulbous nose portrayed on a Jew, yet sometimes a stereotyped bulbous nose is the attribute of an identifiable Jew.'[14] She supports this claim with an image from the Taymouth Hours, an early fourteenth-century English illuminated manuscript, which depicts an event related in the N-Town Nativity and in other sources: when a Jew attempts to attack Mary's bier at the Assumption, he finds his hands irreversibly affixed to it.[15] In this depiction, the Jew's head turns awkwardly to the side to show his bulbous, foreshortened nose in profile, in contrast to the straight and proportional noses of the twelve Christians carrying Mary's bier.

If we look closely at the Stratford carving, we note all of these conventions at play (Illustrations 24 and 25, details of carvings on left and right, respectively, of Illustration 23). Both men have disproportionally large noses, although neither is the classic hooked nose frequently employed in depictions of Jews. The image on the left has a partially hooked nose that appears squashed or foreshortened into an ugly bulbous stub (Illustration 24). In the figure on the right, the ridge of the nose is again curved and foreshortened, but distorted further with a grotesquely large and deep nostril (Illustration 25). Both profiles have oversized eyes set in deep, exaggerated sockets; a prominent, bulging cheekbone further deforms the face of the figure on the left. The carver has also endowed both faces with prominent lips that emphasize and disfigure their mouths. The left-hand figure appears to be grinning, while the opposing figure opens his mouth as if to bare his teeth; grimacing mouths and, in particular, gnashing teeth are frequently employed in the depiction of the Jewish tormenters of Jesus.[16]

In addition, medieval images of Jews often portray them with beards. While facial hair did

---

[11] Ruth Mellinkoff, *Outcasts: Signs of Otherness in Northern European Art of the Late Middle Ages*, vol. 1 (Berkeley, 1993), pp. 211–12.

[12] Bernhard Blumenkranz, *Le Juif médiéval au miroir de l'art chrétien* (Paris, 1966), pp. 96–104.

[13] Mellinkoff, *Outcasts*, vol. 1, pp. 123, 127–8.

[14] Mellinkoff, *Outcasts*, vol. 1, pp. 128, 130.

[15] Lisa Lampert, *Gender and Jewish Difference from Paul to Shakespeare* (Philadelphia, 2004), pp. 133, 225 notes 109 and 110.

[16] James Marrow, *Passion Iconography in Northern European Art of the Late Middle Ages and Early Renaissance: A Study of the Transformation of Sacred Metaphor into Descriptive Narrative* (Kortrijk, 1979), pp. 41–3.

24. Detail of Illustration 23, carving on left.

not always indicate evil, it took on a negative connotation when combined with other disparaging and distorted features, such as noses. Because depictions of devils utilized bestial features such as horns and beards, the application of the latter to representations of Jews provided another means of stigmatization.[17] The demon in the Stratford misericord, while damaged, displays the remnants of a goatish beard along the line of his lower jaw (Illustration 23). The image on the left may also have a beard running along the bottom of his face; because the folds of his hood meet up next to his chin, it is difficult to determine if the extended rim of the man's lower face represents hair or an exaggerated jawbone. The sideburns, cheeks and chin of the figure on the right are carved in a regular, textured manner, giving a clearer

indication of a close beard. In connection with the other distorted features discussed above, the beard on at least one of these figures could have been taken as another indication of Jewish identity.

Finally, the fact that these men are depicted as wearing some kind of head covering also suggests that they are intended to represent Jews. Hats are one of the principal means of establishing Jewish identity in visual representations from the twelfth century on.[18] Jewish 'headgear was multivalent, [and] usually became identifying in context or when accompanied by other characterizing attributes . . . [C]ertain types of Jews' hats

[17] Debra Higgs Strickland, *Saracens, Demons & Jews: Making Monsters in Medieval Art* (Princeton, 2003), pp. 65, 78.
[18] Mellinkoff, *Outcasts*, vol. 1, pp. 65–6.

25. Detail of Illustration 23, carving on right.

. . . were used as stigmatizing signs much earlier than the thirteenth century, and in an English ambience.'[19] While particular types of hats are more commonly associated with Jews, a variety of styles is used in their portrayal; among these is the hood.[20] Both figures in the Trinity carving wear what appears to be a type of soft, folded hood. This type of headgear appears in a number of English manuscripts dating from the thirteenth and fourteenth century that contain marginal caricatures of Jews.[21] One image of a Jew with a folded or flat hood appears in the 1240 King's Remembrancer Memoranda Roll next to an order that the wax of Jewish charters be put in a chest (Illustration 26).[22] Here the hood folds towards the front of the head, and the Jew is depicted in profile with a beard, pronounced hooked nose and distorted eye. The 1277

Essex Forest Roll also contains the profile image of a hooded Jew in the margin next to an account of a case in which Colchester Jews were prosecuted under the Law of the Forest for chasing a doe

[19] Mellinkoff, *Outcasts*, vol. 1, p. 91.

[20] Mellinkoff, *Outcasts*, vol. 1, p. 67.

[21] Cecil Roth, 'Portraits and Caricatures of Medieval English Jews', in *Essays and Portraits in Ango-Jewish History* (Philadelphia, 1962) pp. 22–5 at 23–4. While these images are more carelessly rendered, as caricatures they are more likely to betray immediate, unthinking visual stereotypes. Thanks to Lena Orlin for suggesting this point.

[22] Presumably the Jews used a particular type of wax to seal their loan documents; it might have been kept in the locked chest or *archa* in which such papers were customarily preserved. Roth, 'Portraits', p. 24; M. T. Clanchy, *From Memory to Written Record, England, 1066–1307* (Cambridge, MA, 1979), p. 51.

26. Marginal drawing of hooded Jew in the King's Remembrancer Memoranda Roll,
Henry III (1240).

through the streets of the city (Illustration 27). The clerk recording the proceedings included a depiction of Aaron, son of Leo, who was present in court to stand bail for one of the accused. The man's hood surrounds his face with the peak hanging at the back of his head; his eye and mouth are disproportioned and large, and his outsized nose is hooked, flattened and indented at the top. The badge in the shape of the two tablets of the law affixed to Aaron's lower garment confirms his Jewish identity; laws required English Jews to mark their outer garments in this fashion throughout the thirteenth century.[23] The caption above the image identifies its subject as 'Aaron, fil' diaboli', son of the devil.[24]

MEDIEVAL DEVILS

This reference to the devil brings us back to our Stratford carving and its inclusion of the devil between the profiles of the Jews. The association of Jews with the devil has been established by numerous scholars, most notably Trachtenberg,

but also, in a predominantly English context, Fisch, Felsenstein and Gross.[25] Trachtenberg argues that the New Testament and early Church Fathers elaborated a logic by which Jews are allied or identified with the devil: 'The two inexorable enemies of Jesus, then, in Christian legend, were the devil and the Jew, and it was inevitable that the legend should establish a causal relation between them.'[26] In the Gospel of John, Jesus identifies Jews, not as

---

[23] See Solomon Grayzel, *The Church and the Jews in the XIIIth Century* (New York, 1966), pp. 60–70 and Cecil Roth, *A History of the Jews in England* (Oxford, 1964), 3rd edn, pp. 95–6.

[24] Roth, 'Portraits', p. 24.

[25] Joshua Trachtenberg, *The Devil and the Jews: The Medieval Conception of the Jew and its Relation to Modern Antisemitism* (New York, 1966); Harold Fisch, *The Dual Image: The Figure of the Jew in English and American Literature* (New York, 1971); Frank Felsenstein, 'Jews and Devils: Anti-Semitic Stereotypes of Late Medieval and Renaissance England', *Journal of Literature and Theology*, 4 (1990), 15–28; John Gross, *Shylock: A Legend and Its Legacy* (New York, 1992).

[26] Trachtenberg, *Devil*, p. 20.

27. Marginal drawing of hooded
Jew in the Essex Forest Eyre (1277)

associated or identified with Antichrist. According to the ninth-century Archbishop of Mainz, Rabanus Maurus, in rejecting Jesus as the Messiah, the Jews in fact await the coming of the Antichrist: ' "The Jews dream of the coming of their Christ, whom we know to be the Antichrist".'[29] Other theologians, including Thomas Aquinas and Albertus Magnus, develop this idea further, explaining that 'Antichrist will be born in Babylon, of the tribe of Dan, will proceed to Jerusalem, where he will be circumcised, and will easily persuade the Jews that he is their long-awaited Messiah.'[30] Popular considerations of this topic imagined an 'antithetical parallel between Antichrist and the Christ, making the first the child of a union between the devil and a *Jewish* harlot – in deliberate contrast to the son of God and a Jewish virgin'.[31] This genealogy renders Antichrist both the son of the devil and Jewish by virtue of his mother's religion, thus merging Jew and demon. Trachtenberg also explores representations of the Jewish Antichrist in medieval visual and dramatic art.

Medieval sermon stories or exempla similarly develop the assumed relationship between Jews and devils by depicting them together in a number of tales. In the *Index Exemplorum*, a comprehensive list of motifs found in medieval exempla, Frederic Tubach lists six topoi in which Jews are represented with devils. Most of these portray the Jew as a magus able to call up demons and consult with them. In one narrative, a Jew conjures a demon in the appearance of the Virgin Mary; in two others a Jew invokes demons to inform him of the seducer of his daughter.[32] The most popular and

children of Abraham or of God, but of the devil: 'You are from your father the devil, and you choose to do your father's desires' (John 8:44). Here, John presents the relation as familial, and depicts the Jews as willing agents of the devil; he anticipates our thirteenth-century caricaturist, who identifies Aaron as the devil's offspring. In Revelations John suggests that Jews serve the devil by worshipping him in the 'synagogue of Satan' (Revelations 2:9, 3:9), a claim Chrysostom iterates when he states that ' "Jews do not worship God but devils".'[27]

The medieval articulation of the concept of Antichrist provides another means by which this relationship was ramified. A type of parody or inversion of Jesus, Antichrist is the leader of Satan's earthly forces. As understood through New Testament references, he 'takes on a distinct eschatological significance as Christ's principal opponent at the time of his Second Coming'.[28] Trachtenberg traces the trend by which Jews were

27 Quoted in Trachtenberg, *Devil*, pp. 20–1.
28 David Lyle Jeffrey, ed., *A Dictionary of Biblical Tradition in English Literature* (Grand Rapids, 1992), p. 44.
29 Trachtenberg, *Devil*, pp. 32, 224 n. 2.
30 Trachtenberg, *Devil*, p. 34.
31 Trachtenberg, *Devil*, p. 35. Interestingly for Trachtenberg, Mary's Jewishness does not register, while the harlot's does, as indicated by his italicization of the term indicating her religious identity.
32 Frederic C. Tubach, *Index Exemplorum: A Handbook of Medieval Religious Tales* (Helsinki, 1969), p. 219 #2794; p. 220 #2800, 2803–43; p. 136 #1663; p. 277 #3572.

widely recounted story is that of Theophilus, a good priest who was slandered and as a result loses his office. Desperate to repair his reputation, he asks a Jewish magus to summon the devil for him. Satan promises to restore Theophilus to his former position in exchange for his soul; the priest agrees to this bond, which he confirms in a parchment signed with his blood. However, after returning to his prior status, he repents of his sin and prays to the Virgin Mary; she releases him and miraculously returns the bond. Theophilus confesses and burns the bond, but dies shortly thereafter.[33] As Joan Gregg notes, various versions of this story accord greater or lesser responsibility to the Jew

in medieval manuscripts from England, France, and Germany... In a French version the Jew poses as Theophilus's friend and ally while actually being the instrument of his delivery into Satan's clutches; an English narrative in a collection of virgin miracles dilates on the Jew as 'a most wicked Hebrew soaked in all kinds of wickedness, who had already drowned many faithless men in the chasm of perdition'.[34]

In these versions, Jews serve as allies with the devil, sharing the common goal of destroying Christian souls.

Medieval visual representations intimate this allegiance by depicting Jews as resembling devils. The physical similarity emphasizes their shared identity as enemies of Jesus, a concept Trachtenberg traces to the New Testament and subsequent Christian discourses:

Thus, the tradition of a union between the two arch opponents of Christ seeped deeply into Christian thought... the devil and the Jew joined forces, in Christian belief, not only in the war against Jesus during his life on earth but also in the contemporaneous war against the Church and its civilization.[35]

As noted above, negative images of Jews depicted them with beards and distorted facial features – particularly hooked noses, but also deformed mouths and eyes; portrayals of devils also commonly share these attributes. Mellinkoff observes that Christian artists deployed these derogatory traits to depict evil figures; Debra Strickland demonstrates a tradition dating from antiquity that interpreted large,

misshapen or hooked noses and beards as signifying a range of sinful behaviours.[36] In this illustration of the Theophilus legend, included in a series of images depicting Miracles of the Virgin in a late thirteenth-century English Apocalypse, the artist establishes a correspondence between the devil and Jews by representing both with similar features (Illustration 28). While many versions of the legend include one Jewish magus, this depiction portrays three Jews and a devil approaching and surrounding the cleric. All of the antagonists, both devil and Jews, have distorted eyes, large, variously hooked noses and grotesquely wide, open mouths with reddened lips, bared teeth and beards; the three Jews all wear hats. The image presents the faces of the evil characters, as discussed earlier, in profile, in contrast to the conventional, symmetrical, clean-shaven features of the priest, which appear in three-quarter profile. In the depiction of the three figures on the left, as in our misericord carving, the artist positions two Jews on either side of a devil; here the demon holds or touches the cloaks of the Jews, indicating their collusion in the plot to destroy Theophilus's soul.

As Trachtenberg argues, Christian theological discourses – scripture, polemics and sermons – and visual images indisputably construct a malign and dangerous association between the devil and the Jews.[37] However, a consideration of a fuller range of Christian views of Satan reveals that this relationship is not exclusive. Devils are connected not only to other 'infidels' and sinful Christians, but also to Jesus himself. If we return to the evidence of Christian scripture, we find the devil is

---

33 Alfred Fryer, 'Theophilus the Penitent as Represented in Art', *The Archaeological Journal*, 92 (1935), 287–333 at 287–9.

34 Joan Young Gregg, *Devils, Women, and Jews: Reflections of the Other in Medieval Sermon Stories* (Albany, 1997), p. 216.

35 Trachtenberg, *Devil*, p. 20.

36 Ruth Mellinkoff, *Antisemitic Hate Signs in Hebrew Illuminated Manuscripts from Medieval Germany* (Jerusalem, 1999), pp. 23–7; Strickland, *Monsters*, pp. 77–9.

37 It is also important to note, as Narin Van Court argues, that medieval images and texts represent Jews in multiple ways, not always negatively; 'Socially Marginal', pp. 298–308, *passim*.

28. Jews and devil encouraging Theophilus to sell his soul; Apocalypse, Lambeth Palace Library

most frequently associated not with the Jews, but with his main antagonist, Jesus. All four gospels, but especially Luke and Matthew, relate numerous exorcisms that Jesus performs for people possessed by demons. As in medieval exempla portraying Jews and demons, scripture presents Jesus, in addition to resisting the three temptations of Satan, as having the power, albeit divine and beneficent, to control the actions of the devil. Eliseo Diamico argues that the New Testament's portrayal of Jesus serves as the model for later depictions of the magus or conjurer who has supernatural powers. He suggests that Matthew 4:8–9, when Satan tempts Jesus with worldly power, constitutes one of the most important prototypes of diabolical pacts to be found in biblical literature. Furthermore, given Jesus's popularity as a miracle-worker and exorcist, as well as his instructions to the Apostles to heal the sick, raise the dead, and expel demons

(Matthew 10:8–9), it is not difficult to understand the way some of the examples set forth through his own acts were to be emulated by other luminaries. Some of the latter, who in centuries to come became known as magi, acquired, more often than not, the reputation of being in league with the devil, much in the same way as Jesus did when the Pharisees accused him of being linked to Beelzebub (Matthew 12:24–5).[38]

The Pharisees are quick to notice and criticize Jesus's frequent association with the devil, as evidenced by their accusation that he casts out demons through the power of the devil Beelzebub (Matthew 9:34, 12:24; Luke 11:15). Medieval texts iterate this accusation; Ekbert of Schönau's

---

[38] Eliseo Frank Diamico, 'The Diabolical Pact in Literature: Its Transition from Legend to Literary Theme' (Ph.D. dissertation, University of Michigan, 1979), p. 2.

twelfth-century Passion treatise, the *Stimulus amoris*, in its depiction of the Jews' condemnation of Jesus, presents their accusation in the scriptural speech of the Pharisees: ' "This is not a man of God. Through Beelzebub, prince of demons, he casts out demons; he has a demon. He misleads the multitudes".'[39] Although Christian believers would dismiss this claim of the Pharisees, Jesus's power over demons is analogous to and probably more widely disseminated than that of the Jews.

Moreover, medieval exempla include many more stories associating devils with sinful Christians than with Jews, as further consideration of Tubach's *Index Exemplorum* confirms. Of the exempla dealing with Jews, discussed above, only six include the devil or demons and only one involves a pact with the devil – the Theophilus tale in which the Christian, not the Jew, makes the pact. Even in this case several versions of the tale omit the Jew and present Theophilus contacting the devil directly, as in one fifteenth-century English translation of Etienne de Besançon's *Alphabet of Tales*.[40] In contrast to the six tales depicting devils and Jews, over 140 different motifs represent devils with Christians, including seven pacts with the devil. One of these tales, that of the recording demon Tutivillus who writes down and collects in his sack the idle words spoken by Christians in church, appears in over thirty iterations, including the *Alphabet of Tales*. While some versions of this story target lay sinners, others focus on monks who garble the words of the mass.[41]

Similarly, medieval graphic and plastic arts frequently figure Christians as damned or accompanied by devils. In numerous representations of damnation, demons accompany Christian sinners to hell. Portrayals of heretics, heterodox students of philosophy and even clergy also occasionally associate them with the devil.[42] While Sarah Lipton is primarily interested in analysing intolerant representations of Jews in *bibles moralisées*, she also considers images

establishing the interrelationship of heretical exegesis, heretical vice and devil . . . [In one illustration] a cleric

holds up an open book and raises his finger in exposition while a demon whispers into his ear. In this image . . . a new idea appears: clerics who appear to be orthodox may actually create heresy and corrupt their congregation through false . . . interpretation of Scripture.[43]

Thus even ostensibly learned Christians, clergy and lay, are associated with the devil, a view that taps into the Theophilus legend and contributes to the later narratives of Faust, a doctor of divinity.[44]

Another context in which Christians accused their co-religionists of collusion with the devil emerged in medieval polemics on ecclesiastical reform, as well as in conflicts between church and state. Beginning in the eleventh century, popes and emperors accused each other of association with the devil in representing his earthly agent, Antichrist, either as a forerunner or as Antichrist himself. Contrary to Trachtenberg's account, the predominant medieval view associated the Church with demonic forces:

it was the Papacy itself and the institutional church as a whole which came to bear the brunt of the accusation. More and more groups, distressed by what they perceived to be widespread corruption and worldliness

---

[39] Quoted in Thomas H. Bestul, *Texts of the Passion: Latin Devotional Literature and Medieval Society* (Philadelphia, 1996), p. 83.

[40] Etienne de Besançon, *Alphabet of Tales: An English 15th Century Translation of the Alphabetum narrationum of Etienne de Besançon, from Additional MS. 25,719 of the British Museum*, ed. Mary Macleod Banks (London, 1904, 1905; Ann Arbor, 1997), http://name.umdl.umich.edu/AlphTales, pp. 318–19.

[41] Tubach, *Index*, pp. 133–4; Margaret Jennings, 'Tutivillus: The Literary Career of the Recording Demon', *Studies in Philology*, 74 (1977), 1–95, at 8, 10–34 *passim*.

[42] Sara Lipton, *Images of Intolerance: The Representation of Jews and Judaism in the Bible Moralisée* (Berkeley, 1999), pp. 82–111 *passim*.

[43] Lipton, *Intolerance*, p. 109.

[44] A widespread example of an image associating devils with Christians is that of the above-mentioned recording demon, Tutivillus, who appears in numerous visual representations in Western Europe. See Michael Camille's, 'The Devil's Writing: Diabolic Literacy in Medieval Art', *World Art: Themes of Unity in Diversity*, ed. Irving Lavin, vol. 2 (University Park and London, 1989), pp. 354–60 at 354.

within the Roman Church, identified the church, and frequently the popes themselves, as the apocalyptic Antichrist.[45]

In his analysis of four thirteenth-century Apocalyptic commentaries, David Burr notes that the authors tended to minimize the Jews' role, and focused instead on the threat posed by contemporary ecclesiastics and perhaps even the pope: 'those concerned with searching the Apocalypse for evidence of the antichrist tended to think the danger lay not outside the church but within it, that the antichrist would receive less help from Jews than from bishops'.[46] In particular, heretical groups such as the Cathars, Albigensians, Waldensians, Hussites and, in England, Lollards most frequently and fully develop the connection between Catholic Church and its leaders with the devil.[47] The late fourteenth-century 'Twelve Conclusions of the Lollards' in criticizing priestly orders, identifies the tonsure as 'þe leueree of antecryst' and decries the blessing of wine, bread, wax, et alia in the church as 'exorcismis . . . [and] þe uerray practy[s] of nigromancie . . . [W]e sen no þing of chaunge in no sich creature þat is so charmid but be fals beleue, þe whiche is þe principal of þe deuelis craft.'[48] Wycliff's followers suggest that monks, rather than serving Jesus, wear the livery of their true master, Antichrist, and perceive the consecration of foods or objects used in the church as equivalent to incantations of black magic inspired by the devil.

THE MERCHANT OF VENICE

While the pernicious association of Jews with devils in medieval religious discourses and visual images was not exclusive, *The Merchant of Venice* nevertheless focuses on this particular strand of medieval demonization in its frequent association or equation of the devil with Shylock, Tubal or other male Jews.[49] Antonio dismisses as devilish Shylock's citing of the Bible in support of his 'thrift': 'The devil can cite Scripture for his purpose' (1.3.94).[50] The Jew's failure to understand the truth of the scripture is likened to or is a version of the devil's perversion of holy writ. Other characters

in the play share the assumption of a nexus between Jews and the devil. For example, Launcelot claims Shylock 'is a kind of devil' and 'the very devil incarnation', perhaps even worse than the actual devil whose advice the servant follows in leaving his Jewish master (2.2.19, 21–2). Jessica acknowledges that her 'house is hell' (2.3.2), although she does not go so far as to compare her father to the devil. Shylock's entrance onto the stage in Act 3 is introduced by Solanio, who fears lest 'the devil cross [his] prayer, for here he comes in the likeness of a Jew' (3.1.17–19). When Shylock damns Jessica's flight, Salerio sarcastically concurs: 'That's certain, if the devil may be her judge' (3.1.29); here Shylock behaves like a devil in judging his daughter so harshly. Tubal is also associated with the devil, as

---

45 Jeffrey, *Biblical Tradition*, p. 45.

46 David Burr, 'Jews in Four Thirteenth-Century Apocalypse Commentaries', in *Friars and Jews in the Middle Ages and Renaissance*, ed. Steven J. McMichael and Susan E. Myers (Leiden and Boston, 2004), pp. 23–38 at 26–7, 29, 36. Burr acknowledges that the illuminated Apocalypse manuscripts, produced for a lay audience, did emphasize the Jews' role: 'the close identification of Jews and the antichrist in illuminated Apocalypses might be explained by suggesting that the latter were produced with polemical intent, aimed by anti-Jewish clergy at a segment of the laity that could do the Jews substantial damage. Beyond this it is worth noting that, unlike illuminated Apocalypses, commentaries were . . . written by clerics for clerical consumption. It would have been one thing for a cleric to criticize the *praelati* in a commentary and quite another for an illustrator to decide that the laity should see the minions of the antichrist wearing, not Jews' caps, but mitres . . . Thus any work aimed at a lay audience might have some reason to stress external rather than internal enemies' (pp. 36–7).

47 See Christopher Hill, *Antichrist in Seventeenth-Century England* (London and New York, 1971), pp. 7–8 and Nathan Johnstone, *The Devil and Demonism in Early Modern England* (Cambridge, 2006), p. 29.

48 Anne Hudson, *Selections from English Wycliffite Writings* (Toronto, 1997), pp. 25–6.

49 Jessica is excluded from this association; I have explored the gendering of Jewish identity elsewhere: M. Lindsay Kaplan, 'Jessica's Mother: Medieval Constructions of Jewish Race and Gender in *The Merchant of Venice*', *Shakespeare Quarterly*, 58 (2007), 1–30.

50 All quotations from Shakespeare are taken from *The Norton Shakespeare*, eds. Stephen Greenblatt *et al.*, 2nd edn (New York and London, 2008).

introduced by Solanio: 'Here comes another of the tribe. A third cannot be matched unless the devil himself turn Jew' (3.1.65–6). He implies that the Jews may be worse than demons, since the devil would have to convert to Judaism to match this incomparable pair. But we may also have a verbal picture of the misericord carving here, with the two Jews joined by a devilish third (Illustration 23).[51]

Another means by which the play constructs the Jew's connection to the devil is in its apparent assimilation of some elements of the Theophilus tale.[52] In Shakespeare's rendering, however, the Jew does not provide access to the devil, but stands for the devil himself. Antonio, a weak analogue for Theophilus, seems to enter into this bond with some knowledge of his creditor's demonic association, as in the medieval legend. The trial scene completes the Jew's identification with, if not transformation into the devil. Bassanio begs Portia to 'Wrest once the law to your authority. / To do a great right, do a little wrong, / And curb this cruel devil of his will' (4.1.210–12). He does not call his adversary by name, but simply identifies him as a devil. Shylock's desire to collect his bond puts him in the position of Theophilus's devil; in essence both seek the death of their debtors. Bassanio offers to forfeit his life, his wife and the world to save Antonio: 'I would lose all, ay, sacrifice them all / Here to this devil, to deliver you' (4.1.281–2). Shylock is again referred to as the devil, here thwarted not by the Virgin Mary, but by Portia. Granted, Portia, a cross-dressing, law clerk impersonator who marries at the play's end, seems a far cry from the Blessed Virgin. However, her cover story of awaiting Bassanio's return in prayer and contemplation at a neighbouring monastery suggests an odour of holiness that is somewhat realized in her pleas for compassion and her success in saving Antonio's body, if not his soul. Mary epitomizes intercession and mercy, and Portia verbalizes these values in her extended speech on the quality of mercy. In successfully extracting the bond and nullifying its contents, Portia in effect performs Mary's role while Shylock plays that of the devil in the Theophilus legend.

Nevertheless, as in the case of the scriptural and medieval evidence considered above, not all of the play's references to the devil associate him with Jews. In fact, Portia makes the first allusions to the devil in her deprecatory consideration of her suitors. In order to avoid being chosen by the excessively drunken German suitor, she would instruct Nerissa to 'set a deep glass of Rhenish wine on the contrary casket; for if the devil be within and that temptation without, I know he will choose it' (1.2.80–3). This suggestion is somewhat nonsensical, since the suitor cannot know what is in the casket before choosing it, but the implication appears to be that his desire for drink is so strong that he would knowingly choose damnation in order to be able to drink. The Prince of Morocco, described in the stage direction accompanying his entrance as a 'tawnie Moore', is linked by Portia with the devil because of the darkness of his skin colour: 'If he have the condition of a saint and the complexion of a devil, I had rather he should shrive me than wive me' (1.2.109–10). While some critics have argued that complexion could refer to 'temperament', the context does not support this reading. This comparison establishes a contrast between the inner condition and the outer complexion; clearly, skin colour is referenced here. The devil and demons are frequently described as black-skinned in patristic literature

---

[51] This may be proverbial, as Shakespeare uses it again in Queen Margaret's speech:

> Mischance and sorrow go along with you!
> Heart's discontent and sour affliction
> Be playfellows to keep you company!
> There's two of you; the devil make a third,
> And threefold vengeance tend upon your steps.
>
> (*2 Henry VI*, 3.2.303–6)

However, I have not found this form in early modern proverb lists, so it may be an invention of the author. On the other hand, the Lambeth Theophilus illustration creates a similar trio of a devil placed between two Jews.

[52] For the idea that the Theophilus legend operates as a source for *The Merchant of Venice*, see Jeffrey, *Biblical Tradition*, p. 203 and Diamico, 'Diabolical Pact', p. 157.

and are represented in dark colours in medieval illustrations.[53] Like Jews, Muslims and Africans were also associated with the devil in patristic, medieval and early modern texts.[54]

But national, racial and religious others are not the only ones associated with demons. Harkening back to the scriptural and literary examples considered above, Shylock reformulates the association of the Jewish sorcerer and the devil in his reference to pork as 'the habitation which your prophet the Nazarite conjured the devil into' (1.3.28–9). The stunning choice of the verb 'conjure' transforms the act that Jesus performs in the gospels of Matthew 8:28–2, Mark 5:1–13 and Luke 8:26–33 from an exorcism to an invocation of demons. Shylock's identification of the founder of Christianity as a demon-conjurer, puts him in the company of the Pharisees, Jesus's antagonists in the New Testament, a fitting comparison for a character who expresses hatred for Christians in the play. Nevertheless, these lines confirm Diamico's point that Jesus stands as a model for devil-conjuring magi.[55] They also affirm that Jesus has dealings with the devil, something that the play never overtly suggests in relation to Shylock. While he is called a devil by Christians, and ruthlessly seeks Antonio's death, neither Shylock, nor Tubal for that matter, ever addresses or associates himself with Satan.

Furthermore, Shylock is not the only character in the play to link Christians with devils. Launcelot voices an extended, imaginary colloquy between his conscience and 'the fiend', pondering departure from Shylock's service. The devil tempts Launcelot to abandon his master, a disobedient and morally repugnant action from an early modern perspective, while his conscience urges him to remain with Shylock. However, Launcelot reasons that in his circumstance, staying with the master poses greater spiritual danger than leaving:

To be ruled by my conscience I should stay with the Jew my master, who, God bless the mark, is a kind of devil; and to run away from the Jew I should be ruled by the fiend, who saving your reverence, is the devil himself. Certainly the Jew is the very devil incarnation; and in my conscience, my conscience is but a kind of hard conscience to offer to counsel me to stay with the

Jew. The fiend gives more friendly counsel. I will run, fiend. My heels are at your commandment. (2.2.17–25)

Launcelot's choice to remain or depart seems to be one of weighing the lesser of two evils: staying with Shylock means submitting to a Jew, a type of devil or his relation (kind signifying kin) versus being ruled by the devil himself in following his advice. The servant concludes that Shylock is the devil incarnate, the definition of the Antichrist, and that staying with him would be worse than giving into the devil's temptation. While Launcelot's conclusion serves to identify Shylock as the embodiment of the devil, it also represents the Christian as obeying the fiend's 'commandment' instead of God's. On the one hand, this episode contrasts the devil and the Jew in rewriting the Theophilus narrative by excluding the Jewish mediator and presenting the Christian as entering independently into his own deal with the devil. We should recall that while Jessica might liken her house to hell, Launcelot is identified as the 'merry devil' who populates her abode. On the other hand, Launcelot in effect identifies Shylock as Antichrist, reiterating the medieval association of this figure with the Jews.

If Shylock is the most consistently demonized character in the play, we still cannot say that he is exclusively so. The devil should serve to distinguish the damned and the saved, Jews and Christians, but its use in the play worries attempts to construct and maintain this difference: 'Which is the merchant here, and which the Jew?' (4.1.169). By characterizing Jesus as a conjurer of demons, even if intimated blasphemously by a Jew, the play opens up the possibility that Christians as well as Jews can be in league with the devil. These moments would seem to mitigate this aspect of the play's

---

[53] See Philip Mayerson, 'Anti-Black Sentiment in the *Vitae Patrum*', *Harvard Theological Review*, 71 (1978), 304–11 and Strickland, *Monsters*, pp. 68–71, 74.

[54] See Ania Loomba, *Shakespeare, Race and Colonialism* (Oxford, 2002), p. 27, Ania Loomba and Jonathan Burton, eds., *Race in Early Modern England: A Documentary Companion* (New York, 2007), p. 114, and Strickland, *Monsters*, pp. 80–6.

[55] Diamico, 'Diabolical Pact', p. 2.

anti-Semitism insofar as Jews have not cornered the market on the diabolical and do not hold, in this regard, a position of evil entirely distinct from Christians.[56] And yet, when compared to other early modern deployments of the demonic, we see that despite the play's association of the devil with Christians, its repeated emphasis on the concept of the demonic Jew is anomalous in its time. As James Shapiro observes, 'by the late sixteenth century the widespread medieval identification of Jews and the devil had virtually disappeared in England . . . a nation that had broken with its Catholic past'.[57]

EARLY MODERN DEVILS

The polemical exigencies of the Reformation shift vilifying attacks away from Jews, and focus them on a more formidable opponent: the Catholic Church. As Christopher Hill explains, 'With Luther and the adoption of Lutheranism as a state religion in many countries, the doctrine that the Pope is Antichrist, hitherto mostly associated with disreputable lower-class heretics, acquired a new respectability.'[58] In addition to his writings on this subject, Luther published the famously scandalous collection of Lucas Cranach's woodcuts entitled *Depiction of the Papacy* (1545), ensuring that the association of the pope with the devil would reach a popular audience. This piece of anti-papal pictorial propaganda consisted of nine or ten derogatory images, several of which depict the pope and papacy in a demonic context.[59] In his analysis of this text, Robert Scribner notes that 'Luther spent a good deal of his career as a Reformer attacking the papacy both as the Antichrist and as a product of the Devil. It was fitting then [that] the sheet entitled "The Origin of the Pope" should show him being born of the Devil.'[60] In addition to Luther, all the leading continental reformers – including Calvin and Melanchthon – identified the pope or the papacy with Antichrist.[61]

This rehabilitation and development of the heretical concept of the diabolical papacy was enthusiastically redeployed in England, where a version of it had emerged in the Lollard movement. As Nathan Johnstone observes:

[56] The association of Jews with devils does not extend to Shakespeare's other plays that represent the demonic, such as *Macbeth* or *1* and *2 Henry VI*, or to iterations of the Vice figure, such as Iago or Aaron.

[57] James Shapiro, *Shakespeare and the Jews* (New York, 1996), p. 33. He is largely correct in this point, though *Merchant* is the exception that proves his rule. One might argue, as G. K. Hunter does, that *The Jew of Malta* also continues the medieval Jewish-devil equation. Hunter points out that the *Glossa Ordinaria* identifies the biblical Barabbas as the son of the devil in contrast to Jesus; 'so Barabbas is to be interpreted as *Antichristi typus*' and suggests references elsewhere to *The Chester Play of Antichrist* and to hellmouth, in Barabbas's final descent into a boiling cauldron. G. K. Hunter, 'The Theology of Marlowe's *The Jew of Malta*', *Journal of the Warburg and Courtauld Institutes*, 27 (1964), 211–40 at 214, 233–5. John Parker similarly identifies Barabbas with Antichrist, but barely registers the former's Judaism. Parker brilliantly demonstrates how Christian tradition and Marlowe's play stage the virtual equivalence of Antichrist and Christ. See John Parker, *The Aesthetics of Antichrist* (Ithaca, 2007), pp. 193–209. However, none of the Christians in *The Jew of Malta* identify the Jew with the devil. Ithamore does identify Barabbas as a devil twice: 3.3.18 and 3.4.54–5. On the other hand, Ithamore and Barabbas characterize Christians as devils four times: 1.2.154; 1.2.338–40; 4.1.190; 5.1.41. The crux at 4.1.19 in the Quarto, in which Barabbas expostulates, 'Catho diabola', may refer to Abigail, whose apostasy he currently laments; is she a Catholic she-devil? We should also recall that Marlowe offers an early modern figure as the play's explicit source of villainy: Machiavelli, or *Macheuil* in the Quarto's spelling. All references to Christopher Marlowe, *The Jew of Malta*, ed. Richard W. Van Fossen (Lincoln, NE, and London, 1964).

[58] Hill, *Antichrist*, p. 9.

[59] Robert Scribner, *Popular Culture and Popular Movements in Reformation Germany* (London, 1987), p. 278.

[60] Scribner, *Popular Culture*, p. 283. This image portrays the pope's birth as a defecation emitted from a female demon. Three other images emphasize the diabolical nature of the papacy: the image of the so-called 'Papal Ass', a grotesque figure comprised of a mixture of human and animal parts, employed the monstrous, as the embodiment of sin, to make this association with the devil (who was frequently depicted with bestial features) (Scribner, pp. 285–6; Strickland, *Monsters*, pp. 61–5); the image entitled 'Digna merces papae satanissimi et cardinalium suorum' (the just reward of the most satanic pope and his cardinals) depicts the pope and three cardinals hung on a gallows while their souls are carried off by demons; and the final image of the series, entitled 'Regnum Satanae et Papae' (the reign of Satan and the pope) depicts an ass-eared pope enthroned on hellmouth and surrounded by devils. The German caption which accompanies

The study of the Devil in early modern English culture begins with the Reformation, or more precisely, with the understanding of Satanism that emerged out of Protestant attempts to comprehend the corruption of traditional Catholicism. As the will to reform in England gathered pace, Protestant polemicists targeted not only specific clerical abuses but the Roman faith as a whole. They adopted a long-established heretical association of the Pope with Antichrist, and behind Antichrist lay the Devil, the guiding hand of apocalyptic subversion.[62]

In early modern England the devil was primarily associated with the pope or 'papistry'. Hill documents the scope of this construction: 'in the century which separates Archbishop Cranmer from Archbishop Abbott (1533–1633), the old medieval heresy that the Pope was Antichrist had been almost officially accepted by the Church of England'.[63] Not only did leading Elizabethan bishops and archbishops such as Jewell, Aylmer, Richard Cox and Sandys espouse the view that the pope or papacy represented Antichrist, but laymen as diverse as Lord Burghley, Ralph Holinshed and even King James VI, who argued as much in his 1588 commentary on Revelations, did as well. Poets also take up the idea; most notable in the late sixteenth century is Edmund Spenser's 'Booke of Holinesse', the first volume of *The Faerie Queene*, which draws on Protestant readings of the book of Revelations to depict Catholicism in various demonic guises. The decades spanning the end of the sixteenth century saw the publication of numerous and lengthy texts on the subject.[64]

If the association of Catholicism with the devil was ubiquitous, it did not constitute a consensus; beginning in the 1590s, and during the same period which saw increasing publication on this subject, dissenting voices begin to call this virtual article of faith into question.[65] By the early decades of the seventeenth century, a diversity of opinions about Antichrist and the devil sprouted in religious polemic. In addition to the continued belief that the pope was Antichrist, moderate Protestants felt that remnants of Antichrist remained in the Church of England, more radical separatists thought that Antichrist

pervaded the entire English church, while conservative factions questioned the identification of Catholicism with the devil.[66] Roman Catholics obviously took a very different view on the matter in the course of the Counter-Reformation. In the wake of the Reformation's aggressive identification of Catholicism with the devil, defenders of the Roman Church and the papacy responded by re-emphasizing the idea of the demonic Jew, formulated in the medieval period.[67] Protestants did not wholly abandon the association of Jews with the devil; as William Perkins explained in a sermon on Revelations preached in 1595: 'the Iewes, that were once a most famous people... are now become the Sinagogue of Sathan ... but now for their vnbeleefe they are cast off from God'.[68] Nevertheless in this case and in so many others, the example of the Jews was frequently cited as an object lesson in order to demonstrate the more disturbing case of the Catholics or even radical Protestant sects:

when ... [the Jews] remained obstinate, reiecting and persecuting both [the Apostles] and their doctrines then they ceased to bee a church of God, and became the synagogue of Sathan... Whereby we see...a church of God becommeth no church, when they embrace an heresie against the foundation of religion ... Hence we

---

it reads: 'Here sits the pope in the name of all devils; now it is plain that he is the true Antichrist foretold in Scripture' (Scribner, *Popular Culture*, pp. 290, 292–5, 298).

[61] Hill, *Antichrist*, p. 9.

[62] Johnstone, *Devil*, p. 26.

[63] Hill, *Antichrist*, pp. 31–2.

[64] Hill, *Antichrist*, pp. 11, 19–20.

[65] Hill, *Antichrist*, p. 33. It should of course be noted that in early modern England the devil was also widely associated with witches, criminals, the theatre, internal political factions, foreign enemies, average Protestants and even with the godly, who were understood as particularly victimized by the devil's temptations. See Johnstone, *Devil*, pp. 1–26 passim. However, Catholicism was most prominently linked with the devil in the period.

[66] Hill, *Antichrist*, p. 62.

[67] Hill, *Antichrist*, pp. 178–9.

[68] William Perkins, *A godly and learned exposition or commentarie vpon the three first chapters of the Reuelation. Preached in Cambridge by that reuerend and iudicious diuine, maister William Perkins, Ann. Dom. 1595* (1606), p. 103.

may learne, first, what we are to thinke and iudge of the church of the papists, of the Libertines and Anabaptists, familie of Loue, and such like.[69]

Scriptural Jews could be cited to elucidate the workings of the devil, but in an officially *judenrein* England, contemporary Jews were of much less concern to reformers than Christian adversaries on the right or the left.[70]

Concerns about the devil and his power continued to loom large in the transition from the medieval to early modern period in England as did preoccupation with Antichrist, particularly in the wake of Reformation religious upheavals, which led many to believe they were living in apocalyptic times. While some early modern English texts considered the relationship of the Jews to the devil and Antichrist, most understood the diabolical threat as located within one or more of the various Christian sects, or even, in the face of Ottoman military and economic power, Islam.[71] The association of Catholicism with the devil was not a consensus in early modern England, but polemical debates on the identity of Antichrist and the demonic were primarily focused on the pope and the Roman Church and secondarily on intra-Protestant religious conflicts as well as political debates that roiled seventeenth-century England. Jews continue to represent a type of sinful behaviour, and the most virulent medieval view still circulates, but authors tend to use the example of biblical Jews to condemn the practices of contemporary Christians. In fact, many of the attacks directed against Jews in the medieval period – such as charges of idolatry or blindness in terms of understanding the Bible's true meaning – are repurposed by early modern authors and applied to Catholics or radical Protestants.[72]

The *Merchant of Venice*'s emphasis on the more virulent medieval construction of the demonic Jew is certainly due to more than one factor.[73] This association of the devil and the Jew does not depend on Shakespeare interpreting the misericord carving as I have or even on his having viewed it. As I have demonstrated, a wide array of medieval representations of demonic Jews, visual

and verbal, exists to this very day; certainly some or more of these circulated in the period in which the play was composed. Although I can't definitively prove that the misericord carving influenced Shakespeare's depiction of the male Jews in the play, I can however suggest that this proximate example of one of the more negative medieval constructions

69 Perkins, *A godly and learned exposition*, p. 102; see also Johnstone's discussion of this passage, *Devil*, pp. 53–4.

70 On the question of Protestant views on the Jews in relation to Antichrist, Hill comments: 'In most protestant versions, on the other hand, despite occasional reference to "Antichrist and his synagogue", the Jews play a much less sinister role: their conversion indeed is the prelude to the fall of Antichrist and to the millennium... Much controversial protestant energy was therefore spent in proving that Antichrist could not be a Jew, and that he had already come' (*Antichrist*, pp. 179–80).
     Shapiro demonstrates that the unofficial presence of Jews in early modern England caused little alarm: 'in case after case the English show little surprise or concern at the discovery of Jews living in their midst' (*Shakespeare*, p. 76).

71 In light of the considerable economic military power of the Ottoman empire in the early modern period, Islam was also associated with Antichrist: 'In Mediterranean countries the idea that the Turk was Antichrist naturally had some popularity. In England... Aylmer and Foxe were prepared to add [the 'Turk'] to the Pope as Antichrist, and many followed them' (Hill, *Antichrist*, p. 181).

72 A number of the accusations against Catholicism mirror earlier allegations about Judaism: idolatry, justification by works, necromancy, carnality and ignorance. See Peter Lake, 'Anti-Popery: The Structure of a Prejudice', in Richard Cust and Ann Hughes, eds., *Conflict in Stuart England: Studies in Religion and Politics, 1630–1660* (London, 1989), pp. 72–105 at 74–83: 'it is tempting to observe, paraphrasing Sartre's remark about anti-semitism, that if popery had not existed Protestants and, in particular Puritans, would have had to invent it' (p. 83). The most scandalous image in Luther's broadside, the papal 'Sow-ride', intentionally associated the papacy with the antisemitic '*Judensau*' motif, as noted in Scribner, *Popular Culture*, pp. 291–2.

73 For example, see John Cox's arguments that Shakespeare's plays, in contrast to those of his contemporaries, tend to draw on more traditional representations of the devil; 'Devils and Power in Marlowe and Shakespeare', *Yearbook of English Studies*, 23 (1993), 46–64 and 'Stage Devilry in Two King's Men Plays of 1606', *Modern Language Review*, 93 (1998), 934–47. However, he makes no mention of Jews in his book, *The Devil and the Sacred in English Drama, 1350–1642* (Cambridge, 2000).

of Jewish identity may account for Shakespeare's decision to depict Shylock and Tubal as types of the devil. Furthermore, given other contemporary representations of the devil and the range of available views of Jews, this article shows that Shakespeare chose to emphasize a particularly hostile tradition of medieval anti-Jewish representations. While the *Merchant of Venice* also represents a wider association of the devil with Christians, the play is anomalous in the period in its insistent correlation of the Jew with the devil. In contrast to most other early modern texts, and especially to literary discourses, this play perpetuates the medieval view of contemporary, not biblical, Jews as confederates of the devil. In doing so, Shakespeare was clearly swimming against the dominant current in restaging a particularly deleterious construction of Jewish evil.

'IMAGINARY PUISSANCE': SHAKESPEARIAN THEATRE AND THE LAW OF AGENCY IN *HENRY V, TWELFTH NIGHT* AND *MEASURE FOR MEASURE*

ERICA SHEEN

Piece out our imperfections with your thoughts:
Into a thousand parts divide one man,
And make imaginary puissance.
Think, when we talk of horses, that you see them,
Printing their proud hoofs i'th' receiving earth;
For 'tis your thoughts that now must deck our kings
(*Henry V*, Prologue 23–8)[1]

There is an unusually close relationship between the information we use to date the writing of *Henry V* and the kind of ideas with which its critics have chosen to approach it. Written at a time in Shakespeare's career associated with the opening of the Globe and his increasing visibility in print, on the one hand it elicits commentary on questions of dramatic authorship; on the other, the association between the reference to Essex's expedition to Ireland at the beginning of Act 5 and its subject matter as a 'war play' cues a concern with what Katherine Eggert has described as 'the relations between literature and hegemonic political power'.[2]

Dennis Kezar has combined the two approaches in a reading of the play that examines 'the theatre's institutional distribution of agency and responsibility'. For Kezar, the participatory spectatorship invoked in the Prologue articulates an 'authorial dissolution' inevitably attendant upon the collective conditions of theatrical representation.[3] He finds the 'fullest exploration' of this dissolution in 4.1, Henry's disguised conversation with Michael Williams. He is right to point out that this scene has a reflexive function: as he puts it, Henry 'displace[s] accountability from the King's "cause" (4.1.127) onto the guilt of the soldiers who perform it:

intentionality bleeds from the author to the errant actor'. He is also right that it is Henry, not Williams, who makes the 'jump' in this discussion from material to spiritual concerns, thus enabling the displacement to take place. But I do not think his emphasis on the 'disavowal of authorship' helps us characterize the precise questions of agency addressed by this play.[4]

I have suggested elsewhere an institutional approach to Shakespeare that attends to the work individual plays do to enable particular sets of circumstances within the overall development of Shakespearian theatre.[5] I have argued that we must attend to institutional and legal questions in combination – particularly in research that takes its starting point from law, where there is a tendency to subordinate the institutional interests of theatre to those of legal history. Bradin Cormack, for instance, discusses *Henry V* in a superb study of 'early modern literature... deeply engaged... with the *technical production* of the legal

I am grateful to Colette Gordon, Constance Jordan and Kate McLuskie for discussion and encouragement. This article is dedicated to Lily, who died while I was writing it.

[1] All references to Shakespeare's plays are taken from S. Greenblatt, W. Cohen, J. Howard and K. E. Maus, eds., *The Norton Shakespeare* (New York, 1997).
[2] Katherine Eggert, 'Nostalgia and the Not-Yet-Late Queen: Refusing Female Rule in *Henry VI*', *ELH*, 60:3 (1994), 523.
[3] Dennis Kezar, 'Shakespeare's Guilt Trip in *Henry V*', *Modern Language Quarterly*, 61 (2000), 446, 457.
[4] Kezar, 'Shakespeare's Guilt Trip', 458, 459.
[5] Erica Sheen, *Shakespeare and the Institution of Theatre: 'The Best in this Kind'* (Basingstoke, 2009); see especially Chapter 1, pp. 1–18.

order'.[6] Brilliant as his analysis is, I believe that such an approach – to Shakespeare, at least – needs reconsideration. Shakespeare's plays certainly do engage, deeply, with contemporary legal culture; but as far as 'production' is concerned, particularly 'technical' production, they are always and above all engaged with the production of theatre. The questions they raise about law, and the answers they themselves give to these questions, must be approached in terms of the work a particular play or group of plays does on behalf not simply of a general institution of theatre – in the spirit of New Historicism – but specifically the Chamberlain's/King's Men in the particular circumstances in which they were working at the point of a play's or plays' first production in (a) particular theatre(s). In this essay I will consider the presentation of legal and theatrical principles of agency in *Henry V*, *Twelfth Night* and, to a lesser extent, *Measure for Measure*.[7] I will argue that the treatment of these ideas in works written for the new Globe from 1599 to 1603/4 articulates a structural transformation of the status of the professional player and, arising from that, a qualitative transformation of the terms on which these particular players presented the experience of theatre to their audiences, and of the political values associated with that experience. This is not simply a claim for preeminence: as I have also argued elsewhere, Shakespeare and the Shakespeare company's presentation of their work as 'the best in this kind' manifestly predates the opening of the Globe. But with the opening of the new theatre in 1599, there are significant changes in the ideas Shakespeare's plays present about whose interests that pre-eminence serves.[8]

To start, I return to Henry's conversation with Michael Williams in *Henry V* 4.1. As Kezar points out, Williams concentrates on material issues.[9] Although he introduces the idea of 'dying well', his primary concern is the question of the king's accountability for actions undertaken by a subject on his behalf: 'it will be a black matter for the king that led them to it – who to disobey were against all proportion of subjection' (134, 137–8). It is Henry who pushes the conversation towards

spiritual questions, but the examples he provides serve to emphasize the argument he is avoiding by doing so: 'a son . . . by his father sent about merchandise . . . a servant under his master's command transporting a sum of money' (139–43). These are relationships we would describe as forms of legal agency. The law of agency – as it is now called – deals with commercial relationships in which one person (the 'agent') acts in the name and on behalf of another (the 'principal') to set up and carry out some form of (usually) contractual undertaking or agreement. Legal agency has certain

---

[6] Bradin Cormack, *A Power to Do Justice: Jurisdiction, English Literature, and the Rise of Common Law, 1509–1625* (Chicago, 2007), p. 12; Cormack's italics.

[7] Katherine Rowe discusses the concept of agency in *Dead Hands: Fictions of Agency, Renaissance to Modern* (Stanford, 2000), especially in her 'Introduction', pp. 17–28. Whilst her concern, like mine, is with a notion of 'agency for another', her approach draws on analytic philosophy rather than law, notably 'a concept of autonomous moral agency still perceived in terms of obedience to a separate authority that is not entirely coincident with the self' (20). For an application of legal traditions of thinking about agency to Renaissance drama, also referenced by Rowe, see A. R. Braunmuller, in 'Second Means: Agent and Accessory in Elizabethan Drama', in A. L. Magnusson and C. E. McGee, eds., *The Elizabethan Theatre XI* (Ontario, 1990), pp. 177–202.

[8] In what follows I assume that *Henry V*, as written for performance, included the Choruses. I should therefore acknowledge Richard Dutton's account of arguments to the contrary (Richard Dutton, '"Methinks the Truth Should Live from Age to Age": The Dating and Contexts of Henry V', *Huntington Library Quarterly*, 68 (2005), 173–204). Dutton has reservations about the 'self-sustaining certainty of editors and critics that the folio text does represent what was written in 1599, so much of which attaches to the supposed Essex allusion' (202). He sees this allusion as anomalous in Shakespeare's work, and prefers to date the material that includes it 'from after the decisive Battle of Kinsale (1601) rather than from 1599, and therefore to celebrate Mountjoy rather than Essex' (Abstract). His conclusion, that 'a true historical close reading of the play is impossible' (201), is uncontroversial. But attempts at true historical readings should surely give more attention to institutional factors than is the case here. If it is possible to base both an argument about dating and a reading of the play on a general assumption that contemporary audiences were familiar with 'international politics of the era', I hope I can at least advance a case for the somewhat different approach that follows.

[9] Kezar, 'Shakespeare's Guilt Trip', p. 458.

distinctive features. Through the agent, the principal is considered to be privy to, and therefore bound by, agreements made on his or her behalf: that is to say, despite the fact that s/he has not participated in the negotiations in person, s/he is not what in law is referred to as a 'stranger'. Correspondingly, despite the fact that she or he *has* so participated, the agent is not held personally liable for the agreements s/he makes on behalf of the principal. On the other hand, both the principal and the agent are bound by a fiduciary relationship of trust and confidence, the principal to allow the agent to work on his or her behalf, the agent to pursue the best interests of the principal without seeking personal advantage. This unusual situation draws on what is known as the 'fiction of identity of principal and agent', expressed by the Latin maxim *qui facit per alium facit per se*: s/he who acts through another does the act him/herself. As in both of Henry's examples, this legal fiction makes it possible for a contracting party to carry out transactions at a remove – something we may associate with the modernity of a commercial world increasingly characterized by what Anthony Giddens has described as time-space distanciation.[10]

It should be pointed out, however, that there was no such thing as a 'law of agency' in the late sixteenth and early seventeenth centuries; it was not until the late seventeenth and eighteenth century that a body of law described as such came into being. In the 1590s, legal thinking about agency had little more to go on than Christopher St German's statement of a principal's accountability for an agent in the Second Dialogue of *Doctor and Student*, chapter 42, where St German asks 'whether a man shall be bounden by the acte or offence of hys servaunt or offycer': 'he that is a gouernour is bounde for the offence of hys offycers . . . for it shalbe his defaute that he wolde chose such servantes'.[11] He does not pursue the kind of question about the obligations of the agent that would underpin the development of a law of agency in the later seventeenth and eighteenth centuries: thus, for instance, in *The York Buildings Co. v. Mackenzie* in 1795, Lord

Chancellor Loughborough provided a statement that would become a standard formulation in legal textbooks:

A person who is an agent for another undertakes a duty in which there is confidence reposed. He undertakes a duty which he is bound to execute to the utmost advantage of the person who employs him. An agent may be employed by any one or more persons, and such an agent may purchase. Brokers purchase every day, but they can take no advantage by it. The bargain must be perfectly fair and equal, at the best price, because they are placed in a situation, in which they are bound in the first instance, to act against their own advantage, and for the advantage of their employers. And if they sacrifice that interest and advantage, with a view of profiting and taking the interest of it to themselves, the purchase will be liable to be set aside, the advantage will not come to themselves, and the breach of confidence will not avail them.[12]

Sixteenth-century common law was of course familiar with cases in which agreements between contracting parties were negotiated by a third party; but if they came to law, they were characteristically assimilated into the doctrine of consideration, the *quid pro quo* principle increasingly used to test the enforceability of promises. This meant both that in circumstances in which it could not be demonstrated that a principal had given consideration for a promise, s/he would indeed be considered a stranger, and therefore not bound; *and* that there was neither any obligation for the agent to pursue the best interests of his principal, nor a legal framework by which to test claims that s/he had

---

10 According to Anthony Giddens, *The Consequences of Modernity* (Stanford, 1990), p. 18, the social interactions of premodern societies are largely confined to local contexts of interaction. Modernity disembeds such interactions by 'fostering relations between "absent" others, locationally distant from any given situation of face-to-face interaction'.

11 T. F. T Plucknett and J. L. Barton, eds., *St German's Doctor and Student*, Selden Society 91 (London, 1974), pp. 265–6.

12 Alexander Wedderburn, 1st Earl of Rosslyn, Lord Chancellor Loughborough, in Thomas S. Paton, *Reports of Cases Decided in the House of Lords upon Appeal from Scotland, from 1753–1813*, vol. 3 (Edinburgh, 1853), p. 398. This formulation subsequently appears in *Ross on Commercial Law* (1858) and *Kerr on Fraud and Mistake* (1868), amongst others.

not done so. This approach meant that questions of privity – who could be said to be 'privy' to an agreement – were restricted to the 'parties only' position that came to characterize English contract law from then on, and that the question of trust between agent and principal had no legal status. Legal historian Vernon Palmer usefully summarizes the situation I have outlined up to this point:

The word 'agency', as a term of art, was to remain unknown to the common law as late as Blackstone. It was first introduced to the English scene near the close of the Formative Period by Lord Nottingham and from then on it was utilized frequently by 18th century chancellors. Nevertheless, the essential characteristic of modern agency – the legal power to alter the principal's legal relations with third parties – had been recognized long before, and therefore, the legal idea played a role in the Formative Period. It is true that the early bases were extremely narrow. Agency was the exception, not the rule of contractual intercourse. If the principal strayed beyond narrowly recognized bounds, he was simply a stranger to the contract. Even to apply the terms principal and agent in this period requires some sacrifice of terminological accuracy in the interest of convenience. When originally introduced, agency was simply a branch of master and servant, whereas today, master and servant is a branch of agency.[13]

Pointing out that 'contemporary terminology was actually a mélange of such terms as attorney, factor, deputy, servant and bailiff', Palmer adds in a footnote, 'in the 16th century, agency was not a received term. The word "servant" did not even appear in its commercial sense until the time of Marlowe and Shakespeare, e.g., *Henry V*, Act IV, scene I.'[14] He provides no line number, but his reference is clearly to Henry's 'a servant under his master's command transporting a sum of money' (4.1.142–3).

Vague as the idea of 'the time of Marlowe and Shakespeare' is, Palmer signals an historical correlation between the emergence of a commercial idea of service and the development of professional theatre in the 1590s that is fundamental to my argument. Operating formally under a system of patronage but not financially supported by or bound to a patron's economic or political interests,

the player may be seen as an exemplary instance of a form of commercial service making the historical transition from the master/servant framework to the modern paradigm of principal and agent. Shakespeare's work marks this transition.[15] Before 1598, in plays such as *The Two Gentlemen of Verona*, *The Taming of the Shrew* and *A Midsummer Night's Dream*, his representations of theatre and theatricality are broadly based on a conception of theatre as unpaid (or at least not explicitly paid) service within the traditional master/servant hierarchy (this is not to say that they do not challenge that position; simply that it is the cultural framework within which they are situated). By

---

13 Vernon V. Palmer, 'The History of Privity – The Formative Period (1500–1680)', *The American Journal of Legal History*, 33:1 (1989), 28. Nottingham was Lord Chancellor from 1673 to 1682; Loughborough, above, was one of the '18th century chancellors' to whom Palmer refers.

14 Palmer, 'The History of Privity', p. 28 n.96. Palmer is undoubtedly correct in his observation about the term 'agency', which does not appear in legal contexts until the 1650s. The word is, however, familiar in the early 1600s in the *OED*'s sense 1a: 'the process of acting as an agent; the position, role, or function of an agent, deputy, or representative': *Oxford English Dictionary (OED) Online*, 3rd edn, www.oed.com/view/Entry/3851 (accessed 19 September 2012). Similarly, the term 'agent' is in use from the early 1500s in the *OED*'s sense 2a: 'a person who acts as a substitute for another; one who undertakes negotiations or transactions on behalf of a superior, employer, or principal; a deputy, steward, representative; (in early use) an ambassador, emissary': www.oed.com/view/Entry/3859 (accessed 19 September 2012). Shakespeare used 'agent' throughout his career, from *Two Gentleman* and *2 Henry VI*, to *Cymbeline*, *Winter's Tale* and *Henry VIII*. Whilst in his hands it frequently denotes a position of service, it almost invariably does so in contexts that open up the social and political complexities that lie at the intersection of the master/servant and principal/agent paradigms. For an alternative account of the history of the term 'agent', see Rowe, *Dead Hands*, pp. 17–28.

15 Rowe, *Dead Hands*, p. 221 n.8, notes that Lawrence Danson addressed questions of theatrical professionalism in relation to Webster in the 1997 SAA Seminar 'Early Modern Drama and the Question of Agency': 'Danson reads Bosola's divided role as an agent for himself and an agent for others as a reflection of Webster's intense concern with the changing nature of patronage and professional service in this period.' I have not had access to this material.

contrast, *Much Ado About Nothing*, written 1598–99, around the time of the construction of the Globe but probably before its opening, pits principal/agent roles undertaken by social equals, even superiors, against explorations of instrumentality within the traditional master/servant hierarchy, and in doing so pushes its characters towards revelations about theatrical agency that begin to give shape to a new conception of theatre. When Claudio falls in love with Hero, the Prince offers to woo her on his behalf, but Don John encourages Claudio to suspect his motives:

> 'Tis certain so, the Prince woos for himself.
> Friendship is constant in all other things
> Save in the office and affairs of love.
> Therefore all hearts in love use their own tongues.
> Let every eye negotiate for itself,
> And trust no agent.   (2.1.152–7)

At this stage in the action, a determination to 'let every eye negotiate for itself' may seem a recipe for successful spectatorship – particularly given its consonance with contemporary developments in the law of contract. But when Claudio pursues this approach, in the episode reported by Borachio in 3.3 ('know that I have tonight wooed Margaret, the Lady Hero's gentlewoman, by the name of Hero' (126–7)), the results are disastrous. It becomes clear that letting the eye negotiate for itself does not produce the best results: as Claudio must learn by the end of the play when he accepts 'Leonato's brother's daughter' as his wife without seeing her face, a favorable outcome requires a combination of theatrical agents and agencies, willingness to let them work for you and, perhaps above all, trust that the appearances they create will ultimately prove to be in your best interests.

The Chorus in the Prologue of *Henry V* provides what can be seen as a programmatic statement for such a conception of theatrical agency. As such, it should be seen less in Kezar's terms as a 'dissolution' of authorial responsibility than as the point at which authorship materializes within the emerging conception of commercial service (which may well be the historical precondition for conceptions of authorial rights and literary property). It marks the point at which *this* writer and *this* company, in *this* theatre, undertook to act, not as servants to a political master, but as agents to their audience's principal. The Chorus's dynamic direction of his audience's 'imaginary puissance' – 'Think, when we talk of horses, that you see them' (25, 26) – configures this historical moment with supreme confidence. Always an important presence within the spatial dynamics of Shakespearian theatre, Shakespeare's horses had hitherto functioned to extend the fictional world of the play into an off-stage space conceived as continuous with, or an extension of, the stage itself. Thus in *The Taming of the Shrew*, 'Petruccio is coming... his horse hipped, with an old mothy saddle and stirrups of no kindred, besides, possessed with the glanders and like to mose in the chine' (3.2.41–7); in *Love's Labour's Lost*, 'Was that the King that spurred his horse so hard / Against the steep uprising of the hill?' (4.1.1–2); and perhaps most impressively, the named horses in *Richard III* and *Richard II*, white Surrey (5.5.17/131; 5.7.13) and roan Barbary (5.5.67–94), where whole sequences of references evoke extended dramatic locations on the battlefield at Bosworth and in London. By contrast, the *Henry V* speech stresses the *discontinuity*: the fact that the implied location, where the horses *are*, is distanced from the spectator and therefore requires an act of theatrical agency to access it on his or her behalf. Rather than seeing the author as 'dissolving' in a corporate ethos of collaboration, we should note how forcefully his poetry *works with* the 'we' who 'talk', to direct the spectator's eye and mind (Shakespeare invokes the connection between them throughout plays of this period), first, to an imagined whole – '*think*... that you *see them*' – then to a 'close-up' which configures this intellectual address with sensory effects of visual and aural proximity: 'Printing their proud hoofs i'th' receiving earth'.

The best way I can think to describe the trust generated by this theatrical agency is to compare it with an episode in Eisenstein's *Strike* (1925). As a troop of mounted soldiers confront a crowd of angry workers, a child wanders amongst the restless horses; the camera follows, taking the spectator directly beneath the animals' legs. The sense of physical danger that arises from the position of this shot feeds into the mounting emotion of confrontation, and thus into the spectator's participation in the dialectical aesthetic by which his or her experience of film is drawn into political thought.[16] In a similar way, Shakespeare takes the spectator's imagination to a position close enough to feel and hear the weight of the horses' bodies and the rhythm of their movement. But here the effect of distanciation creates a pleasurable sense of safety, allowing the spectator, first, to receive this experience at the hands of skilful agents and, second, in so doing to occupy a position from which to proceed to an intellectual engagement with its political context. In the lines that follow, the authority of this negotiating eye, and the trust it invites from the audience, is enhanced by an allusion to parliamentary representation: 'For 'tis your thoughts that now must deck our kings, . . . for the which supply / Admit me Chorus to this history' (Prologue, 28, 31–2). David Dean has described supply, the parliamentary provision of revenue to the Crown raised by taxation, as 'the major single reason for calling parliament between 1584 and 1601'. It was required 'to meet the crown's ordinary as well as extraordinary expenses', primary amongst which in the parliament of 1597–8 was Essex's expedition to Ireland. Receiving a vote for treble subsidies, the Queen acknowledged the affection her subjects had thereby shown not only for herself but also 'for the defence of this Realme'.[17] The mere fact of Essex's military action in 1599 might be less significant to our understanding of *Henry V* than this popular investment – fiscal and imaginative – in the negotiations with Elizabeth by which it came into being. In 1598–9, invoking the audience's 'imaginary puissance' in terms of the notion of supply dynamically affiliates the Chamberlain's Men's prestigious new theatre to late Elizabethan parliamentary culture and its ethos of public participation.

From this position, just as the players are agents for the spectators' experience of the play, so the play is an agent through which, like Michael Williams at Agincourt, these spectators can confront

'princes . . . and monarchs' (Prologue, 3, 4) and call on them to account for their actions. A theatrical version of the fiction of identity of principal and agent – 's/he who acts through another, does the act him/herself' – is thus strongly represented in Williams's refusal to allow Henry to abuse this fiction, first by pretending *not* to be himself (notably in the hard-hitting discussion about trust between monarchs and subjects in 4.1.202–10), then by reversing the position and insisting on the privilege of sovereignty:

Henry. How canst thou make me satisfaction? . . . It was ourself thou didst abuse.
Will. Your majesty came not like yourself. You appeared to me but as a common man . . . And what your highness suffered under that shape, I beseech you take it for your own fault, and not mine, for had you been as I took you for, I made no offence therefore. I beseech your highness, pardon me. (4.8.42–51)

When Williams subsequently replies to Fluellen's conciliatory offer of 'twelve pence' – 'I will none of your money' (58, 62) – he could be responding either to Fluellen or to Henry's previous instruction to Exeter to 'fill this glove with crowns, / And give it to this fellow' (52–3). In practice, the two are one and the same, since Fluellen's spat with Williams arises from his unwitting assumption of an agent's role in Henry's earlier 'bargain' with Williams, within which Henry has falsely represented Williams to him as a French supporter and 'enemy to my person' (4.7.143–4). As Williams's last words in the play, the line 'I will none of your money' has something of the force of Malvolio's 'I'll be revenged on the whole pack of you' (*Twelfth Night* 5.1.365) or, better still, Isabella's silence at the end of *Measure for Measure*: an unreconciled refusal of Henry's attempt to master him. His insistence on the right to be given theatrical images that truthfully acknowledge the

---

[16] See Sergei Eisenstein, 'A Dialectic Approach to Film Form', in *Film Form: Essays in Film Theory*, ed. Jay Leyda (New York, 1949), pp. 45–63.

[17] David Dean, *Law-Making and Society in Late Elizabethan England: The Parliament of England, 1584–1601* (Cambridge, 1996), pp. 35, 37, 56.

distance between king and subject, and on a form of theatre that will act on the audience's behalf across that distance, establishes a very strong reading of the act of supply. As such, it has considerable bearing on the way we understand the affiliation, both symbolic and real, between the Globe and the machinery of political representation at the end of Elizabeth's reign. In the course of the 1597–8 parliament, on 26 November 1597, an anonymous MP noted that: 'the eyes of the poor are upon this Parliament . . . this place is an epitome of the whole realm: the trust of the poor committed to us, whose persons we supplie, doth challenge the furtheraunce of their releife'.[18] Across the parliaments of the 1580s and 1590s, the word 'supply' would become a familiar term in debates about subsidy and the consensual (or otherwise) process by which subsidies were imposed. In March 1593, Bacon spoke of the 'manner of supply' which 'may be by Levy or Imposition, when need shall most require; so when her Majesties Coffers are empty, they may be filled by this means'.[19] Twelfth Night reflects the way the theatrical supply of imagined persons evokes this vital parliamentary function: as Orsino says of Olivia, 'How will she love when . . . liver, brain and heart / These sovereign thrones are all supplied and filled / Her sweet perfections with one self king' (1.1.34–8)). Orsino is himself, of course, the 'self king' he has in mind, and both his romantic aspirations and their inevitable frustration may echo the now long-past question of an Elizabethan royal marriage. But in the event, it is Viola/Cesario/Sebastian who supplies and fills Olivia, and the process by which s/he does so asks and answers very precise questions about the relations between theatrical agency and the law.

Perhaps Shakespeare's most remarkable achievement in the art of plotting, Twelfth Night offers an elaborate counterpoint of master–servant/principal–agent relations at every level of action, framed with statements of trust in dramatic temporality that identify the play as agent to the audience just as Viola is agent to Orsino: 'what else may hap, to time I will commit' (1.2.56, where 'commit' has the legal sense of 'to entrust'); 'O time,

thou must untangle this, not I. / It is too hard a knot for me t'untie' (2.2.38–9). In Viola's creation and enactment of 'Cesario', Shakespeare coordinates an image of the player with a commercial idea of service; indeed, he presents this coordination as the only solution to the problems created by the breakdown of the traditional family structures which have hitherto supported both Viola and Olivia. The play takes pains to emphasize the steps by which this situation is put in place. Initially, the service Viola seeks is a form of domestic retreat: 'O that I served that lady, / And might not be delivered to the world / Till I had made my occasion mellow / What my estate is' (1.2.37–40). Olivia's reclusion puts this option out of reach, precipitating Viola's decisions both to disguise and to work for Orsino. Earlier plays – notably Two Gentlemen of Verona – had presented the onstage performance that underpins its leading woman's part as a form of service; indeed, Two Gentlemen anticipates Twelfth Night in its use of the disguised female servant as the agent for his/her master's courtship of another woman. But Twelfth Night develops the presentation of this service as paid employment in a quite new and different way. We are told how successful Cesario is: 'If the Duke continues these favours towards you, Cesario, you are like to be much advanced. He hath known you but three days, and already you are no stranger' (1.4.1–3) – and the term 'stranger' here alerts us to the fact that Cesario's actions as agent explore the complex questions of privity that would inform legal conceptions of the role. From the outset, Orsino sees Cesario's agency as a theatrical fiction of identity of principal and agent: a player offering Olivia a performance of himself, on his behalf:

---

[18] Oliver Arnold, 'Mapping England in the Early Modern House of Commons', in Literature, Mapping and the Politics of Space in Early Modern Britain, ed. A. Gordon and B. Klein (Cambridge, 2001), p. 26.

[19] 'Journal of the House of Commons: March 1593', in Sir Simonds d'Ewes, The Journals of all the Parliaments during the reign of Queen Elizabeth (1682), 479–513, online at www.british-history.ac.uk/report.aspx?compid=43724 (accessed 9 September 2012).

... unfold the passion of my love,
Surprise her with discourse of my dear faith.
It shall become thee well to act my woes –
She will attend it better in thy youth
Than in a nuncio's of more grave aspect.

(1.4.23–7)

Viola responds to Orsino's commission with an undertaking to 'do my best' (39): an expression we might associate on one hand with the not yet legally thinkable idea of an agent's obligation to pursue the best interests of his principal, on the other with the competitive drive of Shakespearian theatre as 'the best in this kind'.[20] The fact that Viola does her best so well, in both spheres of activity, is responsible for everything that follows, including the happy ending.

The terms of Viola's employment incorporate a significant element of time-space distanciation. She is the character in this action who travels, both in the original shipwreck, and in her subsequent incessant movement between Orsino's and Olivia's households. It might be objected that Orsino sent others to do his courtship for him before she arrives, but they have evidently made no progress with their negotiations. What makes the difference is Viola's, and then Cesario's, assumption of the role of the player, and with it the possibility that in her/his hands Orsino's business might finally succeed. This possibility precipitates a transition within their relationship from the master/servant hierarchy to the social equality of principal/agent: 'Prosper well in this / And thou shalt live as freely as thy lord, / To call his fortunes thine' (1.4.37–9). Viola's response to Orsino's commission anticipates precisely what would become the defining legal characteristic of the principal/agent relationship – the potential it holds for a conflict of interests:

I'll do my best
To woo your lady – [*aside*] yet a barful strife –
Whoe'er I woo, myself would be his wife. (39–41)

It is of course the question (in Lord Loughborough's words) whether this agent has executed his/her duty to the utmost advantage of his/her principal, or sacrificed that advantage with a view of taking the interest of it him/herself, that becomes decisive at the climax of the action.

Orsino's sense that Olivia will 'attend' more to Cesario's representation of him than to himself in person proves correct. From the outset, Cesario calls on the combined theatrical agencies of writing and performance, and, like the Chorus in *Henry V*, showcases their complementary professional energies. In this respect, the first scene between Viola and Olivia, 1.5, has similarities with the Player's scene in *Hamlet* 2.2. Viola tells Olivia that the speech she has prepared is 'excellently well penned' and that she has 'taken great pains to con it' (1.5.154–5), but since, like Hamlet, she only ever *begins* the speech (like Hamlet, twice), and then breaks off into *extempore* conversation about the performance with her audience, Viola's author, like that of 'Aeneas' Tale to Dido', remains unnamed, absorbed into the charismatic engagement between player and spectator. Within a matter of lines, we become aware that, in 'doing her best', Viola has already gone well past the point where she is able to act in Orsino's interests – as he conceives them, at least. Paradoxically, this theatrical fiction of identity of principal and agent, which Orsino envisages as the precondition for her success, is precisely the reason for her failure: as Olivia puts it, 'Not too fast. Soft, soft – / Unless the master were the man' (1.5.263–4). The potential violence precipitated by Orsino's discovery of Cesario's apparent action on his own behalf –

[Since] I partly know the instrument
That screws me from my true place in your favour...
Him will I tear out of that cruel eye
Where he sits crownèd in his master's spite.

(5.1.117–24)

– is prefigured in Sir Andrew's challenge to a duel. This remarkable episode brings to the surface of the action a confrontation between principles of agency and the contractual framework of consideration. Not coincidentally, the figure over which

---

[20] *A Midsummer Night's Dream*, 5.1.208.

323

this confrontation takes place is an offstage horse – although here again 'offstage' is hardly an adequate term to describe the dramatic space occupied by Sir Andrew's grey Capulet.

Toby has made it obvious from the outset that the whole point of his encouragement of Sir Andrew's 'courtship' of Olivia is to sponge off him, in the same way that Iago will later sponge off Roderigo in *Othello*, and for exactly the same reasons (*Fabio.* 'This is a dear manikin to you, Sir Toby.' *Toby.* 'I have been dear to him, lad, some two thousand strong or so' (3.2.45–7)). But when he accepts Sir Andrew's commission to offer Cesario grey Capulet in exchange for an agreement *not* to fight, their relationship changes significantly: it begins to exhibit the characteristics of a fully developed legal principle of agency. Viola's determined effort at the beginning of 3.4 to give Orsino the full benefit of her exertions in the face of Olivia's declaration of love (*Olivia.* 'What shall you ask of me . . . That honour, may upon asking give?' *Viola.* 'Nothing but this: your true love for my master' (3.4.187–9)) is juxtaposed with Sir Toby's assumption of the role of agent for his friend. In the dialogue that follows, the words 'offence', 'motion' and 'remedy' signal the fact that the play's engagement with these ideas is becoming explicitly legal:

Sir Andrew. Let him let the matter slip and I'll give him my horse, grey Capulet.
Sir Toby. I'll make the motion . . . [*Aside*] Marry, I'll ride your horse as well as I ride you.

Enter Fabian and Viola [as Cesario].

[*Aside to Fabian*] I have his horse to take up the quarrel, I have persuaded him the youth's a devil . . .
Sir Toby. [*to Viola*] There's no remedy, sir, he will fight with you for's oath sake. . . .
Viola. [*to Sir Andrew*] Pray, sir, put your sword up if you please.
Sir Andrew. Marry will I sir, and for that I promised you I'll be as good as my word. He will bear you easily and reins well. (3.4.254–490)

We should note how precisely Shakespeare marks off each stage in the development of this negotiation. Toby's acceptance of the role of agent

is followed, first, by an aside to the audience signalling that he intends to appropriate the horse for himself – 'I'll ride your horse as well as I ride you' – and then by his aside to Fabian saying that Andrew has promised him the horse as payment for negotiating a truce: 'I have his horse to take up the quarrel.' It comes as no surprise that Toby lies to his friends – but something more interesting is going on here. To explain it, I must refer, as I think Shakespeare does, to *Lucy v. Walwyn* (1561), a leading case in the rise of the doctrine of consideration.

In *Lucy v. Walwyn*, Thomas Lucy of Charlecote in Warwickshire sued successfully for the loss of a bargain purportedly negotiated on his behalf by Simon Walwyn:[21]

Thomas Lucy brought an action on the case against Simon Walwyn, gentleman, and complained that, whereas King Philip and Queen Mary I by letters patent dated 5 March 1555 demised the manors of Hampton Bishop and Hatton in Warwickshire, to John Swyfte for 16 years; and the plaintiff desired to purchase them, and had great faith in the defendant because of the long fellowship and familiarity between them, and knew that the defendant was also a great friend of Swyfte: the plaintiff, 12 February 1556 at Charlecote, Warwickshire, earnestly requested the defendant to do his utmost to purchase Swyfte's interest for a reasonable sum of money; and then and there promised the defendant, for his labour to be bestowed in procuring the interest, to pay all his expenses and give him a gelding worth 100s. (or 100s. in cash) immediately upon purchase of the interest; and thereupon the defendant (afterwards on the same day) in consideration that the plaintiff would pay all his expenses and give him a gelding or 100s., as aforesaid, faithfully

---

[21] It's worth remembering that there are points of contact between Shakespeare and Thomas Lucy – some factual, some apocryphal. Charlecote, about four miles east of Stratford-upon-Avon, is the estate in which (according to Nicholas Rowe) Shakespeare was caught stealing deer and rabbits as a young man. Lucy, who became Sir Thomas in 1565 and died in 1600, was an aggressive anti-Catholic who harassed the Arden family after Edward Arden's arrest and execution. He is said to be the model for Justice Shallow in *The Merry Wives of Windsor* (1599–1600) – a play full of the atmosphere, personalities and situations that later took shape in the subplot of *Twelfth Night*.

promised the plaintiff and undertook that he would do his utmost to obtain Swyfte's interest as quickly as he could; nevertheless the defendant did not perform this undertaking, but purchased the manors for himself on 1 March 1556. Walwyn pleaded that on 13 February 1556 . . . and always thereafter until 1 March he did all he could to obtain the manors for the plaintiff, but Swyfte utterly refused to grant them to the plaintiff; and that 1 March Swyfte sold his interest to the defendant, so that he could not possibly obtain it for the plaintiff from Swyfte.[22]

When it was argued at King's Bench, the case hung on the question of the status of the horse as consideration – the *quid pro quo* offered to Walwyn for his efforts on Lucy's behalf. In an argument that seems to anticipate the contrived logic of Sir Toby's machinations, Walwyn's defence argued:

that there ought to be *quid pro quo* in an undertaking, and that the undertaking was that if he laboured and obtained the lease he would have a gelding, and so if he did not obtain the lease it could be said that he did not have a gelding and therefore no undertaking. In reply, it was argued for the plaintiff that 'that is not so, for the gelding is not only in return for the obtaining but for the labour mixed with the obtaining'.[23]

Lucy's argument prevailed, thereby establishing the principle of consideration as the test for contractual undertakings in the future: as John Baker has put it, 'from this point the English law of contract might be said to be consensual'.[24]

But it's obvious that the horse is not the issue here: it only *becomes* the issue because it's an argument lawyers can use to win the case. Even as it does, it becomes clear that what really matters is something completely different, something for which there was no legal test: the fact that Walwyn broke his friend's trust and pursued his own interests. Sir Toby's lie to Fabian works in exactly the same way: it serves to introduce the question of consideration only to emphasize the fact that a completely different set of principles is at stake. In fact, this episode exposes what may be said to be elided by *Lucy v. Walwyn*, may even be seen as a reflection or comment on it: the fact that principles of agency – both in the image of theatrical

enterprise with which the plays under discussion here work so hard to associate themselves, and in society at large – are excluded, or displaced, by this limiting contractual framework. In its insistence that we respond to this episode on the terms of agency rather than consideration, Andrew's aside to Viola at the climax of this episode emphasizes the point: 'for that I promised you I'll be as good as my word. He will bear you easily and reins well.' Obviously, the primary effect of this exchange is comic: because, like Walwyn, Toby has not fulfilled his obligations as an agent, Viola has no idea what he is talking about. But once again something important is going on. Offering what is effectively a warranty that his horse is sound, Sir Andrew affirms his willingness as principal to be bound by the undertaking *he* believes Sir Toby has made on his behalf. Shakespeare was undoubtedly aware, as most of his audience would have been, that cases about unsound horses – of which Petruccio's mount is a superb specimen – recur in the legal literature on warranty, from *Aylesbury v. Wattes* (1382) and *Garrok v. Heytesbury* (1387) onwards. In *Chandelor v. Lupus* (1604), a few years after *Twelfth Night*, we learn that 'everyone in selling his wares will affirm that his wares are good, or the horse which he sells is sound, yet if he does not warrant them to be so it is no cause of action'.[25]

Given how comical, even pathetic, he is, why is Andrew given this meticulously crafted opportunity to show he can be trusted? Why, in fact, does he have a good horse with a Shakespearian name in the first place? After all, the purposes of the plot would have been equally well served by an anonymous beast, like the one in *Lucy v. Walwyn*, or indeed the gelding mentioned by Ford in *The*

[22] KB 27/1198, m. 183, in J. H. Baker and S. F. C. Milson, *Sources of English Legal History: Private Law to 1750* (London, 1986), p. 485.

[23] Gell's reports, MS from Hopton Hall, fols. 154v, 158v, in Baker and Milson, *Sources*, p. 486.

[24] J. H. Baker, *An Introduction to English Legal History*, 3rd edn (London, 1990), p. 331.

[25] *Chandelor v. Lupus* (1604), Cro. Jac. 4, pl. 4, in Baker, *Introduction to English Legal History*, pp. 376–7 and n.13; Baker and Milson, *Sources*, pp. 507–22.

Merry Wives of Windsor ('I will rather trust a Fleming with my butter . . . or a thief with my ambling gelding than my wife with herself' (2.2.265–8)). There are only two other named horses in Shakespeare's plays and both of them belong not just to kings in history plays, but to kings about to die the epoch-changing deaths that define the dramatic direction of those plays. Richard III's white Surrey carries his master into battle and dies with him there; Richard II's roan Barbary breaks his master's heart when he carries Bolingbroke to his coronation 'so proudly as if he disdained the ground':

> That jade hath eat bread from my royal hand;
> This hand has made him proud with clapping him.
> Would he not stumble, would he not fall down –
> Since pride must have a fall – and break the neck
> Of that proud man that did usurp his back?
>
> (5.5.85–9)

In contrasting ways, both horses embody traditional values of mastery and service, trust and loyalty. As servants, they are defined by their relation to their master and expected to maintain that position to the point of self-sacrifice (Richard II would rather Barbary fell than ride well for Bolingbroke).[26] By comparison, grey Capulet is a truly modern horse. He appears in the action *only* at the point at which he is about to be transferred to another owner, an action Andrew follows up with a guarantee (as in *Chandelor v. Lupus*) that Capulet will ride as well for this new owner as he has done for him – can, in fact, be trusted, like Viola, to do his best whomever he serves.[27] Like the war horses of *Henry V*, grey Capulet thus provides an imaginative focus for the audience's thoughtful engagement with principles of agency that structure both the play and the experience of watching it – which is presumably why he has a name that makes us aware that that experience is, precisely, 'Shakespearian'.

As this might suggest, the conception of theatrical agency I have been discussing is so central to Shakespeare's work in this period that it might be seen as something like a brand, where

this term is used in modern intellectual property law to describe

a 'promise of an experience' [which] conveys to consumers a certain assurance as to the nature of the product or service they will receive and also the standards the supplier or manufacturer seeks to maintain. Brands are therefore reputational assets based on powerfully held beliefs; they drive the understanding of value in a product or company, and, perhaps most importantly, customer loyalty.[28]

These ideas – the promise of an experience; reputational assets; customer loyalty – can be invoked to explain structural continuities between plays which cannot be defined as a group in any of the usual ways, such as genre. Thus *As You Like It* showcases the theatrical agency of 'Ganymede's' performance, for Orlando, of 'Rosalind' – a consummate theatrical realization of the fiction of identity of principal and agent. When this performance brings Orlando to the point where he can 'live no longer by thinking', Ganymede offers to 'labour' 'to do [him] good' by [setting] Rosalind 'before your eyes tomorrow' (5.2.45, 59). In *Hamlet*, Hamlet himself, whose response to the Tragedians of the City demonstrates a fine spectator's capacity for 'imaginary puissance', is only able to become a son who 'acts' for his father (as in Henry's conversation with Williams) when he becomes an agent in his own play ('Ere I could make a prologue to my brains / They had begun the play' (5.2.31–2)). The term 'brand' may seem anachronistic for a period of social history which had no formal legal

---

26 It should be noted that Richard himself recognizes that his expectation of loyalty from Barbary is unrealistic: his speech continues, 'Forgiveness, horse! Why do I rail on thee, / Since thou, created to be awed by man, / Wast born to bear?' (5.5.90–2). This apostrophe, and the act of un-naming on which it is based, should, I think, be seen as a bitter disavowal rather than a kind of biological realism.

27 In this respect, grey Capulet is a dramatic counterpart to Feste, whose 'freelance' behaviour earns him his employer Olivia's distrust (see 1.5.1–3; 36).

28 'What is a Brand?', *Intellectual Property Office* (UK Government), www.ipo.gov.uk/types/tm/t-about/t-whatis/t-brands.htm (accessed 17 September 2012).

conception of intellectual property, but it helps us to approach this structuring principle as a form of value rather than a 'theme' or representation. To describe in such terms the conception of theatre that emerges from Shakespeare's work at this time is to identify it as the basis of the institutional consolidation of the company, particularly its efforts to create and maintain an audience: that is to say, a body of spectators that attended the Chamberlain's Men's productions regularly (probably in preference to others), knew Shakespeare's plays *as* Shakespeare's plays, associated them with a particular quality of theatrical experience and dramatic knowledge, and valued them highly both as personal experiences and as reliable frames of reference for the world outside the theatre.

Approaching this conception of theatre on these terms helps us to assess the importance of what happens when it begins to change. If the horses of *Henry V* and *Twelfth Night* provide an imaginary focus for the theatrical agency that take shape in these plays, their assimilation into metaphor in *Measure for Measure* could be said to illustrate its disintegration. Recognizing the 'tyranny' of Angelo's new position, Claudio describes 'the body public' as 'A horse whereon the governor doth ride, / Who, newly in the seat, that it may know / He can command, lets it straight feel the spur' (1.2.136–9).

This analysis is confirmed by the Duke in the next scene, when he tells the Friar, 'We have strict statutes and most biting laws, / The needful bits and curbs to headstrong weeds' (1.3.19–20).[29] First performed in 1604 after the company had become the King's Men, *Measure for Measure* is arguably even more preoccupied with relations of agency than the Elizabethan plays I have looked at so far; it also offers the most developed account of the relationship between agency and supply. But it dismantles the values so carefully accumulated around these terms in the earlier plays. Here, the concept of agency is discredited by its identification with Angelo:[30]

I would the Duke we talk of were returned again; this ungenitured agent will unpeople the province with

continency... The Duke yet would have dark deeds darkly answered: he would never bring them to light (3.1.405–10)

– and the notion of supply is divorced from its affiliation with public political culture and subsumed into the secret machinations of princely prerogative, where its meanings are redirected from questions of political representation towards secrecy and private gratification. Thus, Angelo is 'elected' by the Duke 'our absence to supply' (1.1.18), where 'election' refers misleadingly to an autocratic decision imposed on his subjects with no popular consultation; the Duke instructs the Friar to 'supply me with the habit, and instruct me / How I may formally in person bear / Like a true friar' (1.3.46–8), where the agency devolved onto the

---

[29] Katherine Eisaman Maus, the play's editor in the *Norton Shakespeare*, usefully glosses 'weeds': 'since 'bits and curbs' are parts of bridles, many editors emend 'weeds' to 'jades' or 'steeds', but the OED records several instances of 'weed' as a slang term for a worthless horse' (*The Norton Shakespeare*, 2035 n.2). In her Introduction, she further suggests that Vincentio 'recalls an image from Plato, who compared the desiring part of the soul to a useful but refractory horse, which the rational part of the soul needs to keep strictly bridled and under firm control' (2022).

[30] *Troilus and Cressida* might be included in this analysis. Like *Measure*, it identifies one of its leading characters, Pandarus, as an agent in terms that are primarily negative: 'O world, world, world! – thus is the poor agent despised... Why should our endeavour be so desired and the performance so loathed? What verse for it?' (Epilogue, 5.1.33/6–31/9). It is however worth noting both that Pandarus's role was considered one of the play's primary attractions and that the play may not have been performed at the Globe, despite entries in the Stationers' Register to the contrary. As the Norton Shakespeare edition notes, the second version of the 1609 Quarto 'announces "THE Famous Historie of Troylus *and* Cresseid", goes on to emphasize their love and Pandarus' role and omits any mention of performance. That omission is developed in a new prefatory epistle, which calls the play a comedy, appeals to elite literary taste by saying that it was never acted in a public theatre, and implies that publication is unauthorized' (1832–3). If that is the case, a stand-off between public spectatorship and 'elite literary taste', paralleling the stand-off between the Greeks and the Trojans, may underpin the relation between theatricality and commercialism that informs the play as a whole, and the Pandarus character in particular.

disguised player acting on behalf of a principal in *Twelfth Night* is re-appropriated by the principal himself; and Mariana connives with this 'true' friar and Isabella to 'supply thee [Angelo] at thy gardenhouse / In her imagined person' (5.1.205–9). She thus completes the process whereby 'supply' is dissociated from a conception of theatrical agency publicly engaged on behalf of its audience, and repositioned as a covert operation staged by a sovereign who systematically misrepresents himself and his actions. This misrepresentation is directed not just to the immediate participants but to 'society' as a whole, and nowhere more than in the final scene, with its staged parody of the parliamentary process of private petition ('if any crave redress of injustice, they should exhibit their petitions in the street' (4.4.7–8)).

While there are striking similarities between *Henry V*'s strategic use and subsequent exposure of disguise, *Measure* allows nothing like the challenge to such behaviour offered by Michael Williams (however you read his last line). And where *Twelfth Night* exposes the limitations of 'consensual' principles of contract in favour of a trust-based model of social and theatrical participation, *Measure* promotes an ethos of contract conceived as the imposition of contradictory obligations by an all-knowing sovereign on the unknowing and the unwilling. Thus Claudio, condemned by a law that has not been applied for fourteen years, describes it as 'just' (1.2.103), despite the fact that he also sees his relationship with Juliet as 'a true contract' (l. 122); and Angelo, despite the fact that he tells the Duke he is not ready for the office imposed on him (1.1.47–9), denounces himself in absolute terms as spiritually corrupt when he turns out to be right (2.2.67–191). The issues of trust and reciprocity discussed above have no part in the world of this play. If St German's simple account of the fiction of identity of principal and agent was inadequate to the subtle explorations of agency in *Henry V* and *Twelfth Night*, *Measure for Measure* appears to offer a vision of society within which such an account would present itself as a blinding revelation.

This gives us an important indication as to what an appropriate critical response to this play might

be. Like Henry in *Henry V*, the Duke in *Measure for Measure* creates a spiritual ethos that displaces his own responsibility for the events of the play. But unlike *Henry V* the play also closes down the theatrical machinery that would enable a confrontation of this displacement from within the action. It's easy to see why it has attracted Foucauldian readings, and why it continues to be read primarily in cultural or representational terms as a staging of Jacobean absolutism.[31] But I would argue that such readings *reproduce* the Duke's dematerialization of theatrical agency; that is to say, *they themselves* displace from the play its primary institutional engagement with the agency of Shakespearian performance and spectatorship. Clearly, *Measure for Measure* heralds changes in that agency that will be as fundamental to an understanding of plays written *after* 1603–4 as those that took place in the mid-1590s were to the plays discussed here. Shakespeare appears to re-appraise the late Elizabethan sense of theatre as agent to its audience's principal that became so definitive of his work for the Lord Chamberlain's Men in their inaugural years at the Globe. His first work for the King's Men appears to break the affiliation between parliamentary and theatrical agency displayed in *Henry V* and to dismantle the rich network of social, political, legal and theatrical agencies put so brilliantly in place by *Twelfth Night*. Was this dismantling an act of loss or disillusion? Was it politically cynical, a King's

---

[31] Most notably in a series of highly influential readings associated with New Historicism in the 1980s: see in particular Jonathan Goldberg, *James I and the Politics of Literature: Jonson, Shakespeare, Donne and their Contemporaries* (Baltimore, 1983), especially Chapter 5, 'Social Texts, Royal Measures: Donne, Jonson and *Measure for Measure*'; Leonard Tennenhouse, *Power on Display: The Politics of Shakespeare's Genres* (London, 1986), especially Chapter 3, 'The Theatre of Punishment: Jacobean Tragedy and the Politics of Misogyny'; Steven Mullaney, *The Place of the Stage: License, Play, and Power in Renaissance England* (Ann Arbor, 1988). Tennenhouse reads *Measure for Measure* as a member of a group of plays called the 'Jacobean disguised ruler plays', approaching them as an active strategy within the authorization of Jacobean power. For a recent discussion of these readings, see Kevin A. Quarmby, *The Disguised Ruler in Shakespeare and his Contemporaries* (Farnham, 2012).

Man's willingness to concede his company's hard-won autonomy to a new political master? Or was it simply a conceptual shift towards a new understanding of the relations between social and theatrical agency, a shift that would in its turn precipitate formal innovations that would redefine the 'Shakespearian' dimension of Shakespeare's plays in the remaining, Jacobean, years of his career?

It is not within the scope of this article to answer these questions, but I can indicate at least one of the directions an answer would take. *All's Well That Ends Well* is ostensibly linked to *As You Like It* and *Twelfth Night* in its treatment of the 'woman's part'; but Helena is more like Vincentio than Rosalind or Viola, or even Isabella or Mariana, in that she is a fully-fledged principal, not an agent, and in this respect a precursor of the women of the tragedies. Thus, even if Vincentio's re-appropriation of agency on behalf of the principal seems to suggest some kind of rapprochement with Jacobean absolutism, it is a formal precondition for an institutional quantity in the later plays that modern criticism has associated with a quite different, even opposing set of values, such as those associated with contemporary feminism: the development of a mode of characterization that decisively shifts Shakespeare's women away from their reliance on the comic woman's part and reflexive theatricality. It may, however, be as reductive to see these characterizations in emancipatory terms as it is to read Richard II's un-naming of roan Barbary as a form of biological realism: one of the reasons it can be important to take an institutional rather than cultural approach to Shakespeare's work is that it can encourage us *not* to impose our conceptual systems onto his. My more limited aim here has been to think about a specific period in his working life and to offer an account of the social, political and theatrical values his plays created at that point for his company and their audiences. My other aim has been to think through the way we apply vital interdisciplinarities, like law and literature. I have argued that, in *Henry V* and *Twelfth Night*, Shakespeare took principles of agency beyond the frameworks within which they were currently addressed in sixteenth-century law and that, in the process, he identified the kind of questions that would inform their subsequent formulation as a body of law. Obviously, such a position requires caution: a suggestion that Shakespeare was 'ahead of his time' would be even more problematic than the idea that his plays were engaged with the production of the legal order. But we can, I think, confidently conclude that it is precisely in its role in the institutional development of Shakespearian theatre that the conception of theatrical agency I have been discussing here should be seen as itself an agent in the historical process by which a society that could imagine a law of agency came into being.

HAMLET AND EMPIRICISM

JAMES HIRSH

From the beginning to the end of his career, Shakespeare dramatized myriad ways in which a search for the truth can go wrong. Characters jump to erroneous or unjust conclusions as a result of invalid premises; wishful thinking; fearfulness; some other emotion; ethnic, religious, or class prejudice; misogyny; some other application of a stereotype to an individual; some other form of conventional thinking; narrow-mindedness; a failure of imagination; a simplification of a complex issue; rationalization; illogicality; misleading, inadequate, or false evidence; and so on. Such problems are highlighted in the title of *The Comedy of Errors*, one of Shakespeare's earliest plays. In the Induction to *Henry IV, Part 2* the personification Rumour boasts of his sovereignty over the minds of the 'multitude' (19), but the following scene dramatizes that aristocrats are no less likely to be swayed by rumours that seem to confirm their hopes or fears. Intellectual errors make characters vulnerable to deceptions perpetrated by other characters, with sometimes comic, sometimes tragic consequences. The cryptic elements that Maria cleverly includes in a forged letter lure Malvolio into focusing his intellectual energies on the *meaning* of those elements rather than on the more fundamental issue of the letter's *authenticity*. Iago deceives Othello not by fabricating a massive amount of false evidence but by exploiting habits of thought that predispose Othello to accept trivial and dubious pieces of evidence as conclusive. Some characters fail to test hypotheses rigorously or fail to ask themselves subsidiary questions of crucial importance to their overall enquiry. Shakespeare was fascinated by the convoluted thought processes that allow a person to deceive himself. The process by which Leontes talks himself into jealousy on the basis of flimsy evidence is dramatized in the opening scene of *The Winter's Tale*, one of Shakespeare's last plays.

Noting that Shakespeare frequently depicted characters who arrive at erroneous conclusions, some commentators have erroneously concluded that Shakespeare was a radical sceptic who believed that drawing inferences from evidence is an inherently futile endeavour. As already indicated, in almost all cases characters arrive at erroneous conclusions *not* after rigorously testing ideas against evidence but rather by *failing* to do so. That human beings often make computational errors is not evidence that arithmetic is an inherently futile endeavour. Gloucester and Edgar jump to erroneous conclusions about one another not because truth is inherently unknowable but because neither adequately tests the validity of Edmund's testimony and supposed evidence. If they had, they would have quickly determined that Edmund's evidence was bogus. To his credit, Gloucester does not excuse his error by claiming that truth is inherently unknowable.

Confusion occasionally arises about the relationship between empiricism and scepticism as a result of a failure to distinguish crucially different kinds of scepticism. Far from being incompatible with scepticism, empiricism actually entails one specific kind. An empiricist doubts a theory unless and until it has been proven by reliable and conclusive evidence. An empiricist is also prepared to revive doubt about a theory that has in the past been confirmed by evidence if newly uncovered evidence calls the theory into question. It is only the extreme form of scepticism – which regards all theories as equally doubtful, regardless of the amount or quality of evidence supporting them and which therefore regards a search for or consideration of evidence as a futile endeavour – that is at odds with empiricism. Recent research has established (on the basis of substantial evidence) that there was a revival of this absolute form of scepticism in the Renaissance. Some accounts of this revival convey the impression that absolute scepticism was the only alternative to unquestioning faith. Millicent Bell, for example, asserts that in Shakespeare's age 'doubt and credulity – or faith – contested in the mind', and she projects this dichotomy onto Shakespeare: 'in the four great tragedies . . . the will to belief in universal coherence and meaning struggles, often unsuccessfully, against skepticism'.[1] This is misleading in at least two ways. In the first place, rather than being fundamentally in conflict, unquestioning credulity and absolute scepticism share a fundamental characteristic: they are both forms of self-imposed blindness. Each regards a search for evidence as pointless. Blind scepticism has often been used, paradoxically, as a stalking horse for blind faith. Erasmus in *The Praise of Folly* and Montaigne in the 'Apology for Raymond Sebond' argued that the absolute doubtfulness of human understanding should lead one to place one's absolute faith in God. A second reason that the positing of a simple conflict between blind faith and blind scepticism in the Renaissance is misleading is that it ignores or downplays evidence of a third epistemological position, empiricism, that is espoused or exhibited in the works of some prominent figures in the period. In promoting empiricism, Francis Bacon emphatically rejected absolute scepticism: 'The doctrine of those who have denied that certainty could be attained at all has some agreement with my way of proceeding at the first setting out, but they end in being infinitely separated and opposed.'[2] An empiricist doubts but searches diligently for relevant evidence and ceases to doubt if conclusive evidence is found. A radical sceptic simply doubts.

Bacon was by no means the first advocate of empiricism. It had been advocated and practised by some individuals since ancient times. Thales argued that physical phenomena have physical rather than supernatural causes and that an understanding of those causes should be sought in careful observation. Hippocrates made a similar argument about diseases in particular. In the sixteenth century Copernicus argued that the earth was a satellite of the sun, as demonstrated by astronomical evidence that was more simply explained by a heliocentric system than by the geocentric system with its makeshift epicycles. Machiavelli arrived at an understanding of politics not by deductive reasoning but by the careful analysis of the behaviour of actual politicians. William Gilbert's landmark work of observational and experimental science, *De Magnete* (*On the Magnet*), was published in 1600, at roughly the time Shakespeare was writing *Hamlet*. Lorna Hutson has called attention to 'the rapidly developing sophistication of evidential concepts in English canon law' during the sixteenth century. Legal proceedings 'increasingly involved the exercise of discretion, judgment, and a sense of how to weigh evidence' by 'ordinary people' who served as members of juries. Awareness of evidential concepts 'was socially pervasive' and 'resulted in the investigative procedures of the common law acquiring a new cultural centrality and moral exemplarity'.[3] When Clarence asks the men sent by Richard to murder him, 'Where is the evidence that doth accuse me?' (*Richard III*, 1.4.178), Shakespeare reinforced a connection in playgoers' minds between evidence and justice and a corollary connection between a lack of evidence and injustice.

---

[1] Millicent Bell, *Shakespeare's Tragic Skepticism* (New Haven, CT, 2002), pp. 15, 4.

[2] *The New Organon* (1620), translated from Latin into English, in Bacon, *Works*, ed. James Spedding *et al.* (1863), repr. in *Francis Bacon: A Selection of His Works*, ed. Sidney Warhaft (New York, 1965), pp. 325–92, Book I: Aphorism xxxvii, p. 335.

[3] Lorna Hutson, *The Invention of Suspicion: Law and Mimesis in Shakespeare and Renaissance Drama* (Oxford, 2007), pp. 3, 5. I am grateful to Sarah Higginbotham for drawing my attention to this valuable study.

Shakespeare not only provided intriguing, complex and subtle depictions of characters engaged in the elementary and nearly inescapable human activities of gathering evidence and making inferences but placed playgoers in situations that called upon them to exercise their own abilities to draw inferences from evidence. Placing playgoers in situations that resemble situations confronted by characters is a characteristically Shakespearian manoeuvre.[4] The present article will focus on a few of the ways in which *Hamlet* dramatizes these issues.

Shakespeare devoted a surprising amount of stage time (over 70 lines) to an episode in which Polonius sends Reynaldo on a mission to find out if Laertes is misbehaving in Paris. This episode is inconsequential to the plot of the play but highly relevant to a major theme of the play, how individuals gather and interpret evidence. Polonius instructs his operative to seek out acquaintances of Laertes and to tell each of them lies about Laertes's supposed misbehaviour.

> Wherefore should you do this? . . .
> You laying these slight sullies on my son, . . .
> Mark you, your party in converse, him you would
>   sound,
> Having ever seen in the prenominate crimes
> The youth you breathe of guilty.   (2.1.37–44)

The method Polonius devises to generate evidence about his son's possible misbehaviour undercuts the reliability of the evidence generated. When Reynaldo tells his 'party in converse' about fictional misbehaviour of Laertes, even if that interlocutor is unaware of any actual misbehaviour by Laertes, he is liable to make something up simply to keep up his side of the 'converse'. Furthermore, this party is likely to pass on to other acquaintances of Laertes the lies told him by Reynaldo. When Reynaldo gets around to sounding those young men, they are likely to repeat what they have heard on the grapevine. Two predispositions that make Polonius vulnerable to intellectual error are exhibited in the following passage:

> And thus do we of wisdom and of reach
> With windlasses and with assays of bias
> By indirections find directions out.   (63–5)

Polonius's vanity about his own 'wisdom' deters him from subjecting his plan to rigorous scrutiny. Since he thought of the plan and he is wise, it follows, as the night the day, that his plan is wise. He fails to think through its implications and ramifications. A second psychological trait that predisposes Polonius to err is his tendency to give undue credence to evidence obtained surreptitiously. Rather than employing deception and spying as a last resort, Polonius employs them as the first resort. Polonius's overconfidence in his own judgement and in surreptitious methods blinds him to the obvious problems with his evidence-gathering methodology.

Later in the same scene Polonius formulates the hypothesis that Hamlet's madness is the result of his thwarted love for Ophelia. Although playgoers know this hypothesis is false, it is not utterly groundless. The possibility is suggested by Hamlet's behaviour in Ophelia's closet and a letter in which he declares 'I love thee best' (2.2.121). Acknowledging that this evidence is merely suggestive, not conclusive, Polonius devises an experiment to test the hypothesis. He proposes that he and the King eavesdrop on an encounter between Hamlet and Ophelia. The implied reason that Polonius does not rely on Ophelia's ex-post-facto account of such an encounter is that he does not regard her as a reliable witness. In 1.3 he denigrated her as 'a green girl' (101). Polonius assumes that a young, inexperienced, naive female will not detect the possibly subtle signs of love that the wise old patriarch Polonius has convinced himself will be evident in Hamlet's behaviour. Polonius has himself partly to

---

4 For other examples of this technique, see Stephen Booth, 'On the Value of *Hamlet*' in *Representations of Elizabethan Drama*, ed. Norman Rabkin (New York, 1969), pp. 139–76, and '*King Lear*', '*Macbeth*', *Indefinition, and Tragedy* (New Haven, CT, 1983); James Hirsh, 'Laughter at *Titus Andronicus*', *Essays in Theatre*, 7 (1988), 59–74, repr. in *Shakespearean Criticism*, 134 (2010), 150–8; James Hirsh, '*Othello* and Perception' in '*Othello*': *New Perspectives*, ed. Virginia Mason Vaughan and Kent Cartwright (Madison, NJ, 1991), pp. 135–59, repr. in *Shakespearean Criticism Yearbook 1991: A Selection of the Year's Most Noteworthy Studies*, ed. Ralph Berry *et al.* (Detroit, 1993), pp. 276–86.

blame for another reason that Ophelia might fail to confirm his preconception. He has raised her to be modest and diffident. In the present circumstance those supposedly admirable female traits might prevent her from acknowledging or even perceiving signs that the Prince of Denmark is madly in love with her. Additional factors in Polonius's decision to construct an eavesdropping situation are his sheer love of surreptitious intelligence gathering and his assumption that such techniques are inherently more reliable than more direct means.

From his eavesdropping position in 3.1 Polonius overhears Hamlet refer to 'The pangs of disprized love', but merely as one undistinguished item in a list of misfortunes that human beings are liable to experience:

> Th' oppressor's wrong, the proud man's contumely,
> The pangs of disprized love, the law's delay,
> The insolence of office. (73–5)

In his encounter with Ophelia, Hamlet does not play the conventional part of a pathetic, lovelorn suitor that he played in Ophelia's closet and instead berates her, issues an angry tirade about the incompatibility of beauty and honesty, and sends her off to a 'nunnery' (123). Even in the face of strong counter-evidence, Polonius nevertheless maintains his pet theory:

> But yet I do believe
> The origin and commencement of this grief
> Sprung from neglected love. (179–81)

Shakespeare provides sufficient evidence for playgoers to realize why Polonius clings to his theory despite disconfirming evidence. Under normal circumstances, a prince would be married to a foreign princess or a very high noblewoman in order to forge a political alliance between the two families. Under normal circumstances, therefore, a love affair between the Prince of Denmark and the daughter of a Danish court official could not result in marriage. It is precisely this consideration that prompts Polonius in 1.3 to instruct Ophelia to end her relationship with Hamlet. If Hamlet's madness is the result of thwarted love for Ophelia, however, the situation radically changes. In

that case, the most promising way to cure Hamlet would be to unthwart his love, to allow Hamlet to marry Ophelia. If that were to occur, Polonius would be in line to become the progenitor of kings. In *Macbeth* Shakespeare dramatizes how powerful such a motive might be. Banquo does not share with his fellow thanes either the prophecies of the Weird Sisters or his conviction that Macbeth murdered Duncan because to do so might disrupt the prophecy that he himself would be the forebear of kings. Just as Malvolio's wishful thinking leads him to see anything Olivia does as a sign of love for him, Polonius's wishful thinking predisposes him to see anything Hamlet does as evidence that he is mad for Ophelia. Polonius never gives voice to this motive, but the tenacity of his conviction coupled with vividly dramatized features of his personality (his egotism, pretentiousness, concern for family honour, etc.) constitutes sufficient evidence for playgoers to make the inference. Polonius's adherence to his pet theory in the face of counter-evidence illustrates a principle later formulated by Bacon: 'what a man had rather were true he more readily believes'.[5] Acutely aware that Ophelia's personality traits might lead her to miss or to misconstrue significant pieces of evidence, Polonius is ironically blind to the degree to which his own wishful thinking makes him vulnerable to misinterpreting evidence. By dramatizing Polonius's foolish maintenance of a theory in the face of strong counter-evidence, Shakespeare encourages playgoers to learn from Polonius's mistakes.

The King also seeks to discover the cause of Hamlet's apparent madness. His public motive is simply an avuncular/step-parental concern about his nephew/stepson's wellbeing. If the cause of Hamlet's insanity is discovered, something might be done to cure it. But Claudius has an implicit ulterior reason for wanting to determine Hamlet's state of mind. The political situation at the outset of the play is that King Hamlet has recently died and his brother has succeeded to the throne. In these circumstances it is likely that the old king's

---

[5] *Organon*, I: XLIX, p. 338.

son and namesake feels aggrieved at not having succeeded his father as King. The current King would be foolish not to consider the possibility that the Prince might be plotting to take from the current occupant the throne that the Prince might feel is rightfully his. Hamlet is an obvious potential rival for the crown around whom anyone discontented with King Claudius's rule might rally. Rivalry for a crown is a recurring theme in Shakespeare's English history plays that were first performed in the decade leading up to *Hamlet*. Claudius is dramatized as a shrewd Machiavellian politician. From his perspective, the most important question that Polonius's experiment might answer is not whether Hamlet is madly in love with Ophelia but whether he poses a threat.

Hamlet's tirade during his encounter with Ophelia provides the King with evidence that Hamlet is indeed dangerous:

I am very proud, revengeful, ambitious . . . Those that are married already – all but one – shall live.

(126–7, 150–1)

On the basis of what he has overheard, Claudius dismisses the love hypothesis and even the madness hypothesis:

> Love? His affections do not that way tend,
> Nor what he spake, though it lacked form a little,
> Was not like madness . . .
> And I do doubt the hatch and the disclose
> Will be some danger. (165–70)

Claudius lacks a key piece of evidence relevant to an understanding of Hamlet's state of mind: that Hamlet has encountered a spirit who claimed to be the ghost of his father and who accused the King of murder. Claudius has no reason to suspect that such an extraordinary event has occurred. In light of the evidence available to him, the King's conclusions are astute. Hamlet openly declares that he possesses the very traits that would make him a threat to the King. If the son of a king acknowledges that he is 'ambitious', a prudent inference by the current occupant of the post is that the son is impatient to become King himself. If the ambitious son of a king who did not inherit his

father's throne acknowledges that he is 'revengeful', a prudent inference by the current occupant of the throne is that the son contemplates retaliation against the current occupant for having stolen the throne that the son expected to inherit as a matter of course. In 1.2 Hamlet exhibited bitterness that the marriage of the King and his mother ended the grieving period for his father prematurely, so the King has reason to take personally Hamlet's cryptic assertion that 'Those that are married already – all but one – shall live.' From the King's perspective, a sane Hamlet, governed by coolly rational self-interest, is 'dangerous'. That in a given instance a villainous character draws a reasonable inference from evidence does not discredit empiricism. That in a given instance an intelligent person might use his intelligence in the commission of a crime does not discredit intelligence. In his initial response to what he has overheard, Claudius inadvertently lets Polonius a little too much into his confidence. The King does not want Polonius to realize that he is motivated by fear of an all-too-sane rival for the throne rather than by concern for a mentally ill family member. So Claudius quickly retracts his too-revealing rejection of the madness hypothesis: 'Madness in great ones must not unwatched go' (3.1.191).

Just as Polonius and the King seek evidence to ascertain what is in Hamlet's mind, Hamlet seeks evidence to ascertain what is in the King's mind. Recognizing the possibility that the spirit he has seen may be the devil, Hamlet devises an experiment, one of the most famous in cultural history, supposedly to test the validity of the Ghost's accusation: 'The play's the thing / Wherein I'll catch the conscience of the King' (2.2.606–7). This experiment is fundamentally and conspicuously flawed in multiple ways. The initial premise is a theory of audience response:

> I have heard that guilty creatures sitting at a play
> Have by the very cunning of the scene
> Been struck so to the soul that presently
> They have proclaimed their malefactions. (591–4)

It is not likely that a cold-blooded murderer and adept politician, well-practised in masking his emotions in public, would, in reaction to a play that depicted a crime similar to his own, be unable to prevent himself from proclaiming, 'Stop the show! I can't stand it! I confess! I am guilty of a similar crime!' This initial premise of Hamlet's experiment is later dramatized as invalid when, in response to the play-within-the-play, the King does not in fact proclaim his malefaction. But no sooner had Hamlet articulated his initial experimental premise in 2.2 than he revised it. Realizing how unlikely it would be that the King would proclaim his guilt, Hamlet immediately and drastically lowers the bar of proof.

> I'll observe his looks,
> I'll tent him to the quick. If a but blench,
> [that is, I'll apply pressure as if to a wound. If he
>   but flinch,]
> I know my course.   (598–600)

This is a bogus test for the obvious reason that many playgoers who are innocent of murder flinch at theatrical depictions of murders. Flinching at a depiction of a murder would much more likely be the result of a playgoer's *squeamishness* than the result of guiltiness. If the King flinches in response to the dumb show or to any other element of the performance, his reaction would be a red herring since *guiltless* creatures sitting at a play sometimes flinch in response to dramatized murders. The bar of proof in Hamlet's revised experiment is as preposterously low as the initial bar was preposterously high. Hamlet sets the bar so low that it will enable Hamlet to convict the King – whom he hates for having 'whored' his mother and for having 'Popped in between th'election and [Hamlet's] hopes' (5.2.65–6) to succeed his father as king – merely if the King reacts to a dramatized murder as many playgoers who are not murderers react. Shakespeare understood audience response as profoundly as anyone who has ever lived, so there is no chance that Shakespeare himself believed in Hamlet's preposterous theory that flinching at a crime depicted in a play is proof of one's guilt of a similar crime.

As if all this were not enough to discredit Hamlet's experiment, it is quite evident that *the King does not even flinch* in response to any element of the performance. The evidence for this is that Hamlet becomes increasingly desperate to provoke a reaction. Frustrated that the performance itself has not provoked even a flinch by the King, Hamlet tries to get a rise (so to speak) out of the King in reaction to his own speeches and actions. He perpetrates a series of escalating provocations. From the point at which he identifies the murderer of Gonzago as the 'nephew of the King' (232), any reaction by Claudius might be a sign of his fear of his nephew. The King eventually does storm off, but not until Hamlet has turned the performance into a fiasco by his repeated interruptions that show flagrant public disrespect for the King, the presiding figure at the royal command performance. Hamlet's own behaviour provokes a reaction that the performance failed to provoke. His experiment generates no valid evidence in regard to the King's guilt much less proof beyond a reasonable doubt.

Shakespeare set up multiple profound analogies between the bogus experiments of Hamlet and Polonius. Just as Polonius is predisposed to regard almost anything Hamlet does as a sign of love, Hamlet is predisposed to regard almost anything the King does as a sign of fratricidal guilt. Polonius's predisposition is his wishful thinking about becoming the progenitor of kings. Hamlet's predisposition is his intense hatred of the man whose guilt or innocence he is supposedly trying to determine. Just as the method Polonius devises to generate intelligence about his son contaminates the evidence generated, Hamlet's intrusion into his badly designed experiment contaminates the evidence. Like Polonius, Hamlet is vain about his cleverness and discernment and as in the case of Polonius this makes him vulnerable to intellectual error.

Despite multiple, varied and obvious ways in which his experiment is invalidated, Hamlet regards it as a complete success: 'I'll take the Ghost's word for a thousand pound' (3.2.274–5). A few minutes after gloating about the supposed success of his experiment, Hamlet mocks Rosencrantz and Guildenstern for thinking they can pluck out the heart of his mystery. This is profoundly ironic since Hamlet has just convinced himself, on the basis of a flawed theory and trumped-up evidence, that he has plucked out the heart of the King's mystery.

Nonetheless, the vast majority of post-Renaissance commentators have assumed that Shakespeare wanted playgoers to accept without question the validity of Hamlet's theoretical premise and experimental methodology. Most commentators do so presumably because Hamlet is the apparent hero, and at conventional plays playgoers are supposed to accept unquestioningly the validity of whatever theory the hero concocts and whatever methods the hero employs. One glaring problem with this assumption is that *Hamlet* is demonstrably not a conventional play. It is thought-provoking to a daring, almost unprecedented degree. It relentlessly encourages playgoers to think through the implications and ramifications of everything it contains no matter where those implications and ramifications might lead. One of the themes the play probes most thought-provokingly is how human beings gather and interpret evidence. It is not credible that the author of such a play was blind to the egregious flaws in Hamlet's experimental methodology. It is not credible that this author expected playgoers to recognize the flaws in Polonius's experiment but hoped that they would not notice the even greater number of even more egregious flaws in Hamlet's experiment. Nor is it credible that the author who would soon dramatize Othello's acceptance of a flagrantly low bar of proof of Desdemona's guilt expected playgoers to regard as legitimate the equally low bar set by Hamlet for proof of the King's guilt.

To explain why the King does not respond to the dumb show in the way predicted by Hamlet's theory, W. W. Greg argued that Claudius did not murder King Hamlet in the manner described by the Ghost.[6] J. Dover Wilson argued that the King must have been engaged in conversation and so did not observe the dumb show.[7] In his analysis of the Mousetrap, Stanley Cavell argued as follows:

There seem to be . . . putting aside the currently disfavored hypothesis of textual anomaly that deletes the dumb show, only two possibilities besides Greg's: (1) The king did not see the dumb show . . . or (2) the king saw

and has his conscience caught but was able to suppress the external manifestation of this capture until the repetition of the scene of poisoning accompanied by words.[8]

Cavell disowns knowledge of a possibility far more likely than either of the two he articulates: that Hamlet's theory is simply invalid and that the King eventually storms off not in response to the 'repetition of the scene of poisoning accompanied by words' but in response to Hamlet's increasingly rude disruptions. Cavell accepts as a premise not to be questioned that Shakespeare wanted playgoers to accept unquestioningly Hamlet's theory that a person's (eventual) flinching at a theatrical depiction of a murder is 'the external manifestation' of the person's guilty conscience, proof positive that the person is a murderer.

A few commentators have recognized that the Mousetrap does not prove the King's guilt but have drawn faulty lessons. Graham Bradshaw used the invalidity of the Mousetrap as the centrepiece of his chapter on *Hamlet* in *Shakespeare's Scepticism*, the main thesis of which is that Shakespeare engaged in 'radically sceptical "thinking"'.[9] But the fact that a character in a play employs conspicuously faulty methods of enquiry in no way suggests that the dramatist was a radical sceptic. Rigorous empiricists are as intent as radical sceptics on exposing faulty methods of enquiry. The exposure of faulty premises and methodology was a key component of Bacon's establishment of an empirical regime of enquiry. Steve Roth also recognized that '*the mousetrap doesn't work*' but applauds Hamlet for not letting that failure affect his conviction that the King committed fratricide: 'Hamlet's achievement lies in his ability to adopt that illusion not in the face of "true knowledge", but in despite of

---

[6] W. W. Greg, 'Hamlet's Hallucination', *Modern Language Review*, 12 (1917), 393–421.

[7] J. Dover Wilson, *What Happens in 'Hamlet'*, 3rd edn (Cambridge, 1951).

[8] Stanley Cavell, 'Hamlet's Burden of Proof', *Disowning Knowledge in Six Plays of Shakespeare* (Cambridge, 1987), pp. 179–91, 180–1.

[9] Graham Bradshaw, *Shakespeare's Scepticism* (New York, 1987), especially pp. x–xi, 104, 114–17, 121.

knowing that he can never truly know.'[10] In Roth's view, if you lack reliable evidence, it is commendable to convince yourself that a person you hate has committed murder.

The soliloquy in 3.3 in which Claudius expresses a desire to repent for having murdered his brother opens up a chasm between Hamlet's epistemological situation and that of playgoers. Even though *playgoers* are provided with conclusive evidence that the King committed fratricide, Hamlet does not, as a result of the Mousetrap, acquire evidence to justify *his* conclusion that the King has committed that crime. This differential is profoundly important. In the absence of genuine evidence to corroborate the testimony of a witness whose reliability is doubtful, Hamlet manufactures bogus evidence to frame a man whom playgoers know is guilty on the basis of evidence unavailable to Hamlet. It would be unjust for a police officer to fabricate bogus evidence to implicate a person in a crime *even if the person is actually guilty.* Hamlet behaves unjustly in convincing himself of the King's guilt on the basis of a bogus theory and trumped-up evidence. The play is in part the tragedy of a man who makes up his mind. The contrast between genuine and bogus evidence ironically becomes an explicit issue in 3.3 when in a soliloquy the King imagines a heavenly tribunal:

> There is no shuffling, there the action lies
> In his true nature, and we ourselves compelled...
> To give in evidence.   (61–4)

Hamlet's earthly trial/experiment did not in fact compel the King to give in evidence of his guilt, and it is Hamlet who has engaged in 'shuffling'.

Shakespeare was clearly fascinated by the processes by which people form hypotheses, gather or generate evidence supposedly to test their hypotheses, and interpret the evidence accumulated. As indicated above, most of the investigations he depicted go wrong. This is not surprising since how things go wrong is usually more dramatically interesting than how things go right. Almost all of these investigations go wrong as a result of outright errors on the part of the investigators. In

highlighting *mistakes* made by investigators, Shakespeare anticipated Francis Bacon, a key figure in the establishment of modern scientific empiricism. Bacon observed that 'it generally happens that men make their trials carelessly'.[11] In *The Proficience and Advancement of Learning* (published in 1605, only four or five years after the first performance of *Hamlet*) Bacon categorized and analysed intellectual errors to be avoided. Some of the specific intellectual errors he describes resemble those dramatized in *Hamlet*. The Queen's critique of Polonius, 'More matter with less art' (2.2.96), would be echoed by Bacon, who condemned the common failing of scholars 'to hunt more after words than matter'. Polonius and Hamlet (as well as Malvolio, Othello, and Leontes) exhibit what Bacon would describe as a 'facility of credit and accepting or admitting things weakly authorized or warranted'. Polonius is distracted from a disinterested search for the truth by the glittering prospect of becoming the progenitor of kings. Bacon deplores the tendency of a 'proud mind' to become distracted from a disinterested search for the truth by the prospect of material rewards, as Atalanta was distracted by a golden ball.[12] In *The New Organon* Bacon describes the 'four classes of Idols which beset men's minds', one of which is the following:

The Idols of the Cave are the idols of the individual man. For every one (besides the errors common to human nature in general) has a cave or den of his own, which refracts and discolours the light of nature, owing either to his own proper and peculiar nature ... or to the differences of impressions, accordingly as they take place in a mind preoccupied and predisposed.[13]

---

10 Steve Roth, 'Who Knows Who Knows Who's There? An Epistemology of *Hamlet* (Or, What Happens in the Mousetrap)', *Early Modern English Studies*, 10 (2004), para. 9 and 26.

11 *Organon*, I: LXXX, p. 349.

12 *The Proficience and Advancement of Learning* (1605), in *Bacon: A Selection*, pp. 198–271; 223, 227, 235.

13 *Organon*, I: XXXIX, p. 335; and I: XLII, p. 336. There are similarities between the errors and Idols described by Bacon and some of the 'cognitive biases' catalogued by psychologists in recent decades. See, for example, David Kahneman *et al.*,

This would be an accurate description of intellectual infirmities exhibited by Polonius and Hamlet (as well as those exhibited by Malvolio, Othello, and Leontes), each of whom allows his personal preoccupations and predispositions to cloud his judgement. Polonius clings to an erroneous theory in the face of strong counter-evidence. Hamlet clings to a theory unjustified by the evidence he trumps up.[14] As indicated above, Bacon's acute awareness of the myriad ways an enquiry can go wrong did not lead him to absolute scepticism. His detailed accounts of intellectual errors were not intended to bring discredit upon 'learning' but rather to cleanse it of impediments and distractions. Similarly, the frequent depiction of intellectual errors committed by characters in Shakespeare's plays is not evidence that Shakespeare thought that the rigorous testing of ideas is futile.

In addition to depicting characters whose skills in gathering or generating evidence, assessing the reliability of evidence, and drawing reasonable and just inferences are put to the test, *Hamlet* frequently challenges playgoers to exercise those same skills in trying to answer questions raised by the dramatic action. As indicated above, Shakespeare provided enough evidence for playgoers to arrive at valid conclusions about the invalidity of the experiments conducted by Polonius and Hamlet. The artistic strategy of challenging playgoers to exercise their skills in assessing evidence was not unique to Shakespeare. As Lorna Hutson has noted, sixteenth-century revenge tragedies often made an 'intellectual appeal to the audience as *lay judges*, thus throwing the emphasis simultaneously on to the audience's intellectual capacity to puzzle out what the plot presents as "evidence" and on its ethical arbitration of what that evidence implies'.[15]

As noted above, the King's explicit references to his crime of fratricide in a self-addressed speech in 3.3 provide playgoers with conclusive evidence that the accusation made by the Ghost in 1.5 is true. Some playgoers may be tempted to regard this validation of one of the Ghost's assertions as evidence that the other assertions made by the Ghost, including in particular its assertion that it is a spirit

undergoing purgatorial discipline, are also valid. As Shakespeare demonstrates in this play and in others, however, a person who tells the truth about one issue might lie about another matter. Indeed, one of the most common strategies of con men is to obscure a lie by burying it under a mound of truthful assertions. If the gull tests some assertions and finds them to be truthful, he is likely to accept the remaining assertions, including the lie, without verifying them. Just as the devil can quote scripture, a con artist or devil can tell the truth about one issue as part of a strategy to deceive, mislead, or manipulate. Iago employs this tactic. The validity of a person's assertion in regard to one matter does not constitute conclusive proof of the validity of other assertions by the person. This principle is applicable not merely in situations in which a person might be lying. It is a fundamental principle of scientific methodology. A scientist who provides evidence that conclusively demonstrates the validity of one theory is not thereafter given a free pass. To be accepted by other scientists, *every subsequent assertion* by the scientist must be *independently* proven by conclusive evidence. In most non-scientific fields of study scholars are held to a similar standard.

In the case of the Ghost, it seems unlikely that a spirit undergoing a moral purification process approved by Jesus, who urged people to turn the other cheek, would be given an overnight pass to demand that a relative exact revenge. It is more likely that the Ghost is an evil spirit using a truth to tempt Hamlet to commit a damnable sin. As indicated above, Hamlet does not have conclusive evidence of the King's guilt. If Hamlet kills the King on the basis only of the dubious testimony of the Ghost and the bogus evidence of the

---

eds., *Heuristics and Biases: The Psychology of Intuitive Judgement* (New York, 2002).

[14] These analogies do not constitute evidence that Bacon wrote the plays attributed to Shakespeare but raise the possibility that Bacon's understanding of the ways that enquiries can go wrong may have been informed in part by having seen or read some of Shakespeare's plays that vividly dramatize such errors.

[15] Hutson, *Invention of Suspicion*, p. 69.

Mousetrap, he would be killing a fellow human being *without a valid justification*. Ironically, Hamlet would be guilty of murder even though the King is actually guilty. One further possibility that I have not seen mentioned by any critic is that the Ghost is *both* the spirit of Hamlet's father *and* a spirit from hell. If Old Hamlet died in a state of sin and was damned, he would have become a servant of the devil wholly committed to the project of increasing the population of hell even if that meant tempting his own son to commit a damnable crime. In a play devoted so intensely to depictions of the acquisition and evaluation of evidence, it is not coincidental that playgoers are placed in the situation of having to recognize and assess explicit and implicit pieces of evidence relevant to the issue of the Ghost's identity.[16]

The fact that evidence to answer some questions conclusively cannot be discovered or generated does not discredit empiricism. It merely demonstrates that empiricism has limits. That there are some cases in which conclusive evidence is unavailable does not mean that evidence should not be actively sought or carefully analysed in other cases. That Shakespeare does not supply sufficient evidence for a playgoer to make a certain determination about the identity and status of the Ghost is not evidence that the play does not supply conclusive evidence in other cases. Some critics have argued that *Hamlet* is fundamentally interrogatory and that it generally fails to answer questions it raises.[17] In fact, if a play failed to supply evidence to answer conclusively a large proportion of the questions it raises, playgoers would cease to waste their time and intellectual effort in pondering questions. Such a play would quickly become tedious. Rather than provoking thought, it would actually deter thought. *Hamlet* provides evidence to answer conclusively most of the intriguing questions it raises. In some of these cases the answers are explicit (the King's long soliloquy in 3.3 establishes that he murdered his brother). In other cases Shakespeare withheld an explicit answer but provided evidence that conclusively *implies* a particular answer (such as the implied answer to the question: why does Polonius cling so tenaciously to the

theory that love for Ophelia is the cause of Hamlet's madness?). The authorial act of implication is a challenge to playgoers to exercise their powers of inference. Among the empirical skills Shakespeare calls on playgoers to exercise is the ability to distinguish between those questions for which sufficient evidence is available to make a conclusive inference and those questions for which such evidence is lacking. *Hamlet* is intensely intriguing for this reason. If in many cases the play supplies evidence that conclusively but *implicitly* answers a question, playgoers are encouraged to be constantly on the alert for possibly relevant but implicit evidence and constantly engaged in exercising their powers of inference to the utmost.

In the role of Hamlet in William Davenant's late-seventeenth-century adaptation of the play, Thomas Betterton performed the 'To be, or not to be' speech as the sincere expression of Hamlet's sublime innermost thoughts,[18] and ever since the age of Davenant and Betterton commentators have assumed that Shakespeare designed the speech to be a genuine soliloquy. In order to maintain this orthodoxy, commentators have had to ignore the following plentiful, conspicuous, varied and unambiguous evidence.

(1) Shakespeare located the passage in the midst of an eavesdropping episode. Polonius and the King plan to eavesdrop on a meeting between Hamlet and Ophelia in an effort to find out what is troubling him.

(2) Hamlet does not wander into this locale by accident but rather by the command of the man he suspects of having already murdered one Hamlet. Only 26 lines before Hamlet

---

[16] Notable commentaries on the Ghost include Wilson, *What Happens*; Eleanor Prosser, *Hamlet and Revenge*, 2nd edn (Stanford, CA, 1971); and Stephen Greenblatt, *Hamlet in Purgatory* (Princeton, NJ, 2001).

[17] Most notably, Maynard Mack, 'The World of *Hamlet*', *The Yale Review*, 41 (1952), 502–23; and Harry Levin, *The Question of 'Hamlet'* (Oxford, 1959).

[18] For evidence of this, see, for example, *The Diary of Samuel Pepys*, ed. Robert Lanham and William Matthews (Berkeley, CA, 1970), vol. 5, p. 320.

enters, the King tells Gertrude, 'we have closely sent for Hamlet hither' (3.1.31).

(3) Hamlet is quick to regard anyone associated with the King as an enemy agent. In the preceding scene, simply because his one-time friends Rosencrantz and Guildenstern hesitated when asked if they were 'sent for' (2.2.276, etc.), Hamlet declared in a soliloquy figuratively addressed to them but actually guarded from their hearing in an aside, 'Nay then, I have an eye of you' (292), that is, 'I see you for what you are, agents of my enemy.'

(4) In 3.1 when Hamlet arrives at a place in which he has reason to expect the presence of agents of his enemy, his onetime sweetheart Ophelia is in full view.

(5) Hamlet knows that Ophelia is the obedient daughter of the chief henchman of his enemy, and in the course of his tense conversation with her later in 3.1 Hamlet treats her as if she had committed an act of dishonesty.

(6) In sharp contrast to every one of Hamlet's genuine soliloquies elsewhere in the play, during which he focuses intently on his personal situation, the 'To be' speech is utterly impersonal.

(7) The 'To be' speech contains a passage glaringly at odds with the most memorable experience of Hamlet's life. He refers to 'death' unequivocally as 'The undiscovered country from whose bourn / No traveller returns' (3.1.80–2) even though he has encountered an apparition claiming to be just such a traveller.

(8) In 1.5 Hamlet told Horatio and Marcellus that in future he will 'put an antic disposition on' (173). This disposition is 'antic' not in the modern sense of 'playful' but in the 'morbid' sense intended by Richard II when he applies the epithet to Death (*Richard II* 3.2.158). Alert Renaissance playgoers would have assumed that, from 1.5 onward, Hamlet will put on this morbid disposition *whenever Hamlet knows or suspects that anyone he regards as an agent of the King is present*. In 2.2

Hamlet puts on this act for Polonius and then for Rosencrantz and Guildenstern. In the latter case he actually uses the word 'disposition' (2.2.300). In the 'To be' speech Hamlet exhibits the same morbid disposition that in the preceding scene he put on for agents of his enemy.

(9) Elsewhere in the play Hamlet mocks Polonius for his meddlesomeness.

(10) A short while after finally acknowledging the presence of Ophelia in 3.1, Hamlet abruptly and incongruously asks her, 'Where's your father?' (132).

(11) Elsewhere in the play, Hamlet takes gleeful pride in the cleverness of his plots and counterplots.

(12) English Renaissance drama contains a vast number of eavesdropping episodes, which occur in plays of all types. Many of these episodes are intricate, and many are subtle. In some episodes characters who have reason to suspect that eavesdroppers are present, as Hamlet has when he arrives at the location to which he has been summoned by his enemy, take the opportunity to mislead the eavesdroppers.

(13) In some episodes in late Renaissance drama a character pretends to speak to himself but actually allows another character to hear his speech in order to deceive the other character about his frame of mind. In *Lear* 1.2, for example, Edmund notices the approach of his brother Edgar and pretends to speak to himself in order to mislead Edgar into believing he is philosophically 'melancholy' (*History* 2.130; *Tragedy* 1.2.132), fatalistic, and therefore incapable of action, when in fact he has already set in motion a plan of action against his brother. When Hamlet arrives onstage in 3.1 of *Hamlet*, the obedient daughter of the henchman of Hamlet's enemy is in full view. Before acknowledging her presence, Hamlet expresses a philosophical melancholy and conveys the impression that he is incapable of action, when in fact he has already set in motion a plan of action against his enemy.

The situation in *Lear* is a greatly condensed replay of the situation in *Hamlet*.

(14) As a resourceful and daring writer, Shakespeare frequently used the artistic technique of implication. In the words of Lorna Hutson, 'Shakespeare's innovation . . . was to develop an inferential dramaturgy . . . in order that audiences should infer the details of times, places, motives and intentions with a more vivid and spacious imaginative power than direct representation could ever master.'[19] In 3.3 of *Othello* Iago and Othello enter in time to witness Cassio take leave of Desdemona. Shakespeare expected playgoers to realize on their own that, when Iago says, 'Ha! I like not that' (33), he pretends to speak only to himself but actually allows Othello to hear what he is saying in order to mislead his enemy about his state of mind. Shakespeare expected playgoers to make this inference because they know (a) that Iago is intent on deceiving the man he hates and (b) that what Iago says conflicts with what playgoers know about the character. Iago never explains his tactic in a genuine soliloquy. In a supposedly self-addressed speech while in the presence of the obedient daughter of the henchman of his hated enemy, Hamlet declares that no traveller returns from the bourn of death even though he has encountered such a traveller. In this case playgoers know (a) that Hamlet is intent on deceiving those he regards as agents of his enemy about his actual state of mind and (b) that what he says in his supposedly self-addressed speech conflicts with the experience of the character. Playgoers capable of recognizing the obvious implication of the situation in *Othello* were capable of recognizing the obvious implication of the situation in *Hamlet*.

(15) Although he was supremely eloquent himself, Shakespeare did not sentimentalize eloquence. He frequently dramatized the profound and disturbing fact that no level of eloquence guarantees the sincerity of the speaker.[20]

This is a mere sampling of the evidence that I have catalogued in a series of articles and a book.[21] The one and only reasonable inference to be drawn from this huge body of evidence is that Shakespeare intended playgoers to infer that Hamlet pretends to speak to himself but actually allows those he regards as agents of the King (the obedient Ophelia, who is in full view, and her meddlesome, presumably eavesdropping father) to hear the speech in order to mislead them and ultimately the King about Hamlet's state of mind, to convince his enemy that he is incapable of action and so poses no threat. If the King himself is also eavesdropping, so much the better. Just as Iago allows Othello to overhear a feigned soliloquy in a feigned aside, Hamlet allows Ophelia and any eavesdroppers who may be present to overhear his feigned soliloquy in a feigned aside ('Soft you, now, / The fair Ophelia!' (3.1.90–1)' to give them the false impression that only at this point has he noticed Ophelia's presence. Having encountered countless elaborate and subtle eavesdropping episodes in other plays, experienced Renaissance playgoers needed to notice only one or two of the many clues, all of which point in one and only one direction, in order to infer that the 'To be' speech is a feigned soliloquy. External evidence demonstrates that Renaissance playgoers did indeed make the inference that the speech is a feigned soliloquy.[22] After cleverly misleading agents of his enemy about his state of mind, Hamlet cannot control his anger at Ophelia for participating in a plot against him and in the process of berating her reveals that he is capable of violent action.

That the 'To be' speech was designed to be recognized as a feigned soliloquy is the only

---

19 Hutson, *Invention of Suspicion*, p. 309.
20 See James Hirsh, 'Eloquence in Shakespearean Drama', *Allegorica*, 27 (2011), 71–91.
21 Such as 'The "To be or not to be" Scene and the Conventions of Shakespearean Drama', *Modern Language Quarterly*, 42 (1981), 115–36; *Shakespeare and the History of Soliloquies* (Madison, NJ, 2003); and 'The "To be, or not to be" Speech: Evidence, Conventional Wisdom, and the Editing of *Hamlet*', *Medieval and Renaissance Drama in England*, 23 (2010), 34–62.
22 See Hirsh, 'Conventional Wisdom', pp. 47–50.

explanation that makes sense in light of the relevant evidence. The conventional, sentimental post-Renaissance cliché that the 'To be' speech is the sincere expression of Hamlet's sublime innermost thoughts simply does not make sense in light of many elements of the play, Shakespeare's dramatic practices and English Renaissance stage conditions. The notion that all these pieces of evidence point in one and only one direction by sheer accident rather than by authorial design is patently absurd. Indeed, it is hard to imagine that any author has ever included a larger number of mutually reinforcing clues to lead playgoers or readers to a single inference.

Rather than trivializing the passage, the recognition that it is a feigned soliloquy creates profound and disturbing dramatic ironies. For example, instead of being the meditation of a character so breathtakingly lofty in spirit that he fails to notice the conspicuous presence of his former girlfriend in the location to which he has been summoned by his deadly enemy, the speech is one of many in Shakespeare's plays in which a character uses magnificent eloquence in an attempt to mislead other characters.

Playgoers in Shakespeare's age were not disabled from drawing the correct inference, as post-Renaissance playgoers and readers have been, by pervasive cultural indoctrination insisting that the speech represents Hamlet's innermost thoughts. Since the late seventeenth century, countless editors, commentators, teachers and purveyors of popular culture have all reinforced the dogma. Countless actors in the role of Hamlet have conveyed the impression that the speech is sincere without realizing that they were performing the adaptation created by Davenant and Betterton rather than Shakespeare's version. Long before a person ever reads or sees the play, he or she has already been made certain that the 'To be' speech represents Hamlet's sublime innermost thoughts.

Although individual commentators have tried to explain away one or two of the many pieces of evidence in isolation (Coleridge: 'surely it were easy to say that no traveller returns to this world, as to his home, or *abiding-place*'),[23] no upholder of the post-Renaissance theory that the speech is sincere has ever forthrightly confronted the entire catalogue of relevant evidence because to do so would result in a huge, embarrassingly ramshackle collection of makeshift rationalizations, with a separate, independent rationalization needed to explain away each particular piece of evidence. They would resemble the epicycles invented to prop up Ptolemaic geocentrism. The very bankruptcy of the orthodox position, its indefensibility in an open debate, has prevented the issue from becoming a controversy. In a recent entire book on the 'To be' speech, Douglas Bruster declared that he 'benefited' from my research,[24] but there is no evidence of this in the book. He discusses the passage as if its sincerity were beyond question. He does not attempt to refute my argument or to confront the relevant evidence. An account of the plentiful, conspicuous, varied and unambiguous evidence demonstrating that the most celebrated passage in Shakespeare's works was designed to be recognized by playgoers as a feigned soliloquy has been conspicuous by its absence from the pages of *Shakespeare Quarterly*. No editor of *Hamlet* has ever corrected the false impression about the speech that is maintained by pervasive cultural indoctrination. Nowhere in *Approaches to Teaching Shakespeare's 'Hamlet'* (published by the Modern Language Association) are teachers alerted to the untenability of the conventional post-Renaissance assumption about the most famous passage in the play.[25] Scholars who disregard the immense body of evidence that conflicts with the time-honoured cliché that the 'To be' speech is a transparent representation of Hamlet's innermost thoughts resemble Polonius, who ignores evidence that conflicts with his pet theory about Hamlet's madness, although (to be fair to Polonius) the amount of evidence in conflict with his pet theory, though

---

[23] Samuel Taylor Coleridge, as cited in *Hamlet*, ed. Horace Howard Furness (New Variorum edition, repr. Mineola, NY, 2000), I. p. 214.

[24] Douglas Bruster, *To Be or Not To Be* (London, 2007), p. 105.

[25] Bernice Kliman, ed., *Approaches to Teaching Shakespeare's 'Hamlet'* (New York, 2002).

substantial, is miniscule compared with the vast amount of evidence in conflict with the post-Renaissance assumption that the 'To be' speech represents Hamlet's innermost thoughts.

Most intellectual fields of study are solidly based on empirical research. When a theory in one of these fields is proposed, it is rigorously tested against the relevant evidence as a matter of course. If evidence is uncovered that refutes a long-standing and deeply entrenched theory, the theory is discarded. Genuine advancement of learning occurs in such fields because the rigorous testing of ideas against evidence winnows out erroneous theories. In such fields the search for the truth is a trial-and-error process.[26] Literary and cultural studies, on the other hand, are still beset by one of the classes of Idols described by Bacon in 1620.

Lastly, there are Idols which have immigrated into men's minds from the various dogmas of philosophies . . . These I call Idols of the Theatre, because in my judgement all the received systems are but so many stage plays, representing worlds of their own creation after an unreal and scenic fashion . . . Neither again do I mean this only of entire systems, but also of many principles and axioms . . . which by tradition, credulity, and negligence have come to be received.[27]

In literary and cultural studies, demonstrably erroneous principles and axioms are not discarded as a matter of course and persist to clutter up discourse in the field and to obscure theories that have been verified by rigorous testing. This is illustrated by the fact that decades after the post-Renaissance cliché that the most famous passage in world literature represents Hamlet's innermost thoughts was proven false by published evidence, the cliché is still as widely accepted as ever. As Barbara Herrnstein Smith has remarked, 'In the confrontation between belief and evidence, belief, as we know, is no pushover.' In the face of plentiful, conspicuous, varied, and unambiguous evidence disproving the orthodox belief in the sincerity of the 'To be' speech, a literary scholar unwilling to relinquish the belief merely has to exercise the option of falling back on what Smith calls 'epistemic self-privileging',[28] that is, regarding one's own opinion as *self*-evident, as transcending any need to be rigorously tested against evidence, and requiring any opposing theory to meet an impossible burden of proof.

The evidence presented here demonstrates not merely that Shakespeare was an empiricist himself but that he attempted to induce an empirical frame of mind in playgoers. The evidence shows that he designed *Hamlet* to hone the empirical skills of playgoers by vividly dramatizing failures of characters to test their theories rigorously and by placing playgoers in situations that call upon them to engage in the process of drawing inferences from evidence. It is not Shakespeare's fault that in a particular case Davenant and Betterton obscured his intention and led subsequent playgoers, readers and scholars astray.

---

[26] Notable discussions of evidence and inferential reasoning within or across disciplines include the following: John Henry Wigmore, *The Science of Judicial Proof*, 3rd edn (Boston, 1937); Robin W. Winks, *The Historian as Detective: Essays on Evidence* (New York, 1969); Jonathan Cohen, *The Probable and the Provable* (Oxford, 1977); David A. Schum, *Evidential Foundations of Probabilistic Reasoning* (New York, 1994); William Twining, *Rethinking Evidence* (Oxford, 1990); and Peter Lipton, 'Evidence and Explanation', *Evidence*, ed. Andrew Bell *et al.* (Cambridge, 2008), pp. 10–28.

[27] *Organon*, I: XLIV, p. 337.

[28] Barbara Herrnstein Smith, 'Belief and Resistance: A Symmetrical Account', *Critical Inquiry*, 18 (1991), 139–53, 142.

'LET ME SEE WHAT THOU HAST WRIT': MAPPING THE SHAKESPEARE–FLETCHER WORKING RELATIONSHIP IN *THE TWO NOBLE KINSMEN* AT THE SWAN

VARSHA PANJWANI

The trouble started once Shakespeare began to be disillusioned with the new theatrical fashions. Then, his eyesight began to fail him. Under such dire psychological and physical conditions, he had no choice but to collaborate with an excited John Fletcher. *The Two Noble Kinsmen* was the product of these unhappy circumstances. This is the scenario *For All Time* offered its audiences.[1] This play, premiered at the Theatre by the Lake, Keswick, in 2009, demonstrates that the narrative of a disagreeable collaboration between a tired Shakespeare and a zealous Fletcher has proved persistently popular. Very little seems to have changed since Horace Howard Furness Jr's 1920 play, *'The Gloss of Youth': An Imaginary Episode in the Lives of William Shakespeare and John Fletcher*, which also presented an imaginative account of Shakespeare and Fletcher working together on *The Two Noble Kinsmen*. Furness's Fletcher is keen to work with Shakespeare. 'Let me see what thou hast writ', he says, and proceeds to read and critique Shakespeare's work on the opening scene. He at first admires Shakespeare's turn of phrase, but soon discovers that he cannot approve of all his dialogue. 'Tush, Will, this that follows is but idle stuff!', he declares, before adding that 'it will not do at all'. While Fletcher is happy to discuss and collaborate, surly Shakespeare is not too keen. Shakespeare *'tears the sheet across and drops it on the floor'*. 'I cannot, nor I will not write at *thy* behest', he declares, *'looking fixedly at Fletcher'*.[2]

A less earnest, more tongue-in-cheek version of this narrative was presented by Anthony B. Dawson in 1988 in a very short dialogue. Dawson

imagines Shakespeare's colleagues, John Heminges and Henry Condell, forcing collaboration on a Shakespeare who was becoming too obscure for comprehension by the general public. Heminges has already 'talked to Fletcher', who is 'willing to work with [Shakespeare]', but he worries that this willingness will not be mutual, and with good reason. Shakespeare is initially exceedingly reluctant and difficult to persuade. On learning their designs, he exclaims, 'Fletcher! But I taught the wretch everything he knows, and all he can do is pisspot imitations and flights of sentiment. You must be kidding.' After some consideration, however, Shakespeare gives in because he admits that 'my heart's not in it any more – guess I should take a bit of rest'. In this version, Shakespeare would not have collaborated with Fletcher if he was not 'bored' and had not 'lost his zest', as Condell puts it.[3]

A number of twentieth- and twenty-first-century playwrights have perhaps been drawn to imagine the writing process behind *The Two Noble Kinsmen* because 'we know less than we would like about [Shakespeare and Fletcher's] working habits:

---

[1] Theatre by the Lake, *For All Time*, by Rick Thomas, dir. Stefan Escreet, Stephen Joseph Theatre, Scarborough, 14 November 2009.

[2] Horace Howard Furness Jr, *'The Gloss of Youth': An Imaginary Episode in the Lives of William Shakespeare and John Fletcher* (Philadelphia, 1920), pp. 14, 15.

[3] Anthony B. Dawson, *'Tempest* in a Teapot: Critics, Evaluation, Ideology', in Maurice Charney, ed., *'Bad' Shakespeare: Revaluations of the Shakespeare Canon* (London, 1988), pp. 63, 64, 63.

we do not know how the two men put the plays together . . . the precise division of labour, or how they came upon their sources and plots'.[4] The title-page of the 1634 first quarto of *The Two Noble Kinsmen* declares that the play is written by 'the memorable Worthies of their time; Mr John Fletcher, and Mr William Shakespeare',[5] and an entry in the Stationers' Register in the same year reads 'Entred for his Copy vnder the hands of Sir Henry Herbert and master Aspley warden a TragiComedy called *the two noble kinsmen* by John Fletcher and William Shakespeare'.[6] The title-page and the entry insist on joint attribution, but are silent on the material facts of the play's creation; beyond these two pages, there is no surviving evidence in the form of prompt-books, manuscripts, or anecdotes from the period that can illuminate the exact nature of this creative partnership. Yet, in all three versions discussed above, the working relationship between the co-authors is imagined as necessary and strained. Concomitantly, their jointly written play has been victimized as 'pressurised' hack work resulting from an 'all-night quill-bashing session'[7] or, by Dawson's Shakespeare's own admission, 'a big yawn', with a few scenes thrown in by him to spice it up.[8]

Twentieth- and early twenty-first-century critical commentary, too, has continued to see inconsistencies in the play and attributed these to friction, or at least failure of communication, between the playwrights. Eugene Waith's 1989 Oxford Shakespeare edition reveals his assumptions about joint authorship when he declares that 'one is bound to be *surprised* by how close and efficient the collaboration was' (emphasis mine). His recognition of this closeness and admission that the 'work of the two playwrights is tightly interlaced' does not stop him from identifying the author of each scene in his notes and blaming inconsistencies in stage directions and characterization on the division of labour between the collaborators. Typical notes include comments such as, 'Shakespeare probably wrote the first scene, while Fletcher almost certainly wrote the second. Shakespeare need not have known exactly how Fletcher would begin his part.'[9] This gives the impression that the authors

did not align their work carefully at best or were at cross-purposes at worst. Eight years later in 1997, Lois Potter's Arden Shakespeare edition concedes that 'when a play is known to be the work of two authors, it is tempting to attribute inconstancies and uncertainties of tone either to disagreements between them or to breakdowns in the collaborative process', but itself falls prey to this temptation when it reads uncertainties in stage-directions as a symptom of 'the change from one writer to another'. Potter again seems to be torn by opposite impulses when she decides to 'refrain from identifying the assumed author of each scene'[10] in her edition, yet expresses a desire to see the 'ultimate deconstructionist production, where Shakespeare and Fletcher watch the play from opposite sides of the stage, each nodding approvingly as his own lines are spoken' in an article published one year before her edition.[11] Brian Vickers, more confident and assertive in *Shakespeare, Co-Author*, is convinced that 'the co-authors' of this play 'had not seen each other's drafts'.[12]

These narratives of Shakespeare–Fletcher collaborations have recently come under the spotlight of mainstream criticism. In 2010, Arden published *The Double Falsehood*, edited by Brean

---

[4] Clare McManus and Lucy Munro, 'Introduction: Shakespeare and Fletcher, Fletcher and Shakespeare', *Shakespeare*, 7:3 (2011), 253.

[5] John Fletcher and William Shakespeare, *The Two Noble Kinsmen* (London, 1634).

[6] Edward Arber, ed., *A Transcript of the Registers of the Company of Stationers of London, 1554–1640*, 5 vols. (Various locations, 1875–1894), p. 290.

[7] Alfred Hickling, rev. of *For All Time*, dir. Stefan Escreet, *The Guardian*, 4 August 2009, www.guardian.co.uk/culture/2009/aug/04/for-all-time-review, accessed 10 March 2012, paras. 1, 3.

[8] Dawson, '*Tempest* in a Teapot', p. 64.

[9] Eugene M. Waith, ed., *The Two Noble Kinsmen* (Oxford, 1989), pp. 63, 62, 109.

[10] Lois Potter, ed., *The Two Noble Kinsmen* (London, 1997), pp. 6, 26, 34.

[11] Lois Potter, '*The Two Noble Kinsmen* in 1993–94', *Shakespeare Quarterly*, 47:2 (1996), p. 203.

[12] Brian Vickers, *Shakespeare, Co-Author: A Historical Study of Five Collaborative Plays* (Oxford, 2002), p. 442.

Hammond.[13] This play is claimed to be an adaptation of Shakespeare and Fletcher's lost play, *Cardenio*. In 2011, the Royal Shakespeare Company (henceforth the RSC) mounted a production of *Cardenio*, as reimagined by Gregory Doran, to launch their newly refurbished Swan theatre.[14] Together these two events have led to a renewal of interest in the Shakespeare–Fletcher teamwork and its creations. Various productions (such as *Double Falsehood* at the Union Theatre, Southwark)[15] and critical works (the most notable being the special issue of the journal *Shakespeare* on Shakespeare–Fletcher collaborations)[16] reflect this resurgence of interest.

While these current critical trends promise a more sophisticated reading of the Shakespeare–Fletcher endeavour, the latest edition of *The Two Noble Kinsmen* for New Cambridge Shakespeare reverts to Waith's model, when it alerts readers that 'in the Commentary of this edition the authorship of each scene is given'; the notes deliver the promise by faithfully identifying who wrote what at the beginning of each scene. This results in a fractured reading experience and reinforces the assumption made in the edition's introduction that 'the authors neither much discussed the play while it was in progress nor much exchanged manuscript'.[17]

The Two Noble Kinsmen has also failed to secure a settled place in the repertoire. It was not included in *The World Shakespeare Festival* in 2012 and was given only a single rehearsed reading in *The Royal Shakespeare Company Complete Works Festival* in 2006–7. In this article, I seek to draw attention to the fact that this cycle of renewed interest and reverting to old paradigms creates a feeling of *déjà vu*, for there was a moment in twentieth-century history that could have brought about a change in outlook towards Shakespeare and Fletcher's jointly written works. This event was the opening of the RSC's Swan theatre in 1986, which was launched with a Shakespeare–Fletcher collaboration, *The Two Noble Kinsmen*. In the following sections, I analyse the mixed achievement of this landmark production. On the one hand, its direction proved that what has been considered hastily patched up is, in fact,

carefully crafted but, on the other hand, the event failed to raise the profile of either the play or the Shakespeare–Fletcher collaborations – a step that should have been the logical result of the play's newly proven theatrical vitality. While the exact way in which Shakespeare and Fletcher collaborated on *The Two Noble Kinsmen* may never be uncovered, I argue that the 1986 production proved that there is a greater possibility of this working relationship having been a productive one than the reviews of the time, and the sketches and critical attitudes above, seem to suggest. Using the video recording, the prompt-book, rehearsal diaries, published interviews, the programme and publicity for the show, I aim to discuss this missed opportunity at length, in the hope that my article may prompt fresh thinking about the way in which we imagine the Shakespeare–Fletcher collaboration to have worked.

AN OPPORTUNITY PRESENTS ITSELF

When the RSC inaugurated its new theatre, Trevor Nunn, the joint artistic director at the time, declared in the opening production's programme that the Swan was committed to 'presenting the rarely or never-seen work of [Shakespeare's] contemporaries'.[18] Barry Kyle, the director of the first production, also pointed out to Paul Taylor, who interviewed him for *The Spectator* before the opening night, that the new playhouse would 'act as a space in which some of

---

[13] Brean Hammond, ed., *Double Falsehood, or, The Distressed Lovers* (London, 2010).

[14] Royal Shakespeare Company, *Cardenio*, Re-imagined by Gregory Doran, dir. Gregory Doran, The Swan, Stratford-upon-Avon, 14 November 2011.

[15] See Peter Kirwan, 'Chasing Windmills: An Identity Crisis in *Double Falsehood* at the Union Theatre, Southwark', *Shakespeare*, 7:3 (2011).

[16] *Shakespeare*, 7:3 (2011). See note 4 above.

[17] Robert Kean Turner and Patricia Tatspaugh, eds., *The Two Noble Kinsmen* (Cambridge, 2012), pp. 5, 4.

[18] Royal Shakespeare Company, Programme/Text of the Production of *The Two Noble Kinsmen*, dir. Barry Kyle, programme commentary by Simon Trussler (London, 1986).

those plays to which the public has in the past been most resistant . . . can be explored and reappraised in productions which may persuade the public of their virtues'.[19] These rationales prompted the choice of the jointly authored and rarely staged *The Two Noble Kinsmen* as the opening production for the new theatre. With significant media attention focusing on the opening of an RSC venue dedicated to displaying the virtues of neglected plays and playwrights, it was a great opportunity for Barry Kyle's production to prove both the dramatic potential of *The Two Noble Kinsmen* and the potency of the Shakespeare–Fletcher partnership responsible for its creation. Watching the production in the Shakespeare Centre Library convinced me that Kyle's direction succeeded in attaining the former aim.

While scrutinizing the production, I recollect being on my guard to notice all the inconsistencies that critics claim to have detected in this co-authored play and I distinctly remember how I realized that these supposed inconsistencies were necessary for building complex and nuanced characters in performance. As one of the play's most vocal detractors in recent years, Vickers asserts that 'it is just at the transition point where the co-author takes up the story that we notice a second hand at work'.[20] Vickers refers to the moment when Theseus, the ruler of Athens, has defeated Thebes, and Palamon and Arcite have become prisoners of war. The daughter of their Jailer tells the audience that '[Palamon and Arcite] have no more sense of their captivity than I of ruling Athens.'[21] Vickers complains that, when Fletcher takes up the quill from Shakespeare shortly after this, he presents the heroes as 'anything but Stoic', which is 'contrary to what Shakespeare had the Jailer's daughter prepare us for'.[22] Indeed, when Palamon and Arcite start talking, they complain bitterly about being imprisoned, but this does not seem problematic in the RSC production. Imogen Stubbs as the Jailer's Daughter made it impossible for the audience to miss that her account of the two kinsmen is more about the Jailer's Daughter's feelings than about reporting Palamon and Arcite's actual mental condition.[23] As the scene

began, Palamon and Arcite were in a prison or cage suspended mid-air centre stage while Stubbs was positioned downstage centre, facing the cage, trying to catch a glimpse of these men by standing on tiptoe. As she moved towards the Jailer and the Wooer (her suitor), the prompt-book informs us that she still had to indulge in 'looking up acting'.[24] Stubbs then inflected her lines about the kinsmen's bravery in the face of adversity with such rapture that it provided the right provocation for the Wooer's laconic (perhaps jealous) remark: 'I never saw 'em'.[25] This production demonstrated that the gap between the Jailer's Daughter's report and Palamon and Arcite's discourse, described as a problem of co-ordination by Vickers, leads an audience to grasp the extent of the Jailer's Daughter's adoration of these young gentlemen. Thus, if we believe Vickers that Fletcher did take over from Shakespeare at this point, he did so without disrupting the play or causing a modern actor or director any anxiety about a contradictory impulse in the text.

In discussing the discrepancy between the Jailer's Daughter's description and the subsequent depiction of Palamon and Arcite, I have only

---

[19] Paul Taylor, 'Stratford's New Swan'. 3 May 1986. Collected in *Royal Shakespeare Company Collections: Theatre Records: Series A*: 129–30 (26 April 1986–19 Oct 1986): 41.

[20] Vickers, *Shakespeare, Co-Author*, p. 493.

[21] Royal Shakespeare Company, *The Two Noble Kinsmen*, dir. Barry Kyle, Prompt-book for Swan Theatre (1986), ts. RSC/SM/1/1986/TWN2, The Shakespeare Centre Library and Archive, Stratford-upon-Avon, p. 27. I am using the prompt-book for all quotations of the play, as this allows precision in the description of the performance; the page numbers refer to the second prompt-book as it contains more details of stage business. The source for my description of the performance is Royal Shakespeare Company, *The Two Noble Kinsmen*, dir. Barry Kyle, Video recording of the performance at Swan Theatre (1986).

[22] Vickers, *Shakespeare, Co-Author*, pp. 492, 493.

[23] I deliberately use actors' names for major roles to draw attention to the fact that the actors (in collaboration with their director) have chosen one of the various available performance alternatives of the lines. In other words, decisions about interpreting the lines in this manner are unique to this production.

[24] *The Two Noble Kinsmen*, Prompt-book, stage manager's mark-up note facing p. 26.

[25] *The Two Noble Kinsmen*, Prompt-book, p. 27.

mentioned one part of the dissonance that Vickers finds between what he believes is the work of two authors not working in accord with one another. According to him, Fletcher's presentation of Palamon and Arcite contradicts not only the Jailer's Daughter, but also Shakespeare's portrayal of the heroes earlier in the play: 'while Shakespeare presented the cousins as fiercely moral, condemning a corrupt society and its tyrant in energetic verse, Fletcher allows his heroes to indulge their griefs for fifty-five plangent lines'.[26] The RSC production, instead of shying away from the difference of attitude shown by the protagonists in these scenes, embraced and emphasized it. When we first saw the cousins in this production (in the scene assumed to have been written by Shakespeare), they were at Kendo practice. Maintaining a respectful distance between them, they delivered their lines about Thebes' corruption with a touch of anger, but otherwise remained in perfect possession of their temper. They sat on opposite sides of the stage, discussing contemporary politics, and deploring the corruption of their ruler, with logical precision and moral reasoning, but without betraying much emotion. When we next saw them talking to each other (in a scene usually attributed to Fletcher), they appeared more vulnerable. With their hands in shackles, cramped in a hanging prison-cage, Gerard Murphy (as Palamon) was restless, and Hugh Quarshie (as Arcite) seemed as if he had resigned himself to his fate. Murphy delivered Palamon's opening lines, 'Where is Thebes now? / Where is our noble country? / Where are our friends and kindreds?' in a tone of pathetic desperation. He hurried through the first two questions as if compelled to voice his dark thoughts. In the third question, he put pressure on each of the words, thereby conveying an increasing frustration at the fact that the answers to these questions could not provide any hope. Finally, Quarshie interrupted Murphy's urgent and nervous speaking with a loud and emphatic 'No, Palamon, / Those hopes are prisoners with us.' He then singled out the two 'heres' in 'here we are, / And here the graces of our youths must wither' by raising his volume on those words as if trying to reconcile himself to the dreadful reality of being in this place and what it entailed.[27] While Murphy slowed his delivery to portray a man evoking a supposedly ideal past now beyond their grasp, Quarshie achieved a similar effect in his lines, painting a vivid picture of unfulfilled promise.

The production's programme encourages the audience to read the contrasts between the 'fierce moralists' of the first scene and the emotionally indulgent kinsmen of the latter scene as symptoms of the 'cussedness and complexity inseparable from the human condition under stress'.[28] Ian Herbert, in his review, interpreted these supposed inconsistencies as psychological depth. He found that Murphy and Quarshie's arc from being 'playful at kendo practice' to 'quarrelling in their prison cage' allowed these 'magnetic young actors' to 'evoke all the strength of male bonds forged through the shared experience'.[29] It is clear, therefore, that both actors used the two 'jarring' scenes in the script to map the psychological landscape of the protagonists under changing circumstances. Thus the transition point which, according to Vickers, 'has troubled many readers for the evident discrepancy in values between it and Shakespeare's scene' caused no confusion for the actors and viewers.[30]

If the second act with its contrasts has troubled some readers, then others have declared that the two plots of the play are misaligned. It is surprising to note that Kyle was one of these critics. He declared that 'the relationship between the Theban story and the sub-plot . . . is the most difficult relationship' in this play.[31] His pronouncement is unexpected, because one of the highlights of his production was that everything in the sub-plot of

[26] Vickers, *Shakespeare, Co-Author*, p. 493.

[27] *The Two Noble Kinsmen*, Prompt-book, pp. 28, 29.

[28] *The Two Noble Kinsmen*, Programme/Text, p. 14.

[29] Ian Herbert, rev. of *The Two Noble Kinsmen*, dir. Barry Kyle, *Review*, 16 May 1986, Collected in *Theatre Record: 7–20 May 1986*, 540.

[30] Vickers, *Shakespeare, Co-Author*, p. 493.

[31] Barry Kyle, 'The Director in the Swan: Barry Kyle', in Ronnie Mulryne and Margaret Shewring, eds., *This Golden Round: The Royal Shakespeare Company at the Swan* (Stratford-on-Avon, 1989), p. 74.

the Jailer's Daughter falling in love with Palamon during his captivity and running mad for his love was shown to echo the main-plot involving the two noble kinsmen tragically falling in love with Emilia and entering into a fatal contest in which the loser has to die. This was achieved by accentuating the parallels between Emilia and the Jailer's Daughter. It is worth recounting some of the scenes in detail in order to appreciate just how strongly the two plots mirrored each other in this production. This mirroring effect was conspicuous in 4.2 and 4.3. In the first of these scenes, Emilia tries to decide between Palamon and Arcite and cannot do so. The quarto stage direction requires Emilia to enter 'alone, with 2. Pictures' of her two suitors.[32] In this production, two tapestries (or silk cloths) flanked either side of the stage, depicting the profiles of Palamon and Arcite. A single white bed with a pillow on either side was placed downstage centre. Amanda Harris (who played Emilia) exhausted herself in trying, and failing, to decide between the two suitors, and then lay back on the bed. When a Messenger, Theseus and Pirithous entered to discuss arrangements for the fatal tournament between the suitors, she still lay on the bed. Theseus stood upstage and, as the Messenger, dressed in black, described Arcite's companion, he glided towards Harris's right, trailing red symbolic silk behind him. Then Pirithous, all in white, described Palamon's comrade, and he too trailed red silk behind him. Harris all this while was half awake, writhing, agonizing, twisting, and turning in her bed, and all she could do was shakily ask, 'must these men die too?'[33] Theseus, ignoring Harris's consternation, expressed enthusiasm about the prospect of the grand fight, and then all of them, except Harris, exited. After a brief black-out, Harris woke up as if from a dream, looked around and let out a chilling cry. A rehearsal diary for the production dictates how this idea was labelled and performed. In a rehearsal note, this scene is dubbed a 'nightmare scene' and, among sound and technical cues, the note elaborates that Harris is 'in some sort of nightmare'.[34]

The transition to the next scene was swift. As Harris began to leave, a corridor from the bed to the exit was lit, and she met Imogen Stubbs entering. Immediately after Harris left, Stubbs lay down on the bed which Harris had occupied and which had not been moved. Now the audience saw the Jailer's Daughter twisting and turning on the same bed. If one managed to miss the visual chime of Emilia and the Jailer's Daughter lying on the same bed, occupying the same position, then the rest of the blocking reinforced this impression. While the Doctor stood upstage, the Jailer sat on her right (in black) and the Wooer on her left (in white), paralleling the white and black of the Messenger and Pirithous in the previous scene. The stage picture and the blocking enforced the similarities between the emotional states and plights of Emilia and the Jailer's Daughter. It is as if Emilia's nightmare had turned into reality and she had become 'mad'. The production's final tableau was also arresting in this regard. Michael Ratcliffe of *The Observer* described how the performance 'ends with two brides confronting one another: the jailer's daughter (Imogen Stubbs), mad in raggedy muslin, and Emilia, horribly sane, in elegant mourning black'.[35]

PUBLICITY: MISSING THE OPPORTUNITY

While the stage was thus being set for fresh revelations about the achievements of a Shakespeare–Fletcher collaboration, the production's publicity took a surprising turn. In theorizing his experience of directing the play, Barry Kyle undermined his efforts towards resuscitating it by echoing the orthodox view that Shakespeare and Fletcher's joint authorship was unsuccessful. In the director's note

---

[32] Fletcher and Shakespeare, *The Two Noble Kinsmen* (London, 1634), 62v, 4.2.s.d.

[33] *The Two Noble Kinsmen*, Prompt-book, p. 98.

[34] Royal Shakespeare Company, *The Two Noble Kinsmen*, dir. Barry Kyle, Rehearsal Notes (1986), ts. RSC/SM/2/1986/95, The Shakespeare Centre Library and Archive, Stratford-upon-Avon, p. 23, note 7.

[35] Michael Ratcliffe, rev. of *The Two Noble Kinsmen*, dir. Barry Kyle, *Observer*, 11 May 1986, Collected in *Theatre Record: 7–20 May 1986*, 539.

to the production, he first recognized that 'The Two Noble Kinsmen has for a long time been a victim of speculation about its joint-authorship', but he then reinforced this victimization by adding that 'scholars have observed the play seems not to have had a final revision by the authors. I agree with that.' He elaborated that the play contained 'loose ends', and that there was 'stray material by both writers which doesn't contribute to the joint effort' and therefore had to be cut.[36] Finally, in an article written in 1989, in which Kyle reflected on the experience of directing the play, he cemented these opinions by claiming that The Two Noble Kinsmen 'is a heterogeneous play, not a homogeneous play. It shows evidence of more than one hand.'[37]

The reviewers picked up the cue offered by Kyle's programme note and insisted on seeing an even greater fissure between the smooth production and the co-authored play's supposed inconsistencies. They alleged that the flaws of the play were plastered over by Barry Kyle's direction and re-shaping of the text on the one hand, and the actors' talent on the other. Clive Hirschhorn of the Sunday Express, for instance, was convinced that 'Kyle transforms a hodge-podge of a play into palatable theatre',[38] and Jack Tinker, in two separate reviews, opined that 'on paper, not much recommends the piece apart from its (disputed) authorship',[39] and that, therefore, Kyle's was a 'splendid production of a less than splendid play'.[40] Christopher Edwards, in The Spectator, specifically selected 'the similarity between Arcite and Palamon' as 'one of the main failings in the play's characterisation', but defended Quarshie and Murphy, who 'engage us from the start with their individuality'. He contended that 'it is a measure of the actors' achievement that we are made to believe on stage what we find unsatisfactory and slightly absurd on the page'.[41] Michael Coveney agreed in The Financial Times that Quarshie and Murphy had 'found depth of characterisation where really there is none'.[42] A detailed examination of the cuts in the prompt-book, however, reveals that the actors and the director simply chose one particular way of presenting the text rather than attempting to compensate for any failings in the play.

Edwards and Coveney applauded the actors for lending individuality to Palamon and Arcite, but the original text demands no less from its performers, as it clearly distinguishes between the two knights from their very first scene. In 1.2, which takes place in Thebes before the war, Palamon is at pains to explain the difference between Arcite's grievance and his own. He contradicts Arcite's bleak outlook that Thebes is full of 'temptings in't' and his claim that 'not to swim / I'th' aid o'th' current were almost to sink'. He points out that they can exercise more control over whom they chose to follow:

> 'Tis in our power – '
> Unless we fear that apes can tutor's – to
> Be masters of our manners. What need I
> Affect another's gait, which is not catching
> Where there is faith.

Palamon elaborates on this theme until he reaches the one complaint that 'rips [his] bosom / Almost to th' heart's', and Arcite infers that this cause is

---

36 Barry Kyle, 'Director's Note', in Royal Shakespeare Company, Programme/Text of the Production of The Two Noble Kinsmen, dir. Barry Kyle, programme commentary by Simon Trussler (London, 1986), p. 5. The gulf between Kyle's directing in which he realized the merits of the play and the director's note where he plays down the role of the effort by Shakespeare and Fletcher to craft a coherent play leads him to make other contradictory claims, including that the play is, in fact, a 'compound' and not a 'mixture' and that this is due to the strong 'voice of Shakespeare' in the play, p. 5.

37 Kyle, 'The Director in the Swan', p. 74.

38 Clive Hirschhorn, rev. of The Two Noble Kinsmen, dir. Barry Kyle, Sunday Express, 31 May 1987, Collected in Theatre Record: 21 May–3 June 1987, 658.

39 Jack Tinker, rev. of The Two Noble Kinsmen, dir. Barry Kyle, Daily Mail, 9 May 1986, Collected in Theatre Record: 7–20 May 1986, 539.

40 Jack Tinker, rev. of The Two Noble Kinsmen, dir. Barry Kyle, Daily Mail, 27 May 1987, Collected in Theatre Record: 21 May–3 June 1987, 661.

41 Christopher Edwards, rev. of The Two Noble Kinsmen, dir. Barry Kyle, Spectator, 17 May 1986, Collected in Theatre Record: 7–20 May 1986, 540.

42 Michael Coveney, rev. of The Two Noble Kinsmen, dir. Barry Kyle, Financial Times, 27 May 1987, Collected in Theatre Record: 21 May–3 June 1987, 659.

their 'uncle Creon'. Only the last two lines were retained in this production, so the audience was made aware that Creon was a source of Palamon's vexation, but the lines in which he explains that it is not the corruptness of the city per se but its tyrant ruler which troubles him were cut. It is Palamon who points out that their 'services stand now for Thebes, not Creon', when they hear about Theseus's attack on the city. Thus, there is a difference between the political stance of Palamon, who is against the ruler of Thebes, and of Arcite who is keen to leave Thebes, 'where every evil / Hath a good colour; where every seeming good's / A certain evil'.

A difference in temperament between the two heroes is also inherent in the text. Whereas Palamon stresses that they can resist being subdued to the general corruption, Arcite thinks that their problem can only be solved by fleeing Thebes, 'where not to be even jump / As [Thebans] are, here were to be strangers, and / Such things to be, mere monsters'.[43] If an actor were in a production where these lines had not been cut, he might have conveyed how, in striking contrast to Palamon, Arcite fears being tainted by the corruption of the world. It was appropriate for this production to lose the lines that posit a difference in the moral stance of the cousins, as the casting, physicality and mannerisms of the leading actors in themselves made clear distinctions between their characters. While the director and the actors can be credited for realizing the latent possibilities in the text, they cannot lay claim to improving a 'flawed' text through their cuts or acting.

The prompt-book also reveals that the visual echoes between Emilia and the Jailer's Daughter were suggested to Kyle by the language of the original text. Michael Billington, who found this aspect of the play intriguing, was reluctant to praise the original text. In his *Guardian* review he declared that Kyle 'even manages to excavate a hidden theme suggesting the play is as much about female desperation as masculine competitiveness'.[44] Tracing the cuts in the prompt-book, it is easy to discern that there is nothing 'hidden' about this theme, and that Kyle's only change was substituting

visual pictures for verbal echoes. One deletion worth noting is in Emilia's long soliloquy in the scene discussed above, where she is trying to choose between Palamon and Arcite, to put an end to the fatal tournament. The following lines have been cancelled in the prompt-book and were not spoken by Harris in performance:

> . . . if my brother but even now had asked me
> Whether I loved, I had run mad for Arcite;
> Now if my sister, more for Palamon.
> Stand both together. Now come ask me, brother –
> Alas, I know not! Ask me now, sweet sister;
> I may go look.[45]

No significant plot point is furthered by these obliterated lines, as, throughout the speech, Emilia veers between the two men, but a verbal resonance between Emilia's condition and the Jailer's Daughter can be heard here. Emilia imagines that if she were forced to make her choice she could easily find herself 'running mad' for either of them; the Jailer's Daughter *does* run mad for Palamon. The language linking the main-plot and the sub-plot becomes redundant in this production, as we have already been shown the madness shared by the paired women via the use of set and blocking. Imogen Stubbs reveals that she 'did a lot of work in rehearsal on the connections between the Gaoler's Daughter and Emilia'. She adds that 'the two basically have the same problem'.[46] Whatever problems the two heroines share, the fact that their roles were written by two authors who did not check for artistic irregularities in their play is one problem that they do *not* share.

That the plot and sub-plot are dependent on one another in the original text is further manifested by the fact that others have realized the correspondences between the Jailer's Daughter and Emilia

43 *The Two Noble Kinsmen*, Prompt-book, pp. 13, 14, 15, 17, 14.

44 Michael Billington, rev. of *The Two Noble Kinsmen*, dir. Barry Kyle, *Guardian*, 10 May 1986, Collected in *Theatre Record: 7–20 May 1986*, 538.

45 *The Two Noble Kinsmen*, Prompt-book, p. 96.

46 Imogen Stubbs, 'Acting in the Swan: Imogen Stubbs', in Mulryne and Shewring, eds., *This Golden Round*, p. 109.

after rehearsing the play. Lois Potter describes another production which was a part of the 1994 Oregon Shakespeare Festival at Ashland. Directed by Nagle Jackson, the final scene, once again, drew parallels between the two women. In the production's last moment, only Palamon and Emilia remained on the stage as the Jailer's Daughter entered, 'still mad, in her dirty wedding dress. For a moment the two women looked at each other, touching each other's faces.'[47] Thus, the specific shades of the relationship between Emilia and the Jailer's Daughter will differ in every production, but these two stagings flesh out visually what is already apparent in the script.

In the instances discussed above Kyle took advantage of a directorial opportunity presented by the dialogue and translated it into a visual stage picture, but he certainly did not fill in cracks in the play through his cuts.[48] Similarly the actors enhanced what is already present on the page. When the reviewers realized that the play actually worked on stage, instead of revising the orthodox view of an unsuccessful co-authorship, they credited Kyle and the actors with lending uniformity to an unsophisticated play through the visual coding, judicious pruning and fine acting. There have been other occasions, however, where the play's joint authorship has been given due credit and publicized in a more positive light, but these have been rare. One such instance was when Hugh Richmond (who produced *The Two Noble Kinsmen* at the University of California in 1979) stated that the play was deliberately chosen 'for exploring the adverse affects [sic] of its supposedly divided authorship'. After the experience of producing the play he was unable to trace any such adverse effects and concluded that 'the play has a unique stage effect, a ruefully humorous pathos for which it has been dexterously, consciously, and systematically designed by its author(s)'. He reinforces his praise of the play's joint authorship by declaring that 'the issue of divided goals or methods is not relevant to performance of the play, which reflects a consistent rhythm of feeling independent of the varied authorship assigned to particular scenes. In staging there is no easily detected divergence stylistically.'[49]

Richmond, therefore, was refreshingly happy to give the meticulously crafted play a joint accreditation.

Gavin Bantock, who directed the play for the English Drama Group at Reitaku University, Tokyo, went even further. This production took place just two years after the Swan production and imagined the play's writing process as a truly collaborative one. The director presented onstage both the play and the imagined process of writing the play. The entire play was framed by having Shakespeare and Fletcher on stage discussing and planning the play together. Potter (who is my primary source of information about this production) observes with some surprise that the writers 'had a remarkably amiable working relationship'.[50]

However, the alternative narratives of the Shakespeare–Fletcher collaboration that emerged from these university drama experiments did not, unfortunately, enjoy the media attention that was lavished on the 1986 RSC production, which every major newspaper covered. It was disappointing, therefore, that, despite the discovery that *The Two Noble Kinsmen* is a theatrically engaging play, both Kyle and the reviewers exhibited a reluctance to examine the implications that this finding has for the perception of Shakespeare and Fletcher's jointly authored plays. As the sketches of Dawson and Thomas, and the recent critical commentary on the play discussed in my introduction, establish, critical and popular imagination continues to paint this Shakespeare–Fletcher co-authorship as forced, despite the theatre's having demonstrated that the play resulting from this partnership was the result of systematic mapping rather

---

47 Lois Potter, 'Introduction', in Potter, ed., *The Two Noble Kinsmen*, p. 95.

48 See Peter Holland, 'Style at the Swan', *Essays in Criticism*, 36:3 (1986), pp. 193–209, for the view that excessive focus on visuals detracts from an engagement with the play itself.

49 Hugh Richmond, 'Performance as Criticism: *The Two Noble Kinsmen*', in Charles H. Frey, ed., *Shakespeare, Fletcher, and The Two Noble Kinsmen* (Columbia, 1989), pp. 181, 183.

50 Lois Potter, '*The Two Noble Kinsmen* Onstage: A Postscript', *Shakespeare Quarterly*, 48:2 (1997), p. 226.

than 'hack-work'. Suzanne Gossett reached a similar conclusion after seeing a production of *Henry VIII* (another work usually credited to Shakespeare and Fletcher) at Shakespeare's Globe. She felt that 'we can trust both Shakespeare and Fletcher to know what they are doing',[51] and I argue that perhaps, for once, it is worth imagining that they could be trusted to write another good play together.

---

[51] Suzanne Gossett, 'Review of Shakespeare and Fletcher's *Henry VIII* (directed by Mark Rosenblatt) at Shakespeare's Globe, London, 2 August 2010', *Shakespeare*, 7:3 (2011), 327.

SHAKESPEARE PERFORMANCES IN ENGLAND (AND WALES) 2012

CAROL CHILLINGTON RUTTER

5 January 2012. On the library desk in front of me I've got the latest issue of *The Stage*. Self-described, it's the 'weekly for the entertainment industry', and on its front page, a photo captioned 'Artistic director Dominic Cooke' above the headline 'Royal Court to lose Cooke' pictures the man himself: greying, beefy, slightly jowly. When, I wonder, did the once-young Turk (and one-time Royal Shakespeare Company associate director) get so middle-aged and so well fed? Is there a subtext to the announcement that he is 'to step down' from the Court in 'April 2013' to 'focus on freelance work'? What does it mean that the Court's head administrator is also leaving – to start work as deputy executive director under the two Nicks (Hytner and Starr) who run the National Theatre? And is it significant that what *The Stage* isn't reporting is that Cooke is already doing some high-profile free-lancing? He's in rehearsals at the National, directing his first show there, *The Comedy of Errors* with Lenny Henry playing one of the Antipholuses. Insider gossip is touting this production (with the media attention it will garner through the casting) as Cooke's audition piece to claim the top job at the NT when Hytner retires. (Is it just coincidence, then, that his 'trusted' top lieutenant is getting into post on the South Bank first? Or is the move the first step in a take-over?) Be that as it may, Hytner's exit, murmured for next year, is rapidly in this new year *un*-murmured.

So Cooke may be at a loose end. But it's not only Cooke who's on the move. Back two months, the RSC's artistic director, Michael Boyd, announced he'd be leaving the company – in order, he said, 'to spend more time with my actors'. Since then emails have circulated, like one (from a bloke) subject-lined 'The king of Stratford is dead... Long live the ...', with the message: 'So the book is open on Boyd's replacement. Dominic Cooke is currently odds-on favourite at 3/1. Rupert Goold, 9/2, is worth a flutter. Or will it finally be a woman? Oh, hang on. I know the answer to that one. No.' But 'No' with a difference, because Greg Doran (not even listed by the computer screen bookies, though the in-house candidate), appointed RSC artistic director designate in April, immediately brings on board Erica Whyman from Northern Stage in the new RSC role of deputy artistic director. Sighs of relief: Doran is not just a safe pair of hands with a twenty-five-year-long track record at the RSC; he has also, during the Boyd regime, produced the company's most consistent run of work (*All's Well that Ends Well*, 2003, *The Taming of the Shrew/The Tamer Tamed* double bill, 2003, *A Midsummer Night's Dream*, 2005, *Hamlet*, 2008), even as he's thrown the RSC some curve balls (*Cardenio*, 2011, for one). But if relief, also little gasps of surprise: Whyman's appointment promises to shake up the place, bringing to the RSC someone who doesn't look or talk like the RSC, someone who thinks outside the company's corporate and creative box, someone interested in new wave performance, digital performance, next generation performance, international theatre; someone who, from her experience at Northern Stage, knows how to run an outward-facing arts organization; someone who puts difficult questions to directors, critics and technologies, like 'What is the point of having an

RSC if we don't do something interesting with it?' Someone who may suggest an answer to the question Susannah Clapp is asking, in March, in *The Observer*, 'Why does the RSC make the Bard so boring?'

Spectating on these to-ings and fro-ings, am I watching the top of the UK theatre industry engaged in an inter-institutional game of musical chairs? It feels like it. Michael Grandage stepped down as artistic director of the Donmar on New Year's Day, his farewell production, *Richard II* with Eddie Redmayne. Josie Rourke (his one-time assistant in Covent Garden) back-tracked across London from her current post, the top job at the Bush Theatre, to slip into Grandage's still-warm seat, leaving the vacancy in Shepherd's Bush to be filled by Mandani Younis (artistic director of Freedom Studios, Bradford, Yorkshire).

Of course, musical chairs is not the most energetic sport UK theatre will participate in this year. There's the small matter of 'London 2012', the Olympic razz-ma-tazz that, opening in July, will stop short of putting William Shakespeare into lycra and trainers and onto the starting blocks but will otherwise make him the front runner in London's 'Cultural Olympiad', staged concurrently with the Games. Will will speak first in the opening ceremonies of the Games: via Caliban voiced by Kenneth Branagh playing Isambard Kingdom Brunel, to tell the world that 'This isle is full of noises / Sounds and sweet airs that give delight and hurt not'. (Also 'clouds' waiting to 'open': although, miraculously, the wettest summer in living memory will suspend diluvial operations for the fortnight of the Games.) Will will also fill venues up and down the kingdom, with the 'World Shakespeare Festival' stretching from Newcastle to Brighton, Edinburgh to Cardiff. He will turn up, between April and June, at the Globe where his 37 plays will be staged in 37 languages (a marathon relay – 'Globe to Globe' – reported on elsewhere in this *Survey*). He will also appear in the basement of London offices vacated by the BBC and in the vast empty space of Hangar 858 (RAF St Athan, Wales), as well as in his usual places: on the Olivier, Swan, Donmar, Almeida,

Courtyard and RST stages. Not the Olympic Games themselves will cover as much ground this year as William Shakespeare. But like the Games, 'Shakespeare 2012' will produce as much pain as pleasure, as much abject defeat as soaring triumph, as many tears as shouts of joy. He'll sail over crossbars spectacularly. And he'll fall off apparatus, trip over hurdles, land flat on his face with ignominious, resounding splats. I begin with a couple of 'also-rans'.

HISTORIES

As the last twenty minutes of the RSC's *King John* bopped, rocked and staggered brainlessly on I wished that whatever poison the Mad Monk had administered John he'd share with me. I wanted out of my misery. This production began with a cross-cast Bastard (Pippa Nixon in multi-coloured diamond pattern leggings, converse trainers, gym slip and hoodie) appearing solo on stage, gurning the audience, producing a plectrum from under her tongue, striking an exaggerated Elvis Presley pose, then picking out single, tin-eared notes on a ukulele that resolved themselves ear-gratingly into 'Land of Hope and Glory'. It ended with John (Alex Waldmann) in jeans and sweat-stained singlet, gut-clutching, dying, caught in a sudden lighting change that, backed with Madcon's remixed hip-hop version of the Bob Gaudio classic 'Beggin', transformed him into a boy-band discodancer, sliding, clapping, stomping: danse macabre as karaoke Shakespeare. Was the Bastard a modern-dress court jester? Was 'England' a comedy club, and this, open mic night for amateur stand-ups? Were we watching 'King John: The Office Party'? Was the director Maria Aberg's 'concept' for *John* to ignore any of the big ideas Shakespeare searches in this roller-coaster history of ideological, temperamental and personal switch-back – 'big ideas' being so 'last century' – and to play *John* instead as a series of flashy production numbers interrupted by speech deliberately lampooned (as by Blanche, a blonde bimbo in miles of pink tulle whose manner of speaking in that li'l bitty girl's voice left men gaping, open-mouthed: what *was* she saying???) or delivered by actors who sounded like they were employed in a call centre? A 'concept' built on distractions, vacuousness and superficiality, making crass connections with today's spin-doctored politics and, in this royal 'jubbly' year celebrating Elizabeth II's sixty years on the throne, the nation's frenzied 'jubbly' merry-making? As my rhetorical questions suggest, at the centre of this production I saw a repulsive cynicism.

The place (designed by Naomi Dawson) looked like a high street bank. The Swan stage was covered with industrial-weight, geometric patterned brown-and-beige carpet that ran upstage to a flight of steep steps (set with corporate office plants in corporate plant pots) behind which, held in place with taut netting, was a wall of beach-ball sized balloons: pink, green, purple, aqua. You realized with a kind of rising aesthetic horror the basic design conceit: all the costumes that came on stage from little Arthur's bow-tie to sixty-something Lady Faulconbridge's motorcycle leathers to Queen Elinor's mutton-dressed-as-lamb Jackie Collins's satin day suit were colour co-ordinated to the balloons. And the further theatrical horror (viz. Chekhov's dictum on stage guns) that *of course* they would have to explode from their capture. And they did. Dozens of them. Shortly after the interval. And proceeded to bounce around the set for another hour and a half, completely out of synch with either speech rhythms (balloons don't do iambic pentameter) or the tightening tensions of the story, constantly upstaging actors and needing to be batted out of the way, imposing upon the actors distracted physical parallel play that couldn't be contained in any way by the narrative they were otherwise performing.

The cross-casting – playing the Bastard not *by* a woman but *as* a woman – might have looked good in HR terms. (Though inventing a 'new' woman's part in a history play well-endowed with meaty roles for women looked gratuitous, not least, given that the direction of the other women looked designed to throw their parts away. Was anybody in this production besides Nixon and Waldmann actually directed?) Theatrically, it was a disaster. It made nonsense of the inheritance controversy

that stands at the top of Shakespeare's play troping the other inheritance controversies that factionalize national and international politics; made nonsense, too, of all the other rivalries and hustlings for influence among the male power-brokers. In any case, the opening debate between Faulconbridge brother and sister was played for farce (lots of body language, the writing lost in shrugs and grimaces) anticipating a world in which no idea from paternity to monarchy to fidelity to honour would be anything more than a joke. But worse was to come. More strange business, improvised extra-textually by way of further production numbers, transformed what emerged as the central relationship, between John and the Bastard, into a weird love story: the Bastard opened the second half singing huskily down a mic the title song to Wasner's 'Civilian' (sample lyrics: 'I am nothing without pretend'; 'I am nothing without a man'; 'I wanted to give you everything' and 'love you like my mother's mother's mother did'). Never mind that, if you followed the play's opening scene, you knew the Bastard must be John's niece, and this invented intimacy, incest. Because by this time, a further casting mash-up had been performed: the Bastard morphed into Hubert. But hang on, don't these two roles actually talk to each other in Shakespeare's play? And hadn't we just seen this female Bastard, face, hands and neck smeared in blood, shrieking with glee, throwing down the decapitated head of Austria as her trophy? Surely that rather tedious young whippersnapper Arthur maundering on about his eyes wouldn't have given her a second's pause before she took them out with the heated spit.

Some of what didn't hang together here at the basic level of coherent storytelling wasn't just silly but deeply offensive. The blame-shifting scene (4.2) that has John making Hubert not just the instrument but the inspiration for Arthur's death ('Hadst not thou been by / . . . This murder had not come into my mind') was here played upon the Bastard's woman's body across a hundred lines of dialogue, starting as ugly verbal abuse then escalating to full sexual assault, finishing with her flat on her back, legs spread, John thrusting into her as his hands mauled her breasts and crotch. Seconds later though, her revelation – 'Young Arthur is alive' – prompted instant recovery and a laugh line from him, 'Forgive the comment that my passion made / Upon thy feature.' The rape simply vanished, Hubert morphing back into an amnesiac I-wanted-to-give-you-everything-Bastard who was John's best buddy and cheerleader and, latterly, hysterical chief mourner. John died sprawled in the Bastard's arms, she cradling him, shrieking out the play's final speech like some demented Cleopatra. But surely this was the production's most cynical gesture of all, to stage her grief as 'true' and to make it a valediction to, and validation of, an 'England' that would triumph (Land of Hope and Glory-wise) as long as 'to itself' she should 'rest but true'? This, when what we'd been shown was a truth-emptied England, a shabby, tawdry, venal, corrupted England, an England whose elite displayed about as much 'truth' in their public lives as our own tribe of wind-changing politicians and shyster bankers.

There were, however, three reasons to see this *King John*. First, Susie Trayling's Constance who, every time she came on stage, reclaimed the play for dignity. Second, Paola Dionisotti's cross-cast, fastidious and camp papal legate Pandulph in black trouser suit, dark glasses and beret, a kind of Mother Teresa meets Machiavelli as arranged by Monty Python and, with paradoxical aplomb, taking the play's God business utterly seriously. Third, Jacob Mauchlen's Arthur of Brittany who sat with hands clamped miserably over ears while the grown-ups rowed, then in an awful moment played as in a nightmare, twice, fell forward to his death as a body double toppled headlong backwards from off the top of the stairs into a void.

John has an astonishing line, a near-monosyllabic line, very near the end of the play, as he's dying, his bowels eaten by poison: 'Now my soul hath elbow-room.' Back at the start of rehearsals, in the first read-through of the script, when Waldmann got to that line, surely it should have given him and his director pause, told them what kind of play they were in? From what I saw on stage, they didn't listen.

This same company of actors, with the addition of Jonjo O'Neill in the title role, played *Richard III* alongside *King John* in a Swan season billed 'Nations at War' – although 'war' was an evacuated concept, having more to do with boardrooms and trading floors than battlefields. Was this *Richard* the production Susannah Clapp had in mind when she asked the question 'Why does the RSC make the Bard so boring?'

Directed by Roxana Silbert, designed by Ti Green, it had no style and no ideas, set anywhere and any-when on a blank canvas of distressed silver-painted wood, like faux aluminium siding, panelled upstage in sections that could open as doors or windows. The Duchess of York (Sandra Duncan) was dressed like Maggie Thatcher; Margaret (Paola Dionisotti), in Japanese martial arts gear; the Mayor (Edmund Kingsley) was a joke petty bureaucrat flapping around goofily in a Captain Hook cape and Nelson bonnet wide enough to launch the *Victory*; Dorset (Simon Coombs) and Grey (Iain Batchelor), jumped up spivs in orange satin and electric blue; Brian Ferguson's Buckingham a whining Scot. O'Neill's Richard was first Ian McKellen (in leather trenchcoat) then Napoleon Bonaparte. Then, tugging acres of coronation robes, sitting dwarfed on a 'throne' that looked borrowed from centre court Wimbledon, he was one of those comic megalomaniacs in A. A. Milne as illustrated by Shepard: Bad Sir Brian, perhaps. Nothing in this world mattered. But yet it was Very Serious Stuff. So said the deeply portentous music score that kept kicking in: ostentatious brass, pizzicatos and heavy bowing from cellos, a film-sized composition that sounded like it was auditioning for the remake of *Psycho*.

Such as they were, the production effects were either derivative (like the opening family photo-call, out of Loncraine, or the 'memory wall' to the dead princes, with teddy bears from Uncle Richard, out of Knee-High's *Cymbeline*) or acts of actorly desperation. Dionisotti did her best to drum up some metaphysics in a flatly secularist world where people mouthed words like 'God' and 'evil' (the way the boys at Barclays or the *Sun* or on the trading floor of Citibank use those words) but clearly didn't believe in either – or in retribution. So Margaret's curse ritual (a routine of foot stomps, head shakes, arm thrusts) didn't come out of any local reality, but felt, bizarrely, like a moment of anthropology, a native American rain-dance, perhaps.

O'Neill's silly Richard was headed for detention, not damnation: an insolent overgrown schoolboy with a Tintin quiff and a grinning face you wanted to slap who played for cheap laughs, many of them solicited from the stalls. 'You're going to love this', he joked with the front row part way through the opening soliloquy; later, after 'plots have I laid', double-taking with the audience, to add, 'Oh YEAH!', with a grin (showing rotten teeth: too many trips to the tuck shop). I was not amused. But then, I'm never amused by actors who think they're cleverer than Shakespeare or who have so little professional discipline that they leave the play to indulge their own meagre personalities. I wanted this Richard frog-marched off to the headmaster's office – and left there. (Note to the incoming RSC directorate: please can you look at the bad actor habits that have become rife in the company over the past decade – starting with the ad libs, like the one from *John* that interrupted the drunken wedding, 'Oh shit! it's the legate of the Pope!' – and *get rid of them*. You can use O'Neill as a case study.)

Still, there were two reasons to see this *Richard*. First, the women (Dionisotti, Duncan, Siobhan Redman as Queen Elizabeth) telling their dead in 4.4. Their voices were 'crazed' with 'So many miseries' that they are nearly 'mute' – until they begin on the comparative body-count, and then lament turned into the verbal equivalent of sharded glass shoved into soft tissue: 'I had an Edward...'; 'I had a Rutland...'. The seismic shift on stage was palpable. Watching this 'society' of 'sorrow' we were finally looking at some adults, not gormless adolescents, and some real acting. The pain, grief, hatred they shared across memory was electrifying as performance, terrifying as story. Dionisotti's Margaret squatted, mocking the Duchess with a re-play, birthing 'From forth the kennel' of her 'womb' the 'hell-hound that doth hunt us

all to death', hauling from her crotch the misshapen abortion that she held up, Richard, monster baby.

The second, Lynton Appleton's brief appearance as Prince Edward, facing his Uncle Richard, saying evenly that he feared 'no uncles dead', then answering buffoonish Richard's throw-away joke, 'Nor none that live, I hope' with utter moral seriousness, 'An if they live, I hope I need not fear.' For a single moment, we saw an alternative world to the slapstick charnel house of O'Neill's jigging and mugging.

I've never been so delighted so see a Richmond, a virile and properly boyish performance from Iain Batchelor, whose appearance meant that Richard's end was (finally) in sight. But I took away another thought. Not one reviewer, if they even noticed it, batted an eye at O'Neill playing Richard in his native Belfast accent. Twenty years ago, when Barrie Rutter dared to play Yorkshire Richard in a Yorkshire accent, you'd have thought he was relaunching the Wars of the Roses. In one respect, then, this production is to be celebrated. 'We've come a long way, baby.'

At the Globe, the in-house contribution to the 'Globe to Globe' festival (with its array of other-language Shakespeares and radical 'local' interpretations from around the world delivered to the South Bank) was an entirely uncontroversial Elizabethan costume-drama *Henry V*, set on a near bare stage, taken back (after seasons of extensions and scenic additions) to original plans – except for a frame of ladders that pushed the balcony out to just behind the stage pillars, with stairs giving directly onto the stage. Offering punters plenty of doublets, codpieces, leather jerkins and laced-up bodices, Dominic Dromgoole (directing) and Jonathan Fensom (designing) took the measure of this year's tourist audience. They gave them heritage Shakespeare, and sell-out audiences – it was easier to get a ticket to the Olympics than this *Henry V* – ate it up. Jamie Parker (returning from the *Henry IV*s in 2010) played a decent Hal-turned-Harry who actually needed to be convinced to go to war in France and who, turning away from the miracle of the near-bloodless (English blood, that is) victory at Agincourt, suddenly folded over and wept.

There were some fine touches. Brid Brennan, in cap, sagging ruff and soiled apron, played the Chorus as a left-over from the Boar's Head days. Her rousing 'Now all the youth of England are on fire!' was deliciously deflated by the entrance of Pistol (Sam Cox), Nym (David Hargreaves) and Bardolph (Paul Rider), a crew of clapped-out geriatrics that amongst them couldn't summon enough of a spark to light a squib. Olivia Ross as French Katherine, danced her way through the English lesson – but stopped dead when she heard in the distance the trumpets of war. What they meant registered on her face. She gazed, shaken, on her father. And the young actor, Kurt Egyiawan, is certainly someone to watch: beautiful to look at, as the Dauphin, and with a voice, articulation and clarity, to listen to for hours. But there was also over-acting (a screeching Mistress Quickly from Lisa Stevenson) and the kind of Globe-branded crassness that makes everybody but smutty schoolboys groan: did we have to hear the Salic law expounded by a cleric straining on a close-stool? Did it clarify the offstage story or merely mystify it to have Falstaff's corpse lowered over the balcony and trundled off in a barrow? That shrouded body-bag was *surely* too small to hold a 'tun' of Falstaff 'humours'. Or had he shrunk, in banishment? At the Boar's Head, not all England was large enough to contain his fantasies. Now, a little, little grave would do it.

Much more ambitious *Henry V*s were on offer elsewhere. Theatre Delicatessen is an outfit that collaborates with stakeholders in the commercial sector to take over their empty or disused buildings and turn them into performance spaces where ensembles who are dedicated to exploring text-based theatre create 'immersive' spectator experiences. Their *Henry V*, directed by Roland Smith, designed by HalfCut and Katharine Heath, occupied the vacated basement of the old BBC on Marylebone Gardens. Several rooms were mocked up as a low-ceilinged, subterranean bunker in (notionally) a current conflict (Afghanistan, perhaps) where the claustrophobic central space was set, at one end, with a mess table with

squaddies – this was the modern British Army: women, too, wore desert combat uniform and the red berets – playing poker and patience (the definitive war game?) amongst a clutter of sandbags and bits of kit; the other end, the chaplain's office where, in front of a field altar, he was confessing a man in uniform who would turn out to be Harry the king. Corridors leading off took spectators in the pre-show to wander through the triage room, the comms room (stage management in this production being installed – a great insider joke – in an old BBC studio amidst junked recording gear that crackled with distant voices, lines from *Richard II*), and soldiers' bunkrooms, past pin-ups, slumped flak jackets, half-written letters, poignant traces of young lives. One squaddie had by his bed a copy of Shakespeare's sonnets, another, an English–French dictionary.

The immersive experience was neither in-yer-face nor coercive, but a slow burn that established the audience space and the actor space as shared space. (We sat next to them at the mess table or on sandbags.) It gave spectators plenty of time to ponder, from the installation, from the material details collected there, why we go to war, what we're staking, going to war, before a couple of squaddies came crashing into the mess, bellowing out the tune to 'ENJOY YOURSELF – it's later than you think' as they head-and-body butted each other in a physical game half way between rave dancing and one-on-one combat only to hit the deck, along with the whole outfit, as deafening strafing overhead and the terrifying noise of explosions sent them diving for cover in a blackout that was pitch, total, instant sensory deprivation. All you could hear was shallow breathing, strangled by hearts in mouths. Then out of the silence, a single match was struck, 'O, for a muse of fire' began, and from that pin-prick, light spread. Immersive theatre here gave spectators a little touch of terror in the night; something like a simulation.

Theatre Delicatessen is a young company, bulked up with veterans like the excellent Liam Smith who doubled Pistol and the French King – and appeared to have experienced a personality transplant in the shift between roles. Smith's Pistol was ugly,

29. *Henry V*, 3.7, Theatre Delicatessen, Marylebone Gardens, directed by Roland Smith. Chris Polick as Dauphin. Photograph © Lorna Palmer.

leering, mean, opportunistic; coming upon the soldier laid out on the mess-table-turned-triage-station, he glanced back over his shoulder, then looted the body; his French king was slightly book-ish, tentative, peering at a world that seemed to perplex him: a very fine pair of performances. The youth needed more vocal technique, to take more workmanlike pleasure in Shakespeare's writing and what it's equipping them to do. But they were led by the excellent Philip Desmeules as a Harry, not much older than the lads flying Apaches and patrolling in Helmand in the real British army. A vulnerable Harry, knowing he had no real chance before Harfleur, his fear palpable. (That speech about how he'd lay waste to the city? Pure poppy-cock, bluster!) A Harry with a deep conscience whose need for prayer on the eve of Agincourt was as real as his anguish, sitting around a camp-fire with other soldiers, gossiping, when he learned how the lads he commanded viewed the massacre they faced. A Harry who made us laugh, with more diplomatic fakery: discovering, having started the wooing scene stumbling over 'je', when he got to 'la plus belle Katherine du monde', that he actu-ally spoke French (as the actor does) like a native. This was a steadfast Harry, a Harry committed to the right decision for England and the kingdom, whose personal tragedy, praying 'O God of battles . . . ', was knowing that his right decision would cost Englishmen their lives.

What this young company did best was to pro-duce fine physical performance detail. The English lesson was conducted on some kind of juddering military transport (a helicopter, perhaps). Kather-ine (Laura Martin-Simpson: feisty, strong-jawed; and formidable when she doubled as 'Commander' Gloucester) and Alice (Jessica Guise), being flown behind the retreating front lines to safety, were

30. *Henry V*, 3.4, Propeller, Hampstead Theatre, directed by Edward Hall. Chris Myles as Alice, Karl Davies as Princess Katherine.

wedged up against the exhausted bodies of sleeping French troops whose arms and lolling heads they used as props ('de fingre', 'de nick'). The French 'brag' scene ('Would it were dawn!') was played over a board game – 'Risk'. Agincourt was one Boy (tiny Zimmy Ryan, cross-cast), crouching in the dark, hands over ears, quailing, as explosions overhead shook the bunker. At the end, the final 'frame' left me thinking 'Yet the pity of it, . . . O, Iago the pity of it'. Chorus (Alexander Guiney) swept one final look around the place, wearily slung his rifle over his shoulder – and walked off. That silent exit – into the next theatre of war? – told a whole world.

The yet-to-be realized potential I'm seeing in Theatre Delicatessen's youth comes full-on in Propeller, the pleasure of a Propeller production being the way this all-male company is as powerful and inventive textually as physically. Their *Henry V* showed them at full, irreverent throttle – the

'serious play' of their creative anarchy simply showing up the kind of thing the RSC was getting up to in *Richard* and *John* as witless and embarrassingly puerile. There wasn't a duff speaker among them, so you constantly heard as brand new lines like Exeter's 'For if you hide the crown / Even in your hearts, there will he rake for it' and the Boy's 'they stole a *fire shovel*' (a delicious performance by Karl Davies, who'd double Katherine: his Boy, a gawky kid in a grey hoodie, short trousers, skateboarder knee pads and horn-rimmed glasses who'd ball up into a hedgehog at the noise of battle).

This production's premise was 'suppose'; the conceit, that *Henry V* is a memory play, re-enacted by a bunch of modern-dress English squaddies (desert combat gear, dog tags, sweat-stained singlets) caught up in the pointless, deeply-unglamorous and suicidal civil war, the Wars of the Roses, that's followed Harry's death, using reminiscence nostalgically to look back, to re-present the glory days of English heroism when war was good, clean fun, bashing the French. A dirty dozen in a foot patrol came through the audience, singing a Pogues classic, the one with the disturbing lyrics about 'arms and legs . . . scattered all around' and 'a pair of brown eyes . . . looking at me'. Spectators had already encountered these bizarre strangers out-of-place in the foyer, balaclavas over faces, mingling, shouldering past them and their pre-show cappuccinos: soldiers or terrorists? Liberators or occupiers? These male bodies who were going to war for us: did we want to know them? This pre-show show was signature Propeller.

The stage they mounted and collapsed on looked like a box of dried blood: red camouflage curtains lined the walls. There were some ammunition crates that would produce 'magic objects' as props – a squaddie finding in one a crown that prompted 'O, for a muse of fire', then, passed around, turned them all, sharing line after line, into the Chorus. These crates would double as tables, altars and, their lids held up in front of rocking, tensed troops, the prows of D-Day landing craft hitting the beaches of France. Centre stage there was a double-decker mobile cage with a platform on top (that would serve Harry's sentries – and executioners), set with a couple of trash-cans, and a flagpole flying the St George Cross. Around the set's perimeter ran high-level gantries with access ladders onto the main stage. Designed by the consistently brilliant Michael Pavelka, this was a set that made for constant, non-stop traffic, continuous play, built of component parts that could be taken apart and rearranged to produce different perspectives on men and war, not least when the solid-looking blood walls, backlit, dissolved and let spectators see, as it were, behind the rhetorical surface of the story: another place; another time.

A remount of the original production that launched the company fifteen years ago (and that is now aimed at an ambitious project, a couple of years hence, to stage a full Propeller history cycle under the title *Bloodline*), this *Henry* remembered itself. As in the original, this was the soldiers' story. Members of the squaddie-Chorus-as-national-storyteller were constantly on stage,

stepping out of the crowd into the foreground, pulling on over their fatigues and unwashed faces extra kit: a surplice for the archbishop (Gunnar Cauthery), a bomber jacket for Exeter (Chris Myles), skirts for the cross-dressed Nell and Kate that turned them into history's boys (and girls) and into the multiple parts they played, continuously doubling. Pistol, Nym and Bardolph (Vince Leigh, Finn Hanlon, Gary Shelford) were standard-issue English lager louts, baseball-bat-wielding 'warriors' in football shirts. Mistress Quickly (Tony Bell) wore ice-cream cone falsies and a wedding dress made of army surplus parachute silk. Katherine (Karl Davies), in white-face and cropped boy's hair, pouted in front of a mirror, painting on bee-sting lips, and posing when soldiers sauntered through, asking for her photo and autograph, then (fully dressed) climbed into a bathtub with her Collins dictionary to take her English lesson. Chris Myles, doubling a sturdy, lip-pursing Alice in blue French WAC uniform (sensible shoes, skirt, beret) played her with his Exeter moustache still in place. (For Propeller, the conceit when they cross-dress is never to impersonate women; the conceit is theatrical and performative, the lads always role-players, playing parts.) Throughout, the strains of 'La Vie en Rose' and 'Chanson d'Amour' competed with 'London Calling' and 'Land of Hope and Glory', walls of sound covering scene changes, the noise of pounding feet and banging weapons turning the space into a sound box for the military, and sound-mixing sentimentality and jingoism into a backing-track for swaggering brutality.

But fifteen years on, there was change, too, most significantly, a change in tone. Now, there was less swagger, more interrogation, less raw testosterone, more investigation of, curiosity about, masculinity, launched when the box that Exeter opened presented to the English king a pair of tennis balls. They looked like outsized testicles. Faux manliness. A French joke. Simultaneously, the trash bins on the platform above were noisily upturned, spilling – ejaculating? – balls, dozens of them, *hundreds* of them – onto the stage. Those balls troped Harry's business in this production, from 'sport' to deadly earnest, delinquent Hal to 'mirror of all

Christian kings'. The route was not straightforward.

Dugald Bruce-Lockhart's Henry wasn't one of the boys. He appeared from somewhere else, as if a memory conjured by the Chorus, in splendid dress uniform, to sit on his throne, the fingers of one hand impatiently drumming, listening to clerics tediously expound Salic law to give him the 'yes' he needed to reach the decision he'd already made. A heroic decision? Or not? When he'd taken his seat, he'd been showered in red poppies. (And his initial dazzle was instantly undercut by the visual cross-cut to beer-swilling Pistol's raucous shenanigans.) Later, when he appeared in the field in battle-stained fatigues – now very much one of the boys – the weapon he carried was the axe so recently used on Cambridge (Richard Dempsey) and Grey (Nicholas Asbury). Still later, he steeled himself to give the signal for Bardolph's execution (like all the violence in this production, gut-wrenching, but displaced: Exeter 'confessing' Bardolph, then snapping his neck; upstage, a punching bag beaten viciously with a baseball bat while downstage the victim mimed the beating). But then he had to endure the smirking Montjoy (Nicholas Asbury), who'd witnessed the court martial, turning on his heel, exiting, but first handing him a tennis ball. In physical set-ups like these but also in what he made of Shakespeare's writing Bruce-Lockhart's performance constantly caught the bi-focality of this play. 'Once more unto the breach . . . ' was full-throated; 'upon the king', enraged, bitter; 'we few, we happy few' almost absurdly rousing, making geese lions ready to rush the cannon's mouth. And 'not today, O Lord, / O not today . . . ' showed a bare-stripped soul frankly bargaining with his maker.

And then at the end when the 'acceptable' and bloody violence of war had given way to the 'acceptable' and delicious violence of wooing, and the future looked won, martially and maritally, the Chorus took it all away: Henry handed his crown to Kate, who, as he exited upstage into the past, shed skirts, morphing back into the present-day squaddie, sharing out the story of what happened next with his also-morphing colleagues. A story of death. Of loss. Of the magic child Harry imagined:

the future child of civil war. And as the Chorus resumed its part, a final hymn began. 'Requiem': remember. It swelled, and swelled: the astonishing beauty of the voices counterpointing what we'd seen, the violence, the destructiveness, the awfulness of men at war. That harmony: this, too, men could do.

Propeller gives you the kind of total theatre you get in parts elsewhere – as in Michael Grandage's farewell production at the Donmar, *Richard II* which looked terrific (designed by Richard Kent) but fizzled out in its central casting: Eddie Redmayne.

The intimate rectangle facing spectators was set to look like an oak-framed hall in the Middle Temple – or an architectural rendering of the Wilton Diptych. A balcony spanned the width of the stage; behind, carved wood panels suggested a rood screen burnished with gold (that deadened, the dazzle killed when the lights dimmed); the walls were washed with peeling gold, like a Byzantine icon; the whole effect sumptuous, gorgeous – and the place, empty except for incense lying like fog and a throne, centre, occupied by a body, crowned, motionless, eyes closed. Meditating? Proleptically a tomb sculpture? The image of monarch as divinity? The first court entrance had courtier after courtier ostentatiously genuflecting to this 'idol'.

But then the King stood up – and gave the game away. Redmayne was a skinny-kid David Bowie in medieval costume: epicene, high-cheekboned, with botoxed-looking lips, a smile half way between sneering and loonishness fixed on his face, and one of those drawling Eton voices that puts everything into 'quotation marks' – and Shakespeare's all-poetry *Richard* ploddingly into prose. Recruited back to theatre from film, his lungs aren't fit for theatrical purpose: he (Redmayne) kept running out of breath and dropping ends of lines which I struggled to read as Richard literally running out of royal steam. Playing him as an all-surface 'luvvie' might have worked if, in the second half of the play, his Richard had found something interior, another kingdom, to explore; but he never got beyond petulant self-pity to self-awareness; never was anything but outside himself: never found himself groping around the manky prison-under-the-skin. As his glorious fantasizing ('know'st thou not / That when the searching eye of heaven is hid . . .') was tosh, so his discovery of what might have been himself stripped – 'I live with bread' – was just childish whining ('when I'd prefer a jam sandwich'). His 'little, little grave' made spectators bark with laughter. There were things to admire here: Richard's obvious fascination with the volley of treason accusations in 1.1; and the devastating cynicism of the banishments in 1.3, requiring oaths ('never' to 'write, regreet, nor reconcile') he says are for the good of the state but here were coldly self-serving.

The best of this production, though, was first, Ron Cook's pint-pot York, eyes swivelling like emergency lights working on top of a police car, knowing how close everyone was getting to speaking treason, wanting to keep his son (a decent but flat-line Bolingbroke from Andrew Buchan) from suicidal indiscretion. When he finally exploded in 2.1 ('Seek you to seize and grip . . . Hereford's rights? . . . You pluck a thousand dangers on your head!'), the family terrier was a metamorphosed hound of the Baskervilles, leaping for the king's throat. Second, Michael Hadley's John of Gaunt, whose death was coming to him too soon. He was palsied, but urgent; really was 'a prophet new-inspired', knowing this was his last word, his last breath, and that he was *going to say it all*, at speed, at volume, his final gasp a dragon's roar, 'This England' backed not by Elgar but Mahler. Third, against the 'wwww-orms' and 'write sorrowwww on the bosom of the earth' mannerisms of Redmayne's speaking, the flat simplicity of the Welsh Captain's (Phillip Joseph) reportage: 'The bay trees in our country are all withered.'

In one respect it was a smart decision to make this summer's Globe *Richard III* an 'original practices' production, to put it in 'authentic' early modern dress, and thus to corral it in a long-ago, redundant past. Because next door, the huge screen-on-the-green outside Tate Modern that spectators passed on the way to the Globe was showing, live, the London 2012 Paralympics – and those athletes would have made any modern-dress

Richard's thoughts on disability ('scarce half made up') sound like whining self-indulgence. In every other respect, though, this production (directed by Tim Carroll, designed by Jenny Tiramani) showed 'original practices' as a dead end. It's not just that men in ruffs and farthingales impersonating women were grotesque: like James Garnon's drag-act Duchess of York, doing 'old lady' walking, scuttling across the stage, beetle-browed, the spitting image of another scowl-faced Duchess, from *Alice Through the Looking Glass*. Nor was it the fundamental mismatch between stage and yard: the fact that whatever the actors claimed to be doing in terms of 'original practices' on the stage, we in the audience weren't 'original' spectators; so we weren't looking at *Richard* as Shakespeare's spectators did, in our time, but as a rather pretty period costume drama. ('Pretty' not least because everybody in Globe 'original practices' productions is always wearing brand-new clothes. But that's just daft – and why would Richmond go to war in full court dress?) It's a dead end to my mind because none of the actors belonged in the clothes. They may have been dressed for the part. But the behaviours they were producing from inside their early modern doublets and hose are resolutely postmodern. So they didn't act the part.

Take Mark Rylance's Richard, apparently designed 'after' the portrait of the king in London's National Gallery (pork-pie hat, tunic, shoes, not calipered boots, stringy hair hanging to his shoulder; with a significant addition not from the portrait, a tiny withered left hand in a sleeve pinned to his chest). But this Richard was neither the soldier, the lover nor the villain. (Maybe a memory of Rooster Byron in *Jerusalem*?) He hemmed and hawed, affected a stammer – or aphasia ('I . . . I . . . I . . . that am not . . .'), repeated half lines as though he were in one of Beckett's alzheimer scenarios, mugged the audience, coming out of the play to perform detached business as though he were always standing outside the part, quoting Shakespeare, and *badly*. I've rarely heard so much 'approximate' Shakespeare, speeches thrown away, cue jumping, and clean forgetting of text. Worst of all, in a production that cut Margaret

31. *Twelfth Night*, 5.1, RSC, Royal Shakespeare Theatre, directed by David Farr. Sandy Grierson as Priest, Jonathan McGuinness as Orsino, Kirsty Bushell as Olivia, Emily Taaffe as Viola/Cesario. Behind: Kevin McMonagle as Feste, Jan Knightley as Antonio, Felix Hayes as Fabian, Sargon Yelda as Valentine, Ankur Bahl as Curio.

(because the crowd in the pit wouldn't know who to make of the cursing crone?) Rylance's Richard conveyed no sense beyond secular solipsism. He was a buffoon, comic after a geriatrically maundering fashion. But never dangerous. Never evil – or capable of radiating what the play requires of Richard, the kind of deep destructiveness that shows us what human nullity looks like. When, I wondered, did Rylance get so forgettable?

COMEDIES

Under the strap line 'What Country Friends Is This?' the RSC put together a 'Shipwreck Trilogy' of comedies this season, cross-cast from an ensemble of eighteen actors working on an adaptable set designed by Jon Bausor to look like a ship forced aground in a storm. Its blackened,

splintered deck ran downstage; its aft was heaved up behind as though the hull had broken amidship; as though its stern would fold into the prow. Far upstage, the smoky brick back wall, inset with a massive iron-frame skylight, half porthole, half cathedral rose window, seemed to remember an industrial Victorian past, a railway station perhaps. What looked like a giant steel girder, or the arm of one of those cranes that tower over building sites in London today, ran diagonally out across the stage at lighting rig level. One downstage corner was cut away to look like a giant aquarium: at stage level, a rock pool; below, you were looking (that is, if you were sitting in Row D, as I was) into a subaquatic world of sunk castaways and drownings, objects sea-swallowed (though some would be, literally, 'cast' again). This space was re-furnished for each play: with a massive, washed-up

32. *The Tempest*, 4.1, RSC, Royal Shakespeare Theatre, directed by David Farr. Sandy Grierson as Ariel.

shipping container in *The Tempest* (directed by David Farr) and an Ozymandias-like fallen statue, headless, just one breast discovering its female form (a wrecked bowsprit? Setebos?). For *Twelfth Night* (Farr again), with the stuff of a dotty, once-elegant seaside hotel, stuck in the 1930s (both furniture *and* habitants), decorated with the flotsam and jet-sam of many sea-storms, equipped with two bits of apparatus that would have mighty consequences for the playing: upstage right, a 'first generation' open, art nouveau grille-work cage-lift that moved with stately unhurriedness, putting its occupants on display as it delivered them to the lobby; upstage left, just beyond the registration desk (that was set with a dinosaur-sized 1970s PC and intercom but backed with a wall of vintage pigeon holes for hotel messages) was a revolving door. For *Comedy of Errors* (directed by Amir Nizar Zuabi), the stage-side aquarium was reproduced in a second one,

onstage, used for waterboarding Egeon. This *Errors* was set in the shipping warehouses of the bad-ass docklands (Bausor maybe thinking of *The Wire*) of some totalitarian state.

The shipping container was practically the only trick in Farr's *Tempest*. Some tempests start with Prospero raising the storm; some, with Ariel. This tempest, if not the work, was the concern of Miranda (Emily Taaffe), a crop-haired waif in her father's cut-down trousers, cinched at the waist, who sat huddled at a rough table, scraping let-ters onto a school slate, but then lifted her head hearing the sound of rising wind. She consulted a clock on the desk, climbed up onto her chair and crouched there, staring out, as disembodied voices shouted 'Mayday, mayday!' Lights inside the con-tainer came up; its 'wooden' sides became trans-parent; inside, as in a fish-bowl, the Neapolitan voyagers experienced the violence of the storm until 'We split! We split!' froze the action on the human wreckage. Blackout. Miranda's hurt voice called 'If by your art . . . ' and lights came partially up in the box, showing a fraught figure, plastered up against the surface, struggling, like a drowning body fighting the murky water that was choking him, until the container burst open and Prospero staggered out, hobbling as though every bone in both legs had been broken and healed badly. He was in a wrecked business suit, so worn to tatters that the tailor's canvas of the inner-lining showed through on one lapel. Bald, gaunt, he looked like a death's head. He had no robes, no book, no 'art', except the box, which operated as the magic door onto his black, white, and grey island; operated also as the chamber-sized theatre of his performances.

But after this spectacular 'prologue', when Prospero got down to the business of telling Miranda her back-story, there were no more tricks. Just a father – with something he had to say. A telling-and-listening exercise. Jonathan Slinger's Prospero was damaged goods. 'Twelve years – *twelve years*': the repetition wasn't an intensifier, but staggered wonder. Struggling to make sense of the past, Slinger constantly found new rhythms in the narrative that made the story new. (The ready joke about Miranda's parentage, for instance, that other Prosperos make smutty, for Slinger was no joke, but a choked reminiscence of his dead wife: he wore a wedding ring.) 'Brother' was chewed between clenched teeth; 'my library', a marker of loss. He let us in to the full range of emotions he would use later, from rage to humiliation and self pity, to love, showing here such gentleness for his daughter, and (unlike the semi-detached Prosperos of Ralph Fiennes last year or Stephen Dillane the year before) a father focused on his child, listening to her, hugging her: a deeply human Prospero.

But you knew he was serious about his revenge – and didn't blame him. The garish colours the castaways imported, still in their wedding clothes, and the whore-pink stilettos the cross-cast Sebastian (Kirsty Bushell) persisted in wearing *on sand* were reason enough to hang them all. There was amusing funny business from Bruce Mackinnon's

Stephano and Felix Hayes's Trinculo (though I worry that Hayes is going to get stuck in his Forrest Gump routine, playing every part like a child with learning difficulties). Amer Hlehel's Caliban was, like Slinger's Prospero, a very human monster: no sign of deformity – so perhaps only his step-parentage from Prospero, his education and nurture, accounted for his malignity. I wondered, though, how to 'read' the actor's heavy Palestinian accent, the voice some would hear as the terrorist's (here, perhaps, a justified terrorist?). Together, Taaffe's Miranda and Solomon Israel's Ferdinand were wonderful children just stepping into adulthood – he, astonished to hear his language; she amazed at the beauty of humankind.

But for me the great revelation of this *Tempest* was Sandy Grierson's Ariel, who entered, like Prospero, 'drowning', through the magic box: his master's doppelganger, dressed like his twin. Grierson has one of those faces that's as beautiful and mask-like as the moon in children's book illustrations, and he has a soft Scottish accent. His Ariel was a companion performance to last year's Little Angel/RSC puppet Caliban: his form human but his gestures, his looks, the tilt of his head, listening, slightly odd, mechanical, like an automaton's, yet alert, like a dog. 'Doing' the storm for Prospero, he was balletically animated, diving and dividing, catching phrases of the story that he physically embodied before, at the end, finishing, simply closing down, turning off like a PC shutting applications, attending to his cuffs, fixing his moon-face to hear next instructions. So: a machine, a puppet. But never cold or alienating: warm, engaging. An Ariel who was fascinated by mankind, *so curious* about what it might mean to be human! He mimicked human gestures (of, for example, grieving Ferdinand, arms in a knot, as though by doing the business Ariel might feel the emotion). He pulled the invisible strings that made the masque; 'performed' as a statue clothes-horse, wearing the 'trash' that diverted the drunken would-be revolutionaries on the way to kill Prospero; froze on Caliban's line about all the spirits hating Prospero: paused, turned, considered, wondered. While Prospero spoke of the 'baseless fabric' of the 'vision', he stood trapped in the box, behind, sweeping up after the show. This Ariel, head shaking, clearly expected 'No' to 'Do you love me, master?' and was puzzled by his master's deeply emotional 'DEARLY'; expected more 'NO!', sitting next to Prospero, observing, all the while shaking his head, 'If you saw them you would grow tender'; expected rebuke on 'Mine would were I human' – a line that turned only on the genuine impossibility of his ever knowing what 'human' could be. At the end, coming upon Prospero newdressed for Milan, Grierson's Ariel examined the suit, its lining, the buttons. Curious to the last. Freeing him, Prospero undressed Ariel. Took off the look-alike uniform that had made them both slaves to the past. Ariel vanished. And you knew that this Prospero, speaking the Epilogue in the glare of reality, the houselights full up, would never recover from that loss.

The lines that evidently framed David Farr's *Twelfth Night* (cast from the *Tempest* ensemble, played on the basic *Tempest* set) were Sebastian's, from late in the play, 'Or I am mad, or else this is a dream: / . . . If it be thus to dream, still let me sleep!' Upstage, in deep shadows, the broken, heaved-up stern of Bausor's shipwreck was made up to look like a sprawling bed set at a dangerous angle: on it, a figure, asleep; above it, a vintage tropical room fan; beside it, a cabinet, a rolltop bath-tub, all outsized, slightly wonky, 'dreamed' (so when the fan blades started rotating, they made you think of the propeller on a submersible). Downstage was the lobby of a seaside hotel trapped in a time-warp (Olivia and Orsino were dressed like Bacall and Bogart; the interlopers, Sebastian and Viola, like Jedward). There was a grand piano (its lid, set like a shrine to a dead brother with a black-bordered portrait), an antique globe, a chessboard, the manually operated lift, the revolving door, with its murky panels made of yellowing – or waterstained – industrial plastic, that troped the activity in Illyria and came brilliantly into its own, late on, as Olivia wailed behind furious Orsino exiting to do mischief on Cesario, and already half way through the revolve, 'HUSBAND!' – the two of them 'revolving' right back round, into the thick

of things! 'HUSBAND?' Centre stage, an iron pillar thrust up into the flies gave the impression of a periscope, or a lighthouse: a lamp on top flashed red when the storm that opened the action began, but around its base was a leather banquette.

The event that kicked this place of suspended animation into action was a *coup-de-théâtre*. In blackout, we heard the roar of breakers on the sea, a tempest crashing, then, caught in a spotlight on the downstage pool, a lung-filling gasp for air as a head broke water, arms hauling a body up onto land like a beached mermaid where one line came out – 'What country friends is this?' – before the shipwrecked girl collapsed in a foetal curl while behind her lights came up on 'If music be the food of love . . .' (Later, another coup would see that other woman's figure, the one on the bed tossing and turning then sitting bolt upright as, following his sister through the water, Sebastian surfaced downstage, crawled onto land and lay there, motionless: Olivia somehow dream-knowing him in Illyria.) This production caught the heart-broken misery of the play without being miserable. It saw twin trajectories: the women were occupied with death and how to remember love (set up a shrine, dress up like your brother); the men, with desire, and the vanity of their self-absorbed fantasies (the down-gyved braces the Count wore in his first entrance predicted some braces on yellow stockings to come).

Viola/Olivia; Orsino/Malvolio: these were the real twins of this *Twelfth Night*. Particularly fine was Kirsty Bushell's cougar-esque Olivia whose move from grief-exhaustion to hyperactive lust was registered in her coiffure, the way her sleek french roll unravelled to hot mess. The kiss she planted on Cesario at the end of 3.1 shocked them both. It was just awful – and as Cesario fled and she wailed after him 'Yet come again! . . .', she was a human shipwreck, humiliated by desire, the sound of her heaving sobs closing the first half.

By then, of course, the clowns Shakespeare plants as decoys in the middle of *Twelfth Night* were outrageously making mayhem: Nicholas Day's unsavoury greasy-haired Belch, a humanoid Moby Dick in Hawaiian print shirt who illustrated how 'dear' he'd been to Aguecheek by flourishing his purloined credit cards; Kevin McMonagle's Feste, a washed up Buddy Holly (jelly roll quiff, black rim glasses, purple plaid suit) toting around a portable electric Casio keyboard that began every song with a drum 'fill in'; Bruce Mackinnon's bumbling Hooray-Henry Aguecheek always one step – and prop – behind the plot; Cecilia Noble's ample Maria radiating female (and racial) indignation. And Jonathan Slinger's Malvolio.

I haven't been wrong in past *Survey*s to moan about Slinger's Richard II, Richard III, Macbeth. I realize now, however, that what's been wrong is the line of parts. Slinger is a very fine *comic* actor: witness his Puck in Doran's *Dream* (2005) and Fluellen in Boyd's *Histories*. Here, he played Malvolio as the super-serviceable hotel manager (shiny lapel badge on elephant grey pinstripe suit), awful blonde toupee side-parted and combed over crown, little Hitler moustache. He had a habit of tugging his ear and straining his head stiffly on his neck like a tortoise with a muscle pull while he rolled his tongue around his inside bottom lip as though dislodging a toffee, preparing to speak. His pencil grin emitted 'hee hee hee' instead of laughter. His way with Shakespeare's writing was calculating, as though he was counting every iamb in every pentameter, a meter reader. How pleased he was with his first 'performance', putting down Feste! How crushed by Olivia's rebuke ('sick of self-love')! How jolted by the poke in the stomach his mistress gave him, as though 1000 volts had shot through him! How pretentious, chasing after the 'peevish boy' who'd left an unwanted ring, driving the 'For Management's Use Only' motorized service buggy. And how utterly, painfully ludicrous, the vision of him in yellow pvc stockings, S/M black leather braces (exposing girly nipples), posing pouch (with lots of Malvolio bulging over the sides) – and suit jacket. It wasn't a pretty sight. And the visual gag, Malvolio descending by the lift, played for a long, long, long time. More humiliating was the exit: crawling up the stairs (by now the cross-gartering had cut off all blood to his feet), exposing behind lardy, wobbling, leprously white naked buttocks.

At the end, his entrance stopped cold the hot, raunchy rave-up disco dancing (that had Olivia straddling Stephan Hagan's dishy Sebastian). Malvolio was barefoot. Barechested. His toupee on backwards. He was furious – but righteous: 'You can say *none* of this.' He swung his head in indignant 'No!' as Olivia explained – until the penny dropped. He froze. Silence. The revenge he promised was vitriolic. There was no indulgence at the end – though you got the feeling that Olivia knew what it felt to be as humiliated as he'd been and would find repair. There was just Feste's simple song, sung straight to the audience with his keyboard on his knee – about rain and the 'every day'.

Completing the 'Shipwreck Trilogy', Amir Nizar Zuabi's *Comedy of Errors*, set in a grim shipping warehouse stacked with containers where some of the import/export traffic was human, had Antipholus/Syracuse (Jonathan McGuinness) and his Dromio (Bruce Mackinnon) jimmied out of a wooden crate by a shadow-hugging Merchant (Kevin McMonagle) who, shoving money and passports into their dazed hands, made it clear in furtive whispers how dangerous it was for foreigners in Ephesus. Really? Surely we were in comic territory! Because as he scuttled off, the warehouse sprang into bizarre life as 'The Mart'. The lid on a crate in the background lifted an inch. Bug-eyes looked out. The top came off. A black man in traditional Nigerian dress climbed out. Took stock. Eye-balled the flummoxed Syracuseans. Dashed off. Noise. They swivelled. To see *another* stowaway emerge from the box. And another – a whole tribe of them, like rabbits out of a hat. The last was festooned with the kind of cheap football jerseys and fake designer handbags that the touts-out-of-Africa peddle on the Rialto in Venice.

But despite the hilarity of this gag, and the periodic swerves this production made into Goons slapstick, the director clearly wanted his *Comedy* to do much darker work, to investigate the brutality of people-trafficking and the plight of refugees in flight from murderous despots who land in even more brutal totalitarian regimes. So Ephesus was an Athens-under-the-generals police state, not full of mountebanks and cozeners, but AK-47 toting thugs (Solomon Israel, Amer Hlehel) in dark glasses who patrolled streets that were governed by a psychopath Solinus (Sandy Grierson, not so much a different performance as a different actor, from his Ariel) whose opening line, spoken down a publicity-seeking microphone – 'Merchant of Syracuse, plead no more' – was a sick joke, given that, at that moment, Egeon's head was being held underwater. The long opening backstory was delivered between bouts of waterboarding – a huge aquarium centre stage (another black joke) standing proxy for the sea that had swallowed Egeon's lads.

This production was 'torture comedy'. The interval came as Antipholus/Syracuse, determining 'I'll be straight away', looked round to see a gang of black-robed hooded figures (medieval flagellists, or KKK men) in front of gun-slinging police frogmarching the Nigerian stowaway towards arrest, then forcing him to his knees, putting a gun to his head, laughing, offering the gun to Antipholus (who stood paralysed in terror), then swinging it back to their victim's head. Blackout. Later, en route through Ephesus to Shakespeare's comic ending, Solinus would be presented an object wrapped in the kind of black plastic farmers use for silage. A single foot would protrude. The Nigerian's. The body bag would be hung up, by the ankle, on a meat hook; a trophy picture taken, with Governor Solinus beside it beaming as the photographer's bulbs popped.

But torture isn't funny. And its use as 'entertainment' here made me politically deeply angry (smoke coming out of my ears, not how I normally drive home from The Comedy of Errors). Because the other half of this production was farce: cupcake-in-the-face jokes with a shrieking Adriana (Kirsty Bushell) and prissy Luciana (Emily Taaffe) and chase scenes with an 'aren't-fat-girls-funny' Nell (Sarah Belcher) wielding a giant, phallic courgette. (A scenario made grotesque by its object, Felix Hayes's Dromio/Ephesus, who had the speech and gestures of a retarded child – the joke being that he had the sexual instincts historically attributed to the idiot? Some joke.) But poor Sandy Grierson. He

must have got whiplash every performance doing that reversal at the end that volte-faced his General Gaddafi Solinus into Father Christmas!

One (limited) pleasure of this Comedy, however, was watching the theatre machinery operate. The thing stretched diagonally above the playing space that I thought looked like the arm of an industrial crane ('decoration' in the other two plays) finally here earned its keep. As an industrial crane. It delivered the shipping crates centre stage. Also the 'domestic interiors'. The Antipholus household – a fully furnished and peopled open-sided platform – was swung into place like cargo trussed up in longshoreman's chains. If just watching it made my stomach flip-flop, I wonder how the actors on board the flying apparatus felt.

Production gimmickry was high on the list of attractions in the National Theatre Comedy of Errors, too. If this was Dominic Cooke's bid for the NT's top job, he clearly wanted to demonstrate that he knew how to use the theatre's toys – all of them. Ephesus was a world in constant motion, the Olivier stage's two rim revolves keeping things moving. The opening scene (Cooke's production opened long before Zuabi's, both coincidentally quoting images that could have come from The Wire) was set around grey, rusting, dripping dockland warehouses, the kind you walk past on your way from London Bridge Station down the South Bank; Solinus (Ian Burfield) was a bad-ass thug; his 'minders', sloping, sneering toughs munching curling sandwiches as Egeon (a heart-rending performance by Joseph Mydell) began his story, which was going to end in a gangland rub-out.

Then, mid-narrative, the action exploded. 'History', the back-story, came to life. Enter Egeon's young African self. Enter his young African bride. Enter their 'baby' twins, made out of her head wrap. Enter the poor couple – their babies, rags; their adoption by 'rich' Egeon a moment of utter poignancy as, handed over, the lengths of cloth unravelled, emptied out, in the poor woman's arms. Then the storm cracked; the three storeys of the warehouse became a giant climbing frame for people fleeing disaster; a helicopter hovered overhead, bungling the rescue, winching only half the family to safety. End of narrative. Revolve. Giving 'Downtown Ephesus', the façade of a street cafe. Revolve. Giving 'The Phoenix', aka chez Antipholus, a flash apartment between two tottering decayed tenements, where Luciana and Adriana foot-tapped impatiently on the balcony amongst potted plants. Revolve. Shop fronts – some of them knocking shops. Revolve. Pool Hall. Revolve. Harley Street clinic door (doubling as the nunnery). Not just teeming with activity (there would be a chase scene involving an ambulance crossing the stage), this Ephesus was teeming with *people*. Last year Propeller played *Comedy* with fourteen actors; this company doubled that, and featured a perambulating street band (with accordion) sound-mixing Ephesus into a mash-up of east and west by singing British pop in Romanian.

So there was plenty of visual interest. But very little laughter – the audience simply not struck on the funny bone by the zany absurdity of what they were watching (nor, indeed, heart-cracked by the loss-making effort of the plot). And I think that was because this *Comedy* never hit a comic rhythm: the problem with all the 'production' was that actors had to move at the pace of the machinery; the machinery simply couldn't keep up with them – or what Shakespeare's manic pace sets in motion *after* Egeon's grief-frozen back-story. That said, Lenny Henry's wide-eyed, Nigerian-accented, straight-off-the-boat-from-darkest-Africa Antipholus, with his stocky, football-jerseyed side-kick Dromio (Lucian Msamati), were a terrific double act, entirely convincing, big eyes *even bigger*, being 'spooked', and using a hilarious homebred voodoo routine to ward off the local 'witches', who were actually rent-boys and prozzies. (I wondered though: wouldn't Adriana have noticed that her husband, between breakfast and dinner, had experienced a voice transplant? *Nobody* in Ephesus talked 'l-daht'!) Henry is one of the UK's best-loved stand-up comics, his initiation into Shakespeare via *Othello* in 2009 a revelation shown here not to be a one-performance wonder. Constantly inventive physically – and he's a big man, so his gestures read to the back of the auditorium – he played

Antipholus/Syracuse as an open-faced naif. He had no idea he'd landed in the city's red light district; that the latest to 'salute' him – wonder! – 'As if I were a well-acquainted friend' (a six-footer in platform high heels and PVC miniskirt) was the street's transsexual touting for work.

Equally good was the parallel double act of Adriana (Claudie Blakley) and Luciana (Michelle Terry), a pair of bottle-blonde Essex imports marooned in Villa Bling who weren't going to put up with men behaving badly without a fight. The leap Blakley's Adriana made onto the pool table (having tracked her wayward husband down to that address) in her seven-inch stilettos, skidding across the baize to immobilize the wrong man as she grabbed his crotch, had every man in the theatre groaning. How could you do that to *a pool table*?

Back at the RSC and outside the 'Shipwreck Trilogy', Roxana Silbert directed in the Swan a best-forgotten Star-Wars-Meets-Bondage-Beds-R-Us *Measure for Measure* that dressed Raymond Coulthard's Duke as Captain Kirk and had Mrs Overdone (Annette McLaughlin) as a sleazy dominatrix running a kinky sex joint where men undressed to thongs (Paul Chahidi's Lucio looking overwhelmed with embarrassment) had to squeal orgasmically through 1.2 as their bottoms were smacked ('If the duke [thwack] with the other dukes [thwack] come not to composition with the Duke of Hungary... [thwack, thwack, "eeeeeh!"]'). This was a production I'd guess the excellent Jamie Ballard (Angelo) and Jodie McNee (Isabella), both wasted here, won't be admitting on their CVs. He was made into a 'mini-me' version of the Duke, same space uniform, leather belt suggesting bondage corset; she, quite painfully ugly – so no 'wimple fantasy' here, rather, a frump in a shapeless dress and tight headscarf that scraped back her hair, accentuating her hooked nose, while her working hands, demonstrating the ecstatic/obsessive quality of her speech, pawed the air like claws or clasped themselves in the kind of poses tortured saints strike in martyr portraiture.

Silbert's 'ideas' were either textually crude (tarts doubling nuns; a joke resurrection, the Duke popping up out of a coffin carried in a funeral procession by comic-gothic hooded monks) or gob-smacking in their theatrical crassness. Two of her actors actually came on stage and played a pair of lamps, magically turned on when the Duke snapped his fingers; and one later returned as a garden fountain – running with water.

Coulthard's Duke was Paul Daniels reimagined for panto: mugging the audience as he did sleight-of-hand tricks that pulled commissions out of thin air, warrants from up his sleeve, switched invisible sound systems on and off. But if he could do magic, why not just 'magic' a clean-up of Vienna? Why go through the charade of seeing 'what our seemers be'? (The answer to that gave us a retro-reading of *Measure*, a reading I thought died out forty years ago: that *Measure* is all the omniscient Duke's show, all a test, that's he's always in control, pulling the strings.) The worst of the waste of such fine actors as Ballard, McNee and Chahidi was that they'd come to this *Measure* straight from *Written on the Heart*, commissioned by the RSC for the Swan from David Edgar to celebrate the quatercentenary of the King James Bible, a play built on theological argument, doctrinal hair-splitting, debate-to-the-death over lexical minutiae, the politics of 'the word' and its translation, performed as a series of heads-to-heads. These actors had been in training, were *ready* for what Shakespeare gives them in *Measure*. And Silbert evidently had not a clue what the play was about.

Equally disastrous was the experiment in arranged marriages that brought together the Wooster Group (cast as Trojans) and the RSC (Greeks) to produce a *Troilus and Cressida* that by anybody's reckoning was a grotesque misalliance. Left high and dry by Rupert Goold who abandoned the project some days before rehearsals were due to begin, the RSC company, let by Scott Handy (Ulysses) very sensibly, it appears, went for survival rather than suicide, and borrowed a past production off the shelf. They quoted liberally from Cheek by Jowl's 2008 *Troilus* (Handy a former CbyJ boy), then pushed CbyJ's irreverence much further. So Handy was Ryan Kiggell's wire-rim spectacled Ulysses, but wearing Kiggell's air of

diffidence like full-body armour, who, offering the 'Order' speech, took the biggest political risk of his life; ending it, collapsed in a panic attack, sucking his inhaler. Zubin Varla's Thersites was Richard Cant's transvestite Captain Klinger-reimagined-by-Noel-Fielding, now a double amputee (faking it) in a wheelchair, a long-wigged raver whose mini-skirt kept flashing the manhood it was too short to cover (and who'd speak his final speech as he defiantly stripped himself naked, dumping his 'uniform', exiting the play AWOL, head high, prim, pushing his wheelchair). Aidan Kelly's Ajax, crashing around in big boots, was a doltish muscle-bound roaring boy in a tattooed latex body suit that bulked out his six-pack like a kid's plastic 'Hulk' toy. Joe Dixon's Achilles, a languishing narcissist, was always just out of the sauna, on a masseur's gurney – until he appeared in a whore-red dress. (Why? The borrowed in this production may momentarily have saved actors' lives; ultimately, nevertheless, it was deadly.)

The American half of this *Troilus* had the Wooster Group exhibiting their trademark practice: actors miked up (their voices not just amplified but their earpieces conducting a competitive soundtrack into their heads); TV monitors elevated over the corners of the stage playing alternative narratives that actors' eyes were glued to, their automaton-like gestures prompted by, responding to the film; a flat-toned delivery that, by comparison, would make a ticker-tape machine sound interesting; and a design conceit that patched together cultural ideas into an obscene cartoon: here, disintegrating clichés of nostalgic American self reference. The 'Trojans' were Native Americans, as much cultural constructs as 'Indians', mythologized human artifacts evidently trapped in an image of what the future would say about them. So there was a tepee on stage, like a post-modern survivor from reservation days (clearly fake: waste materials held together with bulldog clips) surrounded by plastic junk (an office chair on castors), stereotypical stuff (a wagon wheel, dream catchers, lacrosse sticks), fakery (a mobile campfire).

I tried to meet this production on its own terms: to appreciate the gimmicks as an actorly methodology for 'presence-ing' performance, for being always in the moment, for breaking apart theatrical 'naturalism', to see the theatrical 'event' not as product but evolving 'project', and ourselves not as spectators watching a realized performance but participants in public rehearsal.

But I failed. My American childhood kept getting in the way. I found Wooster's white boys (ostentatiously 'pale faces') playing Indians politically obnoxious. Of course, their 'buckskin' leggings, their straight black wigs (one actor was bald-domed in a latex wig, as though he'd been scalped, another was in 'squaw' plaits), their gunked-up gum-boots were spectacularly fake, made of styrofoam, latex and plastic. So no doubt I was meant to read the stage with a sense of post-modern irony: to see two doomed cultures, both loaded with memorial 'trash', in conversation with each other across the millennia; white boys playing with identity, trying to interrogate stereotypes inherited from their national, mythologized past. For me it didn't work. I heard their voices as though learned from reruns of *The Lone Ranger*, where the side-kick, called Tonto ('Stupid'), the magnificent Jay Silverstone, ran the whole role on one line, 'Huh, Kimosabe'. If these Wooster lads need to work on their inherited guilt and anxieties they should find another vehicle than Shakespeare. He's too big for their footling-ness.

One design detail did hit the mark. Where plains Indians would have worn on their backs animal hides as trophies, the heads (buck, buffalo, bear) giving them their Apache names, these Trojans carried around latex 'skins' of slaughtered Greeks. The classically-shaped dead heads were bound Janus-wise, to their own, so the live/dead faces looked in opposite directions. Ironically, then, the Trojans became human plinths supporting Greek sculpture, their 'trophies' the dead weight of the invader's culture. That said, given the relentless ugliness of what I was looking at, I found the self-satisfied claim in the programme – that the designer's primary material, styrofoam, would 'never decompose' – utterly depressing.

Another RSC experiment had slightly better success. Transporting Messina to modern Delhi and employing a full Asian cast led by television star Meera Syal of *The Kumars* (Beatrice) and Paul Bhattacharjee (Benedick), Iqbal Khan directed a post-colonial *Much Ado about Nothing* that made sense of the play's military discourse in terms of contemporary India's international peace-keeping deployments. Equally, Tom Piper's set, a traditional, balconyed two-storey stucco Delhi house, brilliantly established the play's 'upstairs/downstairs' structure. Above, lived Leonato's household: thoroughly modern Hero (Amara Karan) and Margaret (Chetna Pandya), girls in skin-tight jeans and sassy hair-dos who came in laden with purchases from high-fashion outlets. Below, literally holding up the new Indian elite, in traditional dress, and spilling out into the yard under a massive banyan tree, cooking, plaiting hair, pounding washing, remainders from colonial rule, were Dogberry's household (Simon Nagra), husband to the cross-cast Verges (Bharti Patel), who hilariously drilled her underlings like some aspirational subaltern trained on B-grade movies. Here, dhobi-wallahs met mobile phones. (Secretly, though, I was disappointed, when they appeared, that Dogberry and the Watch weren't Tusker et al. from *Staying On*, ex-pat leftovers of the British Raj who might have neatly reversed John Barton's casting of the gormless crew from 1976: no doubt an in-joke too far.)

The problem with this production was that Khan wasn't much interested in Shakespeare's writing, what he referred to in rehearsal (I had this from more than one actor) as 'that lyrical shit'. Mostly, then, dialogue went for nothing, there being almost no spark between Syal's chain-smoking Beatrice and Bhattacharjee's winningly bookish Benedick (who kept blurting out truths before he could stop them). Instead, Khan created alternative performance narratives – like the one played out while a Bollywood version 'Sigh No More' was sung. Tiny Anjana Vasan, credited as 'Maid' but acting like Balthasar's (Raj Bajaj) kid sister, was shoved, resisting, into the centre of the song, presented as dance partner to Sagar Arya's Claudio. But then, like kids do, she not only got into the swing of things, she started making an exhibition of

33. *The Taming of the Shrew*, 3.3, RSC, Royal Shakespeare Theatre, directed by Lucy Bailey. Lisa Dillon as Kate, David Rintoul as Gremio, Sam Swainsbury as Hortensio.

herself. Claudio backed off, disconcerted. Big-brother Balthasar finally dragged her away, threw her to the ground, shamed her: so, a prolep-tic stand-in for Hero. She continued, throughout the rest of the eavesdropping scene, to pull focus, her 'business' downstage in the competitive nar-rative much more fascinating than anything poor Benedick was doing, hiding on the balcony. Not only did this sort of thing distract, it added *days* to the production – which ran 3.5 hours when I first saw it.

One big point was brilliantly made by Khan's concept. When thoroughly modern Hero entered, as from 2012, to be married, she had been cap-tured for 1812. She appeared covered: in scar-let, silver-embroidered wedding sari, veil, laden with head-dress, bangles, rings, gold, an exhi-bition of tradition walking into patriarchy's self-legitimating ritual. The stakes could not have been

more spectacularly on show, the reversal – 'give not this rotten orange to your friend' – more appallingly, misogynistically brutal.

In Khan's Messina, misogyny shocked because it felt like a great gob of poisonous phlegm hawked up and spat into Hero's lovely face. In the Padua of Lucy Bailey's *Taming of the Shrew* it was the standard demotic, as unremarkable as spit on the pavement. But because Bailey contrived to make Kate's town both 'real' and 'dream' space, she found a way for spit to function (also) as love juice.

The stage (designed by Ruth Sutcliffe) was made up like a male supremacist's fantasy, as a gigantic, lumpy bed, covered with a brown canvas sheet, enormous bolsters sprawling its width and floor-to-ceiling hangings behind, a bed that would function as battleground and wrestling mat and make for hilarious under-cover chases, but that would also double (the headboard – as in a dream – transformed: the hangings parting to reveal ancient oak-panelled city gates; the pillows becoming stones; the sheets, a dusty road leading into Padua) as a sun-drenched public piazza where crowds gathered for gossip and local viewing of notorious spectacles. The pre-show acoustic set us in 1940s Italy, with a sexy, playful *Godfather* backing track, its instruments – clarinet (Dai Pritchard), accordion (Maurizio Minardi), mandolin (George Hadjineopyhtou), trumpet (Andrew Stone-Fewings), euphonium (Richard Henry), percussion (James Jones) – composing the town band that would give the down-at-heel loungers who'd later be hanging around the hot noonday piazza, the jeerers and leerers, the finger pointers, something to do.

The production's first beat, however, was a dark sequence from nightmare. A burst of activity behind the backlit bed-hangings showed giant shadows lurching drunkenly across the bar of a public house in an uproar of inebriated noise. Then Sly (Nick Holder) spilled out – a human hog, slovenly, obese, grunting – with the Landlady (Aicha Kossoko) right behind him, a honking Black Maria of a female, hair piled up 40s-style, with menacing hips and mouth wide enough to out-talk any tinker, who, when he toppled into his alcohol coma, bared what nightmare produced as canine fangs, the rest of her clientele swarming out to join her, savaging the fallen Sly like hounds that the Lord (a peasant landowner, Italian-style), entering in the nick of time, had his men (pleated trousers, flat caps, white shirts, braces, broken shot-guns) haul off. So this production's violence was imagined from the first. It was pack activity, bestial, human. Here, the shrew would be just one exhibit in a local zoo managed by handlers who knew how to break stubborn beasts – and how to kill to eat.

And what a zoo! Gavin Fowler's Lucentio, a preppie, book-clutching geek in horn-rimmed spectacles, was breathless with excitement, literally spinning with anticipation arriving at the university (his wide-boy, greaseball Tranio (John Marquez) with his Bronx/Bergamo accent, distinctly less so). Lucentio's first encounter with the locals, however,

left him gawping (and in a love-spin). A procession entered, led by an acolyte swinging incense, a priest, Baptista (Terence Wilton), meticulously dressed in a sharp suit, the padrone, but hunched, bewildered by humiliation; Bianca (Elizabeth Cadwallader), dripping with yellow curls and saccharine smiles, in front of a tiny, bare foot woman in black, her hair looking like pigeons nested there, yoked in a scold's fiddle. Kate (Lisa Dillon) performed her penance silently, sweet piety, gazed at by the town: David Rintoul's out-of-Jonson foxy, posturing Gremio (side-parted hair plastered to skull, pencil moustache), Sam Swainsbury's permanently baffled Hortensio (a beautiful performance that held the slapstick centre of this production together). But once the fiddle was lifted, Dillon's Kate grabbed it, turned it on the crowd, swung it like a scythe mowing down men who jumped for cover. Their impotence, falling all over each other, was comic; her rage, fierce, ugly, restless; their obvious inability to control her, serious. This Kate was a sociopath in a town too small to give a sociopath any place to hide.

She was also capable of nasty abuse. At the top of 2.1, she stepped through the city pedestrian gate, lounged against the wall like a tart awaiting custom, swigged from her hip flask, lit a fag. Her hair was still a mare's nest. Bianca struggled out – mouth gob-stopped pig-wise with an apple, cheeks painted in livid red circles, her top lip graffiti-ed with a moustache. Her hands and feet were bound, so she tripped over the gate's threshold, rolled down the street, hopped across the piazza begging for mercy. The performance was hilarious – but also hurt; and Kate, hatchet-faced, dragging on that fag, gave Bianca no quarter.

When Dillon's Kate met her match in Petruchio (David Caves), I never doubted she could hold her own. He was a man made to her violent measure, who head-butted his servant then used him as a human battering ram; as rangy and raw-boned as an Irish wolf-hound that looked like it had been sleeping rough with Grumio (Simon Gregor). They were an improbable couple, the longshanks master dressed out of some 1940s charity shop reject pile; the servant, a Fellini grotesque with rubber lips and a collapsible face, a mini-Hercules, spoiling for a fight. Their brutish parallel play to Kate's sisterly knockabout (and the same ludicrous discrepancy in size) set up the terms of the wooing. She'd been thrown out the gate – which slammed behind her and refused to open when she stood there banging on it. So she took up her characteristic position, sullen, silent, fag in hand. Meanwhile, he'd turned, clapped eyes on her, and caught his breath on a 'Whoooaaa' that measured a heart-stopping missed beat – not 'in lurrrrve' but utterly intrigued by the hardcore hostility facing him – before launching into 'Good morrow, Kate'. His Irish accent made 'Kate' both a joke and menacing. When he insulted her with a crude gag, she walloped him. He responded with a balled fist and a punch only just pulled. When he off-loaded the news that 'will you, nill you, I will marry you', she planted her feet as wide as her pencil skirt would allow, and pissed a long stream of contempt. Open-mouthed, Petruchio was *thrilled*. The audacity of it! And they kept raising the ante on each other: Petruchio showing up to the wedding stripped to the waist, in Dionysiac grape-cluster codpiece, graffiti-ed 'Kate + Petruchio' across his back; she (no advance on the hair, still chain-smoking) flattening the locals against the city walls with her roar 'I WILL BE ANGRY'; he sweeping her up, all macho protection, arms pinned to her sides – 'Fear not sweet wench, they shall not touch thee' – enveloping her in something that looked awfully like a salted horsehide, and galloping her off over his shoulder to married life.

The miracle was that this married couple actually found a shared space to be married. She spent her time in his wreck of a household in her wrecked linen wedding suit and a pair of dingy drooping socks evidently borrowed from one of the men. Watching. Listening. As little 'persuaded' by Petruchio's aspirational programme ('He that knows better how to tame a shrew . . .') as we in the audience. Still, she was intrigued – an echo of him earlier – by the gorgeous song her husband sang for her. For this Kate and Petruchio, the road home sun/moon episode was no big 'brain change' moment. She wasn't cowed. Didn't

capitulate. Instead, still raging, she connected to a Petruchio willing to take her, and whatever she brought, take whatever 'shame' she felt, and have her 'lay it on [him]'. Given that astonishing generosity, who cared what you called 'it'? These two arrived home wearing the taming visibly upon them, both (still) wrecked, nothing resolved. The wager was the biggest gamble of Petruchio's life, a 'win' that, right until the end, looked like the opposite. For Kate gave her big speech smoking yet another fag, not pretty, not haloed in an aura of light. Not transformed. But somehow *informed*. Somehow recognizing something – that registered when she dumped the fag into spluttering Hortensio's champagne, leaving her hand free to open to offer her husband. Petruchio was the one transformed by wonder: kneeling, taking her hand. Fast married.

Then the pair of them exploded into action, made a dash for the door, and beyond it, to BED, tearing off each other's clothes. A little while hence, under cover of a lighting change, it would be groaning Sly who'd wake to stagger home to bed. But in the 'real' space of dream, we knew Kate and Petruchio were somewhere tangling the sheets – and the image satisfied. The bed that troped a town might just be big enough for this pair.

After this big-hearted, ballsy and unsentimental *Shrew* that showed Lucy Bailey gloriously back on form, the Globe's *Shrew* this season (directed by Toby Frow) needs to be noticed only as potboiler Shakespeare: a crowd-pleaser in early modern dress (except for the stupendous mistake, in period costume terms – if the production sets up those rules, doesn't it have to play by them? – of Simon Paisley Day's Petruchio turning up to his wedding in striped slops, tumescent codpiece, and bare-assed naked buttocks showing scrawny flanks). Samantha Spiro's Kate was conventionally pretty, conventionally feisty; Paisley Day (first playing drunken Sly of the Induction, in modern sports gear staggering through the yard howling abuse before passing out on stage) was conventionally disgusting – and, conventionally, he doubled Petruchio. There were conventional jokes (Sly pissing on the stage pillar;

a depressive Eeyore of a Grumio (Pearce Quigley), regularly kicking a bucket). And a deeply conservative reading that had the oddball pugilists falling in love at first sight and the audience bursting into applause at the end when Kate, prostrating herself, offered not just her hand but her whole body beneath her husband's foot. Still, there was excellent supporting work here from Joseph Timms, a deliciously dopey Lucentio, locked like a heat-seeking missile onto his inevitable pratfall, and from Jamie Beamish, producing here much more disciplined work than last year's at the RSC, a Tranio with dangerous eyeballs and a trick of hitching up his lip till it met his nostril.

While the RSC was busy, in only its second season in its new theatre, using comedy to figure out the workings of their thrust stage (and discovering, for instance, its design limits, like the fact that spectators in the side galleries couldn't have had a clue what was going on in Prospero's 'magic box' or Olivia's 'dream bedroom' because they couldn't see them), other companies were doing what they do best, making big impacts with limited means. Two of my favourite stage images this year came out of Northern Broadsides' touring production of *Love's Labour's Lost* (director: Barrie Rutter; designer: Jessica Worrall). The first had Navarre (Owen Findlay) arriving in a space bathed in golden light set minimalistically with four yellow wooden curved benches, a music stand holding what was clearly a hefty legal document, an industrial hand-trolley piled high with fat, leather-bound tomes, behind him, at the exits, tree branches (providing the sense that he'd come to a space carved out of woods, like the bottom of a chestnut walk where the gardener had arranged a place for conversation or restful poetry). Navarre was carrying a cello. Which he proceeded to straddle and play. Wobblingly – a delightful enacted metaphor for the earnestness, the high-mindedness of his tutorial aspiration, no less than its chasteness: the cello the only 'girl' who'd be coming between his legs for the next three years. But also a suggestion of how far his academicians had to go before they'd ever get close to anything like a Grade 8 certificate in music *or* philosophy. The second stage image simply had

Matt Connor's Berowne in the overhearing scene perched up a vintage ladder, inches from love-turned-inside-out Navarre's rapturous trial reading of the homework he'd set himself on his new, alternative syllabus.

Mostly audiences can hum along with over-familiar Shakespeare scripts. *Love's Labour's Lost's* is one we have to listen to. Hard. It's built on long, poetic periods (Berowne's 'I forsooth in love' doesn't take breath for fifteen lines), stuffed with rhyming couplets, 'flowers of fancy...jerks of invention', and in-jokes for an in-crowd. (Though Shakespeare, presciently, wrote a line for the future, and for the 'out-crowd'. Roy North's Dull, in Yorkshire bobby's uniform, as taciturn as a plate of mushy peas, paused half-a-beat behind Holofernes (Barrie Rutter, as officious as a Bradford town clerk), fussily rebuking him: 'Thou hast spoken no word all this while!' 'Nor', Dull replied, 'understood none neither'. Broadsides' first night audience reacted with a corporate yelp and spontaneous applause.)

The joy of this production was that it savoured this 'pedantic' writing (while leaving it to the audience's ears to hear Shakespeare's simultaneous satire on a 'feast' that would bloat Gargantua). It found a visual analogue to the verbal stylishness in Worrall's ravishingly stylish Noel-meets-Gertie 1930 costumes – slinky satins in royal blue, emerald, flame red, eau-de-nil, bias-cut gowns, halter dresses, jumpsuits, padded (or bare) shoulders for the women; for the men, saddle brogues and sharp Leeds-tailored three-piece suits, pockets stuffed with silk handkerchiefs whose colours predicted their mating games. And as the lads (Jos Vantyler/Longaville; Kelsey Brookfield/Dumaine with Connor and Findlay) played the space like an up-market baiting-ring-cum-chess-board, posturing against the encircling walls, or ricocheting off them like national league ice hockey players smacking against bumpers, leaping onto the benches, later hiding behind them then exposed as they slid balletically away, so they played with Shakespeare's verse. Characteristically for this company, the Yorkshire voice was the 'artless'-sounding instrument for punching out artful couplets like 'O,

34. *Love's Labour's Lost*, 4.3, Northern Broadsides, New Vic Theatre, directed by Barrie Rutter. Owen Findlay as King, Matt Connor as Berowne, Jos Vantyler as Longaville.

what a scene of foolery have I seen, / Of sighs, of groans, of sorrow and of teen.'

Backing the glittering (and gormless) toffs were a second-eleven that widened the angle on male dopeyness: huge, permanently gaping Costard (Adam Fogarty) in clodhopper boots, trousers the size of a circus tent belted with a girth strap for a Clydesdale; simpering Boyet (Andy Cryer) with his precise fingers, patent leather hair and silly moustache; Armado (Andrew Vincent), a strutting piece of Toledo steel turned (by love) bent bow; his sidekick, Moth (Dean Whatton), half his size and hilarious as Hercules strangling – and *strangling* – the snake; Holofernes visibly recoiling, stung, hearing bad Latin.

The women (Princess/Sophia Hatfield; Rosaline/Catherine Kinsella; Maria/Hester Arden; Katherine/Rebecca Hutchinson) simply ran rings around the lot of them. Beautifully arch, with a superior tilt to the chin and an out-riposting habit of answer, Hatfield's Princess's iciness nevertheless pointed to a defrost button that any moment could switch on. Equally, Kinsella's pertness, her mockery as Rosaline was as without edge or sarcasm as Berowne's was, outing his friends. Still, the women were the ones to hold the male project of 'love's labours' seriously to account. Navarre's assignment to Berowne to come up with some 'proof' that 'Our loving [is] lawful and our faith not torn' was an exercise in the perversion of learning, producing rhetorical invention to make good heresy, to legitimate the breaking of vows. What kind of scholars *were* they in this 'academe'? Clearly, boys behaving badly who'd earn Holofernes-as-Judas-Maccabeus's show-stoppingly hurt rebuke on their wisecracking interruption of the 'Nine Worthies': 'This is not generous. Not gentle. Not humble'. Clearly, they were ones the women needed to take in hand, to put to the test, to teach their alternative (female) syllabus. Perjury in men isn't acceptable. And word games may flourish in tutorials – but not in real life. They can't underpin a 'world without end bargain'. Ending unresolved, this *Love's Labour's Lost* nevertheless ended with glorious harmony, the full company's voices, first solo, then layering

on top of each other, singing of 'daisies pied and violets blue'. But it also ended with a celebration of the company, this, Broadsides' twentieth year producing some of the most robust Shakespeare anywhere on offer, by guest-casting Mercade, the spoiler who comes on with death notices at the end, everywhere they toured, with a local veteran Broadsider, brought on in a cameo for the night.

The images that stuck in my mind from Broadsides' *Love's Labour's Lost* were in tight focus, close-ups capturing character. There were plenty of those in Terry Hands's Theatr Clwyd *As You Like It*, too, but the picture that really stuck from that production was both epic and visually beguiling. It caught the location change from Court to Arden, rendering architecturally a thought-shift that transported exiles (and spectators) across a landscape of the mind.

The opening scenes were set in a tight black-and-silver space (designed by Mark Bailey) that felt elegantly, neoclassically French. A narrow verge of black floorboards ran the width of the forestage. Along it, an avenue of silver columns, suggesting a Louis Quinze orangery, perhaps, was backed with floor to ceiling sweeps of white gauze drapes. The effect was austere, formal, artificial: a feeling of interior space placed out-of-doors. Menacing, too. Lit from above, the columns cast deep shadows that dropped the pillars across the ground in black gashes, like wounds. This horizontal strip was Orlando's whole world, and Alex Felton made him a gangling, tousle-haired lad paralysed not by ambition, by talents wasted, but by grief for a father dead, one sensed, not years but *days*. Even when he got his big brother in a headlock (Daniel Hawksford; dressed like Thomas Jefferson in black frock coat, periwig, tricorn hat; radiating hauteur across the word games – 'make you'/'mar you' – he inflicted), it wasn't because he wanted to hurt him but because he wanted to make him listen. This same strip marked the Court limits of Celia (Antonia Kinlay) and Rosalind's (Hedydd Dylan) world: cousins in mourning black, the kind of huge-skirted, cinch-waisted dresses that squeeze the air (and protest) out of a woman's lungs; performing aimlessness, Rosalind threading the columns,

35. *As You Like It*, 1.2, Clwyd Theatr Cymru, Hopkins Theatre, directed by Terry Hands. Alex Felton as Orlando, Kai Owen as Charles. Behind: Michael Geary as Le Beau, Dyfrig Morris as Duke Frederick, Hedydd Dylan as Rosalind, Antonia Kinlay as Celia, Christian Patterson as Touchstone.

searching vacancy; Celia right behind; their word games, antidotes to depression, interrupted by a parade of Dickensian grotesques. Christian Patterson was a Touchstone of Falstaffian girth, the black-and-silver diamond pattern on his waistcoat scaled to the size of floor covering. Beside him, Michael Geary's diminutive frockcoated Le Beau was like something ornithological that you'd hang on a Christmas tree: a pouter pigeon who hopped with little balletic moves; who had jelly roll curls across his head anchored at the nape of his neck with a floppy bow; who, helping Orlando into his jacket after the disastrous triumph of the wrestling, gave his advice conspiratorially, cheeks puffing; who later took the hint to flee the court. Shrugging off accusations of conspiracy, he'd been lifted off his mincing feet and shaken silly by the enraged duke. (He'd arrive in Arden minus

festooned coat but in wildly unsensible shoes.) Played against the flat screen surface of the opening design, performances embodying such narrative density as these constantly suggested a 3-D world – that was actually revealed when the drapes flew out and we were looking deep into darkish Arden, where snow patched the ground, at bare trees glazed silver in misty light, the 'natural' equivalent of the black-and-silver Court and literally framed by that Court. Because for some long seconds, before the columns, too, flew out, spectators had to 'see' Arden through the Court's structures, 'liberty', 'banishment', freedom, repression nicely superimposed.

If that image problematized any easy difference between Court and Country, still, in Arden, they did things differently. It wasn't just the delight in silliness, the way, for instance, having arrived

36. *As You Like It*, 2.1, Clwyd Theatr Cymru, Hopkins Theatre, directed by Terry Hands. Daniel Hawksford as First Lord, Robert Blythe as Duke Senior, (behind) Kai Owen as Forester, and Paul Morgans as Amiens.

hauling not just all the luggage but Celia on his back, Touchstone unceremoniously dumped the lot, only (with his first free step) to tread in something objectionable (a hoary gag), but then – a new joke – to reach out and find something to hand to wipe his shoe, a bit of paper (*paper*? Touchstone didn't miss a beat) stuck on a tree. Or the way that the 'real' shepherds, Silvius (Sion Pritchard) and Phoebe (Katie Elin-Salt), were fantastic figures off French porcelain. Or the way the rage-sweating, hyperactive, mountainous Duke Frederick (Dyfrig Morris) resurfaced, at half-speed, in Arden as a very 'special' William, a great big lubberly lad in a rustic smock who, instructed to put on the hat he held in his hand, followed its journey through the air, gazing upward like a turkey feeling rain, and nearly toppling over backwards; or reaching desiring arms for Audrey (Elin Phillips) in slow motion managed always to close them on empty air.

It was the way Arden embraced its own sententiousness – was unafraid, in 'nature', of artifice – that gave the verse, Arden's 'native' speech, currency. So Daniel Hawksford (metamorphosed Forest Lord) made the account of the sobbing deer, so often a distracted anthology piece, wonderfully urgent reportage. And Philip Bretherton, unlike so many Jaques of recent memory (who've treated it like some geriatric celebrity kinsman, now in his dotage, that they're embarrassed to introduce) made each of the men in the 'Seven Ages' both visible and accountable: men you could *see*, men you'd want to talk to, to question.

This was the most complete account of *As You Like It* I've seen in years, the central couple, utterly winning, playful, making the poetry of the wooing *happen*, the supporting parts cameos fitting together like facets on a crystal. It showed me something I'd never seen before, the way

Touchstone's riff on poetry ('if a hart do lack a hind'), coming just after Rosalind's first encounter with tree-dropped verses, acts structurally as the ante-masque to the masque, the front-of-cloth performance to the performance, the proleptic mockery (on 'prick', Touchstone rolled up his script into a penis and flourished it at Ganymede) of the profoundly serious stuff to come that clears away derision to make space for wonder. It's Mercutio on Mab before Romeo meets Juliet. And in this Arden, it worked a treat.

Watching Propeller's all-male touring production of *The Winter's Tale* I felt like I was meeting for the first time an old friend I'd only ever known as a pen-pal. This was a revival from 2005 (*ShS* 59) that, without seeing it, I'd written about in *Shakespeare and Child's Play*, now completely recast, with the original directorial concept unchanged but a wholesale redesign by Michael Pavelka – illustrations of which can be seen elsewhere in this *Survey*.

Production elements from 2005 remained in place: the stream of sand spilling from the flies as from some cracked cosmic timepiece into the child's wagon below while 'TICK/TOCK/TICK/TOCK' beat a hollow tattoo; the space populated by toy androids and a boy (Ben Allen) in pyjamas (who'd watch most things in Bohemia, play the 'exit pursued by a bear' stage direction with his teddy, reappear as Perdita in Sicilia, and again, as his dead boy-self, unforgiving of his father at the end, blowing out the last candle, to leave Leontes in the dark). Here again, the company played the sheep herded by Karl Davies's delightful, deeply idiotic Young Shepherd (in headgear that looked like a haberdasher's take on 'boiled brains'). Then they became the human-esque backing vocals to the scratch band at the sheepshearing – 'The Bleatles'.

But the look of this *Winter's Tale* was new and gave actors a different vocabulary of space to play with. The design for Bohemia put them in a world of cool, chic, polished steel, at once glamorous and nightmarish in the mirror images it distortingly caught. Above a half wall, a full moon, zinc-grey, rose, a perpetual reminder of those 'nine changes of the watery star' that tell the time for Leontes, troping, too, supposed female inconstancy. And

lunacy – the 'idle' 'lunes' of a brainsick king. Sicilia, then, basked under the exploding colours of a sunburst canopy: noisy, jostling, competitive, argumentative, where Autolycus (Tony Bell, as ever, irrepressible) would manage to pickpocket the Young Shepherd not just of his pockets' contents but the pockets themselves – right down to his underpants, and would arrive at the sheep-shearing a wolf, head to toe, in a fur coat, and where Polixenes (Nicholas Asbury) and Camillo (Chris Myles) would arrive among the locals 'disguised' as Baden-Powell with his side-kick Scout Mistress (in uniform, sash, plaits, beret, butterfly-net – and moustache). As always, the continuous doubling in a Propeller production brought into anarchical alignment roles that make for dangerous doubles, not just Mamillius/Perdita but Hermione/Dorcas.

The best of this production was the central triangle. Robert Hands's Leontes, stricken, flipped from 'brother' to 'sluiced neighbour' in a single beat of *tremor cordis*, a spasm of heart attack. 'Nor night nor day no rest' put us inside his head; behind him, as he stood downstage half undressed, his courtiers, upstage, ran fingers around rims of brandy glasses, producing a weird humming that mixed with their *sotto voce* mutterings, whisperings, the gossip the king's brain heard, making him the cuckold he feared. Then calmly, on 'say that she were gone, / Given to the fire', he took the Hermione photograph he was holding, had been examining, and touched its corner to the candle beside him, watched it curl, turn her beauty into monstrous ugliness, fall to ash – all observed by wakeful, grief-rocking Mamillius. Later this Leontes would batter his wife with relentless accusations ('You had a bastard . . . Thy brat . . . '), then collapse, howling, when the revelation of her death arrived. It was delivered by a Paulina – Vince Leigh – who had no time for either Leontes's 'weak-hing'd fancy' or his too-late repentance. One of the great benefits of the cross-casting of this part was that this Paulina had the physical size and strength to match the speech Shakespeare gives her: savaging Leontes in 3.2 she was biting, sarcastic, every line a knife, happy to make Leontes Saint Sebastian by shoving another bitter blade into the wounded body, not apologetic even on 'I do repent', which was rather toxically ironic. Against these two exemplars of male and female choler, Richard Dempsey's gorgeously dignified Hermione was, from the first, in her statuesque poses the nation's icon of graciousness – cool, but miraculously, 'she's warm', too. The evenness of her 'Adieu, my lord' from 2.1, 'I never wish'd to see you sorry; now / I trust I shall' visibly lodged in her husband's heart the pang it would suffer for the next sixteen years. Shakespeare performance doesn't get much better than this.

TRAGEDIES

Where was Hamlet hanging out in 'World Shakespeare' year? If he was German and directed by Thomas Ostermeier, in a dirt pit (where his dad had recently been interred in a black joke funeral that had the prince clownishly wrestling with the coffin, unable to get the too-big box into the too-small hole) backed by what looked like a high table set in front of gold bead curtains at a cheap and nasty 1990s hotel wedding peopled by the cast of a particularly sleazy production of *Cabaret*. He'd hang out with five other actors who'd double all the parts, which would mean that Ostermeier could flog his idea (yawn) that Hamlet (Lars Eidinger) 'sees' his mother (Judith Rosmair, blonde wigged, grinding to karoake) in Ophelia – and would give Rosmair the undoubted professional opportunity of being brutalized in one part after the other in multiple sequences that denied her a voice while griming her face with filth or gobbing it with spit. And would mean that Horatio (Sebastian Schwarz, also playing Guildenstern, the Player King and Gravedigger) would spend the first scene like an extra in the gourmandizing sequence in *Tom Jones*, sitting at table, compulsively stuffing his face with the cold 'baked meats', scoffing piles of chocolate pudding (that looked like the culinary equivalent of the *Scheisse* people kept talking about), but would never be alone with Hamlet, would never stand as his ally in a place of repose or trust or relief. And would mean that Hamlet himself – Eidinger a cross between bloated Keith Moon at his most strung-out and low-browed Claudius in Asta Nielsen's 1920 silent film, a fat slob with lank hair in a rumpled suit, his 'disposition' always 'fr/antic' – would have free scope to improvise German Shakespeare (through or sometimes beyond Marius von Mayenburg's script) in lines (surtitled) like (to Rosencrantz and Guildenstern) 'Leave me alone. I have to deliver a monologue now' or (to Polonius about his daughter), 'Fuck, fuck, fuck the cunt' or swinging out into the audience to crawl over seats and bait them – 'What should I do? You know what's going to happen!': the duel. But would also mean he'd come back, doubling the Player/Porn Queen, stripped to tiny panties, in high heels and stockings, skinny as a lath in a rabbit skin, in the Murder of Gonzago opposite Horatio-doubling-Player-King-in-jockstrap-and-crown, before (in full audience view) climbing back into his sag-breasted latex fat suit (yup: fat suit) to re-present the world-famous prince spectacularly de-glamorized.

Was I meant to feel shocked? Affronted? Indignant? Repulsed? I wasn't. I was impressed with individual images, like Hamlet, drenched by the 'rain' he was making as he flailed a hose pipe around the dirt pit, his mouth a rictus, his shockingly brilliant blue eyes strobing, his face almost dissolving under the coursing water, staggering like a soul in torment, the crown wedged upside down on his head, its prongs stabbing into his brain. But mostly I was just bored by old-hat devices (back projections, mic delivery, heavy metal, post-modern textual carve-ups and playerly nudge, nudge, wink, winks) exhibiting adolescent Berlin beer cellar antics. I stayed the whole 165 minutes. There was no option: no interval.

If Hamlet was English and directed by Ian Rickson, he was in the secure wing of a psychiatric unit, an R.D. Laingian 'urban home', the 'social cradle' that located psychosis in the 'family nexus'. (The core text here might have been Laing's *Sanity, Madness and the Family* with its analysis of the lies families tell as projections of their 'normality'.) Spectators entered this 'home' (designed by Jeremy Herbert) through the dim, back corridors of the Young Vic, past grim rooms mocked up as

'Chapel', 'Library' (forlornly: torn paperbacks in a cardboard box), rooms stacked with left luggage (suitcases of a vintage that must have meant their being deposited decades ago) and boxes of dog-eared paper hospital records, consulting rooms (doors shut), an exercise cage where two fencers were limbering up, finally, a glass-walled controlled-access office with metal table and filing cabinet, intercom prominent, giving out, through electronically controlled metal doors (that would later slide a metal wall down the façade) onto open space, what felt like the institution's gymnasium. There seemed to be piles of sports apparatus, a basketball hoop, a score board – but maybe that was some surveillance device, a red buzzer, blue flashing lights. The effect of sports 'play' was bizarrely disturbed by the fact that, crossing this space, we had to walk around chairs set out in an 'encounter group' semi-circle past a coffin poised on pit-props over a grave. The first beat of Rickson's production, like Ostermeier's, was old Hamlet's funeral. But there was nothing comic about the wrestling with the past that this English Hamlet – Michael Sheen, an over-aged, perpetual student with rucksack, battered suitcase, staring eyes and electrocuted hair – performed at the graveside. He lunged forward, recovering his father's massive greatcoat that had dressed the coffin like a tomb effigy, embraced it, seemingly tried to shrink into it. (Later, encountering his father's 'ghost', he'd morph into the 'perturbed spirit', personify Laingian 'ontological insecurity', roar Dad's report at his stand-in, Horatio (cross-cast, Hayley Carmichael).)

As things proceeded in Clinic Elsinore I kept having flashbacks to Sebastian in Illyria, wondering 'am I mad?' or 'is she mad?' or 'is everyone mad?' Was Polonius (Michael Gould) a health professional – or patient? He looked normal enough. (But then, they all did, in their three-piece suits and so on until you noticed, then became fixated on the oddity that their clothes had too many buttons and belts and loops and fasteners: insane!) But the more you saw of Polonius, the more you realized he was as empathy-stunted as a gravedigger's spade, a candidate for psychiatric treatment. So the 'therapy' he looked to be conducting might

actually have been role-play: as when he got to be the 'doctor' muttering his notes ('Though this be madness, yet there is method in't') into his dictaphone while his 'patient' sat nose to nose with him. Gertrude (Sally Dexter) was palpably mad. Wasn't she? One of her first appearances had her ransacking the fish-bowl office looking for what fish-cold Claudius (James Clyde) would, coming behind her, administer: pills, sedation that kept her from knowing too much – 'as kill a king'? Or that anchored her on the safe side of a mental precipice – that her manic depressive son, careering into one of his highs, seemed intent on pushing her off? Sheen's Hamlet (the self-styled MC in a crude music hall set-up) made *The Mousetrap* a pornographic command performance for Gertrude – blindfolded, bewildered, forced into lewd intimacy with flexi-tube S&M toys that worked her over. 'Horrible, horrible, most horrible.'

That Clyde's Claudius, the evidently nerveless consultant psychiatrist administering this NHS madhouse was (handy-dandy: which is the doctor, which the loon?) on the point of cracking up, didn't surprise me. (It was inspired direction that Hamlet, slouched concealed in a heap beneath the sightline of the glass office window, hearing the evidence of Claudius finally breaking, trashing his office, could, reaching up a hand to manipulate the dial on the intercom that communicated with the gymnasium/clinic, cut in and out of his uncle's speech, bringing 'my offence is rank' into and out of hearing, so that Claudius's 'confession' was never complete, never guilt-purging.) Much more painful was watching the mental wrecking of Ophelia (a superb performance by Vinette Robinson) who wound up here mind-blasted, in a hospital gown, strapped to a wheelchair, hollow-eyed, singing, a zither on her lap, fingers bloody from raking them over, and over, and over the metal strings. Her funeral produced Rickson's most shattering image. The gym's central floor square was ponderously hoisted aloft, revealing below a massive sandpit, a vast grave, into which Ophelia, delivered on a stretcher, was lowered then shovelled over with sand, interred, left when the scene moved on. Only then (a thud marking the moment), the corpse shockingly inhaled, a reverse death-rattle: Ophelia sat up, shook free the grave, and weirdly returned to life as the water-fly Osric. Here, we saw, the clinic hovered over the grave, the dead occupied the living, and in this Elsinore, there was nothing either live or dead but thinking made it so.

Compared to the bad-boy insanity of Eidinger's Hamlet or the autistic dementia of Sheen's, the geriatric madness of two very different Lears looked to have settled into its opposite, into an appearance of sanity. Indeed, the true appalling-ness of John Shrapnel's Lear at the Tobacco Factory was that, at his maddest, he acted as though his actions were sane, giving us a Lear in Jacobean dress that somehow spoke to today's politics: the insane sanity of life in the present. Bullet-headed, squat, strutting pigeon-breasted on short legs like Juno's 'paycock', Shrapnel's Lear was an old man. He had a white beard. But he also had a much younger man's sergeant-major's voice that rattled out words like cannon balls or with a mock sententiousness ('*crawl* towards death') that had everyone laughing at the absurdity of the idea. The volume of that voice disowning Cordelia (Eleanor Yates) blasted the rest of the family into a huddle, then, aimed straight at her, but answering Burgundy's mortified palterings over the promised dowry, stripped her, the vocal equivalent of Nitromors, to the 'NOTH-ING!' she'd offered her dad. In the storm, the hovel, the war, captivity, this voice never weak-ened, never demanded pity, even asking for a but-ton to be undone, even running out of its last breath. That, even so, he *was* a man 'more sinn'd against than sinning' was entirely due to the fact that his daughters – all three of them – had his DNA in spades and could match him in familiar abuse: Goneril (Julia Hills) turning 'sister' into a snake's hiss; Regan (Dorothea Myer-Bennett, who looks like porcelain but talks like titanium), next cast-ing for Lady M, washing her hands in Gloucester's (Trevor Cooper) blood; Cordelia erupting, furious, into observations she aimed at dad on the 'glib and oily art'.

Directed by Andrew Hilton, designed by Har-riet de Winton, this was 'concept-lite' Shake-speare: nothing in the production, for instance,

took up the intriguing set of ideas offered in the publicity poster, which showed a vintage rocking horse alongside a jack-in-the-box. Still, the straight telling of the story in the Factory's tiny space where eye-satisfying costumes carried the work of design on actors' backs (Goneril in red brocade, Cordelia in ivory 'betrothal' silk, Edmund (Christopher Staines), tight-curled, pearl ear-ringed) meant that nothing got in the way as words like 'father', 'son', 'child', 'kind' ricocheted around the space, *heard*, as were lines like 'Is man no more than this?', and 'What a difference of man and man!' (Does *Lear*, this production simply asked, find out difference or equivalence?) The tight focus in the narrow room made *Lear*'s grotesque moments of 'wrong' revelation all the more excruciating – those awful moments of ironic conjoining that spell separa-tion in this play, the inability to tell, to take off the disguise, to make things better: like Glouces-ter telling disguised-as-Caius-Kent about Kent and about Edgar while Edgar-as-Mad-Tom stood by; or Lear telling blind Gloucester about his 'good' son Edmund, who'd arranged the blinding, over-heard by the 'bad' son who'd just saved his life. The memorable moments were simply so: a William Camden-esque figure (there to record on parch-ment the division of the kingdom?), hunched at a desk, taking down the family brawl instead; Kent (Simon Armstrong at his solid best), during the Lear/Tom exchange in the hovel, standing in his heavy wool cloak, leather bonneted, head slung low like Crow in the rain, figuring the sorrow of this story; Lear (while soldiers ran, stage right, to save the captive king and Cordelia) suddenly present, stage left, his dead daughter slung like a sack over his shoulder.

At the Almeida, directed by Michael Atten-borough, Jonathan Pryce reversed Lear's mental state. His Lear appalled because, at his sanest, he was stark mad. Shaggy, grizzled both of beard and hair, his huge frame bulked out with layers of leather and wool in a faux-modern medieval design (by Tom Scutt) that mixed tabards, sur-coats, cloaks and trousers, set against stark archi-tecture, a five-faced façade of plain rough brown brick, to locate the play in a primitive Britain, pre-civilization, Pryce's Lear was used to having space around his person. Attenborough (like Grandage at the Donmar a couple of years back) read *Lear* as a chamber play; opened the action with Shakespeare's first line; and went for immediate story (not back-story). The way Gloucester (Clive Wood) and Kent (Ian Gelder) glanced over their shoulders as they exchanged urgent gossip and jumped when Edmund (Kieran Bew) entered; the way the family mustered, flustered through side doors; the way the king appeared behind the central double doors that slid open, standing like Darth Vader framed in flooded light; the way he physically placed two daughters on the map (Zoe Waites, a hair-triggered Goneril, Jenny Jules, a pushy Regan) as he gave them their portion, and ground a deep kiss onto their lips to seal the inheritance by seeming to allude to an incestuous past 'love'; the way, interrupted in his rage by Kent, he froze, unbelieving, not just at his subject's defiance, but *his subject's hand on his arm*: all this told spectators how this kingdom operated. But so did Cordelia's stance. 'Nothing-ed', she (Phoebe Fox) stood, staring out, refusing tears. Commanded 'Out of my sight', she folded arms across chest and didn't budge.

And so did the distraction that was already detouring this big Lear's authority into a mental cul de sac: the way, from the first, he constantly fumbled at the buckles on his chest, trying to open the fastenings, get air, catch his breath; the way the eyes, under shaggy brows like a pair of ancient scavenger crows ready to dive, seemed to lose focus. For this Lear, the storm was less a physical, elemental exposure than a nightmare journey through nightmare: made of light, not water, thrown up in a wall of blinding whiteness from the foot of the stage, that Lear wanted to tip himself over as suicidally as Gloucester over Dover cliffs, while the Fool (a beautifully dry Geordie Trevor Fox) hauled him back, struggling to hold on to a mind pitched into the abyss. At the place where other Lears find madness, on Dover beach, Pryce's Lear had been so long a resident of this state that he behaved there like Richard II at Pomfret: populating a virtual kingdom with virtual subjects – priest, bowman, apothecary – by playing all the parts himself.

While I could have done without the directorial silliness (accounting in the programme for a credit to a 'Magic Consultant'?) of the green shoot that grew out of the stage floor and leafed just before the interval – trite, sentimental, and deeply premature for Britain on the mend – mostly it appeared that Attenborough stayed out of his actors' way, let them get on with the business of getting to workmanlike grips with this script. Perhaps because I saw in Pryce's performance a Lear who began where the bereft, child-changed king normally finishes up, I never felt he went the journey through devastation that has him clinging to Cordelia at the end like wreckage. The performance I found most remarkable was Wood's as Gloucester. There was a delicacy and nuance in his acting that I'd not seen in a string of his previous roles: listening, reacting, paying hard attention; anticipating by his physical recoil the pain of the blinding-to-come when he simply heard of his first son's betrayal; sagging, the break of the heart more killing than the anguish in the eyes, after the blinding, learning of the true betrayer; but needing no pity, indeed, barking with laughter when the mad king encountered him on Dover beach and mocked him: 'Dost thou squiny . . . ? . . . blind Cupid, I'll not love.'

Excusing himself to the opening committee of the British Museum's 'Shakespeare: Staging the World' exhibition Simon Russell Beale apologized that he was occupied that night with other business for the 'World Shakespeare Festival', across the Thames, opening *Timon of Athens* at the National Theatre, a production that ironically conducted parallel play with, even mirrored, the BM's gala reception. Beale as the lavish-spending philanthropist kicked off Shakespeare's story of patronage-gone-wrong by opening (to photographers' popping bulbs, reporters' scribbling and sycophants' fawning) an exhibition in something that looked very like the BM gallery, among champagne sippers dressed exactly in one venue like those in the other (and with one notable charlatan at 'Staging' Shakespeare standing dummy for all the charlatans in Athens). The NT's onstage gallery was ostentatiously blazoned the 'TIMON ROOM'. (Its centre-piece should, though, have given its sponsor pause: it was a floor-to-ceiling El Greco canvas of Christ driving the money changers from the Temple. In a set change, the painting would convert to a window looking out on the City with the HSBC building prominently logoed in the mid-distance.)

Directed by Nicholas Hytner as a screamingly obvious secular parable for our times and designed by Tim Hatley on the Olivier revolve to bring a sequence of London niche cultures circling into view, this *Timon* imagined the disaffected clustering around Alcibiades (Ciarán McMenamin) as the anti-capitalist, anti-City protesters who'd so recently been camping out in tents and benders in St Paul's churchyard, and the 'wilderness' of Timon's exile as burnt-out Tottenham after last summer's riots. For Beale, Timon might have previewed a future Lear. A wonder-plumbing line like 'To Lacedaemon [changed to 'distant Sparta'] did my land extend' in that hollow voice that Beale can produce from somewhere around his knees, it's so low, felt like premonitions of 'I gave you all' while his bafflement (grinding his fist into his stomach, feeling the quotidian in the extreme) at flesh's insistent claims which nevertheless force the body that's in mental shut-down to scrabble in the dirt for roots – 'That nature, being sick of man's unkindness / Should yet be hungry' – anticipated 'Is man no more than this?'

But if a pre-play of Lear, then a coming-of-age of Beale's Thersites from 1990. That other Greek's utter disillusion was grounded in a comic miscalculation, imagining he was acting in a script by Homer but discovering himself actually an extra in *Up Phrygia*. So Thersites's misanthropy was hilarious. Timon's was tragic. Because Beale's Timon *learned* his disillusion, and spectators had to endure his learning: running the gauntlet of his clamouring creditors in 3.4, coming down the revolve, ashen, blood-drained, hair-blown, sweating, astonished to realize they'd 'Cut my heart in sums'. Breathless, he was shocked, *amused*, to discover 'They have e'en taken my *breath* from me!'

Relentless, the learning was excruciating: watching him, in the second banquet scene visibly grow stranger to his 'guests'; his rant propelling the walls to fly out, the revolve to start turning, himself to start walking destination-less into an empty black void, pausing to vomit (sick of their ingratitude?) before disappearing round the revolve to reappear striding straight down it to deliver the great vituperation prayer (4.1) that had him stripping himself to nakedness by throwing down wallet, keys, credit cards. Seeing him walk into dystopian, *Blade Runner* London like a dosser, pushing a supermarket shopping trolley spilling his worldly possessions: scrounged plastic garbage bags ripped open for food. Watching him beaten up – but worse, made to cringe, to play the self-parodying joker to parry the violence that still came. As spectator sport, it was practically unbearable.

This *Timon* was a one-man show, but it was also a show with a big part for a crowd that produced terrific support work from Deborah Findlay (Timon's long-suffering Steward), Hilton McRae (acid-tongued Apemantus, hunkering down with Timon in a concrete bunker to trade bitter laughs), Paul Bentall (a frightful big-city banker, Lucullus), and Ciarán McMenamin (doubling Alcibiades with a Hooray-Henry 'Actor' taking Lucius's lines). At the end, the City crowd closed like water over Timon's dead memory. Alcibiades-of-the-anti-capitalist-protest made peace with the schmoozers and Armani-suited horse-leeches who, bleeding Timon white, had literally consumed him. Changed from urban guerilla combat gear into Armani corporate uniform to look like them, Alcibiades sat at a table facing a bank of microphones, read out the epitaph, then turned to face the TV lights to speak his ingratiating capitulation ('I will use the olive with my sword') to the forces represented by the logos you could see through the window in the distance on the skyscrapers behind him.

Beale took his curtain call in his filth-streaked bloody face, which somewhat wiped the smug grin off the chops of Alcibiades's freeze-framed, celebrity ending, and kept in mind that early observation of Apemantus which functioned like economic analysis (and which should be inscribed across every plutocrat's forehead where he'll see it daily when he shaves): 'He that loves to be flattered is worthy o'th'flatterer.' And, I'd like to hope, will go the way of Timon.

Conceding Beale his stellar performance, a young director friend of mine nevertheless complained about the production that for all it attempted anything theatrically challenging, its thinking might have been sketched out in two minutes on the back of a napkin. At least, I countered, its topicality registered some need to do this play *now*. Which was more than could be said for Daniel Evans's *Macbeth* at the Sheffield Crucible (Evans winning my 'turkey' award for the most pretentious and factually inaccurate director's note in a programme this year). He had fine actors in Geoffrey Streatfeild (Macbeth) and Claudie Blakley (Lady Macbeth). He had a workable design (by Richard Kent, vaguely 'period' costumes and a jumped-up version of Trevor Nunn's set from 1976: circles inside circles, with the innermost inscribed with runic patterns like a maze cut into bog-turf that would later rise, become the banquet table). What he produced with these materials was an Art-of-Coarse-Acting *Macbeth*. I admit that my heart sank when I saw 'Hecate' announced in the cast list. I admit too that attending a half-term matinee was like watching *Macbeth* from the backseat of the school bus. But the kids around me were pretty shrewd viewers: their restlessness, their snorts, their guffaws were spot-on responses (and only 'being grown-up' prevented me from joining in). They shrieked at the opening plunge into blackout; sniggered when Macbeth, on 'Bring forth men children only', grabbed his wife's crotch; hooted when Banquo's ghost (David Ganly) shot up through the banquet table; went silent when the assassin initiated the rape of Lady Macduff (Sophie Roberts) by shutting her up: bashing out her brains against a stone. Crass director/designer/actor choices abounded: giving Lady Macbeth Bride of Dracula red-eyed make-up for the coronation and real water and real bells chiming for the sleepwalking (she's hallucinating the past, stupid!); bringing on Hecate (Christopher Logan) like something out of Inigo Jones, in a feathered masquing costume; allowing Andrew Jarvis (Duncan/Old

Man/Siward) to play every part like some actor laddie impression of Donald Wolfit; having Macbeth not just supervise the slaughter of Macduff's (John Dougall) household in 4.2 but 'save' his last surviving child – and refuse to hand him over to the assassin: a baby he'd carry, cradle, nurse, address in 5.3 ('Bring me no more reports') until 'signifying *nothing*' (5.5) finally prompted the adoptive father's hand-over into the child-killer's clutches.

Still, my guess is that, in an otherwise forgettable *Macbeth*, the kids won't forget the final stage picture: Macbeth's head jammed on a pole, eyeballing Malcolm (Joseph Drake). I hope they'll remember not just 'sights' but words and lines as actors performed them: the sheer human cost of wrongdoing contained in the way Streatfeild spoke Macbeth's terrible exhaustion ('I 'gin to be aweary of the sun') or the 'O, O, O' of Blakley's Lady Macbeth, the sound of heartstrings stretching, thinning, snapping.

There was nothing back-of-the-napkin about Gregory Doran's RSC *Julius Caesar*. Doran assembled a powerful black cast of actors, workshopped the play, then developed what they'd learned into a full, all-black production that set *Caesar* today, in a fictional East Africa (designed by Michael Vale), in accents that gave political currency (and dangerous edge) to the sarcasm of lines like 'this man / Is now become a god!' and 'what meat doth this our Caesar feed / That he is grown so great?' You knew exactly who Jeffery Kissoon's Caesar was when he entered his national 'forum' – a brutalist, crumbling, poured-concrete football stadium, wrecked by war (or just shoddily built, falling apart), that bizarrely 'remembered' its ancient prototype – in a white linen desert suit, languidly flicking across his shoulders a horse-tail fly whisk, his wife (Calpurnia: Ann Ogbomo) three steps behind him in Yoruba *gele* (and in front of him, showing its head above the top of the stadium, facing away, a monumental statue of the man himself). Moments earlier the place had been heaving with a slum crowd on holiday (an army of RSC volunteer 'extras' who'd rehearsed themselves: just brilliant!): women in traditional headwraps and mismatched UN care-package hand-me-downs; men in random

37. *Julius Caesar*, 3.1, RSC, Royal Shakespeare Theatre, directed by Gregory Doran. Paterson Joseph as Marcus Brutus, Cyril Nri as Caius Cassius, Theo Ogundipe (behind) as Soothsayer.

football shirts, Nikes, toting banners, playing drums, kora; singing, dancing, stomping. Think *Sarafina!* Or *Hotel Rwanda* in party-political mode, before the bodies start piling up. Clearly, they were 'idle', 'countrymen' who were both politically infantile and superstitious: a Soothsayer, near-naked, covered in ash scored with tribal signs, directed their activity. Clearly, they needed strong leadership, and from a black elite who'd

rehabilitate their credulous worship of a totalitarian demagogue; who'd follow up serious debate on assassination as a legitimate form of self-determination – 'It must be by his death' – with mob-murder; who'd make 'progress'. Next stop: *Breakfast with Mugabe*.

The satisfaction of this production was to see in one place, working to such effect three generations of black British actors, huge talent our

Shakespeare theatre needs, next casting not just of Aaron, Othello and Cleopatra but Romeo, Lear, Leontes, Hermione, Falstaff, Rosalind and any English king or queen. Here, what they did was to inhabit their parts with an immediacy that made the characters' self-contradictions the material of the play's political debate, *living* matter. Paterson Joseph's Brutus was that most dangerous of political idealists: utterly winning, genuine, heart placed in the centre of his being – and brain totally disconnected from the rhetoric rolling out of his mouth. I've never seen that scene with Portia (Adjoa Andoh) played so powerfully, and to such screamingly frustrated anti-climax when the wife who deserved to be heard as his equal was fobbed off with delay: 'go in awhile'. WHY wouldn't he listen? He'd listened to Cassius: but then this Cassius (Cyril Nri) ground him down like casava in a mortar. Antony (Ray Fearon) was his psychological opposite: as blandly complacent at the beginning as Brutus was anxious, his permanent cool smile a kind of leer; after the funeral, that leer twisting into a snarl: satisfied that Rome should turn on Rome and savage Romans. Why, oh WHY did Brutus grab Cassius's bloody hand, prevent his fellow assassin from finishing the job, the killing that Antony, stood over Caesar's corpse, invited: 'Live a thousand year, / I shall not find myself so apt to die'?

The strength at the top of this company went all the way through the ranks: little Lucius (Simon Manyonda), exhausted, couldn't keep his eyes open; recruited as a child-soldier, he didn't know which way up to hold his rifle.

Still, nagging away were questions: wasn't the concept of this production, well, *racist*? Didn't it simply circulate white stereotypes of blackness, the aspirational democrat doomed by incipient dictatorship, primitivism, and superstition, and black democracy by savage violence? (Cinna-the-Poet was murdered by 'necklacing', a tyre put round his neck and torched.) Or did it represent important pro-activism by the RSC en route to actual, as against token, colour-blind casting? (Later in the year, a perfect storm would break over Greg Doran's head when he managed to cast only three Asian actors in an otherwise all-white *The Orphan*

of Zhao, billed 'the Chinese *Hamlet*'; two of them playing dogs.) I can't answer my questions. But I'll be fascinated to watch how the new RSC artistic director's casting policies develop. Watch this space.

I began this year's Olympics-inspired 'Shakespeare 2012' review marathon with the 'also-rans'. I end with gold, a production, on paper, that looked like it wouldn't get off the starting block, announced as (Brecht welded to Shakespeare) *Coriolan/us* played in the wilds of Glamorganshire, directed by Mike Pearson and Mike Brookes for National Theatre Wales in an empty RAF hangar where the set would consist of a transit van, a caravan (for 'in-door' scenes) and a couple of clapped out autos; where the audience would follow the action as it grouped and regrouped and pulled them from one end of the vast expanse to the other; and where the whole thing would be simultaneously filmed both by zip cameras (the kind used in sports events) whizzing along an overhead cable and by hand-held camera operators snaking in and out of the action (and audience), the filmed images thrown up on huge screens suspended from the hangar's curved ceiling that would allow spectators to cut from action to reaction, to see *here* and *there*, immediate, distant, to be in the moment, and in the same moment, detached, watching events as already captured by the media, *mediatized*.

It sounded like my idea of theatrical hell. Like another night with the Wooster Group.

But it was absolutely thrilling. Beat 1: as the massive, battered hangar sliding-door slid open and the 300-strong sell-out crowd who'd been huddling outside, buffeted by a Welsh wind driving straight down the open valley, surged forward, we met ourselves coming toward us. In black and white. We were being filmed. We were being projected, onto the big screen on the far wall and on two smaller screens closer to us. We looked like refugees. Or an army of invasion. We were the 'Rome' who'd be making this play. We were 'on'. We were 'epic'. The 'us' of *Coriolan/us*.

Beat two: a white transit van raced down the concourse, screeched to a halt. Doors flew open. 'Citizens' (John Rowley, Gerald Tyler) in scruffy beards and duffel coats sprang out. We clustered

38. *Coriolan/us*, 3.2/3.3, National Theatre Wales, Hangar 858 RAF St Athan, directed by Mike Pearson and Mike Brookes. Richard Harrington as Aufidius.

round. They began a harangue. We backed off. But wanting distance from the ugly snarl ('chief enemy of the people') and baseball bats, we couldn't get it. The cameras were weaving through us. The screens were throwing up close-ups on faces, mouths. We could see down the throats of the Citizens' fury.

Meanwhile, competing images were showing up on other screens. Caius Martius (who had the stance, the moves, the body of a middle-weight boxer, pitched slightly forward, leading with his right shoulder: Richard Lynch) was limbering up. He didn't 'do' patrician. His claim to status was not what he looked like, in non-U, broken down knee-length leather coat, rather, the disdain he radiated. When he started speaking, his voice was an animal growl low in the throat; words rattled round him like the gravel builders throw into cement mixers at the end of the day to scour it. People talked noise, never conversation. His 'What's

the *matter?*' parley with the Tribunes (Chris Jared; Nia Gwynne, a smirking one-woman rage-ignition system, niggling and baiting Martius to murderous fury, but always just managing to keep a human shield between herself and him) was conducted knee to knee in the back of the van. Later, while, in the foreground, the Tribunes manipulated the plebs and 'fixed' the second 'What's the matter?' scene, images of Martius, wedged between mother and mentor in the caravan, reacting to Menenius's (Matthew Thomas) pleas for him to deal 'mildly', were simultaneously screened overhead. Still later, he heard the ambassadors from Rome slumped in the front seat of his Audi, Aufidius (Richard Harrington: a pitch-perfect performance, political antennae finely tuned) at the wheel, staring stonily straight ahead while cameras shoved up against the windows caught their faces, projected them to public media view, as Menenius, cramped in the

39. *Coriolan/us*, 2.3, National Theatre Wales, Hangar 858 RAF St Athan, directed by Mike Pearson and Mike Brookes. Richard Lynch as Coriolanus, John Rowley and Gerald Tyler as Citizens.

back seat, wheedled and bargained and sweated and slunk away defeated, slamming the door behind him.

This space was big enough to build a no-man's land between warring Corioli and Rome: narrowly spaced 8-foot-high parallel grey breeze-block walls making a rat's run where the battle was fought like urban guerilla war, around blind corners, scaling and leaping verticles, past burnt out cars. Big enough, then, to stage explosive action-man sequences.

But space worked here, too, paradoxically to foreground the terrible internalized isolation of uncompromising individuals in a play that doesn't explore it in soliloquies: Caius Martius alone at the far end of the hangar. Body seemingly suspended in emptiness. Then, later, Aufidius in deep shot. Discovering the loneliness of coalition with Coriolanus. Making his mind up. In Lynch and

Harrington *Coriolanus* had unusually thoughtful protagonists: and thinking was what they did as they covered distance, speaking. The rest of the eleven-strong company kept the pace moving pell-mell, two hours of uninterrupted, headlong Shakespeare (Brecht's part, it turned out, material added in the crowd scenes). Most impressive of all, in a space that was a sound engineer's acoustic night-mare, which meant that actors were miked and spectators issued headphones, these actors delivered Shakespeare with such clarity of diction and assertive shaping of phrase – the music of their Welsh voices here issuing exclusively from the brass and tympani sections of the orchestra – that I didn't bother with my set. When Rhian Morgan's Volumnia turned her verbal fire first on the sloping-off Tribunes then her truculent son, she was a dragon whose roar could've been heard in Cardiff.

With that account of my exhilarating dash after *Coriolan/us* I end the year's review marathon. Except that, like all distance runners, I need to warm down with a last jog round the review track. So my final lap will consider a production that doesn't strictly qualify among this year's main events, a Shakespeare spin-off, the Dmitry Krymov Laboratory's re-mix of a play we were told (in Russian, with surtitles) that we'd been getting wrong *for years*, billed *A Midsummer Night's Dream* (*As You Like It*). Tonight, said the front man ('Quince'?) for the troupe of men and women in overalls (cack-handed scene-shifters who, in a pre-show, had just made comic mayhem hauling across the stage a Herne's-oak-sized fake tree that first got stuck then fell apart to their touch, to be dumped backstage; and following that, a National-Trust-House-sized garden fountain, spewing water, similarly carted, similarly dumped: expectations of scenic 'realism' introduced only to be given the elbow, *tonight* we'd see the *real* story.

A whistle blew. The workers mustered. Stripped off their overalls. Climbed into formal gear, white ties, tails, but tatty. They stood, incongruously, in plimsolls. Stood so long to attention waiting that one fell flat on his face. Another, *sotto voce*, asked, 'Are we?' Was answered, 'Yes.' 'When?' 'Tonight.' 'What time?' 'Soon.' 'What's it called?' 'Pyramus and Thisbe.' 'And who is Pyramus?' 'You.' While behind them was screened a Brechtian notice:

The mechanicals are discussing Shakespeare's creative works. Now they are moving on from his early works to discuss the later ones. Opinions differ. They are paying particular attention to the poetic language that features in certain works by the great author – its phonetic and semantic structures. Their conversation touches upon the broad spectrum of versification issues – a comparative study of the Elizabethan poets' textual structures and contemporary inclinations is being undertaken. The conversation touches upon the problems of the contemporary theatre . . . the temperament of the artistic director and that of his wife. The humane qualities and the creative potency of each are discussed . . . They dwell particularly on an artistic director's fidelity to the highest principles . . . his honesty . . . his generosity . . . and the kindness of the artistic director's spouse. The untranslatable wordplay, together with the use of local dialects demonstrate the mechanicals' deep knowledge of Shakespeare's creative works, his essential Englishness.

The real story, then, the one Shakespeare didn't properly tell, was the story of Pyramus and Thisbe that tonight the Mechanicals would perform to an audience who, wandering across the stage, elegantly dressed, aristocratic (like Romanov left-overs), bored, took their seats in what they disdainfully saw as an unfinished theatre. They'd constantly interrupt. Their mobile phones would ring. (Within minutes we other spectators would *hate* them.)

It was out of these unpromising materials that the Mechanicals re-created from 'papers found in the Lubiankya' the history 'of real people on earth': discovering Pyramus and Thisbe to be 20-foot tall puppets, assembled of mismatched materials ranging from wickerwork to soldered metal to porcelain (for Thisby's doll's head). One hand padded. The other, articulated meccano. They were monsters. They were miracles. And the company – all of them practitioners from the Moscow Theatre School of Dramatic Art, their art combining clowning, acrobatics, magic, dance, circus stunts, and a running scenario with a dog – manipulated the puppets in glorious *lazzi* that had them wooing (Pyramus's erotic excitement registered in an erection inflated with a bicycle pump) then coming to grief over a mistaken identity. When puppet-Pyramus saw what he took to be Thisby's bloody mantel, he reeled back in horror, grief literally taking him apart, arms, legs, head flying off, then reassembling; flying off again. Each time he reassembled, his face had aged, from youth to old man. His hulking hands scooped up the mantel, pushed it into a little pile. Arranged over it a black umbrella, as if to keep rain off his beloved. Took the sword. Stabbed himself through his wicker chest. Fell. I wept!

This was physical performance at its most glorious. And it ended not in tears but laughter. There was a bergomask! That brought on principals from the Bolshoi! In *Swan Lake*! Then, after they'd all taken their bows, including Venya, the dog, and disappeared, 'Quince' dashed back on to retrieve the humble wooden block that had wedged open the trap that had exposed the lighting gear that had illuminated the stage to enable the actors to make it all happen. He'd need it for 'next time'. I pondered that wedge. And its relation to other humble 'starting' blocks that had enabled so much spectacular human activity this year. London 2012. World Shakespeare. The jamborees, the razz-ma-tazz were great fun. But in the last analysis, what was unforgettable came down to a number of simple wedges – and the extraordinary performances that got started from them.

PROFESSIONAL SHAKESPEARE PRODUCTIONS IN THE BRITISH ISLES JANUARY-DECEMBER 2011

JAMES SHAW

Most of the productions listed are by professional companies, but some amateur productions are included. The information is taken from *Touchstone* (www.touchstone.bham.ac.uk), a Shakespeare resource maintained by the Shakespeare Institute Library. Touchstone includes a monthly list of current and forthcoming UK Shakespeare productions from listings information. The websites provided for theatre companies were accurate at the time of going to press.

ALL'S WELL THAT ENDS WELL

Shakespeare's Globe Company. Shakespeare's Globe, London, 27 April–21 August.
www.shakespeares-globe.org
Director: John Dove

ANTONY AND CLEOPATRA

Royal Shakespeare Company. Swan Theatre, Stratford-upon-Avon, 3–24 March.
www.rsc.org.uk
Director: Michael Boyd
Antony: Darrell D'Silva
Cleopatra: Katy Stephens

Rose Theatre, Bankside, London, 9 March–2 April.
www.rosetheatre.org.uk
Director: David Pearce

Creation Theatre Company. Said Business School, Oxford, 8 July–3 September.

www.creationtheatre.co.uk
Director: Helen Tennison
Caesar and Mardian doubled.

AS YOU LIKE IT

Royal Shakespeare Company. Roundhouse Theatre, London, 13 January–5 February.
www.rsc.org.uk
Director: Michael Boyd

Rose Theatre Company. Rose Theatre, Kingston, 18 February–26 March.
www.rosetheatrekingston.org
Director: Stephen Unwin
Rosalind: Georgina Rich
Touchstone: Michael Feast

Shakespeare's Globe Company. Shakespeare's Globe, London, 17 May–26 August and tour.
www.shakespeares-globe.org
Director: James Dacre
Played with female Jaques, doubled with Phoebe.

Royal Exchange Company. Royal Exchange Theatre, Manchester, 29 June–6 August.
www.royalexchange.org.uk
Director: Greg Hersov
Rosalind: Cush Jumbo

Chester Grosvenor Park, Open Air Theatre, Chester, 7 July–21 August.
www.grosvenorparkopenairtheatre.co.uk
Director: Nikolai Foster

THE COMEDY OF ERRORS

Sell A Door Theatre Company. Greenwich
Playhouse, Greenwich, 25 January–20 February.
www.selladoor.com
Director: Bryn Holding

Shakespeare at the Tobacco Factory. Tobacco
Factory, Bristol, 24 March–30 April; Northcott
Theatre, Exeter, 3–14 May.
http://sattf.org.uk
Director: Andrew Hilton

Propeller Theatre Company. Hampstead Theatre,
London, 23 June–9 July and tour.
www.propeller.org.uk
Director: Edward Hall
All male company.

Stafford Festival Shakespeare. Stafford Castle,
23 June–9 July.
www.staffordfestivalshakespeare.co.uk

National Theatre Company. Olivier Theatre,
Royal National Theatre, London,
1 November–1 April 2012.
www.nationaltheatre.org.uk
Director: Dominic Cooke
Antipholus of Syracuse: Lenny Henry

Adaptation
Told by an Idiot. The Roundhouse, London,
21 December 2010–1 February; Royal
Shakespeare Theatre, Stratford-upon-Avon,
26 March–2 April.
www.toldbyanidiot.org
Director: Paul Hunter
80-minute version aimed at younger audiences.

CYMBELINE

Fluellen Theatre Company. Grand Theatre,
Swansea, 4–6 October.
www.fluellentheatre.co.uk
Director: Peter Richards

HAMLET

National Theatre Company. Olivier Theatre,
London, 30 September 2010–9 January and UK
tour.
www.nationaltheatre.org.uk
Director: Nicholas Hytner
Hamlet: Rory Kinnear

Icarus Theatre Collective. Harrogate Theatre,
Harrogate, 1–5 February and touring from
Autumn 2010–May.
www.icarustheatre.co.uk
Director: Max Lewendel

Guildford Shakespeare Company. Holy Trinity
Church, Guildford, 11–26 February.
www.guildford-shakespeare-company.co.uk
Director: Caroline Devlin

Northern Broadsides. New Victoria Theatre,
Newcastle-under-Lyme,
25 February–19 March and tour.
www.northern-broadsides.co.uk
Director: Conrad Nelson
Hamlet: Nicholas Shaw

Shakespeare's Globe Company. Shakespeare's
Globe, London, 23 April–9 July and small-scale
tour.
www.shakespeares-globe.org
Director: Dominic Dromgoole
Hamlet: Joshua McGuire

Stamford Shakespeare. Rutland Open Air
Theatre, Tolethorpe Hall, Little Casterton,
5 July–27 August.
www.stamfordshakespeare.co.uk

Galleon Theatre Company. Greenwich Theatre,
London, 13 September–9 October.
www.galleontheatre.co.uk
Director: Bruce Jamieson

Young Vic Company. Young Vic Theatre,
London, 28 October–21 January 2012.
www.youngvic.org
Director: Ian Rickson
Hamlet: Michael Sheen

Set in a psychiatric institution.

Bard in the Botanics. Botanic Gardens, Glasgow, 15–20 July.
Director: Jennifer Dick

Adaptation
Five Truths
59 Productions, V&A Museum, London, 12 July.
Director: Katie Mitchell
Performer: Michelle Terry
Video installation. Five reworkings of Ophelia's mad scene.

Royal Shakespeare Company Young People's Shakespeare. CLORE Learning Centre, Stratford-upon-Avon, 9 September and tour.
www.rsc.org.uk
Director: Tarell Alvin McCraney
70-minute adaptation.

Schaubühne Berlin. Barbican Theatre, London, 1–4 December.
Director: Thomas Ostermeier
Hamlet: Lars Eidinger
A loose adaptation in German with English surtitles.

Hamlet: 1603
Vital Signs Theatre Company. White Bear Theatre, Kennington, London, 26 April–22 May.
www.whitebeartheatre.co.uk
Director: Imogen Bond
Production of the First Quarto.

Hamlet, the Clown Prince
Company Theatre Mumbai. Northern Stage, Newcastle-upon-Tyne, 8–12 March; Warwick Arts, 16–19 March; Hackney Empire, 23–26 March.
Director: Rajat Kapoor
Performed by a company of clowns 'in English and Gibberish with no surtitles'.

Hamlet the Comedy
Oddsocks. Nottingham Arts Theatre, Nottingham, 3–4 January and UK tour.

www.oddsocks.co.uk
Director: Andy Barrow

Hamlet! – The Musical
Eleanor Lloyd Productions. Royal & Derngate Theatre, Northampton, 6–21 May; Richmond Theatre, Richmond, 24–28 May and tour.
Director: Ryan McBride
Composer: Alex Silverman
Revival of 2010 Edinburgh Festival production.

Hamlet House of Horror
Westminster Theatre Company. The Edinburgh Playhouse at the Hawke and Hunter, Green Room, Edinburgh, 1–31 August.
www.hamlethouseofhorror.com
Shakespeare's play in gothic vaudeville style, employing mime, satire and the original music of The Horror House Band.

Kupenga Kwa Hamlet
Watermill Theatre & Two Gents Productions. Tara Studios, London 7–9 June; Arena Theatre, Wolverhampton, 12 October.
A cast of two from Zimbabwe playing all the roles.

Ophelia
RSH Productions. the Spaces on the Mile, Edinburgh, 15–27 August.
Adaptor: Hugh Janes
A retelling focusing on Ophelia.

Rosencrantz and Guildenstern Are Dead
Chichester Festival Theatre. Festival Theatre, Chichester, 20 May–11 June; Haymarket Theatre, London, 16 June–20 August.
www.cft.org.uk
Director: Trevor Nunn
Playwright: Tom Stoppard

'Tis in My Memory Locked: An Adaptation of Hamlet
The Second Earth Theatre Company (USA company). C Venues, C eca, Edinburgh, 3–29 August.
A monologue accompanied by an on-screen Ophelia.

Wittenberg
Gate Theatre, London, 24 August–1 October.
www.gatetheatre.co.uk
Director: Christopher Haydon
Playwright: David Davalos
Hamlet prequel.

Ballet
Northern Ballet. West Yorkshire Playhouse,
    20–24 September.
www.northernballet.com
Choreographer and Director: David Nixon
Set in Nazi-occupied Paris.

HENRY IV, PART 1

Peter Hall Company. Theatre Royal, Bath,
    7 July–13 August.
Director: Peter Hall
Falstaff: Desmond Barrit
Hal: Tom Mison
Henry IV: David Yelland

HENRY IV, PART 2

Peter Hall Company. Theatre Royal, Bath,
    7 July–13 August.
Director: Peter Hall
Falstaff: Desmond Barrit
Hal: Tom Mison
Henry IV: David Yelland

HENRY V

Company Boudin. Salisbury Arts Centre,
    Salisbury, 1 October; Opera House, Buxton, 4
    October; Studio Theatre, Hull Truck Theatre,
    Hull, 18–19 October.
www.buxtonoperahouse.org.uk
Director: Andy Burden
Four soldiers take on all the roles.

Propeller Theatre Company. Yvonne Arnaud
    Theatre, Guilford, 9–12 November and UK
    tour to August 2012.

www.propeller.org.uk
Director: Edward Hall

JULIUS CAESAR

Royal Shakespeare Company. Roundhouse
    Theatre, London, 6 January–5 February.
www.rsc.org.uk
Director: Lucy Bailey

Adaptation
Thrice Three Muses. The Dell,
    Stratford-upon-Avon, 17 July; Bristol
    Shakespeare and Edinburgh Festivals.
http://thricethreemuses.webs.com
A gender reversed production set among
    Amazonian tribes.

KING JOHN

Richmond Shakespeare Society. The Mary
    Wallace Theatre, Twickenham, 5–12 March.
www.richmondshakespeare.org

KING LEAR

Donmar Warehouse. Donmar Warehouse,
    London, 3 December 2010–5 February and
    tour.
www.donmarwarehouse.com
Director: Michael Grandage
Lear: Derek Jacobi

Royal Shakespeare Company. Roundhouse
    Theatre, London, 21 January–4 February;
    Royal Shakespeare Theatre,
    Stratford-upon-Avon, 7 March–2 April.
www.rsc.org.uk
Director: David Farr
Lear: Greg Hicks
The first production presented in the refurbished
    Royal Shakespeare Theatre.

West Yorkshire Playhouse, Leeds,
    23 September–22 October.
www.wyp.org.uk

Director: Ian Brown
Lear: Tim Piggott-Smith

Adaptation
Contemporary Legend Theatre. Royal Lyceum,
    Edinburgh, 13–16 August.
www.eif.co.uk
Director: Wu Hsing-Kuo
One-man show presented in the style of Peking
    Opera. Performed in Mandarin with English
    surtitles.

MACBETH

Custom & Practice. Harrow Arts Centre, Harrow,
    8–16 March and tour.
www.custompractice.co.uk
Directors: Suba Das and Rae Mcken

Lazarus Theatre Company. Blue Elephant
    Theatre, Camberwell, London,
    22 March–16 April.
lazarustheatrecompany.webs.com
Director: Ricky Dukes

Candy/King Productions with Celtic Kiss.
    Greenwich Playhouse, London, 5 April–1 May.
Director: Scott Le Crass
Adaptor: Eamon McDonnell
All black cast, set in Africa.

Royal Shakespeare Company. Royal Shakespeare
    Theatre, 18 April–6 October.
www.rsc.org.uk
Director: Michael Boyd
Macbeth: Jonathan Slinger
Lady Macbeth: Caroline Martin

Belt Up Theatre. House of Detention,
    Clerkenwell, London, 18 April–8 May.
Director: Alexander Wright
All male promenade production with a cast of
    four.

River Productions. Charlton House, London,
    23 April–1 May.

www.riverproductionsuk.com
Directors: Paul Christopher and Michael Mooney
With the witches cast as children.

Liverpool Everyman and Playhouse. Everyman
    Theatre, Liverpool, 12 May–4 June.
www.everymanplayhouse.com
Director: Gemma Bodinetz
Macbeth: David Morrissey
Lady Macbeth: Julia Ford

Jadis Shadows. The Norbury Theatre, Droitwich
    Spa, 14 May; Old Joint Stock Pub Theatre,
    Birmingham, 19–20 May and tour.
www.jadisshadows.com

Sprite Productions. Ripley Castle, Harrogate,
    North Yorkshire, 21 June–10 July.
www.spriteproductions.co.uk
Director: Charlotte Bennett

Icarus Theatre Collective. New Town Theatre,
    Edinburgh, 5–28 August and tour until Feb-
    ruary.
www.icarustheatre.org
Director: Max Lewendel

Hiraeth Artistic Productions. Upstairs at the
    Gatehouse, London, 9–14 August; Barons
    Court Theatre, London, 20 September–
    9 October.
www.hiraeth-theatre.co.uk
Director: Mary Clare O'Neill

Platform 4. Nuffield Theatre, Southampton,
    20–22 September and tour to February.
www.platform4.org

Mooted Theatre Company. 41 Monkgate
    Theatre, York, 28 September–8 October.
www.mootedtheatre.com
Director: Mark France

Baz Productions. The Crypt, St Andrew's
    Church, Holborn Viaduct, London, 18
    October–5 November.
www.bazproductions.co.uk
Director: Sarah Bedi

Adaptation
Dunsinane
Royal Shakespeare Company and National
    Theatre of Scotland. Royal Lyceum,
    Edinburgh, 14 May–4 June; Citizens Theatre,
    Glasgow, 7–11 June; Swan Theatre,
    Stratford-upon-Avon, 15 June–2 July.
www.rsc.org.uk
Playwright: David Greig
Director: Roxana Silbert
A sequel set in the immediate aftermath of
    Shakespeare's play.

Oddsocks. Holmewood Hall, Peterborough,
    12 June and tour until August.
www.oddsocks.co.uk

Macbeth in the Blitz
Workspace Theatre Company. The Space,
    London, 26–28 January.
www.space.org.uk
Play-within-a-play in which a group of actors
    stage *Macbeth* to raise morale during the
    London Blitz.

Out, Damned Spot
Not Stalking Productions. Etcetera Theatre,
    London, 10–12 August.
Playwright and Performer: Emma Hutchins
A prequel.

Opera
Royal Opera House. Royal Opera House,
    London, 24 May–18 June.
www.roh.org.uk
Director: Phyllida Lloyd
Composer: Giuseppe Verdi

MEASURE FOR MEASURE

Roar Theatre. The Lion, 132 Stoke Newington
    Church Street, London, 19 June–7 July.
Director: Bryony Hope

Shakespeare at the George. George Hotel,
    Huntingdon, 21 June–2 July.

www.satg.org.uk
Director: John Shippey

Rose Theatre Trust. Rose Theatre, London,
    4 November–4 December.
www.rosetheatre.org.uk
Director: Brice Stratford

Royal Shakespeare Company. Swan Theatre,
    Stratford-upon-Avon, 17 November–10 March
    2012.
www.rsc.org.uk
Director: Roxana Silbert
Vincentio: Raymond Coulthard
Isabella: Jodie McNee

THE MERCHANT OF VENICE

Derby Live. Derby Theatre, Derby,
    4–26 February.
www.derbylive.co.uk
Director: Pete Meakin

Royal Shakespeare Company. Royal Shakespeare
    Theatre, 13 May–4 October.
www.rsc.org.uk
Director: Rupert Goold
Shylock: Patrick Stewart
Portia: Susannah Fielding
Set in modern day Los Angeles.

Adaptation
Shylock
Assembly Theatre. Assembly Hall, Edinburgh,
    10–29 August and tour.
Playwright: Gareth Armstrong
Performer: Guy Masterson
Written from the perspective of Tubal.

THE MERRY WIVES OF WINDSOR

Oddsocks Theatre Company. Borough Theatre,
    Abergavenny, 6 December and tour to January
    2012.
www.oddsocks.co.uk
Director: Andy Barrow

A play-within-a-play set in a television studio with the audience watching the Television Repertory Company's 1957 production of *The Merry Wives of Windsor*.

Opera
York Opera Company. Theatre Royal, York, 15–19 November.
Composer: Otto Nicolai
Director: Clive Marshall

A MIDSUMMER NIGHT'S DREAM

Gameshow. Broadway Theatre, Lewisham, 2–27 February.
www.gameshow.org.uk
Director: Matthew Evans
A cast of four.

Headlong Theatre Company with Hull Truck. Nuffield Theatre, Southampton, 3–19 February and tour.
www.headlongtheatre.co.uk
Director: Natalie Abrahami

The Faction. Brockley Jack Pub, London, 31 May–18 June and tour.
www.thefaction.org.uk
Director: Mark Leipacher

Chapterhouse Theatre Company. The Festival Theatre, Hever Castle, 4 June and tour to September.
www.chapterhouse.org

The Lord Chamberlain's Men. Scarborough College, Scarborough, 7 June and tour to September.
www.tlcm.co.uk
Director: Andrew Normington

Bard in the Botanics. Botanic Gardens, Glasgow, 24 June–9 July.
Director: Gordon Barr

Iris Theatre, St Paul's Church Gardens, Covent Garden, London, 2 July–5 August.
Director: Dan Winder

Tomahawk Theatre Company. Oxford Castle Courtyard, New Road, Oxford, 4–16 July.
www.tomahawktheatre.co.uk

Goodmann Productions. Studio, Courtyard Theatre, London, 5–10 July.
goodmann-productions.co.uk
Director: Petina Hapgood

Roar Theatre. Abney Park Cemetery, Stoke Newington, 12–31 July.
Director: Owen Lewis

Royal Shakespeare Company. Royal Shakespeare Theatre, Stratford-upon-Avon, 29 July–5 November.
www.rsc.org.uk
Director: Nancy Meckler

Pell Mell Theatre Company. New Diorama Theatre, London, 1–7 August.
theatrepellmell.wix.com
Director: Natalie York

J2 in association with Southwark Playhouse. Bermondsey Square Hotel, London, 8–23 August.
Director: Jayne Dickinson

Get Over It Productions. Upstairs at the Gatehouse, London, 25–28 August.
All female company.

Filter Theatre Company with the London Snorkelling Team. Curve Theatre, Leicester, 31 October–5 November and tour to August.
www.filtertheatre.com
Director: Sean Holmes

Adaptation
Actors, Eat No Onions!
Somesuch Theatre Company. Hexagon Theatre, Midland Arts Centre, Birmingham, 17–19 June.
www.somesuchtheatre.com
Playwrights: Deirdre Burton and Tom Davis
Oberon and Titania 40 years later and in the world of ordinary people.

Ill Met by Moonlight
Moon Fool in association with Trestle Unmasked.
  Trestle Arts Base, St Albans,
  28 February–17 March and tour.
www.moonfool.com

In Your Dreams
Woolton Irregulars. Greenside, Edinbugh,
  22–27 August.
Playwright: Jeanie Jones
Comic version focusing on the Mechanicals in an
  amateur dramatics setting.

Pocket Dream
Propeller Theatre Company. Southbank Centre,
  London, 30 April–14 May.
Director: Edward Hall
60-minute version for younger audiences.

Shakespeare 4 Kidz. Cliffs Pavilion,
  Southend-on-Sea, 31 January and tour to April.
www.shakespeare4kidz.com

Opera
The Fairy Queen
English Touring Opera. Opera House, Buxton,
  20 October; Northcott Theatre, Exeter,
  17 November.
Composer: Henry Purcell

English National Opera. Coliseum, London,
  19 May–30 June.
www.eno.org
Composer: Benjamin Britten.

MUCH ADO ABOUT NOTHING

Bury St Edmunds Company. Theatre Royal, Bury
  St Edmunds, 10–26 February.
www.theatreroyal.org
Director: Abigail Anderson

Shakespeare's Globe Company. Shakespeare's
  Globe, London, 21 May–1 October.
www.shakespeares-globe.org
Director: Jeremy Herrin
Benedick: Charles Edwards
Beatrice: Eve Best

Sonia Friedman Productions. Wyndham's
  Theatre, London, 1 June–3 September.
www.wyndhams-theatre.com
Director: Josie Rourke
Benedick: David Tennant
Beatrice: Catherine Tate

Rain or Shine Theatre Company. Mannington
  Hall, Saxthorpe, Norfolk, 3 June and tour to
  August.
www.rainorshine.co.uk

Theatre Set-Up. Oakhill Park Arena, East Barnet,
  5 June and tour to August.
www.ts-u.co.uk

Principal Theatre Company. Capel Manor,
  London, 21 June–2 July and small scale tour.
www.principaltheatrecompany.com

Immersion Theatre Company. The Courtyard
  Theatre, London, 2–25 August.
http://immersiontheatre.co.uk
Director: Charley Ive

Mapa Mundi/Theatr Mwldan. Theatr Mwldan,
  Cardigan, 29–30 September and tour to
  November.
www.mappa-mundi.org.uk

Adaptation
Much Ado About Nothing – The Dogberry Diaries
Spin-Off Theatre. Henderson's Vegetarian
  Restaurant & Arts Venue, Edinburgh,
  11–13 August.
Re-told by Dogberry.

OTHELLO

Swivel Theatre Company. Barons Court Theatre,
  London, 1–20 February.
http://swivel-live.co.uk

Custom/Practice. Rose Theatre, Bankside.
  5–30 July.
www.rosetheatre.org.uk
Director: Suba Das

DugOut Theatre. Zoo Roxy, Edinburgh,
    5–20 August.
www.dugouttheatre.com
Director: George Chilcott

Sheffield Crucible Theatre, Sheffield,
    15 September–15 October.
www.sheffieldtheatres.co.uk
Director: Daniel Evans
Othello: Clarke Peters
Iago: Dominic West

Nuffield Theatre & Yellowtale Theatre.
    Greenwich Theatre, London,
    10–12 October and tour.
Director: Robin Belfield
A cast of three.

ACS Random Theatre. Chelsea Theatre
    1–12 November.
www.acsrandom.co.uk

New London Company. The Lion and Unicorn
    Theatre, London, 6–18 December.

PERICLES

Adaptation
Pericles Re-imagined for Everyone aged 6 and Over
New Shakespeare Company. Open Air Theatre,
    Regent's Park, London. 2–23 July.
http://openairtheatre.org
Director: Natalie Abrahami
An adaptation focusing on Marina and combining
    Shakespeare, pirate adventure and pantomime.
    Cast of six.

Bard in the Botanics. Kibble Palace Glasshouse,
    Glasgow, 20–30 July.
Director and Adaptor: Gordon Barr
90-minute version with a cast of three.

RICHARD II

Shakespeare at the Tobacco Factory. Tobacco
    Factory, Bristol, 10 February–19 March.

http://sattf.org.uk
Director: Andrew Hilton
Richard: John Heffernan

Donmar Warehouse, London,
    1 December–4 February.
www.donmarwarehouse.com
Director: Michael Grandage
Richard II: Eddie Redmayne

RICHARD III

Old Vic Company. The Old Vic, London,
    18 June–11 September.
www.oldvictheatre.com
Director: Sam Mendes
Richard: Kevin Spacey
The final production of the Bridge Project.

Propeller Theatre Company. Hampstead Theatre,
    London, 22 June–9 July and tour.
www.propeller.org.uk
Director: Edward Hall
Richard: Richard Clothier
All male Company.

Adaptation
Now is the Winter
Alarum Theatre Company. Iambic Arts Theatre,
    Brighton, 21–23 May and Edinburgh Fringe.
www.alarumtheatre.co.uk
Playwright: Kate Saffin
Monologue by Richard's servant.

ROMEO AND JULIET

Royal Shakespeare Company. Roundhouse
    Theatre, London, 30 November
    2010–1 January; Royal Shakespeare Theatre,
    Stratford-upon-Avon, 3 March–2 April.
www.rsc.org.uk
Director: Rupert Goold
Juliet: Mariah Gale
Romeo: Sam Troughton

Pilot Theatre Company. Unicorn Theatre,
London, 2–12 February and small scale tour.
www.pilot-theatre.com
Directors: Marcus Romer and Katie Posner

The Octagon Theatre, Bolton,
3 February–5 March.
www.octagonbolton.co.uk
Director: David Thacker

Innerleithen, Traquair House, Peebleshire,
1–10 June.
www.shakespeare-at-traquair.co.uk
Director: Kath Mansfield
A cast of over fifty combining professional and
community actors in a promenade
production.

Lodestar Theatre Company. St George's Hall,
Liverpool, 25 August–10 September.
www.lodestartheatre.co.uk
Director: Max Rubin

Night Light Theatre Company. Manchester,
18–20 October and tour.
www.nightlighttheatre.co.uk
Combining live actors and puppets.

Fluellen Theatre Company. Grand Theatre
Swansea 10–13 November.
www.fluellentheatre.co.uk
Director: Peter Richards

Adaptation
Boxed Romeo & Juliet
Box Clever Theatre Company. The Round at
The Dukes, Lancaster, 7–8 April.
Aimed at younger audiences. 50-minute version
followed by audience workshops.

Ballet
English National Ballet. Coliseum, London,
5–15 January.
www.ballet.org.uk
Composer: Sergei Prokofiev
Choreographer: Rudolf Nureyev

Bolshoi Ballet. Hippodrome, Bristol,
14–15 February.
Composer: Sergei Prokofiev

Russian State Ballet of Siberia. Malvern Theatres,
Malvern, 2–3 March; Regent Theatre,
Stoke-on-Trent, 17–19 March.
Composer: Sergei Prokofiev

Peter Schaufuss Ballet. The Congress Theatre,
Eastbourne 23–24 May; London Coliseum,
London, 11–17 July.
www.schaufuss.com
Composer: Sergei Prokofiev

The Royal Ballet. The O2 Arena, London,
17–18 June.
www.roh.org.uk
Composer: Sergei Prokofiev
Choreographer: Kenneth Macmillan

THE TAMING OF THE SHREW

Immersion Theatre. Courtyard Studio, London,
1–20 February.
http://immersiontheatre.co.uk
Directors: Rupert Holloway and James Tobias

Cut to the Chase Theatre Company. Queen's
Theatre, Hornchurch, 11–30 April.
www.queens-theatre.co.uk
Director: Bob Carlton
Set in the Wild West.

Clwyd Theatr Cymru. Anthony Hopkins
Theatre, Mold, 6 May–4 June.
www.clwyd-theatr-cymru.co.uk
Director: Terry Hands

Heartbreak Productions. Jephson Garens,
8–9 June and tour to September.
www.heartbreakproductions.co.uk

Chapterhouse. Aberglasney Gardens, 16 June and
tour to September.
www.chapterhouse.org

Festival Players. Pitmedden Garden,
Aberdeenshire, 3 August and tour.
www.thefestivalplayers.co.uk

Royal Shakespeare Company Young People's
Theatre. Swan Theatre, Stratford-upon-Avon,
24 September–15 October.
www.rsc.org.uk
Director: Tim Crouch

Southwark Playhouse. Southwark Playhouse,
London, 4–29 October.
www.southwarkplayhouse.co.uk
Director: Robert Norton-Hale

THE TEMPEST

Cheek by Jowl & Chekhov International Theatre
Festival. The Barbican, London, 7–16 April
and small-scale tour.
www.cheekbyjowl.com
Director: Declan Donnellan
In Russian with English surtitles.

Principal Theatre Company. Coram's Fields,
London 22 July–5 August.
www.principaltheatrecompany.com
Director: Paul Gladwin
Aimed at younger audiences.

Mokwha Repertory Company. Edinburgh
Theatre Festival, King's Theatre, Edinburgh,
13–16 August.
www.mokwha.co.kr
Director: Tae-Suk Oh
Performed in Korean with English surtitles.

Hammerpuzzle Theatre Company/PBH's Free
Fringe. Gryphon Venues at the Point Hotel,
Edinburgh, 15–27 August.
www.hammerpuzzle.co.uk

Antic Disposition Theatre Company. Middle
Temple Hall, London, 20 August–
3 September.

www.anticdisposition.co.uk
Directors: John Risebero and Ben Horslen

Theatre Royal Haymarket. London,
27 August–29 October.
www.trh.co.uk
Director: Trevor Nunn
Prospero: Ralph Fiennes

AJTC. Mill Studio, Yvonne Arnaud Theatre,
Guildford, 15–17 September and tour to July
2012.
www.ajtctheatre.co.uk
Director: Geoff Bullen
Cast of two.

Jericho House. St Giles, Cripplegate, London,
21 September–22 October with a preceeding
tour of Israel and the West Bank.
www.jerichohouse.org.uk
Director: Jonathan Holmes

Adaptation
The Isle Is Full of Noises
Wilton's Music Hall, London, 7–9 September.
Director: Kalma Streun
Puppeteer: Phillip Plessman

The Magician's Daughter
Little Angel, in association with the Royal
Shakespeare Company. Little Angel Theatre,
9 April–15 May, 4 June–10 July.
www.littleangeltheatre.com
Playwright: Michael Rosen
Director: Peter Glanville
Puppet show featuring warring Ariel and Caliban
who are reconciled by Prospero's
granddaughter.

*Tempests – An Adaptation of Shakespeare's The
Tempest*
Re-STAGE. The Old Penny Lodging
House, Berwick-on-Tweed,
22–25 September.
www.restage.org.uk
A sequel exploring events after the courtiers leave
the island.

TIMON OF ATHENS

Gentleman Jack Theatre Company. The Crypt of
St Paul's Church, Bristol, 1–5 November.
http://gentlemanjacktheatre.com

TITUS ANDRONICUS

Inside of Out Theatre Company. Barons Court
Theatre, London, 7–12 June.
Director: Tanith Linden
All female cast.

Action to the Word. C venues – C, Edinburgh,
13–29 August.
www.actiontotheword.com
Director: Alexandra Spencer-Jones

Purple Coats Theatre. Contemporary Urban
Centre, Liverpool, 1–3 September.
http://purplecoatproductions.com
Director: Calum Green

Adaptation
The Tragedy of Titus
Headlock Theatre. theSpace, Edinburgh,
15–20 August.
http://headlocktheatre.co.uk
50-minute version.

TWELFTH NIGHT

Another Way Theatre Company. The Space,
London, 21 December 2010–8 January;
Hoxton Hall, London, 10–13 January.
www.anotherwaytheatre.co.uk
Director: Chris Chambers

National Theatre. Cottesloe Theatre, London,
11 January–2 March.
www.nationaltheatre.org.uk
Director: Peter Hall
Viola: Rebecca Hall
Toby Belch: Simon Callow
Practical Productions. Pavilion Theatre,
Bournemouth, 20 January and tour.

www.practicalproductions.co.uk
Director: Harry Denford

New Century Theatre Company. Studley High
School, Studley, 11 March and tour to
May.
www.newcenturytheatre.com

Illyria Theatre Company. Hutton-in-the-Forest,
Penrith, 21 June and tour to September.
www.illyriatheatre.co.uk
Director: Oliver Gray

Ludlow Festival. Ludlow Castle, Shropshire,
25 June–9 July.
Director: Charlie Walker-Wise
Malvolio: John Challis

Red Rose Chain. Theatre in the Forest.
Rendlesham Forest, 27 July–28 August.
www.redrosechain.com

Horsecross Arts. Perth Theatre, Perth,
30 September–15 October.
www.horsecross.co.uk
Director: Rachel O'Riordan

Original Theatre Company. Yvonne Arnaud
Theatre, Guildford, 3–4 November and tour to
December.
www.originaltheatre.com
Director: Alastair Whatley

New London Company. The Lion and Unicorn
Theatre, London, 7–17 December.

Adaptation
I, Malvolio
The Egg, Bath, 5–8 October; Bristol Old Vic,
Bristol, 22–26 November.
Playwright and Performer: Tim Crouch
Retold from Malvolio's perspective.

THE TWO GENTLEMEN OF VERONA

Rash Dash. Royal & Derngate Theatre,
Northampton, 30 September–22 October.

www.rashdash.co.uk
Director: Matthew Dunster

THE WINTER'S TALE

Stamford Shakespeare. Rutland Open Air
Theatre, Tolethorpe Hall, Little Casterton,
14 June–20 August.
www.stamfordshakespeare.co.uk
Director: Ken Walsh

Mercury Theatre, Colchester. Mercury Theatre,
Colchester, 23 September–8 October.
www.mercurytheatre.co.uk
Director: Sue Lefton

POEMS AND APOCRYPHA

Cardenio
Royal Shakespeare Company, Swan,
Stratford-upon-Avon, 14 April–6 October.
www.rsc.org.uk
Director: Gregory Doran
Adapted from Cervantes and Theobald's *Double
Falsehood*. The inaugural production in the
refurbished Swan Theatre.

Double Falsehood
MokitaGrit Theatre Company. Union Theatre,
Southwark, London, 21 January–12 February.
Director: Phil Willmott
Playwright: Lewis Theobald

Love
Rough Winds. St John's Church, Edinburgh,
10–21 August.
A two-hander exploring love through extracts
from the Sonnets.

Love is my Sin
Swan Theatre, Stratford-upon-Avon, 7–8 January;
Rose Theatre, Kingston, 14–16 January.
Director: Peter Brook
Performers: Michael Pennington and Natasha
Parry
A play adapted from 31 sonnets.

The Rape of Lucrece
Makin Projects Production. Playhouse,
Salisbury, 25–26 January and tour to January
2012.
www.therapeoflucrece.co.uk
Performer: Gerard Logan

Royal Shakespeare Company. Swan Theatre,
Stratford-upon-Avon, 30 March–2 April.
www.rsc.org.uk.
Directed: Elizabeth Freestone
Performer: Camille O'Sullivan

MISCELLANEOUS

Being Shakespeare
Trafalgar Studio 1, London, 22 June–23
July.
Performer: Simon Callow
Director: Tom Cairns
Playwright: Jonathan Bate
Based on the life and works of Shakespeare.

Call Mr Robeson
Tayo Aluko & Friends. Yvonne Arnaud Theatre,
Guildford, 24–26 November.
Playwright: Tayo Aluko
Director: Olusola Oyeleye
A review of Paul Robeson's life.

Cleo Laine: Shakespeare & All That Jazz. Leicester
Square Theatre, London, 16 April.

*The Complete Works of William Shakespeare
(Abridged)*. New Red Lion, London,
16 March–7 May.
Director: Henry Filloux-Bennett
Revival, originally performed by the Reduced
Shakespeare Company.

The Course of True Love
1623 Theatre Company. Courtyard at Cromford
Mills, 6 August; Barn Theatre at Smallhythe
Place, 24 September.
www.1623theatre.co.uk

Director: Ben Stiller
Featuring selected love scenes.

*The Distant Near (Shakespeare and Bengal's
Bard)*
Bangla Theatre / Mamunur Rashid. The Spaces
on the Mile, Edinburgh, 22–27 August.
Playwright: Shahidul Mamun
One-man show exploring the relationship
between Tagore and Shakespeare.

I, Elizabeth
The Spring Arts and Heritage Centre, Havant,
30 April and tour.
Playwright: Rebecca Vaughan
Director: Guy Masterson
Adapted from the speeches, letters, poems and
prayers of Elizabeth I.

Love's the Thing
368 Theatre Company. Old Ship Hotel Regency
Room, Brighton, 22, 29–30 May.
An evening combining Jane Austen and
Shakespeare.

My Friend William
Rocket Theatre. Marlborough Theatre, Brighton,
14–16 May.
www.rockettheatre.co.uk
Playwright and Performer: David Platt
One-man show.

The School of Night
Sticking Place, Gilded Balloon Teviot, Edinburgh,
14–18 August.
www.thestickingplace.com

Playwright: Ken Campbell
Improvised show based on Shakespeare themes.

Shakespeare's Monkeys
Under Dogs Company, Laughing Horse @ The
Three Sisters, Edinburgh, 14–28 August.
Director: David Richardson
Comedy sketch show based on the output of the
infinite number of monkeys.

*Speak of Me As I Am – A Conversation with Ira
Aldridge*
Royal Exchange, Manchester, 17–18 October.
Playwright: Maureen Lawrence
Performer: Wyllie Longmore
One-man show.

The Tragedian
Riverside Theatre, London, 6 June–2 July.
Playwright and Performer: Alister O'Loughlin
Director: Miranda Henderson
One-man show about the life of Edmund Kean.

'Tis I, Shakespeare the Brit
Five One Productions. C Venues, C eca,
Edinburgh, 3–29 August.
www.five-one-productions.com
A humorous exploration of authorship issues.

Anne Boleyn
Shakespeare's Globe Company. Shakespeare's
Globe, London, 8 July–21 August. Revival of
2010 production.
www.shakespeares-globe.org
Director: John Dove
Playwright: Howard Brenton

THE YEAR'S CONTRIBUTIONS TO
SHAKESPEARE STUDIES

I. CRITICAL STUDIES
reviewed by CHARLOTTE SCOTT

LOOKING FOR SHAKESPEARE

From this year's London Olympics, to the anniversary of Shakespeare's death in 2016, the Shakespeare production line will be in perpetual motion. In 2012, to coincide with the Olympics, we are presented with a global Shakespeare, a multicultural, internationally aware Shakespeare whose 'imaginary universe', according to Jonathan Bate and Dora Thornton in *Shakespeare: Staging the World* (the catalogue accompanying the British Museum's latest exhibition), 'extends across the known planet and tunes into a global conversation' in which he produces 'a panoramic theatre of the world'. This all-encompassing, liberal, proleptic Shakespeare brings us into the brave new world of anniversaries and the protean face of England's cultural capital. The heightened attention that Shakespeare will receive over the next few years shows how we are always in the process of making 'Shakespeare': an irrepressible becoming that shapes and reshapes our own preoccupations with his work. Graham Holderness's *Nine Lives of Shakespeare* is a witty exploration of this mutable subject, who, like the best characters in fiction, absorbs our own fantasies into the history of his possible lives. Holderness's premise is a very clever one: Shakespeare biographies have always been made according to a standard recipe – a pinch of fact and a vast amount of subjective projection. Holderness's project is to separate out these ingredients, expose the compo-

nent parts for what they are (tradition and myth), and then build upon the facts in the form of nine possible lives.

Among these possibilities we meet the corpse of Susanna, dug up from the crypt in Holy Trinity Church, Stratford, with a manuscript next to her decomposed cheek; and Shakespeare the actor-director (a figure reminiscent of Jonathan Miller), who instructs his actor: 'You are Aeneas, narrating the story of Troy to Dido: a man telling a tale. And yet you are not Pyrrhus, but John Lowin, a player, standing here on the stage of the Globe . . . You must feel these characters, Pyrrhus, Aeneas, John together at the same time'. Observing the consistent development of speculation into tradition, Holderness amplifies the history of creativity in Shakespeare biography through his own flagrant rewritings of enduring assumptions. Alongside Shakespeare in love (with any number of people – except his wife), we have Shakespeare the butcher/poacher; Shakespeare the Catholic, and Shakespeare the troubled lover, devouring the Jamaican nurse, Mary Seacole. Most of the Shakespeares present here do not retain any resemblance to the Elizabethan playwright, filtered as they are through multiple styles, historical periods and creative mutations. Holderness is at his most artful and indeed most compelling when he enters into the style of other writers. Taking Conan Doyle as his inspiration, for example, he recasts Holmes's last stand through the story of 'The Adventure of Shakespeare's Ring', in which the inscrutable detective meets Oscar Wilde in a hunt for the thief of a ring inscribed with the initials 'W. S'. Here, Holderness blends the gay narratives of Wilde, Wriothesley and Holmes himself. Conflating novels and biography, quotations and facts, Holderness deconstructs the distinctions between creative and life writing. But his point is not only to gesture at the literary text as a radically fluid and unstable form; he also highlights the wonderfully egocentric nature of writing itself and the ways in which both reading and writing are creative acts. Whether we read, interpret, interpolate or rewrite, the relationship between text and reader is always in a process of definition. Holderness is never censorious, but he is often playful, exposing his fellow biographers as occasionally narcissistic and frequently partial. This, he concedes, is the result of little evidence and a great deal of speculation, fantasy and wish-fulfilment.

Holderness's penultimate 'life' of Shakespeare is in fact his death and in this essay the author creates an extraordinarily emotive account of the body fighting to both stay and depart. Importing Lear's rages and Fitzdottrel's fits, Holderness imagines Shakespeare dying as a terrible struggle on the threshold between faith and doubt, pain and relief:

Slowly his hand moved down from his forehead, traversing his body to his chest, then up again to his left shoulder, and over to the right. The sign of the cross. The priest absolved him, and commended his soul to God. Through the mist of incense he could see three women, bowed and grieving, like weeping queens conducting the dying Arthur to Avalon. His pain had gone, and with it his fear.

Let it come. The readiness is all.

These are not really 'lives' (or deaths) of Shakespeare, imagined or otherwise, but often very clever, and very moving, exercises in creative writing in which the facts in question go through so many mutations that the life stands as an isolated fiction of contemporary ingenuity. The book's structural logic is very helpful as it sets out to

establish the differences between fact, myth and tradition, as it also playfully exposes the egoism of the modern biographer.

Holderness's demystification of the biographer's ego is fascinating but it also sets up expectations that he can somehow depart from the biographical model and provide a new – albeit fictional – Shakespeare that is at once plausible and exciting. What the *Nine Lives of Shakespeare* reveals, however, is that this is not in fact possible. The interpolations and dreams of Rowe, Schoenbaum, Honan, Wells, Greenblatt, Greer, Duncan-Jones, Ackroyd and Bate are necessary to make sense and a sensation of a Shakespeare we need but cannot ultimately know. Neither is it possible, as this book shows, to write Shakespeare biography without incorporating insights from the plays or poems. While the hunt for traces of 'the real William Shakespeare' will continue to preoccupy scholars, the works in which he resides will always be more fascinating. Holderness's range is impressive and his experience as a poet and novelist is always in evidence: he can write through the styles of Conon Doyle and Ernest Hemingway; he adapts to the pornographic and the lyrical, the suggestive and the explicit with equal skill; and he can bury allusions so deep that Shakespeare is, in the end, lost in translation.

As is increasingly evident in the best of recent biographies (including Ian Donaldson on Jonson, Andrew Hadfield on Spenser and Natalie Zemon Davis on Leo Africanus) informed speculation is important and indeed, according to Zemon Davis, absolutely necessary. For without the endeavours of such biographers we would have little to animate our imaginative reconstructions of the early modern worlds. In *The Truth About William Shakespeare: Fact, Fiction and Modern Biographies*, David Ellis takes an apparently similar tack when he begins with the assertion that his 'is a book as much about biography as Shakespeare'. What follows, however, is a rather desultory trawl through the kind of well-trodden material that Holderness recounts. For Ellis, however, the question is 'What was he [Shakespeare] like?' This is a question that fills me with dread. Like Holderness, Ellis attempts to take on contemporary biographers of Shakespeare but, unlike Holderness, he does so through a range of analogies that left me weary – international athletes, television programmes and American courtroom dramas, for example – but the point seems to be that with so little material to go on how can we continue making silk purses out of sow's ears (or 'bricks without straw', to use Ellis's analogy)? So, as Ellis suggests, biographers resort to the plays to find confessional moments from the playwright, an 'autobiographical "I" in the Sonnets' or dramaturgy from *Hamlet*. Working through 'biographers, over-interpreting the small number of available facts' we move seamlessly into the question of Catholic Shakespeare, Shakespeare growing up, married Shakespeare, gay Shakespeare, and so on and so on. Inevitably Ellis concedes that we can only ever speculate somewhere between the probable and the possible: an act which he ultimately observes as inherent to the nature of writing itself. For Ellis, the lack of documentation is not a limitation but liberation, since no life is recorded intact. Ellis's book is an attack on both historicism and academic imperialism. For him, biography is a 'messy compromise', muddled by quasi-historical access and contemporary perspectives: 'The relevance of [James] Shapiro's insistence on the dangers of thinking of Shakespeare's private life as modern does not, therefore, seem especially acute when the information available hardly affords us the opportunity for thinking about it at all.'

Nicholas Fogg proposes another biography under the title of *Hidden Shakespeare*, in which he constructs a traditional account of the poet-playwright's life through a combination of fact, supposition and liberal recourse to the plays and poems. The unfortunately named Fogg relies on a rather random selection of (predominantly) out-of-date scholarship and so the sense in which this book is presented as revelatory is somewhat misleading. Fogg situates Shakespeare alongside his contemporaries: Jonson, who 'never fulfilled his huge potential', and his apparent 'sense of inferiority made him condescending about what he perceived as his friend's [Shakespeare] lack of classical scholarship'. As this quotation suggests, Fogg falls foul of what Holderness calls a 'clear pattern' of 'ideological inflections', creating a fantasy Shakespeare (complete with personal library) and 'the most articulate man who ever lived'. Irrespective of the attraction of such speculative assertions, Fogg's account is often misleading.

Among such dim reflections, however, Lois Potter's *The Life of William Shakespeare: A Critical Biography* shines like a good deed in a naughty world. Following a conventional chronological structure, Potter builds a thoughtful and nuanced account not only of Shakespeare's 'life' but of the development of early modern life, including playing companies, educational structures, social history and, of course, theatre. Her careful, often wry and unerringly intelligent account provokes new thinking in an otherwise bloated field. Writing on the prescriptive structures of education through religious creed and schoolroom practices she observes:

The object of both religion and education was to ensure uniformity of belief and practice. The boy who would become a classic example of 'original genius' was about to receive an education designed to prevent him from being original in any way.

Such subtle reflections make Potter's biography original, amusing and wholly engaging. She moves between the Shakespearian playtext and the humanist curriculum with perfect ease, identifying themes, terms or transitions that would come to define the playwright's work. We are not encouraged to read these as idiosyncratic instances of Shakespeare's 'genius', but as wider cultural imperatives of a post-Reformation investment in civic pride and institutional reform. Her 'suppositions' often gesture towards modern psychotherapy, sociology or Darwinism, but all of them provide sensible speculations or intriguing observations. While the first half of the book follows a more obviously biographical structure, the second follows the chronology of the plays. The 'might have', 'could have', 'possibly' or 'perhaps' that define so many Shakespeare biographies manifest in Potter's book as genuine reflections rather than flights of fancy. Potter's own humanity comes across and supports her testing of potential theories as to

Shakespeare's movements. Drawing on the lives and works of Shakespeare's contemporaries, Potter creates a vivid picture of the development of Elizabethan theatre through collaboration, censorship, spectacle and the growing awareness of what the audience 'ought to want as Christians and what they wanted as theatrical experience'. The 'critical' nature of this biography emerges throughout in Potter's fluent and wide-ranging allusions to the plays and poems. Unlike most biographies she does not follow the formula of, say, 'John Shakespeare was a glover so here are some references to gloves in Shakespeare's plays' (exemplified by Anthony Holden and Peter Ackroyd's more commercial biographies). Rather, Potter's excursions into the works provide discursive backgrounds for the exploration of, among other things, collaboration, playing companies, chronicle, controversy and whatever current anxieties were preoccupying Londoners. Potter's lack of sensationalism is immensely rewarding; she writes about love, sex, birth, death, fear and tragedy with a profound interest in human life rather than literary affect. This is a biography for those who love the works, as much as the possible life of their author.

HUMANIST SHAKESPEARE

Away from the strictly biographical, however, Shakespeare's life continues to inflect and inform the studies of his works. Lynn Enterline's *Shakespeare's Schoolroom: Rhetoric, Discipline, Emotion* interrogates the ways in which rhetoric – as both a formal style and a method of imitation – produces a set of learning conditions that are simultaneously theatrical, punitive and rewarding. For Enterline, humanism is not an early modern fantasy about the past but an evolving practice of animating language through form, body and emotion, which results in a compelling synchronicity between the school and the theatre, pedagogy and performance. Within this model she identifies the apparently complicit nature of these institutions in their reliance on punishment, latency (a psychoanalytic term that is resonant for both early education and acting), sexuality and

discipline. The book aims to 'bring evidence about the minutiae of daily life in sixteenth-century schoolrooms to bear on Shakespeare's representation of character and emotion and investigate, in turn, what his rhetorical and meta-rhetorical portraits reveal about the institutional curriculum and pedagogical practices that made them possible'. Within these terms Enterline isolates how forms of rhetoric produce as well as describe the affect that they seek to explain. For example: 'the affective intensity allied to verbal and visual interplay implicit in ekphrastic display might have been of considerable social value'. Beginning with an exposition on the state of Elizabethan schoolrooms, she evaluates the role of punishment and imitation in the classroom, asserting that the child's emotional life 'became part of an ongoing "internal audition" derived from early experiences in an institution where one's voice, body, gestures, and emotions came to make sense – became socially legible to oneself and to others – in relation to a hierarchical distinction between audience and actor, judge and speaker, master and student'. Enterline goes on to explore her argument within the context of some of Shakespeare's dramatic schoolrooms and their corollaries. Her chapter on *The Taming of the Shrew* establishes the role of punishment (in all its emotional, sexual and corporeal manifestations) within the context of teaching; and in *Venus and Adonis* she explores rhetoric as a form of emotional surrogacy, as characters and speakers adopt passions through figures of persuasion. Crucial to Enterline's argument is an exposition of gender and the ways in which performing and imitating allow us access to a pedagogic and parental dynamic in which '*Venus and Adonis* becomes particularly suggestive for an anti-foundational theory of sexuality's incessant challenge to normative gender ideologies'. The 'link between persuasion and sexual violence' is further developed through *The Shrew*. Central to Enterline's enquiry is a perceived discrepancy between 'theory and practice in schools' in which the creation of authority is dependent on consent or force. One of the problems that this presents, however, is the attempt to uncover such discrepancies whilst simultaneously relying on the texts that deny them. It is within this context that *The Shrew* offers Enterline access to an otherwise ideologically constructed schoolroom: 'Katherine engages in the kind of exercise in public argument, in other words, that masters commonly demanded a schoolboy perform effectively – without reference to a boy's actual convictions.' Learning and performing, words and emotions, become part of an endless cycle of deferred meaning in which the idea of reality or even conviction itself becomes ever more attenuated. What this seems to suggest, however, is that the self, however it may be defined, is always capable of making the distinction between imitation and assimilation; and that there lies – deep in all of us – some kind of essential being who is able to resist the community of coercion that governs our affective lives. The final chapter extends the discussion about 'imitation as a disciplinary practice' through 'portraits of grief' in *Hamlet*, *Lucrece* and *The Winter's Tale*. Within the terms of the book's wider interest in imitation as a form of hegemony through which the subject is coerced, convinced or resistant, Enterline observes the 'social categories' defined by classical texts. Differentiating between the father and mother tongue, she traces the distinctions between the popular and the elite as they were propounded in the schoolroom:

The meta-rhetorical production of character and affect in Hecuba's 'sad shadow' indicates that the regime of Latin rhetorical training forged eloquence in schoolboys by way of disciplinary structures (both real and imaginary) that involved more than one party.

The fantasy of the Other, or an other, returns us to the pedagogic practices by which children learned to express themselves within the controlled conditions of the classroom. These conditions, Enterline suggests, support the distance 'between speaking and being' that was to become so central to Shakespeare's work. Reading carefully for the oppositions to ideologically inscribed practices, Enterline demonstrates 'Shakespeare's fractious indebtedness to the Latin grammar school's disciplinary regime – or perhaps his fine-tuned ear for its internal contradictions'. *Shakespeare's*

Schoolroom is lucid and engaging. The blend of psychoanalysis, post-structuralism and historicism is deftly handled; and the section on Mamillius is beautifully expressed.

Armed with a similarly diverse methodology, Holger Schott Syme turns his attention to practices of law and the role of testimony – written and oral – in the development of theatre. *Theatre and Testimony in Shakespeare's England: A Culture of Mediation* sets out to explore the early modern creation of 'a phantasmagorical reality' through forms of representation which were governed – indeed produced – by deferral and mediation. Mediation, as the title suggests, is the driving principle of Syme's book, and for him this term represents a fundamental force in the development of Shakespeare's theatre, wherein impersonation, representation, description, projection and deferral are all embodied discourses of presence – and, of course, absence:

In this profound reliance on a logic of deferral (the locus of authority is neither the actor's body nor the playwright's script, and yet both), the theatre encapsulated the larger cultural trope of authority-through-transmission or mediation.

This 'larger cultural trope' feeds neatly into the law and how testimony, jury, trial and court records belong to a system (as it were) of witness, reconstruction and verification. Syme's work enters into an increasingly articulate debate within Shakespeare studies as to the role of physical presence in the construction of cultural hegemony. Central to this debate is the imaginative reconstruction of 'truth' as well as fulfilment (legal, theatrical, social) in the development of civil institutions. For Syme such structures depend on an apparently negotiable distance between illusion and reality: a distance that can be denied, amplified and reconstituted:

Ultimately neither the visual nor the verbal can claim final authority, although both are variously positioned in ways that suggest an absolute certainty about where truth lies. Object and body, narrative and rhetorical artifice are thus engaged in the very same circular give-and-take of endless deferral that also formed the basis of the theatre's own reality-making power.

Following through on this argument, Syme unpacks the courtroom dynamic in order to expose ideas of justice as they are represented by jury and testimonial. Within these terms, he looks at the oath and the material practices through which truth is reconstructed by legal authorities, so that the witness becomes an 'invisible source of authority whose most significant gesture is the oath proclaiming that what the jury hears is what was spoken before a magistrate, months ago, miles away'. Focusing on Edward Coke's prosecution of Essex, Syme explores the uses of testimonials in court and interpretative processes they produce, which can 'be associated with the principles of humanist reading, which were likewise based on systematic selection and redeployment of isolated passages, sentences and words, [which] similarly harnessed a model of authority that endlessly oscillated between readers and texts, and also had the future production of new texts and verbal performances as its ultimate goal'. In this way, reading becomes a model of abstraction and selection by which the material becomes meaningful only within the terms in which it is reiterated. Such observations have clear implications for the theatre and the relationship between author, script and actor as it is enabled by the dramatic performance: 'Courtroom and theatre has this commitment to an "as if" in common. While they strove to get as close to the real as possible, they nevertheless approached actuality asymptomatically, without ever truly wishing to achieve it.' Within these terms Jonson becomes an intriguing figure of apparent resistance: someone who obstructed theatre's ability to achieve 'terrifying credibility'. Such a 'bewitching effect', Syme argues 'blocked access to the kinds of responses Jonson explicitly strove for: aesthetic judgement, moral reflection, reasoned critique – all reactions, in other words, that depend not on immersion but on detachment'. The idea of mediation – the presence of a voice, body or script through which words pass from one source to another – continues to inform Syme's understanding of both text and performance. Tracing different forms of mediation through testimonials, possessions (as in demonic) and stage-play opens up the possibilities of interpreting stagecraft. This is not, however, Syme suggests, an era in which there was a 'crisis of representation'. The book asserts quite the contrary: in respect of Richard II's deposition scene, Syme notes: 'What might appear mere word play in fact points to a significant historical and structural relation. The logic of mediation which governed the use of legal depositions in Elizabethan and Jacobean criminal trials closely resembles that which Shakespeare and Holinshed elaborate as they engage the complex and problematic connections between writing, speech, and authority.' The final chapter deals with the reported scene of reunion in *The Winter's Tale*. Arguing against critical convictions that such offstage action retains the audience's energy for the *dénouement*, Syme argues that presence is no more convincing than absence: 'In forcing us to listen to Paulina and the other characters, the statue scene simultaneously forces us to ignore or reframe our own perceptions – our own visual experiences – and encourages us to access the world of the play through the sense of others: presence is suspended in representation.' Syme's book is ambitious and, in parts, highly sophisticated, but it is occasionally overstated. There is a tendency to amplify its originality at the expense of constructing a linear narrative. The chapters cover such a range of material and methodologies that they can appear restless or in search of their own affirmation (evidenced by the repeated recourse to 'in other words' or 'put another way'). Nevertheless, *Theatre and Testimony* makes an important contribution to the ways in which we think about words and bodies on the early modern stage.

The recognition of knowledge through a complex debate between evidence and doubt is pursued with great skill in *Fictions of Knowledge, Fact, Evidence and Doubt*, edited by Batsaki, Mukherji and Schramm. Although this book takes a longer view, from the sixteenth to the nineteenth centuries, the chapters on the early modern period offer exceptional insights into the production of an epistemic debate in humanist, religious and scientific literature. Barbara Shapiro, to whom Syme's work is indebted, sets up the context for reading 'matters of fact' and the historically nuanced ways in which the idea of 'fact', as well as the assertion of 'beyond reasonable doubt', informed 'institutional anxiety'. For our period, however, Lorna Hutson, Kathryn Murphy and Subha Mukherji provide lucid contributions to the contested sites of knowledge and the ways in which experience and doubt inform a developing poetics of selfhood. Hutson's essay specifically engages with Shakespeare and 'the emergence of theatrical realism' through inference. Here there is a clear dialogue with Syme's work, but Hutson's attention to 'character' and the questions of motive and circumstance provide a compelling avenue into the role of narrative in the suggestion of both motive and action. Like Enterline, Hutson focuses on the humanist curriculum but she casts the teaching of narrative – or *narratio* – in forensic terms. Exploring the 'imagined presence' of persons through humanist constructions of *enargeia*, *evidentia* and *copia*, Hutson develops her argument through an interrogation of what constitutes circumstance and perception – or to borrow the modern phrase 'narrative glue'. Exploring instances of conjecture and inference within Shakespeare's drama, Hutson develops an argument for the role of circumstantial evidence in the creation of character – and motivation. In implicit dialogue, and occasionally argument, with Hutson's essay, Subha Mukherji's 'Epistemic Plots and the Poetics of Doubt' explores the ethically double-edged nature of probability in Shakespearian as well as post-Shakespearian drama. Focusing on plots of trial, it shows how the impulse to know or ascertain – whether scientific, legal, or more broadly epistemological – can slip into, or be overtaken by, a desire to craft that is ethically dubious. Through a focus on *The Winter's Tale*, the Shakespearian part of this essay offers an original and historicist insight into Shakespeare's use of improbability in his late work, showing how it illuminates the interface between secular and theological ideas of trial, evidence and assent. Overall, the essay establishes Shakespeare's intervention in an emergent 'poetics of doubt' across what may now seem disparate areas of thinking on the condition of knowledge, and the ends and means of knowing: law, theology, natural philosophy and imaginative literature. This is suggestive at once of popular drama's participation in a larger discursive culture centred on investigation and discovery, and of the affective awareness that informs early modern culture's engagement with epistemic processes in human affairs.

Quoting from a recent edited collection, Hutson observes 'Character has made a comeback' and in Raphael Lyne's *Shakespeare, Rhetoric and Cognition* we notice a version of that comeback. Here, however, it is mediated through a careful and lucid focus on language study, not as the platform for a grand narrative of early modern epistemology, but as the province of thought. In this book, Lyne addresses some of Shakespeare's most complex speeches, exposing their component parts and the ways in which networks of meaning are constructed across rhetorical figures and tropes. Attending to the unfashionable study of character, form and a discrete text, Lyne proposes that 'rhetoric could be a science of thinking even before it is a science of speaking'. To that end, he rehabilitates the characters who 'can only think in words, or perhaps in the implications of their words', arguing that: 'For Shakespeare, at key moments, rhetoric comes to look like a problem-solving process whose goal is to make sense of things that are not easily made into sense.'

For me, this has always been the point of Shakespeare: that his poetry and plays give us access to ways of making sense of the ineffable. Why, this book asks, do we reach for metaphors at moments of emotional crisis – or, to take refuge in Nietzsche – do 'we possess nothing but metaphors'? Lyne's point, however, is not the discrepancy between words and things, but the ways in which rhetoric becomes, for Shakespeare, a heuristic enterprise and how by attending to both the problems and their resolutions (or lack of them) we can observe a mind in motion – or a thought in action. This is not a teleological process but one in which 'patterns and resemblances arise in the course of storytelling, character development, and mimesis, and from within that set of motives they offer out their implications'. Lyne is proposing that we take notice of character (something that has fallen out of undergraduate studies) and 'give characters a large stake, and great credit, for their words and what they represent'. Discussing *Hamlet*, Lyne states: 'Hamlet's tropes at times seem not to persuade anyone, even himself, and instead they seem to be devoted to mustering and arranging thoughts.' Suggesting that Hamlet displays 'a kind of cognitive re-booting', Lyne examines how metaphor serves the speaker, enabling him or her to explore as well as express a plurality of thought, thereby enhancing 'the vertiginous sensation of reading something that is working on so many levels at once'.

In a recent BBC programme on Shakespeare Germaine Greer declared: 'Shakespeare doesn't tell you what to think. He says "think".' Perhaps an obvious, but certainly fundamental point, it is one that resonates with Lyne's work. Largely focusing on metaphor and synecdoche, Lyne aims to 'map out ways in which thinking works'. Thinking is a vast and often murky process that lurches towards comprehension through signs that are at once familiar and sympathetic. Observing the ethics of philology, Lyne notices the ways in which rhetoric is believed to work upon the listener and why metaphor 'should give pleasure'. Concentrating on the development of meaning through rhetorical practice, its history, use and effect, Lyne uncovers how the mind has been taught to express itself, if not necessarily to find resolution. Ophelia's speech 'O what a noble mind is here o'erthrown!' displays 'failed recognition' since, despite the heuristic model, her tropes are 'scrambled', 'disordered' and various, to the extent that she cannot reconstruct a Hamlet – her Hamlet, our Hamlet. This is not a value judgement but a point to 'reconcile a technical close reading with the immediacy of drama, by reconsidering what a trope might convey'. Cognitive theories provide Lyne with a useful model because they engage with meaning-making across a network of effects which do not presuppose cohesion or resolution. Applying his thesis to *A Midsummer Night's Dream*, *Othello*, *Cymbeline* and the Sonnets, Lyne tackles some of the most complex and rewarding speeches in these plays. This book is a beautiful example of the values of

close-reading and literary analysis. On Titania's reflection on Oberon's 'forgeries of jealousy', for example, observing 'fairy insouciance' and an 'angry moon', he locates the speech as 'poised so delicately within and outside a maelstrom of agency in the unnatural-natural world'. Lyne displays a great affinity with the images and tropes through which he traces cognitive rhetoric and releases the reader from any expectation of closure through the sheer pleasure of attending to the words in play. On Iago's search for the circumstances in which he can falsely lead Othello to 'the door of truth', Lyne notices the mobility of such a metaphor, since 'The door admits and excludes. This ambiguity is revelatory in that it tells us a poetic truth about truth, but it is also part of an obfuscatory scheme within the fiction.' Iago, he states, 'causes Othello epistemological problems by means of these tropes'. Such insights remind the reader that character is always in the process of becoming through the very terms through which it is mediated: 'The ensign is able to invade the thought processes by which his general comes to terms with the world, and thus is able to change his whole relationship to it.'

Iago's domestic violence belongs to a sophisticated form of mental rewiring, wherein he is capable of hating the very thing he would not kill. The final chapter on the Sonnets brings many of the book's wider concerns together in its pursuit of the 'construction of effectual thoughts'. Within these terms 'metaphor is a medium of progress as well as deferral'. In other words, where is Shakespeare's language going and how does it get there? Or, 'why Macbeth says pity is like a new-born babe'. Lyne's book returns our attention to the ways in which cognitive rhetoric can expose 'dazzling insights into emotion' and the complex and not always consolatory ways Shakespeare 'takes language and mimesis beyond the simplistic implications of a mirror being held up to nature'.

In contrast to the networks of cognition that Lyne presents through his close analysis of Shakespeare's rhetoric, James M. Bromley turns our attention to the body in *Intimacy and Sexuality in the Age of Shakespeare*. Here Bromley sets out to extend our understanding of intimacy by expanding the spheres through which we recognize both proximity and sexuality. Rejecting any notion of fixed categories, Bromley proposes that we consider 'alternatives to marriage and coupling' those of the 'erotic, non-erotic, cross-gender, and same-gender relations' as within the bounds of the 'intimate sphere in the Renaissance'. The fluidity of these relations, Bromley indicates, urges us to re-evaluate the values through which we appreciate as well as identify early modern relationships. Within this context, Bromley traces the changing conceptions of both marriage and friendship and the ways in which the understanding of those relationships is redefined in order to accommodate competing versions of intimacy. Bromley's approach is guided by psychoanalysis as well as historicism and seeks to open up the often narrow, modern recognition of intimacy, by examining how 'it was possible to think of affective relations in multiple ways in the Renaissance'. Bromley argues, however, that the changing conceptions of marriage that sought to narrow the intimate sphere within the period also gave rise to a 'textual circulation of knowledge about alternatives to this narrower version of intimacy'. To that end the book explores 'failures of intimacy', challenges 'posed to marriage, inwardness, and futurity posed by anal pleasure', masochism, 'communal relations in convents' and cross-racial and same sex relations. The texts in play are wide-ranging and include the works of Marlowe, Lady Mary Wroth, Shakespeare, Middleton and Greene. In his attempt to expose the value of these multiple spheres of intimacy, however, Bromley seems to take it for granted that they are essentially exclusive and independent. It left me wondering why intimacy, erotic pleasure and non-erotic pleasure cannot, for example, exist within marriage, as well as without it?

Most of the time he is convincing and almost always engaging. Some of the insights are overstated and somewhat dubious: as when he suggests a healthy scepticism for historical homogeneity but then goes on to suggest that 'if everyone already agreed with Tilney about marriage and behaved accordingly, *The Flower of Friendship* would not exist'. This statement strikes me as somewhat at odds with the kind of historical sensitivity that this book claims to rest upon.

Similarly concerned with the disruption of conventional boundaries is Jenny C. Mann's *Outlaw Rhetoric: Figuring Vernacular Eloquence in Shakespeare's England* which offers an engaging discourse on the subject of the English vernacular and how the vulgar tongue grew up both alongside and in defiance of its classical precedents. Mann develops a methodological approach to her subject in which vernacular English becomes outlaw rhetoric by virtue of its development as 'discursive errancy', belonging to an idea of place in which 'spatialized social transgression' takes effect. To this end, the figure of Robin Hood becomes a significant image in establishing her argument, where 'the situation of vernacular English rhetoric . . . [becomes] an outlaw itself, roaming the margins of the classical tradition'. Out of this image of Robin Hood Mann defines the development of English language through the translation of classical rhetoric into stories, which in turn become 'a characteristic feature of vernacular literary production'. Understanding this translation as producing a series of outlaw figures, or digressions, Mann pursues the development of an emergent vernacular as on the 'margins of classical rhetoric' but one which produces a 'distinctively English eloquence in the early modern period'. Within these terms place becomes a central feature of her argument, as a metaphor for digression, but also in the development of a 'common' English rhetoric 'yoked to the local countryside'. To this end, vernacular guides 'collectively seek to render "England" the proper subject matter of vernacular rhetoric'. Drawing on the work of scholars on both nationhood and rhetoric, Mann presents an attractive argument for the unique development of a vernacular tradition in which style takes precedent over invention. Deviating from the traditional emphasis on classical Latin manuals, Mann discovers the vernacular rhetorical manual as concerned with 'outlandish figures of speech, disorderly forms that foreground the difficulty, if not impossibility, of making classical figures "speak English"'. Focusing on both form and content of the English rhetorical manual, Mann pursues her argument through the 'common' tongue, weale, or land, drawing parallels between land and language in the anxieties of form, containment, use and possession. Identifying 'vagrant figures of speech' as transitional forms that mediate between 'classical precept and vernacular grammar', Mann explores 'the process of accommodation – the means whereby the figure is made "at home" in English'. Setting such disorderly figures within the context of key texts – *The Faerie Queene*, *A Midsummer Night's Dream*, *Arcadia* and *Epicoene*, for example – Mann follows the transition from interruption to assimilation. Intertextual and taxonomic, the book situates English vernacular at the centre of early modern systems of identity and expression which are rooted in place as well as practice. Sometimes the figurative images for digression read like rhetorical devices and tend to blur the significance of the claims, but *Outlaw Rhetoric* builds on a developing relationship between linguistics and cultural geography and is an important contribution to this field.

SHAKESPEARE IN PARTS

The Oxford Handbook of Shakespeare provides an up-to-date and comprehensive survey of many of the major themes in current Shakespeare studies. The collection includes 40 new essays which are wide-ranging and provide an in-depth analysis of the historical contexts in which Shakespeare was working, as well as including some finely tuned and detailed interpretations of language, manuscripts and print culture and the developing conditions of Elizabethan theatre. Kinney's introduction is a lesson in compressed biography. Providing a neat structural logic to both Shakespeare's life and work, he focuses on what he perceives as certain patterns in both Shakespeare's life and work: conflict crescendos in Act 3, for example, and developing dramatic characters around the strengths of his acting companies. Kinney presents us with a highly rounded author who has the insight and capacity to pre-empt as well as harness his own strengths: 'He juggled all his roles in the Lord Chamberlain's Men with those of characters and events in his life.'

All the usual topics are here – authorship, collaboration, global Shakespeare, textual circulation, theatre practice, language, gender, readership and nationhood. Essays on social history provide comprehensive overviews, particularly Ian Archer on the economy, who gives a nuanced account of the economic changes of this period, paying attention to the often over-simplified interpretations of the shift from feudalism to capitalism. Archer's 'economy' is broad and includes a focus on the role of the theatre in the development of London's economy. For Archer, however, and contrary to a number of essays in this volume which present Shakespeare as a budding entrepreneur, Shakespeare is less interested in making money and more interested in the ethical implications of money itself. On *Troilus and Cressida*, Archer writes: 'Indeed the language of commerce in the play perhaps functions as a critique of devalued human relationships, which on the surface after all is the matter of the play, rather than the pervasive language of commodification being intended as an indicator of the corrosive nature of capitalism.' Janet Clare is equally good on censorship and, like Archer, provides a more nuanced account of the process than is conventionally represented. She identifies different forms and processes of censorship (the literary and dramatic, for example) and the discrepancies between official and evidentiary practice.

Alongside the essays which focus on historical contexts, there are some glittering vignettes into Shakespeare's craft. Two essays on Shakespeare's language particularly stand out, and deserve a more detailed consideration here. Matteo Pangallo's explanations of sound, rhythm and rhyme are beautifully thought through and elegantly expressed. Situating the development of blank verse within the context of the period, Pangallo explores the often competing ways in which the form was both used and abused. Tracing how the structure of the verse affects meaning, he observes the ways in which such effects are reflected through individual and shared lines, and many of the dramatic and poetic gestures that we often take for granted in reading. Attending to metrical flexibility, Pangallo observes that it 'echoes spoken

English, but it has the added benefit of contributing rich ambiguity to the reading, allowing actors to make various choices that, while upheld by the verse, can greatly change the nuanced meanings of the exchange'. Much of his essay is indebted to the work of George T. Wright, but it is also sensitive to current trends in criticism as well as student expectations and pedagogical practice. Pangallo's affinity for his subject is evident in his sensitivity to the medium in which he is working and the musical range that governs the inflection of the spoken word. Like Raphael Lyne, Pangallo understands that language can not only produce emotion but represent it too. Lynn Magnusson's essay on language is characteristically accomplished: fluent, thoughtful and wide-ranging. Central to Magnusson's piece is an examination of the ways in which the increasingly sophisticated tools of analysis developed by contemporary criticism has, paradoxically, anaesthetized modern readers, making them 'short-sighted' about 'important kinds of difference'. Focusing on what she calls 'miscomprehension sequences' in *The Merry Wives of Windsor*, Magnusson suggests that we make an effort to 'recognise and accommodate the separate horizons shaping our own linguistic understanding and that adumbrated in the text'. In both *Love's Labour's Lost* and *The Merry Wives* the 'portrayal of the heterogeneity of the linguistic community' provide valuable support for her claim that:

These interactions function both as moments of language acquisition and adjustment for individuals and as contributions to the flux or the creative changes in the language. In these microcosms of linguistic change and innovation, the play assesses the collaborative participation of the entire community, including its least educated members, in the making and transforming of English.

In a section focusing on Mistress Quickly, Magnusson explores the misplaced critical value in the term malapropism. Engaging in a more sophisticated understanding of orality allows us to understand the character's word-use less as a sign 'of the linguistic insecurity or anxious struggle to conform that sociolinguistics identify as hypercorrection. Her word coinages or adaptations may supply

comedy, but they are also resourceful – even creative risk-taking – use of language.'

Centring on the more complex identities of figurative patterns, Catherine Bates's essay on the Sonnets presents an argument for the role of lyrical poetry as distinct from Shakespeare's drama. Focusing on the role of readership in the formulation of Shakespeare's authorial identity, Bates makes a clear distinction between the forms:

Unlike the playwright, the poet need not fear that his words would be wasted on the unappreciative multitude – 'caviar to the general', as Hamlet put it – for he was directing his words far more pointedly at a target audience: the discerning few (*Venus and Adonis* was caviar to the cognoscenti).

Although Bates's argument goes against much important recent criticism on the lyrical affinities between drama and poetry, not to mention the nature of authorship itself, her section on the Sonnets presents a number of through-line arguments which are both convincing and attractive, although not especially subtle. Her matter-of-fact tone is refreshing: on the problems of art, for example, she writes, 'Art cannot "be" in the same way as the beloved, precisely because it is fixed and does not change. It can survive death but it does not live (memorial art always has the whiff of the mausoleum about it).' She not only considers Shakespeare's poetry as distinct from the drama, in ambition and reception, but she also presents a writer who is actively shaping – if not necessarily controlling – his own career.

Most of the essays in this collection are thematic and to that end they present a large amount of material in a relatively general way. James Marino's chapter on 'Middle Shakespeare', however, is highly engaging for its attention to ingenuity and stagecraft. For Marino, 'The Chamberlain's Men could promote themselves by promoting Shakespeare; they appreciated the market value of artistic innovation.' His exploration of the middle phase presents Shakespeare as actively working through and beyond the expectations of Elizabethan drama. To that end, Marino situates the playwright within the context of his contemporaries to show the ways in which Shakespeare was rewriting old plays for new audiences: 'The resulting works leap-frogged the Admiral's Men's dramaturgy, turning pre-Marlovian chestnuts into post-Marlovian experiments.' Further discussions of phases in Shakespeare's career are developed by Adam Zucker on 'late Shakespeare' and David Bevington on 'early Shakespeare'. Both essays are well-pitched and discursive. Bevington pays particular attention to the history plays and situates the drama within the wider context of theatre in the 1590s. Elegant and concise, Bevington makes sense of the apparent appetite for dramatic history at the end of the sixteenth century. Alan Somerset's essay on local records is more expansive than the title suggests, discussing frauds and fraudsters and the impacts and legacies of those who have tampered with the archives as well as created and promoted them. Jane Hwang Degenhardt expands our horizon from the public records offices of England to the East and the influences that Africa, the Levant and the Far East exercised on European trade, culture and development. But even 'within this cross-cultural Renaissance', she writes, 'England assumed a belated and struggling role'. Tracing 'the effects of global commerce' in Elizabethan England, Degenhardt examines anxieties about alien figures, including the rise of foreign merchants and the deportation of Spanish and Portuguese Moors. Looking at Shakespeare's representations of cultural boundaries through cartography, objects and metaphors, she goes on to focus specifically on *Twelfth Night* and the (albeit anachronistic) 'geopolitics' of Illyria. Understanding Illyria as a border country between East and West, Ottoman and Christian empires, Degenhardt reads Viola's disguise as a version of the castrated slave: a eunuch who is de-sexualised, rather than bi-sexualised, which 'offered a form of protection for female vulnerability, [as] it also conveyed anxieties about masculine vulnerability'.

In contrast to the border Shakespeare, however, is Ton Hoenselaars's world Shakespeare, which extends our attention to Shakespeare's afterlife and how his works have been reproduced and appropriated in translation, performance history and by

divergent cultures. Hoenselaars ends with an ethical question that might have been better at the beginning, rather than the end, of this otherwise neutral book: 'amidst the profiteering and trading that characterize the Shakespearean afterlives, we should also continually ask ourselves if and how traditional humanist values survive or cede to new modes of engaging with Shakespeare'.

The grand narratives of empire, law, nationhood, republicanism and religion are addressed through attentive readings of historical context and the ways in which parochial, personal and institutional expectation shaped Shakespeare's theatre. Rebecca Lemon's survey of the law identifies the wider boundaries of this term, to include the institutions, practices, language and training that supported the multiple legal systems and the multiple courts. Attending to the ways in which Shakespeare's plays reflect legal philosophy as well as specific codes, Lemon focuses on such issues as succession, sovereignty, investment and, of course, Shylock's bond. Andrew Hadfield's essay on republicanism addresses some of the key questions surrounding the term and how (and indeed if) we can trace versions of a republic in early modern political culture. Focusing on humanist appropriations of Cicero, Hadfield explores the values, ideologies and geographical centres of the republic and the ways in which they were expanded, celebrated and contested in Shakespeare's plays.

Whilst much of this collection follows the conventional structures of a 'handbook' or 'companion' there are some notable additions. Tzachi Zamir's essay on 'philosophy' tackles the ambitious task of identifying and explicating the philosophical in Shakespeare's work, which as he suggests, is no mean task: 'While such lofty speculations immediately come to mind when thinking of Shakespeare and philosophy, when one actually attempts to think through such a linkage in a specific textual moment, one comes up with very little.' Indeed, identifying Shakespeare's apprehension of life as a 'poor player' or an existential impasse is part of what makes his work continually resonant to anybody interested in the quality of life, as well as mercy. Yet, as Zamir goes on to explore, apprehending such philosophical questions as whether it is better to suffer an unhappy life or enter into the unknown requires that we understand the conditions under which such questions arise: 'May we know what necessary and sufficient conditions are being presupposed with regard to "life" and "acting" when Macbeth identifies "life" with a poor player?' Such sententious embellishments, however, are, as he suggests, 'spice for the bookish' rather than 'independent philosophical arguments'. Similarly rejecting the contextualizing of Shakespeare's work within the foundational narratives of Christian humanism, stoicism or scepticism, Zamir goes on to warn his readers against happily historicizing Shakespeare's philosophical utterances and thereby relegating 'his philosophical significance to the history of philosophy (and not one of its grander moments at that) rather than making him a partner in contemporary thought'. Focusing instead on Sonnet 71, Zamir explores the complex relations between emotion and language as suggested by the 'descriptive, expressive, and generative elements' of the poem. Understanding the sonnet as 'the means whereby an evolving sentiment is being progressively created before us', Zamir demonstrates an affinity with Lyne and the ways in which the poems promote a heuristic enterprise. Concentrating on the paradoxes of Sonnet 71's 'love' Zamir moves from the particular questions of grief and desire to the complex formulations of proposition, truth and recognition. Teasing out the interrelations between mindscape and material reality, he suggests that 'the poetic articulation is only *partly* a description that conforms to what one imprecisely senses to be the case in another's love'. In this way 'art' becomes a heightened instance of experience, which in turn supports the reader's 'imaginative participation' in the poetic articulation: 'Such is the route whereby poetry is able to generate not truth, but a *potential* truth.' Shakespeare's capacity to 'metamorphose weak and marginal movements of thought and feeling into moments of heightened awareness' does not, however, lead Zamir into understanding Shakespeare as universalizing human experience. On the contrary, the work

of critics, he suggests, is to open up the text to the possibility of multiple experiences and how these may advance our understanding as well as our knowledge. Lars Engle's chapter on pragmatism responds to Zamir's challenge to Shakespeare criticism to engage more fully with the epistemologies of close reading in such a way as to not be demonized as 'regressive'. Engle's attention to 'truth' as a continually mutating dialogue between experience and knowledge leads him to *Macbeth* and how the play 'offers a dramatic meditation on the relation among broader ideas of causal influence and on the future-orientated idea of meaning as practical consequence that is at the heart of pragmatism'. Engle and Zamir offer a fresh and inquisitive contribution, challenging critical fashions and re-engaging with the ethical and epistemological duties of scholarship. Asking such questions as 'Is it possible, for instance, to be good in the play's [*Macbeth*] Scotland?' Engle confronts the kinds of moral binaries that have dropped from critical view. Many of the grander (and indeed ethical) narratives of truth, knowledge and experience are developed in subtle and persuasive ways in other books considered here, notably those by Enterline, Lyne and Symes.

While Zamir and Engle consider some of the metaphysical implications of Shakespeare's plays, Frederick Kiefer examines the materiality of aesthetics and production in his essay on architecture. Concentrating his essay on some of the most impressive houses of the period – Hardwick Hall, Wollatton Hall, Longleat – Kiefer attends to how these houses redeploy classical architecture as well as exceed the contemporary expectations of a domestic building. Revealing how architects adopted classical features to modern forms, Kiefer demonstrates the extent to which symmetry (often concealed) governed both beauty and utility. Kiefer discusses both exterior and interior, including decoration, tapestries, plasterwork and the frieze, within which Hardwick Hall 'provides...an aesthetic paradigm expressive of Elizabethan and Jacobean culture'. Linking such aesthetic paradigms to pageantry, plays and masques, Kiefer demonstrates the extent to which art and architecture shaped the drama of the age.

SHAKESPEARE'S HISTORY

One of this year's undoubted gems is Janette Dillon's *Staging Shakespeare's History Plays*. As part of the Oxford Topics it is a brief but brilliant book, full to the brim with penetrating insights, cleverly orchestrated narratives and a glorious range of textual, dramaturgical and interpretative material. Dillon is masterly at putting what is often treated as discrete historical moments into a wider framework of theatrical genesis. Focusing on the full range of the histories, including the frequently neglected *Henry VIII* and *King John*, Dillon explores the multifaceted nature of these plays. The book presents the reader with a stage populated by the clamorous voices and bodies of Shakespeare's history characters, from which Dillon pulls out people, props, stage directions, asides, speeches and interactions for a 'close up'. Moving through the spatial arrangement of scenes, and the implicit codes of status and service they present, she demonstrates the rich texture of even the briefest scenes. Attending to the scrivener in *Richard III*, for example, a scene which is frequently cut, she observes the function of this moment:

he is invented and embodied by an actor for this scene only for a particular purpose. It is not he, but what he has to say that matters; but giving him physical embodiment on the stage gives the audience a picture to hold in their minds of an ordinary man holding a paper, registering a moment of insight: he sees through Richard's deceits and says so.

Dramatizing the writing of history as an unreliable account of forced testimony, the scrivener points to the instabilities of the very form it represents. But part of the strength of this book is its attention to the smaller voices that so easily get lost amid the grand speeches of their eponymous characters. Drawing on an ongoing and discursive relationship between history and dramaturgy, Dillon applies our minds to the roles of emblems and images in the orchestration of interconnecting narratives. On which side of a king a character sits, or whether they are below or next them, for example, or the mutation of Henry's glove into Williams's money bag; how they cradle their loved ones, carry severed heads or sit in a chair not only imparts valuable information but performs or disrupts forms of ceremony. Dillon's themes are more wide-ranging than their titles suggest: domestic space, for example, extends beyond the home and into moments of intimacy, such as Arthur and his gaoler in *King John* or the uncomfortable familiarity between Anne and Sands in *Henry VIII*. Similarly extensive is her section on the soliloquy which moves beyond the grand musings of central characters to audience asides, and even those self-reflective moments that occur in the middle of an assembled company. Dillon's great skill is making you read the spaces (as well as bodies and objects) between the lines. Alerting us to the subtle ways in which language performs direction – something Dillon calls the 'close up' – the book demonstrates the ways in which language draws the audience in and out of the theatrical space, even beyond the scope of the projected audience:

Unlike Richard III, who uses soliloquy to make a collusive relationship with the audience, out of sight and hearing of other characters in the play, Richard II seems to make no distinction between private and public space. He assumes the whole public sphere as his private domain; and the egotism of this assumption is as monstrous in its way as the egotism of Richard III's determination to ride roughshod over all others to get what he wants.

Equally perceptive is her attention to the 'closing perspective': the last lines, rhyming couplets or exits of a scene which imperceptibly draw the reader/audience into a specific frame of mind. Her section on history and providence examines ghosts (manifest or imagined), prophecy and curse in the projection of history. Addressing Shakespeare's development of the history play she observes the mutation of prophecy into something altogether more rational, something more like self-awareness or pragmatism. The concluding chapter focuses almost exclusively on *Henry VIII* and the competing visions, quite literally, of the dying Katherine and incumbent Anne. Throughout this play, Dillon argues for the presence of the chair of state as a powerful, conflicted and often terrifying image of authority that seeks to both destabilize and anticipate forms of rule. This is a very good book, clear, concise, fluent and immensely skilled. Perhaps too skilled – Dillon's ability to range so fluently between all these plays occasionally collapses the distinctions between them. But perhaps that is her point: the stagecraft and the statecraft of these plays extend way beyond the chronicles they report.

Once again, *Richard II* remains the most written about history play this year and alongside Dillon's and Syme's accounts of the play, Jeremy Lopez's fronts a new edition of critical essays. Lopez's introduction focuses on poetic form and the ways in which the play 'is fundamentally informed by critical attitudes toward and questions about the efficacy of poetry'. In contrast to Dillon's attention to Richard's egotism and his apparent inability to distinguish between self and state, the first half of this collection offers predominantly historicized accounts of the play's relationship to kingship, succession, theatrical production, print, representations of the domestic and the politics of periodization (both early modern and modern). James Siemon begins the collection with a focus on the 'utterance' and an emphasis on what he calls 'tonality'. Reading the play within the multiple, and often competing forms of communication (and miscommunication), presents us with a 'tangle of languages, values and utterances' which Siemon seeks to explore within the historicized context of Shakespeare's theatre. Within these terms he concentrates on the competing languages of the 'monarchical republic' and the literature of tears which appear to both collude with and undermine the very values they seek to express. Roslyn Knutson extends Siemon's 'tangle of languages' beyond the play and into questions of both genre and what she calls 'repertorial commerce'. Writing about the larger networks of plays in the repertory system, Knutson shifts the focus away from the artistic to the commercial. Her point here is that by

positioning *Richard II* within the wider context of history plays in performance we can understand the ways in which the commercial theatre capitalized on – and created – an appetite for the chronicle play. Melissa E. Sanchez's chapter confronts the play's relegation of women. Contesting the critical perception of women as 'invisible' or strategically marginalized, Sanchez argues for a re-evaluation of female agency in the play. Setting Kantorowicz's naturalization of the (male) political body in dialogue with Judith Butler's attention to the 'zone of uninhabitability' in which the female body has historically resided, Sanchez asks that we reconsider the critical binaries so often attributed to the play – public and private, political and domestic, emotional and rational – and observe the extent to which Shakespeare amplifies 'the presence of women far more than . . . [his] source texts . . . . [to register] forms of political agency that go beyond official enfranchisement'. To this end, Sanchez thinks about both 'common and noble women' and powerfully argues for a reconstitution of the ways in which 'women *have* mattered', as well as been marginalized. Bridget Escolme's essay implicitly builds on this argument as she examines Fiona Shaw's performance of the king and the ways in which Shaw's performance troubled many critics of the show. Quoting a number of reviews, Escolme identifies a deep uneasiness about Shaw's performance that begins in accusations of infantile eccentricity but moves towards more aggressive intimations of mad woman in the attic. Attending to both versions of the production – film and stage – Escolme explores the divergent expectations of the stage and the screen and the ways in which 'female theatricality' can be so easily interpreted as 'mental illness'. Arguing that film endorses a greater 'psychological subtlety', Escolme identifies Shaw's stage Richard as disrupting the rituals and allegiances upon which critical perceptions of (male) kingship have depended. Margaret Shewring, on the other hand, focuses on the last twenty years of the play in performance, and the ways in which it has been variously politicized and interpreted during the '*zeitgeist* crucial to the mind-set of those experiencing the new millennium'. Shewring asks us to consider how can we 'find a timely performance style and interpretation that takes us forward, back to Shakespeare?'

Taking us forward, and also back, to Shakespeare is Paul Menzer's essay on Marlowe, in which he considers the anxiety (or lack of it) of influence between these two writers. Menzer traces the critical traditions which seek to sanction a relationship (chummy, antagonistic or competitive) between the playwrights through either allusion or biography. For Menzer, both are speculative and rest on a dualistic perception of the authors: 'Marlowe is our anti-Bard, the croaking raven of Deptford to Shakespeare's Avonian swan. Independently, they fascinate, but together, they hypnotize.' Menzer's project in this chapter, which he pursues with great verve and tenacity, is to demonstrate that 'Marlowe's plays did not merely dent Shakespeare's, they battered them – and . . . bettered them.' For Menzer, it is Shakespeare's 'failure' to assimilate Marlowe that renders him unique: 'In concentrated encounters with Marlowe (and others), moments where he was essentially being as unlike himself as possible, Shakespeare produces the incommensurate inconsistencies at the heart of so many of his plays' mysteries.' In pursuit of his thesis, Menzer goes on to explore the relationship between *Richard II*, *Edward II* and *Faustus* in which he observes Shakespeare's random importation of Marlowe as providing moments of complexity or opacity that have since been hungrily devoured by literary critics. There is a simpler response, Menzer suggests, in regard to Bolingbroke's borrowed condemnation of the caterpillars: 'the problem has no solution because Bolingbroke's charge *makes no sense*'. Menzer offers an alternative model for Shakespeare's borrowing which he calls 'fan fiction' in which 'Shakespeare and his contemporaries repurposed theatrical effects without much troubling themselves to distinguish their contributions from their literary antecedents.' Menzer's thesis is not revelatory: scholars have frequently acknowledged 'borrowing' as endemic to pre-copyright periods, but his irreverence and wit is refreshing.

In contrast to the recent proliferation of essays on *Richard II*, David Margolies's *Shakespeare's Irrational Endings* turns our attention to the frequently neglected 'problem plays'. Here Margolies begins with the observation that 'The discomfort Shakespeare creates for the audience in the Problem Plays is not a heuristic device; it reflects irritation with corruption, hypocrisy, injustice and other evils of his society but it is not a casual effect – it is intentional.' Understanding this irritation and 'negativity' as 'Shakespeare's own', Margolies goes on to interrogate this collection of plays through their contradictions which are seen as integral to the nature of theatre itself, a medium which, he suggests, cannot be reduced to discrete forms of word-play or expectations of naturalism. Beginning with 'nobody's favourite play', *All's Well that Ends Well*, the book engages with a discourse of 'inconsistency and strained credibility' through which we can relinquish our need for emotional response or naturalism and discover 'the hand of the artificer'. Margolies's point is that by attending to 'dislocations and deferrals' (to borrow Susan Snyder's phrase) we can discover in these troubling plays a richly rewarding and 'slippery value'. Such values are nowhere more evident, the book suggests, than in the dislocation between form and content, between our expectations and our experience. Including *Othello*, *Much Ado*, *Troilus*, *Measure* and *The Merchant of Venice* in this collection, Margolies pursues an argument against the expectations of naturalism and the disturbances (emotional, narrative, structural) that cause doubt – a healthy doubt he implies which raises questions about the world in which Shakespeare's audience lived. Contrary to conventional criticism, Margolies observes in Shakespeare's drama a move from the particular to the general, in which 'Irony became ever more appropriate, growing from incidental occurrences to the point where it characterised the structure of the whole play and developed into social critique.'

SHAKESPEARE IN PRACTICE

In *Costuming the Shakespearean Stage: Visual Codes of Representation in Early Modern Theatre and Culture*, Robert I. Lublin moves our focus from the word to the image. This book seeks to explore the ways in which costume functioned – symbolically, sexually and socially – on the Elizabethan stage. Taking his cue from Peter Stallybrass and Anne Rosalind Jones's *Renaissance Clothing and the Materials of Memory* (although not extending it), Lublin attends to the multiple process of exchange and identification through which clothing became visually representational. Lublin's work offers a welcome focus on theatre history and the codes of meaning embedded in sartorial effects. In its attempts to rationalize these codes into interpretative packages, however, it tends towards oversimplification. On women, for example, Lublin writes that 'It was almost impossible for a woman's visual presentation to suggest anything other than immorality' on the basis that she is damned if she wears make-up and damned if she doesn't. But he then goes on to say that 'Characters were not understood merely according to whether they wore a beard or not, whether they wore cosmetics or not.' This kind of writing runs throughout the book. However, Lublin's book offers a decent enough introduction to the subject. Moving through gender, social status, ethnicity and faith Lublin attends to the clothed body as a visual text which Elizabethan audience members were highly capable of reading. Within his argument, the body and its clothing become supplementary (if not always sympathetic) theatrical devices.

Equally invested in the dynamics of the theatrical space is Tim Fitzpatrick's *Playwright, Space and Place in Early Modern Performance: Shakespeare and Company*. Here, like Lublin, the focus is on the ways in which dramaturgy – or for Fitzpatrick, convention – encodes certain expectations from both player and audience. Attending to the specifics of stage space – exits, entrances, trapdoors, vertical posts, gallery or tiring house – Fitzpatrick argues for a re-evaluation of the ways in which the text and the stage govern, dictate or promote specific direction. Following the ways in which the dialogue directs stage directions, Volpone peeping 'over' the curtain rather than through it, for example, Fitzpatrick reconstructs not only the resources of the Elizabethan playing space but also the ways in which those resources are translated from production to production. Distinguishing between 'space' and 'place' to indicate the importance of both performance area and offstage preparations for those areas, the book highlights the complex choreography that makes up early modern theatre. Although Fitzpatrick doesn't explicitly defer to the work of either Henri Lefebvre or Emrys Jones the book sets out to explore the ways in which both scenic form and space can choreograph audience response. Fitzpatrick unpacks the various techniques used by playwrights (and actors) to create and develop networks of theatrical meaning, examining the various effects of signifier, sound, prop, signified and physical direction within the play-text. Central to this thesis are the roles of exits and entrances, stage doors and concealment spaces and the importance of paying attention to the effects such references, actions or structures have on a play. The book's rather old-fashioned pedagogical structure is well thought-out and reassuring, as Fitzpatrick guides the reader through a narrative of dramaturgy from the commonsense (divergent exits as signs of separation) to the more complex and codified signifiers of actors' 'movement patterns'.

In *Shakespeare's Memory Theatre: Recollection, Properties, and Character*, however, Lina Perkins Wilder focuses on the objects of the stage and the ways in which visual (and suggested) forms promote and perform recollection. Attending to the organization of certain mnemonic devices she argues that 'In Elizabethan and Jacobean London, theatre provides a model for remembering more elaborately conceived and more detailed than any theatrical memory structure seen in Continental memory treatises.' Although strangely reticent on Cicero, the book offers a thoughtful exploration of the multiple ways in which divergent forms of remembering informed and affected the development of Shakespeare's craft. Examining the art of memory through objects and place, Wilder traces the valuable ways in which stagecraft supported images of both absence and presence in its guided reconstruction of both narrative and performance. Sensitive to gender and discipline, the book acknowledges the powerful extent to which

'Shakespeare's memory theatre is in part a space in which thought becomes physical and in which physical objects become the conduits for thought'. Engaging with the power of rhetoric to imaginatively reconstruct material objects, Wilder notes that 'For every skull or handkerchief that brings the "past" of the play into its staged present, there are objects whose deeply felt physicality is entirely a matter of language, not a material fact.' Pursuing practices of memory for both audience and actors, Wilder examines the relationships between memory and production, coercion and collaboration.

Interrogating collaboration within a different context, however, is James Marino, whose *Owning William Shakespeare: The King's Men and their Intellectual Property* begins with the assertion that copyright and editing 'entered history together'. He goes on to make a compelling and convincing argument for the collaborative status of Shakespeare's plays both before and after they entered the realm of the Chamberlain's Men. Building on the now largely accepted thesis that drama is essentially and almost always collaborative, Marino goes further by establishing the contexts – and expectations – of playwrighting in the early 1590s. Reviewing the long cherished critical traditions in which authorial intention remains the guiding principle (or an 'impossible goal') of editing Shakespeare's plays, Marino focuses on the ways in which both theatre and performance have shaped the production and possession of texts, including the claim that 'textual variants should be considered as signs of continued and appropriate possession'. Beginning in 1594, the book traces the 'long collective career' of the plays that entered repertory authorless and ended as Shakespeare's. Focusing on the thorny issues of revision, 'foul papers' and 'memorial reconstruction', Marino explores the extent to which such tags have distorted our perceptions of early modern play writing. Rehearsing some of the prevailing attitudes to composition and textual production, he reveals how far modern bibliography is dependent on anachronistic assumptions about not only the status of playwright and player but the role of playing companies and printers in establishing rights. The book attends to the King's Men and their 'aggressive business strategies' in the ways they 'deployed Shakespeare's name to secure their property claims'. Exploring how the use of Shakespeare's name became a strategic way to lay claim to certain plays, Marino shows how the King's Men devised a form of intellectual property rights. Intriguingly, however, the point is not that it's 'Shakespeare' or even an original script but that it belonged to a playing company dependent on revision and rewriting to retain their rights to the play. Attending to *King Lear*, *The Taming of the Shrew*, *Hamlet*, *Henry V*, *Sir John Oldcastle* and a number of other plays, Marino carefully traces the various ways in which the texts of these plays have manufactured a sense of a 'lost original'. Writing of the Chorus's 'wooden O', Marino observes that 'The Folio text of *Henry V* gives the readers words that make no sense, that have no referent, outside the context of the Southwark playhouse . . . The reader is not allowed to forget that this play was meant to be staged, so that the text is only a poor substitute for a poor substitute.' Pursuing the collapse of exclusive performance rights through the Civil War Marino notes that 'the theatre no longer provided Shakespeare's copy to the press, but the other way around'.

CAPITAL SHAKESPEARE

David Landreth's *The Face of Mammon: The Matter of Money in English Renaissance Literature* is one of this year's most compelling books. Setting out to explore both the substance and the image of money, Landreth argues that 'English Renaissance writers use coined money to present matter itself as a basis of social meaning.' Redefining the critical relationship between subject and object, Landreth focuses on the ways in which coins generate forms of authority that are simultaneously transparent and instrumental. The very nature of money and its capacity to inhabit both material and ontological planes creates a fascinating discourse for the analysis of early modern value – economic and social. Attending to strategies of debasement, minting and stamping, Landreth shows the competing roles that money played in the imaginative reconstructions of early modern life. Thinking through the nature of things, the values of substance (extrinsic and intrinsic) and the invisible journeys that money makes from hand to hand, in credit, loan and payment the sheer concept of the coin comes to occupy a profoundly important space in the analysis of social and economic relations. Central to Landreth's thesis is the relationship between materiality and metamorphosis, and it is this that makes the argument so wide-ranging and compelling. Examining the ethical complexities of the potential of money – its destiny of circulation and the problems of avarice – in *The Faerie Queene*, Landreth considers 'the matter of memory' and 'the objects that generate histories'. In *The Merchant of Venice*, he focuses on the play's 'obsessive ambivalence towards coins', a state he calls 'disavowal' in which mystification and demystification are in continual operation to render money both essential and irrelevant. In *Measure for Measure* he explores the relationships between pleasure and representation, and the peculiar authority, even iconography, of the 'angel' (a purer coin without the imprint of the monarch). His chapter on Donne attends to the premise 'that in early modernity, people and money shared certain ontological conditions'. The methodological ambitions of this book sometimes lead to dense explications of the philosophical relations between substance and self: while these are almost always compelling they are sometimes so intricate that they are hard to unravel. The meaning of money outside its context of trade or exchange extends to the very corners of the social self. Whether in resistance, disruption, identification or acquisition the matter of Mammon is always in the process of remaking the values of value.

BOOKS REVIEWED

Yota Batsaki, Subha Mukherji and Jan-Melissa Schramm, eds., *Fictions of Knowledge, Fact, Evidence and Doubt* (London, 2012)

James Bromley, *Intimacy and Sexuality in the Age of Shakespeare* (Cambridge, 2012)

Janette Dillon, *Staging Shakespeare's History Plays* (Oxford, 2012)

David Ellis, *The Truth About William Shakespeare: Fact, Fiction and Modern Biographies* (Edinburgh, 2012)

Lynn Enterline, *Shakespeare's Schoolroom: Rhetoric, Discipline, Emotion* (Philadelphia, 2012)

Tim Fitzpatrick, *Playwright, Space and Place in Early Modern Performance: Shakespeare and Company* (Farnham, 2011)

Nicholas Fogg, *Hidden Shakespeare: A Biography* (Stroud, 2012)

Graham Holderness, *Nine Lives of Shakespeare* (London, 2011)

Arthur Kinney, ed., *The Oxford Handbook of Shakespeare* (Oxford, 2012)

David Landreth, *The Face of Mammon: The Matter of Money in English Renaissance Literature* (Oxford, 2012)

Jeremy Lopez, ed., *Richard II: Critical Essays* (London, 2012)

Robert I. Lublin, *Costuming the Shakespearean Stage: Visual Codes of Representation in Early Modern Theatre and Culture* (Farnham, 2011)

Raphael Lyne, *Shakespeare, Rhetoric and Cognition* (Cambridge, 2011)

Jenny C. Mann, *Outlaw Rhetoric: Figuring Vernacular Eloquence in Shakespeare's England* (Ithaca, 2012)

David Margolies, *Shakespeare's Irrational Endings: The Problem Plays* (Basingstoke, 2012)

James Marino, *Owning William Shakespeare: The King's Men and their Intellectual Property* (Philadelphia, 2011)

Lina Perkins Wilder, *Shakespeare's Memory Theatre: Recollection, Properties, and Character* (Cambridge, 2010)

Lois Potter, *The Life of William Shakespeare: A Critical Biography* (Oxford, 2012)

Holger Schott Syme, *Theatre and Testimony in Shakespeare's England: A Culture of Mediation* (Cambridge, 2012)

2. SHAKESPEARE IN PERFORMANCE
reviewed by RUSSELL JACKSON

This year's books cover a wide range of topics, from the specifics of stage practices in Shakespeare's theatres to the cultural exchange that takes place when the plays are reworked by directors outside the dominant Anglo-American film industry and, in a thought-provoking and often moving account, the aesthetic and political dimensions of a production of *Love's Labours Lost* in Kabul.

Mariko Ichikawa's *The Shakespearean Stage Space* examines early modern play texts for evidence of 'the relation between onstage and offstage spaces and . . . the audience's awareness both of the imaginative world created by the play and the wood, lath and plaster reality of the playhouse itself – that is to say, the balance between fiction and theatre' (1). The results of her discussion of dozens of examples can be represented concisely by the table of different meanings attached to the terms 'enter' 'within' and 'above' which is included in the book's Conclusion. This is not an exhaustive list, as the author points out, but it does illustrate (in her concluding words) 'the great achievement of early modern playwrights and players' in making 'full use of both the separation and the connection between onstage and offstage spaces and of the versatility of the stage structure so as to present a truly remarkable variety of fictional events and situations' (157).

In the course of her six chapters Ichikawa addresses many problems still encountered by directors working in theatres – particularly black-box, in-the-round or thrust – where getting bodies offstage or managing the traffic in overhearing scenes have to be accomplished without the subterfuges that might conceal the means used. In this respect, such questions as the status (fictional or actual) of stage doors in Shakespeare's playhouses have implications for our understanding of the aesthetics as well as the mechanics of plays. (When, in effect, is a door not a door?) They also bear directly on the decisions made by modern editors who are called on to indicate stage action, however conservatively, where the directions of the origi-

nal texts are inadequate or appear to be misleading. A guiding principle, appropriately enough, is pragmatism: audiences were able to follow where the players led them. At times, though, something more specific may be involved in such phrases as 'in his orchard'. Ichikawa suggests that the patterned walks and plots of the enclosed Elizabethan garden may have been suggested by the manner in which (for example) Brutus paced up and down in his scene with the conspirators (*Julius Caesar*, 2.1). The point is certainly arguable, but here, as in a handful of other cases, there is a danger of extrapolating stage behaviour too directly from the signals that the audience may have received by other means: Malvolio, after all, can use the whole of a stage in any number of ways as he luxuriates in imagined prosperity before he stumbles on the letter that will be his undoing. And doors may well be imagined offstage as well as being on occasion represented literally by the 'flanking doors' available in the rear wall, so that it is hardly necessary for Brutus to follow Ligarius off, indicating, Ichikawa suggests (127), his commitment to the conspiracy by leaving by the outer door of his own house when he bids his visitor farewell. When it is suggested (98) that 'for all we know' it may have been 'quite common for an actor waiting for his entrance to be visible some lines before his actual entrance', the further speculation that 'the audience might not have cared about the fact that he was wholly or partly visible' begs a number of questions. Specifically, one wonders how this can be related to overhearing scenes, in which the visibility of an actor unseen (or unheard) by those on stage is clearly significant; and whether there was a limit to the potential for 'switching off' or varying the interpretation of 'on' and 'off' stage space. It is true that 'one cannot over-emphasize the flexibility of the early modern stage, which could remain neutral and also, when desired, become specific' (120), but here we (and the actor) seem to be pushing at the limits of this versatility. The experiences and anxieties of Peter Quince and his players suggest that

Shakespeare and his audience relished the dizzying potential of a (relatively) empty space.

However, such moments reflect the value of Ichikawa's intervention in discussions shared by theatre practitioners, historians and editors. At times her work might have benefited from fuller consideration of the experiences of the first of these, and of the wider debates among theoreticians and historians of the phenomenology of performance, but this would have jeopardized its sharpness of focus and acuity of argument. Grounded in formidable research in the voluminous commentary on these matters, as well as in careful study of the texts themselves, this is a valuable overview of an important dimension of the semiological richness of early modern theatre.

Shakespeare in America, by Alden T. Vaughan and Virginia Mason Vaughan, in the Oxford Shakespeare Topics series, traces the growth of what is now a formidable and varied Shakespeare industry from its earliest 'toehold' (15) on the continent in the mid-1700s. The authors are anxious to identify the distinctive nature of American Shakespeare, and by and large succeed in this aim, although the traits of earnest nineteenth-century educational endeavour and the drawing of moral lessons from the works can be found in the British commentaries, anthologies and editions as well as their transatlantic equivalents. Early in the nineteenth century America's 'lack of scholarly originality' is attributed to the absence of the 'tools' of scholarship in the form of early editions and other materials and of a 'community of scholars for debating new findings and theories and encouraging each others' endeavours'. An important element of the authors' narrative in *Shakespeare in America* is their tracing of the process by which, with the founding of world-class libraries and other institutions and the professionalizing of English studies in universities and colleges, the United States progressed from a state of affairs in which 'many Americans read and watched the plays; very few studied them' (55) to the international standing at the end of the twentieth century of the constituency represented by the Shakespeare Association of America.

In the theatres of the new millennium, the establishment (and defence) of an American way of playing Shakespeare has been hotly debated. The decentralized and vigorous 'Festival Shakespeare', its roots traced to an American tradition of 'locally based programming' (179), together with the absence of major subsidized companies on the British and European models, have fostered varied and innovative approaches. In their discussion of this and of 'Popular Shakespeare' the authors provide a concise introduction to a complex topic. Earlier periods present a less clearly defined picture. Distinctions between English and American acting styles were one of the contributing factors – in the rivalry between Forrest and Macready – to the agitation that led to the Astor Place riots. Nevertheless, the presence of many British actors on American stages, either as visitors or as permanent or semi-permanent residents, means that a specifically North American 'school' of acting, at least in Shakespeare, is not easily defined. Greater diversity, and a sense of Shakespearian performance beyond the dominant Anglo-Saxon culture came towards the end of the century. A chapter on 'Multicultural Shakespeare' describes the tension between assimilation and apartness in African-American performance (legally segregated until the middle of the twentieth century) and Yiddish theatre. In the latter, *Hamlet*, *Othello* and *Romeo and Juliet* were 'adapted to meet their audiences' needs, accentuating conflict between the generations and the challenges faced by outsiders' (111). In *The Merchant of Venice*, the first of the plays to be translated, Jacob Adler, arguably the greatest tragic actor of the Yiddish stage, modelled his sympathetic Shylock on Henry Irving's. African-American and Latino Shakespeare, until recently neglected or subordinated to the Anglo-Saxon 'mainstream', also receive their due, with emphasis on their political context as well as their aesthetic achievements. Although *Shakespeare in America* does not foreground a political agenda, it draws attention throughout to Shakespearian performance and study as existing within the nation's political and social culture.

An iconic figure in African-American Shakespeare is the subject of Bernth Lindfor's two-volume biographical study of the 'African Roscius' Ira Aldridge (*The Early Years, 1807–1833* and *The Vagabond Years, 1833–1852*). The first sentence indicates the mystery that is to be explored. 'Ira Aldridge was not African.' In most respects the work supersedes *Ira Aldridge: The Negro Tragedian* by Herbert Marshall and Mildred Stock, published in 1958.[1] The second of Lindfors's volumes ends in 1852, so Marshall and Stock remain the source in English for access to accounts of his travels after that date. Born in New York in 1807, Aldridge pursued an international career that took him far beyond the restrictions of his native land's segregated theatres and involved the fashioning of an identity almost as exotic as that described by Othello, one of his signature roles. His repertoire extended beyond Shakespeare's Venetian Moor to encompass other tragic and comic heroes (and villains) of colour, and outsiders of one hue or another. (He also played some leading roles in whiteface.) He was famous for delivering comic songs as well as dramatic impersonations, and was fêted and honoured in Britain and Ireland, Western Europe, Russia and Poland. He died on tour in Łodz in 1867. Aldridge's career consisted for the most part of endless touring either as a star performer appearing with local companies, or with a small company of actors in a 'grand cultural and dramatic entertainment'. Even when actors were beyond the point in their career where, as a member of a stock company, they might be called on to be 'up in' an unfamiliar role with no more than a day's notice, the routine was punishing. On one occasion in Hull, Aldridge 'performed twenty-four times in ten nights in fifteen different roles' (*Early Years*, 200). Lindfors has assembled a formidable array of documentation that allows him to shed light on the actor's early days in New York, to unravel the fictions with which he rendered his background more glamorous, and to follow him on his arduous tours. Reviews and plot summaries are quoted at length, which may not always make for a smooth read, but effectively provides an anthology of nineteenth-century national and provincial dramatic reviewing. It also furnishes

outstanding examples of racial attitudes, ranging from the welcoming of the actor as evidence that men and women of colour were susceptible of civilizing influences, to out-and-out racist abuse. It was difficult to find acceptance simply as a powerful and sophisticated actor, and race would inevitably be a factor in praise as well as dispraise throughout Aldridge's career, especially in Britain.

In March 1848, when he returned to London after an absence of some fifteen years, the *Era* remarked on the favourable reception he had received on his last visit in terms that summarize the factors that might have weighed against him: 'the novelty of a man of colour representing Shakspere's [*sic*] intellectual heroes so as to meet the serious approval of critics, and the extraordinary circumstances of Mr Aldridge (although a black) taking his stand in the profession as a gentlemen and a scholar, capable of receiving the poet's creations, and portraying his thoughts in a display of histrionic art' (*Vagabond Years*, 137). In countering adverse criticism, such comments implicitly accept prejudice as the normal, expected response to such ambitions: how extraordinary that a black man could do all this! But this pales in comparison with the virulent racism that had already contributed to the failure of the actor's earlier attempt to gain a secure footing in the principal metropolitan theatres. Gilbert Abbott À Beckett, editor of *Figaro in London*, had taken the trouble to launch an attack while Aldridge was appearing in Denbigh, publishing a derisive account of the performances of 'a stupid looking, thick lipped, ill formed African', an incompetent 'stage-struck chip off an alleged royal block' whose presumptions should be punished (*Early Years*, 229, 230). À Beckett's was not the only voice raised in similar language against the actor when he appeared at Covent Garden in 1833, but the satirist preened himself on the part his 'relentless tomahawk' played in banishing 'that miserable nigger whom we found in the provinces imposing on the public by the name of the *African Roscius*' (*Early Years*, 257).

---

[1] Herbert Marshall and Mildred Stock, *Ira Aldridge: The Negro Tragedian* (London, 1958).

For better or worse, Aldridge himself cultivated the sense of difference by fabricating far-fetched accounts of his lineage, claiming descent from 'Princes of the Foulah Tribe', and (as Lindfors observes) 'engaging in an illicit but entertaining form of ethnological show business' (*Early Years*, 184). On a less elevated level, he played on the distance between his own achievements and common expectations by appropriating the comedian Charles Mathews's parody in *A Trip to America* (1824) of a black Shakespearian actor ('To be or not to be, dat is him question'). His appearing as the comic slave Mungo in the popular farce *The Padlock*, and 'introduction' in that and other entertainments of the song 'Opossum up a Gum Tree' further complicate the matter: Aldridge, who had billed himself initially as 'Mr Keene', courted danger in the self-promoting strategies of his early career. Elaborate – and, by all accounts, tiresome – curtain speeches in verse and published biographical sketches contributed to the aura of distinction and distinctiveness. A paradoxical effect of Lindfors's accumulation of detail and lengthy citation of commentary is that the book becomes livelier when he moves from the long-winded encomiums of the right-thinking to the violent abuse of characters like À Beckett. Another paradox of Aldridge's life, though, is that after his departure from the United States in late 1824 or early 1825, he never played again in the country of his birth. (Playbill puffery would later announce him as being about to return to his fictional homeland, but he never visited Africa.) Consequently, Aldridge's status as an icon of black American Shakespearian performance has to be qualified: he exemplifies the restrictions laid on people of colour in the early nineteenth century, and the efforts that had to be made by him and others – including James Hewlett, leading actor at the African Theatre in New York in the early 1820s and, Lindfors argues (51), his one possible role model as a black tragedian. A recent and highly acclaimed theatrical revisiting of Aldridge should be noted. In the autumn of 2012 *Red Velvet*, a play about Aldridge by Lolita Chakrabati, was produced at the Tricycle Theatre in London. Michael Billington in *The*

Guardian (17 October 2012), wrote that the play 'open[ed] up a fascinating subject' and that Adrian Lester's performance as Aldridge 'whet[ted] the appetite' for his Othello at the National Theatre in 2013: 'What is striking about Lester's performance is its emphasis on the novelty of Aldridge's approach: it was his insistence on direct physical and emotional contact with his Desdemona, as well as his colour, that caused consternation. But Lester also brilliantly shows that Aldridge's innovative realism was accompanied by nineteenth-century gestural acting; so when he says of Desdemona's handkerchief that "there's magic in the web of it", his hands weave a pattern in the air.'

Lindfors establishes Aldridge as an important figure on the nineteenth-century Shakespearean stage, significant for reasons beyond his colour and representative of the experiences of many touring tragedians. Another important adjustment to interpretations of the period, even more far-reaching is proposed convincingly by Stuart Sillars in *Shakespeare, Time and the Victorians*. In the second chapter of this major study, Stuart Sillars demonstrates the ways in which two illustrated editions, those of Charles Knight and 'Barry Cornwell' (the pseudonym of Bryan Proctor), exemplify 'the dual axes of Victorian Shakespeare activity, its concern with temporal location within history and its construction of time, in duration, rhythm and accent, through its unfolding in the theatre and the book' (51). At the centre of Sillars's thesis is an illuminating reading of the visual and critical evidence for the elaborate 'revivals' presented at the Princess's Theatre by Charles Kean. He reassesses by examination of designs and prompt-book illustrations the ways in which their 'visual manipulation of the temporal unfolding of the . . . action' of the plays was more sophisticated than has been suggested by the habitual characterization of the actor-manager as privileging irrelevant and pedantic pictorial detail at the expense of the drama. In a detailed analysis of one 'episode' in particular – the entry of Bolingbroke and the defeated Richard into London in *Richard II* – Sillars demonstrates the dynamics of the scenography and staging as interpretative strategies: 'Shakespeare is at the heart of

Kean's visual theatre: this is neither empty spectacle nor simple historical re-enactment, but a far more subtle interweaving of the play, the historical events, and the idea of Shakespeare as the true presence of national identity' (128). Later chapters carry the argument forward with examinations of the status of graphic evidence – engraving and photography – that records or reflects the performances after the event, and move to a reassessment of subsequent Shakespearian productions and works of graphic art.

Starting appropriately with discussion of Henry Courtney Selous's painting *The Opening of the Great Exhibition*, which typifies 'the concern to see the present through the past, to give it validation through its innate superiority while acknowledging its dependence on heroic precedent and tradition' (1), Sillars identifies the Victorian view of history as 'essentially a dialogue in which the present examined the past and sought its own identity' (5). Although the concept may not be entirely novel, it has not hitherto been pursued with comparable breadth of view or richness of evidence. Due acknowledgement is made to the groundbreaking work of W. Moelwyn Merchant, Martin Meisel and others, and there is a strong sense of the author's engagement in dialogue with other commentators as well as with the primary material. In his treatment of the latter, he is concerned not simply with the status of prints and photographs as evidence in a literal, direct sense – how reliable is a studio photograph as a depiction of an actor's performance? – but as expressions of cultural ethos and acts of interpretation in their own right. Here, as in the pursuit of its argument, *Shakespeare, Time and the Victorians* is a suggestive work, pointing to new lines of enquiry in its analyses of paintings, illustrations and stage performances.

The generous defence of Charles Kean as a producer and director *avant la lettre* – his not altogether stellar acting does not figure here – suggests his kinship with the methods of filmmakers, equally adept at substituting visual for verbal effects with interpretive intent that has not pleased every critic. Some early films, such as the brief scene of King John's death enacted by Herbert Beerbohm Tree or the episodes from *Richard III* performed on the Stratford stage by F. R. Benson's company, are effectively animated versions of the illustrations in Victorian editions: the inclusion in *Richard III* of the aftermath of the battle of Tewkesbury and the murder of the princes in the Tower, never shown in Benson's production of the play, and the presence of intertitles quoting the play but not always corresponding to lines seeming to be spoken by the actors, reinforce the sense of an 'extra-illustrated' edition printed on celluloid. In another kind of cross-fertilization of moving and still pictures, it is arguable that the quotation (a Victorian would have written 'realization') of Millais's painting of Ophelia in Olivier's 1948 film of *Hamlet* has extended the influence of the painting.

Volume XI of the *Great Shakespeareans* series is edited by Daniel Albright, and offers accounts of Shakespearian operas by Hector Berlioz, Giuseppe Verdi, Richard Wagner and Benjamin Britten. Peter Bloom's essay on Berlioz is helpfully methodical in its organization, enumerating the composer's engagements with the dramatist play-by-play, and following Shakespearian references through the criticism, memoirs and letters. Berlioz's description, in his *Mémoires*, of his encounter with an English company's performances of Shakespeare in Paris in 1827, is a familiar document: 'the supreme drama of [his] life' led to his (disastrous) marriage to the actress Harriet Smithson, the composition of *Roméo et Juliette*, major elements of the *Symphonie Fantastique* – the poet wandering in the fields as the composer had done under the influence of Smithson and Shakespeare – and much else besides. His responses to artistic stimulus were characteristically extreme, even without the additional erotic element provided by Smithson's acting. Not one to stint in demonstrations of enthusiasm, in 1859 he wrote to his sister Adèle: 'recently I was rereading Shakespeare's *Julius Caesar*; I became literally furious with admiration, I pounded my head, I pulled my hair . . . I am passionate about passion' (27).

Bloom traces the Shakespearian dimension in Berlioz's music beyond *Roméo et Juliette*, where only orchestral music without singing can encompass the lovers' first meeting and the balcony scene, via the more conventionally operatic *Béatrice et Bénédict*, and the act of homage to Shakespeare in *Lélio*, into *Les Troyens*, where the duet 'Nuit d'ivresse et d'extase infinie' that ends Act 4 brings Lorenzo and Jessica's scene in 5.1 of *The Merchant of Venice* into the Virgilian context. Here the grown-ups are allowed to sing the *scène d'amour* that the Veronese teenagers had to leave to the orchestra, but as the act ends their ecstasy is ominously qualified by the appearance of Mercury with his chilling and laconic repetition of 'Italie!' Bloom's commentary on these and other works is sharpened by the kind of felicitous phrasing that characterizes the volume editor's own writing: in the Carthaginian sentinels' sceptical remarks in Act 5 of *Les Troyens* about the Trojans' mission ('Par Bacchus! Ils sont fous avec leur Italie . . . ') the 'levity' of the music, its effect likened by Bloom to that of the gravediggers' scene in *Hamlet*, is enhanced by 'a simulacrum of regularity that in the end reflects Berlioz's lifelong allergy to everything in music that is "expected"' (64–5).

A corresponding lifelong disposition in Wagner – its manifestations less striking than Berlioz's constant sounds of surprise, now that the erstwhile 'music of the future' has been embedded in the aural expectations of the present – seems to have contributed to the eccentric choice of *Measure for Measure* as the basis for his only fully 'Shakespearian' opera, *Das Liebesverbot* (1836). Performed in its entirety only once during the composer's lifetime, it resurfaced in 1922 when a vocal score was published. (A full score appeared in the following year.) David Trippett notes that the autograph score has been missing since 1945, 'after it had been in the possession of one of the opera's more notorious fans, Adolf Hitler' (142).[2] The early opera did not have the same status as *Rienzi*, *Parsifal* or the *Ring* cycle in the dictator's personal pantheon, but the story of a 'ban on love', set now in Palermo, may well have found a niche there. There is a clue in the revolutionary spirit evinced in Luzio's championing of carnival in the face of the prohibition not only of brothels and extra- and pre-marital sex but also alcohol by the Duke of Sicily's strait-laced deputy, the German regent Friedrich

(Angelo). Trippett identifies the relevance of Luzio, no longer the play's lazily urbane rake, as a leader of popular revolt, to the politics of the 1830s and the romantic rebellion of 'Young Germany', which the authorities responded to with persecution that sent Wagner and others into exile. In more immediately musical (or musical-political) terms, Wagner was in revolt against what he considered trivial prettiness and the quest for (in Trippett's phrase) 'sanctimonious profundity' in the operas of Weber and other Germans, which he contrasted with the freely acknowledged lyrical sensuality of the Italians. Hence the opposition between the Prussian Friedrich and the Sicilian realm he rules. 'It seems', writes Trippett, 'that stimulated by Shakespeare's Isabella, Wagner spun the opera's sexual-social narrative out of a perception of hypocritical Puritanism within German musical style' (151). Among its intriguing adjustments in the plotting and *dramatis personae* (including the renaming of Pompey Bum as Pontius Pilatus), the absence of any character corresponding to the Duke from the onstage action makes Isabella the instigator of the bed-trick and enhances the sense of her agency.

Beyond *Das Liebesverbot*, appropriately enough the main focus of the essay, traces of Shakespeare are identified in other operas, possibly including *Tristan und Isolde* (*Antony and Cleopatra*) and *Die Meistersinger* (the midsummer night, 'Johannisnacht'). His enduring enthusiasm for Shakespeare, and the family evenings at home in Wahnfried, the family villa in Bayreuth, spent reading aloud even such less popular plays as *Titus Andronicus*, suggest that, unlike Berlioz, for Wagner the influence went deep but did not reveal itself directly or on a grand scale in music and drama. The juxtaposition of these two essays is an opportunity for comparison of two very different varieties of the

---

2 Hitler acquired *Das Liebesverbot*, along with other autograph scores, in two leather-bound volumes, a gift (brokered by Winifred Wagner) from the Confederation of German Industry on the occasion of his fiftieth birthday. See Joachim Köhler, *Wagner's Hitler: The Prophet and his Disciple*, translated and introduced by Ronald Taylor (Cambridge, 2000), pp. 13–14.

Romantic temperament. Seth Brodksy, in 'Britten as Another: Six Notes on a Mystic Writing Pad', delivers a persuasive account of *A Midsummer Night's Dream*, tracing intricate internal cross-references in the opera as well as its relationship with the composer's other work, its citations of operatic precedents and the sophisticated parodic vein of *Pyramus and Thisbe*. Brodsky's writing, at times dauntingly (and on occasion, jauntily) recondite, is also rewarding: the diagram with which he represents the 'operas within an opera' and their cross-connections is a *tour de force* of graphic exposition.

Albright's own essay on Verdi complements those of his contributors with an incisive account of the dramatic and musical craft and power of *Macbetto*, *Otello* and *Falstaff*. His writing, here as in his *Musicking Shakespeare* (2007), constantly impresses with its acuteness of musical analysis and arresting aesthetic judgements wittily expressed. The duet that ends the first act of *Otello* is 'more appropriate for a golden wedding anniversary than for two newlyweds. There is no urgency in it, it takes place in a crystal Elysium of melody' (118). In *Macbetto*, 'Lady' – Verdi's designation of the character throughout – 'infects Macbeth's imagination by echoing him' when he returns from the battlefield and his encounter with the witches:

She attempts to regularize his musical discourse, to fetch him out of a traumatic realm of minor keys, diminished chords, black cadences, sudden silences and hesitations, fragmentary phrases, oracular ambiguities, into a straightforward, major-key domain of resolute action. (91)

Albright delivers some of the brightest and best metaphors in the critical business, valid because they make a vivid connection with the experience of listening and the shape of the musical drama. He points out that the two great scenes in this opera, the Act 1 duet and the sleep-walking scene, 'have a texture quite distinct from normal Italian operatic practice: they seem assembled out of musical pebbles and rocks, with a peculiar sort of continuity that's more like the flow of gravel from a dump truck than the flow of a river' (86). Writing of this kind, supported by exemplary scholarship, sends the reader back to the score and the CD player (or the opera house) with a renewed zest.

Volumes in *The Great Shakespeareans*, a pricey series destined inevitably for the 'institutional' market, are less likely than *Verdi's Shakespeare: Men of the Theatre* by Gary Wills to reach that much-sought-after customer 'the intelligent general reader'. This is unfortunate, because (with the possible exception of Brodksy) Albright's contributors write in a style that is accessible to the non-specialist. Wills, a well-informed enthusiast and experienced writer but not an academic, starts from the unexceptionable and not altogether novel proposition that as well as being 'creative volcanoes', both composer and dramatist were 'mainly...men of the theatre, engaged in the companies they worked with, active at each stage of the production of the plays and operas that filled their lives...Theirs was a hands-on life of the stage, not a remote life of the study' (4). The working conditions of Shakespeare's theatre are sketched in, as are Verdi's dealings with singers, managements and collaborators. Wills acknowledges that with Shakespeare we have little to go on in matching roles to known performers, whereas Verdi's careful instructions to singers and others are lavishly documented.

This does not claim to be a work of original scholarship: for Verdi, Wills relies on the very full documentation provided by established secondary works, and this element of his book is a sensible introduction to the operas, directing the reader to the detailed critical and historical commentaries on which it draws. For Shakespeare and his theatre, many of the sources cited are not as up-to-date, and the speculative nature of the writing becomes less secure. The engaging suggestion that in *The Winter's Tale* Autolycus might have been pursued offstage by a young polar bear is welcomed (6) with an enthusiasm that has not been widely shared – Andreas Höfele, in his recent study of animals in Shakespeare's theatre, concludes that, unlike the use of a canine actor as Crab in *The Two Gentlemen of Verona*, 'the case of the bear...is far less clear'.[3] Richard Burbage's proven ability to deliver complex soliloquies is not decisive evidence for his having played Iago rather than Othello, and is at best a plausible proposition when compared to the very full documentation of Verdi's choices in casting *Otello* with tenors in both corresponding roles. Nor is Burbage's ability to sing – not after all so rare an accomplishment in a professional actor – a clear indication that some (or indeed any) of the snatches of rhyme in Hamlet's part would be sung (108). Even if these were standards from the back catalogue of the Elizabethan hit parade, has anyone ever *tried* singing some of Wills's suggestions, such as 'To a nunnery, go' or 'For if the sun breed maggots in a dead dog, being a good kissing carrion'?

As the book progresses, Wills has fewer points to make about Shakespeare and more on Verdi. He has a sympathetic and well-informed ear for nuances in recordings, including those by singers who had performed in the premieres of *Otello* and *Falstaff*, but his translations of the words set by the composer are sometimes eccentric. When the merry wives – the traditional version surely more appropriate than 'conspirers' for 'comari' (gossips, cronies or godmothers) – exclaim against the 'mostra' (monster) who has written them the love-letter(s), 'weirdo' seems weakly rather than arrestingly modern, and 'Falstaff immenso! / Falstaff enorme!' the glorifying exclamations of the knight's henchmen, suffer some diminution when the second line becomes 'outsize Falstaff!' (202, 194). Nevertheless, Wills's book serves as a useful introduction to Verdi's wonderfully precise and intimate engagement with vocal and dramatic performance, to such insights as his insistence that in casting *Falstaff* the producer should not 'meddle with artists who want to sing too much and express feeling and action by falling asleep on the notes' (184), or his favouring Marianna Barbieri-Nini over the more comely Eugenia Tadolini for 'Lady' because he wanted a performer who will be 'ugly and evil' with a 'harsh, stifled and hollow (*cupa*) voice'. The eminent English critic Henry Chorley observed that 'unsightly is a gentle adjective as applied to her case' (31–2). With appropriate warnings in respect of its treatment of evidence for Shakespeare's theatrical circumstances

the book can be recommended to those encountering Verdi's Shakespeare for the first time. It also includes in one of its notes a prize anecdote featuring Kenneth Tynan and Roman Polanski. At the premiere of the latter's 1971 film of *Macbeth*, Wills asked the director whether he did not think that, despite his presentation of Lady Macbeth sleepwalking in the nude, 'the witch [*sic*] references to gown and taper' might not be important: 'He referred me to his artistic adviser standing by, Kenneth Tynan, who blithely assured me that Shakespeare would have done the scene nude except for the fact that his Lady Macbeth was a boy.' Wills remarked (one hopes, with intentional irony) that he had been in Scottish castles, 'whose interiors are cold and wet even in summer, and they hardly invite anyone to nudity' (54).

Nick de Somogyi's *Shakespeare on Theatre* is a brisk and well-informed survey of the playwright's utterances (through his works and characters) on the theatre practice of his day. Not a 'contribution to Shakespeare studies' in the sense of a work of primary scholarship, the book is nevertheless reinforced with ample quotation from other contemporary sources. It can safely be recommended to undergraduates and to those 'intelligent general readers' presumably addressed but poorly served in the Shakespearian parts of Wills's *Verdi's Shakespeare*. Any book that can cite Sondheim alongside Jonson, and has room in its chapter epigraphs for an exchange from *North by Northwest* and lyrics by Noël Coward and Howard Dietz, has to be worth the whistle.[4]

This important readership is served in a different way by *Sweet William: Twenty Thousand Hours with Shakespeare*, in which Michael Pennington writes from experience as an actor and reader, with an

---

[3] Andreas Höfele, *Stage, Stake and Scaffold: Humans and Animals in Shakespeare's Theatre* (Cambridge, 2011), p. 30.

[4] The Hitchcock scene is that between Roger Thornhill (Cary Grant) and Phillip Vandamm (James Mason), and begins with the latter asking 'Has anyone ever told you that you overplay your various roles rather severely, Mr Kaplan?' Dietz's lyric is from 'That's Entertainment' (in *The Band Wagon*, 1952) and celebrates the scene 'Where a ghost and a Prince meet, / And everyone ends in mincemeat.'

eye for detail and a lively appreciation of poetic as well as theatrical effect. Always an engaging writer, Pennington often makes the kind of observation that frames a character or situation in a novel manner. He suggests that Falstaff 'is part of an ongoing English tradition – the disreputable regimental type who passes as a gentleman in peace, the rake who can step up to the line in a national emergency. Evelyn Waugh must have loved him' (89). Up to a point: Falstaff may be 'competent to lead a platoon into battle', but the recruits he musters for the battle of Shrewsbury are hardly likely to put the fear of death into the enemy and were put together by means worthy of Waugh's least admirable military wide boys. Nevertheless, the evocation of Waugh – to which one might add Anthony Powell – is felicitous. Troilus's language 'crackles with military static' – 'Why should I war without the walls of Troy?' – and *Coriolanus* is 'pre-eminently a play of politics and war, one of the greatest, but it would be less so if it were not also a story of love – and not entirely of its absence' (249, 255). In the passages of the book where he discusses his experiences with productions and companies, Pennington is no less succinct: the English Shakespeare Company, which he co-directed with Michael Bogdanov, 'was based on a conviction that everything in Shakespeare, however beautiful, is full of argumentation, and every line a point of view in a transfixing debate' (154). 'Shakespearean acting has largely become a matter of finding out how real you can be without screwing up the verse' (146). Pennington is an expert and appreciative critic of verse speaking, recalling the sound of Shakespeare in his youth, with 'a brisk and genteel prettiness in the women' (Celia Johnson in *Brief Encounter*) and 'a sound that was generally staunch, officer-class and heterosexually sensible' for the men (Cyril Raymond as her husband). By way of contrast Gielgud (whose Hamlet was recorded for radio in 1948) 'stood outside fashion':

A miracle of speed and feeling, his is the only [recorded] performance which sounds as if it comes from a deep place within him and that he will perish if he doesn't let

it out. His secret was less the fabled beauty of his sound than the visceral force that made its beauty possible. (138–9)

Pennington's accounts of plays are larded with acute references to performers and performances, open to argument (in the spirit of the ESC) and forceful in invective when occasion demands it. In the context of Menenius's fable of the belly, the present Coalition government's infliction of cuts on arts funding is observed to be a stage in working down an alphabetical shopping list of 'national enterprises to hack them down in turn – C for Culture, E for Education, H for Health, P for Pensions' (302). The energy and generosity of spirit of *Sweet William* make for an exhilarating and often illuminating read.

The Edinburgh Companion to Shakespeare and the Arts, edited by Mark Thornton Burnett, Adrian Streete and Ramona Wray, brings together thirty essays divided into six groups, addressing Shakespeare and 'the book' (poetry, novels, anthologies, biography and 'textual Shakespeare'), and Shakespeare in music, on stage and in performance, in the context of 'youth culture', 'visual and material culture' and 'media and culture.' These titles indicate a degree of potential cross-fertilization, with the final section presumably requiring its 'and culture' because the internet is added to film, television and radio. The essays on performance – theatre, film, etc. – have much to offer, although the decision on the part of some authors not to provide an overview of the topic suggests that the volume's claim to be a 'companion' needs some qualification. In 'Shakespeare and Opera', for example, Adrian Streete gives a valuable account of Verdi's *Otello* in terms of cultural and political analysis, with particular focus on the vocal interpretations of the title role as reflections of racial attitudes evidenced in nineteenth-century performances of Shakespeare's play as well as the recorded or reported approach of singers. The 'chronology of Shakespearean operas' and exemplary works of 'musicological critique' are indeed 'easily available elsewhere' (145). However, a reader approaching the topic for the first time may not find as much help here as a 'companion' might be expected to provide. Streete does embed his discussion of *Otello* in deft and expert discussions of the range of Shakespearian operas, but this is very much a second (perhaps, third) port of call after the interested reader and listener has found those chronological and analytical works. Christie Carson's 'Shakespeare and the Modern Stage' and Andrew James Hartley's 'Shakespeare and Contemporary Performance Spaces' do not survey the whole scope of their respective topics, but are valuable for shrewd and provocative commentary. Hartley gives a fascinating and valuable account of the range and nature of the (very) numerous spaces, institutions and cultural contexts of American Shakespearian performance. He starts from the proposition that a focus on space 'gets us away from that conservative and essentialist notion of the magical, orthodox power of the text being generically broadcast throughout the world, inoculating the larger culture with the assumed value(s) of the monolithic "Shakespeare"' (333).

Like Streete's, these essays can be required reading for students, but the desire (in many respects, laudable) to avoid the chronicle approach suggests that they will need to be contextualized by more conventional work of that kind. In fact, some of the volume's other essays present a stimulating combination of the two approaches: a fresh approach to historical overview marks out Susan Greenhalgh's historical survey of the unduly neglected field of Shakespeare on radio, and there are stimulating essays by Stephen Purcell ('Shakespeare on Television') and on filmed Shakespeare by Judith Buchanan, Ramona Wray and Anne-Marie Costantini-Cornède. Purcell's essay includes the suggestion – in the light of the 'quotation' of the other medium in Baz Luhrmann's *Romeo+Juliet* and Michael Almereyda's *Hamlet* – that 'perhaps it is only a matter of time before Shakespeare on television becomes just as much about television as it is about Shakespeare' (534). As well as providing an historical overview, this is effectively a position paper, a stimulus to further enquiry. Some contributions that are not exclusively or primarily concerned with performance have implications

for approaches to it – in particular, Kevin J. Wetmore Jr on 'Shakespeare for Teenagers' and Mike Jensen on Shakespeare in comic books. One tension – or dynamic, to put it more positively – that emerges in this and other recent publications is that identified by Carson in her comparison of two British theatre companies: 'I would suggest that the [all-male] Propeller company provides a more "local" Shakespeare for a new British audience while the Globe Theatre [on the Bankside] provides "global" Shakespeare for an international popular audience' (315). This uneasy relationship between the close and the distant, and the question of authenticity (to what, for whom?) is reflected in the ways 'the last two years of the twentieth century show an exhausting attempt to address a festival audience while also maintaining established audiences in international centres, particularly in New York and Tokyo' (323). Like Hartley's wariness about the export of the 'magical, orthodox power of the text', Carson's observation acknowledges a brave new world while being wary of the dangers of a bland new globalization. Are we in danger of devising an extravagant and wheeling Shakespeare of everywhere and nowhere, or is this in fact a desirable transformation of expectations and a new-found freedom?

For those who do not read or speak Russian, hearing Boris Pasternak's translation of *Hamlet* on the soundtrack of Grigori Kozintsev's 1964 film will probably have been their only encounter with the poet and novelist's direct engagement with Shakespeare. In 'Pasternak's Shakespeare in Wartime Russia', his contribution to *Shakespeare and the Second World War: Memory, Culture, Identity*, Aleksei Semenenko identifies the patterns in the Russian author's work that draw on and contribute to 'his' Shakespeare, 'a certain mythological theme that can be generally described as a plot in which the messiah-like hero sacrifices himself for the sake of an approaching epoch that can be traced in poems, translations (including *Hamlet*) and the novel *Doctor Zhivago*' (152). Shakespeare was 'a sort of an artistic mirror that, in the times of oppression and war, revealed and made more palpable the essential motifs of Pasternak's own *oeuvre*' (156). Other essays examine the place of Shakespeare's works in the mythologizing efforts of regimes – notably Mussolini's Italy and the cult of the Roman imperial past – or, in the case of post-war Poland, the difficulties of accommodation with a deeply troubled and tragic past. Katarzyna Kwapisz Williams, in 'Appropriating Shakespeare in Defeat: *Hamlet* and the Contemporary Polish Vision of War', describes an adaptation of *Hamlet*, performed in and around 'a real battlefield and a war grave'– the memorial to the dead of the Warsaw uprising – an event and a location that express a national dilemma, 'the self-image of Poles as simultaneously betrayed victims and heroes' (287). Neither re-enactment nor documentary, and involving veterans of the conflict, this performance touched on raw nerves. The same might be said of the productions of *The Merchant of Venice* in Israel and Palestine discussed by Mark Bayer in 'Shylock, Palestine, and the Second World War', an essay that reaches beyond the immediate period in question and addresses the sources of the seemingly ever-present conflict between the Jewish and the Palestinian states. Shylock also figures, as one might expect, in the account by Werner Habicht of 'German Shakespeare, the Third Reich, and the War', and Zeno Ackermann's discussion of specific productions in 'Shakespearean Negotiations in the Perpetrator Society'. Given the fact (Ackermann points out) that some prominent German-speaking interpreters of Shylock had been Jewish, Nazi cultural policy encountered major problems in appropriating the play: 'as a figure of difference [Shylock] simultaneously unsettled and ratified the fantasies of the Nazis. This is why the administrators of National Socialist cultural policy were so cautious about allowing Shylock to appear on the stage – and, at the same time, it is why they were so eager to make him serve their ends' (46). The 1943 production at the Burgtheater in Vienna, with Werner Krauss as the Jew, was far from being a simple matter of hate-culture of the kind common in the more rabid Nazi press and manifest in such exhibitions as 'The Eternal Jew'. Ackermann identifies the ways in which the production 'built on and ratified the pastness of the Jewish presence in Austria

and Germany'. Perhaps the most chilling comment on it is that of Siegfried Melchinger, in a review for the *Neues Wiener Tagblatt* that queasily invokes the Brothers Grimm: 'Behind the Jew we can see the wicked man of the fairy tale, the unearthly man-eater, the bogey man, who, just like the witch, will finally have to be shoved into the oven' (55).

Other essays in the volume address similarly uncomfortable Shakespearian events, including the performances of the same play by Polish prisoners-of-war, and Tibor Egervari's play *The Merchant of Venice in Auschwitz*, three versions of which have been given in Canadian theatres. Shakespearian productions in the relative safety of unoccupied countries are discussed in other essays on Shakespeare in wartime Stratford-upon-Avon; the work of the formidable Nancy Hewins's all-female touring group the Osiris Players; and Maurice Evans's *GI Hamlet*. Alexander C.Y. Huang describes an extraordinary site-specific *Hamlet* in a Confucian temple during the Sino-Japanese war, and Ryuta Minami offers intriguing evidence of an unusual appropriation in 'Shakespeare as an Icon of the Enemy Culture in Wartime Japan, 1937–1945'. The last of these compares and contrasts with the Nazis' dilemma of claiming Shakespeare as one of their own while at the same time having to disown or distort aspects of his work that fitted badly with their ideology. The picture that emerges from the collection is one of global Shakespeare in a world at war, a history of equivocal emotions and, in some quarters, downright equivocation.

Mark Thornton Burnett's *Shakespeare and World Cinema* deploys a range of sophisticated interpretative strategies in an account of Shakespeare films from outside the dominant Anglo-American industry of production and distribution. In doing so, Burnett breaks new ground in the study of Shakespeare on screen, in which Anglophone productions have predominated to the exclusion of all but a handful of films in other languages and cultures. The reasons for this are easily identified: before a film reaches audiences beyond its immediate regional context, backers must be found not only for production but also for distribution, the latter forming a major portion of the costs.

Even when a DVD has been produced, it may disappear unexpectedly from the 'local' market, let alone from the list of films available internationally. This unreliable and effectively one-way traffic in 'international' cinema hinders access to notable films for even the most assiduous of researchers – among whom Burnett must be acknowledged as a leader – let alone for students. The account of these problems in the 'Epilogue' reinforces the readers' gratitude to the author, while confirming their frustration at not being able to see the films he has analysed, and being denied a dialogue between their own experiences and those of Burnett by market forces. The general points of principle and argument, however, are persuasive, and are informed by detailed examinations of the cultural work done by the films.

An instance where, having seen the films in question, I feel able to take the measure of Burnett's critical responses and insight, is the discussion in Chapter 4 ('Shakespeare, Cinema, Asia') of *The Banquet* (dir. Xioaogang Feng, 2006) and *Prince of the Himalayas* (dir. Sherwood Hu, 2006). Only the first of these two *Hamlet*-derived films has achieved international distribution, despite the acclaim that greeted *Prince of the Himalayas* at international festivals. *The Banquet* benefited (Burnett points out) from its kinship with 'recent blockbuster martial arts movies – such as *Crouching Tiger, Hidden Dragon* (dir. Ang Lee, 2000) – that, drawing upon chivalric and operatic motifs, remodel eastern heroism for audiences around the world' (125). *Prince of the Himalayas*, refashioning its Shakespearian material to somewhat similar effect, is set in Tibet in a period safely removed from familiar and potentially controversial arguments concerning Chinese occupation of the region (which indeed is not identified by its modern designation in the title or within the movie), but has unmistakable resonance with them. In both films, 'A Shakespearean presence is felt not so much through citation . . . but through revision: *Prince of the Himalayas*, for instance, becomes a tragedy of forgiveness rather than revenge' (127). Burnett does not himself make the point, but one might add that this suggests kinship with the radical reshaping of the *Hamlet* material in Asta Nielsen's

1920 version of *Hamlet*, with its regendered Prince and the transformation of Gertrude into a willing accomplice of the villainous Claudius.[5]

Burnett alerts the reader to the danger of assuming that a 'correct' reading of the films can be arrived at by appealing to a simplistic assumption that in their region of origin all audiences respond in the same ways. In his 'Introduction' he observes that the 'Shakespearean imprimatur' does not 'guarantee cross-cultural veneration', and notes that in China some audiences laughed at the stilted dialogue 'and the intertextual resonances of actors familiar from earlier comic roles' (11). Anglophone viewers are likely to take on trust any details of the societies depicted in either film, accepting them as historically correct even when they are not, and assuming that if their significance is not clear, this should not be taken as a failing on the part of the filmmakers. Burnett takes pains to go beyond this response, identifying the films' cultural contexts as well as the fictional worlds depicted in them, and assessing the relationships between the two: who is speaking to whom and to what purpose.

An example of historical indeterminacy in *Prince of the Himalayas* is the identification of Hamlet/Lhamoklodan's 'rejection of worldliness' – the 'trappings, and suits' – with the Buddhism that the film's largely fictional representation of shamanistic religion would appear to predate (141). Although he eschews the outward signs of present-day Buddhism, with their local political significance, the director effectively suggests its ethics in the thinking of the central character. At another level, though, such issues as loyalty, allegiance, the tradition by which an individual learns from a master to acquire skills and the close identity of meditative techniques with (for example) swordplay, are familiar to audiences outside Asia, and their absorption into such popular sagas as the *Star Wars* series has probably contributed to the readiness with which

---

5 Authorship of this film has been attributed variously to Svend Gade and/or Nielsen herself. The project was initiated by the actor, and Gade and Heinz Schall should both be credited as directors: see liner notes to the Deutsches Filminstitut DVD of the restored film (2011).

Crouching Tiger, Hidden Dragon and similar films have been welcomed internationally.

A complementary perspective on 'global' Shakespeare and insight into another kind of cultural exchange are presented by *Shakespeare in Kabul*, by Stephen Landrigan and Quais Akbar Omar in a vivid and often moving description of challenges and eventual triumph. Along the way, it reveals the distance in understanding between even the most enlightened and ambitiously benevolent Western theatre-workers and the society they are anxious to enrich with their own cultural offerings. It is teatime in Kabul, during rehearsals for *Love's Labour's Lost*, in the summer of 2005:

Besides providing time for fighting and the pleasure of complaining, the tea breaks gave the actors an opportunity to talk among themselves. A frequent topic was Shakespeare. Everything about him was new to them. Being in a play was new to several of them. Many of the actors were new to each other . . . One day as we were pouring tea, Shah Mohammed asked the group, 'Who wants to share his impressions on Shakespeare?' (95)

Quais Akbar Omar, the translator, assistant director and channel of communications (often tactfully adjusted) between the Afghan actors and their French director, Corinne Jaber, manages to avoid starting the discussion by taking a bite out of a cake.

Nabhi Tanha, may his sons be blessed, took over the conversation . . . [He] spoke like a thoughtful and well-educated *mullah*. He drew himself up and started using his hands to amplify his points. His hands are very finely boned. He moves them with great grace. They speak eloquently by themselves, but Nabhi Tanha, who usually talks in the Kabul street dialect, was matching the language of his gestures with very formal and poetic Dari. His eyebrows would rise to emphasise words he thought were important and make him look very wise. 'Shakespeare brings utter silence into your consciousness. The way he uses words, they rush like a small river from somewhere far away, and bring sadness and happiness, restlessness and restfulness into you. They make you feel sorry for yourself and everyone else, and vice versa. The words leave you motionless, and take you into a deep, pensive silence.' (96)

Shakespeare in Kabul describes many moments like this – in and around rehearsal and performance – where the encounters with Shakespeare are both emotional and complex. Nabhi Tanha concludes, with regret, that 'doing Shakespeare is a waste of time', because 'Shakespeare plays with words, while our people played with guns for the past three decades'. One of the women in the group, Sabah Sahar, observes that in speaking Shakespeare's words 'you have to think of the words you say before they come out of your mouth, and ask yourself if they are worth saying', a contrast with 'these crazy politicians we have' (96). Producing *Love's Labour's Lost* presents its own difficulties, from the anxiety that the enforcing of the men's oath might evoke the strictures of the Taliban, to the very concept of romantic love, or even the sight of men and women touching each other, enjoyed in Bollywood romances but outside the personal experience of the actors and their audience. In a country without a real (or recent) tradition of theatrical performance, despite the popularity of films and television, the actors needed to learn the fundamentals of rehearsal: 'But we did that yesterday. Why do we want to do it again?' (135).

Then there are delicate negotiations to be made on- and offstage with fundamental rules of etiquette in this sophisticated society. Jaber had to be protected from some of the consequences of these, such as the instinctive impulse to guide an actor off the stage by gentle physical pressure. The actors, Quais explains, 'would look at me with unhappy eyes that asked "Why is she pushing me?" Pushing Afghans is an excellent way to start a fight. I would quickly explain what she was doing, but by the time I did, Corinne was already speaking to another actor, and I had to catch up on that conversation' (134). Jaber's background is as multicultural as they come: born in Munich to a German mother and Syrian father, she learned English in Canada when the family emigrated there, and after they returned to Germany, 'at eighteen . . . took herself off to Paris, learned French, became an actress and soon found herself at the Bouffes du Nord working with Peter Brook and a company of actors from nearly every part of the world' (28). Although the challenge of Shakespeare in Kabul was seen by her as 'an extension of her life and work', motivated to a degree by her desire to see women performing there in public, even a person who had directed *The Dybbuk* in India and adapted *Antony and Cleopatra* for seven actors would be challenged by the new task.

Shakespeare in Kabul – supplemented by the web site that accompanies it[6] – gives a striking picture of the production itself, not least in the beauty of the costumes and the settings against which it was performed, but the most important dimension of the book is its account of the cultural exchange that it documents, and its picture of a society whose diversity in languages (as well as dialects) and traditions is easily lost sight of in the narratives of 'insurgency' and conflict that dominate the Western news media. At the end of the book, the men and women of the company engage in a *shehr jangi*, a 'poetry battle', capping each other's quotations, taking up the challenge to recite poems by their favourite authors that begin with a specific letter of the alphabet. It ends with neither the men nor the women emerging as clear winner. 'And that is how our production of *Love's Labour's Lost* ended: on a wave of sublime poetry and fierce competition' (224). It is not the end of the story: Jaber returned to Kabul in each summer in the three years following, and in 2010 she was invited to bring her actors to London in 2012 for the Globe to Globe festival. *Richard II* was proposed: '"Afghans don't do tragedy", Corinne told them. "*The Comedy of Errors*?" they asked. "Let's talk", she replied' (229).

WORKS REVIEWED

Albright, Daniel, ed., *Great Shakespeareans Volume XI: Berlioz, Verdi, Wagner, Britten* (London and New York, 2012)

Burnett, Mark Thornton, Adrian Streete and Ramona Wray, eds., *The Edinburgh Companion to Shakespeare and the Arts* (Edinburgh, 2011)

Burnett, Mark Thornton, *Shakespeare and World Cinema* (Cambridge, 2013)

Ichikawa, Mariko, *The Shakespearean Stage Space* (Cambridge, 2013)

Landrigan, Stephen and Quais Akbar Omar, *Shakespeare in Kabul* (London, 2012)

Lindfors, Bernth, *Ira Aldridge: The Early Years, 1807–1833* and *Ira Aldridge: The Vagabond Years, 1833–1852* (Rochester, NY, 2011)

Makaryk, Irena P., and Marissa McHugh, *Shakespeare and the Second World War: Memory, Culture, Identity* (Toronto, Buffalo, London, 2012)

Pennington, Michael, *Sweet William: Twenty Thousand Hours with Shakespeare* (London, 2012)

Sillars, Stuart, *Shakespeare, Time and the Victorians* (Cambridge, 2012)

de Somogyi, Nick, *Shakespeare on Theatre* (London, 2012)

Vaughan, Alden T., and Virginia Mason Vaughan, *Shakespeare in America* (Oxford, 2012)

Wills, Garry, *Verdi's Shakespeare. Men of the Theater* (New York, 2011)

---

[6]   www.shakespeareinkabul.com/annex

3. EDITIONS AND TEXTUAL STUDIES
reviewed by SONIA MASSAI

A large number of the contributions I have selected for inclusion in this article are devoted to reconstructions of *Cardenio*, 'Shakespeare's lost play', and to Lewis Theobald's *Double Falsehood*, alternatively regarded as an adaptation loosely based on it or as a fake. The flurry of essays, journal articles, reviews and books published in 2011 and early 2012 is directly related to two crucial events: the publication of Brean Hammond's 2010 edition of *Double Falsehood* as part of the Arden Shakespeare series and Gregory Doran's production of *Cardenio* as part of the 2011 season which marked the formal reopening of the Royal Shakespeare and Swan Theatres in Stratford-upon-Avon and the 50th birthday of the Royal Shakespeare Company. The exceptional endorsement bestowed on Theobald's play and on Doran's production by these two formidable institutions has clearly catalyzed creative and scholarly efforts. The ensuing debate has produced no definitive answers as to what modes of textual and theatrical transmission, if any at all, might link *Double Falsehood* to a manuscript play called 'The History of Cardenio', which an entry in the Stationers' Register dated 9 September 1653 attributes to 'Mr Fletcher. & Shakespeare', or to two court productions of a play called 'Cardenno' and 'Cardenna' and staged by the King's Men in May and June 1613. However, this recent revival of interest in *Cardenio* has generated some of the most exciting investigative textual criticism published over the last twelve months.

THE YEAR OF CARDENIO

Foremost among recent contributions to the *Cardenio / Double Falsehood* debate are one essay by Gary Taylor and two by Tiffany Stern. Both scholars focus on the scanty documentary evidence mentioned above but they reach diametrically opposed conclusions. As Taylor puts it, he falls into the camp of 'those content to live probabilistically' (17) and takes his distance from the 'radical skeptics', who are not prepared to join the dots in quite the same way as he does. Radical scepticism is undoubtedly what Stern does best in the context of this debate. In her own words, she offers no answers but highlights problems that 'can question the solutions of others' (2011: 129). When it comes to the Stationers' Register entry of 1653, for example, Stern points out that 'The History of Cardenio, by Mr. Fletcher. & Shakespeare' is listed under 'F' for Fletcher and that the full-stop after 'Fletcher' suggests that '& Shakespeare' might be an afterthought or even a disingenuous attempt to capitalize on Shakespeare's reputation, given that the same entry includes other apocryphal plays. Taylor rebuts that Fletcher was Moseley's best-selling playwright and that he would have been prepared to invest in a play solely authored by him, as suggested by his efforts to track down the manuscript of Fletcher's *The Wild Goose Chase*, which he had been unable to include in his 1647 Folio edition of Beaumont and Fletcher's plays. Taylor adds that, had Moseley, 'or the person who sold him the manuscript, wanted to increase *The History of Cardenio*'s marketability . . . the obvious name to add would have been Francis Beaumont's', not Shakespeare, given that '"Beaumont and Fletcher" were the most successful and prestigious double act of the seventeenth century' while 'the names of Fletcher and Shakespeare had been paired only once before, on the title page of *The Two Noble Kinsmen*' (20). Taylor's probabilism would seem to outweigh Stern's scepticism, at least on this occasion, and especially as Taylor points out that '[t]he exact phrase "The history of *Cardenio*" had appeared, before 1653, only once: in [the] translation of *Don Quijote* published in London in 1612', which is generally taken to have served as the main source for the *Cardenio* play staged by the King's Men in 1613. However, when Taylor and Stern consider the records of the court performances registered in the royal treasury accounts for the year 1613, Stern's objection that '"Cardenno" occurs at the point in the list [of plays performed at Court] where titles of plays give way to titles of heroes' and that the second record refers to a 'playe . . . called Cardenna', as in the 'County of *Cardena*' (2011: 556–7), pushes Taylor over the edge: 'Is "Cardenna" the same play as "Cardenno"? Radical scepticism will say no. After all, there might have been two plays, one called "Tweeddledeedo", and the sequel called "Tweeddledeeda"' (23).

The crux of the matter, though, is not the existence of a lost play (or plays) called 'The History of Cardenio' or 'Cardenno' or 'Cardenna', which is documented by the royal treasury accounts and the Stationers' Register, but the relation between this lost play and the manuscript play which Lewis Theobald first advertised as having come into his possession in 1726 and which he then claimed to have published the following year as *Double Falsehood*. Theobald actually mentions owning several manuscripts of the same play in the preliminary materials prefaced to the 1727 edition of *Double Falsehood*. Stern believes that Theobald is unlikely to have owned one or several early manuscripts, including the oldest one, which he claims had been penned by Restoration prompter John Downes. Firstly, there are no documents recording their existence, either pre- or post-Theobald. Secondly, none of Theobald's contemporaries seem to have seen them and Theobald never mentioned them in his scholarly work, including his edition of Shakespeare's *Works* published in 1733. Thirdly, Theobald first advertised his ownership of a manuscript play by Shakespeare when he published *Shakespeare Restored* (1726), a fierce attack on Pope's 1725 edition of Shakespeare's *Works* and a bold bid to become the next editor of Shakespeare. What better enticement for the Tonsons, the publishers of all major eighteenth-century editions of the *Works*, than the alluring prospect of adding a lost play to the Shakespeare canon? Stern also suggests that, if Downes, who worked with William Davenant and Thomas Betterton, had indeed copied an early manuscript play, at least partly by Shakespeare, the three men, who went to great lengths to advertise and to feed their passion for Shakespeare, would not have kept quiet about it. Having questioned the likelihood that Theobald ever owned a Shakespearian manuscript, Stern makes one further important point (which is discussed at greater length in her 2012 essay in *The Quest for Cardenio*): had Theobald owned such a manuscript, he was far more likely to use the story-line while radically rewriting the dialogue because he found it difficult to devise original plots but enjoyed writing in the style of the writers he edited and admired – and he edited both Shakespeare's *Works* in 1733 and Beaumont and Fletcher's *Works*, which was published posthumously in 1750. Stern therefore concludes that 'forgery is a more likely possibility than has been conceded' (2011: 592) and that, even assuming that Theobald did own a manuscript play descended from Fletcher and Shakespeare's *Cardenio*, the likelihood is that very little of what the earlier playwrights had written survives in *Double Falsehood*.

Instead of trying to counter her multiple and cogent objections, Taylor attempts to trump Stern by proving that at least some passages in *Double Falsehood* cannot be attributed to Theobald or to Theobald writing in the style of Fletcher or Shakespeare. Taylor brilliantly points out that 'nine consecutive words in *Double Falsehood* 4.2 contain five unique parallels to four different passages in the Fletcher scene of *Barnavelt*' (47), a play which has survived in a unique manuscript copy first published in 1883. Since, as Taylor stresses, '[n]either Theobald, nor any of his contemporaries, refers to the play, its authorship, or the existence of this unique manuscript', we can safely assume that Theobald was not imitating it (46). No similar data set exists for Shakespeare and Taylor must rely on style alone to identify Shakespeare's contribution to *Cardenio*. He makes the strongest case for some linguistic features in *Double Falsehood*, including one of the lines ridiculed by Pope, 'None but itself can be its parallel' (3.1.17), which, he claims, is in fact eminently Shakespearian. By building on the few traces of Fletcher and Shakespeare he has identified in *Double Falsehood*, Taylor has 'unadapted' Theobald's *Double Falsehood* and has produced a fully reconstructed version of *The History of Cardenio*, where Cardenio and Lucinda (Julio and Leonora in *Double Falsehood*) jostle for attention with Don Quixote and Sancho Panza!

I should stress that Taylor and Stern agree in at least one important respect, namely that, since the documentary evidence is so sparse, more stylometric analysis needs to be carried out to identify not only Fletcher and Shakespeare, but also Theobald, in *Double Falsehood*. This type of analysis has been championed primarily by MacDonald P. Jackson and by Richard Proudfoot. Their work has so far produced only marginally encouraging results. While Jackson concludes that 'Theobald probably did work from a manuscript (or manuscripts) descended from a *Cardenio* written jointly by Shakespeare and Fletcher, but scarcely a line of Shakespeare's verse survives intact into *Double Falsehood*' (161), Proudfoot, slightly more optimistically, believes that 'there are reasonable grounds for believing that Theobald's play is indeed the sole surviving version of "*Cardenio*" and doubts that 'the whole thing was fabricated by Theobald himself' (163). As one of the general editors of the Arden Shakespeare, Proudfoot is clearly at pains to justify the inclusion of *Double Falsehood* in this series. Proudfoot's stylometric method is persuasive in its own right. However, his claim that the reactions of those who have objected to its inclusion in the Shakespeare Arden series are 'obsolete in assigning to a modern series of editions a level of authority about attribution of authorship to which it has no pretensions' seems strikingly understated.[1]

By far the most enjoyable overview of the controversy is Gregory Doran's *Shakespeare's Lost Play: In Search of Cardenio*. Doran's book is witty, entertaining and packed with insights into the creative process that led to the staging of his reconstructed version of *Cardenio* in April 2011. His book will appeal to textual scholars because it shows how a great director and scholar of Shakespeare and early modern drama identifies and integrates textual traces of Fletcher and Shakespeare into his own work. Particularly addictive are Doran's serendipitous (textual) discoveries, as he travels across Europe and North America, in search of clues as to what may survive of *Cardenio* in Theobald's play. The reader walks with Doran into rare book shops, where, on one occasion, he stumbles upon a reprint of Shelton's 1612

translation of *Don Quixote*, or gets to peer over his shoulder as he reads Fletcher in the 1812 edition prepared by Henry Weber: 'So I sit on the Tube, flicking through these wonderful old tomes, which smell of damp cellars, with their flaky spines, and torn marbled end-papers, their pages foxed and blotched and wavy, and am transported' (110). More crucially, the textual scholar who embarks with Doran on his search for 'Shakespeare's lost play' gets to share his suggestive insight that even a heavily 'unadapted' version of Theobald's play, like his own, smacks more immediately of Fletcher than of Shakespeare, 'particularly in the character of the two fathers' (76). Doran also gives tantalizing leads to the textual scholars who care to follow him on his quest: is it possible, he wonders, that Gabaleone, the Savoyard Ambassador to the Court of James I who had arranged the match between the late Prince Henry and the Savoyard Infanta, Maria Apollonia, and in whose honour the play was revived in May 1613, might have taken a presentation copy of the play back to Turin 'for the poor Infanta to treasure?' Of course, Doran admits, there

---

[1] All the essays discussed so far, except for Stern (2011), are included in Carnegie and Taylor's *The Quest for Cardenio*, a superb collections of essays to which I cannot do sufficient justice here. I should however at the very least note that this collection includes twelve short essays and reviews on theatrical reconstructions of *Cardenio*, including Taylor's *The History of Cardenio*, Stephen Greenblatt's 'Cardenio Project', Gregory Doran's *Cardenio*, and productions of *Double Falsehood*, as well as essays on the intertextual links between Cervantes, Continental European versions of 'The History of Cardenio', and adaptive traditions in the work of Shakespeare and his contemporaries. Also worth mentioning is ' "This orphan play": *Cardenio* and the Construction of the Author', an interesting essay by Richard Meek and Jane Rickard, included in the special issue of *Shakespeare* devoted to Shakespeare and Fletcher and edited by Clare McManus and Lucy Munro in 2011. Meek and Rickard point out that, although early modern playwrights often wrote collaboratively, the paratextual materials prefaced to early modern printed playbooks tend to advertise their authorship as singular. They therefore qualify the recent tendency to understand collaboration both as a widespread practice in early modern theatrical culture and as a dominant model of textual production (273) and remind us that the current obsession with (Shakespearian) singular authorship is actually not a new phenomenon but has its roots in the early modern period itself.

is 'probably little point . . . in launching a search of the ducal libraries for evidence of its survival. But such a thing is possible' (54). Doran's extraordinary ability to establish connections between texts, people and places hardly ever overrides the historical accuracy of his account of his extraordinary quest. One exception occurs when he writes about his visit at Stationers' Hall and he takes a minute to think that 'it must have been in a room on this site four hundred years ago, that the representatives of the twelve companies charged by King James to produce a new translation of the Bible had met together to review the whole book' (100). Stationers' Hall, which had been housed in a former Church building in the Southwest corner of St Paul's Precinct, was actually relocated to rented premises in Milk Street, off Cheapside, between 1606 and 1610, when the translation of the King James Bible was in full swing. It was only after 1610 that the Stationers' Company moved to Abergavenny Hall, which, though largely destroyed in the Great Fire of 1666, has served as the Company's headquarters ever since.

SHAKESPEARE IN LOVE: THREE NEW EDITIONS OF *THE TWO NOBLE KINSMEN*, *ROMEO AND JULIET*, AND *THE SONNETS*

Written by Shakespeare and Fletcher around the time when *Cardenio* was first performed, *The Two Noble Kinsmen* has been newly edited by Robert Kean Turner and Patricia Tatspaugh for the *New Cambridge Shakespeare* series. This generous and thought-provoking edition completes the series, which was launched in 1984 under the general editorship of Philip Brockbank. Brian Gibbons succeeded him in 1994 and has seen the series through to completion, along with one of the series' associate general editors, A. R. Braunmuller. They should be warmly congratulated on overseeing such a splendid project. In keeping with one of the distinctive features of this series, *The Two Noble Kinsmen* offers an enlightening critical overview of the play's reception on the

stage, with a focus on the main professional productions since 1973 (31–51). Particularly useful is the detailed discussion of the prompt-book used for the York Festival production of 1973, which transferred to the Open Air Theatre at Regent's Park the following year. Barry Kyle's 1986 Royal Shakespeare Company production is rightly singled out as marking a turning-point in the reception of the play on stage, because for the first time both those who worked on this production and those who reviewed it focused more on its prominent features, including its emphasis on ritual and pageantry and the significance of its female characters, both in the plot and in the sub-plot, rather than on the contested attribution of individual scenes to Shakespeare or Fletcher or on similarities with other better-known Shakespearian plays. Particularly effective is the closing paragraph in the introduction, as it sums up 'the distance *The Two Noble Kinsmen* has travelled from its revival in 1928, when [director Andrew] Leigh described it as "essentially a story of medieval chivalry rather than Greek legend", to 2002, when [director David] Lathan claimed it as "really a young people's play, about maturity and growing up"' (51). Eight out of the ten illustrations included in the introduction are stunning production photographs, which add invaluable visual details to this lively and informative section of the introduction. Extremely clear and helpful are other parts of the introduction devoted to a discussion of the 'craftsmanship' of Shakespeare and Fletcher as adapters of their primary source for their main plot, Chaucer's *Knight's Tale* (7–16) and the complexities of Shakespeare's late style (23–8).

The same impetus to clarify seems to have driven the preparation of the text of the play, which is still less familiar than most of the other plays in the Shakespeare canon and undoubtedly riddled with stylistic complexities and a few challenging textual cruces. The Cambridge editors intervene more frequently than some of their immediate predecessors to emend their source text, the first quarto of 1634 (Q). They, for example, replace 'fury-innocent' with 'ev'ry innocent' in Emilia's notoriously difficult lines in Q: 'This rehearsall / (Which fury-innocent wots well) comes in / Like old importments bastard, has this end, / That the true love tweene Mayde, and mayde, may be / More then in sex individuall' (C3v 26–30). The Cambridge editors take their cue from Henry Weber, who had in turn been inspired by Charles Lamb's conjectural reading in his *Specimens of English Dramatic Poets* (1808). In doing so, they depart from recent editions, like Lois Potter's Arden 3 edition, where 'fury-innocent' is left unaltered but a lengthy commentary note is added to help readers make sense of it. They also depart from other twentieth-century editors who opt for less than straightforward readings, which can, however, be justified on paleographical grounds. The editors of *The Oxford Complete Works*, for example, settle for 'seely innocence' because the letters 's', written as 'ſ', and 'f' would have looked quite similar in secretary hand and the double 'e' could have easily been mistaken for the two minims in the letter 'u'.

The Cambridge editors depart again from their immediate predecessors when they cut a half line at 5.4.76, 'on end he stands', which Q aligns with the second half of the previous line, 'He kept him tweene his legges, on his hind hoofes', on the ground that 'the second line seems intended to replace "on . . . hoofes", which evidently was imperfectly cancelled' (208). While this fairly radical emendation had been conjectured by Frederick O. Waller in 1958, no other editor since then has adopted it. On one other occasion, the Cambridge editors cut the second part of the original entry direction at 2.3.24 – '*Enter .4. Country people, & one with a garloud before them*' – because, they argue, 'the [countryman] with the garland . . . was added to the four countrymen to swell the scene'. 'He has no lines', they add, 'and is omitted from Q's version of the countrymen's *Exeunt* at [line] 78' (109). Other editors have more conservatively attempted to justify the significance of the garland in this scene: Richard Proudfoot, for example, in his Regents Renaissance Drama edition of 1970, explains that garlands were 'used in the May games, either as a prize or to be worn by the May queen' (45). The decision to omit a reference to a potentially significant prop, for the sake of ensuring consistency in the numbers of countrymen featuring in this scene, is quite daring, especially in light of the fact that the number of secondary characters is notoriously unstable in early modern plays.

Quite unusual in an otherwise generously annotated edition is the lack of a commentary note to explain the logic informing a well-established, but by no means universally adopted, emendation, the addition of a half line (in italic) to Arcite's address to Mars, 'Thou mighty one that with thy power hast turned / Green Neptune into purple, *whose approach* / Comets prewarn' (5.1.49–51). More frequent is the omission of square brackets as markers of editorial intervention in stage directions, as with the exit direction at the end of the Prologue, with the editorial direction '*The Queens rise*' at 1.1.37, or around '*and Attendants*' and '*The Queens sing*' at the beginning of 1.5, around '*as morris-dancers*' at the beginning of 3.5, and around '*wearing*' at 5.1.136. Lineation is also occasionally silently rearranged (cf., for example, lines 5.2.27–8, which are printed as one line in Q) and, while indentation is effectively used to indicate what lines are sung and what lines are spoken by the Jailor's Daughter at 3.5.54–66, no typographical marker suggests that the last two lines in 3.4 would seem to be spoken rather than sung by the same character.

In his Arden Shakespeare edition of *Romeo and Juliet*, René Weis carries off the unenviable task of re-presenting one of Shakespeare's most frequently performed and best-known plays to a new generation of readers with great aplomb. His introduction is refreshingly insightful and genuinely instructive. Weis's exuberant prose style is at its best when he expounds on aspects of Italian culture or the play's rendering of its Italian setting. Here, for example, is Weis writing about the place of Catholicism in Shakespeare's Verona: '[a]longside orchards groaning with pomegranates and sunbaked streets bursting with prowling hot-heads, [Verona] possesses an abbey garden in which a friar, friend and confidant of both families, gathers herbs' (16). Written in the style of a unified and elegantly argued essay,

Weis's introduction is as beautifully written as it is informative.

Welcome prominence is accorded to Juliet as a fully developed tragic heroine. Weis rightly points out that while the play offers a detailed characterization of Juliet, especially through her relationship with the Nurse, Romeo's upbringing and character are at best sketchy prior to his fateful encounter with Juliet. Weis highlights other ways in which Shakespeare reinforces Juliet's centrality, ranging from her very name, which is linked to the time of year when the young lovers first meet, to the fact that 'Juliet speaks thirteen lines in Act 5, one line for every year of her life, with the thirteenth ending on "die"' (3). Equally enlightening are Weis's comments about the surprising lack of moral judgement in relation to the lovers' suicide, especially in light of the explicitly Catholic setting of the play and the problematic quality attached to suicide elsewhere in the Shakespearian canon, nowhere more prominently than in *Hamlet* or in *The Rape of Lucrece*. Weis helpfully reminds his readers that '[t]he punishment under Elizabethan law for attempting "self-slaughter" was death' (16) and that, nevertheless, 'young love triumphs, it seems, unconditionally in the teeth of doctrinal sanctions against self-murder' (19). By contrast, Weis mentions Arthur Brooke's *Tragical History of Romeus and Juliet*, Shakespeare's main source, where Romeus and Juliet are described as 'a couple of unfortunate lovers, thralling themselves to unhonest desire, neglecting the authority and advice of parents and friends, conferring their principal counsels with drunken gossips, and superstitious friars' (46). Weis's survey of the play's reception is similarly impressive. Worth mentioning are his perceptive insights into Zeffirelli's 1960 Old Vic production and his iconic 1968 film adaptation ('*The Age of Zeffirelli (1960–8)*', 79–85) and Thomas Otway's Restoration adaptation *The History and Fall of Caius Marius*. 'Otway's most enduring departure from Shakespeare,' Weis explains, 'was to allow his lovers to survive long enough after Marius ingests poison to share one last exchange before dying.' However, he adds, '[t]he scene is more Antony and Cleopatra than Romeo and Juliet' (59). I have only very minor, local reservations about Weis's elegant introduction, including his claim that the First Folio 'emancipated Shakespeare from performance' (57), given the popularity of Shakespeare in smaller formats prior to 1623. I was also taken aback by Weis's passing reference to the New Variorum editions as 'mark[ing] the beginning of scholarly editing of Shakespeare' (61). More crucially, I wondered why relatively little attention is paid to the critical reception of the play, with the possible exception of the Romantics, whose main instinct, according to Weis, was to reject the received performance text, as tweaked by their early-to-mid-eighteenth-century predecessors. But, as Weis notes with characteristic insight, '[i]t is a pity that no Garrick emerged to carry the Romantic torch on to the stage' (66).

The text of the play is generously annotated to the standards that have become associated with the Arden Shakespeare editions. The choice of using the second quarto (Q2) as copy-text and to rely on the first quarto (Q1) for its fuller stage directions and for lines which were missing or damaged in the manuscript used as the printer's copy for Q2 is by now established editorial practice. Weis is however exceptionally generous in paying tribute to the fourth quarto (Q4), which was set from an intelligently, if sporadically, corrected copy of the third quarto (Q3). While some corrections, especially to speech prefixes and stage directions, may have originated through consultation of Q1, other corrections, which are unique to Q4, have often been silently adopted by earlier editors. Weis gives the anonymous corrector who prepared Q4 for press his due, when, for example, he ranks Q4's 'shroud' above Malone's 'grave' as the fittest ending to Juliet's line 'And hide me with a dead man in his shroud' (4.1.85), which stops at 'his' in Q2. More could be done, though, especially by editors who are as sensitive as Weis is to the different textual qualities of the early editions, to highlight the composite nature of the text offered to modern readers in scholarly editions like the Arden 3 Shakespeare. Weis's textual notes duly record the frequency with which the early editions are used to supplement or to correct Q2, but typographical markers could also be used to highlight the fact that the received text of *Romeo and Juliet* is effectively a conflation of several source texts rather than a straightforward, modernized version of Q2.

The most original feature of Weis's text is the addition of editorial stage directions. Some of them are particularly useful. Weis, for example, singles out '[*Mercutio's Page*]' among the generic '*and Men*' traditionally added to the first entry direction in 3.1 since Rowe's edition of 1709. Weis's stage direction helps his readers visualize this character, who remains silent throughout this scene but is then addressed by Mercutio when the latter, fatally wounded by Tybalt, sends him to fetch a surgeon. Later in the same scene and throughout his edition, Weis specifies the exact moment when a character dies. In this scene, he adds '[*and dies*]' after '*They fight. Tybalt falls*'. While the phrasing is unique and Weis uses it repeatedly in his edition, the *Oxford Shakespeare* (1986), where this stage direction reads, in a rather more prolix fashion, '*They fight. Tybalt is wounded. He falls and dies*' (3.1.131), should have been acknowledged as a precedent. One other editorial stage direction is worth mentioning because it offers a new reading of Capulet's parting lines at the end of 4.2. Other editors rely on the Folio's '*Exeunt Father and Mother.*' to clear the stage at the end of 4.2, thus allowing Capulet's Wife to witness (and, as she does in some productions, to silently mock) her husband's failed attempt to recall his servants – 'What, ho! / They are all forth.' (43–4) – and to take charge of the wedding preparations, as he has just announced – 'I'll play the housewife for this once' (43). Weis instead takes 'They are all forth' to signal that Capulet has already dismissed all the other characters, including his wife at 4.2.41–2 ('Go thou to Juliet, . . . / Let me alone'). Weis's editorial stage director defuses an opportunity for some light banter at Capulet's expense, which can work well, especially as it anticipates the witty repartee between the Nurse and Capulet in the next scene, where the Nurse calls him a 'cotquean' and urges him to go to bed and leave her and Capulet's wife to take care of the preparations for Juliet's wedding. But Weis's reading of this sequence makes sense and is more in keeping with his copy-text, where the final exit direction signals that Capulet exits alone.

Weis's approach to other textual features in his copy-text and in the other early editions he collates in the textual notes is not entirely flawless. A textual note on the very first page of the text ('THE PROLOGUE] Q2–4, F, Q1') misleadingly suggests that the prologue can be found in all quarto *and* folio editions, which is patently untrue. At 1.1.55, the stage direction '*Enter* BENVOLIO' is square bracketed and the textual note attributes it to Capell, when in fact it originates in Q2. Lineation seems to have caused some problems too. On a few occasions, the textual notes include typos in the transcriptions of the original lineation, which should conventionally reproduce the final word of each line as it appears in the copy-text, including the original punctuation. For example, at 2.1.27–9n 'name' should read 'name.'; at 3.2.34–5n 'fetch' should read 'fetch?'; and at 3.2.85–7n 'Pallace,' should read 'Pallace.' More importantly, line 3.3.68 ('Then mightst thou speak, then mightst thou tear thy hair') and line 3.3.83 ('There on the ground, with his own tears made drunk.') are printed as two lines in Q2. Weis rightly rearranges them into two regular pentameters, but adds no textual notes to record his intervention. Conversely, Q2 prints lines 5.3.128–9 ('It doth so, holy sir, and there's my master, / One that you love.') as one line and Weis rightly but, once again, silently arranges it as one-and-a-half lines of regular verse. On a similar occasion, Q2 prints Peter's lines at 4.5.115–6 ('I will carry no crotchers. I'll re you, I'll fa you. Do you note me?') as verse, breaking after 'I'll fa', while Weis prints them as prose. Once again, Weis makes the right editorial decision, but omits to record it. All other emendations are generally meticulously recorded, except for the pretty straightforward correction from Q2's 'death arting' to 'death-darting' at 3.2.47.

Among other editions published over the last year, *Shakespeare's Sonnets: An Original-Spelling Text*, edited by Paul Hammond for the

University Press at Oxford, stands out for its elegant layout. Each sonnet has facing glosses and, in most cases, vast expanses of surrounding blank space. The luxurious feel of this edition begs the question as to what intended readership the editor and the publisher might have in mind. Though advertised online as being targeted to 'students and scholars of Shakespeare and of Elizabethan verse', it is difficult to see how the current hardback format, priced at £75, can appeal to the former constituency of readers. And yet some features are clearly aimed at a student readership. Particularly useful are some of the appendices. 'Shakespeare's Rhetorical Figures' (425–35), for example, provides definitions and examples of over twenty different figures, ranging from the more familiar (metaphor and oxymoron) to the more obscure (paradiastole or polyptoton), while 'A Rhetorical Analysis of Sonnet 129' (436–7) shows how Shakespeare deploys some of these figures in this sonnet. Three further appendices – 'Shakespeare's Proverbs' (439–45), 'Shakespeare's Complex Words' (447–83), and 'Further Reading' (485–7) – and two short sections at the end of the introduction – 'Reading an Original-Spelling Text' (89–97) and 'A Reader's Guide to Using an Original-Spelling Text' (98–102) – are also clearly aimed at encouraging a younger, wider readership to read the Sonnets as they were printed in the first quarto edition of 1609 (Q). Quite unsettling is the fact that modern spelling occasionally slips into Hammond's analysis of a selection of sonnets in his introduction, especially in light of his reminder that old-spelling preserves rhyming structures and multiple meanings which are otherwise lost in modernized editions (see, for example, Hammond's claim that 'The first quatrain [in Sonnet 48] pivots around two key words, "true" and "use" [read 'vse']', in 'Reading the Sonnets' 49–88). More generally, Hammond's introduction judiciously discourages readers from reading the Sonnets autobiographically or even as 'a story with coherent, naturalistic characters' (49) and urges its readers to approach them as 'a repertoire of scenes and images which helped [Shakespeare] to develop his own ideas about the complex psychology of love and infatuation' (48) instead.

Hammond then contextualizes the Sonnets by considering how they relate to other early modern sonnet sequences and miscellanies, but he overlooks other more broadly cultural contexts (for example, how the clash between older models of vassalage and an emerging market economy inflects Shakespeare's apparently idealized language of love, or how early readers read sonnets and love poetry in the period, a topic merely touched upon in the first section, misleadingly called 'The *Sonnets* and their First Readers', 3–20).

The text of the Sonnets is reproduced from Q 'with minimal intervention' (103). In keeping with current conventions informing old-spelling editions of early modern texts, Hammond removes the long 's' (ſ) and all ligatures, but retains spelling, capitals, italics and punctuation. He also adopts a conservative editorial strategy when it comes to dealing with plain errors in Q. As Hammond explains, he 'admit[s] only the most uncontested emendations' (103) but reproduces Q whenever the correct reading of an obvious error is irrecoverable and possible alternatives are necessarily conjectural. Alternatives are discussed in the glosses and Hammond hopes that 'the occasional pencil alteration will easily generate the reader's preferred text' (103). Accordingly, lines 3 and 4 in Sonnet 12 read 'When I behold the violet past prime, / And sable curls or siluer'd ore with white:'. The relevant gloss records a wide choice of alternatives, proposed by earlier editors, including Malone's 'all silver'd o'er' or Evans's 'o'er-silvered are'. Hammond therefore challenges his readers to experience first-hand the instability of Shakespeare's text, but his editorial approach is occasionally a little more interventionist than his rationale suggests. For example, when faced by the notorious 'their/thy' crux (editors suspect that 'thy' was wrongly misread and set as 'their' fourteen times in Q), Hammond replaces 'their' with 'thy' on seven occasions (46:3, 46:8, 46:13, 46:14, 70:6, 128:11, and 128:14 – incidentally, his gloss for 128:14, where 'thy' occurs twice, does not identify the relevant 'thy'). While Hammond's intervention is justified by the fact that 'their' is often clearly wrong in these three sonnets, I wonder whether all seven occurrences of 'their' are indeed harder to defend than when Hammond decides to leave them unaltered in other sonnets. In Sonnet 70, for example, personal and impersonal modes of address coexist throughout. Only the first line in the first quatrain addresses the 'Boy' directly ('That thou are blam'd shall not be thy defect, / For slanders marke was euer yet the faire, / The ornament of beauty is suspect, / A Crow that flies in heauens sweetest ayre.'). Similarly, one could assume that only the first and the last lines in the second quatrain are addressed to the 'Boy' ('So thou be good, slander doth but approue, / Their worth the greater beeing woo'd of time, / For Canker vice the sweetest buds doth loue, / And thou present'st a pure vnstayined prime.'). The second line, and 'their' within it, can be read impersonally, if 'approue' is not assumed to take 'worth' as its object. Rather than querying Hammond's decision *per se*, this example goes to show how difficult it is to adopt a consistent rationale for editorial intervention in old-spelling editions.

MORE SHAKESPEAREAN RICHES

Three new Shakespeare editions were added to the Norton Critical Editions series in late 2011 and early 2012: *As You Like It*, edited by Leah S. Marcus, *Antony and Cleopatra*, edited by Ania Loomba, and *Hamlet*, edited by Robert S. Miola. A new series, the Evans Shakespeare Editions, was also launched earlier this year. This new series is general – edited by J. J. M. Tobin and published by Wadsworth, at Cengage Learning, formerly the publisher of the Arden Shakespeare series. The first eight volumes in this series are: *As You Like It* (ed. Heather Dubrow), *Hamlet* (ed. J. J. M. Tobin), *Macbeth* (ed. Katherine Rowe), *Measure for Measure* (ed. John Klause), *A Midsummer Night's Dream* (ed. Douglas Bruster), *Richard III* (ed. Nina Levine), *The Tempest* (ed. Grace Tiffany), and *The Winter's Tale* (ed. Lawrence F. Rhu). The new series takes its name from the late Gwynne Blakemore Evans, whose texts, textual notes and textual commentary are reprinted here from the Riverside Shakespeare.

Similarities in the formats of these two series might suggest that the Evans Shakespeare was conceived as a direct competitor of the Norton series. However, the Evans Shakespeare Editions seem predominantly aimed at students or generally interested readers who might be encountering Shakespeare for the first time, as suggested by the fact that these editions include new introductions written by the volume editor and fully cross-referenced to selected extracts from primary and secondary sources. The range of these extracts is also more limited than in the Norton series, where readers are generally ushered into the volume by a short preface which merely whets their appetite for its rich offerings. However, the inclusion of a new introduction in Miola's *Hamlet* suggests a potential convergence between the two series in years to come. The Evans Shakespeare Editions also include a separate introduction fully devoted to the play's performance history, a conspicuous omission in the Norton Critical Editions, possibly because the Norton series accommodates a vast range of world-famous literary texts across different genres and across different periods, languages and cultures. Recent Norton editors have, however, started to include actors' accounts of their approaches to plays and characters, have selected critical essays that focus specifically on theatrical or cinematic responses, or have accorded more prominence to theatrical adaptations, thus closing even further the gap between the two series.

Textually speaking, only the Norton Critical Editions offer newly edited texts and I will therefore confine my comments about individual volumes to this series. The text of *As You Like It*, prepared by Leah Marcus, is impeccably edited and consistently, if sparsely, annotated. Her text is also 'the first', in Marcus's words, 'to preserve folio readings that occasionally ... refer to Rosalind as a "he" rather than a "she".'. In line with her tendency to 'unedit' early modern texts by removing the legacy of a century-long editorial tradition, she argues that 'these anomalies should not be edited out of existence in our texts of the play because they are important clues to the malleability of gender categories for early readers and probably also for Shakespeare's dramatic company, particularly in relation to its central character' (x). The texts of Miola's *Hamlet* and Loomba's *Antony and Cleopatra* are also generally accurate, but I found their editorial approach slightly less consistent than Marcus's. A Folio stage direction in Loomba's edition ('CLEOPATRA *kneels*' at 5.2.110) is, for example, printed and aligned as a verse line. More generally, Loomba's decision to record only 'the most significant departures from the First Folio' (117) is problematic, because her notion of what constitutes a 'significant' emendation is hard to fathom. At 1.2.99, for example, she records replacing 'windes' with 'minds' in 'When our quick minds lie still', presumably on the basis of how similar these words would have looked as written in secretary hand in the printer's copy from which the play was set, but she does not record a near-identical emendation in the same scene, where she replaces 'Saue' with 'Saw' in 'Saw you my lord?' at line 70. A similarly minor inconsistency occurs when Loomba uncharacteristically normalizes the First Folio's 'Makes' to 'Make' at 1.4.48–9 ('Menecrates and Menas, famous pirates, / Make the sea serve them'). Miola's *Hamlet* is generally a very accurate edition of the second quarto of 1604–5 (Q2), with very minor slips. His entry direction at 4.2.2, for example, '[*Enter* ROSENCRANTZ, GUILDENSTERN, *and others.*]' should have read '*Enter* ROSENCRANTZ, [*GUILDENSTERN*], *and others.*' to reflect the fact that Guildenstern is the only character who is mistakenly left out of the original entry direction in Q2. Miola's editorial approach is fairly conventional but occasionally interventionist, given the good quality of his copytext. At 2.2.222–3, for example, where Guildenstern remarks 'Happy in that we are not overhappy. On Fortune's cap we are not the very button' in response to Hamlet's perfunctory 'Good lads, how do you both?' (220), Miola follows most editors in emending Q2's 'lap' to 'cap', but he also emends Q2's viable 'euer happy' to 'overhappy'. I also felt that at least a minimal gloss might have been added to explain why Miola replaces Q2's obscure 'friendly Fankners' with the more accessible, but by no means straightforward, 'French falconers'.

UNSUNG HEROES

Reference sources are labours of love. They take up an inordinate amount of time out of the busy schedules of modern-day scholars and academics and they are paradoxically self-effacing: the better they are, the easier it is to consult them on an ad hoc basis, while remaining blissfully unaware of the Herculean efforts gone into their preparation. Two such magnificent resources are Eric Rasmussen and Anthony James West's *The Shakespeare First Folios: A Descriptive Catalogue*, which they compiled with the help of a dedicated team of researchers (Donald L. Bailey, Mark Farnsworth, Lara Hansen, Trey Jensen and Sarah Stewart), and *British Drama 1533–1642: A Catalogue*, prepared by Martin Wiggin (editor) and Catherine Richardson (associate editor). The amount of new data made available by these two catalogues is so vast that even users who will consult them to check a company attribution or the provenance of any of the known copies of the First Folio will be struck by the range, ambition and thoroughness of each entry and will be lured to browse other entries after completing their searches.

Paul Werstine, who writes a short preface to Rasmussen and West's *Catalogue*, rightly hails it as a 'gift to Shakespeareans' (viii). The *Catalogue* provides detailed descriptive entries of all 232 currently known copies of the First Folio, including the 70-odd copies added by Anthony West's *Census of First Folios* (2003) to Sidney Lee's census (1902). A standard entry includes a new serial number (taken from West's *Census*), followed by the copy's location, its history, provenance, a list of known owners and associated documents, a thorough description of its binding, and a meticulous description of all bibliographical features of each copy, including the number of original leaves present, the condition of the binder's leaves, of the preliminaries and of the text, all manuscript annotations, repairs and damage affecting and not affecting the text, a list of pages in the uncorrected state (i.e. pages which do not appear to include press variants), and watermarks. Different users will find the *Catalogue* helpful for different reasons. As Werstine points out, 'now that this monumental labour is complete, editors can provide Shakespeare's readers with editions of the Folio plays based on fully informed decisions about which printed variant has the highest probability of reflecting the manuscript from which the text was printed' (viii). Even more crucially, though, the *Catalogue* puts the printed book, rather than Shakespeare, centre-stage. The vast majority of information made available by the *Catalogue* sheds light on how the Folio was bought, inherited or stolen, on how early readers made the book their own by annotating, emending, or defacing it with their scribbles, and how each transfer of ownership can help us reconstruct the cultural capital accrued by Shakespeare over the last four centuries. Ultimately, the *Catalogue* fulfils Rasmussen's, West's and their team of dedicated researchers' ambition to make the Folio one of the most-documented books of all time.

Another gift to Shakespearians is Rasmussen's 'companion' book *The Shakespeare Thefts: In Search of the First Folios*. By telling us the extraordinary stories associated with those whose lives, fortunes and scholarly endeavours became inextricably linked with the First Folio, Rasmussen infects his readers with the obsession that drives the 'Folio hunter' and makes them care for copies that have been absconded, stained, vandalized, secreted in vaults, shot (!), or were dragged to the bottom of the Atlantic Ocean by the sinking *Titanic*. The book is packed with cliff-hangers that will amuse the general reader and tantalize the textual scholar. Rasmussen, for example, reports sightings in the 1830s of a copy of the Folio, 'covered with notes in a seventeenth-century hand' (13), in the dilapidated remains of Count Gondomar's palace in Valladolid. This copy, which Gondomar acquired at the end of his stint as Spanish Ambassador at the court of King James I, as his attempts to arrange a match between Prince Charles and the Spanish Infanta finally collapsed, was never recovered, despite several appeals published in literary magazines at the time. Nothing was heard of this copy again, Rasmussen explains, 'until June 16, 2008, when a fantasist showed up in Washington, DC, with a copy of a book he claimed was a First Folio

from Galicia in Spain', where Gondomar had once owned a castle which housed part of his immense library. Although the date is likely to trigger memories of the sad circumstances surrounding the theft and recovery of the Durham copy (West 7), confirmation that the Gondomar copy does indeed remain 'unfound' only comes two chapters later. In the meantime one is left to wonder how much more exciting historical collations in scholarly editions of Shakespeare would become if Gondomar's copy was ever to re-emerge from a dusty attic in Valladolid or Galicia. Rasmussen does not leave readers with an interest in copies that preserve seventeenth-century annotations entirely empty-handed, though. Drawing on West 11, Rasmussen describes another copy now in the holdings of the Glasgow University Library and the annotations most probably added to it by Henry Cary, 1st Viscount Falkland. Annotations next to the list of the principal actors in Shakespeare's company, the King's Men, suggest that the annotator knew some of them and had probably watched them perform. Though not as extensive and as well known as the prompter's notes added by an early hand to the copy of the Folio now held at the University Library in Padua, the annotations in this copy are just as captivating for theatre historians and for textual scholars alike.

Rasmussen's book is immensely enjoyable in its own right but it can also help readers navigate the *Catalogue*, which can seem dauntingly technical to the uninitiated. In fact, the multiple indexes in the *Catalogue* seem to be simultaneously meant to help and to disorient the reader, inviting browsing as much as enabling targeted searches. The serial numbers assigned by West by geographical areas in his 2003 *Census* have produced bizarre gaps and jolts in the *Catalogue* because a number of copies have moved hands, or have been miraculously recovered, or have been more accurately identified since then. Someone unfamiliar with historical ownership of even the better known Folios might struggle to work out why the *Catalogue* lists copies 31 to 35 under Oxford, but omits copy number 33. Normally the Summary Catalogue (Annexe 1 on pages 868 to 872) helps readers identify skipped entries and their new locations (see, for example, West 27, which is noted in the 'Summary Catalogue' as '*27 *See after 188*' and duly found after West 188, because this copy, formerly part of Dr Williams's Library in London, has been in the hands of a private owner in Virginia since July 2006). However, copy number 33 seems to have vanished without a trace, both from its sequential place in the main body of the *Catalogue* and from the Summary Catalogue. If one is already well-versed in Folio ownership, the index of 'Folio Owners' might provide a clue as to where to find entry 33. However, searching this index intuitively under 'Oxford' or 'Oxford University' will only take one as far as West 34 for the copy held at Queen's College. West 33 will remain 'unfound' by users of the *Catalogue* unless one knows that Oriel College used to own a copy of the Folio and then sold it to Sir John Paul Getty in 2002 and searches for it by looking up its former and current owners in the 'Folio Owners' index. Alternatively, one might stumble upon West 33 by moving down the list of copies in the Summary Catalogue, past West 34, West 35, and (!) West 222 (a copy at the Craven Museum and Gallery in Skipton, North Yorkshire, misidentified as a copy of the Second Folio until Anthony West examined it in 2003 and determined that it was in fact a copy of the First Folio minus all preliminaries). I must admit that it took me a while to establish that the location of West 33 in the *Catalogue* is determined by the fact that the Getty collection at 'Stokenchurch' in Buckinghamshire comes alphabetically straight after 'Skipton'. The arrangement of individual entries is only bound to become more counterintuitive when the *Catalogue* is reprinted, given the pace at which copies seem to change hands. The *Catalogue* is, however, bound to become an electronic resource and the shift from print to digital technology will make searches completely straightforward. I will hang on to my printed copy of the *Catalogue*, though: far from putting me off, the quirky quality of the numbering and consequent arrangement of the entries gave me the vicarious pleasure of doing some 'armchair Folio hunting' of mine own![2]

A staggering amount of work has also gone into *British Drama 1533–1642: A Catalogue*. Its main editor, Martin Wiggins, explains that he first started working on this project eleven years before the first two volumes reached the press, the second hot on the heels of the first, in early 2012. Wiggins and Richardson should be very pleased with the outcome of their project to date. The first two volumes of their *Catalogue* offer clear and detailed entries arranged in chronological order for all known and lost plays from 1533 to 1566 and from 1567 to 1589. Each entry includes information drawn from a close analysis of the theatrical and dramatic features of the play, from the bibliographical or paleographical make-up of the extant early editions in print or manuscript, from a survey of relevant early modern documents (Revels Accounts, State Papers, the Stationers' Register, Henslowe's Diary, etc.), and from modern editions and scholarly sources. Basic information about the attribution, composition, early performance(s) and publication of early modern plays is already available elsewhere, primarily in W. W. Greg's *Bibliography of the English Printed Drama to the Restoration*, in Harbage's *Annals of English Drama, 975–1700*, and in Lesser and Farmer's *DEEP: A Database of Early English Plays*, an online resource which combines and updates information found in Greg and Harbage. However, Wiggins and Richardson's *Catalogue* offers a wealth of new data. Worth highlighting are the lists of roles, of variations in the names of characters as they appear in speech prefixes and stage directions, and of 'Other Characters', along with an indication of where these characters are mentioned in the play (the section on *Freewill*, entry 471 in volume 2, includes as many as 86 'Other Characters'!).

---

[2] While it is impossible to check the accuracy of bibliographical descriptions of copies held in so many different locations across the world, I should note that I fortuitously stumbled upon a minor omission in West 179. While the *Catalogue* correctly records the crossing out of the word 'graue' on ff6, it omits to mention that the alternative variant 'shroud' was inscribed by the same hand right next to it.

Wiggins and Richardson's *Catalogue* is already searchable thanks to the multiple indexes of 'Persons', 'Places' and 'Plays' appended to each volume. The *Catalogue* will however become fully searchable as an electronic version to be issued at a later stage by Catherine Richardson and Mark Merry. Users will then be able to search the vast amount of data collected in the *Catalogue* for specific information about props, music, costumes and make-up, or special effects deployed even in the most obscure of plays from the period. The *Catalogue* is therefore bound to have a significant impact both on teaching and research in the fields of Shakespeare and early modern drama. As with Rasmussen and West's *Catalogue*, though, the printed version of Wiggins and Richardson's *Catalogue* will continue to be useful for searches that are better served by the codex form than by the electronic medium. The printed volumes are, for example, ideal for browsing entries chronologically or to get a sense of how many plays survive and how many were lost from any given year throughout the period, thanks to the smart visual coding used for the headings of lost plays (white type on a black background), which makes this category of plays stand out quite dramatically among plays that are extant in their entirety (black type on a white background) or only as fragments (black type on a grey background). Both the printed and the electronic versions of this *Catalogue* will prove immensely useful to scholars and students alike. While I eagerly await the publication of the remaining volumes, I wonder whether the editors have plans to ensure that the electronic version of their *Catalogue* interfaces effectively with other excellent and freely accessible online resources, such as *DEEP*.

RE-ENTER THE AUTHOR,
TRANSLATED, CHANGED, REBORN

Several new essays methodologically informed by recent developments in attribution studies, book history and manuscript studies continue to redress and qualify our understanding of what Shakespeare may or may not have written and how his work was received by its first readers.

Laura Estill, for example, explores the popularity of Shakespeare in the seventeenth century by establishing how a classical proverb, which was rephrased by Shakespeare in *Love's Labour's Lost* as 'Fat paunches have lean pates, and dainty bits / Make rich the ribs, but bankrupt quite the wits' (1.1.26–27), was then reproduced as a free-floating excerpt in print and manuscript throughout the period. While the frequency with which Shakespeare's version of this proverb was reproduced in printed books and manuscript miscellanies attests to 'the popularity of Shakespeare's words', Estill rightly argues that 'the circulation of this couplet' does not necessarily point to Shakespeare's 'status as revered playwright' (48). It is worth pointing out that Peter Stallybrass and Roger Chartier had reached a similar conclusion in a seminal essay published in 2007: 'Shakespeare . . . emerges as a canonical English poet . . . neither through poems nor through his plays but rather through individual "sentences" . . . extracted from his works' (*A Concise Companion to Shakespeare and the Text*, 2007, p. 46). I was therefore surprised not to find at least a passing reference to their work in Estill's essay.

Estill's approach is methodologically exciting and her findings are generally sound and significant, but I did wonder why she underplays the influence of the Shakespearian source, or other literary sources, including Robert Allott's *Englands Parnassus* (1600), where this couplet was first anthologized, or the later authors who quoted it in their work or copied it in their commonplace books. While I would, for example, agree with Estill that the reoccurrence of the variant phrasing in Thomas Walkington's *The Optick Glasse of Humors* (1607) – 'Fat paunches make lean pates, and grosser bitts / Enrich the ribs but bankrout quite the witts' – rules out a direct link with Shakespeare's play or with Allott's poetic miscellany, I am not sure why a *verbatim* reproduction of the Shakespearian phrasing in W. B.'s *A Helpe to Discourse* (1623 edition) should be ascribed to '*knowledge* of Shakespeare's play' (my emphasis) or to 'oral tradition' (41). Given the level of variation associated with oral transmission, consultation of a written source (and why not Shakespeare's play or Allott's miscellany?) would seem to be just as (if not more) likely. By the same token, consultation of Shakespeare's play or Allott's miscellany cannot be ruled out when this couplet was copied in Bodleian MS Rawl. 117 (f. 156 rev.), because the single initial variant 'Fat'/'Full' is in keeping with the well-documented tendency among commonplacing authors to introduce minor variants even when they were copying extracts from written sources. Estill's assumption that the couplet was here 'either copied from memory or from another handwritten source' does not seem entirely justified, especially in light of the fact that, as she points out, the couplet as rephrased in Walkington is copied elsewhere in the same commonplace book (f. 276 rev.), while the near-exact Shakespearian phrasing at f. 156 rev. is followed by another couplet from *The Merchant of Venice*, which presumably does not feature in Walkington. Positing a more direct link with *Love's Labour's Lost* or with *Englands Parnassus* does not undermine but possibly refines Estill's important point that, in the seventeenth century, Shakespeare circulated as a collection of free-floating proverbs, often quoted in non-literary works, and that the commonplacing of Shakespeare was as significant as, or possibly even more influential than, the circulation of his plays and poems in print in establishing his reputation.

One other essay, Peter Kirwan's 'The First Collected "Shakespeare Apocrypha"', focuses on the early circulation of Shakespeare's works in print. Kirwan reconsiders the history and significance of a small volume of plays, which originally belonged to the library of David Garrick and was then broken up in the 1840s, once it had passed into the holdings of the British Museum. By identifying a mistake in the attribution of this volume to the library of Charles II (instead of Charles I), Kirwan dates its original constitution as a gathering of bibliographically independent plays (a so-called nonce collection) to the pre-Restoration period, establishing 1631 as its *terminus a quo*, since two of the quarto plays bound in this volume were reprinted that year. By consulting the catalogue of Garrick's library compiled by George Kahrl and Dorothy Anderson in 1982, Kirwan is also able to prove that the volume, originally inscribed with the title 'Shakespeare, Vol. 1.', included eight plays – *The Puritan*, *Thomas Lord Cromwell*, *The Merry Devil of Edmonton*, *The London Prodigal*, *Mucedorus*, *Fair Em*, *Love's Labour's Lost* and *1 Sir John Oldcastle* – and not just three – *Mucedorus*, *Merry Devil* and *Fair Em* – as previously assumed. Kirwan's reassessment of this volume has significant implications: 'the Charles I volume', as he explains, 'shows that the notion of a Shakespearean "supplement" or "apocrypha" already existed in the Caroline period, taking shape as early as a decade after the publication of the First Folio and implying that the "canon" established by that volume was already unstable in discourse' (600). However, and I am grateful to Kirwan for his comments about my work on the Pavier Quartos, I think the following corollary is suggestive but not entirely apt: '[i]n a manner not dissimilar to the Pavier project, the Charles I volume acts as an authority, not on what Shakespeare wrote, but what could legitimately be read as Shakespearean' (601). The binding of plays into a collected volume for an individual library is different from a publishing project, as Kirwan himself points out, but also, and more crucially, the Pavier project predated the publication of the First Folio and therefore lacks the supplementary quality that Kirwan rightly ascribes to the Charles I volume.

Adele Davidson, the author of *Shakespeare in Shorthand: The Textual Mystery of King Lear* (2009), continues to urge fellow scholars to regard early modern systems of shorthand as one of the modes of transmission through which some early modern plays reached the press. Building on *Shakespeare in Shorthand*, Davidson's essay '"Common Variants" and "Unusual Features": Shorthand and the Copy for the First Quarto of *Lear*' provides further examples of unique or rare spellings in the first quarto of *King Lear* (Q) that can best be accounted for as deriving from the abbreviated writing introduced by John Willis in his shorthand manual called *The Art of Stenographie* (1602). While Davidson's theory provides an attractive ad hoc explanation for some variants in Q, this essay does not strengthen or develop her earlier work, which was deemed by Henry Woudhuysen as 'valuable' but 'finally unconvincing' (*Shakespeare Quarterly*, 62 (2011), 604–9, 607). As a reviewer of *Shakespeare in Shorthand*, Woudhuysen pointed out that 'the major problem with Davidson's argument' stems from her need to 'show that [John] Willis's *Stenographie* is sufficiently developed to allow an expert to transcribe the play in abbreviated writing, yet the system must be sufficiently impractical and inefficient to produce some or many of the huge number of errors and anomalies found in Q' (608). Instead of tacking this methodological problem head on, Davidson's latest essay provides more internal evidence from Q and some circumstantial evidence to prove that shorthand was a familiar technology among Shakespeare's contemporaries and that it was used in transcribing plays.

The circumstantial evidence discussed by Davidson in this essay is suggestive but far from compelling. Davidson, for example, wonders 'what number and types of allusions' to shorthand 'by men with theatrical connections' may 'constitute necessary or sufficient evidence' (327) to ensure that the 'shorthand debate' is not 'prematurely or permanently closed' (326). Two out of three such allusions considered by Davidson in her essay do not add up to 'necessary or sufficient evidence'. As Davidson herself admits, Robert Taylor's allusion to a 'plot' being 'powdred vp' in *The Hog Hath Lost his Pearl* is rather vague and nothing more than an 'image perhaps intimating the reduction of text into small elements in a manner evocative of abbreviated writing' (328n). Similarly, George Chapman's preface to *All Fools* (1605) includes an ambiguous allusion to some unorthodox method of textual transmission – I am assuming that Davidson is referring to Chapman's claim that his work has been published 'without my passport – patch'd with others' wit' – but nothing in Chapman's phrasing suggests that he is alluding to shorthand. Besides, as W. W. Greg explains in his *Bibliography of the English Printed Drama to the Restoration*, this preface, an unsigned sonnet 'To my long lou'd and Honourable friend Sir Thomas Walsingham Knight', is printed on a smaller leaf than the rest

of the playbook, which 'makes it improbable that it belongs to the volume' (347). The third allusion, Thomas Heywood's complaint that 'Some by Stenography drew the Plot' of his 1605 play *If You Know Not Me, You Know Nobody*' is the only isolated (and very well-known) example discussed by Davidson. Without discounting its significance altogether, we should bear mind that Heywood is referring to the 'Plot' of the play rather than the play itself.

Davidson's discussion of early modern references to shorthand in relation to the transmission of sermons into print is similarly ambiguous. Especially problematic is Davidson's analysis of Andrew Wise's output as the stationer who published editions of Thomas Playfere's sermons and some of the best-selling early quarto editions of Shakespeare's plays, including *Richard II*, *Richard III* and *1 Henry IV*. Davidson claims that, when Playfere complains about textual 'reporting' as the method though which one of his sermons was first committed to print, he is referring specifically to a system of shorthand. Davidson does not identify Playfere's sermon, but she must be referring to *The meane in mourning* (STC 20015), which Wise had previously published as *A most excellent and heauenly sermon* (STC 20014, STC 20014.3 and STC 20014.5, 1595). Davidson should at least discount the possibility that Playfere's complaint was disingenuous, since Wise published both the first, putatively defective, edition of this sermon, and the later, 'authorized' editions and entrusted Wise with the publication of another sermon (*The pathway to perfection*, STC 20020, 1596). While this essay does offer additional internal evidence to suggest that some textual features in Q may be linked to shorthand as a method of textual transmission of this play into print, Davidson's discussion of other types of evidence does a disservice to her justifiable interest in the impact of shorthand on early modern drama in print.

Having started this review essay with the quest for the lost *Cardenio*, I am going to end with Helen Hackett's sobering appeal 'to free ourselves of the obsession with finding lost Shakespearean works' (56). Accordingly, she shows that the 'Dial

Hand' poem is not a long-lost epilogue written by Shakespeare for a court production of *As You Like It*, but rather a court epilogue written by Thomas Dekker for *The Shoemaker's Holiday* (53–6). While both plays may have been performed at Court on Shrovetide 1599 (the time of year and the date are recorded in the transcription of the poem first found and attributed to Shakespeare by William A. Ringler and Steven W. May in 1972), internal evidence supports Dekker's rather than Shakespeare's candidacy to the authorship of this poem. Hackett singles out the close resemblance between the poem and the panegyric of Elizabeth in the court prologue prefaced to Dekker's play and then goes on to explain that the encomiastic style of the 'Dial Hand' poem is quite unlike any of the sparse allusions to Elizabeth in Shakespeare's works and very similar to Dekker's thinly veiled homage or explicit references to the Queen in late Elizabethan and early Jacobean works, including *Old Fortunatus* (1599), *The Wonderful Year* (1603) and *The Whore of Babylon* (1605). Jonson, the alternative candidate championed by other scholars, is ruled out by Hackett on the grounds of both internal and external evidence: apparently, when Jonson writes about the same theme of circularity evoked in the 'Dial Hand' poem, 'emphasis is not upon temporal cycles [as in the poem] but upon wholeness and integrity as noble virtues'; and, even more crucially, as Hackett points out, 'Jonson was in disgrace in 1599, making it unlikely that he would have been commissioned to write a court epilogue at this time' (47).

All in all, Hackett's essay is a model of balanced, logical reasoning and well-judged use of the different types of evidence she discusses in it. My only objection, peevish as it may sound, is that, contrary to what Hackett suggests in relation to the epilogue in *Locrine* – 'Stern, following Sonia Massai, believes that the epilogue is "undoubtedly" by Shakespeare' (44) – I have never made such a claim. Hackett (or Stern) might be referring to a recent essay where I pay tribute to C. F. Tucker-Brooke, who, in 1908, argued that 'there is . . . no shadow of a reason why we should not accept as absolute truth the statement of the title-page' in the first edition of *Locrine*, namely that someone whose initials were '*W.S.*' had 'Newly set foorth, ouerseene and corrected' an older play and *probably* written a new epilogue for it. I go on to argue that what is crucial in the context of my own work on early modern dramatic paratexts and the rise of Shakespeare's authorship in print is not 'the authenticity of this epilogue, but the fact that it was ascribed to '*W.S.*' [and] that contemporary readers would have associated those initials with William Shakespeare more readily than with any other known playwrights or writers in the mid-1590s'.[3] My interest, in other words, lies in the significance of this attribution, whether genuine or apocryphal, in the context of the mid-1590s, which is quite a far cry from assuming that I believe this epilogue to be 'undoubtedly' by Shakespeare.

WORKS REVIEWED

Carnegie, David and Gary Taylor, eds., *The Quest for Cardenio: Shakespeare, Fletcher, Cervantes and the Lost Play* (Oxford, 2012)

Davidson, Adele, '"Common Variants" and "Unusual Features": Shorthand and the Copy for the First Quarto of *Lear*', *Papers of the Bibliographical Society of America*, 105:3 (2011), 325–51

Doran, Gregory, *Shakespeare's Lost Play: In Search of Cardenio* (London, 2012)

Estill, Laura, 'Proverbial Shakespeare: The Print and Manuscript Circulation of Extracts from *Love's Labour's Lost*', *Shakespeare*, 7 (2011), 35–55

Hackett, Helen, '"As the Diall Hand Tells Ore": The Case for Dekker, not Shakespeare, as Author', *The Review of English Studies*, 63 (2012), 34–57

Jackson, MacDonald P., 'Looking for Shakespeare in *Double Falsehood*: Stylistic Evidence', in Carnegie and Taylor, *Quest for Cardenio*, pp. 133–61

Kirwan, Peter, 'The First Collected "Shakespeare Apocrypha"', *Shakespeare Quarterly*, 62:4 (2011), 594–601

Meek, Richard and Jane Rickard, '"This Orphan Play": *Cardenio* and the Construction of the Author', *Shakespeare*, 7 (2011), 269–83

---

[3] Sonia Massai, 'Shakespeare, Text and Paratext', *Shakespeare Survey 62* (Cambridge, 2009), pp. 1–11 at 9.

Proudfoot, Richard, 'Can *Double Falsehood* Be Merely a Forgery by Lewis Theobald?', in Carnegie and Taylor, *Quest for Cardenio*, pp. 162–79

Rasmussen, Eric and Anthony James West, *The Shakespeare First Folios: A Descriptive Catalogue* (Basingstoke and New York, 2012)

Rasmussen, Eric, *The Shakespeare Thefts: In Search of the First Folios* (Basingstoke and New York, 2011)

Shakespeare William, *Antony and Cleopatra*, A Norton Critical Edition, ed. by Ania Loomba (New York and London, 2011)

Shakespeare, William, *As You Like It*, A Norton Critical Edition, ed. by Leah Marcus (New York and London, 2012)

Shakespeare, William, *As You Like It*, The Evans Shakespeare Editions, ed. by Heather Dubrow (Boston, MA, 2012)

Shakespeare, William, *Hamlet*, A Norton Critical Edition, ed. by Robert Miola (New York and London, 2011)

Shakespeare, William, *Hamlet*, The Evans Shakespeare Editions, ed. by J. J. M. Tobin (Boston, MA, 2012)

Shakespeare, William, *King Lear*, The Evans Shakespeare Editions, ed. by Vincent Petronella (Boston, MA, 2012)

Shakespeare, William, *Macbeth*, The Evans Shakespeare Editions, ed. by Katherine Rowe (Boston, MA, 2012)

Shakespeare, William, *Measure for Measure*, The Evans Shakespeare Editions, ed. by John Klause (Boston, MA, 2012)

Shakespeare, William, *A Midsummer Night's Dream*, The Evans Shakespeare Editions, ed. by Douglas Bruster (Boston, MA, 2012)

Shakespeare, William, *Richard III*, The Evans Shakespeare Editions, ed. by Nina Levine (Boston, MA, 2012)

Shakespeare, William, *Romeo and Juliet*, The Arden Shakespeare, ed. by René Weis (London, 2012)

Shakespeare, William, *Shakespeare's Sonnets: An Original-Spelling Text*, ed. by Paul Hammond (Oxford, 2012)

Shakespeare, William, *The Tempest*, The Evans Shakespeare Editions, ed. by Grace Tiffany (Boston, MA, 2012)

Shakespeare, William, *The Two Noble Kinsmen*, The New Cambridge Shakespeare, ed. by Robert Kean Turner and Patricia Tatspaugh (Cambridge, 2012)

Shakespeare, William, *The Winter's Tale*, The Evans Shakespeare Editions, ed. by Lawrence F. Rhu (Boston, MA, 2012)

Stern, Tiffany, '"The Forgery of Some Modern Author"? Theobald's Shakespeare and Cardenio's *Double Falsehood*', *Shakespeare Quarterly*, 62:4 (2011), 555–93

Stern, Tiffany, '"Whether one did Contrive, the Other Write, / Or one Fram'd the Plot, the Other did Indite": Fletcher and Theobald as Collaborative Writers', in Carnegie and Taylor, *Quest for Cardenio*, pp. 115–30

Taylor, Gary, 'A History of *The History of Cardenio*', in Carnegie and Taylor, *Quest for Cardenio*, pp. 11–61

Wiggins, Martin, in association with Catherine Richardson, *British Drama 1533–1642: A Catalogue*, vol. I: 1533–1566 and vol. II: 1567–1589 (Oxford, 2012)

INDEX

INDEX

INDEX

INDEX

INDEX

INDEX

INDEX

INDEX